# Ancient Women Writer
# and Rome

*Ancient Women Writers of Greece and Rome* features the extant writings of major female authors from the Greco-Roman world, brought together for the first time in a single volume, in both their original languages and translated into English with accompanying commentaries.

The most cost-effective and comprehensive way to study the women writers of Greece and Rome, this book provides original texts, accessible text-commentaries, and detailed English translations of the works of ancient female poets and authors such as Sappho and Sulpicia. It takes a student-focused approach, discussing texts alongside new and original English translations and highlighting the rich, diverse scholarship on ancient women writers to specialists and non-specialists alike. The perspectives of women in the ancient world are still relevant and of interest today, as issues of gender and racial (in)equality remain ever-present in modern society.

*Ancient Women Writers of Greece and Rome* provides a valuable teaching tool for students of Greek, Latin, and Classical Studies, as well as those interested in ancient literature, history, and gender studies who do not have proficiency in Greek or Latin.

**Bartolo A. Natoli** is Associate Professor of Classics and Women, Gender, and Sexualities Program Affiliate at Randolph-Macon College. He holds a BA in Latin, Greek, and Secondary Education from the University of Richmond, an MEd in Adult Education and Training from Colorado State University, and a PhD in Classics from the University of Texas at Austin. His recent publications include a monograph entitled *Silenced Voices: The Poetics of Speech in Ovid* (2017) and an edited volume entitled *Teaching Classics with Technology* (2019).

**Angela Pitts** is Professor of Classics at the University of Mary Washington. She received her BA in English and Classics from the University of Ohio and her MA and PhD in Classics from the University of Wisconsin-Madison. Angela has published articles in peer-reviewed journals and volumes on a variety of topics ranging from soundscape in Homer's *Iliad* to Sappho's *Nachleben* in antiquity.

**Judith P. Hallett** is Professor of Classics and Distinguished Scholar-Teacher Emerita at the University of Maryland, College Park. She holds a BA in Latin from Wellesley College and an MA and PhD in Classical Philology from Harvard University. She has published widely in the areas of Latin language and literature; women, the family, and sexuality in Greco-Roman antiquity; and the study and reception of classics in the Anglophone world. A former Blegen Visiting Scholar in the Department of Classics at Vassar College and Suzanne Deal Booth Resident Scholar at the Center for Intercollegiate Studies in Rome, Judith has also held fellowships from the Mellon Foundation and the National Endowment for the Humanities. A collection of essays from Routledge—*Domina Illustris: Latin Literature, Gender and Reception* (2013), edited by Donald Lateiner, Barbara Gold, and Judith Perkins—celebrates her academic career.

**Routledge Sourcebooks for the Ancient World**

Recent titles include:

**Pompeii and Herculaneum**
A Sourcebook, 2nd edition
*Alison E. Cooley and M.G.L. Cooley*

**Ancient Rome**
Social and Historical Documents from the Early Republic to the Death of Augustus, 2nd edition
*Matthew Dillon and Lynda Garland*

**Pagans and Christians in Late Antiquity**
A Sourcebook, 2nd edition
*A.D. Lee*

**Greek and Roman Technology**
A Sourcebook of Translated Greek and Roman Texts, 2nd edition
*Andrew N. Sherwood, Milorad Nikolic, John W. Humphrey, and John P. Oleson*

**Italy Before Rome**
A Sourcebook
*Katherine McDonald*

**Sexuality in Greek and Roman Society and Literature**
A Sourcebook, 2nd edition
*Marguerite Johnson*

**Ancient Women Writers of Greece and Rome**
*Bartolo A. Natoli, Angela Pitts, and Judith P. Hallett*

For a full list of titles in this series, please visit https://www.routledge.com/Routledge-Sourcebooks-for-the-Ancient-World/book-series/RSAW

# Ancient Women Writers of Greece and Rome

Bartolo A. Natoli, Angela Pitts, and
Judith P. Hallett

Routledge
Taylor & Francis Group
LONDON AND NEW YORK

Cover Image: © The History Collection / Alamy Stock Photo

First published 2022
by Routledge
4 Park Square, Milton Park, Abingdon, Oxon OX14 4RN

and by Routledge
605 Third Avenue, New York, NY 10158

*Routledge is an imprint of the Taylor & Francis Group, an informa business*



*British Library Cataloguing-in-Publication Data*
A catalogue record for this book is available from the British Library

*Library of Congress Cataloging-in-Publication Data*
A catalog record has been requested for this book

ISBN: 978-0-367-46877-4 (hbk)
ISBN: 978-0-367-46252-9 (pbk)
ISBN: 978-1-003-03172-7 (ebk)

DOI: 10.4324/9781003031727

Typeset in Times New Roman
by KnowledgeWorks Global Ltd.

**This volume is humbly dedicated to the memories of Medea Norsa (1877–1952) and bell hooks (1952–2021)**

# Contents

# List of Figures

# Preface and Acknowledgments

This volume has its genesis in a series of conversations with undergraduate students over the past decade. Invariably, each of these conversations unfolded along quite similar lines. They always began in the context of a discussion of ancient literature—sometimes in the original languages, and sometimes in translation. We would ask students about their knowledge of women writers in ancient Greece and Rome, and they would always respond with the same answer: there was Sappho, of course, but no other writers of note from antiquity. When we responded that, in fact, there were numerous female writers and that the works of more than sixty such writers have survived in some fashion, there always was a mixture stunned silence, audible gasps, and unbridled excitement. After having enough of these conversations, we began to inquire as to why students had such little knowledge of these writers. The scholarship on female writers is rich and impressive in every manner; however, it is quite diffuse and oftentimes difficult to access. To examine just the authors discussed in this volume in translation and in the original would require no fewer than a handful of books, a daunting and expensive task for most students.

Therefore, we set out to craft a volume that aims to make these texts and the major works of scholarship on them accessible to all students, whatever their proficiency in ancient languages. This volume gathers together in one place the works of women writers from the Greek and Roman worlds that have come down to us in the most substantial form. Following an introduction by Judith P. Hallett on the survival and later, gendered interpretations of the ancient Greek and Roman women's writings featured in the volume, Angela Pitts and Bartolo A. Natoli present the Greek and Latin texts in both the original and English translation, with notes, running vocabulary and commentary.The running vocabulary provides entries for less familiar words, but all Greek and Latin words from the texts are included in the glossaries at the end of this volume. The texts of each of the authors are introduced with an introduction to the author and the scholarly debates surrounding her writing. Appendices on disputed texts, Greek dialects, and meter complete the volume. It is our hope that this volume can make these important works accessible for both students of Latin and Greek on the secondary through graduate levels and students of the history of literature and of gender and sexuality who have not yet mastered the ancient languages.

With its student-centered focus, this volume is intended to be a primer for study of these texts, not as a detailed, technical commentary on textual or papyrological criticism, although some of that can be found in the following pages. Instead, for each author, we have included a select bibliography of works that delve into these issues much more deeply than is possible in this volume. We encourage all readers of this volume to explore that scholarship and to gain a deeper knowledge of all of the aspects of these texts.

As is natural for a volume of this sort, there are numerous individuals to thank. First and foremost, our deepest appreciation goes to our coauthor Judith P. Hallett. Throughout the process of compiling this work, we both have been amazed by her expertise and energy. She proved to be an invaluable resource for us as the volume came together, offering sage advice learned through her years of experience, much of which is in full display in her Introduction to this volume. We hope that you, as readers, draw as much knowledge and inspiration from her insights as we have.

Secondly, we would like to thank the actual *raison d'etre* for this volume: our students. Your insightful comments and innovative methods of reading these texts in class and individual discussion have provided us so many insights into what type of volume would aid in student understanding the best. In particular, we thank our student assistants, Grace McIntire, Hannah Hurt, and Miranda Wollen, who painstakingly helped edit, collate, and transcribe many of these texts. This volume would not have been possible without their dedicated efforts.

Likewise, thanks are owed to the tremendous institutional support each of us has enjoyed for the duration of this process. Bartolo would like to recognize his outstanding colleagues in the Classics Department at Randolph-Macon College, particularly Elizabeth Fisher and Thomas Rose, who always were there with steadfast support and friendly critiques during every stage of the manuscript preparation. Angela would like to thank her colleagues in the Department of Classics, Philosophy, and Religion at the University of Mary Washington, and particularly Joe Romero and Liane Houghtalin for their judicious counsel on many matters pertaining to this volume, as well as their constant support.

At Routledge Press, we were lucky to have a tremendous team of editors, all of whom helped us fine-tune this manuscript into its current form; all while providing copious amounts of grace and patience as we developed the volume at the height of the COVID-19 pandemic. We especially thank Elizabeth Risch, Ella Halstead, Amy Davis-Poynter, Suzanne Pfister, and Marcia Adams for their tireless efforts and their patience with the endless emails and corrections that accompany edited volumes. Likewise, we owe a great debt of gratitude to the anonymous readers who reviewed our proposal and who encouraged us to pursue this volume to the fullest extent.

Any shortcomings that remain in the volume are due either to our own collective stubbornness or oversight.

Finally, we would like to thank our families and mentors, without whom this volume would not have been possible. Individually, Bartolo would like to thank his wife, Morgan, to whom he is indebted for her unwavering confidence and patience throughout the many drafts of this work, and his children, Luca, Mira, and Nico, for sharing dad with his books and computer. Angela, who writes in her home positioned on the traditional hunting grounds of the Manahoac Nation, offers gratitude to Lena and David Welker, who have shown by their leadership, friendship, and example the responsibilities attendant upon those who carry into the future the fragile threads of old stories and voices that have nearly been lost. She also offers gratitude to her beloved friends Laura and George Mentore, Anthropologists whose inspiring work has helped to give voice to threatened indigenous communities in the Amazonian rainforests of Guyana so that the next generation can hear the old stories that matter. She would like to express gratitude to her mother, Marietta, and to her sisters, Victoria Pitts and Jennifer Gosetti, for a lifetime of support and inspiration. Finally, she offers her deepest gratitude to Patricia Rosenmeyer for so many reasons, but especially for introducing her to the enchanting poetry of Sappho many years ago.

*B.N.*
*A.P.*
*November 2021*

# Text Credits

## Sappho

1, 16, 31, 44: Voigt, Eva-Maria (ed.). 1971. *Sappho et Alcaeus.* Amsterdam: Polak & Van Gennep.

2: Campbell, David A. (ed.). 1967 and 1982. *Greek Lyric Poetry.* Bristol: Bristol Classical Press, p. 41–42.

58: Obbink, Dirk. 2009. "Sappho Fragments 58-59: Text, Apparatus Criticus, and Translation," in Ellen Greene and Marilyn B. Skinner (eds.), *The New Sappho on Old Age: Textual and Philosophical Issues.* Hellenic Studies Series 38. Washington, D.C.: Center for Hellenic Studies. https://chs.harvard.edu/chapter/2-dirk-obbink-sappho-fragments-58-59-text-apparatus-criticus-and-translation/

16a, "Kypris Song", "The Brothers Poem": Obbink, Dirk. 2016. "The Newest Sappho: Text, Apparatus Criticus, and Translation," in Anton Bierl and André Lardinois (eds.), *The Newest Sappho: P. Sapph Obbink and P. GC inv. 105, Frs. 1-4.* Brill, p. 13–33.

## Corinna

Page, Denys Lionel. 1962. *Poetae Melici Graeci.* Oxford: Oxford University Press.

## Erinna

"The Distaff" = P.S.I. 1090: We have largely used West's (1977) edition, consulting Lloyd-Jones and Parson (1983) in the case of the more controversial supplements suggested by West.

West, M. L. 1977. "Erinna," *Zeitschrift für Papyrologie und Epigraphik* 25: 95–119.

Lloyd-Jones, H. and P. Parsons. 1983. *Supplementum Hellenisticum.* Berlin: De Gruyter, p. 187–189.

Epigrams 1, 2, 3: Gow, A. S. F. and D. L. Page. 1965. *The Greek Anthology: Hellenistic Epigrams, vol. 1.*Cambridge: Cambridge University Press, p. 97–98.

## Moero

Epigrams 1, 2: Gow, A. S. F. and D. L. Page. 1965. *The Greek Anthology: Hellenistic Epigrams, vol. 1.* Cambridge: Cambridge University Press, p. 145.

3: Olson, S. Douglas. 2009. *Athenaeus, The Learned Banqueters, Vol. V: Books 10.420e-11.* Loeb Classical Library 274. Cambridge, MA: Harvard University Press, p. 386–388.

## Nossis

Gow, A. S. F. and D. L. Page. 1965. *The Greek Anthology: Hellenistic Epigrams, vol. 1.* Cambridge: Cambridge University Press, p. 151–154.

## Anyte

1-3, 5-21: Gow, A. S. F. and D. L. Page. 1965. *The Greek Anthology: Hellenistic Epigrams, vol. 1*. Cambridge: Cambridge University Press, p. 35–41.

4: Geoghegan, D. 1979. *Anyte: The Epigrams.* Rome: Edizioni dell' Ateneo & Bizzarri, p. 56.

## Praxilla

Page, Denys Lionel. 1962. *Poetae Melici Graeci.* Oxford: Oxford University Press.

## Melinno

Gutzwiller, K. (2017). "Melinno," in D. Sider (ed.), *Hellenistic Poetry: A Selection.* University of Michigan Press.

## Sulpicia

1-11: Fulkerson, L. (2017). *A Literary Commentary on the Elegies of the 'Appendix Tibulliana'. Pseudepigrapha Latina*. Oxford.

12: *L'Année Epigraphique* 1928.73.

## Sulpicia Caleni

1: Dickison, S. and J. P. Hallett. (2015). *A Roman Women Reader*. Bolchazy-Carducci.

2: Butrica, J. L. (2000). *Sulpiciae Conquestio*. http://www.curculio.org/Sulpiciae/Conquestio.html

3-4: Lindsay, W. M. (1954). *M. Val. Martialis: Epigrammata*. Oxford.

## An Inscription from Pompeii

Courtney, E. (1995). *Musa Lapidaria. A Selection of Latin Verse Inscriptions*. Atlanta, GA: Inscription n. 92.

## Terentia

Stevenson, J. (2005). *Women Latin Poets: Language, Gender, and Authority from Antiquity to the Eighteenth Century.* Oxford.

## Vindolanda Tablets

1: *Tabula Vindolanda* II 291 (http://vindolanda.csad.ox.ac.uk/)

2: *Tabula Vindolanda* II 292 (http://vindolanda.csad.ox.ac.uk/)

## Colossus of Memnon

all: Bernand, A. and É. Bernand. (1960). *Les inscriptions grecques et latines du colosse de Memnon.* Paris.

# Sigla

[...] **Square brackets:** This symbol encloses places in which *words have been lost through physical damage.* Oftentimes, dots are placed within the brackets to mark how many letters have probably been lost (e.g., 2 dots = 2 letters missing, etc.). If letters are placed within the brackets, it indicates the editor's attempt at guessing what letters have been lost.

<...> **Diamond brackets:** This symbol encloses *words and letters that an editor has added.*

(...) **Round brackets:** This symbol encloses *words and letters that have been abbreviated by the original text.*

† **Obelus:** This symbol marks a section of text is clearly corrupted (i.e., there's an error), but the editor does not know how to emend. If only one word is corrupt, the obelus precedes the word. If multiple words are corrupt, two obeli enclose the corrupted words.

# Abbreviations for Journals Cited in This Volume

| | |
|---|---|
| **AJA** | American Journal of Archaeology |
| **AJAH** | American Journal of Ancient History |
| **AJP** | American Journal of Philology |
| **ANRW** | Aufstieg und Niedergang der römischen Welt |
| **AW** | The Ancient World |
| **CA** | Classical Antiquity |
| **CJ** | The Classical Journal |
| **CPh** | Classical Philology |
| **CQ** | Classical Quarterly |
| **CW** | Classical World |
| **GRBS** | Greek, Roman, and Byzantine Studies |
| **HSCP** | Harvard Studies in Classical Philology |
| **QUCC** | Quaderni Urbinati di Cultura Classica |
| **TAPA** | Transactions of the American Philological Association |
| **YJC** | Yale Journal of Criticism |
| **ZPE** | Zeitschrift für Papyrologie und Epigraphik |

# Introduction

## Looking at Ancient Women Writers through Male and Female Lenses

*Judith P. Hallett*

The treasure trove of Greek and Latin literary texts preserved from the Greco-Roman world during what we call the classical era—a period extending from the 8th century BCE through the 4th century CE—contains relatively few works by women writers: a cause of frustration not only to those of us who study classical antiquity but also to those of us interested in women's writings through the ages. It is frustrating enough that these writings by Greek and Roman women preserved from classical antiquity are far, far fewer in number than the writings preserved from that era by Greek and Roman men. It is more frustrating still that this small number of writings by women represents only a portion of the female-authored texts actually produced in classical antiquity. Our ancient sources testify to the existence of many others no longer extant.[1]

We often refer to the extant writings by ancient women available to us today as "having survived" from classical times. By so doing, we imply that these texts somehow possess both energy and agency of their own. That they have pluckily willed themselves to persist physically, withstanding the human and natural calamities that also led to the loss, in their entirety or in substantial part, of innumerable male-authored literary works written in classical times, works ranging from Athenian tragic dramas to Roman historical chronicles. Yes, we often employ the verb "survive" to characterize male-authored literary works preserved from classical times. But its application to ancient women writers is especially apt.

For these ancient women writers, the topic of this volume, include such significant artistic voices as the Greek poet Sappho and the Latin poet Sulpicia. Sappho, who flourished on the island of Lesbos from the late 7th through the early 6th centuries BCE, is renowned for her lyrics about love and desire between women, as our English words "lesbian" and "sapphic" document.[2] The lesser-known Sulpicia, who wrote in the city of Rome during the reign of the emperor Augustus, around 20 BCE, is increasingly valued for her elegiac verses about her illicit sexual liaison with a younger man.[3] Many of us who now read the writings by these and other ancient women, whether in their original Greek and Latin, or in modern translations which do literary

DOI: 10.4324/9781003031727-1

justice to their actual words, find these writings personally meaningful and compelling. And rightly so: these writings, especially but by no means solely the poems of Sappho and Sulpicia, forge strong emotional connections between artist and audience, albeit in different imaginative ways. Such an impression of these women's writings—as powerful in their own right, owing to their ability to reach, and touch, the feelings of readers across the millennia—contributes to the notion that these literary texts have also, and always, possessed the sheer capacity for physical survival, for enduring life-threatening challenges to their very existence.

But in fact we owe the "survival" of these ancient writings by women largely to the labors of men who, from classical times to the present day, have taken pains to preserve what these women wrote. These male "preservationists" viewed, and judged the worth of, these women's writings through their own, male, lenses. Some of these men were themselves authors, whose own works were deemed important in classical times, and preserved as important in later eras, even if their own names and writings may not instantly register with readers today. Thankfully, they made the effort, in their own writings, to quote passages of varying lengths by certain women writers. These men chose to do so because they regarded what these women wrote as noteworthy, for different reasons. In some instances they even extol these women's writings for exemplifying literary excellence, or at least illustrating mastery of their own criteria for artistic accomplishment.

One well-known example of serendipitous preservation by an ancient male writer impressed with a woman's literary achievements is a poem, written in the first person and composed in Sappho's hallmark lyric meter, long referred to as Sappho 1 L-P: L and P are the initials of (Edgar) Lobel and (Sir Denys) Page, two British scholars who published an authoritative edition of poems by Sappho and her male contemporary Alcaeus in 1955.[4] The poem's speaker, who refers to herself as Sappho, addresses the love goddess Aphrodite, seeking her divine aid in pursuing a woman she desires. Sappho's words in this poem were deemed quote-worthy on stylistic grounds, and quoted in their entirety, by Dionysius of Halicarnassus, a Greek historian and rhetorical teacher in Augustan Roman times.[5]

The male author of a 1st-century CE aesthetic treatise entitled "On the Sublime," often referred to as "Longinus", similarly quotes, discusses, and should take most of the credit for preserving another renowned and influential poem, Sappho 31 L-P. Also written in the "Sapphic" meter, it describes her intense emotional and physical reactions to the presence of another woman. His discussion focuses on, and expresses high praise for, Sappho's representation of feelings and her portrayal of conflicting sensations and conditions.[6] Sappho's words in this particular poem also seem to have been echoed by two earlier poets, the 3rd-century BCE Greek Theocritus and the 1st-century BCE Latin Lucretius, who thereby played some part in preserving what Sappho wrote.[7]

More crucially, another Roman poet, Lucretius' contemporary Catullus, translates three stanzas of Sappho's poem into Latin, using Sappho's distinctive meter. Strikingly, its first-person speaker of Sappho's translated words is represented as a man, and addressed in the poem as Catullus. Catullus contributed to the preservation of Sappho's lyrics in other ways, too, most unforgettably by referring to his artistically cultivated female beloved as "Lesbia". A pseudonym metrically equivalent to that of Clodia, this woman's actual name, it pays tribute to the Greek island of Lesbos where Sappho lived, and thereby to Sappho herself, inasmuch as Catullus depicts this woman as—like Sappho herself—a literarily learned aristocrat, endowed with keen emotional sensibilities.[8]

The eleven erotic poems featuring the Augustan poet Sulpicia abound in echoes of earlier Greek and Roman poetry. Among them are the mythic epics of both Homer and Vergil, and the erotic lyrics of both Sappho and her literary devotees Catullus and Horace.[9] Eight are narrated by a first-person speaker, who is twice referred to by the name Sulpicia. Sulpicia's decision to write for the most part in the first person, and to refer to herself by her own name, as Sappho does, merits attention. Several Roman love poets in the generation following Catullus, who wrote, as Sulpicia does, in what is called the elegiac meter, used literarily allusive pseudonyms with the same metrical value, as Catullus did with "Lesbia", for the women whom they portray as their lovers. These male elegists represent these women as involved with them in sexual relationships outside of legitimate Roman marriage, and as responsive to and immortalized by their own writing. Yet, following Catullus' practice, they refer to themselves by their own names.[10]

If indeed the female *inamoratae* who memorably figure in their love elegies were actual rather than fictitious women, these male elegists—Tibullus, Propertius, and Ovid most prominent among them—presumably masked these women's, but not their own, real-life identities owing to the illicit nature of their liaisons: to "protect" these women's reputations in a repressive patriarchal society whose laws granted men much, and women no, sexual freedom. Sulpicia's willingness to acknowledge, and explore facets of her love affair with a man not, and never likely to become, her husband is unusual in this literary and sociocultural context. So is Sulpicia's own reversal of gender norms, inasmuch as she engages in this same literary practice herself, by using a literally allusive pseudonym, "Cerinthus", to hide the actual identity of her own young illicit, male lover. Her name for him would seem to play on the Greek and Latin words for "wax", the physical substance on which love poems were physically inscribed.[11]

Nevertheless, we only have access to the eleven Sulpicia-elegies because they are preserved in manuscripts of poems dating from the early modern period which are attributed to her male contemporary Tibullus, and organized into three successive "poetry books". Other than the Sulpicia-elegies, these manuscripts only contain the work of male Latin poets: Tibullus himself in Books One and Two, other men in Book Three.[12] Ancient sources attest that both Tibullus and Ovid belonged to a literary circle fostered by Sulpicia's maternal uncle and legal guardian, the influential military and political leader Marcus Valerius Messalla Corvinus, one of Augustus' close associates. The inclusion of the eleven Sulpicia-elegies in these manuscripts of Tibullus, as well as literary affinities between her poems and those of Ovid and Tibullus, among them evocations of Catullus' poems, would suggest that this circle included Sulpicia herself too.[13]

It has been argued that Ovid himself evokes the Sulpicia-elegies in his own poetry: an elegy in the third book of his *Amores*; his narratives about the Babylonian lovers Pyramus and Thisbe in the fourth book, and about the artist Pygmalion in the tenth, of his mythic epic *Metamorphoses*.[14] But no other written text from classical antiquity directly quotes Sulpicia's words, much less identifies all or even some of the eleven elegies in Tibullus, Book Three, as her poetry. Indeed, no ancient Roman (or Greek) source other than the eleven elegies in Tibullus, Book Three, ever mentions her. We can extrapolate when she lived and wrote from information about her family members, furnished by a variety of ancient sources, but there is no evidence directly attesting to her existence, much less providing biographical details about her.[15] In this regard, she contrasts sharply with Sappho, to whose work—and life—later Greek and Roman writers frequently refer and, as we have observed, whose lyrics they also both quote and evoke.

There is, however, another of Sulpicia's poems warranting close scrutiny: an eight-line funerary inscription written in Sulpicia's characteristic elegiac meter, datable by its language and spelling to around 20 BCE, when Sulpicia appears to have written her erotic elegies. Unearthed in Rome and recorded in an archaeological publication by an Italian archaeologist named Paolino Mingazzini in 1926, it was identified as Sulpicia's writing by a French classical scholar, Jerome Carcopino, three years later. This inscription commemorates a 34-year-old Greek slave woman who worked as a *lectrix*, female reader, and performer of literary texts, named Petale.[16]

An elaborate pun on the name Sulpicia in the opening lines of this inscription identifies Sulpicia as its author, and indicates that Petale was enslaved by Sulpicia's noble and wealthy family, and given the Latin name Sulpicia Petale in addition to free status when she died. The language of the inscription pointedly evokes the "Distaff", a celebrated poem by the 4th-century BCE Greek female poet Erinna. Here Erinna laments the death of her beloved female friend Baucis, depicting the quintessential female activity of spinning wool to emotionally moving effect. Petale's literary performances for Sulpicia's household, and instruction of Sulpicia herself in Greek and Latin poetry, would help to account not only for Sulpicia's own familiarity with Erinna's poem, but also with Greek and Roman authors such as Homer and Sappho, Vergil, Horace, and Catullus, echoed in the eleven Sulpicia elegies.[17]

Sulpicia's family was also likely to have benefited from the labors of enslaved men who read and performed literary texts, *lectores*, along with this female *lectrix*. Together these male and female slaves would have provided her with the hands-on literary education that equipped her to write verses of funerary commemoration for slave and freed household staffers as well as erotic elegiac poems. But however these slave-instructors divided their labors, this testimony to the existence of a woman poetic expert, whose teaching helped preserve Erinna's and Sappho's words through Sulpicia's writing, deserves recognition.

Not all of the labors exerted, not all of the lenses applied, by men of both classical and later times in preserving ancient women's writings have helped modern-day readers appreciate, or even clearly comprehend, the distinctive linguistic and stylistic strengths, or the sheer emotional power, of the words written by ancient women. For centuries, moreover, male lenses on female writers were dimmed by a failure to understand, and an outright resistance to accept, the sexual scenarios apparently represented in women's texts: in Sappho's case, her emotional attraction to other women; in the case of the aristocratic Sulpicia, her proud involvement, despite a series of major obstacles, in an illicit sexual liaison with a younger male lover. The labors and lenses of the renowned Roman poet Ovid, notwithstanding his membership in Sulpicia's own literary circle, and his professed indebtedness to her uncle Messalla, pose problems of their own for those endeavoring to recover and assess Sulpicia's writing. Ovid adored and identified himself with Sappho, striving to outdo her most eminent Roman literary admirers, Catullus and Horace, in paying her homage. It may be for this reason that he never mentions Sulpicia by name, and only evoked her poetry to criticize and erase it, thereby strengthening his claims over hers to be Sappho's Roman literary heir.[18]

But the labors of modern male scholars to preserve, and explicate, the Sulpicia elegies have shortchanged her poetry too. Most obviously, they have successfully hypothesized that the first five of the eleven Sulpicia elegies are actually the work of a male impersonator, whom they label "the Garland Poet" and "Sulpicia's *amicus*, male friend," on several grounds: that three of the first five poems are not written in the first person; that these five poems are longer and more learned than the second six; and that the first five treat the same themes as the second six, but in a more literarily sophisticated fashion. The conjecture that Sulpicia herself did not compose the first five of these elegies has gained wide acceptance, from female and male scholars alike.[19]

Since no ancient commentator on Sulpicia's poems has been preserved, there is little resistance voiced to this conjecture that attributes those five elegies to a male, on assumptions that can be easily refuted. Less successful, but perhaps not surprising, are more recent efforts to deny that Sulpicia wrote any of the eleven elegies in Tibullus Book 3.[20] While I believe that Sulpicia wrote all eleven of these elegies, and have marshaled a large body of evidence to support my beliefs in a series of publications, I here accommodate the current consensus by referring to "the eleven Sulpicia" elegies—rather than "Sulpicia's elegies"—whenever possible, and avoiding references to her as "author" of the first five.

The scholars responsible for recovering Sappho's heretofore lost writings in modern times—by acquiring, interpreting, and publishing papyrus fragments of her poetry—have for the most part been men. A notable exception is the Italian papyrologist Medea Norsa, who lived from 1877 through 1952. She not only managed to survive the near-extermination of her fellow Jews under Mussolini but also, despite the anti-semitic attacks on her and her work under Italian fascism, hung on as conservator of the papyrus collection at the University of Florence from 1935 through 1949. We are indebted to Norsa for recognizing and publishing a fragment of Sappho subsequently labeled poem 2 L-P, in 1937, the year before Mussolini promulgated his "racial laws" to enforce discrimination against Italian Jews and the native inhabitants of Italian colonies abroad. Discovered on a 3rd-century BCE potsherd, Sappho 2 L-P represents, in sensuous detail, the poet-speaker as summoning Aphrodite to join her and her companions at a temple in an apple grove.[21]

The 1928 discovery, at Oxyrhynchus in Egypt, of a papyrus fragment containing 54 previously unknown lines of Erinna's "Distaff", transformed the study of both that poem and Erinna as a poet. Among the other papyri found at the excavations at Oxyrhynchus, led by two British male scholars, Bernard Grenfell of Oxford University and Arthur Hunt, were fragments by Sappho—discovered in 1897 and 1906—and by another Greek woman poet, Corinna.[22] While women scholars do not appear to have played much if any of a role in originally interpreting and publishing these Oxyrhynchus papyri containing female-authored texts, over the past several decades several female classicists have contributed new and valuable insights to their illumination.[23]

The discovery in 2014 of what have been identified as four new fragments from the same Sappho papyrus by Dirk Obbink, an American scholar based at Oxford University has caused a stir among classics scholars worldwide, by raising questions about the circumstances of where and how this papyrus itself was acquired, and about the accessibility to scholars of this papyrus text itself.[24] Unlike most of Sappho's preserved writings, these lyrics do not adopt her characteristically female-centered perspective, her intense focus on her own and other women's emotional experiences as lovers and brides savoring the beauties of nature. Rather, they depict her as dispensing political advice to her two brothers, performing as an unofficial consultant behind the scenes in male-dominated social territory.

The efforts of this particular scholar to construct a different, nonerotic and indeed non-homoerotic, androcentric, and familial setting for Sappho's utterances prompt legitimate concerns about the agendas of earlier male scholars who published Sappho papyri, and hence aided in preserving her writing. Sir Denys Page, for example, tried to problematize Sappho's expressions of homoerotic passion by claiming there was very little evidence of her engagement in physical sexual activity with other women, a different matter entirely. To this end he cited, only to dismiss as irrelevant, a word in one of the Sappho-papyri that may refer to a dildo: a "sex toy" shaped like the male organ.[25] While ancient sources attest that women accustomed to being penetrated by males in three different orifices were thought to make avid use of such technological implements, this evidence does not suggest the popularity, even the utilization, of dildos among women seeking to obtain erotic gratification from other women.

It goes without saying that women have not enjoyed the opportunities to preserve and interpret the writings by ancient women that have historically been afforded to men. We have no testimony about women in classical antiquity who wrote—and were published—as literary authorities on poetry composed by women. Or about women in subsequent eras who were tasked with producing, and determining the contents of, literary manuscripts as scribes and manuscript editors. In modern times, until a few decades ago, only a few women classical scholars were able to participate in such research projects as excavating for papyri, and interpreting, editing, and publishing papyrological findings. Consequently, the preservation of ancient women's writings, and the lenses applied to these writings, by women differ from male labors, and male perspectives, in this regard.

Nevertheless, while female classical scholars have only begun to join Medea Norsa by assuming leadership roles in the discovery and authentication of papyri containing literary works by women, they have spoken up and spoken out in regard to concerns about the new "Brothers" and "Kypris" papyrus identified as Sappho's writing.[26] In recent years women have also figured prominently in the publication and interpretation of non-literary papyri recording women's voices from ancient times.[27] As we have observed, Sulpicia's poems—both the Petale inscription and the eleven Sulpicia-elegies—seemingly allude to earlier writings by women, specifically by Erinna and Sappho, even if Sulpicia does not quote them directly; her *lectrix* Petale presumably contributed to Sappho's and Erinna's preservation by reciting their verses to Sulpicia. Two British female scholars—Jane Stevenson and Janet Fairweather—deserve particular commendation for directing renewed attention to the Petale inscription in a magisterial 2005 volume on women writing in Latin. The inscription had been neglected by scholars investigating and re-evaluating Sulpicia's poetry for 75 years, perhaps because Carcopino's service as a high-ranking official in the Nazi-controlled Vichy government clouded his scholarly reputation thereafter. Sadly, soon after 2000, the Petale inscription mysteriously disappeared from the courtyard of the elegant Roman apartment building where it had been displayed for decades; fortunately, epigraphic scholars had photographed and recorded its text for posterity before it vanished.[28]

Several female classicists who have translated ancient women's writings in the past few years—Josephine Balmer, Anne Carson, and Diane Rayor come immediately to mind—have earned accolades for providing English renderings that do literary justice to these women's texts.[29] So have a great many women classical scholars who have analyzed these writings from the standpoint of literary and new historicist criticism, by drawing on contemporary feminist and other relevant interpretive theories as well as deep philological and literary historical learning.[30] From a sociohistorical standpoint, these women scholars have illuminated, and strengthened the arguments in favor of accepting, the "transgressive sexual scenarios" associated with Sappho and Sulpicia.

Some of the most insightful literary critics on ancient women's writing are themselves lovers of other women, and thereby able to provide a significant new vantage point—not only in regard to Sappho's representations of love, but also as scholars unheeded and marginalized by those locked into heteronormative perspectives—when interpreting texts about women's homoerotic feelings.[31] But others who do not fall into this category enrich the conversations about these women writers by sharing perceptions derived from studying, and often living, in all-female learning environments, among them secondary schools, colleges, and universities led by women.[32] They offer different, distinctly female lenses, of special value in reassessing what these ancient women's voices have to say to subsequent ages.

## Notes

1. The fifteen Greek and Roman women writers chosen for inclusion in this volume, all of them poets, represent only a fraction of those whose work has been preserved: the anthology of Plante (2004) includes 55 female authors, writers of both poetry and prose; see also the list of Robinson (2019).
2. For Sappho, see, for example, Campbell (1967) 260–285; Hallett (1979); Snyder (1989); DuBois (1995); Most (1996); Rayor and Lardinois (2014) 1–17; and Balmer (2017).
3. For Sulpicia, see, for example, Hallett (2002a), (2002b), (2009a), (2009b), (2010), and (2011); Skoie (2002).
4. Lobel and Page (1955); recent scholars such as Rayor and Lardinois (2014) 151–154, however, often rely on the later texts of Campbell (1967) and Voigt (1971).
5. See, e.g., Campbell (1967) 264–266; Snyder (1997) 7–25; and Rayor and Lardinois (2014) 97–98.
6. See, e.g., Campbell (1967) 271–273; Snyder (1997) 28–44; and Rayor and Lardinois (2014) 108–109.
7. See Campbell (1967) 271 and Prins (1996) 48–53.
8. See O'Higgins (1996); Snyder (1997) 33–38, discussing how Catullus' adaptation of this fragment influenced later interpretations; Hallett (2012) 270–271; and Skinner (2011).
9. See Keith (1997); Hallett (2002a), 2002b(), 2006(), and 2009b(); and Merriam (2006).
10. See Hallett (2012) 270–272 and Fulkerson (2017) 25–27.
11. For Cerinthus see Roessel (1990); Hallett (2009b); and Dickison and Hallett (2015) 108–111 on the use of the name Cerinthus by Horace in *Satires* 1.2; Fulkerson (2017) 30–32.
12. See Fulkerson (2017) 58–59.
13. See Hallett (2010) and (2011); Fulkerson (2017) 27–33.
14. See Hallett (2009b), (2009c), and (2009d).
15. See Hallett (2011) and Fulkerson (2017) 46–53.

16. See Mingazzini (1926); Carcopino (1929); Stevenson (2005) 43–44; Hallett (2009a) and (2010); Dickison and Hallett (2015) 122–126; and Fulkerson (2017) 43 n. 93.
17. See Stevenson (2005) 43–44 and Hallett (2009a) and (2010).
18. So Hallett (2012) 283.
19. On this issue, see, for example, Parker (1994); Hallett (2002a); Skoie (2002); and Fulkerson (2017) 42–43. For a refutation applying the same criteria to Catullus' poems that are used for Sulpicia's, see Parker (2006).
20. See Holzberg (1999); Hubbard (2004-2005); and Hallett (2006b).
21. For Norsa, see Campbell (1967) 268 and Balmer (2017).
22. For Erinna, see Balmer (2012) and, for Corinna, see Campbell (1967) 408–413.
23. The work of Eva-Maria Voigt on Sappho (1971) merits special attention. In the case of Erinna, one might cite Dame Averil Cameron (1969); Marylin Arthur (Katz) (1980); Marilyn Skinner (1982); and Jane Snyder (1989); in that of Corinna, Skinner (1983).
24. Obbink (2016); in 2021, Brill, publisher of the volume in which this chapter appeared—Bierl and Lardinois (2016)—informed its readers that the chapter had been retracted, and supported a statement by the volume's editors. In it, they noted that serious doubts have been raised about the provenance of the papyrus, that Obbink has not responded to questions about the provenance, and that the papyrus itself is inaccessible. For a discussion of the Brothers song and the Kypris song—the lyrics found on the papyrus fragments—see Rayor and Lardinois (2014) 155–163.
25. Page (1955) 144; see the discussion of this word, *olisbos* (which can also mean a type of lyre, Sappho's musical instrument) in Hallett (1979), Snyder (1997) 115 and Power (2017); for the absence of references to dildos in Roman representations of female same-sex erotic behavior, see Hallett (1997).
26. Women occupying leadership positions in the field of papyrology include the immediate past president of the American Society of Papyrologists, Jennifer Sheridan Moss, and AnneMarie Luijendijk, who organized a 2014 ASP summer institute at Princeton University. Among the scholars who contributed interpretive essays about the "Brothers" papyrus when it first appeared are Rayor in Rayor and Lardinois (2014) 155–164; Boedeker (2016); and Mueller (2016). Among those who subsequently raised questions about they were Sampson and Uhlig (2019).
27. Ann Ellis Hanson, Rafaella Cribiore and Sarah Pomeroy are particularly noteworthy in this regard.
28. Fairweather, who is an impressive classical scholar in her own right, worked as the research assistant for Stevenson (2005). On Carcopino, see Hallett (2009a) and (2010).
29. See Balmer (2017); Carson (2003); Rayor (1991) and (with Lardinois) (2014).
30. Along with the 16 women scholars whose pathbreaking essays are anthologized in the two 1996 Green volumes on Sappho, DuBois and Snyder merit special attention for their pioneering books—those by DuBois (1995) and Snyder (1997) about Sappho, Snyder (1989) about Greek and Roman women poets—in the final three decades of the 20th century. Over the past 25 years, male classical scholars have predominated among those publishing about Sappho, a development warranting serious reflection, since this is not the case with scholarship on Sulpicia and Roman female writers, most of which have been written by women.
31. Most notably Snyder (1989) and (1997); Williamson (1995); and Stehle (1996).
32. Among them are Arthur (Katz), Boedeker, Hallett, Lefkowitz, and Snyder, who attended all-women's secondary schools or colleges (and in some instances both).

## Select Bibliography


Arthur, M. B. (= Marilyn Arthur Katz). 1980. "The Tortoise and the Mirror: Erinna PSI 109," *Classical World* 74: 53–65.

Balmer, J. 2012. "Translating Fragments II: Erinna's Distaff": https://thepathsofsurvivalwordpress.com/2012/10/05/translating-fragments-ii-erinnas-distaff. transl. 2018. *Sappho: Poems and Fragments New Expanded Edition*. South Park, Hexham: Bloodaxe Books.

———. 2017. *The Paths of Survival*. Emersons Green, Bristol: Shearman Books.

Bierl, A. and A. Lardinois (eds.). 2016. *The Newest Sappho: P. Sapph. Obbink and P. GC inv.105, Frs. 1-4*. Mnemosyne Supplements Vol. 392, Studies in Archaic and Classical Greek Song, Vol.2, Leiden: Brill.

Boedeker, D. 2016. "Hera and the Return of Charaxos," in *Bierl and Lardinois*: 188–207.

Cameron, A. and A. Cameron. 1969. "Erinna's Distaff," *The Classical Quarterly* 10.2: 285–288.

Campbell, D. 1967. *Greek Lyric Poetry: A Selection of Early Greek, Lyric, Elegiac and Iambic Poetry*. New York, NY: St. Martin's.

Carcopino, J. 1929. "Séance du 30 Janvier," in *Bulletin de la Societe Nationale des Antiquaires de France*. Paris: 84–86.

Carson, A. 2003. *If Not, Winter: Fragments of Sappho*. New York, NY: Knopf Doubleday.

Churchill, L., P. Brown, and J. Jeffrey (eds.). 2002. *Women Writing Latin from Roman Antiquity to Early Modern Europe 1: Women Writing Latin in Roman Antiquity, Late Antiquity and the Early Christian Era*. New York, NY and London: Routledge.

Dickison, S. K. and J. P. Hallett. 2015. *A Roman Woman Reader: Selections from the Second Century BCE through the Second Century CE*. Wauconda, IL: Bolchazy-Carducci.

DuBois, P. 1995. *Sappho is Burning*. Chicago, IL: University of Chicago Press.

Fulkerson, L. 2017. *A Literary Commentary on the Elegies of the Appendix Tibulliana*. Oxford: Oxford University Press.

Greene, E. (ed.). 1996a. *Reading Sappho: Contemporary Approaches*. Berkeley, Los Angeles and London: University of California Press.

———. 1996b. *Re-Reading Sappho: Reflection and Transmission*. Berkeley, Los Angeles and London: University of California Press.

Hallett, J. P. 1979. "Sappho and Her Social Context: Sense and Sensuality," *Signs* 4:447–464.

———. 1997. "Female Homoeroticism and the Denial of Roman Reality," in Hallett and Skinner (eds.), p. 255–273.

———. 2002a. "The Eleven Elegies of the Augustan Elegist Sulpicia," in Churchill, Brown and Jeffrey (eds.), p. 45–46.

———. 2002b. "Sulpicia and the Valerii: Family Ties and Poetic Unity," in Henrik Fich, Gorm Tortzen, Pernille Flensted-Jensen, Adam Schwartz and Thomas Heine (eds.). *Noctes Atticae: 34 Articles on Graeco-Roman Antiquity and its Nachleben. Studies Presented to Jorgen Mejer on His Sixtieth Birthday, March 18, 2002*. Copenhagen, p. 141–149.

———. 2006. "Sulpicia and Her *fama*; An Intertextual Approach to Recovering Her Latin Literary Image," *Classical World* 100.1: 37–42.

———. 2009a. "Absent Roman Fathers in the Writings of Their Daughters: Cornelia and Sulpicia," in S. Huebner and D. M. Ratzan (eds.). *Growing Up Fatherless in Antiquity. Cambridge*, p. 175–191.

———. 2009b. "Sulpicia and Her Resistant Intertextuality," in Danielle van Mal-Maeder, Alexandre Burnier, and Loreto Nunez (eds.). *Jeux de Voix: Enonciation, intertextualite et intentionnalite dans la literature antique*. Special issue of *Echo. Collection de L'Institute d'Archaeologie et de Sciences de l'antiquite de l'Universite de Lausanne*, p. 141–155.

———. 2009c. "Ovid's This Be and a Roman Woman Love Poet," in Barbara W. Boyd and Cora Fox (eds.). *Approaches to Teaching the Works of Ovid and the Ovidian Tradition*. Approaches to Teaching World Literature, Modern Language Association, p. 170–177.

———. 2009d. "*Corpus Erat*: Sulpicia's Elegiac Text and Body in Ovid's Pygmalion Narrative (*Metamorphoses* 10.238-297)," in Thorsten Foegen and Mireille Lee (eds.). *Bodies and Boundaries in Graeco-Roman Antiquity*. Berlin and New York, NY: DeGruyter, p. 111–124.

———. 2010. "Human Connection and Paternal Evocations: Two Elite Roman Women Writers and the Valuing of Others," in Ralph Rosen and Ineke Sluiter (eds.). *Valuing Others in Classical Antiquity*. Leiden, p. 353–373.

———. 2011. "Recovering Sulpicia: The Value and Limitations of Prosopography and Intertextuality," in Jan Nelis (ed.). *Receptions of Antiquity*. Ghent, p. 297–311.

———. 2012. "Authorial Identity in Latin Love Elegy: Literary Fictions and Erotic Failings," in Barbara K. Gold (ed.). *A Companion to Roman Love Elegy*. Malden, Oxford and Chichester: Wiley-Blackwell, p. 269–284.

Hallett, J. P. and M. B. Skinner. 1997. *Roman Sexualities*. Princeton, NJ: Princeton University Press.

Holzberg, N. 1999. "Four Poets and a Poetess or Portrait of the Poet as a Young Man? Thoughts on Book 3 of the *Corpus Tibullianum*," *Classical Journal* 94: 169–191.

Hubbard, T. 2004–2005. "The Invention of Sulpicia," *Classical Journal* 100.2: 177–194.

Keith, A. 1997. "*Tandem Venit Amor:* A Roman Woman Speaks of Love," in Hallett and Skinner (eds.), p. 295–310.

Lefkowitz, M. 1973. "Critical Stereotypes and the Poetry of Sappho," in Greene (ed.). *Reading Sappho*, p. 26–34.

Lobel, E. and D. L. Page. 1955. *Poetarum Lesbiorum Fragmenta*. Oxford: Clarendon Press.

Merriam, C. 2006. "Sulpicia: Just Another Roman Poet," *Classical World* 100.1: 11–15.

Mingazzini, P. 1926. "Iscrizioni urbane inedite," *Bulletino della Commissione Archeologia Communale di Roma* 53: 229–230.

Most, G. 1996. "Reflecting Sappho," in Greene (ed.). *Re-Reading Sappho*, p. 11–35.

Mueller, M. 2016. "Recentering Epic Nostos: Gender and Genre in Sappho's Brothers Poem," *Arethusa* 49: 25–46.

Obbink, D. 2016. "Ten Poems of Sappho: Provenance, Authenticity, and Text of the New Sappho Papyri," in Bierl and Lardinois (eds.). p. 34–54. Retracted by publisher, 2021.

O'Higgins, D. 1996. "Sappho's Splintered Tongue: Silence in Sappho 31 and Catullus 51," in Greene (ed.). *Re-Reading Sappho*, p. 68–78.

Page, D. L. 1955. *Sappho and Alcaeus: An Introduction to the Study of Lesbian Poetry*. Oxford: Clarendon Press.

Parker, H. N. 1994. "Sulpicia, the *Auctor de Sulpicia*, and the Authorship of 3.9 and 3.11," *Helios* 21: 39–62.

———. 2006. "Catullus and the '*Amicus Catulli*': The Text of a Learned Talk," *Classical World* 100: 17–29.

Plante, I. 2004. *Women Writers of Ancient Greece and Rome: An Anthology*. Norman, OK: University of Oklahoma Press.

Power, T. 2017. "Lyric Indecorum in Archaic Mytilene (and Beyond): Sappho F 99 c.1-9 L-P=Alcaeus F 303Aa V," *Turkish Journal of Archaeology* https://dergipark.org.tr/dowload/article-file/429365

Prins, Y. 1996. "Sappho's Afterlife in Translation," in Greene (ed.). *Re-Reading Sappho*, p. 36–67.

Rayor, D. 1991. *Sappho's Lyre: Archaic Lyric and Women Poets of Ancient Greece*. Berkeley, CA: University of California Press.

Rayor, D. and A. Lardinois. 2014. *Sappho: A New Translation of the Complete Works*. Cambridge: Cambridge University Press.

Robinson, E. 2019. "A List of Women Authors from the Ancient World," https://sententiaeantiquae.com/2019/03/08/a-list-of-women-authors-from-the-ancient-world-2/

Roessel, D. 1990. "The Significance of the Name Cerinthus in the Poems of Sulpicia," *Transactions of the American Philological Association* 120: 234–250.

Sampson, C. M. and A. Uhlig. 2019. "The Murky Provenance of the Newest Sappho," *Eidolon*: https://eidolon.pub/the-murky-provenance-of-the-newest-sappho-aca671a6d52a

Skinner, M. 1982. "Briseis, the Trojan Women and Erinna," *Classical World* 75.5: 265–269.

———. 1983. "Corinna of Tanagra and Her Audience," *Tulsa Studies in Women's Literature* 2: 9–20.

———. 2011. *Clodia Metelli: The Tribune's Sister*. Oxford: Oxford University Press.

Skoie, M. 2002. *Reading Sulpicia. Commentaries 1475–1990*. Oxford: Oxford University Press.

Snyder, J. M. 1989. *The Woman and the Lyre. Women Writers in Classical Greece and Rome*. Carbondale, IL: Southern Illinois University Press.

———. 1997. *Lesbian Desire in the Lyrics of Sappho*. New York, NY: Columbia University Press.

Stehle, E. 1996. "Sappho's Gaze: Fantasies of a Goddess and Young Man," in Greene (ed.). *Reading Sappho*, p. 193–225.

Stevenson, J. 2005. *Women Latin Poets: Language, Gender and Authority from Antiquity to the Eighteenth Century*. Oxford: Oxford University Press.

Voigt, E. M. 1971. *Fragmente von Sappho und Alkaios*. Amsterdam: Athenaeum-Polak and Van Gennep.

Williamson, M. 1995. *Sappho's Immortal Daughters*. Cambridge, Massachusetts and London: Harvard University Press.

# Part I

# Greece

# 1 Sappho

None of the women writers of the Greco-Roman world rivaled Sappho's reputation as a poet. That reputation enjoyed extraordinary longevity.[1] Epigrammatists from the Hellenistic period onward called her the "tenth Muse", "a mortal Muse", the "female Homer", and her songs "the daughters of the immortal gods."[2] A story preserved by a 5th-century CE writer is representative not only for what it says about Sappho's reputation, but also for the tenuousness of the story's reliability, mediated as it is through layers of sources that clearly drew from apocryphal myth and legend. The story, recorded by the 5th-century CE Stobaeus, who, in turn, attributed the tale to the 2nd- and 3rd-centuries CE writer Aelian, who, in turn, derived it from an unknown source or sources, placed the 6th-century BCE Athenian law-giver and poet Solon at a drinking party. At this symposium, Solon is said to have heard his nephew sing a certain song of Sappho's. Solon then asked his nephew to teach that song to him. When another guest asked Solon why he would want to learn it, Solon is said to have replied: "So that once I have learned it, I may die."[3] Although this story is certainly favorable toward Sappho, its historicity is highly suspect. What it does reveal about Sappho is the degree to which her lyric compositions were, for centuries, hailed by the *cognoscenti* of the Greco-Roman world as worthy of reverence.[4]

We know very little about Sappho's life with any degree of certainty, but a rich biographical tradition about her arose in antiquity, some of which was no doubt inspired by her poetry. It is probably wise to hold many of the accounts of her life in suspicion, as they often appear to be mediated through unreliable sources, including comedies, in which caricatures, stock characters, and formulaic plot-sequences offered up distortions to generate humor and laughter. Sappho's image appears on several 5th-century Attic vases; and, we know that she was the subject of comic plays in the era of that great comic playwright, Aristophanes. These comedies no doubt provided distorted representations of Sappho—of her poetry and her life—for comic effect.[5] Comedies entitled *Sappho* were authored by the 5th- and 4th-centuries writers Amipsias, Amphis, Antiphanes, Ephippus, Diphilus, Cratinas, and Timocles, and what little we know about these plays generally

DOI: 10.4324/9781003031727-3

comes to us through the 2nd and 3rd- centuries CE writer Athenaeus, who reports, for example, that the comedy by Diphilus represented the lyric and invective poets Archilochus and Hipponax as the lovers of Sappho.[6]

We do not know the exact dates of Sappho's birth and death, but a variety of ancient sources agree that she lived during the late-7th to early 6th-centuries BCE.[7] Sappho mentions Mytilene in her own poetry, and a late-2nd or early-3rd century CE papyrus states that she was born on the island of Lesbos in the city of Mytilene, a city which Strabo called the "metropolis of the Aeolian cities" and cited as being situated 60 stades from the coast of Asia Minor.[8] Mytilene was certainly close enough to the opulent trading hub of Sardis in Lydia, which may, in part, account for the richness of sensorial imagery in Sappho's poems—the incense, golden drinking cups, highly wrought headbands, purple robes, and so forth—that evoke a synaesthetic and luxurious environment. Like many Greek cities in the archaic era, Mytilene experienced great political turmoil arising from conflict between rivaling aristocratic families and their supporters and the tyrants who emerged from those families, such as Pittacus, Myrsilus, and the Cleanactidae (the sons of Cleanax). The poetry of her Lesbian contemporary, Alcaeus, heavily critiques both Pittacus and Myrsilus, and Sappho refers to the "reminders of the exile of the Cleanactidae" in a very fragmentary poem in which she laments that she is not able to supply Cleïs (whom she references in another poem as her *pais*, which can mean either "young girl" or "daughter" in ancient Greek) with a delicately crafted headband, even though a girl with beautiful hair more blonde than a torch-fire ought to have such luxuries.[9]

The chronographical Parian Marble, a monumental inscription dating from sometime *post* 264–263 BCE, claims that Sappho was exiled from Mytilene to Sicily, while Critius the Elder was Archon at Athens (just before 595–594 BCE).[10] It is, however, helpful to keep in mind that the Parian Marble also provides rather precise dating for what we would consider mythical persons and events, such as the rule of Cecrops, Athens's first king, the life of Theseus, the Amazonomachy, and the Trojan War. A much later source (either Ovid or an anonymous imitator of Ovid) veers quite steeply into fiction by imagining an exiled Sappho who spurns the young women she had previously loved out of unrequited passion for the mythical ferryman, Phaon. Rejected by him, this source claims, she committed suicide by hurling herself from a legendary White Rock that has been shown to have mythic connections to the Underworld.[11] Imaginings of her life, her loves, and her death have inspired millennia of poems, plays, novels, operas, and works of art, and she has been represented as a literary genius, a prostitute, a Muse, a schoolmistress, a leader of a religious cult, a seducer of women, the world's eponymous lesbian, and a morose suicidal.[12] That tradition is still going strong. Erica Jong's bawdy (2003) novel, *Sappho's Leap*, depicts a Sappho who is seduced by the poet Alcaeus, becomes involved in political intrigue on Lesbos, is married off to an old man, and leaves Lesbos to embark upon a series of casual, raunchy, amorous adventures with women and men as she journeys throughout the Mediterranean world.

Of Sappho's *actual* life, very little is known. As we noted above, Sappho's poetry twice mentions a young girl and (possibly) daughter, Cleïs, as well as two brothers, Larichos and Charaxos.[13] A variety of ancient sources as early as Herodotus claim that Charaxos, a brother of Sappho, went to Egypt as a wine merchant, where he fell in love with a *hetaira* named Rhodopis or Doricha,[14] and that he spent lavishly to purchase her freedom before returning to Mytilene. Herodotus claims that Sappho rebuked him soundly in her lyric poetry for these actions.[15] Indeed, both brothers are mentioned by name in a papyrus published by the papyrologist Dirk Obbink in 2014. Obbink himself, who claimed that he had gained access to and permission to publish the poem through an anonymous owner of a private collection in London, dubbed the papyrus "P.Sapph.Obbink".[16] The poem's provenance, as well as Obbink's alleged and, if true, profound breaches of professional ethics, has since come under intense international scrutiny.[17] The poem itself, however, at the time of this publication, has not proved to be inauthentic. In it an unnamed speaker—perhaps Sappho herself or a literary version of Sappho—gently chides Larichos for fretting over the expected arrival by sea of Charaxos. One scholar, at least, has rightly urged caution in reading this (or any) poem of Sappho's as autobiographical, since the first-person voice and the expression of "personal" subjectivity are generic hallmarks of lyric poetry, and because in her poetry, Sappho likely presents "a fictionalized self".[18]

Sappho's poems were arranged by Alexandrian scholars into either eight or nine books, possibly according to their meter, in contrast to their organizations of other poets' works (such as those of Bacchylides or Pindar), which were arranged according to occasional context or genre.[19] We know that two of these books consisted of *epithalamia*, or marriage hymns, which may have been composed for choruses. In addition to monodies, that is, songs meant to be sung by a single (rather than a choral) voice to the accompaniment of the lyre (hence, "lyric poetry"), the Byzantine *Suda* encyclopedia claims that Sappho also wrote epigrams, elegies, and iambics, and in the Hellenistic period, at least two epigrams were ascribed to her.[20] Sappho was said to have invented the so-called Sapphic stanza, and the first book of her poetry in the Alexandrian edition (or editions) is known to have consisted of 330 such stanzas, for a total of 1320 lines.[21] She was also credited with the invention of one of the seven principal modes (a mode being an ordered sequence of intervals of tone) of ancient Greek music, the *Mixolydian*, which was characterized by Plato as melancholic. Plato's Socrates suggested banning it (along with all the other modes, save for Dorian and Phrygian) from a utopian *Republic*, since it was the mode most closely associated with plaintive lamentation and dirges.[22] Sappho was both composer and singer, and her poetry would have been passed on orally in both private and public performances long before it was recorded textually.[23] Whether or not

Sappho's music was melancholic is, perhaps, indeterminable, but it was considered to be highly emotive. When reading the text of Sappho's poetry, it is easy to forget that it would have been accompanied by music; we who *read* Sappho's works as *poetry* in the 21st century are bereft of a fair portion of the aesthetic experience of her work.

Much of her poetry is highly allusive to Homeric poetry and the epic tradition. But, whereas epic poetry relates legendary stories of heroes from the mythic past from the perspective of an omniscient, third-person narrator whose voice seldom intrudes into the poem, Sappho's lyric poems allude to such myths to voice interpersonal motives, feelings, experiences, and emotions from one person to another from the subjective perspective of a first-person narrator. References to mythic figures (such as Tithonus, Helen of Troy, and Hector and Andromache) tend to serve as foils or exempla for the personal experiences of the narrator. The name of "Sappho" appears four times, each time in a vocative form of direct address, and each time in the context of dialogue imagined within the poem.[24] Although Sappho names herself in her poetry (in Sappho 1, for example), it is probably wise to view both the first-person voice and the self-naming as evocations of a poetic *persona* that may very well elide fiction, personal (i.e., autobiographic) experience, and the common experiences of women of the upper classes on Lesbos (such as sisters, daughters, wives, and mothers awaiting the homecoming of men at sea, and the sensorial experiences of women involved in erotic and interpersonal relationships, weddings, and religious festivals).[25] In the vast majority of the erotic fragments that have come down to us, a female narrator speaking in first person addresses or identifies another female, sometimes by name, as the object of erotic desire.

Most of what survives of Sappho's songs have come down to us in tantalizing fragments principally through three means: (1) either preserved by other ancient authors who quote her poetry in their own treatises; or, (2) inscribed on Egyptian papyri found by archaeologists both in a trash heap at a site in Egypt called Oxyrhynchus and in the cartonnage (papyrus that was recycled to form a plaster-like wrapping) of Egyptian mummies; or, (3) inscribed on a potsherd found in Egypt and discovered by the Italian papyrologist Medea Norsa (Sappho fr. 2 Voigt). Sophisticated and multispectral imaging and scanning technologies have recently enabled papyrologists to access writings on papyri that are too fragile to handle.

The newest papyrus finds of Sappho, published in 2016 in *The Newest Sappho: P. Saph. Obbink and P. GC inv. 105, Frs. 1–4*, edited by Anton Bierl and André Lardinois (Leiden: Brill), have been mired in controversy and international scandal due to claims of uncertain provenance and questions about the authenticity of the poems published therein. We have placed these poems in Appendix C, along with a summary of the controversies, relevant bibliography about the poems in light of their uncertain provenance, the Greek texts in question, and supplemental grammar and vocabulary notes to assist readers who wish to study them.

While Sappho's poems would have been consulted whole and complete in the libraries of the ancient Mediterranean (including the famous library at Alexandria, Egypt), only two complete poems survive of the approximately 200 surviving fragments that have been attributed to Sappho. There are more surviving fragments of Sappho than any other female poet whose work survives. And, yet, a mere selection of these appears in this volume. We hope that the selections we have provided will give readers the opportunity to be exposed to not only the Sapphic stanzas for which she was so influential, but also the full range of her metrical works. Like any editors of a volume, we have had to make difficult choices, and none of the choices that we have had to make have been as wrenching as choosing between the "immortal daughters" of Sapphic fragments for inclusion here. All of her poems were written in the Aeolic dialect, which some later female poets (like the Roman Julia Balbilla) imitate to communicate their aesthetic and thematic interactions with Sappho's work.[26]

Evidence suggests that direct access to Sappho's poems was probably available until the 4th century CE, when the likes of Himerius and Julian the Apostate, both of whom were pagans, quoted from and paraphrased Sappho's *epithalamia* and appeared to emulate her works directly.[27] After the 4th century CE, however, familiarity with Sappho's works was probably acquired indirectly through handbooks and commentators of other authors, and little evidence can be found for an independent transmission of Sappho's poetry, although the 6th-century CE Byzantine epigrammatist Paulus Silentiarius ludically alluded to her poetry and poetic language.[28] The rise of Christianity may have provided a significant counterweight against its circulation, and some Renaissance scholars even reported through secondhand or thirdhand sources that Pope Gregory VII ordered the burning of Sappho's poetry in 1073 for content that was deemed immoral.

The humanists of the Renaissance rehabilitated Sappho's reputation and once again upheld her as exemplum of classical learning and literary achievement. One striking example may be found within Raphael's 1509 "Parnassus", painted on the interior walls of the *Stanza della Segnatura* in the Vatican Palace opposite the famed "School of Athens". The painting depicts Apollo playing the lyre on Parnassus, the mountain near Delphi sacred to him, surrounded by the nine Muses and by ancient and contemporary poets, including Homer, Dante, Vergil, and Sappho, all engrossed in *sacra conversazione.* Sappho was a popular figure in Neoclassical art, literature, and opera in the 18th century following publications and translations of fragments of her poetry.[29] The painting "Sappho Inspired by Love" which appears on the cover of this volume, for example, by the Swiss artist, Angela Kauffmann, was put on exhibit at the Royal Academy in London in 1775 with the title, "Sappho". In the painting, Cupid, whose quiver lies at his feet, peers over Sappho's left shoulder to gaze upon a composition which the poet holds (along with a stylus) in her right hand. Sappho's head is turned backward to gaze into Cupid's eyes, while she indicates with her left hand the poem's lyrics, which are written in Greek and which obtain from lines 25 to 26 of Sappho fr. 1, translations of which were available in German (Kauffmann's own language) in the early 18th century.

## Select Bibliography

Acosta-Hughes, B. 2010. *Archaic Lyric into Hellenistic Poetry.* Princeton, NJ: Princeton University Press.

Balmer, J. 1992. *Sappho: Poems and Fragments.* Newcastle upon Tyne: Bloodaxe Books.

Bierl, A. and A. Lardinois (ed.). 2019. *The Newest Sappho: P. Sapph. Obbink and P. GC inv. 105, Frs. 1–4: Studies in Archaic and Classical Greek Song, vol. 2.* Leiden: Brill.

Blondell, R. 2010. "Refractions of Homer's Helen in Archaic Lyric," *American Journal of Philology* 131.3: 249–391.

Boehringer, S. 2007. *L'Homosexualité feminine dans l'Antiquité grecque et romaine.* Paris: Les Belles Lettres.

Bowman, L. 2004. "The 'Women's Tradition' in Greek Poetry," *Phoenix* 58, 1/2: 1–27.

Bundy, E. L. 1986. *Studia Pindarica.* Berkeley, CA and LA: University of California Press.

Burris, S., J. Fish and D. Obbink, 2014. "New Fragments of Book 1 of Sappho," *ZPE* 189: 1–28.

Caciagli, S. 2012. "Do the Fragments Lie? Heretic Sappho or Sappho Schoolmistress," *Center for Hellenic Studies Research Bulletin.* https://research-bulletin.chs.harvard.edu/2012/12/21/do-the-fragments-lie-too-heteric-sappho-or-sappho-schoolmistress/

Calame, C. 2001, *Choruses of Young Women in Ancient Greece.* Translated by D. Collins. Lanham, MD: J. Orion.

Campbell, D. A. (ed.). 1967 and 1982. *Greek Lyric Poetry.* Bristol: Bristol Classical Press.

———. 1982. *Greek Lyric: Sappho and Alcaeus. vol. 1.* Loeb Classical Library, 242. Cambridge: Harvard University Press.

Carson, A. 1996. "The Justice of Aphrodite in Sappho 1," in E. Greene (ed.), *Reading Sappho: Contemporary Approaches.* Berkeley, CA: University of California Press, p. 226–232.

———. 1998. "Sappho Shock," in Yopie Prins and M. Shreiber (eds.), *Dwelling in Possibility: Women Poets and Critics on Poetry.* Ithaca, NY: Cornell University Press, p. 223–228.

———. 2003. *If Not, Winter: Fragments of Sappho.* New York, NY: Vintage Books.

D'Angour, A. 2013. "Love's Battlefield: Rethinking Sappho fr. 31," in E. Sanders, C. Thumiger, C. Carey, and N. Lowe (eds.), *Eros in Ancient Greece.* Oxford: Oxford University Press, p. 59–71.

Dale, A. 2011. "Sapphica," *HSCP* 106: 47–74.

Decker, J. E. 2019. "*The Most Beautiful Thing on the Black Earth:* Sappho's Alliance with Aphrodite," in H. L. Reid and T. Leyh (eds.), *Looking at Beauty: to Kalon in Western Greece: Selected Essays from the 2018 Symposium on the Heritage of Western Greece.* Sioux City, IA: Parnassos Press, p. 39–50.

DeJean, J. 1989. *Fictions of Sappho: 1546–1937.* Chicago, IL: University of Chicago Press.

DuBois, P. 1995. *Sappho is Burning.* Chicago, IL: University of Chicago Press.

———. 1996. "Sappho and Helen," in E. Greene (ed.), *Reading Sappho: Contemporary Approaches.* Berkeley, CA: University of California Press, p. 79–88.

Ferrari, F. 2010. *Sappho's Gift: The Poet and Her Community.* Translated by B. Acosta-Hughes and L. Prauscello. Ann Arbor, MI: Michigan Classical Press.

Finglass, P. J. and A. Kelly (eds.). 2021. *The Cambridge Companion to Sappho.* Cambridge: Cambridge University Press.

Freeman, B. C. 1997. *The Feminine Sublime: Gender and Excess in Women's Fiction.* Berkeley, CA: University of California Press.

Freeman, P. 2016. *Searching for Sappho: The Lost Songs and World of the First Woman Poet.* New York, NY and London: W.W. Norton & Co.

Giacomelli (= Carson), A. 1980. "The Justice of Aphrodite in Sappho Fr. 1," *TAPA* 110: 135–142.

Gilhuly, K. 2017. *Erotic Geographies in Ancient Greek Literature and Culture.* London and New York, NY: Routledge.

Gordon, P. 1997. "The Lover's Voice in *Heroides* 15: Or, Why is Sappho a Man?," in J. P. Hallett and M. B. Skinner (eds.), *Roman Sexualities.* Princeton, NJ: Princeton University Press, p. 274–291.

Gosetti-Murrayjohn (= Pitts), A. 2006a. "Sappho as the Tenth Muse in Hellenistic Epigram," *Arethusa* 39.1: 21–45.

———. 2006b. "Sappho's Kisses: Biographical Tradition and Intertextuality in *A.P.* 5.246 and 5.236," *CJ* 102.1: 41–59.

Greene, E. 1996a. "Apostrophe and Women's Erotics in the Poetry of Sappho," in E. Greene (ed.), *Reading Sappho: Contemporary Approaches.* Berkeley, CA: University of California Press, p. 233–247.

——— (ed.). 1996b. *Reading Sappho: Contemporary Approaches.* Berkeley, CA: University of California Press.

——— (ed.). 1996c. *Re-Reading Sappho: Reception and Transmission.* Berkeley, CA: University of California Press.

——— (ed.). 2005. *Women Poets in Ancient Greece and Rome.* Norman, OK: University of Oklahoma Press.

———. 2009. "Sappho 58: Philosophical Reflections on Death and Aging," In E. Greene and M. B. Skinner (eds.), *The New Sappho on Old Age: Textual and Philosophical Issues.* Hellenic Studies Series 38. Washington, D.C.: Center for Hellenic Studies. https://chs.harvard.edu/chapter/11-ellen-greene-sappho-58-philosophical-reflections-on-death-and-aging/

Gronewald, M. and R. W. Daniel. 2004a. "Ein neuer Sappho-Papyrus," *ZPE* 147: 1–8.

———. 2004b. "Nachtrag zum neuen Sappho-Papyrus," *ZPE* 149: 1–4.

———. 2005. "Lyrischer Text (Sappho-Papyrus)," *ZPE* 154: 7–12.

Gubar, S. 1996. "Sapphistries," in E. Greene (ed.), *Re-Reading Sappho: Reception and Transmission.* Berkeley, CA: University of California Press, p. 199–218.

Hallett, J. P. 1982. "Beloved Cleïs," *QUCC* 10: 21–31.

———. 1989. "Female Homoeroticism and the Denial of Roman Reality in Latin Literature," *YJC* 3.1: 209–227.

———. 1996. "Sappho and Her Social Context: Sense and Sensuality," in Ellen Greene (ed.), *Reading Sappho.* Berkeley, CA: University of California Press, p. 125–142.

———. 2005. "Catullan Voices in *Heroides* 15: How Sappho Became a Man," *Dictynna* 2: 1–15.

———. 2009. "Ovid's Sappho and Roman Women Love Poets," *Dictynna* 6: 1–11.

Hammerstaedt, J. 2009. "The Cologne Sappho: Its Discovery and Textual Constitution," in E. Greene and M. B. Skinner (eds.). *The New Sappho on Old Age: Textual and Philosophical Issues. Hellenic Studies Series 38.* Washington, D.C.: Center for Hellenic Studies. https://chs.harvard.edu/chapter/3-jurgen-hammerstaedt-the-cologne-sappho-its-discovery-and-textual-constitution/

Higgins, C. January 9, 2020. "A Scandal in Oxford: the Curious Case of the Stolen Gospel," *The Guardian.* https://www.theguardian.com/news/2020/jan/09/a-scandal-in-oxford-the-curious-case-of-the-stolen-gospel. Accessed 10/11/2021.

Johnson, M. 2009. "A Reading of Sappho poem 58, fragment 31 and Mimnermus," in E. Greene and M. B. Skinner (eds.), *The New Sappho on Old Age: Textual and Philosophical Issues.* Hellenic Studies Series 38. Washington, D.C.: Center for Hellenic Studies. https://chs.harvard.edu/chapter/12-marguerite-johnson-a-reading-of-sappho-poem-58-fragment-31-and-mimnermus/

———. 2013. *Sappho.* Bristol: Bloomsbury.

Jong, Erica. 2003. *Sappho's Leap: A Novel.* New York, NY: W. W. Norton & Company.

Kassel, R. and C. Austin (eds.). 1983–2001. *Poetae Comici Graeci, vols. 1–8.* Berlin: deGruyter.

Knox, P. E. 1995. *Ovid: Heroides: Select Epistles.* Cambridge: Cambridge University Press.

Lardinois, A. 1994. "Subject and Circumstance in Sappho's Poetry," *TAPA* 124: 57–84.

———. 1996. "Who Sang Sappho's Songs?," in E. Greene (ed.), *Reading Sappho.* Berkeley, CA: University of California Press, p. 150–173.

———. 2001. "Keening Sappho: Female Speech Genres in Sappho's Poetry," in A. Lardinois and L. McClure (eds.). *Making Silence Speak: Women's Voices in Greek Literature and Society.* Princeton, NJ: Princeton University Press, p. 75–92.

Lardinois, A. and L. McClure (eds.). 2001. *Making Silence Speak: Women's Voices in Greek Literature and Society.* Princeton, NJ: Princeton University Press.

Lebessi, A. 2009. "The Erotic Goddess of the Syme Sanctuary, Crete," *AJA* 113.4: 521–545.

Lefkowitz, Mary R. 1996. "Critical Stereotypes and the Poetry of Sappho," in Ellen Greene (ed.), *Reading Sappho: Contemporary Approaches.* Berkeley, CA: University of California Press, p. 26–34.

Liberman, G. 2014. "Reflections on a New Poem by Sappho Concerning Her Anguish and Her Brothers Charaxos and Larichos," Paper delivered at F.I.E.C., Bordeaux, August, 2014. (English version). http://www.papyrology.ox.ac.uk/Fragments/Liberman.FIEC.Bordeaux.2014.pdf. Accessed 10/12/2021.

Lidov, J. B. 2002. "Sappho, Herodotus, and the *Hetaira*," *CP* 97.3: 203–237.

———. 2009. "The Meter and Metrical Style of the New Poem," In Ellen Greene and Marilyn B. Skinner (eds.), *The New Sappho on Old Age: Textual and Philosophical Issues.* Hellenic Studies Series 38. Washington, D.C.: Center for Hellenic Studies. https://chs.harvard.edu/chapter/8-joel-lidov-the-meter-and-metrical-style-of-the-new-poem/

Lobel, E. and D. L. Page. 1955. *Poetarum Lesbiorum fragmenta.* Oxford: Clarendon Press.

Mendelsohn, D. Mar. 9, 2015. "Girl, Interrupted: Who Was Sappho?," *The New Yorker.*
Most, G. 1996. "Reflecting Sappho," in E. Greene (ed.), *Re-Reading Sappho: Reception and Transmission.* Berkeley, CA: University of California Press, p. 11–35.
Nagy, G. 1973. "Phaethon, Sappho's Phaon, and the White Rock of Leukas," *HSCP* 77: 137–177.
———. 1974. *Comparative Studies in Greek and Indic Meter.* Cambridge, MA: Harvard University Press.
Norsa, Medea. 1937. "Dai papiri della Società Italiana," *Annali della R. Scuola Normale Superiore di Pisa.* Serie II, vol. 6. Bologna.
Obbink, D. 2009. "Sappho Fragments 58–59: Text, Apparatus Criticus, and Translation," in E. Greene and M. B. Skinner (eds.), *The New Sappho on Old Age: Textual and Philosophical Issues.* Hellenic Studies Series 38. Washington, D.C.: Center for Hellenic Studies. https://chs.harvard.edu/chapter/2-dirk-obbink-sappho-fragments-58-59-text-apparatus-criticus-and-translation/
———. 2014. "Two New Poems by Sappho," *ZPE* 189: 32–49.
———. 2016. "The Newest Sappho: Text, Apparatus Criticus, and Translation," in Anton Bierl and André Lardinois (eds.), *The Newest Sappho: P. Sapph. Obbink and P.GC inv. 105, Frs. 1-4. Mnemosyne Supplements* vol. 392, vol. 2, Leiden: Brill, p. 13–33.
O'Higgins, D. 1990. "Sappho's Splintered Tongue: Silence in Sappho 31 and Catullus 51," *AJP111*.2: 156–167.
Page, D. L. 1955. *Sappho and Alcaeus: An Introduction to the Study of Ancient Lesbian Poetry.* Oxford: Clarendon Press.
Parker, H. 1993. "Sappho Schoolmistress," *TAPA* 123: 309–351.
———. 2005. "Sappho's Public World," in E. Greene (ed.), *Women Poets in Ancient Greece and Rome.* Norman, OK: University of Oklahoma Press, p. 3–24.
Poochigian, A. 2009. *Sappho. Stung with Love: Poems and Fragments.* New York, NY: Penguin.
Powell, J. 2007. *The Poetry of Sappho.* Oxford: Oxford University Press.
Prins, Y. 1996. "Sappho's Afterlife in Translation," in Ellen Greene (ed.), *Re-Reading Sappho: Reception and Transmission.* Berkeley, CA: University of California Press, p. 36–67.
———. 1999. *Victorian Sappho.* Princeton, NJ: Princeton University Press.
Prins, Y. and M. Shreiber (eds.). 1997. *Dwelling in Possibility: Women Poets and Critics on Poetry.* Ithaca, NY: Cornell University Press.
Putnam, M.C.J. 1960. "Throna and Sappho 1.1," *CJ* 56.2: 79–83.
Rabinowitz, N. S. and L. Auanger (eds.). 2002. *Among Women: From the Homosocial to the Homoerotic in the Ancient World.* Austin, TX: University of Texas Press.
Rayor, D. J. 2005. "The Power of Memory in Erinna and Sappho," in E. Greene (ed.), *Women Poets in Ancient Greece and Rome.* Norman, OK: University of Oklahoma Press, p. 59–71.
Rayor, D. J. and A. Lardinois (eds.). 2013. *Sappho: A New Translation of the Complete Works.* Cambridge: Cambridge University Press.
Reynolds, M. 2001. *The Sappho Companion.* New York, NY: Palgrave.
Rissman, L. 1983. *Love as War: Homeric Allusion in the Poetry of Sappho.* (Beiträge zur klassischen Philologie, 157). Königstein/Ts.: Anton Hain.

Roisman, H. M. 2006. "Helen in the *Iliad,* 'Causa Belli' and Victim of War: From Silent Weaver to Public Speaker," *AJP* 127.1: 1–36.
Rosenmeyer, Patricia. 1997. "Her Master's Voice: Sappho's Dialogue with Homer," *Materiali e discussioni per l'analisi dei testi classici.* 39: 123–149.
———. 2008. "Greek Verse Inscriptions in Roman Egypt: Julia Balbilla's Sapphic Voice," *CA* 27.2: 334–358.
Rostein, A. 2016. *Literary History in the Parian Marble.* Hellenic Studies Series 68. Washington, D.C.: Center for Hellenic Studies.
Sabar, A. June, 2020. "A Biblical Mystery at Oxford," *The Atlantic.* https://www.theatlantic.com/magazine/archive/2020/06/museum-of-the-bible-obbink-gospel-of-mark/610576/. Accessed 10/11/2021.
Sampson, C. M. 2016. "A New Reconstruction of Sappho 44 (P.Oxy. X 1232 + P. Oxy. XVII 2076)," *Proceedings of the 27th International Congress of Papyrology: Warsaw, 29 July-3 August 2013.* XXVIII, Warsaw, p. 53–62.
———. 2020. "Deconstructing the Provenances of P.Sapph.Obbink," *Bulletin of the American Society of Papyrologists* 57: 143–169.
Sampson, C. M. and A. Uhlig. Nov. 5, 2019. "The Murky Provenance of the Newest Sappho," *Eidolon.* https://eidolon.pub/the-murky-provenance-of-the-newest-sappho-aca671a6d52a. Accessed 10/11/2021.
Segal, C. 1998. *Aglaia: The Poetry of Alcman, Sappho, Pindar, Bacchylides, and Corinna.* Lanham, MD: Rowman & Littlefield.
Shrenk, L. P. 1994. "Sappho Frag. 44 and the *Iliad,*" *Hermes* 122.2: 144–150.
Skinner, M. B. 1996. "Woman and Language in Archaic Greece, or, Why is Sappho a Woman?," in E. Greene (ed.), *Reading Sappho: Contemporary Approaches.* Berkeley, CA: University of California Press, p. 175–192.
———. 2002. "Aphrodite Garlanded: Erōs and Poetic Creativity in Sappho and Nossis," in N. S. Rabinowitz and L. Auanger (eds.), *Among Women: From the Homosocial to the Homoerotic in the Ancient World.* Austin, TX: University of Texas Press, p. 60–81.
———. 2009. "Introduction," in E. Greene and M. B. Skinner (eds.), *The New Sappho on Old Age: Textual and Philosophical Issues.* Hellenic Studies Series 38. Washington, D.C.: Center for Hellenic Studies. https://chs.harvard.edu/chapter/1-marilyn-b-skinner-introduction/
Snyder, J. M., 1989. *The Woman and the Lyre: Women Writers in Classical Greece and Rome.* Carbondale and Edwardsville: Southern Illinois University Press.
———. 1997. *Lesbian Desire in the Lyrics of Sappho.* New York, NY: Columbia University Press.
Spelman, H., 2017. "Sappho 44: Trojan Myth and Literary History," *Mnemosyne* 70.5: 740–757.
Stehle, E. 1996. "Sappho's Gaze: Fantasies of a Goddess and Young Man," in E. Greene (ed.), *Reading Sappho: Contemporary Approaches.* Berkeley, CA: University of California Press, p. 193–225.
———. 2016. "Larichos in the Brothers Poem: Sappho Speaks Truth to the Wine-Pourer," in A. Bierl and A. Lardinois (ed.), *The Newest Sappho: P. Sapph. Obbink and P. GC inv. 105, Frs. 1–4: Studies in Archaic and Classical Greek Song, vol. 2.* Leiden: Brill. p. 266–292.
Tarrant, R. J. 1981. "The Authenticity of the Letter of Sappho to Phaon," *HSCP* 85: 133–153.

Thornsen, T. S. and S. Harrison (eds.). 2019. *Roman Receptions of Sappho*. Oxford: Oxford University Press.

Thorsen, T. S. 2019. "As Important as Callimachus? An Essay on Sappho in Catullus and Beyond," in T. S. Thornsen and S. Harrison (eds.), *Roman Receptions of Sappho*. Oxford: Oxford University Press, p. 77–98.

Tsantsanoglou, K. 2019. "Sappho 1.18-19 V," *ZPE* 201: 15–16.

Voigt, E.-M. (ed.). 1971. *Sappho et Alcaeus*. Amsterdam: Polak & Van Gennep.

West, M. L. 1970. "Burning Sappho," *Maia* 22: 207–330.

———. 2005. "The New Sappho," *ZPE* 131: 1–9.

———. 2014. "Nine Poems of Sappho," *ZPE* 191: 1–12.

Whitmarsh, Tim. 2018. "Sappho and Cyborg Helen," in F. Budelmann and T. Phillips (eds.), *Textual Events: Performance and the Lyric in Early Greece*. Oxford: Oxford University Press, p. 135–149.

Williamson, M. 1996. "Sappho and the Other Woman," in E. Greene (ed.), *Reading Sappho: Contemporary Approaches*. Berkeley, CA: University of California Press, p. 248–264.

———. 1999. *Sappho's Immortal Daughters*. Cambridge: Cambridge University Press.

Wilson, L. H. 1996. *Sappho's Bittersweet Songs: Configurations of Female and Male in Ancient Greek Lyric*. London and New York, NY: Routledge.

Winkler, John J. 1990. "Double Consciousness in Sappho's Lyrics," in *The Constraints of Desire: The Anthropology of Sex and Gender in Ancient Greece*. New York, NY: Routledge, p. 162–187.

———. 1996. "Gardens of Nymphs: Public and Private in Sappho's Lyrics," in E. Greene (ed.), *Reading Sappho: Contemporary Approaches*. Berkeley, CA: University of California Press, p. 89–111.

Yatromanolakis, D. 1999. "Alexandrian Sappho Revisited," *CP* 99: 179–195.

———. 2001. "Visualizing Poetry: An Early Representation of Sappho," *CP* 96.2: 159–168.

———. 2007. *Sappho in the Making: The Early Reception*. (Hellenic Studies Series 28). Washington, D.C.: Center for Hellenic Studies.

**_Sappho_ 1 Voight = L-P 1**

ποικιλόθρον᾽ ἀθανάτ᾽ Ἀφρόδιτα,
παῖ Δίος δολόπλοκε, λίσσομαί σε,
μή μ᾽ ἄσαισι μήδ ὀνίαισι δάμνα,
πότνια, θῦμον·

ἀλλὰ τυίδ᾽ ἔλθ᾽, αἴ ποτα κἀτέρωτα
τὰς ἔμας αὔδας ἀίοισα πήλοι
ἔκλυες, πάτρος δὲ δόμον λίποισα
χρύσιον ἦλθες,

ἄρμ᾽ ὐπασδεύξαισα· κάλοι δέ σ᾽ ἆγον
ὤκεες στροῦθοι περὶ γᾶς μελαίνας
πύκνα δίνεεντες πτέρ᾽ ἀπ᾽ ὠράνω ‿αἰθέ-
ρος διὰ μέσσω,

αἶψα δ᾽ ἐξίκοντο· σὺ δ᾽ ὦ μάκαιρα,
μειδιαίσαισ᾽ ἀθανάτωι προσώπωι
ἤρε᾽ ὄττι δηὖτε πέπονθα κὤττι
δηὖτε κάλημμι,

κὤττι μοι μάλιστα θέλω γένεσθαι
μαινόλαι θύμωι· "τίνα δηὖτε πείθω
...σάγην ἐς σὰν φιλότατα; τίς σ᾽, ὦ
Ψάπφ᾽, ἀδικήσι;

καὶ γὰρ αἰ φεύγει, ταχέως διώξει·
αἰ δὲ δῶρα μὴ δέκετ᾽, ἀλλὰ δώσει·
αἰ δὲ μὴ φίλει, ταχέως φιλήσει
κωὐκ ἐθέλοισα."

ἔλθε μοι καὶ νῦν, χαλέπαν δὲ λῦσον
ἐκ μερίμαν, ὄσσα δέ μοι τέλεσσαι
θῦμος ἰμέρρει, τέλεσον, σὺ δ᾽ αὔτα
σύμμαχος ἔσσο.

*Meter: Sapphic Stanzas*

—

**ἀθάνατος, -ον:** immortal
**αἰθήρ, –έρος, ὁ:** air (i.e., the bright sky between the heavens and earth)
**ἀΐω:** perceive, hear; takes a gen object when the object is a person; acc. object when the object is a thing
**αἶψα:** quickly
**ἅρμα, -ματος, τό:** chariot
**ἄση, –ης, ἡ:** pain, anguish, distress
**ἀτέρωτα:** at another time
**αὐδή, –ης, ἡ:** voice (of a human being)
**ἄψ:** back again

**δαμνάω:** subdue, conquer
**δηὖτε = δὴ αὖτε:** yet again
**δίννημι (Aeolic) = δινέω (Attic):** whirl, eddy
**διώκω:** pursue, chase
**δολόπλοκος, -ον:** weaver of cunning manipulation or stratagems
**δῶρον, –ου, τό:** gift
**ἐξικνέομαι:** arrive, reach a destination
**ἔρομαι:** ask
**ἔρχομαι, ἐλεύσομαι, ἦλθον:** come, go
**Ζεῦς, Δίος:** Zeus
**ἱμείρω:** desire
**κλύω:** hear
**λίσσομαι:** beg, entreat
**μαίνολης, –ου:** frenzied, maddened
**μάκαρ, μάκαιρα, μάκαρ:** blessed
**μειδιάω:** smile
**μέλας, μέλαινα, μέλαν:** black
**μερίμνα, –ας, ἡ:** care, anxiety, distress
**μέσσω = μέσου (from Attic, μεσός, –ή, –όν): middle**
**ὀνία = ἀνία, –ης, ἡ:** trouble, misery
**πάσχω, πείσομαι, ἔπαθον, πέπονθα:** suffer, endure
**περί = ὑπέρ in Aeolic:** above
**πήλοι = τηλοῦ:** from far away
**ποτα = ποτε:** ever
**πότνια, –ας:** mistress
**πρόσωπον, –ου, τό:** face
**πτέρον, – ου, τό:** wing
**πύκνος, –η, –ον:** thick, close together
**στροῦθος, –ου:** sparrow
**σύμμαχος, –ον:** allied (and, thus, an ally) in battle
**τελέω:** accomplish, make happen
**τυίδε = τῇδε:** here, to this place
**ὑποζεύγνυμι:** yoke; fasten
**φιλέω:** love
**φιλότης, φιλότητος, –ή:** love, affection
**χρύσιος = χρύσεος, –α, –ον:** golden
**ὠκύς, –εῖα, –ύ:** swift, quick

—

**1.–28:** Frequently called the "Ode to Aphrodite," this poem was preserved *in toto* by Dionysius of Halicarnassus (*On Composition*, 173–179), and it is partially preserved on a 2nd-century CE papyrus from Oxyrhynchus, Egypt (Papyrus Oxyrhynchus 2288). The poem would have appeared in the first book of the Hellenistic edition of Sappho's poetry produced at Alexandria. Like all of Sappho's poems, it is written the Aeolic dialect of the island of Lesbos.

The speaking persona of Sappho, in prayer-like supplication, appeals to the goddess Aphrodite to spare her the pangs of desire, to come down from the golden home of her father as the goddess has done before when Sappho has called upon her, and to redress the injustice of unrequited love. Sappho (as narrator) imagines the goddess descending through the air on a chariot drawn by sparrows, appearing in epiphanic solidarity with the speaker, and asking Sappho a series of solicitous questions—why has she called, what has she suffered, what does her heart desire, whom should the goddess persuade into loving, and who has wronged her. The narrator imagines Aphrodite addressing her by name in line 20 (Ψάπφ') and promising to make the object of Sappho's desire an active lover, even if she is unwilling, who pursues rather than flees and gives gifts rather than refusing them. The narrator's imaginative conjuring of past and future assistance ends abruptly at line 25, as the final stanza returns to a mode of supplication, wherein the speaking persona of Sappho begs the goddess to come to her now, to release her from cares, to grant her desires, and to be her ally.

The gender of the participle ἐθέλοισα (line 24) is feminine, making it clear that the object of Sappho's erotic love is female. The structure of triangulation (i.e., between Sappho as speaking narrator, her addressee, Aphrodite, and the unnamed woman whom Sappho desires) is observable, albeit, in different form, in both Sappho 16 (Sappho, Helen, Anactoria) and Sappho 31. The narrator's repetitive use of temporal markers (δηὖτε, lines 15, 16, and 18, and καὶ νῦν, line 25) shifts the scene between past, future, and present and between imagination and current reality. Finally, the complexities of the relationships between Sappho's poetry and Homeric epic, between oral poetry and written textual poetry, between general acoustic echoes of epic language and intentional allusions to Homer, must be considered, as epic resonances abound in the poem.[30] Rissman (1983) argues that the image of Aphrodite in Sappho 1 resonates with three specific episodes in the *Iliad:* as the inspirer of love between Paris and Helen (3.441–446); as a complicit partner in Hera's seduction of Zeus (14. 195ff.); and as an incompetent on the battlefield (5. 348–351 and 428–430). As Greene (1996a) and Decker (2019) have observed, Sappho appropriates military terminology and subverts it to her own purpose. The final words, σύμμαχος ἔσσο (line 28), are especially noteworthy in this regard. Although the noun σύμμαχος does not appear in Homer, it nevertheless evokes divine intervention on the agonistic, Iliadic battlefield (where Aphrodite was not adept) and transfers it to the private, lyric world of subjective perception and erotic love, which Aphrodite champions. Blondell (2010) argues that Sappho 1 parodies this battlefield scene in book 5 of the *Iliad* involving Athena, Aphrodite, and Diomedes.

1. **ποικιλόθρον'**: This unique compound adjective consists of two parts: **ποικίλος, –η, –ον** means "intricately decorated" and implies the craftsmanship of a genius and skilled artisan; **θρον'**, however, has two possibilities. Some scholars read **θρόνος, –ου ὁ** as an elevated chair (usually with

a footstool), seeing a parallel in the Homeric epithet, Ἥρη …χρυσόθρονος ("golden throned Hera", *Il.* 14.153). But, others have argued that Sappho may have adapted the Homeric phrase **θρόνα ποικίλ'** (a *hapax legomenon* from *Il.* 22.441), wherein Andromache is weaving a rich purple robe on which she placed "intricate geometric patterns, figures, or flowers". See Putnam (1960, note 3, p. 82) for a bibliographic history of this discussion. Putnam (1960) argues persuasively that *poikilothron'* must mean a himation with charms embroidered upon it.

**3. ἄσαισι…ὀνίαισι** = (Attic) ἄσαις…ἀνίαις: dat. pl. f.;

**3. θῦμον:** Greek often uses the accusative case to denote the body part affected by the action of the verb.

**5. ἔλθ' = ἔλθε**; 2nd sing. aor. imperative of ἔρχομαι.

**5. αἰ** = (Attic) εἰ

**5. κἀτέρωτα** = καὶ ἀτέρωτα; this is an example of *crasis*, wherein a contraction occurs combining vowels and/or diphthongs from two words.

**6. αἰίοισα** = (Attic) ἀΐουσα: pres., nom., fem., sing., act. part.

**7. λίποισα** = (Attic) λίπουσα: strong (1st) aor., nom., fem., sing., act. part.

**9. ἄρμ'** = (Attic) ἅρμα; as Decker (2019, p. 39) has noted, Sappho "adopts a Homeric voice" but "slyly makes significant switches in content," for example, in the fact that Aphrodite yokes sparrows rather than conventional war horses to her chariot.

**9. ὐπασδεύξαισα** = (Attic) ὑποζεύξασα, from ὑποζεύγνυμι: weak (2nd) aor., nom., fem., sing., act. part.

**9. ἆγον** = (Attic) ἦγον

**10. γᾶς** = (Attic) γῆς

**11. ὠράνω = οὐρανοῦ** (Attic)

**11–12. αἴθερος διὰ μέσσω:** "through the middle aether"

**13. ἐξίκοντο:** strong aor. 3rd pl. act. indic. from ἐξικνέομαι

**14. μειδιαίσαισ'** = (Attic) μειδιάσασα (weak aor., nom., sing., fem., act. part.)

**15. ἤρε'** = ἤρεο (from ἔρομαι): 2nd sing., aor., deponent indic.

**15. ὄττι** = (Attic) ὅ τι: "what thing", "on account of what thing", "for what thing", or "why". Putnam (1960) observes a number of echoes between Aphrodite's questions to the Sapphic narrator and the Iliadic episode (14.195–221 especially) in which Hera seeks Aphrodite's aide in seducing her husband, Zeus. Putnam suggests that the parallels between these lines and Aphrodite's promise of help to Hera (book 14.195–196) in the *Iliad* are "surely more than fortuitious" (p. 81): "in 195–196, Aphrodite declares to Hera: 'Speak out to me what you have in mind. My heart bids me to accomplish it, if I am able to accomplish it and if it is capable of accomplishment' ….The whole symbolic aura … is one of beguiling and seduction. Hera wants to charm Zeus back to her love and draw him away from the battle for a while ….The context of Sappho's poem is so close to this that it barely needs exposition."

**15. δηὖτε** = δὴ αὖτε: *crasis*

**15. κὤττι** = καὶ ὅ τι: also *crasis*; appears again in line 17

**16. κάλημμι** = (Attic) καλέω

**17. θέλω** = (Attic) ἐθέλω
**18. μαινόλαι θύμωι** = (Attic) μαινόλῃ θύμῳ
**18–19. "τίνα...φιλότατα":** The reading is a bit difficult to comprehend here and is muddled by textual difficulties. Is πείθω a first-person sing. act. verb ("Whom do I persuade...") or the proper noun, Πείθω, the goddess of persuasion (i.e., "whom should Persuasion lead into your love?") as some scholars argue? Second, a careful reading must account for the "σάγην" and "ἐς σὰν φιλότατα" in line 19, with "you" seeming to function as the direct object of σάγην = (Attic) σε ἄγειν and σάν (ἐς σὰν φιλότατα) = (Attic) σήν, "your". Some scholars, however, have suggested that the "σ", which is very faint in the actual manuscripts, may actually be a digamma (Fάν), rendering the third-person possessive pronoun (i.e., "her"). Thus, "Whom do I persuade to lead/draw you (in)to your [or "her"] affection?" Or, "whom should Persuasion draw you into your/her love?" Tsantsanoglou (2017) translates, "whom am I to convince again so as even to lead that one into your love?"
**21–23. αἰ:** all three occurrences of αἰ in lines 21–24 = (Attic) εἰ. While one might read in these lines mutual reversal in the roles of pursuing lover and pursued object of desire, Giacomelli (1980, p. 136) notes that this "is not what the Greek words say. Aphrodite's statements contain no direct object." The Sapphic narrator imagines Aphrodite promising, Giacomelli suggests, merely to make the other woman *pursue*, not necessarily to pursue *her*.
**22. δέκετ'** = (Attic) δέχεται
**24. κωὐκ** = καὶ οὐκ (*crasis*): καὶ is best translated here as "even"
**24. ἐθέλοισα** = (Attic) ἐθέλουσα
**25. λῦσον:** weak aor. 2nd s. act. imperative
**25–26. χαλέπαν...μερίμναν** = (Attic) χαλέπων … μερίμνων
**26. ὄσσα** = (Attic) ὅσος, –η, –ον: however many things
**27. ἰμέρρω** = (Attic) ἱμείρω
**27. τέλεσσαι:** aor. act. infin. of τελέω
**27. τέλεσον:** 2nd sing. weak aor. imperative, also from τελέω
**27. αὔτα** = (Attic) αὔτη (intensifying pronoun with σὺ–"you, yourself,...")
**28. ἔσσο** = 2nd sing. pres. imperative of εἰμί

### *Sappho* fr. 2 Campbell (1967) = Voigt 2 = L-P 2

..................................

δεῦρυ μ' ἐκ Κρήτας ἐπ[ὶ τόνδ]ε ναῦον
ἄγνον, ὄππ[ᾳ τοι] χάριεν μὲν ἄλσος
μαλί[αν], βῶμοι δὲ τεθυμιάμε-
νοι [λι]βανώτῳ·

ἐν δ' ὔδωρ ψῦχρον κελάδει δι' ὔσδων
μαλίνων, βρόδοισι δὲ παῖς ὀ χῶρος
ἐσκίαστ', αἰθυσσομένων δὲ φύλλων
κῶμα καταίρει·

ἐν δὲ λείμων ἰππόβοτος τέθαλεν
ἠρίνοισιν ἄνθεσιν, αἰ δ' ἄηται
μέλλιχα πνέοισιν [ ]
[ ]

ἔνθα δὴ σὺ †....† ἔλοισα, Κύπρι,
χρυσίαισι ἐν κυλίκεσσιν ἄβρως
ὀμμεμείχμενον θαλίαισι νέκταρ
οἰνοχόαισον.
......................

*Meter: Sapphic Stanzas*

—

**ἀβρός, –ά, –όν:** graceful, delicate
**Ἀγνός, -ή, -όν:** holy, sacred
**αἰθύσσω:** (usu. in present) set in rapid motion, stir up (*act.*); to quiver, of leaves (*pass.*)
**αἱρέω, αἱρήσω, εἷλον, ᾕρηκα, ᾕρημαι, ᾑρέθην:** take hold of, grasp, seize
**ἄλσος, –ου, τό:** sacred grove
**ἄνεμος, ου, ὁ:** wind, breeze
**ἄνθος, –ους, τό:** blossom, flower
**βῶμος, –ου, ὁ:** altar
**δεῦρο:** here, thither, to this place
**ἔναυλος, –ου, ὁ:** dwelling, shelter, haunt (esp. of the gods)
**ἠρινός, –ή, –όν:** of spring
**θαλία, –ας, ἡ:** good cheer; (in pl.) festivities
**θάλλω, θαλήσω, ἔθηλα, τέθηλα**:** grow, bloom, flourish
**θυμιάω, θυμιήσομαι, ἐθυμίησα, τεθυμίηκα, τεθυμίαμαι, —:** burn incense or to cause to smoke (*act.*); smoking or burning (with incense) (*med.*)
**ἱππόβοτος, –ον (βόσκω):** grazed by horses
**καταίρω/καταέρρω, καταρρήσω, — κατερύηκα, — κατερρύην:** flow, stream, or sink down
**κελαδέω:** make the sound of running water
**Κρήτη, –ης, ἡ:** Crete (island in the Aegean Sea)
**κύλιξ, –ικοξ, ἡ:** wine-cup
**Κύπρις, ιδος, ἡ:** Cypris, an epithet of Aphrodite
**κῶμα, κώματος, τό:** deep sleep
**λειμών, –ῶνος, ὁ:** grassy meadow
**λιβανωτός, –οῦ, ὁ:** incense
**μεῖλιχος, –ον:** gentle, soothing
**μήλινος, -η, -ον:** made of apples or quinces
**μῆλον, –ου, τό:** apple
**νέκταρ, –αρος, τό:** nectar; along with *ambrosia*, the nourishment of the gods
**ὄζος, –ου, ὁ:** tree-branch, part of a branch where the bud sprouts
**οἰνοχόη, -ης, ἡ:** vessel used in the mixing and pouring of wine
**ὅπῃ:** where, in which place, whither

**πνέω, πνεύσομαι, ἔπνευσα, πέπνευκα, πέπνυμαι, ἐπνεύσθην:** breathe, blow
**ῥόδον, –ου, τό:** rose
**σκιάζω:** cast a shadow (*act.*); to be in shade or shadow (*pass.*)
**συμμείγνυμι, συμμείξω, συνέμειξα, συμμέμιχα, συμμέμειχμαι,—:** co-mingle with
**ὕδωρ, ὕδατος, τό:** water
**φύλλον, –ου τό:** leaf
**χαρίεις, -εσσα, -εν:** pleasing, beautiful
**χρύσεος, –α, –ον:** golden, made of gold
**χῶρος, –ου, ὁ:** place, land
**ψυχρός, –ρά, –ρόν:** cold

**1–16:** This fragment of a poem by Sappho survives on a 3rd- and 2nd-centuries BCE potsherd (the so-called "Florentine ostracon") discovered in Egypt and published by Medea Norsa, an Italian papyrologist and philologist who headed the Instito Papirologico Girolamo Vitelli in Florence from 1935 to 1949 and who recognized the poem on the ostracon as belonging to Sappho. The ostracon is now in Florence in the collection of the Biblioteca Laurenziana. The poem most likely obtained from the first book of the Alexandrian edition of Sappho's poetry, which consisted of poems composed in Sapphic Stanzas.

The narrator of Sappho fr. 2 calls upon Aphrodite to abandon her Cretan sanctuary in favor of an apple grove in a meadow where smoking altars fill the air with the fragrance of incense, where cool springs of water murmur, where rose bushes cast shade, where shimmering leaves have a soporific effect, and where flowers bloom and breezes gently blow. There, the speaker bids, the goddess should take up golden cups filled with nectar and take part in the festivities that imply the participation of a group of people.

It is hard to tell whether the incantatory, hypnotic, synaesthetic environment to which the goddess is called is an actual or imagined sacred precinct, but it is certainly appropriate for the goddess of sensuality. Segal (1974) suggests that the personal encounter to which the Sapphic narrator calls Aphrodite imitates the love-magic of the goddess herself, since bringing Aphrodite before one is the best form of a love-charm.

Because this text is so fragmentary and difficult, there is much scholarly debate on its lexicographical details. We have adopted the text of Campbell (1967) due to its accessibility. One might compare the rather significant differences between Campbell's version of the text with those of Voigt (1971) and Caciagli (2012), who published a reading of the text in the *Center for Hellenic Studies Research Bulletin* based on his autopsy of the Florentine ostracon.

**1. δεῦρυ** = (Attic) δεῦρο. Notice that each stanza begins with a locative preposition or adverb, directing the addressee, Aphrodite, "here" and "to this place".

**1. Κρήτας** = (Attic) Κρήτης. Although Sappho does not specify a particular cult site on the island of Crete, archaeologists have discovered a sanctuary to Hermes and an "Erotic goddess" at Syme, Crete. In a survey of the votive offerings found at the site, Lebessi (2009, p. 534) suggests that the rituals presented visually in the votives "come close to the dream-like description of flowering meadows in lyric poetry that witnessed the sexual maturation of the girls of Lesbos and Lydia, as well as the *mixis* between immortals or between morals and deities." Sappho fr. 2 concludes with just such a *mixis* between morals (including the narrator) and Aphrodite. The sanctuary was in use from the Minoan through the 6th and 7th centuries CE; Lebessi notes (p. 537) that although Aphrodite's name is not indicated in writing in association with the sanctuary until the Hellenistic period, her name is probably absent from the 7th and 6th centuries BCE figurines and plaques because the names of divinities are not to be found on such votive offerings until the Classical period.

**2. ἄγνον** = (Attic) Ἁγνόν

**2. ὄππᾳ** = (Attic) ὅπῃ

**3. μαλί[αν]** = (Attic) μήλων

**5. ψῦχρον** = (Attic) ψυχρόν

**5. ὔσδων** = (Attic) ὄζος

**6. μαλίνων** = (Attic) μηλίνων; cool water (perhaps dew?) makes the acoustic sound of trickling down from the branches of apple or quince trees.

**6. βρόδοισι** = (Attic) ῥόδοις. For a discussion of the symbolic significance of roses in Sappho's poetry, see Gosetti-Murrayjohn (2006a).

**6. παῖς** = (Attic) πᾶς

**7. ἐσκίαστ'** = third-person sing. pluperf. pass. of σκιάζω

**9. λείμων** = (Attic) λειμών

**9. τέθαλεν** = (Attic) τέθηλεν

**10. αἰ δ' ἄηται** = breezes; Homer (*Il.* 15.626, *Od.* 4.567) and Hesiod (*Op.* 621) use the phrase ἀνέμων ἀῆται. In Homer and Hesiod, the nouns ἀῆται are first declension masculine, but Sappho employs a feminine form of ἄηται.

**11. μέλλιχα** = (Attic) μείλιχον

**13. ἔλοισα** = (Attic) ἕλουσα

**14. χρυσίαισι** = (Attic) χρυσέαις

**14. ἄβρως** = (Attic) Ἁβρῶς

**15. ὀμμεμείχμενον** = (Attic) συμμεμείχμενον. Aphrodite is a goddess of *mixis*, or comingling. The imagined mingling of the goddess, golden cups, nectar, feasts, and participants in the final stanza parallels the mingling of the sensory elements in the first three stanzas and evokes the role of the goddess in erotic *mixis*. Aphrodite's intimacy with mortals is common in Greek poetry: she is intimate with both Helen and Paris in the *Iliad* (3.441–446) and with Anchises in the *Homeric Hymn to Aphrodite*.

**16. οἰνοχόαισον:** If Campbell's (1967, p. 42) text is correct, this is an Aeolic, aorist imperative of οἰνοχοεύω in Attic, best translated as "pour out the wine". Voigt (1971, p. 33) provides a different rendering in the form of the feminine, nominative participle οἰνοχόεισα, while Caciagli (2012), who published the text in the *Center for Hellenic Studies Research Bulletin* based on his autopsy of the Florentine ostracon, offers [οἰ]νοχόαισα[ι].

### ***Sappho* fr. 16 Voigt = L-P 16**

ο]ἰ μὲν ἰππήων στρότον, οἰ δὲ πέσδων,
οἰ δὲ νάων φαῖσ' ἐπ[ὶ] γᾶν μέλαι[ν]αν
ἔ]μμεναι κάλλιστον· ἔγω δὲ κῆν' ὄττω τις ἔραται·

πά]γχυ δ' εὔμαρες σύνετον πόησαι
π]άντι τ[ο]ῦτ', ἀ γὰρ πόλυ περσκέθοισα
κάλλος [ἀνθ]ρώπων Ἐλένα [τὸ]ν ἄνδρα
τόν [... ἄρ]ιστον

καλλ[ίποι]σ' ἔβα 'ς Τροΐαν πλέοι[σα
κωὐδ[ὲ πα]ῖδος οὐδὲ φίλων το[κ]ήων
πά[μπαν] ἐμνάσθ⟨η⟩, ‿ἀλλὰ παράγαγ' αὔταν
]σαν

]αμπτον γὰρ [
]...κούφως τ [ ]οη.[.]ν
..] με νῦν Ἀνακτορί[ας ὀ]νέμναι-
σ' οὐ] παρεοίσας·

τᾶ]ς ⟨κ⟩ε βολλοίμαν ἔρατόν τε βᾶμα
κἀμάρυχμα λάμπρον ἴδην προσώπω
ἢ τὰ Λύδων ἄρματα κἀν ὄπλοισι
πεσδομ]άχεντας.

].μεν οὐ δύνατον γένεσθαι
].ν ἀνθρωπ[... π]εδέχην δ' ἄρασθαι
[ ]
[ ]
[ ]
[ ]
[ ]
προσ[

ὠσδ[
..].[
.].[.]ωλ.[
τ' ἐξ ἀδοκή[τω.

*Meter: Sapphic Stanzas*

—

**ἀδοκήτος, -ον:** unexpected
**ἀμάρυγμα, –ματος, τό:** sparkling or flashing, particularly of the eyes
**ἀναμιμνήσκω:** (*act.*) call to mind again, remind (+ gen. or acc.); (*med.* or *pass.*) remember
**ἅρμα, –ματος, τό:** chariot
**βῆμα, –ματος, τό:** walk, gait, footfall
**βούλομαι, βουλήσομαι, —, —, βεβούλημαι ἐβουλήθην:** want, wish, be willing; with ἤ, prefer
**ἔραμαι, ἐράσομαι, ἠρασάμην, —, ἤρασμαι, ἠράσθην:** desire passionately, love
**ἐρατός, ή, όν:** beloved, lovely, charming
**εὐμαρής, –ές:** (it is) easy (+ infinitive)
**ἱππεύς, –εως, ὁ:** member of the cavalry; chariot-fighter; horseman
**κάλλος, –ους, τό:** beauty
**καταλείπω, καταλείψω, κατέλιπον, καταλέλοιπα, καταλέλειμμαι, κατελείφθην:** leave behind, abandon, forsake
**λαμπρός, ά, όν:** shining, bright
**Λυδός, ὁ:** Lydian; Lydia is a region of what is now modern-day Turkey
**μέλας, μέλαινα, μέλαν:** black, dark, murky
**μιμνήσκω, μνήσω, ἔμνησα, —, μέμνημαι, ἐμνήσθην:** (*act.*) call to memory, remind (+ gen. or acc.); (*med.* and *pass.*) remind one's self, remember (+ gen. or acc.)
**ναῦς, νεῶς, ἡ:** ship
**ὅπλα, ων, τά:** armor, weapons
**πάμπαν:** (*adv.*, πᾶς, πᾶσα, πᾶν) wholly, altogether
**παράγω, παράξω, παρήγαγον, παραγήγοχα, παρήγμαι, παρήχθην:** lead aside from the right path, lead astray, avert
**πάρειμι (εἰμί):** be present
**πεζομαχέω:** fight on land or foot (i.e., of the infantry)
**πέζος, –η, –ον:** on foot; fighters on foot (as opposed to those on horse or in chariot); infantry
**περ:** (*enclitic particle*), adds force to the word which follows it, in the sense of "very much, much, however"
**περιέχω/περίσχω, περιέξω/περισχήσω, περιέσχον, —, —, —:** surpass
**πλέω, πλεύσομαι πλεύσω, ἔπλευσα, πέπλευκα, πέπλευσμαι, ἐπλεύσθην:** sail
**πρόσωπον, –ου, τό:** face
**συνετός, –ή, –όν:** intelligible, able to be understood
**τοκεύς, –έως, ὁ or ἡ:** parent

—

**1–20:** Preserved on a 2nd-century CE papyrus from Oxyrhynchus, Egypt (Papyrus Oxyrhychus 1231), fragment 16 likely obtained from the first book of the Alexandrian edition of Sappho's poetry, a collection which consisted of probably eight, possibly nine books.[31] We have used Voigt's text (1971, p. 42–43), which supplies very fragmentary and uncertain lines of 21–32. In 2014, Burris, Fish, and Obbink proposed that a newly discovered papyrus (P. GC. inv. 105) contained additional lines of fr. 16, which they cross-examined with the papyrus used by Voigt to produce a fuller rendering. We have placed the text proposed by Burris et al. (labeled as fr. 16a) in an appendix of disputed texts of Sappho for reasons addressed in that appendix.

Fr. 16 opens with a priamel, a 20th-century rhetorical and literary term used to describe an ancient literary formula in which an array of things generally deemed by others to be the best serves as a foil to the true subject of the poem. A priamel in Greek literature usually provides a dyad (as in the opening lines of Pindar's First Olympian Ode) or triad of alternatives, which the speaker rejects in favor of something else. The narrator extols that something else, the true subject of the poem, as preferential to all other things.

Sappho's priamel contains a triad of conventionally epic alternatives (a cavalry, an infantry, and a fleet of ships) organized by distributive clauses (οἰ μὲν ... οἰ δὲ...οἰ δε..., lines 1–2), that others claim to be the best thing on the "black earth." This list of alternatives is followed by a pronoun cap (ἔγω δὲ, line 3) that marks the transition between the list of foils and the speaker's preference, the focal point of the poem, "whatever someone desires" (lines 3–4).[32] Sappho's narrator then asserts that it is possible to make this entirely clear to everyone via the mythical exemplum of Helen, who went to Troy, abandoning a noble husband and forgetful of her dear parents and her child. The clarity of the text falters in the fourth stanza, where the feminine name of Anactoria appears, whose absence (in the fourth stanza) prompts a renewal of the theme of the priamel brought out of the world of epic legend and into the realm of the lived, everyday world of the narrator: the speaker insists that she would rather see Anactoria's lovely walk than all the chariots and infantry of Lydia. Rissman (1983) is right to remind us that the Lydians (whom Homer called the *Maiones*) comprised an essential ally of the Trojans in the Trojan War. Rosenmeyer (1997, p. 143) suggests that the mythical exemplum of Helen in the priamel combines Sappho's "'present' with Homer's 'past' to create ... this double love story." "In Helen," Rosenmeyer (1997, p. 147) suggests, "Sappho might find a mythic female source of inspiration, a strong unsilenceable voice, or more accurately many voices at once, to support her own poetic choices."

Sappho's choice of extolling the exemplum of Helen contrasts starkly with an apocryphal story about the archaic lyric poet Stesichorus, whom Plato (*Phaedrus* 243a) claims was struck blind when he slandered Helen. Recognizing, Plato claims, the cause of his blindness, Stesichorus immediately wrote the following palinode and immediately regained his sight: "This story is not true, you did not go on well-benched ships, you did not reach the Pergamum citadel of Troy."[33]

**1–2. οἰ μὲν...οἰ δὲ...οἰ δε...** = There are no aspirations in the Aeolic dialect, so the smooth breathing marks over each of the definite articles would appear in Attic as rough breathing marks. There is a distributive sense at work ("some ... others ... others ...")

**1. ἰππήων** = (Attic) ἱππέων

**1. στρότον** = (Attic) στράτον

**1. πέσδων** = (Attic) πέζων

**2. νάων** = (Attic) νεῶν. The priamel elements of cavalry, infantry, and ships evokes the catalog of ships and commanders that comprises most of book 2 of the *Iliad*, providing a sense of the grandeur and scale of the besieging Achaean force. Note, however, that Sappho's sympathies appear to align or "ally" with the Trojans: not only did Helen abandon her family to go to Troy out of desire, which the speaker has said is the "most beautiful" thing on the black earth; but, the narrator also claims that she would rather see the walk of Anactoria (lines 15–20) than the armament of the Lydians, allies of the Trojans in the *Iliad* (whom Homer calls *Maiones*). In the logic of the poem, the armament of the Lydians is held up as the foil-ideal that fails against the mental visage of the absent Anactoria's walk.

**2. φαῖσ'** = (Attic) φασί(ν)

**2. γᾶν** = (Attic) γὴν

**3. ἔμμεναι** [Hom.] = (Attic) εἶναι

**3. κῆν'** = (Attic) ἐκεῖνο

**3. ἔγω δὲ** = φημί is the understood verb (dependent upon φαῖσ' in line 3); **ἔγω** provides a pronominal cap that issues the conclusion of the priamel.

**3–4. ὄττω** = (Attic) ὅτου, neut. gen. sing. of ὅστις, ἥτις, ὅ τι. One might observe that the indefinite pronoun that Sappho employs here is neuter. At the conclusion of the mythic exemplum, Sappho re-engages the language of the priamel by extolling the "walk" of Anactoria, presumably as the "most beautiful" thing on the black earth.

**5. πάνχυ** = (Attic) πάντα, used adverbially here

**5. σύνετον** = (Attic) συνετὸν

**5. πόησαι** = (Attic) ποίησαι, aor. act. inf. of ποιέω

**6. πάντι** = (Attic) **παντὶ**

**6. ἀ** = (Attic) **ἡ**

**6. περσκέθοισα** = (Attic) περίσχουσα, aor., nom., fem., sing., act. part. of περιέχω/περίσχω

**7. κάλλος** = not an adjective, but rather the acc. neut. noun (acc. of respect), κάλλος, –ους, τό

**7. Ἐλένα** = (Attic) ἑλένη, Helen, traditionally represented as the 'causa belli' of the Trojan War. She appears in six exchanges in the *Iliad:* Helen and Iris, 3.121–145; Helen and Priam, (3.161–242); Helen and Aphrodite (3.380–420); Helen and Paris (3.421–447); Helen and Hector (6.323–24, 343–368); and Helen's funeral speech for Hector (24.761–776). See Roisman (2006) for a survey discussion of each of these scenes and an analysis of the ways in which the Iliadic Helen exerts increasing agency over the course of the epic, despite the extraordinary constraints placed upon her by the Trojan and Achaean communities. See also DuBois (1996).

**9. καλλ[ίποι]σ'** = (Attic) καταλίπουσα

**9. ἔβα** = (Attic) ἔβη, 3rd s. aor. act. indic. of βαίνω

**9. πλέοισα** = (Attic) πλέουσα

**10. κωὐδε:** (*crasis*) = (Attic) καὶ οὐδέ

**10. τοκήων** = (Attic) τοκέων, like ἱππήων, line 1

**11. ἐμνάσθην** = (Attic) ἐμνήσθην

**11. παράγαγ'** = (Attic) παρήγαγε; lines 12–14 likely contained the subject of this verb, which was, given the context, probably Eros or Aphrodite.

**11. αὔταν** = (Attic) αὐτήν

**13–14. Lines are lost beyond reconstruction.**

**15. Ἀνακτορίας** = gen. sing., Anactoria

**15. ὀνέμναισ'** = (Attic) ἀνέμνησε, of ἀνα-μιμνήσκω (see principal parts for μιμνήσκω in the vocabulary above).

**16. παρεοίσας** = (Attic) παρούσας of πάρειμι

**17. τᾶς** = (Attic) **τῆς**

**17. κε(ν)** [Hom.] = (Attic) ἄν

**17. βολλοίμαν** = (Attic) βουλοίμην, 1st sing. pres. dep. opt.; "I would prefer" + infinitive (see ἴδην, line 19).

**17. βᾶμα** = (Attic) βῆμα

**18. κἀμάρυχμα:** *crasis*; ἀμάρυχμα = (Attic) ἀμάρυγμα

**18. λάμπρον** = (Attic) λαμπρόν

**19. ἄρματα** = (Attic) ἅρματα

**19. ἴδην** = (Attic) ἰδεῖν, aor. infin. of ὁράω

**19. προσώπω** = (Attic) προσώπου

**19. κἀν** = *crasis* (καὶ + ἐν)

**19. ὄπλοισι** = (Attic) ὅπλοις

**20. πεσδομάχεντας** = (Attic) πεζομάχεντας (modifying an understood masc. pl., acc. noun, such as ἄνδρας or (Attic) πέζους). Lydia appears again in Sappho fr. 96 Voigt, as the Sapphic narrator laments that an absent addressee now is preeminent among the Lydians (line 6) just as rosy-fingered moon surpasses all the stars. The speaker notes that the absent woman will remember Atthis with desire (lines 15–17).

**21–32.** The fragmentary nature of these lines makes full rendering difficult. π]εδέχην (line 22) = Attic μετέχειν (to partake of/have a share in something). Perhaps, οὐ δύνατον γένεσθαι (line 21) ("it is not possible") that something or someone (perhaps "ἀνθρωπ[…" of line 22) π]εδέχην (have a share in something and ἄρασθαι (from ἀράομαι), "to pray". Put all together, "but it is not within a person's power to have a share in… but to pray…". See the appendix (fr. 16a) for a proposed rendering of these lines by Burris, Fish, and Obbink (2014) based on cross-readings with new papyrus findings.

**_Sappho_ fr. 31 Voigt = 31 L-P**

φαίνεταί μοι κῆνος ἴσος θέοισιν
ἔμμεν' ὤνηρ, ὅττις ἐνάντιός τοι
ἰσδάνει καὶ πλάσιον ἆδυ φωνείσας ὐπακούει

καὶ γελαίσας ἰμέροεν, τό μ' ἦ μὰν
καρδίαν ἐν στήθεσιν ἐπτόαισεν·
ὡς γὰρ εἰσίδω[34] βρόχε' ὤς με φώνη-
ς οὐδὲν ἔτ' εἴκει,

ἀλλὰ †καμ† μὲν γλῶσσα †ἔαγε†, λέπτον
δ' αὔτικα χρωι πῦρ ὐπαδεδρόμακεν,
ὀππάτεσσι δ' οὐδὲν ὄρημμ', ἐπιβρόμεισι δ' ἄκουαι,

† ἐκαδε† μ' ἴδρως κακχέεται, τρόμος δὲ
παῖσαν ἄγρει, χλωροτέρα δὲ ποίας
ἔμμι, τεθνάκην δ' ὀλίγω 'πιδεύης
φαίνομ' ἔμ' αὔται.

ἀλλὰ πὰν τόλματον, ἐπεὶ †καὶ πένητα†

*Meter: Sapphic Stanzas*

**ἀκοή, -ῆς, ἡ:** ear
**αὐτίκα:** immediately
**βραχύς, -εῖα, -ύ:** brief, short
**γελάω, γελάσομαι, ἐγέλασα, —, —, ἐγελάσθην:** laugh
**εἰσοράω, -όψομαι, -ίδω, -όρακα/-ώρακα, -ώραμαι, -ώφθην:** look at, behold, gaze at
**ἐναντίος, -α –ον:** (+ dat.) opposite to, facing
**ἐπιδεής, -ές/ἐπιδευής, -ές (poetic form):** lacking, deficient in, in need of
**ἐπιρρομβέω:** make a buzzing or whirring sound
**ἔτι:** still, yet
**ἡδύς, -εῖα, -ύ:** sweet
**ἱδρώς, -ῶτος, ὁ:** sweat
**ἱζάνω:** sit
**ἵκω, ἵξω, ἷξον/ἷξα, —, ἷγμαι, —:** come, come upon
**ἱμερόεις, -εσσα, -εν:** charming, inducing desire
**καρδία, -ας, ἡ:** heart
**κατάγνυμι, -άξω, -έαξα, -έαγα, —, -εάγην:** break
**καταχέω, καταχέω, κατέχεα, κατακέχυκα, κατακέχυμαι, κατεχύθην:** (note: the present and the future have the same form) pour, shower down (*act.* and *med.*); be poured over (*pass.*)
**λέπτος, -η, -ον:** fine, thin, subtle
**ὄμμα, -ματος, τό:** eye

**πένης, -ητος, ὁ:** one who works for a living, day-laborer, poor man
**πλησίος, -α, -ον:** near, nearby
**ποία, -ας, ἡ:** grass
**πτοέω, πτοήσω, ἐπτοήσα, —, ἐπτόημαι, ἐπτοιήθην:** flutter, excite (by passion)
**στῆθος, ους, τό:** breast, chest; the seat of feeling and thought
**τρόμος, -ου, ὁ:** trembling, quivering, quaking
**ὑπακούω, ὑπακούσομαι, —, —, —, —:** hear, listen to
**ὑποτρέχω, ὑποδραμέομαι, ὑπέδρακον, ὑποδεδράμηκα, —, —:** run under
**φωνέω, —, ἐφώνησα, —, —, —:** speak, produce a sound
**φωνή, -ῆς, ἡ:** sound, specifically of the human voice
**χλωρός, -α, -ον:** pale, green-yellow
**χρώς, χροός, ὁ:** skin

—

**1.–16:** Fragment 31, consisting of four virtually complete Sapphic stanzas and the first line of a fifth stanza, is one of the more substantial fragments of Sappho's poetry that survives. It comes to us through the intermediary of pseudo-Longinus, the 1st century CE author of a seminal work of literary criticism, Περὶ Ὕψους ("On the Sublime"). In the relevant passage (10.1–10.5), Longinus celebrates the complexity and condensed aggregation of appropriate language and imagery in the poem and praises Sappho's skill at selecting and organizing material so as to convey effectively "the emotions that arise in the madness of erotic love" (τὰ συμβαίνοντα ταῖς ἐρωτικαῖς μανίαις παθήματα). Longinus also compares Sappho's precision and realism with Homer's ability to convey the essence of an experience, demonstrating Homer's skill with a simile in which Hektor is likened to a storm-surging wave crashing upon a ship (10.5 Longinus, discussing *Iliad* 15. 623–628). Barbara Freeman (1997, p. 20) suggests that Longinus identifies in both Sappho and Homer "the ability to select and combine the most disparate elements of an awesome event in order to present a complete, unified portrait of it."

The poem involves an erotic triangulation between the narrator, κῆνος (line 1, "that man"), and the unnamed, female object of the narrator's transfixion, whose gender is made clear by two feminine participles φωνείσας (lines 3–4, "speaking") and γελαίσας (line 5, "laughing"). The fact of the male's proximity to the sweetly speaking and laughing woman produces in the Sapphic narrator a series of cascading physical and synaesthetic experiences. Her heart thumps, her tongue breaks, a thin fire courses under her skin, her eyes fail, her ears ring, her body is covered in sweat, a trembling takes hold, she grows pale, and she seems to herself near to dying. Longinus preserved only part of the poem, which D'Angour (2013) suggests must have continued for several more stanzas, largely on the basis of a comparison with Catullus's 51, Catullus's famous "translation" of Sappho fr. 31. D'Angour argues that Sappho 31 should be read as a construction of passionate desire that, like the battlefield faced by Homeric heroes, offers not only conflict, but also the possibility of confronting and rising above misery and mortal danger. In this construction, *eros* is "just as painful, violent, and potentially fatal as any martial engagement" (D'Angour, 2013, p. 59).

**1. κῆνος** = (Attic) ἐκεῖνος
**2. ἔμμεν'** = (Attic) εἶναι
**2. ὤνηρ** = (Attic) ὁ ἀνὴρ
**2. ὄττις** = (Attic) ὅστις
**2. τοι** = (Attic) σοι
**3. ἰσδάνει** = (Attic) ἵζάνει
**3. πλάσιον** = (Attic) πλησίον
**3. ἆδυ** = (Attic) ἡδὺ
**3–4. φωνείσας** = (Attic) φωνούσης (contracted present participle, fem. gen. sing. act.)
**5. γελαίσας** = (Attic) γελώσης (contracted present participle, fem. gen. sing. act.)
**5. τό:** "a thing which" (τό is the subject of the verb in line 6)
**5. ἦ μάν** = (Attic) ἦ μήν, "truly"
**6. ἐπτόαισεν** = (Attic) ἐπτόησεν
**7. ὡς** = (Attic) ὡς; with εἰσίδω, "when I behold it [that is, the τό of line 5]..." See note 30 for an alternate rendering and interpretation of this phrase.
**7. βρόχε'** = (Attic) βράχυ; βρόχε' ὤς: "as soon as" or "however briefly"
**7–8. φώνη-ς** = (Attic) φωνῆς
**8. εἴκει** = (Attic) ἵκει
**9. καμ** = (Attic) κατά, *tmesis* with ἔαγε
**10. ὐπαδεδρόμηκεν** = (Attic) ὑποδεδράμηκεν
**11. ὄππα** = (Attic) ὄμμα
**11. ὄρημι** = (Attic) ὁράω
**11–12. ἐπιβρόμεισι** = (Attic) ἐπιρρόμβεισι(ν)
**12. ἄκουαι** = (Attic) ἀκοαί
**13. † έκαδε†:** Voigt's rendering, but Longinus's text offered "κὰδ δέ μ' ἴδρὼς κακχέεται," which most editors read as corrupt, largely on the basis of metrical reasons. One codex (P) of Longinus offers έκαδε μ' ἰδρῶς ψυχρὸς κ' ἀκχέεται ("a could sweat pours down me"), but this rendering contains two too many syllables to work. Whatever the construction, the sense of (Attic) κατά seems to be at play (i.e., sweat pours *down me*).
**13. ἴδρως** = (Attic) ἱδρώς
**13. κακχέεται** = (Attic) καταχεῖται (pres. tense, middle voice)
**14. παῖσαν** = (Attic) πᾶσαν
**14. ἄγρει** = (Attic) αἱρεῖ (from αἱρέω)
**14. ποίας** = (Attic) ποίης (a genitive of comparison)
**15. ἔμμι** = (Attic) εἰμί
**15. τεθνάκην** = (Attic) τεθνάναι (perf. act. infin. of ἀποθνήσκω)
**15. ὀλίγω 'πιδεύης** = "lacking a little bit", that is, "a little bit short of" or "nearly". This phrase is working adverbially with τεθνάκην. That is, "I seem to myself to be a little short of dying."
**16. ἔμ'** = (Attic) μοι

**16. αὔται** = (Attic) αὐτῇ. Together, ἔμ' αὔται is a reflexive pronoun in the dative case ("I seem to myself")

**17. πὰν** = (Attic) πᾶν

**18. τόλματον** = a verbal adjective in –τος, τον; the noun it is modifying is πὰν, "everything must be endured" or "everything must be dared"

### *Sappho* 44 Voigt = 44 L-P

……………………………….
Κυπρο [………………….]ας·
κάρυξ ἦλθε θε[………]ελε[…].θεις
Ἴδαος ταδεκα…φ[..].ις τάχυς ἄγγελος
⟨ ⟩
τάς τ' ἄλλας Ἀσίας. [.]δε. αν κλέος ἄφθιτον·
Ἔκτωρ καὶ συνέταιρ[ο]ι ἄγοισ' ἐλικώπιδα
Θήβας ἐξ ἰέρας Πλακίας τ' ἀπ' [ἀϊ]ν⟨ν⟩άω
ἄβραν Ἀνδρομάχαν ἐνὶ ναῦσιν ἐπ' ἄλμυρον
πόντον· πόλλα δ' [ἐλί]γματα χρύσια κἄμματα
πορφύρ[α] καταΰτ[με]να, ποίκιλ' ἀθύρματα,
ἀργύρα τ' ἀνάριθμα ποτήρια κἀλέφαις.'
ὣς εἶπ'· ὀτραλέως δ' ἀνόρουσε πάτ[η]ρ φίλος·
φάμα δ' ἦλθε κατὰ πτόλιν εὐρύχορον φίλοις.
αὔτικ' Ἰλίαδαι σατίναι[ς] ὐπ' ἐυτρόχοις
ἆγον αἰμιόνοις, ἐπ[έ]βαινε δὲ παῖς ὄχλος
γυναίκων τ' ἄμα παρθενίκα[ν] τ..[..].σφύρων.
χῶρις δ' αὖ Περάμοιο θύγ[α]τρες[
ἴππ[οις] δ' ἄνδρες ὔπαγον ὐπ' ἀρ[ματ-
π[ ]ες ἠίθεοι, μεγάλω[σ]τι δ[
δ[ ]. ἀνίοχοι φ[……].[
π[ ]ξα ο[
[verses (perhaps 6 or 7 lines) missing here]
ἴ]κελοι θέοι[ς
]ἄγνον ἀολ[λε-
ὄρμαται [ ]νον ἐς Ἴλιο[ν
αὖλος δ' ἀδυ[μ]έλης [ ] τ' ὀνεμίγνυ[το
καὶ ψ[ό]φο[ς κ]ροτάλ[ων, λιγέ]ως δ' ἄρα πάρ[θενοι
ἄειδον μέλος ἄγν[ον, ἴκα]νε δ' ἐς αἴθ[ερα
ἄχω θεσπεσία γελ[
πάνται δ' ἦς κάτ' ὄδο[ις
κράτηρες φίαλαί τ' ὀ[…]υεδε [..]..εακ[.].[
μύρρα καὶ κασία λίβανός τ' ὀνεμείχνυτο
γύναικες δ' ἐλέλυσδον ὄσαι προγενέστερα[ι
πάντες δ' ἄνδρες ἐπήρατον ἴαχον ὄρθιον
πάον' ὀνκαλέοντες Ἐκάβολον εὐλύραν
ὔμνην δ' Ἔκτορα κ' Ἀνδρομάχαν θεο⟨ε⟩ικέλο[ις.

*Meter: glyconic with dactylic expansion*

—

**ἀβρός, -ά, -όν:** graceful, delicate, pretty, luxurious
**ἄγγελος, -ου, ὁ:** messenger
**ἁγνός, -ή, -όν:** pure, holy, chaste
**ᾄδω, ᾄσομαι, ᾖσα, —, ᾖσμαι, ᾔσθην:** sing
**ἄθυρμα, -ματος, τό:** beautiful object, an adornment
**αἰθήρ, -έρος, ἡ:** sky
**ἁλμυρός, -ά, -όν:** salty, briny
**ἅμμα, -ματος, τό:** clothing
**ἀνακαλέω:** call or summon by name
**ἀναμίγνυμι, -μίξω, -ἔμιξα, —, -μέμιγμαι, -ἐμίχθην:** mix (*act.*); be mixed or mingled together (*pass.*)
**ἀνάριθμος, -η, -ον:** countless, without number, measureless
**ἀνορούω, —, ἀνόρουσα, —, —, —:** verb form found only in the weak aor. in Homer (as here); start up, leap up
**ἀολλής, -ές:** all together, in a crowd, as a horde
**ἄργυρος, -α, -ον:** made of silver
**ἅρμα, -ματος, τό:** chariot
**αὖ:** again, once more
**αὖλος, -ου, ὁ:** a wind instrument consisting of a reed pipe whose sound marginally resembles that of a modern oboe
**ἀϋμήν, -μένος, ὁ:** scent, fragrance, breath
**αὐτίκα:** immediately, at once
**ἄφθιτος, ον:** imperishable, not subject to death
**εἴκελος, -η, -ον:** like (to) or resembling an object in the dat. case
**Ἕκτωρ, -ορος, ὁ:** prince of Troy whose name means "holding fast". He is the "keep" or "stay" of Ilium.
**ἐλέφας, -αντος, ὁ:** elephant; in the neuter form, used as an adjective meaning "ivory".
**ἔλιγμα, -ματος, τό:** anything that twists or wraps, such as a bracelet or lock of hair; probably "bracelet" here
**ἑλικῶπις, -ώπιδος, ἡ:** a distinctively fem. form of the adj. ἑλῖκωψ, -ωπος, ὁ, ἡ. Quick-glancing; with eyes that dart about; bright-eyed.
**ἐπήρατος, -ον:** charming, lovely
**εὔλυρος, -ον:** skilled in the lyre
**εὐρύχορος, ον:** spacious, characterized by wide-open spaces
**ἐΰτροχος, ον:** smoothly-running
**ἡδυμελής, -ές:** sweetly singing
**ἠίθεος, -ου, ὁ:** unmarried young man or youth
**ἡμίονος, -ου, ἡ:** mule (literally, "half-donkey")
**ἡνίοχος, -ου, ὁ:** chariot-driver (literally, "the one who holds the reins")
**ἠχή, ῆς, ἡ:** echo; ringing or returning sound
**θεσπέσιος, α, ον:** divinely sweet, divinely sounding
**ἰάχω:** resound, ring out, shout

**ἱερός, -ά, -όν:** holy, consecrated, filled with divine power
**Ἰλιάδαι, -ων, οἱ:** descendants of Ilos, Trojans
**κασία, -ας, ἡ:** cassia, a spice like cinnamon
**κῆρυξ, κήρυκος, ὁ:** herald, public messenger
**κλέος, τό:** glory, fame, good report. This noun appears only in the nom. and acc. sg. and pl.
**κρατήρ, -ῆρος, ὁ:** a crater—a large bowl used to mix wine with water from which cups were filled
**κρόταλον, -ου, τό:** a percussion instrument consisting of two castanet-like clappers held in one hand and struck together with the fingers of that hand; often used in accompaniment with dancing
**λίβανος, -ου, ὁ:** frankincense
**λιγύς, λίγεια, λιγύ:** clear-sounding, ringing, whistling, or singing
**μεγαλωστί:** adv., far and wide, over a vast space
**μέλος, -εος, τό:** song
**μύρρα, -ας, ἡ:** myrrh, the resinous gum of an Arabian tree
**ὀλολύζω:** cry out loud or ululate with a loud voice, especially of women praying to the gods
**ὄρθιος, -α, -ον:** straight, upright, high-pitched, loud, shrill
**ὁρμάω, ὁρμήσω, ὥρμησα, ὥρμηκα, ὥρμημαι, ὡρμήθην:** urge on, set in motion (*act.*); be eager (*med./pass.*)
**ὀτραλέος, -α, -ον:** used by Hom. and Hes. only as the adv., ὀτραλέως (as here); quickly, readily
**ὄχλος, -ου, ὁ:** crowd, multitude
**πάντῃ:** adv., everywhere, in all directions, from all sides
**παρθένος, -ου, ἡ:** unmarried young woman or girl
**ποικίλος, -η, -ον:** wrought in various colors or patterns
**πόντος, -ου, ὁ:** sea, open water of the sea
**πορφύρεος, -α, -ον:** purple or blood-red
**ποτήριον, -ου, τό:** drinking-cup, wine-cup
**Πρίαμος, -ου, ὁ:** Priam, aged and noble king of Troy
**προγενής, ές (προγενέστερος, -α, -ον = comparative):** elder, born earlier
**σατίνη, -ης, ἡ:** chariot
**συνέταιρος, -ου, ὁ:** companion, comrade
**σφυρόν, -οῦ, τό:** ankle
**ὑμνέω, ὑμνήσω, ὕμνησα, —, —, —:** sing in praise of, celebrate in song
**φήμη, -ης, ἡ:** speech, utterance, rumor, report
**φιάλη, -ης, ἡ:** a flat bowl used for drinking or pouring libations
**χρυσίος, -ά, -όν:** made of gold, golden
**χωρίς:** adv., separately, apart from
**ψόφος, -ου, ὁ:** sound, especially of musical instruments (and, not of the human voice)

—

**1.–34:** Our knowledge of fragment 44 derives from two Oxyrhynchus papyri, P. Oxy. X 1232 and XVII 2076, both of which contain large, lacunose portions. In a cross-study of both papyri, Sampson (2016) has argued that several lines of the incipit (labeled a–c above) and perhaps six or seven lines after line 20 (labeled 20a–g above) are missing. One of these papyri (P. Oxy. XVII 2076) indicates that fr. 44 was the final poem in the second book the Alexandrian edition of Sappho's poetry, and another ancient source (Athenaeus, 11.460d) independently confirms this.

The lacuna at the incipit leaves some traces of the involvement of Aphrodite, who is referenced by her epithet *Cyprian*. When the text picks up again, the Trojan herald Idaeus, part of whose speech is missing, announces that the newlywed couple of Hector and Andromache are arriving by ship (lines 4–8) and catalogs the bridal treasures that accompany the couple (lines 8–10). News of their arrival sweeps through the city of Troy (line 12), and the community prepares to receive them with appropriate pomp and circumstance (lines 13–17). Mostly missing text intervenes (lines 19–22), and the text resumes with a narration of the festivities in Troy celebrating the marriage, including hymns, dancing, musical procession, and a communally sung Paean to Apollo (lines 26–34).

The poem treats the marriage of Andromache and Hector and is composed in a heavily dactylic meter. Its language and narrative style evoke epic poetry and subject matter. While some scholars (Nagy, 1974, p. 138, Rissman, 1983, and Shrenk, 1994, for example) interpret Sappho 44 in light of "Homeric reminiscences that permeate the poem" (Shrenk, 1994, p. 144), particularly the more tragic scenes involving the meeting of Hector and Andromache on the walls of Troy (*Iliad* 6, 369–439), wherein Andromache imagines the enslavement of herself and their son Astyanax should Hector die in battle, Apollo's desertion of Hector immediately before the latter's death (*Iliad* 22, 208–213), and Andromache's lament, inspired by the sight of Hector's corpse being dragged behind Achilles' chariot (*Iliad* 22, 475–515). Spelman (2017) has argued, however, that archaic Lesbian lyric poetry may generally interact with traditional mythic and epic cycle content rather than the *Iliad* specifically. Furthermore, Spelman posits that the wedding of Hector and Andromache would have brought to mind to Sappho's contemporaries a parallel tradition of the wedding of Paris and Helen, the story of which circulated in the lost epic, *Cypria*. A summary of this epic by a 2nd- or 5th-century CE writer named Proclus claims that its events treated the causative circumstances of the Trojan War. Among the events it narrated, so the summary claims, was the union of Paris and Helen: Aphrodite brought Helen and Paris together; after they had intercourse, they loaded up many valuables onto ships and sailed away at night; when they arrived at Troy, Paris Alexander married Helen. As Spelman (2017, p. 752) succinctly observes, "Sappho's poem presents Troy at its happiest but also recalls the occasion which ultimately doomed the city."

**a–c.:** The text is irretrievably corrupted here.

**1. Κυπρο:** The island of Cyprus, whose connections to Aphrodite are frequently evoked in Sappho's poetry. Hesiod (*Theogony*, 173–199) tells the story of her birth, claiming that she arose out of the sea when Cronos castrated his father, Ouranos, and his genitals fell from the sky and mixed with sea foam. The goddess arose out of the foam and drifted first to the island of Cythera and then to sea-girt Cyprus. The *Homeric Hymn to Aphrodite* (#5) opens with an invocation to the Muse, requesting that the song hymn the deeds of "golden, Cyprian Aphrodite" (lines 1–2). Local tradition on Cyprus maintains that Aphrodite emerged from the sea at the sea stack called the *Petra tou Romiou* ("Rock of Romios") near the city of Paphos.

**3. Ἴδαος:** the herald of the Trojan king Priam in the *Iliad* (see *Il.* 3.248, for example).

**3. τάχυς ἄγγελος:** A Homeric formulaic phrase. For discussion of the considerable Iliadic elements in this poem, consult Shrenk (1994), Rosenmeyer (1997), and, more recently, Spelman (2017), who argues that a poetic treatment of the wedding of Andromache and Hector would have brought to mind to Sappho's audience contemporaneous, traditional poetic treatments of the marriage of Helen and Paris.

**4. κλέος ἄφθιτον:** A Homeric phrase. In the *Iliad's* famous "ambassador scene", Achilles uses this phrase (9.413) to describe the glory that will be his in compensation for a short life.

**5. ἄγοισ'** = (Attic) ἄγουσιν

**6. Θήβας ἐξ ἰέρας:** The epithet of "holy" is standard Homeric phraseology, but Homer uses this particular epithet to describe the city of Thebes (*Il.* 3.66).

**6. Πλακίας:** In the *Iliad*, Andromache's father, Aetion, is from Thebes, below wooded Plakia (see 6.395ff.).

**6. [ἀϊ]ν⟨ν⟩άω:** a gen. sing. fem. adjective, meaning something like, "well-inhabited".

**8–9. κἄμματα/πορφύρ[α] καταΰτ[με]να:** "and fragrant, purple robes". Weaving was the province of women in archaic Greek society, and purple dye signaled both luxury and high status. Purple pigment, the most prized and expensive of fabric dyes, derived from the glandular secretions of dead murex snails and was incredibly difficult to obtain. A single gram of the pigment required the secretions of thousands of snails. Pliny (*Naturalis Historia* 9.62.133) claimed that the best time to harvest murex snails was just before the summer solstice when Dog-Star was rising, or else before spring.

**9. καταΰτ[με]να:** fragrant, a compound form related to the Homeric noun ἀϋτμή, ἡ, which means both "breath" and "fragrance" or "scent".

**10. κἀλέφαις:** *crasis;* ἐλέφαις seems to be an Aeolic form meaning "ivory" (see ἐλέφας, -αντος in the vocabulary above).

**12. πτόλιν** = (Attic) πόλιν; the form used here is not distinctly Aeol., but an epicism found in Homer.
**14. αἰμίονοις** = (Attic) ἡμίονοις
**14. παῖς** = (Attic) πᾶς
**15. παρθενίκαν** = (Attic) παρθένων
**16. Περάμοιο** = (Attic) Πριάμου
**19. ἀνίοχοι** = (Attic) ἡνίοχοι
**20. lacuna consisting of an uncertain number of lines**
**21. ἴκελοι** = (Attic) εἴκελοι
**21. ἄγνον** = (Attic) ἁγνὸν
**22. ἀολλε-:** the text is corrupt here, but the word is, in all probability, some form of ἀολλής, -ές
**23. ὀρμαται** = (Attic) ὁρμᾶται
**24. ἀδυ[μ]έλης** = (Attic) ἡδυμελής, -ές
**24. ὀνεμίγνυτο** = (Attic) ἀνεμίγνυτο, imperf. 3rd s. pass. indic.: the "sweet-singing aulos was mingling" with the sound of another instrument, which was probably named within the lacuna. Campbell (1967, 1982, p. 46) suggests it may have been the cithara, a stringed instrument similar to the lyre.
**25. λιγέως:** adv. of λιγύς
**26. ἄειδον:** uncontracted, epic imperfect form of ᾄδω; = (Attic) ᾖδον
**26–29.:** the text is corrupt, but enough is present to give some indication of the general mood and subject of these lines. γελ[ is probably from some form relating to "laughter" or "laughing"; thus, a "divinely sounding echo of laughter" may be the sense here.
**27. ἄχω** = (Doric) ἠχώ; the Doric ἠχώ = (Attic) ἠχή, ῆς, ἡ.
**28. πάνται δ' ἧς κάτ' ὄδοις:** πάνται = (Attic) πάντῃ ("everywhere"); ἧς = (Attic) ἦν or 3rd s. imperf. of εἰμί; ὄδοις = (Attic) ὁδούς.
**30. μύρρα** = (Attic) σμύρνα. I have listed the Aeolic form in the vocabulary since it is etymologically closer to English than the Attic form and, thus, easier to recall. Campbell (1967, 276) notes that Sappho is the earliest writer to mention myrrh, cassia, and frankincense.
**30. ὀνεμείχνυτο:** from (Attic) ἀναμίγνυμι
**31. ἐλελύσδον:** = (Attic) ὠλολύζον (from ὀλολύζω)
**33. πάον'** = (Attic/Ionic) παιόνα, from παιών, -όνος. A paean is a choral song addressed to and celebrating Apollo (or Artemis).
**33. ὀνκαλέοντες** = (Attic) ἀνακαλοῦντες. In Aeolic, the preposition ὄν is equivalent to ἀνά.
**33. Ἐκάβολον** = (epic) Ἐκήβολον, a Homeric epithet of Apollo, as in *Iliad* 1.14, for example. The epithet contains within it two registers of meaning: (a.) "he who shoots from afar" (ἑκάς + βάλλω); and, (b.) "he who attains his aim" (ἑκών + βάλλω). Apollo opposed the Achaeans and heavily supported the Trojan side of the war.
**34. ὔμνην:** = (Attic) ὕμνουν, 3rd pl. act. imperf. indic.

**34. θεο⟨ε⟩ικέλο[ις:** "like the gods"–a Homeric epithet often applied to Achilles, Hector's killer.

### *Sappho* 58[35]

ὔμμες πεδὰ Μοίσαν ἰ]ο̣κ[ό]λ̣πων κάλα δῶρα, παῖδες,
σπουδάσδετε καὶ τὰ]ν̣ φιλάοιδον λιγύραν χελύνναν·
ἔμοι δ' ἄπαλον πρίν] π̣ο̣τ̣' [ἔ]ο̣ντα χρόα γῆρας ἤδη
ἐπέλλαβε, λεῦκαι δ' ἐγ]ένοντο τρίχες ἐκ μελαίναν·
βάρυς δέ μ' ὀ [θ]ῦμο̣ς πεπόηται, γόνα δ' [ο]ὐ φέροισι,
τὰ δή ποτα λαίψηρ' ἔον ὄρχησθ' ἴσα νεβρίοισι.
τὰ ⟨μὲν⟩ στεναχίσδω θαμέως· ἀλλὰ τί κεν ποείην;
ἀγήραον ἄνθρωπον ἔοντ' οὐ δύνατον γένεσθαι.
καὶ γάρ π̣[ο]τ̣α̣ Τίθωνον ἔφαντο βροδόπαχυν Αὔων
ἔρωι φ..α̣θ̣ε̣ισαν βάμεν' εἰς ἔσχατα γᾶς φέροισα[ν,
ἔοντα̣ [κ]ά̣λ̣ο̣ν καὶ νέον, ἀλλ' αὖτον ὔμως ἔμαρψε
χρόνωι π̣ό̣λ̣ι̣ο̣ν̣ γῆρας, ἔχ[ο]ν̣τ̣' ἀθανάταν ἄκοιτιν.

*Meter: acephalous Hipponacteans with double choriambic expansion*[36]

—

**ἀγήραος, -ον:** ageless, without old age
**ἀθάνατος, -ον:** immortal, "without death"
**ἄκοιτις, -ιος, ἡ:** wife, spouse
**Ἀπαλός, -ή, -όν:** soft, delicate
**γῆρας, γήραος, τό:** old age
**γόνυ, γόνατος, τό:** knee
**ἐπιλαμβάνω, -λήψομαι, -έλαβον, -εἴληφα, -εἴλημμαι, -ελήφθην:** seize, attack
**ἔρος, -ου, ὁ:** love, desire
**ἔσχατος, -η, -ον:** furthest, uttermost, extreme
**Ἠώς, Ἠόος, ἡ:** Eos, the goddess of Dawn
**θαμέες, οἱ, dat. θαμέσι, acc. θαμέας, adv. θαμέως:** thickly crowded, often
**θρίξ, τρίχος, ἡ:** hair
**ἰόκολπος, -ον:** violet-colored, draping robes
**λαιψηρός, -ά, -όν:** nimble, quick, light
**λευκός, -ή, -όν:** white
**λιγυρός, -ά, -όν:** clear-toned
**μάρπτω, μάρψω, ἔμαρψα, —, —, —:** seize, reach, catch
**μέλας, μέλαινα, μέλαν:** black
**νεβρίον, -ου, τό:** possibly a diminutive of νεβρός, -οῦ, ὁ, fawn
**ὅμως:** yet, still, nevertheless
**ὀρχέομαι, ὀρχήσομαι, ὠρχησάμην, —, —, —:** dance
**πολιός, -ά, -όν:** grey, grizzled
**ῥοδόπηχυς, -υ:** rosy-armed
**σπουδάζω, σπουδάσομαι, ἐσπούδασα, ἐσπούδακα, ἐσπύδασμαι, ἐσπουδάσθην:** be eager, pursue earnestly

**στεναχίζω:** Epic lengthened form of στενάχω: groan or lament (about an accusative object)
**Τίθωνος, -ου, ὁ:** Tithonus, the mortal husband of Eos (Dawn). Zeus, at her request, granted Tithonus immortal life. However, Eos forgot to ask Zeus to also give her husband eternal youth.
**φιλάοιδος, -ον:** delighting in signing
**χελώνη, -ης, ἡ:** literally, "tortoise shell"; a lyre made from a tortoise shell
**χρώς, χροός, ὁ:** skin, complexion

—

**1.–12:** Rarely does a new find of ancient Greek literature occur, and even more rarely a new find originally composed by a female poet. Even more rarely still does a new find make breaking news. But, when the late Martin L. West, a British philologist and scholar of Classics, published an article in the *TLS: The Times Literary Supplement* entitled, "A New Sappho Poem" (June 24, 2005), containing in it a proposed text and translation of the so-called "Tithonus Poem", Sappho made international headlines.[37]

The poem published in the *TLS* is not *really* "new", in the sense that fragments of it had been published by Lobel and Page (1955) and Voigt (1971) as "fragment 58", deriving their edited texts from: (a) a known papyrus source (2nd century CE P. Oxy. 1787), retrieved from an ancient land-fill in Oxyrhynchus, Egypt by archaeologists B.P. Grenfell and A.S. Hunt during their 1889–1907 excavations; and, (b) the ancient author Athenaeus (15.687b), who quotes part of the poem, as well as other ancient attestations. What made headlines was the fact that the existing, known fragment's substantial lacunae were supplied by newly discovered fragments (called the Cologne Papyrus fragments, or P. Köln inv. 21351 and 21376), enabling papyrologists to study the overlapping texts and produce a complete, whole poem. The Cologne papyrus fragments were acquired in the form of mummy-cartonnage, recycled papyrus covered with gesso and decorative paint and used in ancient Egyptian, mummy-mask funerary art. The papyri used in the cartonnage had originally contained a Hellenistic era (3rd century BCE) collection of literary extracts and were purchased by University of Cologne from an antiquities dealer and then published by Gronewald and Daniel (2004a and 2004b).

The poem offers a first-person, lyric perspective on the experience of descending into old age and may have been composed as a choral song. The first two lines invite παῖδες (young persons whose genders and ages are not specified) to pursue the gifts of the Muses and the "clear-sounding" lyre. The narrator transitions between youthful pursuits and the limitations set upon her in old age by means of a pronominal cap (ἔμοι δ', line 3). The physical changes wrought by age are cataloged (lines 3–6) and then lamented (line 6). A gnomic statement follows, situating the limitations of human beings (line 7) as a prelude to the mythic exemplum of the continually aging Tithonus, consort of the immortal goddess Eos (lines 9–12).

**1. ὔμμες:** = (Attic) ὑμεῖς

**πεδὰ:** = (Attic) μετά (with, among)

**Μοίσαν:** = (Attic) Μουσῶν (gen. pl.)

**2. σπουδάσδετε:** = (Attic) σπουδάζετε

**χελύνναν:** = (Attic) χελώνην

**3. πρίν:** here, used adverbially: "earlier" or "before"

**4. ἐπέλλαβε:** = (Attic) **ἐπέλαβε**

**5. πεπόηται:** 3rd. sing. perf. pass. of ποιέω, "has been made" (i.e., "has become")

**φέροισι:** = (Attic) φέρουσι

**6. τά:** the definite article is often (particularly in the Homeric dialect) used as a relative pronoun. Its antecedent is γόνα. It is being used in the same way in line 7.

**ποτα:** = (Attic) ποτε (once, once upon a time); see also line 9.

**ὄρχησθ':** present, deponent, epexegetical infinitive with λαίψηρ': "quick to dance" or "nimble at dancing"

**7. τά:** see line 6 above, but this time as the object of στεναχίσδω = (Attic) στενάχω, the lengthened epic form of which is στεναχίζω

**κεν:** = (Attic) ἄν (+ optative in an independent clause indicates potential or hypothetical)

**ποείην:** = (Attic) ποιείην, 1st s. pres., act., opt. of ποιέω.

**8. ἔοντ' οὐ δύνατον:** an impersonal construction: "since it is not possible that…"

**9. ἔφαντο:** 3rd pl. imperf. act. indic. of φημί: "they say that" (a traditional way of introducing a myth or story)

**βροδόπαχυν:** = (Attic) ῥοδόπηχυν; in Homer, Eos is ῥοδοδάκτυλος ("rosy-fingered")

**Αὔων:** the Aeolic, accusative form of Ἠώς, or Eos, the goddess "Dawn"

**10. φ...αθ̣ε̣ισαν:** several letters of this word are unclear in the manuscripts. Not enough of this word survives to make sense of it.

**βάμεν':** Aeol. aor. infin. of βαίνω (walk, come, go)

**εἰς ἔσχατα γᾶς:** "to the ends of the earth"

**φέροισαν:** = (Attic) φέρουσαν; Αὔων is the subject of this participle

**11. ὔμως:** = (Attic) ὅμως

***Sappho* 1 Voight = L-P 1**

Immortal Aphrodite on your richly carved throne,
child of Zeus,[38] weaver of deception, I beg you,
do not subdue my heart, mistress,
with anguish and misery,

but come to this place, if ever before
you heard my voice, listening from afar,

and abandoning your father's golden home
you came;

and, having fastened them to your chariot, beautiful, swift
sparrows[39] drew you over the black earth,
wings eddying in a blur as they flew from heaven through the middle
of the aether,

and quickly they arrived. But, you, blessed one,
smiling with your immortal face,
asked what thing, once again, I suffered and why,
once again, I called,

and what thing I most wanted in my frenzied heart
to happen. "Whom, once again, am I to persuade
to draw back into your love-making?[40] Who wrongs you,
Sappho?

For if she flees, she will quickly pursue;
and, if she refuses love-gifts, she will give them;
and, if she does not love, quickly she will love
even if she is unwilling."

Come to me now, too, and release me
from oppressive cares, and however many things my heart
desires to come to fruition, make them happen. And, you yourself,
be my ally in battle.

### *Sappho* fr. 2 Campbell (1967) = Voigt 2 = L-P 2

Come to me from Crete to this holy haunt,
where stands your graceful grove of
apple-trees and where altars are smoking
with incense;

And, here, cool water trickles down from
tree-branches, and the whole sanctuary is shaded
with roses, and sleep pours down from shimmering
leaves;

And, here blooms a meadow where horses graze
...... with blossoms, and the breezes
sweetly blow....
.......

Here, you, Cyprian[41] goddess, taking...
pour luxuriously in golden cups
a wine of nectar[42] mixed with
our festivities.

### *Sappho* fr. 16 Voigt = L-P 16

Some people claim that an armed force of cavalry, others– of infantry,
and, still others–of ships, is the most beautiful thing
upon the black earth. But, I say it is whatever
someone desires.

It is entirely easy to make this clear
to everyone. For, Helen, far surpassing
other mortals in beauty, abandoned
her excellent husband

and went sailing to Troy, remembering neither
her child nor her dear parents, but … led her…
…….
………………………..
…………………
… now remembering Anactoria
who is not here,

I would rather see her lovely walk
and bright, sparkling face
than the chariots and infantry of Lydia
with their weapons.

### Sappho fr. 16a (possibly a continuation of fr. 16)[43]

It is not possible for a person
to be altogether happy. But, it is possible
to pray to have some portion of good things. I myself
know this from experience.

[2–4 stanzas missing]

…………………….. to be
…………………[you walked?] on tip-toes
,… the snow; but she……………
much….

…………………..to depart
……………… for whomever
I treat well, those people in particular hurt
me without warning.

### *Sappho* fr. 31 Voigt = 31 L-P

That man seems to me to an equal of the gods,
whoever sits opposite you,
and being near you, hears you
sweetly speaking

and laughing alluringly, a thing which has made
my heart in my breast leap;
for, when I look on with even the briefest glance,
my voice fails me,

my tongue is broken, a subtle
fire has suddenly run up under my skin,
my eyes see nothing, there is a buzzing
in my ears,

a sweat pours over me, a trembling
seizes all of me, I am paler than grass,[44]
and I seem to myself
just a little short of dying.

But everything must be endured [or dared], [….for even poor person…]

**_Sappho_ 44 Voigt = 44 L-P**

[several verses missing]
Cyprus……
Idaeos[45] came…………………
………… a swift messenger
………………………………
"…the other women of Asia…undying glory;
Hector and his companions are bringing the glancing-eyed woman
from holy Thebes and populous Plakia,
graceful Andromache,[46] on ships over the briny
sea; and they are bringing with them many golden bracelets,
fragrant, purple clothing, objects of rare craftsmanship,
and countless silver goblets and ivories."
So he spoke. And, his dear father leapt up,
and, word went quickly to his family and friends throughout the
   spacious city.
At once, the descendants of Ilos[47] brought their smoothly running
   chariots
led by mules, and the entire multitude of women and unmarried girls
   [with lovely] ankles
climbed on board. But, apart from them the daughters of Priam …
and the men yoked their horses to chariots
…… unmarried men far and wide…
….chariot-drivers….
……………
[several verses missing…]
…………….like the gods
……….holy, as a crowd
eager… to Ilium
and the sweet-singing aulos[48] mingled

with the sounds of the crotala,[49] and the unmarried girls
sang a resounding and pure melody,
and a divinely sweet echo [of laughter?] rose to the heavens....
and there was everywhere along the roads.......
mixing bowls and libation-cups...........
myrrh and cassia and frankincense wafted together
and all of the elder women were ululating,
while the men were ringing out a lovely,
paean to far-shooting Apollo who is skilled in the lyre,[50]
celebrating godlike Hector and Andromache.

**Sappho 58**

Seek after the beautiful gifts of the violet-robed Muses, children,
and the clear-toned lyre that loves singing;
but for me—old age has already seized my once
delicate skin, my black hair has become white;
my heart has become heavy, and my knees no longer support me,
although they used to be nimble as fawns in the dance.
I groan in lament often about this; but what could I possibly do?
A human being cannot be ageless.
For they say that once upon a time, rosy-armed Eos[51]
carried Tithonus away to the ends of the earth [overcome] with desire,
since he was beautiful and young. Yet, grey old age
took him in time, even though he had an immortal wife.

## Notes

1. Strabo (13.2.3) states that Sappho was a "marvel", and that "in all the time of which we have record I do not know of the existence of any woman who could rival Sappho, even in a slight degree, in the elegance of poetry".
2. *Palatine Anthology*, 9.506, 9.66, 9.571, 7.15, 7.407; *Anthology of Planudes* (*A. Pl.*), 1.65. For a discussion of Sappho's representations in Hellenistic epigram, see Gosetti-Murrayjohn (=Pitts), 2006a.
3. The source for this story is rather late, 5th century CE author Stobaeus (3.29.58), a compiler of extracts from various Greek authors. The author to which Stobaeus attributes this apocryphal tale is the 2nd and 3rd centuries CE writer Aelian (frags. 187/190).
4. The 1st century BCE Roman poet Catullus not only imitated Sappho's poetry (especially poems LI, LXI, LXII), but also used the epithet "Lesbia" as a sobriquet for his literary love, no doubt as a tribute to Sappho. In poem XXXV, Catullus calls his poet-friend's new infatuation a "Sapphica puella musa doctor" ("a Sapphic girl more learned than a Muse"). Horace alludes heavily to Sappho's poetry (in *Odes* 1.22 and 4.1, for instance), as do Propertius and Ovid. One scholar has even raised the question as to whether Sappho was as influential to the Roman *literati* as was Callimachus (Thorsen, 2019).
5. Amipsias, for example, an Athenian colleague of Aristophanes, wrote a comedy entitled *Sappho.* Pap. Ox. 2659 fr. 1 coll. 2; see also Pollux 9.138 who cites

the author and title of the comedy in a passing comment about the various synonyms for "loitering" to be found in Attic 5th and 4th centuries texts.

6. Athenaeus 13.599d = Kassel-Austin, 1986, vol. 5, p. 94.
7. Eusebius (3rd cent. CE) dates her floruit to the Olympic year 45.1 (600/599 BCE). The 10th century Byzantine encyclopedia of the ancient Mediterranean world (called the *Suda*) claimed that she was either born or at the height of her career in the 42nd Olympiad (612–608 BCE). Several ancient sources claim that she was a contemporary of the poet Alcaeus (born c. 625–620 BCE) and of the tyrant of Mitylene, Pittacus (c. 650–570 BCE). See, for example, Hermesianax (4th century BCE), *Leontion*, 47–56, which claims (quite anachronistically) that the poets Alcaeus and Anacreon were once rivals for the love of Sappho, but it should be noted that we know of at least one comedy entitled *Sappho* in which the poets Archilochus and Hipponax were represented as Sappho's lovers (a comedy by Diphilus, Athen. 13.599d; See also Kassel-Austin (1986, vol. 5, p. 94). Strabo, likewise, places her in the general timeframe of Pittacus and Alcaeus (13.2.3). Sappho fr. 98b L-P mentions the exile of the sons of Cleanax, a political rival of Pittacus.
8. Strabo 13.2.1–2.
9. Sappho L-P 98(b). See also L-P 132, in which Cleis is both named and referred to as the narrator's daughter.
10. Par. Marmor 36; For a useful text and study of the Parian Marble, see Rostein (2016).
11. Sappho's plunge from the White Rock out of frenzied, unrequited desire for Phaon probably appeared first in comedy and was taken up by Ovid (or "Pseudo-Ovid") in his *Heroides* XV. Menander, fr. 258 K, is the first surviving attestation of this story, and the suicidal leap is mentioned in the introductory anapests of his comedy, *Leukadia*. See also Strabo 10.2.9. For discussion of the association of the "White Rock" and Phaon with the underworld in Greek literature, see Nagy (1973). For the question of the authenticity of the Ovidian "Epistula Sapphus" (*Heroides* XV), see Tarrant (1981) and Knox (1995, p. 12–14). For discussions of the representation of Sappho by Ovid in the "Epistula Sapphus", see Gordon (1997) and Hallett (2005), both of whom argue that Ovid characterizes Sappho in a very masculine way.
12. Margaret Reynolds (2001) compiled a very useful compendium of many of the literary and dramatic representations of Sappho since antiquity, demonstrating how her influence has been coupled with (and sometimes fueled by) speculations about her sexuality, loves, and life.
13. See Hallett (1982) on the question of Cleïs' identity in fr. 132 L-P.
14. The ancient Greek word *hetaera* literally means "companion," and was widely used as a euphemism to describe both free, usually foreign, and enslaved women who entertained and sold sexual favors to men in a variety of transactional and relational contexts.
15. Herodotus 2.134.1–2.135.6. For discussion of these sources, see Lidov (2002).
16. Obbink (2014), note 2.
17. See Higgins (January 9, 2020), Sabar (June, 2020), and Sampson and Uhlig (November 19, 2020) for discussions of the allegations of antiquities theft and fraud facing Obbink for alleged, illicit sales of Oxyrhynchus papyri belonging to the Egypt Exploration Society and housed at Oxford University's Sackler Library. Other fragments from the Oxyrhynchus collection are alleged to have been sold privately by Obbink to purchasing agents of the Museum of the Bible, a museum created by the Green family, the American, evangelical owners of the Hobby Lobby craft-store chain. See also Sampson (2020), whose analysis of metadata of a brochure advertising P.Sapph.Obbink for private

sale all but prove that Obbink's claims of the poem's provenance are patently false.

18. Stehle (2016).
19. Lidov (2009) cautions that the evidence for an Alexandrian edition of Sappho's poetry arranged according to meter is fairly sparse, and is predicated upon ancient attestations that certain meters were found in certain books. Moreover, papyri often show multiple poems in the same or similar meters or stanzas, suggesting a metrical arrangement.
20. *Palatine Anthology (A.P.).* 6.269, 7.489, 7.505.
21. For a discussion of the Alexandrian edition or editions of Sappho's poetry, see Yatromanolakis (1999). He argues that it is likely that more than one edition or collection was made available during the Hellenistic era, and that later biographers of Sappho and encyclopedic compilers, such as the author of the *Suda* (who claims that there were 9 books), would have had a wide variety of source materials (including such editions) to draw from.
22. Aristoxenus named as the source in ps.-Plutarch, *On Music,* 16.1136c considers the Mixolydian mode Sappho's invention. The same work, however (*On Music* 28.1140f), also attributes the invention of the Mixolydian to another great Lesbian musician, inventor, and composer, Terpander. Plato, *Rep.* 3.398d-e.
23. The earliest manuscript containing fragments of Sappho's poetry is the so-called "Cologne" papyrus, which has been found to have a very similar and unique writing style as another manuscript containing anonymous fragments of tragedy and dated to the early 3rd century BCE. For an overview of the paleographical histories of these papyri, see Hammerstaedt (2009).
24. See fragments 1.21, 65.5, 94.5, and 133.2.
25. A point driven home by Stehle (2016, p. 267).
26. See Rosenmeyer, Patricia (2008). Discussing the set of four elegiac poems inscribed by Julia Balbilla on the colossus statue of Memnon in Egypt, Rosenmeyer points out (p. 335), "Elegiac meter is a logical choice for inscriptional verse, but the dialect [Aeolic] is definitely not, and calls out for our attention" as Balbilla uses dialect and style to signal that Sappho is a literary model.
27. 104(b) and 108 Voigt and Julian *Or.* 3.109c.
28. As argued by Dale, Alexander, 2011, esp. pgs. 63–65. For a discussion of Sappho's influence on Paulus Silentiarius, see Gosetti-Murrayjohn (= Pitts) (2006b).
29. The earliest of these was published by Johann Christian Wolf, 1733 (*Sapphus, poetriae lesbiae, fragmenta et elogia quotquot in auctoribus antiquis Graecis et Latinis reperiuntur cum virorum doctorum notis integris*). Hamburg: A. Vandenhoeck. A translation in English was published by Joseph Addison in 1735 in a volume entitled, *The Works of Anacreon* in London by the publisher J. Watts.
30. See Rissman (1983) and Rosenmeyer (1997) for discussions of the complex interplay between Sappho's poetry, Homeric epic, and oral and textual transmission in archaic lyric poetry.
31. For discussion of the Alexandrian edition of Sappho's poetry, Yatromanolakis (1999) is an excellent resource. He argues that there is little reliable evidence to support the existence of a ninth book.
32. A seminal study of priamels may be found in Bundy's (1986) analysis of Pindar's First Olympian Ode, p. 47–59.
33. The Greek text of Stesichorus's palinode, according to Plato's Phaedrus (243a2–243b3): οὐκ ἔστ' ἔτυμος λόγος οὗτος,/ οὐδ' ἔβας ἐν νηυσὶν εὐσέμοις,/οὐδ' ἵκεο Πέργαμα Τροίας.
34. This text is mostly Voigt. However, the emendation of ὡς γὰρ εἰσίδω in line 6 is suggested by Glenn Most (1996), p. 31. Most's rendering makes the object of εἰσίδω ambiguous (this scene? you? that man? the both of you together?). Voigt

has "ὡς γὰρ [ἔς] σ' ἴδω" ("when I look at *you*"). The text is sufficiently corrupt to make either version possible, with significantly differing implications for interpretation of the poem.

35. Text from Obbink (2009).
36. For a discussion of the meter and metrical style of Sappho 58 (also commonly called "The Tithonus Poem"), see Lidov (2009).
37. For overviews of this discovery, see Skinner (2009), Obbink (2009), and Hammerstaedt (2009).
38. In Homer's *Iliad* (5.370-5.371), Aphrodite is the daughter of Zeus by the goddess Dione. In the *Theogony* (176–200), however, Hesiod offers an alternative paternity for Aphrodite, claiming that she originated from the mixing with sea water of the castrated genitalia of the male sky god, Ouranos, or "Heaven", the grandfather of Zeus.
39. Sparrows, as well as doves and swans, were sacred to Aphrodite.
40. Sappho imagines Aphrodite appearing to her and addressing her with the words in quotations. There is some wonderful ambiguity in the original Greek that is worth commenting on here. I have translated the ancient Greek word *philotata* as "love-making", but it has a wide range of meanings, from a more platonic sense ("friendship", "affection") to an erotic one ("sexual love" or "sex").
41. Hesiod's *Theogony* (192–193) claims that Aphrodite first went to the island of Cyprus after she was washed up onto Cythera at her birth (see endnote 1). He also claims, however (198–199), that she is called "Cyprian-born" because she was born on Cyprus.
42. While humans drink wine, nectar is traditionally the exclusive drink of the gods.
43. Lines 1–4 of fr. 16a may be a continuance of fr. 16. Fr. 16a is derived from three papyrus rolls dating from the 1st century to early 3rd century CE. For ancient Greek text and apparatus criticus, see Obbink, Dirk (2016), p. 13–33, esp. p. 19.
44. Translators often render this phrase as "greener than grass," which, in English idiom, suggests an experience of jealousy. However, the Greek actually says "paler". It must be remembered that under the hot Mediterranean sun, grass often turns a pale, yellowish color. While the physical symptoms described in this poem may be the result of jealousy, a careful reading of the poem suggests other possibilities, as well, such as desire.
45. Idaeos is a prominent herald of the Trojans in the *Iliad.* See *Il.* 3.248, for example.
46. Andromache, the wife of the Trojan prince Hector, was the daughter of Eëtion, the king of Cilicia who dwelled in Thebes under Plakia. In the *Iliad* (6.414–430), Andromache pleads with Hector not to face Achilles one-on-one in battle, as that Greek hero slew her father, sacked the city of Thebes, and killed her seven brothers on the same day. "Hector," she pleads, "you are father to me and queenly mother, you are brother and my strong husband. Come now, have pity and remain here on the wall so that you do not make your child an orphan and your wife a widow".
47. The name of "Ilos" is associated in myth with the founding of Ilium (or, Troy). According to Homer (*Il.* 20.215–239), Dardanus, a son of Zeus and founder of Dardania before Troy was established, had a son, Erichthonius, who became the wealthiest of mortals. Erichthonius fathered Tros, who became the king of the Trojans, and among the sons of Tros were Ilos, Assaracus, and Ganymedes (beloved by Zeus and the wine-bearer of the gods). Ilos' son, Laomedon, was king Priam's father.

48. The aulos was a wind-instrument with a double-reed mouthpiece. Although it is often called a "flute" or "double-flute", the aulos bears more affinity to the modern oboe. Two *auloi* were fitted together at the mouthpiece to produce a rich and enchanting double-melody.
49. This percussion instrument consists of two castanet-like clappers held in one hand and struck together with the fingers of that hand; it was often used in accompaniment with the singing and dancing of marriage processions.
50. Sappho uses two epicizing epithets of the god Apollo, *far-shooting* and *skilled in the lyre*. His iconic bow and arrow enable him to be "far-shooting", and the first book of the Iliad depicts the god climbing Mt. Ida, taking aim at animals in the Achaean camp, and hurling forth an arrow that spreads plague among them because King Agamemnon dismissed and insulted a priest of Apollo, Chryses, who came to the Achaean camp to ransom from them his captive daughter. Apollo's role in the *Iliad* is substantial, and he generally supports the Trojans and Trojan Hector, who is abandoned by the god on the battlefield to face a raging Achilles alone.
51. Eos was the goddess of Dawn whose epithets in early Greek literature included "rosy-fingered", "rosy-armed", and "golden-throned". She was the daughter of Helios and the sister of Selene (Moon) and Helios (Sun). The *Homeric Hymn to Aphrodite* (*Homeric Hymn* 5.218ff.) tells the story of her love affair with her mortal lover, Tithonus. According to this source, Eos asked Zeus to make him deathless and immortal. Zeus granted her request, but as she had not thought to ask for eternal youth to attend her husband's immortality, Tithonus grew old endlessly. While he enjoyed youth he lived a sweet life with Eos at the ends of the earth by the streams of Oceanus. But, when the first gray hairs appeared upon his head and beard, Eos kept away from his bed, although she continued to feed him with ambrosia and clothe him richly. But, when his old age advanced to such a state that he could not lift his limbs, she laid him in a room and built doors to shut him in. There he babbles ceaselessly and has no strength in him at all.

# 2 Corinna

Corinna hailed from the *polis* (city) of Tanagra in Boeotia, just over 50 km (about 33 mi.) northwest of modern-day Athens, and one source claims that she was the daughter of father Acheloodorus and mother Procatia.[1] What survives of her poetry gives every indication that it concerned epichoric (i.e., local) legend about founding heroes and minor deities indigenous to Boeotia (the ancestral origins of the local Ptoan oracle, for example, in *PMG* 654 iii.32–41), while adapting Panhellenic myths in broader circulation (such as stories about and the lineage of descendants of the hunter-giant, Orion) in such a way as to connect them to and celebrate their relationship with her own *polis*, thus increasing her locality's prestige among other Greek polities.[2] Indeed, much recent scholarship has centered on fleshing out the blending and merging of Panhellenic and epichoric elements in the fragments of Corinna's poetry that survive.[3] Moreover, her poetry is unique among Greek lyric poets for its use of a distinctive local, Boeotian dialect, one of the three major strains within the Aeolic family of dialects.[4] Even ancient Greek and Roman authors, some of whom wrote handbooks on grammar and meter, occasionally felt moved to explain and comment upon her poetry's Boeotian orthography.[5]

If Pausanias (9.22.3), the 2nd-century CE Greek traveler and geographer, is to be believed, Corinna was buried in a tomb in a conspicuous part of Tanagra, and a painting of her wearing a fillet or headband that signified her victory over Pindar in a lyric poetry contest in Thebes proudly adorned her hometown's local gymnasium. Pausanias attributes her victory to the fact that she composed in an Aeolian dialect which locals could understand, unlike Pindar, who composed in the Doric (more 'international') dialect, which was more commonly spoken in areas like the Peloponnesus, Sicily, Crete, and Rhodes, far from Boeotian Thebes. Pausanias adds that if her likeness in the painting was a true representation, Corinna was "the most beautiful woman of her time," and he seems to suggest that her victory over Pindar may have, at least in part, been attributable to her good looks. While Pausanias plays the role of interpreter of local paintings and statues in his travel writings, and we should, thus, take his views as subjective, they do

DOI: 10.4324/9781003031727-4

give us some insight into how Corinna was perceived not only within her own community centuries later, but also by a visiting, learned, itinerant traveler who gave every impression of being familiar with her name, if not her *oeuvre.*

As to her purported victory over Pindar, a fellow Boeotian, ancient sources claim that she defeated him five times in competitions at Thebes.[6] She is also said to have offered a young and aspiring Pindar critical feedback, counseling him that "making myths" was the business of poetry, and advising him against a compositional focus on embellishments like excessive wordiness, metaphors, melodies, and rhythms. He is said to have taken her advice by generating a poem that mentioned Ismenus, Melia, Cadmus, the race of sown men, Thebe, Heracles, and Dionysus in the space of four lines. Our source states that when Pindar showed the poem to Corinna, she laughed and said that one should sow with the hand and not with the sack.[7] While these sources offer apocryphal legend that ought to be viewed with some skepticism as to their historicity (as one scholar put it, "the *testimonia* are notoriously inaccurate on matters of biographical, historical and geographic detail"),[8] nevertheless, they do indicate that in antiquity Corinna was viewed as a highly competent poet who was a contemporary of Pindar, who rivaled him and bested him in both style and content, and who performed in the same public arena in Boeotian Thebes.[9]

So much for where Corinna lived and, if our sources are to be trusted at all, competed publicly. But, when did she live? On this question, we enter into uncertainty and wade into a great deal of scholarly debate, in which dialect elements of Corinna's poetry, as well as the modality of transmission of epichoric and Panhellenic myths in it, are frequently brought to bear. There are generally two camps. The traditional date for Corinna situates her in the 5th century BCE,[10] the evidence for which rests largely on ancient testimonia linking her with both Pindar and the 6th century BCE, Boeotian, female poet, Myrtis.[11] The *Suda* claims that Corinna was a pupil of Myrtis, whose poetry does not survive despite the fact that she was also reputed to have been the teacher of Pindar. In addition to this connection with Myrtis, the ancient grammarian Apollonius Dyscolus preserves a snippet of a poem in which Corinna's first-person narrator-persona states, "... and, I also find fault with clear-voiced (*ligouran*) Myrtis because she, being a woman, once entered into strife (or competition) with Pindar."[12]

More recently, however, additional evidence has been considered to place Corinna in the 5th century. Larson (2002), who provides a comparative reading of Corinna's mythological subjects against those in Hesiod's *Catalogue of Women* has suggested, in response to those who favor a later date on the grounds that Corinna's genealogical and regional material are characteristic of a Hellenistic author,[13] that "Corinna ... appropriates the genealogical tradition found in a Hesiodic, Panhellenic context, and returns it to its epichoric roots," and that "Corinna's subject matter is very much at home in the fifth century, with affinities to the genealogical epic and the body of epichoric material (essentially lost to us) that made up the sources for such epic." This traditional, 5th century date for Corinna, Larson notes, is made more plausible by the fact that a 4th-century BCE sculpture of Myrtis in the Roman city of Pompeii crafted by the artist Silanion has been identified as such by the art historian Andrew Stewart in a 1998 publication, providing some evidence that Myrtis was well-known by the 4th century BCE.[14]

As hinted above, however, there are detractors who yet argue that Corinna lived centuries later during the Hellenistic age, sometime after 300 BCE.[15] Lobel (1930) and West (1970 and 1990), for example, argued, among other reasons (relating to style, orthography, dialect, meter, language, diction, and content), that the papyrus of her poetry is written in 3rd century BCE Boeotian dialect (not 5th century)[16] and that the so-called "Terpsichore" fragment (*PMG* 655, included in this volume) was composed with the intention of placing it as an introductory poem to a collection of her poetry, a practice which West (1990) argues is not attested before 300 BCE. Until new evidence comes to light or familiar evidence is reexamined in such a way as to provide a conclusive consensus, the debate about when Corinna lived—either 5th century or 3rd century BCE—continues.

Four substantial fragments of poems preserved on papyri survive and are included in this volume, and all of them are in fragmentary state with some illegible portions that have been partially reconstructed by papyrologists and editors.[17] One of them, the so-called "Terpsichore" fragment (*PMG* 655), begins with an invocation of sorts, in which the narrator states, "Terpsichore [summons?] me/to sing beautiful tales/for the white-robed women of Tanagra,/and the city rejoices greatly/at the swallow-song of my voice." The references to Terpsichore (the Muse of lyric or melic poetry), tales or stories, the white-robed women of Tanagra, the city, and the poet's voice all conspire to lead many readers to conclude that this poem was intended to be performed publicly by a singing and dancing chorus of local, young women. Such choral poems, called *parthenia* (literally, "maiden" songs), were common to the melic poetry of the 5th century BCE. Several religious contexts for the performance of her *parthenia* have been proposed, such as a cult festival in honor of the Muses called the Mouseia at Thespia[18] or the Daedala festival in honor of Hera at Plataia,[19] particularly given that another fragment (*PMG* 654.i.12–34) features Hera so prominently in it. Those who argue that Corinna's date is Hellenistic also conjecture that *PMG* 655 may involve conscious archaicizing. In this line of thinking, the poem self-consciously models itself on a 5th-century *parthenion*, but was intended largely for a reading audience rather for performance by a chorus of young women.

In antiquity, Corinna appears to have been known for complex manipulations of local and Panhellenic myth. Corinna's name first appears in Roman literature in the elegies of Propertius (2.3.21), whose narrator's mistress Cynthia dances like Ariadne among the Maenads and sings in the style of Sappho and sets her own poetry in rival with that of "antiquae ... Corinnae."

Heath (2013) has convincingly argued that her "masterly and creative treatment of traditional tales" (p. 163) led Ovid to adopt the sobriquet "Corinna" as both the name of his elegiac mistress in the *Amores* and as a symbol of his elegiac poetry. And, Statius (*Silvae* 5.3.158) characterizes Corinna's poetry as "tenuis" (a translation of the Greek word "*leptos*", meaning particularly fine, delicate, restrained in style, elegant) and "arcana" (hidden, secret, mysterious, probably in reference to the learnedness of her mythography). As Plant (2004, p. 93) points out, Corinna's poetry appeared in edited volumes, and Antipater of Thessaloniki, Clement of Alexandria, and Eustathius all considered her poetry canonical.

## Select Bibliography

Allen, A. and J. Frel. 1972. "A Date for Corinna." *CJ* 68.1: 26–28.

Berman, D. W. 2010. "The Landscape and Language of Korinna," *GRBS* 50: 41–62.

Bintliff, J., et al. 2004. "The Tanagra Project: Investigations at an Ancient Boeotian City and in its Countryside (2000–2002)," *Bulletin de correspondence hellénique*. vol. 128–129, 2.1: 541–606. doi: https://doi.org/10.3406/bch.2004.7366

Campbell, D. A. 1967, 1972, 1976, 1982, and 1990. *Greek Lyric Poetry*. Bristol: Bristol Classical Press.

———. 1992. *Greek Lyric, Vol. IV: Bacchylides, Corinna, and Others*. Cambridge, MA: Harvard University Press.

Clayman, D. L. 1978. *"The Meaning of Corinna's Ϝεροῖα," CQ 28*.2: 396–397.

Collins, D. 2006. "Corinna and Mythological Innovation," *CQ* 56.1: 19–32.

Finglass, P. 2007. *Pindar: Pythian Eleven*. Cambridge: Cambridge University Press.

Heath, J. 2013. "Why Corinna?" *Hermes* 141: 155–170.

———. 2017. "Corinna's Old Wives' Tales," *HSCP* 109: 83–130.

Henderson, W. J. 1995. "Corinna of Tanagra on Poetry," *Acta Classica* 38: 29–41.

———. 1989. "Criteria in the Greek Lyric Contests," *Mnemosyne* 42: 24–40.

Kousoulini, V. 2016. "Panhellenic and Epichoric Elements in Corinna's Catalogues," *GRBS* 56: 82–110.

Larmour, D. 2005. "Corinna's Poetic *Metis* and the Epinikian Tradition," in E. Greene (ed.), *Women Poets in Ancient Greece and Rome*. Norman, OK: University of Oklahoma Press, p. 25–58.

Larson, J. 2002. "Corinna and the Daughters of Asopus," *Syllecta Classica* 13: 47–62.

Lobel, E. 1930. "Corinna," *Hermes* 65: 356–365.

McPhee, B. D. 2018. "Mythological Innovations in Corinna's Asopides Poem (fr. 654.ii-iv *PMG*)," *GRBS* 58: 198–222.

Nagy, G. 1990. *Pindar's Homer: The Lyric Possession of an Epic Past*. Baltimore, MD: Johns Hopkins University Press.

Page, D. L. 1962. *Poetae Melici Graeci*. Oxford: Oxford University Press.

———. 1963. *Corinna*. London: Society for the Promotion of Hellenic Studies.

Plant, I. 2004. *Women Writers of Greece and Rome: An Anthology*. Norman, OK: University of Oklahoma Press.

Rayor, D. J. 1993. "Korinna: Gender and the Narrative Tradition," *Arethusa* 26.3: 219–231.

———. 2005. "The Power of Memory in Erinna and Sappho," in E. Greene (ed.), *Women Poets in Ancient Greece and Rome*. Norman, OK: University of Oklahoma Press, p. 59–71.

Segal, Charles. 1998. *Aglaia: The Poetry of Alcman, Sappho, Pindar, Bacchylides, and Corinna*. Lanham, MD: Rowman & Little.

Skinner, M. B. 1983. "Corinna of Tanagra and Her Audience," *Tulsa Studies in Women's Literature* 2.1: 9–20.

Snyder, J. M. 1984. "Korinna's 'Glorious Songs of Heroes,'" *Eranos* 82: 1–10.

———. 1989. *The Woman and the Lyre: Women Writers in Classical Greece and Rome*. Carbondale, IL and Edwardsville, IL: Southern Illinois University Press.

Stewart, A. 1998. "Nuggets: Mining the Texts Again," *AJA* 102: 271–282.

Vergados, A. 2012. "Corinna's Poetic Mountains: *PMG* 654 col. 1–34 and Reception," *CP* 107.2: 101–118.

West, M. L. 1970. "Corinna," *CQ* 20: 277–287.

———. 1990. "Dating Corinna," *CQ* 40: 553–557.

**Corinna 1 = *PMG* 654.i.12–34**

..................................
]ευ. [..... ] Κώρει-
τες ἔκρου]ψαν δάθιο[ν θι]ᾶς
βρέφο]ς ἄντροι, λαθρά[δα]ν ἀγ-
κο]υλομείταο Κρόνω, τα-
νίκα νιν κλέψε μάκηρα ῾Ρεία

μεγ]άλαν τ' [ἀ]θανάτων ἔσ-
ς] ἕλε τιμάν.' τάδ' ἔμελψεμ·
μάκαρας δ' αὐτίκα Μώση
φ]ερέμεν ψᾶφον ἔ[τ]αττον
κρ]ουφίαν κάλπιδας ἐν χρου-
σοφαίς· τὺ δ' ἅμα πάντε[ς] ὦρθεν·

πλίονας δ' εἶλε Κιθηρών·
τάχα δ' ἑρμᾶς ἀνέφαν[έν
νι]ν ἀούσας ἐρατὰν ὡς
ἕ]λε νίκαν, στεφ[ά]νυσιν
δ. . ]. ατώ. ανεκόσμιον
μάκα]ρες· τῶ δὲ νόος γεγάθι·

ὁ δὲ λο]ύπησι κά[θ]εκτος
χαλεπ]ῆσιν Fελι[κ]ὼν ἐ-
σερύει] λιττάδα [π]έτραν
..... ] κεν δ' ὄ[ρο]ς· ὑκτρῶς
δ.... ] ων οὐψ[ό]θεν εἴρισέ
νιν ἐ]μ μου[ρι]άδεσσι λάυς·

*Meter: See Appendix*

—

**ἀγκουλομήτης (gen., –ου):** (masc. first decl. adj.) adroitly clever; crooked of counsel; wily
**ἀνακοσμέω:** adorn; adorn again
**ἄντρον, -ου, τό:** cave
**αὔω, ἀΰσω, ἤϋσα, —, —, —:** cry out, shout, call upon
**βρέφος, -εος, τό:** infant
**γηθέω, γηθήσω, ἐγήθησα, γέγηθα, —, —:** rejoice (perf. tense often used as present tense)
**ἐξερύω, ἐξερύσω, ἐξέρυσα, —, —:** draw out
**ἐρατός, ή, όν:** desired, lovely
**ἐρείδω, ἐρείσω, ἤρεισα, ἔρεικα, ἐρήρεισμαι/ἤρεισμαι, ἐρείσθην:** attack, push, thrust
**ζάθεος, α, ον:** divine, sacred
**καθεκτός, ή, όν:** in the grip of, held back by, restrained by

**κάλπις, -ιδος, ἡ:** urn, pitcher (in this case, used for collecting votes)
**κρύπτω, κρύψω, ἔκρυψα, κέκρυφα, κεκρύψομαι, ἐκρύφθην:** hide, conceal, cover
**κρύφιος, α, ον:** hidden, concealed
**λᾶας, λᾶος, ὁ:** stone
**λαθράδαν:** secretly; a secret; a thing kept hidden; unknown
**λισσάς, -άδος:** bare, smooth
**λύπη, -ης, ἡ:** pain, grief
**μάκαρ, μάκαρος:** blessed
**μέλπω, μέλψω, ἔμελψα, —, —, —:** to celebrate in song and/or dance
**μυριάς, -άδος, ἡ:** literally, 10,000 (of something); figuratively, countless
**οἰκτρός, -ά, -όν:** pitiable, to be pitied (adv.: pitifully, piteously)
**ὄρνυμι, ὄρσω, ὦρσα, ὄρωρα, ὀρώρεγμαι ὤρεγμαι, ὠρέχθην:** (act.) urge, excite, make (a direct object) to rise up; (med.) arise, rise up
**ὄρος, -εος, τό:** mountain
**πλείων, -ον:** (οἱ πλέονες = nom. pl. m. form): full, complete; in pl., the greater number (of something—in this case, votes)
**στέφανος, -ου, ὁ:** wreath, garland
**τάσσω (Att., τάττω), τάξω, ἔταξα, τέταχα, τέταγμαι, ἐτάχθην:** order, command, bid; draw up in order; array
**τηνίκα:** (adv.) then, at that time
**ὑψόθεν:** (adv.) from above
**χρυσοφαής, -ές:** of shining gold
**ψῆφος, -ου, ἡ:** pebble (placed in an urn) used to cast a vote

—

**12–34:** Composed in a Boeotian dialect that is largely artificial and literary rather than in conformity to a spoken Boeotian dialect of a particular period in time, the poetry of Corinna contains interesting orthography which sparked interest and debate in antiquity that has continued into recent scholarship. See Appendix A for an overview of the specific characteristics of the Boeotian Aeolic dialect. Attic equivalents for dialectical variants and/or tricky morphological identifications are provided in the commentary below.

This fragment of a poem obtained from a papyrus originating from Hermopolis, Egypt (now in Berlin) dated to the 2nd century CE, narrates an otherwise unknown singing contest, judged by the gods, between two anthropomorphized Boeotian mountains—Mount Citaeron (whom Hermes declares the winner) and Mount Helicon (or, "*Welikon*"), sacred to the Muses, who turns out to be a sore loser.

The poem begins at the conclusion of Mt. Cithaeron's song, which tells the story at its climax of the goddess Rheia concealing her infant son Zeus with the help of a mythical people called the Curetes inside a cave to protect the immortal child from his father, wily-minded Cronos, who, according to the poet Hesiod, swallowed each of his children to prevent any one of them from usurping their father. The gods judge the singing contest and award victory to Cithaeron, a loss which Helicon does not take particularly well. Helicon responds in anger by taking a big boulder from itself and hurling it to the ground, shattering it into splinters.

Mount Helicon's song is not preserved in the poem, but the end of Cithaeron's is, and in it the mountain sings the story of Rheia stealing away and hiding her infant Zeus on the island of Crete to save him from his father Cronos. Corinna adapts the traditional story of Zeus's birth as narrated in Hesiod's *Theogony* (esp. lines 453–506) in interesting ways, and a careful study of Corinna's poem will take note of its mythological and literary adaptations.

Since the first eleven lines of the poem are poorly preserved, most editions and translations begin at line 12.

**12–13: Κώρειτες** (Boeotian dialect) = *Κουρῆτες*. The Kouretes (or, the Curetes) were a tribe in Aetolia, afterward expelled by the Aetolians; Meleager's refusal to defend Calydon during the Kouretes' siege of the city is related to Achilles by Phoenix at *Iliad* 9.529–599.

**13. ἔκρουψαν** = ἔκρυψαν (Att.)

**13. δάθιον** = ζάθεον (Att.)

**13. θιᾶς** = θέας (Att.)

**14. ἄντροι** = ἄντρῳ (Att.)

**14. λαθράδαν** = λάθρᾳ (Att.)

**14–15. ἀγκουλομείταο** = gen. of ἀγκυλομήτης, an epithet used by both Homer and Hesiod to describe Cronos (*Il.* 2.205, *Od.* 21.415; *Th.* 18) and Prometheus (*Th.* 546, *Op.* 48).

**15. Κρόνω** = Κρόνου (Att.)

**15. τανίκα** = τηνίκα (Att.)

**17–18. ἔσς** = ἐξ (Att.)

**18. ἔμελψεμ** = ἔμελψεν (Att.)

**19. Μώση** = Μοῦσαι (Att.)

**20. φερέμεν** = present active infinitive of φέρω.

**20. ψῆφον** = ψῆφον (Att.)

**21. κρουφίαν** = κρυφίαν (Att.)

**21. χρουσοφαίς** = χρυσοφαεῖς (Att.)

**22. τὺ** = τοὶ, Ep. and poetic version of nom. Third person pl. pronoun ("they")

**23. Κιθηρών** = Κιθαιρών (Att.). Kithairon (Cithaeron) is a mountain in Boeotia sacred to Dionysus.

**23. πλίονας** = πλέονας (Att.), f. acc. pl. of πλείων, -ον—that is, the full measure of votes. In other words, Cithaeron won the contest of song.

**25. ἀούσας** = ἀύσας (Att.)

**26. στεφάνυσιν** = στεφάνοισιν (Att.)

**27. εκόσμιον** = imperfect, 3rd pl., indic., active, of κοσμέω

**28. τῶ** = τῷ (Att.)

**28. γεγάθι** = ἐγεγήθει (pluperfect, 3rd s., active of γηθέω: "to rejoice"). The pluperfect form of this verb is commonly used in place of the perfect tense to suggest simple past action.

**29. λούπησι** = λύπαισι (Att.)

**29. κάθεκτος** = καθεκτός (Att.)

**30. Γελικὼν** = Ἑλικών (Att.), Mount Helicon, a mountain in Boeotia sacred to the Muses. It is worth noting that Hesiod begins the *Theogony* (lines 1–4) with an invocation to the Muses who dwell on Helicon and who dance and sing around the altar of Cronos. (μουσάων **Ἑλικωνιάδων** ἀρχώμεθ' ἀείδειν,/αἵθ' **Ἑλικῶνος** ἔχουσιν ὄρος μέγα τε ζάθεόν τε/καί τε περὶ κρήνην ἰοειδέα πόσσ' ἁπαλοῖσιν/ὀρχεῦνται καὶ βωμὸν ἐρισθενέος Κρονίωνος.)

**30–31. ἐσερύει** = ἐξερύει (Att.)

**31. λιττάδα** = λισσάδα (Att.)

**32. ὐκτρῶς** = οἰκτρῶς (Att.)

**33. οὐψόθεν** = ὑψόθεν (Att.)

**33. εἴρισέ** = ἤρεισε (Att.)

**34. νιν** = Dor. enclitic, acc. of third person pronoun (like Epic and Ionic μιν) in place of αὐτόν, αὐτήν

**34. ἐμ** = ἐν; **μουριάδεσσι** = μυριάδεσσι (from μυριάς, -άδος)

**34. λάυς** = λάεσι (Att. dat. pl. from λᾶας, λᾶος)

**Corinna 2 = *PMG* 654.iii.12–51**

……………………….
τᾶν δὲ πήδω[ν τρῖς μ]ὲν ἔχι
Δεὺς πατεὶ[ρ πάντω]ν βασιλεύς,
τρῖς δὲ πόντ[ω γᾶμε] μέδων
Π[οτιδάων, τ]ᾶν δὲ δουῖν
Φῦβος λέκτ[ρα] κρατούνι,
τὰν δ' ἴαν Μή[ας] ἀγαθὸς
πῆς Ἑρμᾶς· οὕ[τ]ω γὰρ Ἔρως
κὴ Κούπρις πιθέταν, τιὼς
ἐν δόμως βάντας κρουφάδαν
κώρας ἐννί' ἑλέσθη·
τή ποκ' εἰρώων γενέθλαν
ἐσγεννάσονθ' εἱμ[ιθί]ων
κἄσσονθη π[ο]λου[σπ]ερίες
τ' ἀγείρω τ'· ἐς [μ]α[ντοσ]ούνω
τρίποδος ὥτ [… …. ].
τόδε γέρας κ[εκράτειχ', ἰὼ]ν
ἐς πεντείκο[ντα] κρατερῶν
ὁμήμων, πέρ[οχο]ς προφά-
τας σεμνῶν [ἀδο]ύτων λαχὼν
ἀψεύδιαν, Ἀκ[ρη]φειν·
πράτοι [μὲν] γὰ[ρ Λατ]οΐδας
δῶκ' Εὐωνούμοι τριπόδων
ἐσς ἰῶν [χρε]ισμὼς ἐνέπειν,
τὸν δ' ἐς γᾶς βαλὼν Οὑριεὺς
τιμὰ[ν] δεύτερος ἴσχεν,
πῆς [Ποτ]ιδάωνος· ἔπιτ'
Ὠα[ρί]ων ἁμὸς γενέτωρ
γῆα[ν Ϝ]ὰν ἀππασάμενος·
χὼ μὲν ὠραν[ὸ]ν ἀμφέπι
τιμὰν δ' [ἔλλαχο]ν οὔταν.
τώνεκ' [εὖ τ' ἔγνω]ν ἐνέπω
τ' ἀτ[ρ]έκ[ιαν χρει]σμολόγον·
τοὺ δέ [νου Ϝῖκέ τ' ἀ]θανάτυς
κὴ λού[πας ἄππαυε] φρένας
δημόν[εσσ' ἑκου]ρεύων.'
ὣς ἔφα [μάντις] π[ε]ραγείς·
τὸν δ' Ἀ[σωπός ἀσ]πασίως
δεξιᾶς ἐ[φαψάμ]ενος
δάκρού τ' [ὀκτάλ]λων προβαλ[ὼν
ὦδ' ἀμίψ[ατο φ]ωνῆ·
………………………

*Meter: See Appendix*

—

**ἀγήραος, ον:** without old age, ageless, eternally youthful
**ἄδυτον, ου, τό:** innermost sanctuary of a temple
**ἀμείβω, ἀμείψω, ἤμειψα, —, ἤμειπται, ἠμείφθην:** change; exchange; (med.) answer another person in dialogue; respond
**ἀσπάσιος, -α, -ον:** glad, well-pleased
**ἀτρέκεια, ας, ἡ:** precise or absolute truth; certainty
**ἀμφιέπω, —, ἀμφίεπον, —, —, —:** (verb appears only in pres. and aor. tenses) do honor or reverence to; tend to; go around; be all around; busy one's self about, look after; frequent
**ἀψεύδεια, -ας, ἡ:** truth; utter lack of falsehood; inerrant truthfulness
**γαμέω, γαμῶ/γαμήσω, ἔγημα, γεγάμηκα, γεγάμημαι, ἐγαμήθην:** wed, marry
**γενέθλη, -ης, ἡ:** race, family, line of descendants
**γενέτης, -ου, ὁ:** begetter, parent; ancestor
**γέρας, -αος, τό:** reward, prize, gift, privilege
**δαίμων, -ονος, ὁ, ἡ:** a divine being; god or goddess
**δάκρυ, δάκρυος, τό:** teardrop, tear
**δεξιός, -ά, -όν:** the right side; often used in the fem. to refer to the right hand
**δεύτερος, α, ον:** second
**ἐκγεννάω:** to beget, bear, bring forth
**ἐνέπω, ἐνισπήσω ἐνίψω, ἔνισπον, —, —, —:** to speak or utter; to tell the tale of
**ἔπειτα:** (adv.) thereupon, thereafter, then
**ἐφάπτω, ἐφάψω, ἔφηψα, —, ἐφήμμαι, ἐφήφθην:** bind, make fixed or fast; (med.) lay hold of; reach; touch (+ gen.)
**ἡμίθεος, -ου, ὁ:** demi-god; a being possessed of lesser divine status, such as a minor deity or the offspring of a god and mortal
**ἥρως, -ος, ὁ:** hero; a race of mortals descended from the gods
**ἵκανω (= ἵκω):** (this form of the verb appears only in the pres. and imperf. tenses; the fut., aor., and pft. are all derived from a related form of the verb, ἱκνέομαι) come to, arrive; reach; attain; approach as a suppliant; beseech; supplicate
**ἴσχω:** (reduplicative form of ἔχω and only found in pres. and imperf. tenses) hold; keep
**κρατερός, -ά, -όν:** strong, mighty
**κρατέω, κρατήσω, ἐκράτησα, κεκράτηκα, κεκράτημαι, ἐκρατήθην:** hold sway, hold power over, prevail, conquer, get possession of
**κρατύνω:** with an acc. or gen., take possession of, possess; become master of
**λαγχάνω, λήξομαι, ἔλαχον, εἴληχα, εἴληγμαι, ἐλήχθην:** to obtain by lot, get as one's lot in life
**λέκτρον, -ου, τό:** marriage-bed

**μάντις, -εως, ὁ:** seer, prophet, diviner
**μέδων, -οντος, ὁ:** ruler
**μαντόσυνος, η, ον:** oracular
**ὅμαιμος, -ον:** brother or sister (as substantive); of the same blood
**περίοχος, -ον:** preeminent, superior
**πολυσπερής, -ές:** wide-spread over the earth, fruitful
**προφήτης, ου, ὁ:** seer, prophet
**σεμνός, ή, όν:** holy, solumn, august, reverend
**τρεῖς, τρία:** three
**τρίπους, -ποδος, ὁ:** tripod
**φωνή, -ῆς, ἡ:** voice, sound of the voice
**χρησμόλογος, ον:** oracular
**χρησμός, -οῦ, ὁ:** oracular response; oracle delivered by a prophet, seer, priestess or priest

—

**12–51:** This poem is partially preserved on a papyrus from Hermopolis, Egypt (now in Berlin) dated to the 2nd century CE. Although lines 1–11 are illegible due to the poor quality of the papyrus's preservation, it may be conjectured that the Boeotian river god Asopus, named in line 48, has come to a local sanctuary of Apollo to obtain a prophecy from the seer, Acraephen, the eponymous hero of the Boeotian town of Acraephia, in order to discover the whereabouts of his nine missing daughters.

When the legible portion of the text begins, Acraephen is speaking, and his reply to Asopus's query continues through line 46. The seer informs Asopus that the latter should be glad at heart because the gods Zeus, Poseidon, Hermes, and Apollo have taken the river god's daughters away as consorts. While these daughters are not named, Page (1963, p. 25) conjectures that among them may have been Aegina and Thebe (taken by Zeus), Corcyra and Salamis (by Poseidon), Sinope and Thespia (by Apollo), and Tanagra (the eponymous heroine of Corinna's hometown, by Hermes).

In order to lend authority to his oracular pronouncement, Acraephen offers a mythic back-story detailing the intergenerational inheritance by which he obtained the position of oracular prophet of Apollo (lines 32–41). The legible text unfortunately cuts off just before Asopus's reply, and Page (1963, p. 25) has suggested (based on a reading of the word fragments that remain) that the river god father states that he is pleased with the prophecy and will cease grieving for his lost daughters.

**12. τᾶν πήδων** = τῶν παιδῶν (Att.)—here, daughters (rather than sons)
**12. τρῖς** (and again at line 14) = τρεῖς (Att. acc.)
**12. ἔχι** = ἔχει
**13. Δεὺς πατεὶ[ρ** = Ζεὺς πατήρ (Att.)
**14. πόντω** = πόντου (Att.)

**14. γᾶμεν** = ἔγημεν (Att.)

**15. Ποτιδάων** = Ποσειδῶν (Att. nom.) Doric spelling, indicated in inscriptions at least twice: IG4.211 and GDI 5085.

**15. τ]ᾶν δὲ δουῖν:** "and of two"; both τ]ᾶν and δουῖν are gen. and fem.

**16. Φῦβος** = Φοῖβος (Att.), an epithet of Apollo meaning "Bright"

**16. κρατούνι** = κρατύνει (Att.)

**17. τὰν** = τὴν (Att.)

**17. ἴαν** = μίαν (Att.)

**17. Μήας** = Μαίας (Att. gen. s.); Maia is the eldest of the seven nymphs who make up the constellation Pleiades. She is both the daughter of the Titan Atlas by his consort Pleias and the mother of Hermes, to whom she secretly gave birth in the peaks of Mt. Cyllene in Arcadia. Hermes's father is Zeus. For more on Maia, read the *Homeric Hymn 4 to Hermes.*

**18. πῆς** = παῖς (Att.)

**19. κή** = καὶ (Att.)

**19. Κούπρις** = Κύπρις (Att.), an epithet of Aphrodite, from the island of Cyprus. Having provided an account of the goddess' origins arising from sea foam where the castrated genitalia of Ouranos mixed with sea water, Hesiod (*Theogony* 192) states that she first came to the island of Cythera (and is thus sometimes called "Cythereia") and then to Cyprus. A few lines later (line 199) Hesiod states that she is called "Cyprogenes" ("Cyprus-born") because she was born in Cyprus.

**19. πιθέταν:** poetic dual aorist of πείθω

**19–20. τιὼς ἐν δόμως** = σοῦς ἐν δόμους (Att.)

**20. βάντας** = βάντες (Att.)

**20. κρουφάδαν** = Boeotian adv. "secretly"

**21. κώρας** = κόρας (Att.)

**21. ἑλέσθη** = ἑλέσθαι (Att.) (from αἱρέω: "to take, seize")

**22. τή** = ταί (Att.), Doric for αἱ

**22. ποκ'** = πότε (Att.)

**22. εἱρώων** = ἡρώων (Att., Ionic/epic)

**22. γενέθλαν** = γενέθλην (Att.)

**23. ἐσγεννάσονθ'** = ἐκγεννήσουσι (Att.)

**23. εἱμιθίων** = ἡμιθέων (Att.)

**24. κἄσσονθη** = καὶ ἔσσονται (Att.)

**24. πολουσπερίες** = πολυσπερὲς (Att.)

**25. ἀγείρω** = ἀγήραοι (Att.)

**25. ἐς** = ἐκ (Att.); again at lines 28 and 35

**25. μαντοσούνω** = μαντόσυνου (Att.)

**26. ᾧτ** = ὥστε (Att.)

**27. κ[εκράτειχ'** = κεκράτηκα (Att.). This emendation (κ[εκράτειχ', ἰὼ]ν) suggested by M. L. West, 1970. "Corinna," *The Classical Quarterly* 2.20, p. 287 and preferred by David A. Campbell, 1992. *Greek Lyric, Vol. IV: Bacchylides, Corinna, and Others*. Cambridge, MA: Harvard University Press, p. 32.

**27. ἰώv** = ἐγώ (Att.)
**28. πεντείκοντα** = πεντήκοντα (Att.)
**29. ὁμήμων** = ὁμαίμων (Att.) (ὅμαιμος: "brother, sibling")
**29. πέροχος** = περίοχος (Att.)
**29–30. προφάτας** = προφήτης (Att.)
**30. ἀδούτων** = ἀδύτων (Att.)
**31. ἀψεύδιαν** = ἀψεύδειαν (Att.)
**31. Ἀκρηφειν** = "Acraephen", the name of the speaker, one of the hunter Orion's fifty sons and a prophet of Apollo. There existed a Boeotian town called Acraephia on the western foothills of Mount Ptoon and situated at the edge of Lake Copais. A sanctuary of Apollo Ptoios to the east of the town was frequented by pilgrims from Boeotia and beyond.
**32. Λατοΐδας** = Λητοίδης (Att.), "son of Leto" (i.e., Apollo).
**32–33. πράτοι ... Εὐωνούμοι** = πρώτῳ...Εὐωνώμῳ (Att., πρῶτος, η, ον: "first"). Thus, "to Euonymos first".
**33–34. τριπόδων ἐσς ἰῶν** = τριπόδων ἐκ ἑῶν, "from his tripods"
**34. χρεισμὼς** = χρησμούς (χρησμός: "oracular response")
**35. τὸν δ' ἐς γᾶς βαλὼν Οὐριεὺς** = i.e., Hyreius exiled Euonymous. In Greek myth, Hyreius was the son of Poseidon and the Pleiad nymph Alycone, as well as the eponymous hero of the Boeotian town of Hyria. He was the father of Nycteus and Lycus, both of whom also feature in Theban myth as kings of the city in the generations before Oedipus.
**36. τιμὰν** = τιμὴν (Att.); again at line 41
**37. πῆς [Ποτ]ιδάωνος** = παῖς Ποσειδῶνος (Att.)
**37. ἔπιτ'** = ἔπειτα (Att.)
**38. Ὠαρίων** = Ὠρίων (Att.); a giant and hunter who is featured in many stories of Greek and Roman myth, and particularly Boeotian and Theban myth, including multiple stories involving rape, exile, blinding, and being transformed into a constellation. He is both a panhellenic and a local cultural hero. He is generally considered to be the son of Poseidon, but Ps.-Hyginus (*Astronomica* 2.34) offered an etiological version of Orion's birth story, perhaps to explain the origin of the hero's name [οὖρον means "urine"], in which the hunter was conceived when Zeus and Hermes buried an ox-hide upon which they had urinated so as to provide King Hyreius with a male heir. In a poem addressed to the women of Boeotian Tanagara (*PMG* 55), Corinna again mentions Orion, claiming that he fathered fifty sons after sleeping with the Nymph daughters of the river Cephisus.
**38. ἁμὸς** = ἐμός
**38. γενέτωρ** = γενέτης (Att.)
**39. γῆα[ν Ϝ]ὰν:** γῆα[ν = γῆν (Att.); the Greek possessive pronoun (ὅς, ἥ, ὅν) originally featured a digamma that disappeared in Attic Greek. The phrase may be translated as "his own land".
**39. ἀππασάμενος** = ἀναπασάμενος (Att.), from ἀναπάομαι: "to acquire back, to get back".

**40. χὠ:** crasis for καί + ὁ
**40. ἀμφέπι** = ἀμφέπει (ἀμφιέπω, "to go around, frequent"); i.e., Orion now traverses the sky because he was transformed into a constellation.
**41. ἔλλαχον** = ἔλαχον (Att.)
**41. οὕταν** = ταύτην (Att.)
**42. τώνεκ'** = τῶν ἕνεκα (Att.)
**43. ἀτ[ρ]έκ[ιαν** = ἀτρέκειαν (Att.)
**43. χρει]σμολόγον** = χρησμολόγον (Att.)
**44. τοὺ** = τύ (Att.)
**44. νου** = νυ (νῦν) (Att.)
**44. Fῖκέ** = ἶκε (Att., from ἵκω, a 2nd s. pres. act. imperative, derived from the lengthened form of the verb ἵκανω and related etymologically to the more commonly occurring ἱκνέομαι. See ἵκανω in the vocabulary above). Here, it means something like "come as a suppliant to" or "submit to" and takes a dative object.
**44. ἀ]θανάτυς** = ἀθανάτοις (Att.)
**45. κὴ** = καί
**46. δημόνεσσ' ἑκουρεύων** = "being a father-in-law to gods". δημόνεσσ' = δαιμόνουσι (Att.). ἑκουρεύων = ἑκυρεύων (Att.), "being a father-in-law" and is only found here in extant Greek literature. For this reason, it is not included in the vocabulary above.
**47. ἔφα** = ἔφη (Dor.), from φημί
**47. περάγείς** = πέρ + ἁγής, ές: "all-holy, all-sacred"
**48. Ἀ[σωπός** = the eponymous god of a local river in Boeotia, who has come to the seer Acraephen to inquire as to the whereabouts of his daughters. Among the more famous of his daughters (unnamed, but likely alluded to in lines 12–13) is Aegina, whom Zeus abducted.
**49. ἐφαψάμενος** = aor. mid. participle, from ἐφάπτω
**50. δάκρού** = δάκρύ, a neut., acc. s., poetic form of δάκρυον, -ου, τό
**50. ὀκτάλλων** = Boeotian for ὀφθαλμῶν.
**51. ἀμίψατο** = ἀμείψατο (Att.). This ends the legible portion of the text, just as the river god is about to reply to Acraephen's χρεισμολόγον.

**Corinna 3 = *PMG* 655 fr. 1 (Oxyrhynchus papyrus 2370, c. 200 CE)**

ἐπί με Τερψιχόρα [καλῖ
καλὰ Ϝεροῖ' ἀϊσομ[έναν
Ταναγρίδεσσι λ[ευκοπέπλυς,
μέγα δ' ἐμῆς γέγ[αθε πόλις
λιγουροκω[τίλυ[ς ἐνοπῆς.
ὅττι γὰρ μεγαλ. [
ψευδ [.] σ. [.]αδομε[
. [.]. . ω γῆαν εὐρού[χορον·
λόγια δ' ἐπ πατέρω[ν
κοσμείσασα Ϝιδιο[
παρθ[έ]νυσι κατάρχομη·
πο]λλὰ μὲν Καφ[ισὸν ἱώνγ'
ἀρχ]αγὸν κόσμ[εισα λόγυ]ς,
πολλὰ δ' Ὠρί[ωνα] μέγαν
κὴ πεντεί[κοντ' οὐψιβίας
πῆδα[ς οὓς νού]μφησι μιγ[ί]ς
τέκετο, κὴ] Λιβούαν κ[αλάν
.]. [.. ]θησ[
Ϝιρίω κόραν. [
καλὰ Ϝιδεῖν αρ[
γ]ῆαν ἅν τίκτ[
.]. τέκετο τυ[
.............................

*Meter: See Appendix*

—

**ἀείδω/ᾄδω, ἀείσομαι/ᾄσομαι, ἄεισα/ᾖσα, —, ᾖσμαι, ᾔσθην:** sing
**ἀρχηγός, -ή, -όν:** ancestral hero or heroine; founder; originator
**γαῖα, -ας, ἡ:** earth; land
**γηθέω, γηθήσω, ἐγήθησα, γέγηθα, —, —:** rejoice (perf. tense often used as present tense); rejoice in a dat. object
**ἐνοπή, -ῆς, ἡ:** voice; sound of crying or shouting
**εὐρύχωρος, -ον:** wide-open (of space or land)
**κατάρχω, κατάρξω, κάτηρξα, —, κάτηργμαι, κατήρχθην:** make a beginning of; commence; begin
**κοσμέω, κοσμήσω, ἐκόσμησα, κεκόσμηκα, κεκόσμημαι, ἐκοσμήθην:** adorn; arrange, set in order; embellish
**λευκόπεπλος, -ον:** white-robed
**λόγιος, -α, -ον:** well-versed in stories or tales; eloquent
**μείγνυμι or μίγνυμι or μειγνύω or μίσγω, μείξα, ἔμειξα, μέμειγμαι, —, ἐμείχθην/ἐμίγην:** mix with; join with; have sex with
**νύμφη, -ης, ἡ:** Nymph (goddess of a lower rank); daughter; girl of marriageable age

**ὁράω, ὄψομαι, εἶδον, ἑόρακα ἑώρακα, ἑώραμαι ὦμμαι, ὤφθην:** see, look upon, perceive with the eyes, behold
**πεντήκοντα, οἱ, αἱ, τά:** (indeclinable) fifty
**τίκτω, τέξω, ἔτεξα/ἔτεκον, τέτοκα, τέτεγμαι, ἐτέχθην:** give birth to; bear, produce, beget; engender

—

**1–21:** This fragment from Oxyrhynchus papyrus 2370 was probably composed for a chorus of young women (the "white-robed women of Tanagra") to perform. The poem begins with a modified invocation of sorts, as the narrator (which may be the voice of the poet or the collective voice the chorus) claims that the Muse Terpsichore commands the singing of beautiful tales for the women of Tanagra. The narrator then cites the kinds of stories and performances that delighted the city in times past, including stories about the river-god Cephisus and about Orion and his fifty sons.
**1. Τερψιχόρα** = literally, "delighting in the dance", Terpsichore is the Muse of dance and chorus and is the patron goddess of lyric poetry.
**1. [καλῖ:** this is a conjecture (see Campbell, 1992, p. 36), and if correct, is the equivalent of Attic καλεῖ.
**2. Fεροῖ'** = This is a *hapax*, likely derived from an archaic verb stem, **FερεF-*, from which the verbs εἴρω and ἐρέω originate. The neuter noun form τὰ Fεροῖα probably means "Narratives" or "Tales" (see Clayman, 1978 and Heath, 2017, p. 102–103). The Roman author Antoninus Liberalis (25) mentions Fεροῖα as the title of one of Corinna's books of poetry and states that both she (in a book by that title) and Nicander each told the story of Metioche and Menippe, two Boeotian weaver daughters of Orion who offered to sacrifice themselves to the gods of the underworld by willingly accepting death in order to save their community from a plague epidemic. Having slashed their own throats with their bodkins, the gods transformed these sisters into comets.
**2. ἀϊσομ[έναν** = ᾀσομένην or ἀεισομένην in Homeric (see *Od.* 22.352), the lexical entry of this verb is ἀείδω or ᾄδω.
**3. Ταναγρίδεσσι** = "for the women of Tanagra" (dat. pl., fem.), from Ταναγρίς, -ίδος, ἡ. Tanagra was a city in Boeotia settled beside the river Asopus and built on the remains of a Bronze Age settlement.
**3. λ[ευκοπέπλυς** = λευκοπέπλοις (Att.)
**5. λιγουροκω[τίλυ[ς** = λιγουροκωτίλοις: Another *hapax*, this compound adjective consists of two parts. The first, λιγουρός, -ά, -όν (λιγύς, λίγεια, λιγύ in Att.), relates to the quality and tone of sound, and generally means "clear", "clear-toned", or "sweet" sounding. On the other hand, κωτίλος, -η, -ον, means "chattering" or "babbling" or "twittering", from which the Boeotian name for the swallow (κωτιλάς, -άδος, ἡ, or "twitterer") derives its name. Furthermore, the verb κωτίλλω is frequently used in the sense of "gossiping" or "chattering uncontrollably" or "prattling", and often stereotypically of women's speech. So, it is unclear whether Corinna is

suggesting that she is "clear-toned, swallow-voiced" or a "sweetly prattling". One scholar (Heath, 2017, p. 96) suggests that Corinna's use of λιγουροκωτίλυς is intended to encompass both of these meanings ironically, serving as a "half-facetious nod to the cultural ambiguity" of her role as female poet, by offering up "a female voice—a source of frequent suspicion of and disparagement of women—to public acclaim."

**6–8.** Damage to the papyrus makes much of these lines unreadable.

**8. γῆαν** = γαῖαν (Att.); see also line 21.

**8. εὐρού[χορον** = εὐρύχωρον (Att.)

**10. κοσμείσασα** = κοσμήσασα (Att.); the same dialect idiosyncrasies apply at line 13.

**10. Ϝιδιο[:** the line breaks off here, so part of the word is missing. However, Ϝιδιο- = (Att.) ἴδιος, -α, -ον, meaning "one's own", "distinctive", or "personal". The English word "idiosyncratic" derives (in its initial syllables) from this Greek word. Campbell (1992, p. 37) translates lines 9–10, "and having adorned (with my art?) stories from our father's time …").

**11. κατάρχομη** = κατάρχομαι (Att.)

**12. Καφ[ισὸν** = Κηφισὸν (Att.). Like Asopus, Cephisus is the name of a river in Boeotia and is here personified as a river-god.

**12. ἰώνγ'** = ἔγωγε (Att.), an intensifying form of ἐγώ meaning "I at least" or, "for my part"

**13. ἀρχ]αγὸν** = ἀρχηγὸν (Att.)

**13. λόγυ]ς** = λόγοις (Att.)

**14. 'Ωρί[ωνα]:** Orion, both a Boeotian and Panhellenic hero. See note for line 38, Corinna 654.iii.12–51.

**15. κὴ** = καὶ (Att.); see also line 17.

**15. πεντεί[κοντ'** = πεντήκοντα (Att.)

**15. οὑψιβίας** = ὑψιβίας (Att.), "very mighty" (ὕψι, or "high, lofty" + βία, or "force, strength, might"), modifying πῆδα[ς (line 16).

**16. πῆδα[ς** = παῖδας (Att.). In this case, sons.

**16. νού]μφησι** = νύμφαις (Att.)

**16. μιγ[ί]ς:** a participle (masc., nom., sing., probably present tense) from μείγνυμι or μίγνυμι, a verb which offers plenty of irregular forms and may have derived from μίσγω, a shortened form of the reduplicated μι(μ)σγω (for which, see Smyth 526c).

**17. τέκετο:** this aorist middle form is commonly used when signifying that parents (father and mother) came together to produce an offspring. The epsilon augment, in these cases, disappears, as it frequently does in Homeric poetry. See also line 22.

**17. Λιβούαν** = Λιβύην (Att.), or the nymph Libya

**18.–22.** These lines are too fragmentary to be fully legible.

**18. Ϝιρίω** = εἴρω (I shall tell). See note for Ϝεροῖ' above (line 2).

**20. Ϝιδεῖν** = ἰδεῖν (Att., "to see" or "to look upon"), another verb with a plethora of irregular forms (the aor. act. indic. = εἶδον). For an overview of this common, but irregular verb, see the *LSJ* entry for "ὁράω".

**21. ἆν** = ἦν (Att.)

**Corinna 4 = *PMG* 690 = *P.S.I.* 1174, text by West (1970)**

ΟΡΕΣΤΑΣ

᾽Ά]ας μὲν ὠκιανῶ λιπῶ-
σα π[αγὰς] ἱαρὸν φάος
σελάνας <σ>πάσα[τ᾽ ὠραν]ῷ̣
᾽Ώρη δ᾽ ἐς Διὸς ἄμβροτυ
[νί̣ονθ]η̣ Fέ̣αρος ἐν ἄνθεσι<ν>,
γέγα[θεν δὲ πόνυς πο]δῦν
χορὸς ἀν ἑπτάπουλον [πόλιν.
…………………………

*Meter: See Appendix*

—

**ἄμβροτος, -ον:** immortal, divine
**ἄνθος, -ους, τό:** flower; bloom
**γηθέω, γηθήσω, ἐγήθησα, γέγηθα, —, —:** rejoice (perf. tense often used as present tense)
**ἔαρ (or, ἦρ), ἔαρος (or, ἦρος), τό:** (form appears in both uncontracted and contracted forms in Attic), spring, springtime
**ἱερός, -ά, -όν:** holy, sacred
**νέομαι:** (pres. and imperf. only), come, go
**οὐρανός, -οῦ, ὁ:** heaven, sky
**πηγή, ῆς, ἡ:** font or source of light or water; streams
**πόνος, -ου, ὁ:** toil, labor, exertion
**πούς, ποδός, ὁ:** foot
**σελήνη, -ης, ἡ:** the moon
**σπάω, σπάσω, ἔσπασα, ἔσπακα, ἔσπασμαι, ἐσπάσθην:** draw, pull
**φῶς, φωτός, τό:** light
**χορός, -ου, ὁ:** chorus, choir, band of dancers and singers
**ὥρα, -ας, ἡ:** season; hour

**1–7:** This fragment is included in the *PMG* among the *Boeotica incerti auctoris* (Boeotian fragments of uncertain authorship), but most scholars now attribute the poem to Corinna following West's (1970, p. 278–279) orthographic, metrical, and stylistic arguments. While most of her poems have some kind of connection to Boeotia and its landscape, it is unclear in the few lines that survive how (and if at all) the author will connect Orestes, the son of Agamemnon (from Argos in the Peloponnesus), to Thebes (the site, perhaps, of the poem's performance). It is possible that a connection to the hero's relationship to Phocis (near Boeotia) was spun out, since Orestes spent his youth in exile there.

The poem begins with a setting, illuminating the time of day (Dawn) and season (Spring) when a chorus (line 7) rejoices in dancing at seven-gated Thebes. If this poem was intended to be performed by a chorus, references to time of day (Dawn leaving behind the waters of Oceanus and drawing the moon's light from the sky) may suggest an early morning performance (Finglass, 2007, p. 33–34).

—

1. **᾿Ά]ας:** perhaps Attic ᾿Ἡως (the goddess Dawn) ὠκιανῶ = ᾿Ὠκεανοῦ (Attic), or Oceanus, a son of Ouranos and Gaia, according to Hesiod's *Theogony* (line 133), married to the nymph Tethys and the father of Thetis (*Iliad* 14.302) and of all the Oceanids (*Theogony* 337); the great outer ocean, conceived of as a river that encircles the earth, returning in upon itself. Beyond it is the underworld and realm of Hades, according to Homer (*Odyssey* 11.20–28).

**1–2. λιπῶσα** = λιποῦσα (Att.)

**2. π[αγὰς]** = Dor. for Attic πηγὰς

**2. ἱαρὸν** = ἱερὸν (Att.)

**3. φάος** = φῶς (Att.)

**3. σελάνας:** Aeol. for Att. σελήνης

**3. <σ>πάσα[τ'** = if this emendation is correct, this is an indicative, aorist, middle, 3rd s. without an epsilon augment.

**3. ὠραν]ῷ** = οὐρανῷ (Att.)

**4. ῾Ὥρη** = ῾Ὥραι (Att.), the personified "Hours" (three in number, Eunomia, Dike, and Eirene, daughters of Zeus and Themis), who guard the gates of Mt.

Olympus (*Iliad*, 5.749 and 8.393), the summit of which serves as the home of the Olympian gods.

**4. ἐς** = ἐκ (Att.)

**4. ἄμβροτυ** = ἄμβροτοι (Att.)

**5. [νί͜ονθ]η** = νέονται (Att.), if proposed supplement is correct.

**5. Fέ͜αρος** = ἔαρος or ἦρος (Att.)

**5.** Both [νίονθ]η and Fέ͜αρος contain synizeses. In [νί͜ονθ]η, the iota and omicron should be pronounced as a single syllable; and, the epsilon and alpha in Fέ͜αρος.

**6. γέγα[θεν** = γέγηθεν (Att.)

**6. πόνυς** = πόνοις (Att.)

**6. πο]δῦν** = possibly ποδῶν (Att.). The whole phrase: "… and the chorus delights in the labors of its feet."

**7. ἀν** = ἐν (Att.)

**7. ἑπτάπουλον** = "seven-gated", an epithet of the Boeotian city of Thebes

**8.** The remainder of the poem is illegible.

### Corinna 1 = *PMG* 654.i.12–34[20]

—

.......................... [these lines are illegible in the papyrus manuscript]

................"...the Curetes[21]

hid the divine infant son of the goddess,
stealthfully, from wily-minded Cronos,[22]
when blessed Rheia[23] stole him away

and earned[24] great honor from the immortals."
Thus, he finished his song.
And, forthwith the Muses[25]
commanded the blessed gods
to place their pebbles as secret ballots[26]
into shining golden urns.
And, together they all rose up.

Cithaeron[27] took the greatest share of votes.
Soon, Hermes appeared,
announcing that he [Cithaeron] had earned
the desired victory, and with garlands
... the blessed ones crowned him,
and his mind rejoiced.

But, gripped by unbearable
grief, Mt. Helicon
pulled out a smooth slab of rock, and
...the mountain.[28] Pitifully,
...from above, he hurled it down,
shattering it into countless stones.

**Corinna 2 = *PMG* 654.iii.12–51**

[...............] [these lines are illegible in the papyrus manuscript]
'...of your[29] daughters,
Zeus, the father and king of all, has three,
and three the ruler of the sea, Poseidon,
has made his consorts, and
Phoebus[30] is lord of the beds of two of them,
and one, the noble son of Maia,[31]
Hermes; for Eros
and Cypris[32] persuaded them
to take for themselves your nine daughters
after they'd stolen secretly into your house.
But, in time, their descendants will be born,
a race of heroes and demi-gods,
and they will be ageless and scattered across the earth.
This privilege of the oracular tripod [....
......] out of my fifty mighty brothers,
only I, Acraphaen,
a preeminent prophet of the holy sanctuary,
obtaining as my lot in life

knowledge of what is true and what is false.[33]
For, the son of Leto[34]
granted first to Euonymus[35]
the power to utter oracles
from his own tripods,
but Hyreius[36] exiled Euonymus from the land
and held the honor of that position
as the second in line,
and he was a son of Poseidon. And, then
Orion, my father,
got back this land as his own.
And, while he traverses the sky,[37]
I have obtained this honor.
Because of this, I well know and I speak
an oracle of absolute certainty.
Submit now to the immortal gods
and release your mind's grief,
since you are the gods' father-in-law.
Thus, he spoke, the holy prophet.
And, gratified, Asopos
grasped the seer's right hand,
and, shedding a tear
his eyes, his voice replied thus…
……………………… [the remaining lines are illegible]

**Corinna 3 = *PMG* 655 fr. 1[38]**

Terpsichore[39] [summons?] me[40]
to sing beautiful tales[41]
for the white-robed women of Tanagra,[42]
and the city rejoices greatly at the
swallow-song[43] of my voice.
For, whatever great …
false ………………
……… spacious earth.
And, having arranged
the stories of my ancestors with my own ….
I begin for the maidens.
Many times I arranged in stories
our founder Cephisus,[44]
and many times great Orion[45]
and his fifty high and mighty
sons whom he fathered
in dalliances with Nymphs,
and beautiful Libya
……………………

the girl … I shall tell ….
beautiful to look upon …….
earth whom ………
……… fathered…
…………………… [these lines are illegible in the papyrus manuscript]

**Corinna 4 = *PMG* 690 = *P.S.I.* 1174, prim. ed. Coppola**

*Orestes*[46]

[Dawn?][47], leaving behind Oceanus's
waters, drew the holy light of
Selene from Ouranos.
And, the immortal Hours[48] come
from Zeus among the flowers of spring,
and a chorus rejoices in the workings of its feet
in the seven-gated city.[49]

## Notes

1. A publication of an archaeological field survey and partial excavation of Tanagra may be of interest, as it offers a sense of the size, complexity, environment, and ceramic, architectural, and prehistoric archaeology of Corinna's home *polis*, demonstrating that ancient Tanagra was built on a Bronze Age site. See Bintliff, et al., 2004. The Suda, a much later source (*Sud.* K 2087), states that she was either from Tanagra or Thebes and provides the names of her parents as cited above.
2. In an influential book called *Pindar's Homer: The Lyric Possession of an Epic Past,* Nagy (1990, p. 59–67) argued that Panhellenic poetry (as opposed to epichoric) did not just adapt itself to local audiences by inclusion of myths and stories idiosyncratically peculiar to specific Hellenic localities, but it concentrated "on traditions that tend to be common to most locales and peculiar to none." Epichoric poetry, however, refers to "myth and ritual produced in a local context, cultural material that, whether for reasons of dialect or content, or merely through lack of circulation, did not travel well." (Kousoulini, 2016, p. 82).
3. The scholarship is reasonably vast, but a few recent publications provide overviews of the history of it and offer significant contributions to the discussion by examining Corinna's mythological innovations (both epichoric and Panhellenic), set against Hesiodic and Pindaric versions of myths. See Collins (2006), Vergados (2012), Kousoulini (2016), and McPhee (2018).
4. There were five major dialect-families in ancient Greece (Ionic, Doric, Aeolic, Arcadocypriot, and Attic), and the Boeotian dialect belonged to the Aeolic family, along with the Lesbian (in which Sappho and Alcaeus composed poetry) and Thessalian strains.
5. See, for example, *PMG* 658, 661, 664, 676, and 684.
6. Aelian, *Varia Historia* 13.25 and *Suda* K 2087.
7. Plutarch, *On the Glory of Athens* 4.347f-28a in *Moralia.*
8. Henderson (1989, p. 26).
9. For more on the tradition of rivalry between Corinna and Pindar, see Henderson (1989, p. 32–33), Snyder (1989, p. 42–43), and Larmour (2005, p. 39–48).
10. See Page (1963), p. 65–84, whose edited volume of the fragments of Corinna's poetry is still highly influential and authoritative, for expansion on the traditional

date of Corinna's life. Campbell (p. 408, 1967, reprinted in 1972, 1976, 1982 and 1990) agrees with a traditional date in his edited volume of Greek lyric poetry, but states in his 1992 volume that Corinna's date "is almost certainly 3rd century." Snyder (1989, p. 43–44) also argues for a 5th century date.

11. For more on Myrtis, see Snyder (1989, p. 40–41). All we know of her poetry is the offering of a paraphrase of one poem by Plutarch (also from Boeotia), who cites that Myrtis is the authority for a story about why women were forbidden to enter a sacred grove in Tanagra dedicated to a local hero, Eunostos. Plutarch, *Quaestiones Graecae* 40, in Plutarch's *Moralia.*
12. Also, see *Sud.* K 2087 and *PMG* 664 = Apollonius Dyscolus, *Pronouns* 64b-65a.
13. For example, West (1970 and 1990), Segal (1998), and Kousoulini (2016).
14. Larson (2002), p. 56. See also Stewart (1998), whom Larson cites. Allen and Frel (1972) have also staunchly argued for a 5th century date.
15. Lobel (1930) was the first to place Corinna's date to the Hellenistic period. In addition, West (1970 and 1990), Segal (1998), and Kousoulini (2016).
16. Although, a copyist living in the 3rd century could have transcribed poems that had been transmitted orally for several centuries in a 3rd-century dialect, a point made by Snyder (1989, p. 43).
17. Especially Page (1962), Page (1963), West (1970 and 1990), and Campbell (1967 and 1992). Throughout this text, *PMG* refers to Page (1962).
18. West (1990).
19. Especially Larmour (2005).
20. The most extensive fragments of Corinna's extant poetry are preserved on a papyrus from Hermopolis, Egypt, often called the "Berlin papyrus" (nr. 284), dated to the 2nd century BCE based on its script and spelling. This papyrus was originally published in 1907.
21. The Curetes (or, *Kouretes*): According to ancient sources (Apollodorus i.1.6, for example), the goddess Rheia, mother of Zeus and wife of Cronus, concealed the infant Zeus in a remote cave on Mt. Dicte in Crete, and she entrusted the care of the infant to the Curetes and the nymphs Adrasteia and Ida, who fed him with the milk of a goat named Amaltheia (whose name means "nourisher" in Greek) and honey. There were either three, or five, or nine Curetes.
22. Cronos (or, *Kronos*): In Hesiod's *Theogony* (404-506), Cronos was the patriarch of an early generation of Greek gods called the Titans. Until his son, Zeus, overthrew him, Cronos ruled the cosmos after deposing his own father, Ouranos (or, "sky") by castrating him with an adamantine sickle. Fearing that he would, like his own father, be usurped by one of his progeny, Cronos swallowed each of his children (Hestia, Demeter, Hera, Hades, and Poseidon) as their mother, the Titan goddess Rheia, was giving birth to them. Rheia, however, clandestinely hid her youngest child, Zeus, in a cave on the island of Crete by a ruse. She cleverly wrapped up a stone in swaddling clothes and presented it to Cronos. He, believing the swaddled stone to be the infant Zeus, ate the rock instead of their son. When Zeus came of age, he killed and overthrew his father, who vomited up the stone and each of his swallowed children, the eldest of the generation of gods called the Olympians because they dwell on Mt. Olympus. Zeus assumed the position of patriarch after war ensued between the Olympians and the Titans, who were defeated and cast into Tartarus, followed by a war with the devastating monster, Typhon. Victorious in two wars, Zeus established his reign, power, and authority as father (or, patriarch) of gods and humans.
23. As noted above, Rheia was the wife of Cronos and mother of the Olympian generation of gods. As the daughter of the goddess Gaia (or, *Gē*, "Earth") and the god Ouranos (or, "Sky"), she was also a Titan.

24. The subject of this verb is ambiguous in the Greek and much debated. It could be either Rheia or Zeus, and various scholars have offered arguments for either possibility.
25. Hesiod's *Theogony* begins with an invocation to the Muses (see lines 1-28), "who dwell on great and holy Mt. Helicon" and who "dance with nimble feet around the deep-blue spring and the altar of the mighty son of Cronos". The "Heliconian Muses" (as Hesiod calls them) are nine in number and were the goddesses of song and poetry. Hesiod states (lines 36–38) that they tell true things that are, as they will be, and, as they were long ago.
26. Established in parts of Greece, and especially Athens, by at least the 5th century BCE, secret voting by members of the jury in court was accomplished when each voter deposited a pebble into one of two urns. The urn containing the largest number of pebbles won. Both Snyder (1984, p. 128) and Larmour (2005, p. 30) note that the pebbles used to cast the vote are reminiscent of the stone that Cronus swallows and foreshadow the thousands of small stones that will become of a piece of Helicon himself.
27. One ancient source (Hermesianax of Cyprus, *FGrH* 797 F 2) provides a mythological anecdote about Cithaeron and Helicon. According to Hermesianax, they were brothers of very differing temperaments. Helicon was gentler, kinder, and more respectful of his parents, while Cithaeron, out of greed, killed his own father to obtain his estate and then ambushed his brother and, while hurling Helicon off a cliff, fell off it, too. The gods turned both brothers into mountains. (See Vergados, 2012, p. 105–107 for discussion of this and other sources, wherein he notes that Cithaeron is also associated with local Theban lore in Greek tragedy. Oedipus, for example, was exposed on that mountain as an infant.) Vergados (2012, p. 103) suggests that "the contest between the two Boeotian mountains parallels the 'contest' between the two Boeotian poets" (Hesiod and Corinna). For this reason, Vergados argues, careful consideration of Corinna's "dense network" of Hesiodic references, alongside departures from Hesiod's version of the cosmogony.
28. Given the deception of Rheia in Cithaeron's tale, Larmour (1996, p. 30) notes that Helicon is enraged because he senses it may be a mirroring of trickery and deception in the contest itself.
29. Acraephen (a prophet of Apollo) is addressing a Boeotian river god, Asopus.
30. Phoebus is an epithet of Apollo.
31. Maia was a nymph daughter of the Titan, Atlas, and the eldest of seven sisters who became the constellation Pleiades. She gave birth to her son, Hermes, on Mt. Cyllene in Arcadia. *Homeric Hymn 4 (to Hermes)* depicts her as an introvert who avoided the company of the other gods. Instead, she lived within one of the mountain's deep, shady caves, where Zeus visited her for amorous interludes in the dead of night when he might escape Hera's detection.
32. An epithet of Aphrodite.
33. The ancient Greek says, "laxōn apseudian", which quite literally means "obtaining lack of falsehood." The sense here of this dense, efficient phrase is that the holy prophet of Apollo has as his lot in life to know what is true and what is false, as well as the existential inability to utter prophetic statements that are untrue in any way. His prophecies are, after all, the word and knowledge of the god delivered through him.
34. Apollo is the son of Leto.
35. Little is known about Euonymus, except that is the son of another Boeotian river-god, Cephisus. In another lost poem, Corinna, ancient sources tell us, wrote about his daughters (*PMG* 660).

36. Hyreius, a son of Poseidon and Alcyone, asked the gods to grant him a son and heir (Hesiod, fr. 148b West). Three gods—Zeus, Poseidon, and Hermes—urinated on the hide of a bull that Hyreius had, before burying it, sacrificed in their honor. Out of the buried, urine-soaked bull-hide, Hyreius's son was born, and the gods called him Orion (whose name is etymologically resonant of the Greek verb, *oureō,* meaning to 'urinate' or 'ejaculate'). Collins (2006, p. 25–25) discusses the Hesiodic version of Orion's birth story and suggests that Corinna drew Orion's genealogy from Hesiod. More importantly, Collins notes, is that Acraephaen directly descends father-to-son from four generations of oracular prophets (Euonymous, Hyrieus, Orion, Acraephen). Although the poem elides over the complex network of mythologies relating to the Panhellenic and local Boeotian hero Orion while he roamed the earth, it does reference his transformation into a constellation. "His Panhellenic destiny," Collins (2006, p. 26) offers, "is thus made to accord with his localized Boeotian role, and his future reward of becoming a constellation is specifically connected…to his reconquest of his land and the assumption of its central oracular seat."
37. Orion was a Giant and hunter who lived a tragic and complicated life. Both the Panhellenic and local Boeotian legends about him are too numerous and rich to encompass in their entirety here, so a brief overview of some essentials will have to suffice. By some accounts, he was extraordinarily handsome, but was unlucky in love. Ps.-Apollodorus (*Bibliotheca* 1.25), for example, states that Orion's first wife was cast into Hades by Hera because she vied with Hera for beauty). Hesiod (*Works and Days,* 618–621) alludes to the Pleides, who were transformed into a constellation by the gods to escape the erotic pursuit of Orion. Multiple sources cite that when Orion either courted or tried to rape Merope, the beautiful daughter of King Oenopion, her father got him drunk and put out his eyes as he slept before banishing him. Apollodorus (*Bibliotheca* 1.25) states that Hephaestus, feeling sympathy for the blind, wandering Orion, gave the hunter a guide in the form of a boy named Celadion and told the blind hunter to head east. Orion wandered east until his eyes were healed by the sun-god, Helius. Although there are multiple, complex variants in the mythic tradition accounting for his death, numerous allude to Artemis's anger, either because Orion raped one of her nymphs or because he attempted to rape the goddess herself. He was set into the sky as a constellation after his death.
38. Most of Corinna's poetry was probably performed for choruses of women or unmarried girls of marriageable age, which in ancient Greece was usually in the teen years between 13 and 18. This fragment of a poem, in particular, draws attention to the "white-robed women of Tanagra" whom, we imagine, formed a chorus of such performers. Whether or not the audience consisted chiefly or exclusively of women is a matter that has been debated by scholars. Skinner (1983) argued that Corinna's poetry was composed with a female audience in mind, but then compiled for a broader readership later; Rayor (2005) believes that Corinna's poems were intended for an all-female audience; and, Heath (2017) argues that Corinna composed her poems for a wider audience, while self-consciously playing with language in her poems that draws ludic attention to the anomaly of her status as a female composer of publicly performed poetry and music. The poem, which appears on a papyrus from Oxyrhynchus, Egypt copied sometime in the vicinity of 200 CE, is not entirely legible and contains numerous lacunae.
39. One of the nine Muses, each of whom has province over a particular genre of poetry, Terpsichore (whose name means "delighting in the dance") is the Muse of dancing, of the chorus, and of lyric poetry, which was often sung by

a dancing chorus. One particular kind of choral song is the *partheneios*, or "maiden's song", a lyric poem that was intended to be performed by a chorus of unmarried girls or young women. It has been conjectured that this poem is a *partheneios*.

40. "Me" may refer to the poet Corinna, her poetic persona, or a chorus of performers who sing and dance the song in one collective voice.
41. One Roman author (Antoninus Liberalis, 25) states that "Tales" was the title of one of Corinna's books of poetry.
42. Tanagra was a city in Boeotia and Corinna's home town. The settlement was situated beside the river Asopus, who (as an anthropomorphized deity) features so prominently in PMG 654.iii.12–51.
43. The Greek word (*ligourokōtilos*) translated here as "swallow-song" deserves some comment, as it is a word found nowhere else in extant Greek literature and was likely an invention by Corinna. It is a compound word consisting of two parts: "*ligouros*" (clear, clear-toned, sweet-sounding, or even shrill) refers to the quality of sound of something and is an adjective, which often describes the sound a lyre produces (a "sweet" or "clear-toned" sound of a lyre); the swallow (or, *kōtilas* in the Boeotian dialect) derived its name from the adjective "*kōtilos*" (babbling, chattering, gossiping, prattling, twittering). So, it is unclear whether Corinna is suggesting that she is "clear-toned, swallow-voiced" or a "shrilly prattling". One scholar (Heath, 2017, p. 96) suggests that Corinna intended to encompass both of these meanings ironically, serving as a "half-facetious nod to the cultural ambiguity" of her role as female poet, by offering up "a female voice—a source of frequent suspicion of and disparagement of women—to public acclaim."
44. Cephisus is a river of Boeotia personified here as a deity.
45. See notes 36–37 above for Orion.
46. The son of Agamemnon, the king of Argos and the commander-in-chief of the Greek army in the Trojan War, Orestes is a Panhellenic hero who killed his mother, Clytemnestra, to avenge her murder of his father. Orestes grew up in exile in Phocis, which is near Boeotia.
47. The text is illegible in parts, although Campbell's (1992, p. 58–59) Loeb edition offers helpful supplements. The Greek deity Eos (or, Dawn), rises in the morning sky, leaving behind the waters of Oceanus (the river that encircles the disc of Earth in Greek thought), while she simultaneously draws down the (chariot of) Selene, the Moon, from her journey across Ouranos (or, Heaven/Sky).
48. The personified "Hours" or "Seasons" are the daughters of Zeus and Themis and are three in number, according to Homer. Their names are Eunomia, Dike, and Eirene. They are guardians of the gates of Mt. Olympus (*Iliad,* 5.749 and 8.393), the summit of which serves as the home of the Olympian gods.
49. Around Kadmeia, the acropolis of the Boeotian city of Thebes, were seven gates. In Greek myth, both Argos (the ancestral home of Orestes) and Thebes appear to have been two major sites of power. The tragedies of both Aeschylus and Sophocles treat the legendary fall-out of the tragic king Oedipus, whose two sons, Eteocles and Polyneices, waged an epic civil war over which of them would be king after Oedipus's death. Polyneices, exiled by Eteocles, sought refuge in Argos and returned to Thebes with an army of allies. There were seven leaders among the besiegers, one for each of the seven gates of Thebes, and each gate was defended by seven Theban champions. The defenders carried the day, but Polyneices and Eteocles killed each other in hand-to-hand combat, and a generation later, the *epigoni* (the sons of the seven besiegers) returned and destroyed Thebes.

# 3 Erinna

Erinna's poetry was highly prized in antiquity, and several epigrams articulate the contrasting conceit that although her output was not large (a mere three hundred verses, notes one epigram), her small *oeuvre* was equal to or better than the poetry of many others, even of Homer.[1] One anonymous epigram even proclaims that "as much as Sappho surpassed Erinna in lyric poetry, so Erinna surpassed the hexameters of Sappho."[2] This same anonymous epigram begins, "This is the Lesbian honey-comb of Erinna. Although it is somewhat small, it is flavored with the honey of the Muses."[3] Epigrams about Erinna describe her poetry as "sweet", "more capable than many others", "honied", and "beautiful".[4] Her voice is characterized as "swan-like," and she is called a "young" or "new singer" and a "*parthenos*" (unmarried virgin) and a "honey-bee".[5] The attributions of both sweetness and apian characteristics to poetry and authorship are intermingled tropes that "pervade Greek poetics from its inception.... It is only a matter of time," Saadi Liebert (2010, p. 97) notes, "before the poet himself adopts the persona of the bee, culling his songs from the Muses' gardens to produce poetry that is, as Pindar puts it, 'sweeter than bee-fashioned honey-comb' (fr. 152)."

Also visible in such characterizations is an emerging sensibility in Hellenistic poetry that smallness and miniature of scope, breadth, scale, and size of *opus* are aesthetic qualities to be favored over grandiosity and epicizing poetic enterprises. Erinna's work was apparently well known to Alexandrian, Hellenistic epigrammatists, and as Cameron and Cameron (1969, p. 286) argue, the cornerstone of her reputation among them was a hexameter poem of three hundred lines known as the *Ēlakatē*, or *Distaff*. The Suda's summary of Erinna's life and literary output may derive from such epigrammatic representations of Erinna, as it claimed that Erinna composed a poem called the *Distaff* which consisted of three hundred lines in both the Aeolic and Doric dialects.

Cameron and Cameron (1969) argued rather persuasively that a set of Oxyrhynchus papyrus fragments dated to the 2nd century CE, and published in 1929 by Girolamo Vitelli and Medea Norsa (Vitelli and Norsa, 1929) contain within them remnants of the so-called *Distaff*. The poem is

DOI: 10.4324/9781003031727-5

metrically dactylic hexameter. Although the papyri are badly mutilated, when they are pieced together and partly restored, fifty-four lacunose lines are sufficiently clear to enable a reader to ascertain that the poem, in which the Greek word for "distaff" and other references to carding, spinning, weaving, and wool-working appear, offers a lament for the narrator's beloved childhood friend, Baucis.

Where the partial restorations begin at line 15, the narrator, who names herself in line 38, appears to be in the process of recalling memorable incidents from their childhood, including a game of tag called "torty-tortoise" that centered on themes of transitioning into marriage, childbirth, and domesticity. Other recollections in the spotty text refer to playing with dolls and fear of the shape-shifting, infant-snatching bogie, Mormo. The narrator shifts suddenly to the more recent past, when Baucis abandoned the things of childhood for a marriage-bed. The text is patchy and lacunose, but the narrator switches again to her present circumstances, lamenting that shame prevents her from leaving her house to gaze upon the deceased corpse of Baucis along with other mourning women. In line 38, the word "nineteen" appears, and several ancient sources (such as the anonymous epigram *A.P.* 9.190.4 and the Suda) apocryphally attest that Erinna herself died at the age of nineteen as an unmarried young woman. The remaining and badly damaged text appears to consist of a lament or dirge (the ancient Greek word for which is *thrēnos*), and the few words on the left side of the column that are visible suggest that the dirge involved repeating refrains and invocations of Baucis's name. All in all, the *Distaff* offers a tantalizing fragmentary window through which to catch glimpses of ancient Greek female childhood. Certainly, what comes through, despite the fragmentary nature of the papyri, is an unmistakable sense of profound emotional attachment and bonding formed between two girls in the period between childhood and late adolescence.

The sophistication of what remains of the poem has led one scholar (West, 1977) to the controversial conclusion that it could not have been composed by a girl of nineteen who (based on West's equally controversial reconstructions of the poem) spent so much of her days engaged in wool-working, a characterization echoed in *A.P.* 9.190.5–6 ("working at her distaff out of fear of her mother/and working the loom, she was a servant of the Muses"). This characterization in the anonymous apocryphal epigram does seem to correspond with frequent, but indeterminable, references to wool-working in the papyrus fragments. West's arguments, however, were quickly rebutted (Pomeroy, 1978 and Arthur (= Katz), 1980, for example), and a general scholarly consensus now attributes the poem to Erinna.

We are in a slightly better position when it comes to Erinna's epigrams, of which three survive. Two of these epigrams are funerary, and the setting for both of them is the funerary monument of Baucis. In the first (*A.P.* 7.710), the voice of Baucis from the grave bids her *stele* monument and the Sirens adorning it to proclaim to passersby that its resident was newly married when she died, that she is from the island Tenos, and that her *sunetairis* (friend, companion, beloved) Erinna composed the epigram for her tomb. In the second (*A.P.* 7.712), the funerary monument of Baucis addresses a passerby, inviting that person to proclaim to the god Hades that he is cruel and to read aloud the tomb's inscription proclaiming her wretched fate. Hymen, the god of the marriage ceremony, sang at her wedding accompanied by the very wedding-torches with which her father-in-law lit her funeral pyre. The third epigram (*A.P.* 6.352) celebrates a painting of the girl or woman Agatharchis for its life-like verisimilitude, an aesthetic theme also taken up repeatedly by Nossis. Finally, a four-line hexameter fragment from a papyrus that does not identify authorship was attributed to Erinna by Bowra (1936), but later studies (especially West, 1977) note that its Arcadian dialect elements preclude her authorship.

Of Erinna's life precious little is known apart from what may be gleaned from her poetry, and it is always advisable to keep in mind that poets frequently adopt personae and poetic voices other than their own. The entry for Erinna in the Byzantine lexicon known as the *Suda* claims that she was either from Tenos, Lesbos, Telos (a small island near Knidos), or Rhodes. The suggestion that she was from Lesbos was probably inspired by the epigram mentioned above (*A.P.* 9.190) comparing the "Lesbian honey-comb of Erinna" with the poetry of Homer and Sappho. The Suda also notes, as mentioned above, that she composed a 300-line hexameter poem called *The Distaff* and that she also wrote epigrams prior to her death as a *parthenos* at the age of 19. While the Suda claims that she was a companion and contemporary of Sappho, most scholars dismiss this assertion as apocryphal fiction and date her work to perhaps 400–350 BCE.[6]

## Select Bibliography

Alexiou, M., 1974. *The Ritual Lament in Greek Tradition.* Cambridge: Cambridge University Press.

Arthur (= Katz), M. B. 1980. "The Tortoise and the Mirror: Erinna PSI 1090." *CW* 74.2: 53–65.

Bowra, C. 1936. "Erinna's Lament for Baucis," in *Greek Poetry and Life: Essays Presented to Gilbert Murray on His Seventieth Birthday, January 2, 1936.* Oxford: Oxford University Press, p. 325–342.

Cameron, A. and A. Cameron. 1969. "Erinna's Distaff," *The Classical Quarterly* 19.2: 285–288.

Gow, A. S. F. and D. L. Page. 1965. *The Greek Anthology: Hellenistic Epigrams, vols. 1–2.* Cambridge: Cambridge University Press.

Iles-Johnston, S. 1995. "Defining the Dreadful: Remarks on the Greek Child-Killing Demon," in M. Meyer and P. Mirecki (eds.), *Ancient Magic and Ritual Power.* Leiden: Brill, p. 361–387.

Karanika, A. 2012. "Playing the Tortoise: Reading Symbols of an Ancient Folk Game." *Helios* 39.2: 101–120.

Levaniouk, O. 2008. "Lament and Hymenaios in Erinna's *Distaff*." in A. Suter (ed.), *Lament: Studies in the Eastern Mediterranean and Beyond*. Oxford: Oxford University Press, p. 324–380.

Levin, D. N. 1962. "Quaestiones Erinneanae," *HSCP* 66: 193–204.

Liebert, R. S. 2010. "Apian Imagery and the Critique of Sweetness in Plato's *Republic*," *TAPA* 140.1: 97–115.

Lloyd-Jones, H. and P. Parsons. 1983. *Supplementum Hellenisticum*. Berlin: De Gruyter, p. 187–189.

Mass, Paul. 1934. "Erinnae in Baucidem Nenia," *Hermes* 69.2: 206–209.

Manwell, Elizabeth. 2005. "*Dico ergo sum:* Erinna's Voice and Poetic Reality," in E. Greene (ed.), *Women Poets in Ancient Greece and Rome*. Norman, OK: University of Oklahoma Press, p. 72–90.

Neri, C. 1996. *Studi sulle testimonianze di Erinna*. Bologna: Pàtron.

———. 2003. *Erinna: Testimonianze e Frammenti*. Studi di Eikasmos, 9. Bologna: Pàtron.

Ormand, K. 1999. *Exchange and the Maiden: Marriage in Sophoclean Tragedy*. Austin, TX: University of Texas Press.

Pomeroy, Sarah B. 1978. "Supplementary Notes on Erinna," *ZPE* 32: 17–22.

Rauk, J. 1989. "Erinna's Distaff and Sappho fr. 94," *GRBS* 30: 101–116.

Rayor, D. 2005. "The Power of Memory in Erinna and Sappho," in E. Greene (ed.), *Women Poets in Ancient Greece and Rome*. Norman, OK: University of Oklahoma Press, p. 59–71.

Rehm, R. 2019. *Marriage to Death: The Conflation of Wedding and Funeral Rituals in Greek Tragedy*. Princeton, NJ: Princeton University Press.

Skinner, M. B. 1982. "Briseis, the Trojan Women, and Erinna," *CW* 75.5: 265–269.

Stehle, E. 2001. "The Good Daughter: Mothers' Tutelage in Erinna's Distaff and Fourth-Century Epitaphs," in A. Lardinois and L. McClure (eds.), *Making Silence Speak: Women's Voices in Greek Literature and Society*. Princeton, NJ: Princeton University Press, p. 179–200.

Vitelli, G. and Medea Norsa. 1929. *Papiri greci e latini della Società Italiana* 9: xii–xiii, 137–144.

West, M. L. 1977. "Erinna," *ZPE* 25: 95–119.

**Erinna, "The Distaff" = P.S.I. 1090**

(col. i)

].ν[
]εοι.[ ].
]ε κώρας·
].ι νύμφαι·
] χελύνναν
σ]ελάννα·
χε]λύννα·

].ελῆσ[
]ω.ει·
]θα φυλλοισ[
]αλασσει·
].αννν·
] νίδα πέξα[ι
].[..]υ κυμα[ ]

(col. ii)

λε]υκᾶν μαινομέν[οισι                    π]οσσὶν ἀφ' ἵ[π]πω[ν
..]αι ἐγὼ μέγ' ἄϋσα· φ [                    ] χελύννα
..]χομένα μεγάλας [                    ] χορτίον αὐλᾶς·
ταῦτά τυ Βαῦκι τάλαι[να βαρὺ στονά]χεισα γόημ[ι],
τα]ῦτά μοι ἐν κρα[δίαι]                    παίχνια κεῖται
θέρμ' ἔτι· τῆν[α δ                    ἀ]θυρομες ἄνθρακες ἤδη,
δαγύ[δ]ων τε χ [                    ]ίδες ἐν θαλάμοισι
νύμ[φ]αι ν [                    ]έες, ἅ τε ποτ' ὄρθρον
μάτηρ αε [                    ].ουσιν ἐρίθοις
τηνας ἤλθ [                    ]να ἀμφ' ἁλίπαστον·
αι μικραι σπ [                    ]ν φόβον ἄγαγε Μορ[μ]ώ·
..]. εν μὲν κο [                    ].ατα, ποσσὶ δ' ἐφοίτη
τέ]τρασιν, ἐκ δ' [ἑτέραν ἑτέρας] μετεβάλλετ' ὀπωπάν.
ἁνίκα δ' ἐς [λ]έχος [ἀνδρὸς ἔβας, τ]όκα πάντ' ἐλάλασο
ἅσσ' ἔτι νηπία εἶτά τ' ἐ[μᾶς ἐν(ὶ)] ματρὸς ἄκουσας
Βαῦκι φίλα· λάθας [.].ετ [          ]. 'Αφροδίτα·
τῶ τυ κατακλα[ί]οισα τὰ μὲν …] ἄ[λ]λα δὲ λείπω·
οὐ [γ]άρ μοι πόδες …[.]φ [          ] ἄπο δῶμα βεβάλοι,
οὐδέ σ' ἰδῆν φαέε[σσιν ἔχω νέ]κυν, οὐδὲ γοάσαι
γυμναῖσιν χαίταισιν […  φ]οικίνεος αἰδώς

(col. iii)

δρύπτε[ι] μ' ἀμφὶ πα[ρῆιδας
α..[ . ] δὲ π[ρ]οπάροιθ[εν
ἐννεα[και]δέκατος τ[
''Ηρινν' ε[. .]ε φίλαι πα[
ἀλακάταν ἐσόρει[σα
γνῶθ' ὅτι τοι κ[

ἀμφέλικες γελ[
ταῦτ' αἰδώς μ' α[
παρθε[ν]ίοις· α [
δερκομένα δ' ε. [
καὶ χαίτα μετ[
πραϋλόγοι πολιαί, ταὶ γήραος ἄνθεα θνατοῖς.
τῶ τυ φίλα φο[
Βαῦκι κατακλα[ι
ἂν φλόγα μιν π[
ὠρυγᾶς ἀΐοισα ὁ[
ὦ πολλὰν ὑμέν[αιε
π]ολλὰ δ' ἐπιψαύ[
π]άνθ' ἑνός· ὦ ὑμ[έναιε
αἰαῖ Βαῦκι τάλαιν[α

*Meter: Dactylic Hexameter*

—

**ἀθύρω, —, —, —, —, —:** play, make sport
**αἰδώς, -οῦς, ἡ:** shame; respect; awe; reverence; sense of honor
**αἰαῖ:** an interjection registering grief or astonishment
**ἀΐω, —, ἐπήϊσα, —, —, —:** hear; perceive by hearing; listen to
**ἀλίπαστος, -ον:** sprinkled with salt
**ἄνθος, -ους, τό:** flower; bloom
**ἄνθραξ, -ακος, ὁ:** charcoal
**αὐλή, ῆς, ἡ:** courtyard; enclosed yard wherein domestic animals are kept
**αὔω, ἀΰσω, ἤϋσα, —, —, —:** shout; cry aloud; call out
**βαρύς, -εῖα, ύ:** heavy, grievous, hard to bear, oppressive
**γῆρας, -αος, τό:** old age
**γοάω, γοήσομαι γοήσω, ἐγόησα, —, —:** groan, weep, bewail
**δαγύς, -ῦδος, ἡ:** doll
**δέρκομαι, δέρξομαι, ἔδρακον, δέδορκα, ἐδέρχθην:** look on or at; flash or gleam
**δρύπτω, δρύψω, ἔδρυψα, —, δέδρυμαι, —:** tear
**ἔριθος, -ου, ὁ, ἡ:** day-laborer; worker in wool; weaver; spinsters
**ἠλακάτη, -ης, ἡ:** distaff, the spindle onto which wool or flax is wound for spinning
**ἡνίκα:** then; at that time; when
**θέρμη, -ης, ἡ:** heat; when it is hot; summer heat
**κατακλαίω, —, —, —, —, —:** lament; bewail loudly; weep
**κεῖμαι, κείσομαι, —, —, —, —:** lie; am laid
**κόρη, -ης, ἡ:** girl; young woman
**κορυφή, -ῆς, ἡ:** head
**κῦμα, -ματος, τό:** wave
**λανθάνω, λήσω, ἔλαθον, λέληθα, ἐπιλέλησμαι, —:** forget; escape one's notice; cause to forget

**λέχος, -εος, τό:** bed
**λήθη, -ης, ἡ:** forgetfulness
**μαίνομαι, μανοῦμαι μανήσομαι, ἐμηνάμην, μέμηνα, μεμάνημαι, ἐμάνην:** rage, be enraged; be driven mad; be frenzied
**μεταβάλλω, μεταβαλῶ, μετέβαλον, —, —, —:** change; alter; undergo a change
**νέκυς, -υος, ὁ:** corpse
**νήπιος, ον:** child; childlike; innocent
**νύμφη, -ης, ἡ:** young woman; bride; newly married wife
**ὀπωπή, -ῆς, ἡ:** outward appearance
**ὄρθρος, -ου, ὁ:** daybreak; just before dawn; dawn
**παίγνιον, -ου, τό:** plaything; toy; pet; darling; children's game
**πέκω, —, ἔπεξα, —, —, ἐπέχθην:** comb; card (wool)
**πολιά, ᾶς, ἡ:** greyness of hair; grey hair
**πούς, ποδός, ὁ:** foot
**πραΰλόγος, ου, ὁ, ἡ:** one who is gentle of speech
**προπάροιθε(ν):** adv., in time before; before; before the time of (a genitive noun or phrase)
**σελήνη, -ης, ἡ:** moon
**στοναχέω, —, ἐστονάχησα, —, —, —:** groan, sigh; groan for or over an accusative object
**τάλας, τάλαινα, τάλαν:** suffering; wretched; in a poor or sorry state
**τέτταρες οἱ/αἱ, τέτταρα, τά:** four
**φάος, φάεος, τό:** light, eye
**φλόξ, φλόγος, ἡ:** flame; fire
**φοινίκεος, έα, εον:** blood-red; crimson
**φοιτάω, —,—, —, —, —:** wander backwards and forwards; stalk; roam about
**φύλλον, -ου, τό:** leaf
**χαίτ-η, ἡ:** loose, flowing hair
**χελώνη, -ης, ἡ:** tortoise
**χόρτος, -ου, ὁ:** enclosed space, usually one in which domestic animals are kept or fed
**ὠρυγή, -ῆς, ἡ:** howling or roaring

—

**1–54:** The 2nd century CE, Egyptian papyri fragments discovered at Oxyrhynchus and known as "P.S.I. 1090" provide a substantial and tantalizing glimpse of the poem commonly referred to as the "Distaff". Published in 1929 by the Italian archaeologists Girolamo Vitelli and Medea Norsa, the papyrus fragments contained, when pieced together and partially restored into three columns, fifty-four fairly mutilated hexameter lines that offer a lament for the narrator's childhood friend, Baucis. Several ancient authors attest to a poem by Erinna called the "Distaff", and the Suda claims that Erinna wrote a 300-line hexameter poem by that title. West (1977) controversially argued that the poem is not Erinna's, but rather an anonymous imitation by a male poet of Cos or Rhodes living in the end of the fourth or early 3rd century BCE. His argument largely rested on the supposition that a nineteen-year old girl heavily involved in wool-working at her mother's behest (as articulated in the poem, or at least in the supplements to the poem that West conjectures) would not have had time in the day to become sufficiently well-educated to compose such a sophisticated poem. Rebuttals to West's conclusions quickly followed (Pomeroy, 1978 and Arthur (= Katz), 1980, for example), and a general scholarly consensus now attributes the poem to Erinna.

The first column preserves only a few legible words on the far right-hand margin, among which are allusions to girlhood, childhood games, and weaving. Where the partially legible text of column II begins, the narrator remembers childhood games like the "Tortoise" (see the note at line 5 of the commentary below; see also Arthur (= Katz), 1980 and Karanika, 2012), addressing "wretched Baucis" with a heavy heart filled with grief. Memories of childhood games with dolls and wool-working are evoked, along with the childhood terror of the phantasmagorical bogie-monster, Mormo (line 25), who caused great fear, stalking about on four feet and shape-shifting (lines 26–27). The narrator switches suddenly to the more recent past, remembering that Baucis was recently married (lines 28–30). The early death of her childhood friend causes the narrator great grief, so much so that she finds herself unable to attend the funeral rites (lines 31–35). Column III is much damaged, but there are a few noteworthy words and phrases legible, including the word *enneakaidekatos* (nineteenth), the age at which some ancient sources claim Erinna died (see note for line 37 in the commentary below), as well as her own name (line 38), allusions to maidenhood and old age (lines 43 and 46), a hymeneal wedding song (line 51), and grief-stricken addresses to Baucis (lines 48 and 54). Much commentary on the poem has centered on its author's strategies for formulating a poetic voice (Manwell, 2005) and on its themes of memory (Rauk, 1989 and Rayor, 2005), lamentation and grief (Skinner, 1982, and Levaniouk, 2008), and the play between girlhood and motherhood in a poem mourning the loss of a young bride (Stehle, 2001). See Alexiou (1974) for a seminal study of the ritual lament in Greek literature.

We have largely used West's (1977) edition, consulting Lloyd-Jones and Parson (1983) in the case of the more controversial supplements suggested by West, which we have either suppressed or referenced in the notes below. Other scholars (Levaniouk, 2008, for example) have done something similar, offering a caveat against the assumption of a papyrological rendering, and we have followed a similar course, given that our aim is to provide a reasonably accessible text by which to introduce intermediate readers to the poetry of Erinna.

**1–14:** The badly damaged papyrus yields but a few tantalizing words in the first fourteen lines.

**3. κώρας** = Doric for (Attic) κόρης

**5. χελύνναν** = Aelic for χελώνη (χελώνη is listed in the vocabulary above). See also lines 7 and 16.Bowra (1936, p. 328) recognized that the tortoises and white horses (see line 15 below) refer to a children's game of tag called χελιχελώνη (*khelikhelōnē*). Karanika (2012, p. 102) argues that it may also be a game for *parthenoi*, or young girls entering the traditional age of puberty in which girls married. Pollux (9.125) describes this game, noting that one girl would sit in the middle of other girls, who ran in a circle around her. The runners and the girl sitting in the center would exchange the following responsorial refrain:

χελιχελώνη, τί ποιεῖς ἐν τῷ μέσῳ; ("torty-tortoise, what are you doing in the middle?"—runners)
ἔρια μαρύομαι καὶ κρόκην Μιλησίαν. ("weaving wool and Milesian thread."—center girl)
ὁ δ' ἔκγονος σου τί ποιῶν ἀπώλετο; ("And, your son, how did he die (doing what)?"—runners)
λευκᾶν ἀφ' ἵππων εἰς θάλασσαν ἅλατο. ("He leapt from white horses into the sea."—center girl)

As the girl in the center spoke these words, she would leap up and try to tag one of the runners, who, if caught, would then take a turn as the tortoise in the center. Pomeroy (1978) fleshes out numerous folktale, religious, and cultural associations with the tortoise, showing its resonant affiliations with Aphrodite, the loom, and weaving. Arthur (= Katz, 1980) suggests that the tortoise represents motherhood and domesticity, highlighting various folktales that allude to the tortoise, such as a story told by Servius (commentary on the *Aeneid*, 1.505). The tortoise, Servius relates, was once a *parthenos* who scorned marriage and, refusing to attend Zeus's wedding, remained at home during the celebration. Hermes, in anger at the girl, threw her cliff-edged house into the sea, where she was transformed into a turtle or tortoise who forever carried her house with her. Karanika (2012, p. 103) regards the song as "a scenario of codified initiation into adulthood" that interweaves themes of women's labor (weaving) and death and (pgs. 113–114) "instructed and initiated girls very subtly into the knowledge of adulthood and their future roles ... through a practice that was unassuming, innocent, yet pervasive." She notes (p. 104) that "the presence of such serious themes may seem strange, given that the song is performed in a playful atmosphere, but it is no coincidence, as allusions to work, death, and destruction are pervasive in children's rhymes." She provides the example of "Ring around the Rosie," whose origins lay in plague in medieval England.

**6. σ]ελάννα** = Aeolic for σελήνη (σελήνη is listed in the vocabulary above).

**11–12.** No single word is intelligible in these lines.

**13. πέξα[ι:** an aorist infinitive of the verb πέκω. While this verb is commonly used to reference the combing of hair, it is used here to signify the carding of wool—the combing process by which wool is cleaned of impurities before spinning into thread for weaving.

**14. κυμα:** Page's text (1946, p. 486) reprints a reconstruction first proposed by Stella (1929, p. 835), favored later also by Mass (1934, p. 206), of the fourth (dactyl) and fifth (anceps) metrical feet of the line: ἐς βαθ]ὺ κῦμα ("into the deep wave"). In a close papyrological reading, however, West, (1977, p. 104 and 112) proposed that Stella's reconstruction is incompatible with the traces of letters on the papyrus and instead offers a "speculative" reconstruction of the words occupying the same metrical position: ἄχρι τ]ὺ κῦμα.

**15. λε]υκᾶν** = λευκῶν (Attic). The genitive adjective modifies ἵ[π]πω[ν ("from white horses").Levaniouk (2008) demonstrates that horses, and especially white horses, are strongly associated with weddings, the pre-wedding activities of women, and the White Rock, a leap from which in ancient Greek myth and literature is associated with love, madness, and intoxication. Nagy (1973) discusses this constellation of evocations in relation to an ancient legend holding that Sappho committed suicide by leaping from the White Rock of Leucas out of unrequited love for the mythic ferryman Phaon.

**15. μαινομέν[οισι ... π]οσσὶν:** "with frenzied feet". West (1977, p. 112) offers a neat suggestion for a restoration of the line: λε]υκᾶν μαινομέν[οισιν ἐσάλαο π]οσσὶν ἀφ' ἵ[π]πω[ν. "And, you leapt with frenzied feet from white horses."

**15. π]οσσὶν:** dat. pl. of πούς. See also line 26.

**16. ..]αι ἐγὼ μέγ' ἄϋσα· φ [ ] χελύννα:** West (1977, p. 112) conjectures the following restoration: "αἴ]αῖ ἐγώ" μέγ' ἄϋσα· φα[νεῖσα δὲ δηὖτε] χελύννα, "Aiai,'" I shouted loudly, and once again turned into a tortoise. ἄϋσα = ἤϋσα (Attic).

**17. χορτίον:** diminutive of χόρτος. Homer (*Iliad* 11.774) uses a similar construction (αὐλῆς ἐν χορτῷ) to allude to a farmyard wherein cattle are kept.

**17. μεγάλας...αὐλᾶς** = μεγάλης αὐλῆς (Attic).

**18. Βαῦκι:** the girlhood friend, Baucis, whose death the poet-narrator laments, is addressed in the vocative case four times in the fragments that remain of the poem. See also lines 30, 48, and 54. The repetitive address to the deceased is a familiar feature of laments, and the somber tone of the address is enhanced via the vocative adjective τάλαι[να ("you, poor Baucis...").

**18. στονά]χεισα** = στοναχοῦσα (Attic), a nominative singular, feminine, present tense, active voice participle.

**18. γόημ[ι]** = γοάω (or, when contracted, γοῶ in Attic); in Aeolic, present and imperfect tense verbs that would have contracted forms in Attic are rendered as—μι conjugation forms.

**19. κρα[δίαι** = Doric for καρδίᾳ

**19. παίχνια** = παίγνια (Attic)

**20. θέρμ' ἔτι· τῆν[α δ                    ἀ]θυρομες ἄνθρακες ἤδη:** West (1977, p. 112) proposes: θέρμα' ἔτι· τῆν[α δ' ἄ πρίν ποκ' ἀ]θύρομες ἄνθρακες ἤδη, "still hot; but those (which we once) played are already [burnt to] charcoal".

**20. ἀ]θύρομες** = ἀθύρομεν or ἠθύρομεν (Attic).

**21. δαγύ[δ]ων τε χ [                    ]ίδες ἐν θαλάμοισι:** West (1977, p. 112) proposes: δαγύ[δ]ων τε χ[οροὶ καὶ ἑταιρ]ίδες ἐν θαλάμοισι, "and dances (of dolls?) and girl-hood friends, brides [line 22] in the bedroom".

**21–24.** Page (1946, p. 120) offers the following conjectural restoration: "δαγύ[δ]ων τ' ἐχ[όμεσθα νεαν]ίδες ἐν θαλάμοισι/νύμ[φαι]σιν προσόμοιοι ἀκηδ]έες· ἅ τε πὸτ ὄρθρον/μάτηρ, ἃ ἔ[ριον νέμεν ἀμφιπόλ]οισιν ἐρίθοις,/τήνα σ' ἦλθ[ε κρέας προκαλευμέ]να ἀμφ' Ἀλίπαστον"; and, he supplies this translation for it, "We clung to our dolls in our chambers when we were girls, playing Young Wives, without a care. And towards dawn your Mother, who allotted wool to her attendant workwomen, came and called you to help with the salted meat."

**21. δαγύ[δ]ων:** this word is apparently only attested elsewhere in Theocritus, *Idyll* 2.110 to signify a wax doll used for magical purposes. Dolls made of rags, wool, terra cotta, wax, and ivory were children's playtoys (usually called 'κοραί'), and girls in ancient Greece often dedicated their dolls to Artemis at marriage.

**22. ποτ'** = Aeolic for πρός (Attic); the prepositional phrase, πρὸς ὄρθον, suggests the time of day in which dawn approaches ("towards dawn").

**24. ἀλίπαστον:** there is not enough text remaining to provide sufficient context.

**25.** West (1977, p. 112) conjectures: αἱ μικραὶ σπ[ουδᾶι γε· τόσο]ν φόβον ἄγαγε Μορ[μ]ώ· (and with little haste; such great fear did Mormo bring).

**25. Μορ[μ]ώ:** Mormo was one of several bogie-monsters in ancient Greek folktale whose conjuring by name was intended to frighten children. In Theocritus, *Idyll* 15 (line 40), the monster (in the form of a horse) is invoked by an exasperated mother trying to quieten down her wildly protesting child and make her acquiesce to her wishes. Other such demons included Lamia, Empousa, Gorgo, and Gello. See Arthur (= Katz, 1980, p. 64–65) for a discussion of the significance of Mormo ("she is the fearsome aspect of marriage for young girls") to the themes of marriage, motherhood, and death. See SarahIles-Johnston (1995) for discussion of child-killing demons, including Mormo, in the ancient Greek imagination. Iles-Johnston (p. 367–368 and note 9) suggests that she may have been imagined as a kind of female werewolf; additionally, she discusses the testimony of a scholiast of Aristides, who provided an explanatory note on Mormo, indicating that the demon's very name frightened children and once belonged to a Corinthian woman who ate her own children and then flew away. So, as Iles-Johnston (p. 368) put it, "Mormo bears children but then fails to nurture them successfully to adulthood." Thus, as Arthur (= Katz, 1980) points out, Mormo's phantasmagorical presence in the poem mirrors that of Baucis, who died just after marriage and before full transition to adulthood and motherhood.

**26.** West (1977, p. 112) conjectures: τᾶς ἐν μὲν κο[ρυφᾶι μεγάλ'] ὤατα, ποσσὶ δ' ἐφοίτη, "on her head were large ears, and she wandered on four [line 27] feet."

**27. τέ]τρασιν** = τέτταρσιν (Attic), the dat. pl., masculine cardinal number "four" and modifies ποσσὶ from the previous line. In ancient Greek, the cardinal numbers for one, three, and four are declinable.

**27. ἐκ δ' [ἑτέραν ἑτέρας]:** "from one (form) into another". Page (1946, p. 120–121) reverses the order of the two adjectives (ἐκ δ' [ἑτέρας ἑτέραν]), but the substance of either Page's or West's reconstruction remains constant.

**27. ὀπωπάν** = ὀπωπήν (Attic)

**28. ἁνίκα** = ἡνίκα (Attic)

**28. ἐλέλασο:** pluperfect, 2nd, singular from λανθάνω ("you had forgotten")

**28. τ]όκα** = τότε (Attic), a temporal adverb ("at that time"; "then")

**29. ἅσσ'** = ἅττα (neuter plural of ὅστις)

**29. ἅσσ' ἔτι νηπία εἶτά τ' ἐ[μᾶς ἐν(ὶ)] ματρὸς ἄκουσας:** the conjectural reconstruction is West's (1977, p. 113), "which you, a child then, heard from my mother"). Page (1946, p. 120–123) offers a slightly different rendering: ἅσσ' ἔτι νηπιάσα[σα] τ[εᾶς παρὰ] ματρὸς ἄκουσας, "But, when you went to a man's bed, you forgot all that you heard from *your* Mother, dear Baucis, in babyhood."

**30. λάθας:** Doric form; the Attic equivalent = λήθης. The line is too lacunose to make out the full sense of it.

**31. τῶ:** adv. "therefore"

**31. κατακλα[ί]οισα** = κατακλαίουσα, a present, feminine, nominative singular, active voice participle: "weeping" or "bewailing loudly". In Attic the verb appears as κατακλάω rather than κατακλαίω, but we have elected to cite κατακλαίω in the vocabulary above, since it is listed thus in the *LSJ*.

**32. βεβάλοι** = βέβηλοι: permitted; sanctioned; the adjective has religious connotations that pertain to ground that is allowed to be trodden, and from that meaning extends to that which is permissible. Thus, the narrator's "feet are not permitted" (to go?) "from the house".

**33. ἰδῆν** = ἰδεῖν (Attic), an infinitive form of ὁράω: "nor am I able (ἔχω) to look upon your corpse with my eyes…"

**33. φάεσσι:** dative plural of φάος, φάεος, τό: "light, eye" ("with my eyes"). As the body parts that illuminate the fire and light of life, this noun serves as a metaphor for "eyes". There is a stark contrast here between the illuminating life-force of the narrator and the extinguished life of her beloved friend, Baucis. (Note: the Attic form of the genitive listed in this explanatory note and in the vocabulary above contracts to φῶς.)

**34. γοάσαι:** an aorist infinitive of γοάω, another infinitive (like ἰδῆν) supplementing ἔχω in line

**34. γυμναῖσιν χαίταισιν:** among "the women, their hair loosened". The liberation of women's hair from woven nets, headbands, ties, and other means of securing the hair is a sign of mourning. When Andromache first sees the lifeless body of her husband Hector (*Iliad*, 22. 460–472), she falls backward, gasping for air, and she tears from her head all of the adornments that bound her hair, including her frontlet (*ampux*), snood, (*kekruphalos*), woven headband (*anadesmē*), and a headdress (*krēdemnon*) that had been given to her as a gift from Aphrodite on her wedding day. See also line 45.

**34. φ]οικίνεος αἰδώς:** blood-red shame

**35. δρύπτε[ι] μ' ἀμφὶ πα[ρῆιδας:** at this point, the papyrus in column III is significantly damaged. The subject may be φ]οικίνεος αἰδώς from the previous line, but in the absence of a fuller manuscript, certainty is untenable. Something, however ("blood-red shame"?) "tears at both sides of my cheeks (?)"

**37. ἐννεα[και]δέκατος:** nineteenth. A quatrain epigram by Asclepiades (*A.P.* 7.11) suggests that Erinna, though she was but nineteen, composed "not a lot" (i.e., she was not prolific), but she was more capable "than many others". In the final lines ("may Hades not come to me quickly...") there is the suggestion that she died young. An anonymous epigram (*A.P.* 9.190) claims that Erinna's three hundred lines rival the poetry of Homer, though she was but nineteen at the time of authorship. The Suda claims that Erinna was a nineteen-year old *parthenos* when she died, but was nevertheless judged "equal to Homer." The text is too damaged to illuminate much, but it is likely that either the narrator (who names herself in the next line) is claiming herself to be nineteen-years old at some point in the poem's sequence of events or at the time of composition. Alternatively, Baucis was nineteen-years old at the time of her marriage or passing.

**39. ἀλακάταν ἐσόρει[σα:** ἀλακάταν is Doric for ἠλακάτην ("distaff" or "spindle"); ἐσόρει[σα is a nominative feminine singular participle from εἰσοράω ("looking at the distaff"). Several sources (Suda; the anonymous *A.P.* 9.190 and 7.12, for example), suggest or hint that Erinna composed a poem of 300 lines in both Aeolic and Doric called the ἠλακάτη. See Cameron and Cameron (1967) for a discussion of whether or not this poem is it. They note, "the consensus of opinion thus seems to be that ἠλακάτη as the title of Erinna's lament for Baucis is at least suspicious; if it is a title at all, it is likely to be a scholarly guess, probably Alexandrian. We believe on the contrary that ἠλακάτη, or rather ἀλακάτα, is indeed the title of Erinna's poem, and that it is Erinna's own." If that is the case, our present text is but a fraction of the original poem.

**40. γνῶθ':** an aorist imperative of γιγνώσκω.

**41. ἀμφέλικες:** "coiled around"; the text is too damaged to make out γελ[, but West (1977, p. 113) proposes that perhaps it referenced the name of Gello, another bogie-apparition invoked to frighten children.
**45. χαίτα** = χαίτη (Attic); see also line 34 above.
**50. ὠρυγᾶς ἀΐοισα:** "hearing a howling"; ἀΐοισα = ἀΐουσα (Attic). Verbs of perception take genitive objects. ὠρυγᾶς = (Attic) ὠρυγῆς.
**51. ὑμέν[αιε:** a *hymenaios* is a wedding or bridal song, sung by the bride's retinue as the wedding procession leads the bride to the bridegroom's house.

**Erinna 1 G-P = (*A.P.* 7.710)**

Στάλα καὶ Σειρῆνες ἐμαὶ καὶ πένθιμε κρωσσέ
ὅστις ἔχεις Ἀίδα τὰν ὀλίγαν σποδιάν,
τοῖς ἐμὸν ἐρχομένοισι παρ' ἠρίον εἴπατε χαίρειν,
αἴτ' ἀστοὶ τελέθωντ' αἴθ' ἑτεροπτόλιες·
χὤτι με νύμφαν εὖσαν ἔχει τάφος· εἴπατε καὶ τό,
χὤτι πατήρ μ' ἐκάλει Βαυκίδα, χὤτι γένος
Τηνία, ὡς εἰδῶντι, καὶ ὅττι μοι ἁ συνεταιρίς
Ἤρινν' ἐν τύμβῳ γράμμ' ἐχάραξε τόδε.

*Meter: Elegiac Couplets*

**ἀστός, -οῦ, ὁ:** citizen
**γράμμα, -ματος, τό:** anything written or drawn; inscription
**γένος, -εος, τό:** family; tribe; clan; kin
**ἑτερόπτολις, ὁ, ἡ:** of another city
**ἠρίον, -ου, τό:** tomb
**κρωσσός, -οῦ, ὁ:** an urn holding the cinerary remains of the deceased
**νύμφη, -ης, ἡ:** bride
**πένθιμος, -ον:** made for mourning
**σποδιά, -ᾶς, ἡ:** ashes
**στήλη, -ης, ἡ:** a block of carved stone that serves as a funerary monument
**συνεταιρίς, -ίδος, ἡ:** companion; friend
**τάφος, -ου, ὁ:** grave; tomb
**τύμβος, -ου, ὁ:** tomb; grave
**χαράττω, χαράξω, ἐχάραξα, —, κεχαράγμαι, ἐχαράχθην:** engrave; carve

—

**1–8:** Baucis, Erinna's childhood friend, calls out from the grave, addressing her funerary monument, the Sirens which adorn it, and the funerary urn filled with her own ashen remains, which now belong to Hades. The voice of Baucis from the grave bids each of these to greet passersby and to proclaim that she was newly married when she died, that she is from the island Tenos, and that her *sunetairis* (friend, companion, beloved)

Erinna composed the epigram for her tomb. Rayor (1996), comparing Erinna's focus on the loss of Baucis with Sappho's expressions of loss on departed companions (L-P fr. 16, for example; also, L-P fr. 94 and 96), argues for homoerotic readings. Whereas Sappho, she notes, (p. 66) "invokes memory to express, rejoice in, and continue the life of a community of women," memory in Erinna's poems focuses more intimately on a connection between two beloved friends. Rayor (p. 67) succinctly articulates an important feature of the epigram: "In the last line …. Erinna makes it clear that it is not really Baukis who speaks: Erinna herself wrote the words. The dead cannot speak, the living cannot hear them, and the poet does not know who will read the written record." The "bride of death" is a frequent motif in ancient Greek literature (Rehm (2019) provides a useful reading of this motif in Greek tragedy, for example).

**1. Στάλα καὶ Σειρῆνες:** Στάλα = στήλη (Attic). Both nouns are vocative, as is the possess adjective ἐμαὶ. Funerary stelae were quadrangular or column slabs (often made of marble or limestone) that served as markers for the deceased and had a function similar to that of headstones over modern grave sites. The Sirens are mythical hybrid creatures—part bird, part human female—who enchant sailors with their irresistible songs, luring them to their deaths. The earliest appearance of the Sirens in Greek literature occurs in the *Odyssey*, wherein they are described as perching in a meadow upon a pile of moldering skeletons of those whom their songs bewitched (12.39–54). Statues of these hybrid creatures were common decorative elements of funerary stelae in ancient Greek cemeteries. Gow and Page (1965, vol. 2, p. 283) suggest that the monument referred to in the poem likely consisted of a column with two Sirens perched on top.

**2. 'Αίδα:** Hades, the god who holds dominion over the Netherworld. The form in the text is vocative, but there may be an error in the copying. Gow and Page (1965, vol. 2, p. 283) suggest that a genitive would make the most sense ("belonging to Hades").

**2. τὰν ὀλίγαν** = τὴν ὀλίγην (Attic)

**3. εἴπατε χαίρειν:** "speak a greeting"

**4. αἴτ'… αἴθ'** = Doric and Aeolic for (Attic) εἴτε… εἴτε

**4. τελέθωντ'** = τελέθονται (Attic), from τεθέλω (be). "whether they are citizens or from other cities."

**5. χὤτι = καὶ ὅτι** (elision); syntactically speaking, ὅτι relies upon εἴπατε in line 3. The same construction is found in the second half of line 5 through line 6.

**5. εὖσαν** = Doric, feminine participle (accusative singular) of the verb εἰμί. The equivalent in Attic = οὖσαν.

**6. Βαυκίδα:** Baucis, the childhood friend who died shortly after getting married and named four times (lines 18, 30, 48, and 54) in the *Distaff* poem by Erinna.

**7. Τηνία:** from Tenos, an island in the Cyclades. It is presently called Tinos.
**7. ὡς εἰδῶντι:** a purpose clause, "so that they may know".
**7. ἁ** = ἡ (Attic)
**8. ''Ηριννʼ:** Erinna names herself in this *sphragis* poem, expressing her own role in keeping alive the memory of her beloved *sunetairis*. Whether the epigram was an actual inscription or fictionally so is unclear.

**Erinna 2 G-P = (*A.P.* 7.712)**

Νύμφας Βαυκίδος εἰμί, πολυκλαύταν δὲ παρέρπων
στάλαν τῷ κατὰ γᾶς τοῦτο λέγοις 'Αίδᾳ
'βάσκανος ἔσσ', 'Αίδα'. τὰ δέ τοι καλὰ σάμαθ' ὁρῶντι
ὠμοτάταν Βαυκοῦς ἀγγελέοντι τύχαν,
ὡς τὰν παῖδ' Ὑμέναιος ἐφ' αἷς ἀείδετο πεύκαις
τᾶσδ' ἐπὶ καδεστὰς ἔφλεγε πυρκαϊᾶς,
καὶ σὺ μέν, ὦ Ὑμέναιε, γάμων μολπαῖον ἀοιδάν
ἐς θρήνων γοερὸν φθέγμα μεθαρμόσαο.

*Meter: Elegiac Couplets*

—

**ἀείδω ᾄδω, ἀείσομαι ᾄσομαι, ἤεισα, —, —, ᾔσθην:** sing; praise; celebrate; sing of (an accusative object); the middle voice often has active voice meaning.
**ἀοιδή, -ῆς, ᾠδή, -ῆς (Attic), ἡ:** song
**βάσκανος, -ον:** malicious
**γάμος, -ου, ὁ:** wedding
**γοερός, -ά, -όν:** mournful; wailing; lamenting
**ἐπιφλέγω, -φλέξω, -ἔφλεξα, —, -πέφλεγμαι, -ἐφλέχθην:** kindle; burn
**θρῆνος, -ου, ὁ:** dirge; lament
**κηδεστής, -ου, ὁ:** father-in-law; brother-in-law; a family member by marriage
**μεθαρμόζω/μεθαρμόττω, —, μεθηρμοσάμην, —, —, —:** change from one mode of music into another
**μολπαῖος, -ον:** tuneful
**παρέρπω, —, —, —, —, —, —:** pass by
**πεύκη, -ης, ἡ:** pine-torch; anything made of pine
**πολύκλαυστος, -η, -ον:** much-lamented
**πυρκαϊά, -ᾶς, ἡ:** funeral pyre
**σῆμα, -ματος, τό:** sign; mark; token; letter; writing
**τύχη, -ης, ἡ:** fate (good or ill); fortune
**φθέγμα, -ματος, τό:** voice

—

**1–8:** The funerary monument of Baucis addresses a passerby, inviting that person to proclaim to the god Hades that he is cruel and to read aloud the tomb's inscription, which proclaims her wretched fate—how Hymen, the god of the marriage ceremony, sang at her wedding accompanied by the wedding-torches with which her father-in-law lit her funeral pyre. The funeral *stele* of Baucis then addresses Hymen, commanding him to change the mode of his song from wedding hymns to funeral dirges.

**1. Νύμφας Βαυκίδος:** genitive: "I am the (*stele*) of the bride Baucis"; Νύμφας = Νύμφης (Attic)

**2. πολυκλαύταν** = πολύκλαυστην (Attic)

**2. στάλαν** = στήλην (Attic). See note for line 1 of Erinna 1 G-P = (*A.P.* 7.710).

**2. γᾶς** = γῆς (Attic)

**2. λέγοις:** an optative of wish ("may you say")

**3. ἔσσ'** = εἶ (Attic), 2nd person sing. of εἰμί

**3. σάμαθ'** = σήματα (Attic), the tomb's inscriptional letters. "These letters are beautiful to the one looking upon and announcing…."

**4. ὠμοτάταν:** "cruelest": an accusative, feminine singular, superlative adjective related to the noun ὠμότης ("cruelty"). The passerby, gazing upon, and reading aloud the inscription on the tomb of Baucis, speaks out or announces "the cruelest fate of Baucis".

**5–6.** Baucis's father-in-law lit her funeral pyre with the same torches that were used in her wedding procession. For the irony "bride of death" motif in Greek literature, especially in Greek tragedy, see Rehm (2019).

**5. τὰν παῖδ'** = τὴν παῖδα (Attic);

**5. Ὑμέναιος:** Hymen, the god of marriage, is believed to have been present at weddings and is frequently addressed in wedding songs by the members of a procession leading the bride to the bridegroom's house.

**5. πεύκαις:** pine-torches were symbols of marriage carried in the wedding procession by the mothers of the bride and groom (c.f., Euripides, *Iphigenia in Aulis* 730–734 and *Trojan Women* 315–324).

**6. καδεστὰς** = κηδεστής (Attic)

**6. τᾶσδ'** = τῆσδε (Attic)

**6. ἐπὶ…ἔφλεγε:** tmesis

**7. γάμων:** The *gamos* was the actual ceremony consisting of a procession leading the bride and groom to their home, usually the groom's ancestral home. During the procession of family and friends, Hymeneal songs were sung, while the mothers of the bride and groom acted as torchbearers. See Ormand (1999) for a description of wedding traditions practiced in 5th-century Athens.

**7. ἀοιδάν:** accusative singular. The Attic form would be rendered as a contraction (ᾠδήν).

**8. μεθαρμόσαο:** an aorist middle imperative

**8. ἐς θρήνων γοερὸν φθέγμα:** in ancient Greek literature, a dirge (*thrēnos*) is a funeral song sung antiphonally by a group of mourners and a soloist or soloists. It may be sung over the deceased's body or on commemorative days. They were outward expressions of mourning through oral ritual practice. The earliest examples of *thrēnoi* occur in Homer (*Il.* 18.50–96 and 24.718–776 and *Od.* 24.43–64, for example). SeeAlexiou (1974) for a seminal study of the *threnos.*

**Erinna 3 G-P = (*A.P.* 6.352)**

Ἐξ ἀταλᾶν χειρῶν τάδε γράμματα· λῷστε Προμαθεῦ,
ἔντι καὶ ἄνθρωποι τὶν ὁμαλοὶ σοφίαν.
ταύταν γοῦν ἐτύμως τὰν παρθένον ὅστις ἔγραψεν
αἰ καὐδὰν ποτέθηκ' ἦς κ' Ἀγαθαρχὶς ὅλα.

*Meter: Elegiac Couplets*

—

**ἀταλός, -ή, -όν:** tender; delicate
**αὐδή, -ῆς, ἡ:** human voice; speech
**γράμμα, -ματος, τό:** drawing; painting; picture; written character; letter; writings (pl.)
**ἔτυμος, -η, -ον:** true
**λῷστος, -η, -ον:** best; most agreeable
**ὅλος, -η, -ον:** complete; whole; entire
**ὁμαλός, -ή, -όν:** equal; on a level with
**προστίθημι, προσθήσω, προσέθηκα, —, προστέθειμαι, προσετέθην:** give besides or also; add on; make an addition;
**χείρ, χείρος, ἡ:** hand

—

**1–4:** An ekphrastic epigram offering an appreciation for the verisimilitude of a painted portrait of the female Agatharchis. The narrator-speaker addresses Prometheus, the Titan who was credited with giving humans technical and artisanal skills and punished by Zeus, boasting that there are human beings who are equal to him in the wisdom or skill of their craft. The epigram concludes with an unreal condition offering the conclusion that if the subject of the painting had been given a human voice by the painter, she would be complete. Without a voice, the girl cannot truly come to life, and her representation is, thus, not quite *true* (ἐτύμως, line 3). Another kind of *gramma,* however, the epigrammatic epitaph referred to in Erinna 1 G-P (= *A.P.* 7.710.8), bestows a human voice upon the funeral *stele* and Sirens of Baucis's tomb.

**1. ἀταλᾶν** = ἀταλῶν (Attic)

**1. τάδε γράμματα:** Erinna uses the singular form of this word in another epigram (1 G-P = *A.P.* 7.710.8) to refer to the funereal epitaph she composed for her beloved, deceased friend Baucis. Here, however, in the plural form, the phrase refers to a painting or portrait.

**1. Προμαθεῦ** = Doric for Προμηθεῦ. Several ancient sources (Aeschylus' *Prometheus Bound,* 252, 445–480, for example) attest to Prometheus' role in teaching humans the arts of architecture, writing, husbandry, medicine, prophecy, astronomy, mathematics, and all other useful arts and *teknai* (the skills necessary for artisans and artists to master). Sappho (fr. 207), Ovid (*Met.* 1.81), and pseudo-Apollodorus (1.45) all suggest that Prometheus was credited with the creation of humans by shaping earth and water.

**2. ἔντι** = εἰσίν (Attic)
**2. τὶν** = σέ (Attic)
**3. ταύταν** = ταύτην (Attic)
**3. γοῦν** = Doric for γε οὖν
**3. τὰν** = τὴν (Attic)
**4. αἰ** = εἰ (Attic)
**4. καὐδὰν:** crasis; in Attic, καὶ αὐδὴν.
**5. ποτέθηκ'… κ':** the protasis of a past unfulfilled or unreal condition. ποτέθηκ' = προσέθηκε (Attic) and κ' = ἄν (Attic). "If only whoever painted this girl so true-to-life had also endowed her with a human voice, Agatharchis (would be) complete.

**Erinna, "Distaff" = P.S.I. 1090**

………………………………………… girls
………………………………………… brides
………………………………………… tortoise
………………………………………… moon
………………………………………… tortoise
……………………………………………
……………………………………………
with leaves
……………………………………………
………………………………………… to card [wool]
………………………………………… wave
from white horses (you leapt?) with maddened feet
"Aiai,"[7] I shouted loudly, and you then turned into a tortoise[8]
……………………little yard of a great courtyard;
and, because of these things, poor Baucis, I weep for you, sighing heavily,
these childhood games lie in my heart……….
still warm; but, those (which we once?) used to play are now charcoal,
and (dances of?) dolls and girl-hood friends, brides
in the bedroom………………………towards dawn
mother…………………… wool-workers
them……………………around….sprinkled with salt;
and (with?) little (haste?) …Morpho[9] brought (such great) fear;
… on (her head? were great big) ears, and she stalked about on four
feet, and she shape-shifted from (one) form into (another).

But when (you went into your husband's bed?), you forgot everything
that belonged to childhood, and then, you heard (my?) mother,
dear Baucis; forgetfulness..........Aphrodite
weeping for you, .........the other things I leave behind;
For, my feet .............are not permitted (to go?) from the house,
nor (am I able?) to gaze upon your dead body (with my eyes?), nor to lament
with women who have unbound their hair.... blood-red shame
tears at both sides of my cheeks..................
in earlier times..........................
nineteenth[10].................................
Erinna................dear.......................
looking upon the distaff[11]........................
know that.............................
coiled around (Gello?) ..............................
about these things, shame.... me...............
with maidens...............
looking.....................
unbound hair..................
gentle-speaking grey hairs, the blooms of old age for mortals.
............dear...............
Baucis.......weep............
flame..........her..............
hearing a howling.....................
o Hymenaius[12]..............
many things....................
..........o Hymenaius...............
Aiai, poor Baucis..........................

**Erinna 1 G-P = (*A.P.* 7.710)**

My *stele* and Sirens[13] and mourning urn,
you who hold the little ash belonging to Hades,
say hello to those who go past my tomb,
whether they are my fellow citizens or visitors from other cities;
and say that a tomb holds me, a bride; and, say this, too—
that my father called me Baucis, and my family
is from Tenos,[14] so that they may know, and say also that my friend
Erinna on my tomb wrote this inscription.

**Erinna 2 G-P = (*A.P.* 7.712)**

I am the *stele* of the bride Baucis. As you pass by this mournful
monument, tell this to Hades beneath the earth:
"you are malicious, Hades." These words are beautiful to the on-looker,

who reads aloud Baucis's cruelest fate—
how Hymen[15] sang about the girl among the wedding torches
with which her father-in-law lit the flames of her funeral pyre.[16]
But, you, Hymen, change the mode of your melodious wedding-hymn
into a mournful voice of dirges.[17]

### Erinna 3 G-P = (*A.P.* 6.352)

Delicate hands made this portrait; superior Prometheus,[18]
there are humans who rival even your skill.
If only whoever painted this girl so accurately
had also endowed her with a human voice—Agatharchis would be complete.

## Notes

1. *A.P.* 7.11 and 9.190.
2. *A.P.* 9.190.7-8.
3. *A.P.* 9.190.1-2.
4. *A.P.* 7.11 and 7.12.
5. *A.P.* 7.12 and 7.13.
6. These dates have been proposed by Levin (1962).
7. "Aiai" is a mournful exclamation in ancient Greek.
8. The children's game of *khelikhelōnē* ("torty-tortoise") is a version of a game of tag wherein one child would sit in the center of a group of other children who ran in a circle around the child in the center. The runners would call out to the her, "torty-tortoise, what are you doing in the middle?" The girl in the middle would respond, "weaving wool and Milesian thread." The others would reply, "And, how did your son die?" The center girl, shouting out, "He leapt from white horses into the sea," would leap from the center and try to tag one of the runners. The one tagged would then take her turn in the center. This game is described by Pollux (9.125). Pomeroy (1978), Arthur (= Katz, 1980), and Karanika (2012) have argued that this game reflects numerous folk-tale, religious, and cultural associations with Aphrodite, the loom, motherhood, domesticity, and initiation into adulthood. See also Bowra (1936), who first identified that the tortoises and white horses in the Erinna poem referred to the game described by Pollux.
9. Mormo was one of several shape-shifting bogie-monsters in ancient Greek folklore whose conjuring by name were intended to frighten children. Others were Lamia, Empousa, Gorgo, and Gello. Iles-Johnston (1995, p. 367–368 and note 9) suggested that Mormo may have been imagined as a kind of child-eating, female werewolf who was transformed from a Corinthian women who ate her own children.
10. An epigram by Asclepiades (*A.P.* 7.11) claims that Erinna, though she was only nineteen years of age, was a highly capable poet, even if she was not prolific. The much later Suda claims that Erinna died unmarried when she was nineteen-years old, but was nevertheless judged "equal to Homer." The text is too damaged to illuminate much, but it is likely that either the narrator (who names herself in the next line) is claiming herself to be nineteen-years old at some point in the poem's sequence of events or at the time of composition.

Alternatively, Baucis was nineteen years-old at the time of her marriage or passing.

11. Several ancient sources (the Suda; the anonymous *A.P.* 9.190 and 7.12, for example), suggest or hint that Erinna composed a poem of 300 lines in both Aeolic and Doric called the ἠλακάτη. See Cameron and Cameron (1967) for a discussion of whether or not this poem is it. They note, "the consensus of opinion thus seems to be that ἠλακάτη as the title of Erinna's lament for Baucis is at least suspicious; if it is a title at all, it is likely to be a scholarly guess, probably Alexandrian. We believe on the contrary that ἠλακάτη, or rather ἀλακάτα, is indeed the title of Erinna's poem, and that it is Erinna's own." If that is the case, our present text is but a fraction of the original poem.
12. Hymen is the god of weddings and was invoked in hymns called Hymeneals by a procession of family and friends who led the bride and groom to the home where they will live together as a married couple.
13. A *stele* is a type of grave monument carved from stone. This particular monument likely consisted of an obelisk-style column surmounted with two Sirens that are carved into the monument and rest atop it. Sirens, half-bird, half-female human hybrid beings were common adornments for ancient Greek grave monuments. An urn containing the deceased's ashes lay on or beside the *stele.*
14. One of the northern Cycladic islands in the Aegean Sea.
15. See note 12 above. The mothers of the bride and groom carried pine-torches in that procession.
16. The tragically ironic motif of the "bride of death" is common in ancient Greek literature, and especially in ancient Greek tragedy. In this motif, a young woman dies before she is married; or, she dies too soon after her wedding to enjoy the fruits of marriage. Great importance was placed upon marriage for young women in ancient Greece, and the deaths of maidens and young brides evoked great pathos. See Rehm (2019) for a discussion of this motif.
17. In ancient Greek literature, a dirge (*thrēnos*) is a funeral song sung antiphonally by a group of mourners and a soloist or soloists. It may be sung over the deceased's body or on commemorative days. They were outward expressions of mourning through oral ritual practice. The earliest examples of *thrēnoi* occur in Homer (*Il.* 18.50–96 and 24.718–776 and *Od.* 24.43–64, for example).
18. Promethus was a Titan god who endowed humans with fire and with technologies associated with a variety of domains of knowledge, skill, and craftsmanship. Several ancient sources (Aeschylus' *Prometheus Bound,* 252, 445–480, for example) attest to Prometheus' role in teaching humans the arts of architecture, writing, husbandry, medicine, prophecy, astronomy, mathematics, and all other useful arts and *teknai* (the skills necessary for artisans and artists to master). Sappho (fr. 207), Ovid (*Met.* 1.81), and pseudo-Apollodorus (1.45) all suggest that Prometheus was credited with the creation of humans by shaping earth and water. Zeus punished Prometheus for giving humans fire by chaining him to Mt. Caucasus and setting upon him the continual torture of having his liver pecked out each day by Zeus's eagle. Prometheus's liver would grow back each night. The Titan was eventually freed by Heracles.

# 4 Moero of Byzantium

Only two quatrain epigrams and one 10-line excerpt of an epic or epyllion survive among the otherwise lost lyric, epic, and elegiac *oeuvre* of the Hellenistic poet Moero of Byzantium, whose name appears as both Moero and Myro in a variety of ancient sources.[1]

She was probably born in the last quarter of the 4th century BCE, and the dating of her *floruit* has been estimated between roughly 300 and 280 BCE.[2] Diverse sources from antiquity suggest that she was highly esteemed and influential among the *litterati* and that her excellent reputation had a long afterlife. The epigrammatist Antipater of Thessalonika includes Moero among the nine canonical women poets whom the Muses fed with song (*Anthologia Palatina* 9.26.3). The 2nd-century CE Christian orator Tatian claimed (*Oratio ad Graecos* 33) that statues of both Moero and Anyte had been cast by the sculptor Cephisodotus. And, the 6th-century CE Christodorus of Coptus in Egypt cites that she was the famous mother of the tragedian Homerus of Byzantium and that she renowned in her own right for her skill in epic poetry, at which craft the Muses taught her to excel while she was still a young girl (*A.P.* 2.407–413).[3] One scholar has suggested that this claim may reflect the adoption by Moera of the persona of a preadolescent child in her writings.[4]

Scant details about her personal life are reported by the *Suda*, a 10th-century Byzantine encyclopedia of the ancient Mediterranean world. This source claims that she was either the mother or daughter of the tragedian Homerus of Byzantium; that she was the wife of the learned philologist Andromachus; and, that she composed epic, lyric, and elegiac poetry.

Other sources hint at some of the themes and content of her lost poems. Pausanias, for example, while describing Thebes, notes that Myro of Byzantium claimed that the city's poet-founder Amphion built an altar to Hermes and was rewarded by the god with the gift of a lyre (9.5.8). In a somewhat lengthy discussion commenting on the work of various female poets of antiquity, Eustathius, a late Byzantine commentator of Homer's *Iliad* (2.711), briefly states that Moero composed a hymn to Poseidon. If Parthenius is to be believed (*Erotica Pathemata* 27), the *Arai* (or "Curses")

DOI: 10.4324/9781003031727-6

of Moero treated the story of Alcinoë, a woman who was punished by Athena with love-sickness and committed suicide by throwing herself into the sea after she deserted her husband and children in erotic pursuit of a foreign stranger. One scholar has convincingly argued that the epigrammatist Anyte (whose work also appears in this volume) may have been alluding to and celebrating compositions by her predecessor Moero by incorporating the twin themes of insects and a young girl's grief into an epigram (*A.P.* 7.190) in which a little girl with the sobriquet "Myro" laments the loss of her two songster-pets, a cicada and a grasshopper.[5]

Her two surviving epigrams conform to standard dedicatory motifs as they simultaneously employ innovative language and metaphors: one is addressed to a cluster of grapes that has fallen from a vine beside a temple to Aphrodite, and may be intended to invoke a real grapevine or the image of one in a painting; the other epigram addresses dryads who are appealed to by the narrator to protect one Cleonymus, who has carved for them a statuette in their honor. Both epigrams, within just two economical pair of elegiac couplets each, evoke lush, sacrosanct settings within nature. Her surviving excerpt of ten lines of hexameter from the *Mnemosyne* ("Memory") treats the childhood of Zeus, who grows up secretly and without the cognizance of the other gods in a cave on the island of Crete, where doves and an eagle bring him nourishing nectar and ambrosia.

## Select Bibliography


Gow, A.S.F. and D. L. Page (eds.). 1965. *The Greek Anthology: Hellenistic Epigrams. 2 vols.* Cambridge: Cambridge University Press.

Gutzwiller, K. 1998. *Poetic Garlands: Hellenistic Epigrams in Context.* Berkeley, CA: University of California Press.

———. 2017. "Moero," in D. Sider (ed., *Hellenistic Epigrams: A Selection.* Ann Arbor, MI: University of Michigan Press, p. 405–412.

Pomeroy, S. B. 1977. "*Technikai kai mousikai:* The Education of Women in the Fourth Century and in the Hellenistic Period," *AMAH* 2: 51–68.

Rayor, D. J. 1991. *Sappho's Lyre: Archaic Lyric and Women Poets of Ancient Greece.* Berkeley, CA: University of California Press.

Skinner, M. B. 2005. "Homer's Mother," in Ellen Greene (ed.), *Women Poets in Ancient Greece and Rome.* Norman, OK: University of Oklahoma Press, p. 91–111.

Snyder, J. M. 1989. "Moero," *The Woman and the Lyre: Women Writers in Classical Greece and Rome.* Carbondale, IL and Edwardsville, IL: Southern Illinois University Press, p. 84–86.

White, H. 1980. "An Epigram by Moero," *Essays in Hellenistic Poetry*, 21–25. *London Studies in Classical Philology* 5. Amsterdam and Uithoorn: J. C. Gieben.

**Moero 1 G-P = *A.P.* 6.119**

κεῖσαι δὴ χρυσέαν ὑπὸ παστάδα τὰν ᾿Αφροδίτας,
βότρυ, Διωνύσου πληθόμενος σταγόνι,
οὐδ᾿ ἔτι τοι μάτηρ ἐρατὸν περὶ κλῆμα βαλοῦσα
φύσει ὑπὲρ κρατὸς νεκτάρεον πέταλον.

*Meter: Elegiac Couplets*

—

**βότρυς, -υος, ὁ:** grape-cluster; bunch of grapes
**ἐρατός, -ή, -όν:** lovely, alluring
**κεῖμαι, κείσομαι, —, —, —, —:** lay, lie
**κλῆμα, -ατος, τό:** twig or branch, especially of the grape vine
**κράς, κρατός, τό:** head
**νεκτάρεος, -α, -ον:** fragrant, nectarous
**παστάς, -άδος, ἡ:** colonnade, such as those which ran around temples
**πέταλον, -ου, τό:** leaf
**πίμπλημι, πλήσω, ἔπλησα, πέπληκα, πέπλησμαι, ἐπλήσθην:** fill, fill up (*act.*); fill for one's self, satiate (*med.*); pass., be filled with/of (*pass.*)
**σταγών, -όνος, ἡ:** drop
**φύω, φύσω, ἔφυσά ἔφυν, πέφυκα, —, ἐφύην:** beget, put forth, make grow

—

**1–4:** A quatrain epigram in which the unnamed narrator expresses playful lament at the "death" of a ripe and fallen grape-cluster that will no longer feel the protective embrace of its mother-vine's foliage. The tone is whimsically solemn and hyperbolic.

**1. κεῖσαι…ὑπὸ:** 2nd pers. sing., pres. indic. This brief four-line poem combines both funerary and dedicatory tropes, both of which are standard in epigram. The term ὑποκεῖμαι ("lie under") is part of a specialized vocabulary used in funerary epitaphs, in which the deceased (which is often an object or animal rather than a person) is addressed ("…you lie here…") and her/his/its burial site described by an unidentified speaker. Such poems are frequently playful and literary, requiring readers to imagine or speculate about the identity of the speaking voice, the life and perspective of the deceased, and the funerary setting.

**1. τὰν** = τὴν (Att.)

**2. σταγόνι:** while the "drop" of the grape-cluster is its juice, this noun is used in Greek tragedy to refer to blood (Aeschylus, *Agamemnon*, 1122 and *Libation Bearers*, 399; Sophocles, *Oedipus Tyrannus*, 1278. Significantly, in Euripides' *Bacchantes*, 767, the chorus of Bacchants is described by the messenger as having washed off blood in sacred springs while snakes clean the drops (**σταγόνα**) from their cheeks. Perhaps Moero has this scene in mind, particularly given the reference to Dionysus in her poem. The tone is one of solemn whimsy.

**3. μάτηρ** = μήτηρ (Att.): The speaker imagining separation of the tender grape-cluster from a fragrant and comforting mother is a playful and innovative personification.

**3. περὶ...βαλοῦσα:** tmesis, or the placement of an intervening word or phrase which separates a prefix (περὶ) from the rest of a compound word (**βαλοῦσα**).

**Moero 2 G-P = *A.P.* 6.189**

Νύμφαι Ἁμαδρυάδες, ποταμοῦ κόραι, αἳ τάδε βένθη
  ἀμβρόσιαι ῥοδέοις στείβετε ποσσὶν ἀεί,
χαίρετε καὶ σῴζοιτε Κλεώνυμον, ὃς τάδε καλά
  εἵσαθ' ὑπαὶ πιτύων ὔμμι, θεαί, ξόανα.

*Meter: Elegiac Couplets*

—

**ἀεί:** adv., always, eternally
**ἀμβρόσιος, -α, -ον:** immortal, divine
**βένθος, -εος, τό:** depth, of a body of water
**ἵζω, εἵσομαι, εἷσα/ἵζησα, ἵζηκα, —, —:** (act.) cause to sit; place; set; seat; (med.) set up and dedicate (in honor of the gods)
**κόρα, -ας, ἡ:** daughter
**Νύμφη, -ης, ἡ:** Nymph, or minor goddess presiding over natural phenomena, such as caves, bodies of water, and woodlands
**ξόανον, -ου, τό:** image carved of wood; statue of a deity
**πίτυς, -υος, ἡ:** pine
**πούς, πόδος, ὁ:** foot. This irregular noun has some unexpected forms: πόδι (dat. s.), πόδα (acc. s., not πόδυν as one might expect), and both πόσι and πόσσι (esp. in epic and lyric) for the dat. pl.
**ῥόδεος, -α, -ον:** of or like roses; rosy
**στείβω, —, ἔστειψα, —, —. —:** walk or tread; this verb usually only appears in the present and imperfect tenses
**σῴζω, σώσω, ἔσῳσα, σέσῳκα, σέσῳσμαι, ἐσώθην:** save, preserve
**ὑπαί** = epic form of ὑπό

—

**1–4:** A dedicatory epigram in which Cleonymus gives a statue as a votive offering to the Hamadryads, tree Nymphs, and daughters of a river-god, so that they may protect him.

**1.** There are two instances of hiatus in this completely dactylic hexameter line: (1) between the final syllable of Νύμφαι and Ἁμαδρυάδες; (2) between the ultima of κόραι and αἵ.

**1. Ἁμαδρυάδες:** Nymphs associated with trees. Athenaeus (*Deipnosophistae* 1.78a) claims that there were eight of them (Karya-nut trees, including hazelnut and walnut; Balanis-oak; Kraneia-cornelian cherry;

Morea-mulberry; Aigeiros-black poplar; Ptelea-elm; Ampelos-vines; and Syke-fig), the daughters of Oxylus and Hamadryas. They are said to have the same life span as their trees, and their dwelling places in the forests are often near freshwater rivers and streams.

**1. βένθη:** neut. pl. acc.

**3. χαίρετε καὶ σῴζοιτε:** An imperative greeting (χαίρετε), followed by an optative expressing wish, which functions as a rather condensed prayer addressed to Nymphs. One might notice that, in an otherwise strongly dactylic epigram, the stress laid upon the phrase "καὶ σῴζοιτε" is echoed by the fact that it is the only spondee in the poem not occurring in the final metrical place of the line.

**4. εἵσαθ':** 3rd sing. med. aor. indic. of ἵζω

**4. ὔμμι:** Aeolic and epic form of ὑμῖν

## Moero 3 = Athenaeus, *Deipnosophistae*, 11.491b

Ζεὺς δ' ἄρ' ἐνὶ Κρήτῃ τρέφετο μέγας, οὐδ' ἄρα τίς νιν
ἠείδει μακάρων· ὁ δ' ἀέξετο πᾶσι μέλεσσι.
τὸν μὲν ἄρα τρήρωνες ὑπὸ ζαθέῳ τράφον ἄντρῳ
ἀμβροσίην φορέουσαι ἀπ' Ὠκεανοῖο ῥοάων·
νέκταρ δ' ἐκ πέτρης μέγας αἰετὸς αἰὲν ἀφύσσων
γαμφηλῇς φορέεσκε ποτὸν Διὶ μητιόεντι.
τὸν καὶ νικήσας πατέρα Κρόνον εὐρύοπα Ζεὺς
ἀθάνατον ποίησε καὶ οὐρανῷ ἐγκατένασσεν.
ὣς δ' αὔτως τρήρωσι πελειάσιν ὤπασε τιμήν,
αἳ δή τοι θέρεος καὶ χείματος ἄγγελοί εἰσιν.

*Meter: Dactylic Hexameter*

—

**αἰετὸς, -οῦ ὁ:** eagle, the bird sacred to Zeus

**ἀμβροσία, -ας, ἡ:** ambrosia, the nourishing substance eaten by the gods

**ἄντρον, -ου, τό:** cave

**αὔξω, αὐξήσω, ηὔξησα, ηὔξηκα, ηὔξημαι, ηὐξήθην:** make increase, grow

**ἀφύσσω, ἀφύξω, ἤφυσα, —, —, —:** draw, especially liquids from a vessel with a smaller vessel

**γλαμφηλαί, -ῶν, αἱ:** the maw or jaws of an animal; the beak or bill of a bird

**ἐγκαταναίω, —, ἐγκατενασσα, —, —, —:** make dwell in

**εὐρύοπα, ὁ:** far-thundering; this adjective is used in Homer only in the nominative and vocative, only of Zeus, and usually in the 5th into 6th metrical foot, as it is here

**ζάθεος, -α, -ον:** holy, sacred

**θέρος, -εος, τό:** summer

**Κρήτη, -ης, ἡ:** the island of Crete

**μάκαρ, ὁ, ἡ (gen. = μάκαρος):** blessed, an epithet commonly used of the gods

**μέλος, -εος, τό:** limb
**μητιόεις, -εσσα, -εν:** wise in counsel, clever-minded
**νέκταρ, -αρος, τό:** nectar, the nourishing substance that the gods drink
**οἶδα, εἴσομαι, ᾔδη or ᾔδειν (plup.), —, —, —:** know, know about
**ὀπάζω, ὀπάσσω, ὤπασα, —, —, —:** give, grant
**οὐρανός, -οῦ, ὁ:** sky; heavens
**πέλεια, -ας, ἡ:** dove
**πέτρη, -ης, ἡ:** rock
**ποτός, -οῦ ὁ:** drink, beverage
**ῥοή, -ης ἡ (Doric =ῥοά):** stream, river (usually in the plural)
**τρήρων, -ονος, ὁ, ἡ:** trembling, shy, timorous
**χεῖμα, -ατος, τό:** winter
—

**1–10:** Athenaeus (11.491b) provides this excerpt from a lost epic or epyllion, *Mnemosyne*. Mnemosyne is named in the Hesiod's *Theogony* as the mother of the Muses, who gave birth to her nine daughters on Mt. Pieria after love-making with Zeus (52–54). Like Corinna 1 = *PMG* 654.i.12–34, what survives to us (thanks to Athenaeus) of Moero's epyllion concerns the clandestine raising of infant Zeus on the isle of Crete, where he was hidden to escape the cannibalistic predations of his father, Cronos. The focus of these ingenious lines rests on avian helpers of the young god, who fed him ambrosia and nectar from their beaks. To these birds Zeus gave particular honors: the eagle he made his own bird and the doves to be harbingers of summer and winter (by transforming them into the constellation Pleiades—see endnote 6 below).

**1.** The short final vowel of **τρέφετο** is permitted to be artificially lengthened before liquids, such as the letter-μ, beginning certain words like μέγας.

**1. Ζεὺς δ᾽ ἄρ᾽ ἐνὶ Κρήτῃ τρέφετο μέγας:** the poet Hesiod (*Theogony* 479ff.) attributes the rise of Zeus to preeminence among the Olympian gods through a series of succession myths in which strong sons overthrow tyrannical fathers who feel threatened by their progeny. Ouranos ("Heaven") mates with Gaia/Ge ("Earth") to produce an early race of divinities called the Titans. Fearful of their power to usurp him, Ouranos lays his full weight on Gaia and refuses to separate from her so that their children will remain entombed in earth. Gaia gives an adamantine sickle to her son Cronos, who castrates his father and subsequently rises to power. He, in turn, mates with Rheia, his Titan sister, and she gives birth to the elder Olympians upon whom Cronus, also fearing that his children would one day overthrow him, gorges himself. When Zeus is born, Rheia hides the infant on the island of Crete, giving Cronos a swaddled stone to consume, thereby deceiving him. Zeus grows up in secret in a cave on Mt. Ida on the island of Crete. When Zeus reaches maturity, he overthrows his father and claims his position as patriarch of the gods. This line may intentionally evoke Hesiod, *Theogony* (480): Κρήτῃ ἐν εὐρείῃ τραφέμεν...

**2. ἠείδει:** οἶδα (base - ιδ, "know") is a perfect tense verb with the sense and meaning of the present tense. ἠείδει is, thus, the pluperfect form (3rd sing., act., indic.), but has the sense and meaning of an imperfect tense.

**2. ἀέξω** = Homeric for αὔξω or αὐξάνω

**3. τρήρωνες:** "timorous" is an epithet used of doves in Homer. Moero's presentation of the doves and the eagle (traditionally the messenger of Zeus) as the infant god's caretakers is both innovative and unique, while also allusive to Homer (see notes for lines 4 and 5 below). Callimachus's *Hymn to Zeus,* for example, offers different caretakers—the goat Amaltheia who gave him milk to suckle, bees which produced honey for his food, and nymphs of Mt. Dicte.

**4. Ὠκεανός, -οῦ, ὁ:** Oceanus, Titan son of Ouranos and Gaia and father to all the Oceanids, or marine nymphs. He is conceived of as a great river deity who encircles the earth's disk before returning upon himself. He is the god of all primeval waters and the source for all other bodies of water, which are but tributaries to Oceanus.

**4. ἀμβροσίην φορέουσαι ἀπ' Ὠκεανοῖο ῥοάων:** as Gutzwiller (2017, p. 408) notes in her commentary of this passage, Moero alludes to a scene in the *Odyssey* (12.62–63) in which it is noted that not even the "trembling doves that bring ambrosia to father Zeus" escape the clashing of the Symplegades. Whenever they pass through, the rocks catch one, and Zeus is forced to replace it.

**5. νέκταρ δ' ἐκ πέτρης μέγας αἰετὸς αἰὲν ἀφύσσων:** compare this line with the moment in the *Iliad* in which Hephaestus draws sweet nectar from a krater while his mother Hera smiles and laughs at the conclusion of her son's story about his fall from Olympus, told to his mother as a warning not to challenge Zeus: οἰνοχόει γλυκὺ νέκταρ ἀπὸ κρητῆρος ἀφύσσων, *Il.* 1.598.

**6. φορέεσκε:** Homer often uses imperfect tense verbs ending in - εσκον to suggest customary or repetitive (or "iterative") past action. See Smyth #495.

**7. εὐρύοπα Ζεὺς:** monosyllabic words in the final position of the line are reasonably infrequent in epic. This exact phrase in the same position occurs once in Hesiod's *Theogony* (line 514), while εὐρύοπα Ζῆν occurs at the same position (line 884). Zeus appears as a monosyllabic finale of lines 514, 520, 558, 820, 884, 904, 914 in the *Theogony* in combination with other epithets (μητίετα, 520, 904, 914; νεφεληγερέτα, 558) and one verb (ἐξέλασεν, 820). It is reasonably likely that Moero intended the final two metrical feet of line 7 as an allusion.

**9. τρήρωσι πελειάσιν:** The three prophetess-priestesses at the shrine of Zeus at Dodona were known as the Peliades or "doves"; they will receive the "honor" of being transformed into the constellation of the Pleiades.

**10. θέρεος καὶ χείματος ἄγγελοί εἰσιν:** the Hellenistic poet Aratus states that Zeus ordered the Pleiades to be constellation whose appearance marks the beginning of summer and winter (Aratus, *Phaenomena* 266). In Hesiod, the Pleiades are the sign of the time for plowing (*Works and Days, 383–384*). See also endnote 6 below.

**Moero 1 G-P = *A.P.* 6.119**

You lie beneath the golden colonnade of Aphrodite's temple,
grape-cluster, filled with the juice of Dionysus;
no longer will your mother, embracing you with her lovely vine,
grow her fragrant leaf over your head.

**Moero 2 G-P = *A.P.* 6.189**

Hamadryad Nymphs, river-daughters, immortal goddesses who
eternally tread these depths with your rosy feet,
I greet you and pray that you may keep safe Cleonymus, who
set up for you, goddesses, these beautiful wooden statues under the
pine trees.

**Moero 3, *Mnemosyne* fr. 1 Powell = Athenaeus, *Deipnosophistae*, 11.491b** (surviving excerpt from a lost epic or epyllion)

Great Zeus was raised on Crete, nor did anyone of the blessed gods
know about him; but, he grew in size in all his limbs.
Trembling creatures nourished him in a sacred cave
carrying ambrosia from the streams of Oceanus,
and a great eagle perpetually drawing nectar from a rock
kept bringing drink to clever-minded Zeus in its beak.
After he vanquished his own father, far-thundering Zeus
made the eagle immortal and gave him to dwell in the heavens.
In the same way, he gave honor to the trembling doves,[6]
who are messengers of summer and winter.

## Notes

1. The spelling of "Moiro" (Latinized to "Moero" in this collection) appears in Parthenius' *Erotica Pathemata* 27, Athenaeus' *Deipnosophistae* 11.490e and 491a, in the preface to Meleager's *Garland* at *A.P.* 4.1.5, in an epigram by Antipater of Thessalonika, *A.P.* 9.26.3, and in the authorial ascriptions in the *Greek Anthology* of the two surviving epigrams by Moero (*A.P.* 6.119 and 6.189). Her name appears as "Myro" in Pausanias 9.5.8; Tatian, *Oratio ad Graecos* 33, in her entry in the Suda, and in the commentary by Eustatheus, *Il.* 2.711.
2. For discussions of the dating of her poetry, see Gow and Page (1965, vol. 2, p. 413–414), Snyder (1989), Skinner (2005).

3. Other sources also suggest Moero's prestige. In his preface to an anthologized collection of poems, the poet-editor Meleager states that he wove into his anthology, along with the irises of Nossis and the roses of Sappho, the lilies of both Anyte and Moero (*A.P.* 4.1.5). Both Anyte (*A.P.* 7.190) and the Roman epigrammatist Marcus Argentarius (*A.P.* 7.364) mention Moero's name in connection the theme of the death of a cicada and grasshopper.[3] Parthenius, who reportedly taught the Roman poet Vergil Greek, claims to have summarized Moero's story of Alcinoë (out of her lost poem, *Arai,* or "Curses") in his *Erotica Pathemata*, a collection of epitomes dedicated to the poet Cornelius Gallus.
4. Skinner (2005, p. 105).
5. Skinner (2005, p. 104–105).
6. The three prophetess-priestesses at the shrine of Zeus at Dodona were known as the Peliades or "doves"; the "honor" that Zeus gives to the doves is to transform them into the constellation of the Pleiades.

# 5 Nossis

Nossis was among the earliest Hellenistic poets to envision and transform the artform of epigraphic epigram for literary purposes.[1] She can be dated roughly to 300 BCE on the basis of one of her funerary epigrams (10 GP = *A.P.* 7.414), which posthumously honors Rhinthon, the Syracusian writer of tragi-comical phlyax plays (also called *hilarotragoidia*, or "cheerful tragedies"). Rhinthon lived in the late 4th and early 3rd centuries BCE, and Nossis likely wrote her funerary epigram sometime after his death, though one need not assume that the epigram was composed immediately following his decease.[2] The 12-quatrain epigrams of Nossis preserved in the *Anthologia Palatina* (*A.P.*), one of which (Nossis 12 GP = *A.P.*) may be spurious, give us a tantalizing view into the world of the women of Epizephyrian Locris, a city in the southern region of the Italian peninsula called Magna Graecia, called so because of the region's predominance of Greek *poleis* established during the Archaic period as Greek colonies.

Nossis names herself in three *sphragis* poems (1 GP = *A.P.* 5.170, 3 GP = *A.P.* 6.265, and 11 GP = *A.P.* 7.718). She presents to the reader a persona of herself as an aesthete and as a connoisseur of art (5 GP = *A.P.* 9.605 and 7 GP = *A.P.* 6.354, for example), artistry (3 GP = *A.P.* 6.265 and 6 GP = *A.P.* 6.275), and even drama (10 GP = *A.P.* 7.414). In what may very well have been the closing poem of her original publication, she claims for herself a prominent place in the poetic lineage of Sappho (11 GP = *A.P.* 7.718). The world her poetry evokes is women-centered, and her poems treat themes relevant to the lives of women in her circle, such as desire, sensual aesthetics, intergenerational relationships between female kin, local religious life, and the ways in which votive offerings to goddesses dedicated by women resonated and were appreciated. Marilynn Skinner (2005, p. 129) has suggested that the original audience for her poetry must have been the circle of women in her community, who operated within "a relatively autonomous women's subculture at Locri" in which "an alternate perspective could be generated, nurtured, and transmitted," even within a largely male-dominant culture.[3]

DOI: 10.4324/9781003031727-7

Nossis mentions her hometown of Locris twice (poems 2 GP = *A.P.* 6.132 and 11 GP = *A.P.* 7.718). Located in the modern Italian province of Reggio Calabria overlooking the Ionian Sea, the ancient city of Epizephyrian Locris, according to Aristotle, was founded in 7th century BCE by slaves from the Locrian region of mainland Greece who fled after they had slept with their masters' wives while these husbands were off campaigning at war.[4] The historian Polybius, writing in the Hellenistic period, reported that, on the basis of his own personal visit to Epizephyrian Locris, during which he was given honors by its inhabitants for favors he bestowed upon them, he could confirm the truth of Aristotle's assertion that the nobility of Epizephyrian Locris descended matrilineally from women, not men, and that these nobles, like those of mainland Locris, were said to belong to the "100 Houses".[5] Most scholars suppose that Nossis was a member of the nobility of her community and, thus, a member of one of the "100 Houses," a status that Nossis herself suggests in epigram 3 GP (*A.P.* 6.265), a dedicatory epigram featuring a linen garment dedicated to Hera at a local temple.[6] Snyder (1989, p. 79) points out that Nossis identifies three generations of matrilineal ancestry by "matronymics" in this epigram, identifying its weavers as both "noble" Nossis and her mother Theophilis, the daughter of Cleocha. It is also worth noting that Nossis appears to have obtained a reasonably sophisticated education, since she mentions Sappho and alludes to her poetry, pays literary tribute to the *hilarotragoidia* of Rhinthon, and composes quaint, elegant, stylized, and innovative quatrain epigrams intended for literary consumption.[7]

Several historical accounts pertaining to the noble women of the "100 Houses" being selected for temple prostitution and "sacrificed" to the goddesses Athena and Aphrodite are worth mentioning in an introduction to Nossis and her poetry, particularly given the extraordinary attention Nossis gives to votive offerings dedicated by women to the local temple of Aphrodite. One of her epigrams, for example, (4 GP = *A.P.* 9.332) highlights a statue of the goddess dedicated by the prostitute Polyarchis, whom Nossis acknowledges in quite a positive light as having enjoyed great wealth from the physical beauty of her body.

A variety of historical accounts attest to mainland Locrian virgins being offered as *hierodoulai* ("sacred slaves") to a temple of Athena at Troy as a way to expiate the community at large for the crime of Ajax Oileus, a Locrian whom legend accused of raping Cassandra, the Trojan princess and priestess of Apollo, in Athena's temple during the sack of Troy. According to these sources, the noble 100 families throughout mainland Locris offered up as *hierodoulai* young, unmarried, virgin girls to the goddess to prevent disease and destruction from descending upon the whole Locrian community as the result of the wrath of the goddess.[8] While historical sources suggest that this form of communal sacrifice was suspended in the mid-4th century BCE, one source claims that it was resumed during the first half of the 3rd century BCE.[9]

Examining the historical evidence of Locrian *hierodoulai* descended from the "100 Houses," Adolfo J. Domínguez (2007) has demonstrated quite clearly a connection between practices in mainland Locris and the practice of temple prostitution in the temple of Aphrodite at Epizephyrian Locris on the Italian peninsula, calling it a "re-enactment of an old ritual in a colonial environment." Historical sources tend to focus on two major incidents in which temple prostitution in honor of Aphrodite occurred, in both instances to ward of the total destruction and enslavement of the entire community. The first instance occurred in 477 BCE, perhaps, and, if true, within the living memory of Nossis's grandmother's mother or grandmother. The historian Justin reports (21.3.1) that when hard pressed against Leophron, the tyrant of Rhegium, the Epizephyrian Locrians vowed to prostitute their virgins at a festival of Venus if they would only be victorius.[10] Domínguez (2007) rightly argues that this vow, or *votum*, was viewed as a sacrifice to prevent total destruction of the city and enslavement of the entire community, a process widely known in the Greek world as *andrapodizing*. Kathy Gaca's (2010) study of *andrapodizing* argues that it consists of a military force sacking a city, slaying some or all of the male population of a city, particularly those who are armed, and enslaving the survivors, mostly women and children. Sexual violence occurred at every stage of *andrapodization*.

The second incident connecting Epizephyrian Locris to temple prostitution occurred between 356–347/6 BCE, perhaps within the living memory of Nossis's mother, Theuphilis, and possibly that of Nossis herself. When the unpopular and cruel tyrant of Syracuse, Dionysius II, was deposed and forced into exile, he took refuge in Epizephyrian Locris, where he set himself up as the city's tyrant. When the Lucanians, an aboriginal tribe of southern Italy, threatened to reduce and did reduce other cities on the southern peninsula (Cumae, Neapolis, and Poseidonia)[11] to total destruction and enslavement, Dionysius recommended, according to Justin (21.3.3–7), that the Locrians send the wives and daughters of the aristocracy (i.e., from the "100 Houses") to the temple of Aphrodite dressed in their finest clothing and jewels. From these women, 100 would be selected by lot to offer themselves as *hierodoulai* in sacred prostitution to the goddess for a period of one month. However, all of the men of the community would swear an oath beforehand not to touch any of *hierodoulai*. When the aristocratic women arrived at the temple for selection by lot, Dionysius's soldiers robbed the women of their jewelry and likely committed sexual violence against them. Strabo (6.1.8) reports that the Locrians took their vengeance out on Dionysius upon his two daughters and wife after the tyrant returned to Sicily and the Locrians captured them on military campaign. Dionysius had named his daughters Arete ("Excellence"), Dicaeosyne ("Righteousness") and Sophrosyne ("Prudence") as potent symbols of the political and ethical virtues he claimed to espouse.[12] Strabo (6.1.8) reports that the Locrians refused to release them on any terms. Instead, the Locrians prostituted his wife and daughters, strangled them, burned their bodies, ground their bones, and sank their ashen remains into the sea.

The important thing to keep in mind here with regard to the poetry of Nossis, if our sources are to be trusted, is the collective support of temple prostitution as the option of last resort within her community in the century leading up to Nossis's lifetime. As Domínguez (2007, p. 419) put it, "the fear of enslavement was still strong enough in Locri to persuade them to give their consent, albeit with guarantees, to the reenactment of a ritual that many would have considered a relic of the past." Moreover, those whom the community offered up as sacrificial temple prostitutes were members of Nossis's own social class. Thus, it may be that Nossis's poems reflect not just a positive expression of erotic desire and the aesthetic beauty of high-class *hetairai* and their votive offerings. It is entirely possible that her poems intentionally preserve or evoke within her community the cultural memory of the religious function of prostitutes as *hierodoulai*, and, thus, as saviors of the community. Epigram 2 GP = *A.P.* 6.132 celebrates the weapons captured by Nossis's fellow Locrians in their skirmishes with the native Bruttians with whom the Locrians were long involved in hostilities. Such celebration is not just an adoption and display of heroic, masculine values. The defeat of hostile indigenous tribes of Italy averted both the prospect of enslavement by an invading force, as well as the need for the community to exact more urgent sacrifices of Nossis's own circle of girls and women, as it may have done in 477 BCE and in the 340s–350s BCE. The statue of Aphrodite in epigram 4 GP (*A.P.* 9.332), given as a votive offering by Polyarchis in gratitude for the wealth she has enjoyed, happens to be metonymically consonant with the offering of aristocratic women of Epizephyrian Locrian for prostitution to the goddess in exchange for the welfare and continued prosperity of the city itself.

The surviving poems of Nossis appear in the *A.P.*, a collection of Greek epigrams collated in the early 10th century CE by Costantine Cephalas. A substantial portion of the *A.P.* was excerpted by Cephalas from an earlier anthology of Greek epigrams which does not survive, Meleager's *Stephanos* or *Garland*, which dates to about 100 BCE. Meleager's anthology, as Gutzwiller (1997b, p. 169) notes, eventually replaced poetry books by individual authors in becoming the principal source for the transmission of ancient Greek epigram. The title of Meleager's *Garland* derived from a network of metaphors employed in the proem of that work (1 GP = *A.P.* 4.1) in which the Muses identify Meleager, his dedicatee Diocles, and each of the authors in the collection as a flower or plant woven into the "garland".[13] The poetic proem is composed in elegiac couplets of alternating hexameter and pentameter lines and contains a total of 58 lines in which 47 epigrammatists whose epigrams appear in the volume are named. The first ten lines of that poetic proem deserve attention in this collection of women's writings, particularly with regard to the way in which they characterize the epigrams Meleager selected for inclusion from Nossis's poetry:

> Muse beloved, to whom are you bringing this all-fruited song,
> or, who wove this garland of poets?
> Meleager created it, but for glorious Diocles
> he labored to offer it as a gift and keepsake.
> He wove into it many white lilies of Anyte, and many lilies of Moero,
> and small flowers of Sappho, but they are roses,
> and the narcissus, heavy with the clear songs of Melanippides,
> and the wine-flower of the grape-vine of Simonides,
> and here and there he wove in the sweet-smelling blooming iris
> of Nossis, for whose tablets Eros melted the wax.
>
> (Meleager 1 GP = *A.P.* 4.1–10)

Meleager characterizes Nossis chiefly as a love-poet, for whom the god Eros himself melts the wax of her writing tablets. Included in Meleager's collection is a lovely quatrain that probably served as the preface to the original publication of Nossis's poetry. In it, Nossis proclaims that "Nothing is sweeter than *eros*..." and that those to whom Aphrodite has not given favor do not know "what kind of flower are her roses" (Nossis 1 GP = *A.P.* 5.170).[14] Another epigrammatist in the *A.P.*, Antipater of Thessalonika, characterizes Nossis as "female-tongued" and Sappho as "the female Homer" in an epigram that catalogues nine female poets, among whom are Praxilla, Moero, Anyte, Erinna, Corinna, and Telesilla (*A.P.* 1.65).[15] In general, then, we get the picture from Hellenistic epigram of Nossis as an esteemed poet whose *oeuvre* focused on erotic themes, Aphrodite, and women-centered experiences.

Nossis was caricaturized in the comic sketches of Herodas (3rd century BCE) in a sexual and derogatory manner. In his sixth mime, two female characters, Metro and Coritto, discuss a beautifully crafted dildo that Coritto had purchased from a cobbler and which had been stolen. Coritto claims that it is now possessed by "Nossis, daughter of Erinna." (6.20). As Warwick (2020) points out, most scholars believe that this is intended to be a satirizing joke on the poets Nossis and Erinna. Warwick argues that this scene and another in Herodas involving dildo-related humor concerning Nossis and Erinna (7.57–58) represent misogynistic, metapoetic attacks on the contemporary popularity in the Hellenistic period of poetry written by women.[16]

## Select Bibliography

Balmer, J. 1996. *Classical Women Poets.* Newcastle upon Tyne: Bloodaxe Books.
Barnard, S. 1978. "Hellenistic Women Poets," *CJ* 73.3: 204–213.

Bowman, L. 2004. "The 'Women's Tradition' in Greek Poetry," *Phoenix* 58. 1/2: 1–27.

Cazzaniga, I. 1972. "Nosside, nome aristocratico per la poetessa di Locri?," *Annali della Scuola Normale Superiore di Pissa. Classe di Lettere e Filosofia* Serie III, 2.1: 173–176.

Corrente, G. 2017. "The Phlyax Plays: Performative and 'Political' Dimensions of an Original Form of Mediterranean Theatricality," in H. L. Reid, D. Tansi, and S. Kimbell (eds.), *Politics and Performance in Western Greece: Essays on the Hellenic Heritage of Sicily and Southern Italy.* Sioux City, IA: Parnassos Press, p. 55–68.

Deardon, C. 2004. "Sicily and Rome: The Greek Context for Roman Drama," *Mediterranean Archaeology: Festschrift in Honour of J. Richard Green* 17: 121–130.

Degani, E. 1981. "Nosside," *Giornale Filologico Ferrarese* 4: 43–52.

Domínguez, A., J. 2007. "Fear of Enslavement and Sacred Slavery as Mechanisms of Social Control among the Ancient Locrian," in A. Serghidou (ed.), *Fear of Slaves, Fear of Enslavement in the Ancient Mediterranean = Peur de l'esclave, peur de l'escalvage en Méditerranée ancienne: discours, representations, pratiques: actes du XXIXe colloque du groupe international de recerche sur l'esclavage dans l'antiquité.* Franche-Comté, p. 405–422.

Fountoulakis, A. 2000. "The Artists of Aphrodite," *L' Antiquité Classique* 69: 133–147.

Gaca, K. 2010. "The Andrapodizing of War Captives in Greek Historical Memory," *TAPA* 140: 117–161.

Gosetti-Murrayjohn (= Pitts), A. 2006. "Sappho as the Tenth Muse in Hellenistic Epigram," *Arethusa* 39.1: 21–45.

Gow, A. S. F. and D. L. Page. 1965. *The Greek Anthology: Hellenistic Epigrams. vols. 1-2.* Cambridge: Cambridge University Press.

Gutzwiller, K. J. 1997a. "Genre Development and Gendered Voices in Erinna and Nossis," in Y. Prins and M. Shreiber (eds.), *Dwelling in Possibility: Women Poets and Critics on Poetry.* Ithaca and London, p. 202–222.

———. 1997b. "The Poetics of Editing in Meleager's Garland," *TAPA* 127: 169–200.

———. 1998. *Poetic Garlands: Hellenistic Epigrams in Context.* Berkeley, CA: University of California Press.

Hallett, J. P. 1979. "Sappho and Her Social Context: Sense and Sensuality," *Signs* 4:447–464.

Hōschele, R. 2007. "The Traveling Reader: Journeys through Ancient Epigram Books," *TAPA* 137.2: 333–369.

Jaeger, M. 2006. "Livy, Hannibal's Monument, and the Temple of Juno at Croton," *TAPA* 136.2: 389–414.

Jendza, C. 2020. *Paracomedy: Appropriations of Comedy in Greek Tragedy.* Oxford: Oxford University Press.

Jenkins, I. and D. Williams. 1985. "Sprang Hair Nets: Their Manufacture and Use in Ancient Greece," *AJA* 89.3: 411–418.

MacLachlan, B. C. 1995. "Love, War and the Goddess in Fifth-Century Locri," *AW* 26: 205–223.

Mari, M. 1997. "Tributo a Ilio e prostituzione sacra: storia e reflessi sociali di due riti femminili Locresi," *Rivista di cultura classica e medioevale Iuglio-Dicembre*, 39.2: 131–177.

Mitchell, L. G. 2012. "The Women of Ruling Families in Archaic and Classical Greece," *CQ* 62.1: 1–21.

Parker, H. N. 2004. "An Epigram of Nossis (8 GP = *A.P.* 6.353)," *CQ* 54.2: 618–620.

Piqueux, A. 2006. "Le corps comique sur les vases ≪phlyaques≫ et dans la comédie attique," *Pallas* 71: 27–55.

Plant, Ian. 2004. *Women Writers of Ancient Greece and Rome: An Anthology.* Norman, OK: University of Oklahoma Press.

Pomeroy, Sarah B. 1977. "Technikai kai Mousikai: The Education of Women in the Fourth Century and in the Hellenistic Period," *AMAH* 2: 51–58.

Skinner, Marilyn B. 1987. "Greek Women and the Metronymic: A Note on an Epigram by Nossis," *Ancient History Bulletin* 1.2: 39–42.

———. 1989. "Sapphic Nossis," *Arethusa* 22: 5–18.

———. 1991. "Aphrodite Garlanded: Eros and Poetic Creativity in Sappho and Nossis," in de Martino, F. (ed.), *Rose di Pieria. Bari: Levante Editore*, p. 60–81.

———. 1996. "Woman and Language in Archaic Greece, or, Why is Sappho a Woman?" In Ellen Greene (ed.), *Reading Sappho: Contemporary Approaches.* Berkeley: University of California Press, p. 175–192.

———. 2001. "Ladies' Day at the Art Institute: Theocritus, Herodas, and the Gendered Gaze," in A. Lardinois and L. McClure (eds.), *Making Silence Speak.* Princeton, NJ: Princeton University Press, p. 201–222.

———. 2005. "Nossis *Thelyglossos*: The Private Text and the Public Book," in E. Greene (ed.), *Women Poets in Ancient Greece and Rome.* Norman, OK: University of Oklahoma Press, p. 112–138.

Snyder, J. M. 1989. *The Woman and the Lyre: Women Writers in Classical Greece and Rome.* Carbondale, IL and Edwardsville, IL: Southern Illinois University Press.

Warwick, C. 2020. "Nossis' Dildo: A Metapoetic Attack on Female Poetry in Herodas's Sixth *Mime*," *TAPA* 150: 333–356.

## Nossis 1 G-P = *A.P.* 5.170[17]

Ἅδιον οὐδὲν ἔρωτος, ἃ δ' ὄλβια δεύτερα πάντα
ἐστίν· ἀπὸ στόματος δ' ἔπτυσα καὶ τὸ μέλι.
τοῦτο λέγει Νοσσίς· τίνα δ' ἁ Κύπρις οὐκ ἐφίλασεν
οὐκ οἶδεν τῆνας τἄνθεα ποῖα ῥόδα.

*Meter: Elegiac Couplets*

—

**ἄνθος, -εος, τό:** bloom, flower
**ἔρως, ἔρωτος, ὁ:** desire, love
**ἡδύς, ἡδεῖα, ἡδύ:** pleasant, sweet
**μέλι, -ιτος, τό:** honey; anything sweet; eloquence
**ὄλβιος, -ον:** wealthy; rich; prosperous; happy; blessed
**ποῖος, -α, -ον:** of what kind?
**πτύω, πτύσω, ἔπτυσα, ἔπτυκα, —, ἐπτύσθην:** spit out; spit; spew
**ῥόδον, -ου, τό:** rose
**στόμα, -ματος, τό:** mouth; mouth as the organ of speech; and, thus, voice

—

**1–4:** Like all of the surviving epigrams of Nossis, this poem is a quatrain (i.e., consisting of two couplets and, thus, four lines). It is characteristic of a *sphragis* or "seal", a poetic motif in which an author names herself or himself, particularly in a prologue poem intended to introduce a volume of poetry, or in an epilogue poem, in which an author identifies herself for posterity as the author of the completed collection. *Sphragis* poems are often allusive and self-referentially meta-poetic, and they frequently draw attention to the literary tradition within which they are operating by offering agonistic and programmatic claims of authority. Generally regarded as a prologue to her lost collection of poems, Nossis 1 G-P, as Skinner (1989, p. 7) put it, "invokes Sappho as a primary poetic model." Allusions to Sappho 16 and 55, wherein the narrator claims that no one will remember an unnamed woman after she dies since she has had no share of "βρόδων τὼν ἐκ Πιερίας" (the "roses of Pieria"—the Pierian Spring near Mount Olympus and sacred to the Muses), dominate Nossis's epigram and signal both her indebtedness to Sappho as a poetic model and engagement with her predecessor's themes and style.[18] Nossis may also have in mind Sappho fr. 113.

**1. Ἅδιον** = Doric for ἥδιον, the comparative adverb of ἡδέως, from the adjective ἡδύς, ἡδεῖα, ἡδύ; comparative adjectives and adverbs may take a genitive object of the thing compared, as here with ἔρωτος. There are subtle nods to Sappho in this poem. Compare, for example, the opening priamel of Sappho L-P 16 with lines 1–2 of Nossis 1 G-P.

**2. ἔπτυσα:** an onomatopoeic verb.

**2. τὸ μέλι:** that is, even honey tastes awful in comparison to erotic desire. Perhaps Nossis has in mind Sappho fr. 113, μήτε μοι μέλι μήτε μέλισσα ("neither the honey nor the bee for me,"), a fragment which the modern poet H.D. used as a launch for her own lovely poem, "Fragment 113," which begins: "Not honey,/nor the plunder of the bee…".Skinner (1989, p. 9 and note 12) also sees possible allusions to Pindar's epinicians.

**3. ἁ** = ἡ (Att.)

**3. ἐφίλασεν** = ἐφίλησεν (Att.)

**4. τῆνας:** Gow and Page (1965, vol. 1, p. 151) supply a crux (†κῆνα τ'†) which has been solved by Degani (1981). Commentators have debated the identity of the referent of this pronoun, but most now accept Degani's suggestion that it refers to the poet herself (1981, p. 51–52), and that ἄνθεα (line 4) is a figurative metaphor for her poems. τῆνας is the Doric form of the Aeolic κῆνας and the Attic ἐκείνης.

**Nossis 2 G-P = *A.P.* 6.132**

ἔντεα Βρέττιοι ἄνδρες ἀπ' αἰνομόρων βάλον ὤμων
  θεινόμενοι Λοκρῶν χερσὶν ὕπ' ὠκυμάχων,
ὧν ἀρετὰν ὑμνεῦντα θεῶν ὑπ' ἀνάκτορα κεῖνται
  οὐδὲ ποθεῦντι κακῶν πάχεας οὓς ἔλιπον.

*Meter: Elegiac Couplets*

—

**αἰνόμορος, -ον:** fated to a sad end; fated to doom
**ἔντεα, -ων, τά:** weapons; armor; shields
**θείνω, θενῶ, ἔθεινον, —, —, —:** (act.), strike; dash; (pass., only in pres. and imperf.), stricken; dashed
**κεῖμαι, κείσομαι, —, —, —:** (only in pres., imperf., and fut.); lie; be placed (regularly used instead of the perfect passive of τίθημι; see Smyth #791)
**πῆχυς, -εος, ὁ:** arm; the part of the arm from the elbow to the middle finger
**ποθέω, ποθήσω, ἐπόθησα ἐπόθεσα, πεπόθηκα, πεπόθημαι, —:** desire; long for; miss
**ὑμνέω, ὑμνήσω, ὕμνησα, —, —, —:** sing of; celebrate; celebrate in hymns
**ὠκυμάχος, -ον:** swift in battle

—

**1–4:** This epigram imagines the sentiment of shields which have been affixed to a temple wall to celebrate the Locrian victory over the Brettioi. As Skinner (2005, p. 123) observes, the final line of this quatrain reverses a standard trope in play since Homer (e.g., Achilles's horses grieving for Patroclus on the battlefield)—wherein the war-horses or the weaponry of a fallen warrior grieve their owner's death.
**1. βάλον** = ἔβαλον (Att.); that is, the Brettioi threw away their shields.
**1. Βρέττιοι:** The Brettioi or Bruttians were an indigenous people of southern Italy (the heel) who threatened the autonomy of other Greek settlements in southern Italy.
**2. ὠκυμάχων:** This is the only surviving instance of this adjective in Greek literature.
**3. ὑμνεῦντα** = ὑμνοῦντα (Att.); the subject of this participle is ἔντεα from line 1; that is, the shields cast off from the Brettioi celebrate the martial excellence of the Locrians.
**3. ἀρετὰν** = ἀρετὴν (Att.)
**3. θεῶν ὑπ' ἀνάκτορα:** literally, "under the lord of the gods", this phrase indicates that the shields of the Brettioi have been placed inside a temple of a male deity.
**4. ποθεῦντι** = ποθοῦσι (Att., which is a contraction of ε+οντσι), it is a third-person pl. pres. indic. The lost shields do not miss their previous owners.
**4. κακῶν:** cowardly (rather than a general "evil" or "bad")
**4. πάχεας** = πήχεας (Att.)

**Nossis 3 G-P = *A.P.* 6.265**

῞Ηρα τιμάεσσα, Λακίνιον ἃ τὸ θυῶδες
  πολλάκις οὐρανόθεν νισομένα καθορῇς
δέξαι βύσσινον εἷμα τό τοι μετὰ παιδὸς ἀγαυᾶς
  Νοσσίδος ὕφανεν Θευφιλὶς ἁ Κλεόχας.

*Meter: Elegiac Couplets*

—

**ἀγαυός, -ή, -όν:** noble, illustrious
**βύσσινος, -η, -ον:** made of linen
**δέχομαι, δέξομαι, ἐδεξάμην, δέδεγμαι, εἰσ-εδέχθην:** receive; accept
**εἷμα, -ματος, τό:** garment, robe
**θυώδης, -ες:** smelling of incense, fragrant
**καθοράω, κατόψομαι, κατώρα, καθεώρακα, κατῶπμαι, κατώφθην:** look down upon; perceive; regard
**νίσομαι/νίσσομαι:** (usually in the present or imperf.), come; go
**οὐρανόθεν:** from heaven
**πολλάκις:** often, many times, frequently
**τιμήεις, -εσσα, -εν:** honored, esteemed
**ὑφαίνω, ὑφανῶ, ὕφηνα/ὕφανα, ὕφαγκα, ὕφασμαι, ὑφάνθην:** weave; create

—

**1–4:** A *sphragis* epigram commemorating the dedication of a linen robe woven by Nossis and her mother, Theuphilis as a votive offering to the temple of Hera on the Lacinian promontory near Croton in southeast Italy.

**1. τιμάεσσα** = τιμήεσσα (Att.)

**1. Λακίνιον:** Gow and Page (1965, vol. 2, p. 437) identify this temple as that of Hera on the Lacinian promontory southeast of Croton on the cape which is now called the Capo Colonna, whose modern name derives from a single remaining Doric column of its temple to Hera Lacinia, which originally boasted 48 Doric style columns. The temple was six miles from the city of Croton in southeast Italy. Adorning it were marble decoration roof-tiles, a pediment sculpture of Parian marble, and a famous painting of Hera by the artist Zeuxis. Livy (24.3.1–9) called the temple "more famous" (*nobilius*) than the city and sacred to all the surrounding peoples (*sanctum omnibus circa populis).* He describes a grove at the sanctuary surrounded by a dense wood of silver-fir trees and having a pasture in its center wherein cattle sacred to Juno could feed untended by shepherds. Livy claims that the flocks were never molested by humans or wild animals and provided great profit to the temple. With that profit was fashioned a column of solid gold dedicated to the goddess, and the temple was highly regarded both for its wealth and for its sanctity (*inclitumque templum divitiis etiam, non tantum sanc-*

*titate fuit*). Livy also claims (28.46.15–16) that Hannibal erected an altar beside the temple when the Carthaginian's army spent the summer in its vicinity weighed down by the afflictions of hunger and a disease epidemic. For more on the temple of Juno (i.e., Hera) at Croton, see Jaeger (2006).

**1. ἅ** = ἥ (Att.); see also line 4

**2. νισομένα** = νισομένη (Att.)

**3. δέξαι:** the infinitive is occasionally used in lieu of a second-person imperative to express a command, especially in poetry, as here. See Smyth #2013.

**3. ἀγαυᾶς** = ἀγαυῆς (Att.)

**4. Νοσσίδος:** gen. of the poet's name. Here, we learn the names of Nossis's mother and maternal grandmother, as three generations of women are highlighted in the final summary line of the quatrain.

**4. Κλεόχας:** genitive

**Nossis 4 G-P = *A.P.* 9.332**

ἐλθοῖσαι ποτὶ ναὸν ἰδώμεθα τᾶς Ἀφροδίτας
  τὸ βρέτας ὡς χρυσῷ δαιδαλόεν τελέθει.
εἵσατό μιν Πολυαρχὶς ἐπαυρομένα μάλα πολλάν
  κτῆσιν ἀπ' οἰκείου σώματος ἀγλαΐας.

*Meter: Elegiac Couplets*

—

**ἀγλαΐα, -ας, ἡ:** beauty; splendor
**βρέτας, -εος, τό:** wooden image of a god or goddess
**δαιδαλόεις, -εσσα, -εν:** cunningly crafted; intricately wrought
**ἐπαυρέω, ἐπαυρήσομαι, ἐπηυρόμην, —, —, ἐπαυρέθην:** (act.) partake of, share in a thing; (med.) reap the fruits; enjoy the benefit of a thing
**ἵζω, εἵσομαι, εἷσα/ἵζησα, ἵζηκα, —, —:** (act.) cause to sit; place; set; seat; (med.) set up and dedicate (in honor of the gods)
**κτῆσις, -εως, ἡ:** property; wealth; possessions
**ναός, νεώς, ὁ:** temple; innermost part of a shrine
**σῶμα, -ματος, τό:** body
**τελέθω:** (cognate with τελέω, τέλλω, and πέλω; τελέθω appears chiefly in the present tense), come into being; to be; to exist

—

**1–4:** The unnamed narrator of this epigram calls upon a group of women to go with her to the temple of Aphrodite so that the group may gaze upon a statue of the goddess placed there as a dedicatory offering by the courtesan Polyarchis in gratitude for the wealth she accrued from her beautiful body. Of course, the reader is also invited to go on that journey and participate in the imagined gaze.[19]

The specific temple of Aphrodite (the goddess of erotic love and, thus, prostitution) referenced in the poem is unclear and unnamed, but the world of the poem suggests that inside it is a particularly fine wooden statue adorned with gold. Of equal curiosity and interest, perhaps, to the speaker and addressees is its dedicator. See Domínguez (2007, esp. note 57) for a survey of archaeological research that indicates a substantial cult of Aphrodite was present in Epizephyrian Locris.

**1. ἐλθοῖσαι** = ἐλθοῦσαι (Att.)—notice the gender and number of this participle, which indicate that the addressee is a group of women and/or girls.

**1. ποτὶ** = πρὸς (Att.)

**1. ἰδώμεθα:** from εἶδον, which serves as the aorist form of ὁράω; the base ἰδ- supplies a great many forms of the verb in Attic. In the middle voice, this verb means to "see" or "behold" (with one's own eyes); the unnamed (female) narrator of this epigram includes herself in the hortatory expression (the verb is first person plural subjunctive) as she addresses a group of fellow females (which is determined from ᾿Ελθοῖσαι), among whom is, presumably the reader.

**1. τᾶς ᾿Αφροδίτας** = τῆς ᾿Αφροδίτης

**3. Πολυαρχὶς:** lines 3–4 suggest that Polyarchis, the woman who paid for the erection of a partially gilt wooden statue of Aphrodite, is a prostitute whose gift to Aphrodite is made out of gratitude for the wealth she has earned from the profits of her trade. See the introduction for Nossis in this volume for a discussion of historical sources that indicate that in Epizephyrian Locris, sacred prostitution of aristocratic women constituted a form of community sacrifice to avert the brutal consequences of defeat in war. It may be that Nossis celebrates the women associated with the cult of Aphrodite in her community.

**3. ἐπαυρομένα** = ἐπαυρομένη (Att.)

**3. πολλάν** = πολλήν (Att.)

**4. οἰκείου:** here, the adjective functions as a synonym of ἴδιος, -α, -ον, meaning "her own"

**Nossis 5 G-P = *A.P.* 6.275**

χαίροισάν τοι ἔοικε κομᾶν ἄπο τὰν ᾿Αφροδίταν
ἄνθεμα κεκρύφαλον τόνδε λαβεῖν Σαμύθας,
δαιδάλεός τε γάρ ἐστι καὶ ἁδύ τι νέκταρος ὄσδει·
τούτῳ καὶ τήνα καλὸν ᾿Άδωνα χρίει.

*Meter: Elegiac Couplets*

—

**ἀνάθεμα, -ματος, τό:** dedicatory offering; anything dedicated; votive offering

**δαιδάλεος, -α, -ον:** cunningly crafted; intricately wrought

**ἔοικε:** (an impersonal verb), it is fitting; it is right (that an accusative object do the action of an infinitive)

**ἡδύς, ἡδεῖα, ἡδύ:** sweet; pleasant
**κεκρύφαλος, -ου, ὁ:** hair-net
**κόμη, -ης, ἡ:** hair; locks of hair
**ὄζω, ὀζήσω, ὤζησα, ὤζηκα, —, —:** smell of; smell sweet
**χαίρω, χαιρήσω, ἐχαίρησα, κεχάρηκα, κεχάρημαι, ἐχάρην:** rejoice in; take pleasure in; delight in
**χρίω, χρίσω, ἔχρισα, κέχρικα, κέχριμαι, ἐχρίσθην:** anoint; anoint with oil or perfume

—

**1–4:** The narrator (unnamed) celebrates another dedicatory object to Aphrodite—a hair-net placed there by Samytha. Like most votive offerings celebrated in Greek epigram, the object is intricately wrought and highly redolent of the oils with which Samytha perfumes her hair. This same perfume either Samytha or Aphrodite uses to anoint Adonis, the goddess's exceptionally handsome consort.

**1. χαίροισάν** = χαίρουσάν (Att.)

**1. κομᾶν** = κομῶν (Att.)

**1. τὰν ᾿Αφροδίταν** = τὴν ᾿Αφροδίτην (Att.);

**1–2.** Aphrodite is the object of the impersonal verb ἔοικε and the accusative subject of λαβεῖν in line 2. The object of λαβεῖν (as well as the participle χαίροισάν) is κεκρύφαλον, to which ἄνθεμα stands in apposition. Placed into English word order, lines 1–2 would be reflected thus: ἔοικε τὰν ᾿Αφροδίταν χαίροισάν λαβεῖν τόνδε κεκρύφαλον ἄπο κομᾶν Σαμύθας (as an) ἄνθεμα.

**2. ἄνθεμα** = ἀνάθεμα (Att.); the vocabulary above lists ἀνάθεμα.

**2. κεκρύφαλον τόνδε:** The *kekruphalos* references a finely worked hair net made of sprang fabric. *Kekruphaloi* were probably woven manufactures made by hand on the loom. Jenkins and Williams (1985, p. 416) argue that the spinning and production of small textiles like hair-nets probably occurred in the brothels of 5th-century Athens and were also probably frequently fashioned by *hetairai* (prostitutes) for personal use and for sale to supplement their earnings.

**2. Σαμύθας** = Σαμύθης (Att. gen.), the name of the girl or young woman who dedicated the hair-net as a votive offering.

**3. ἁδύ** = ἡδύ (Att.)

**3. ὄσδει** = ὄζει (Att.)

**4. τούτῳ:** "with this" sweet-smelling nectar, i.e., the same nectar used to perfume the hair-net.

**4. τήνα** = Doric for ἐκείνη (Att.); grammatically, the antecedent of this demonstrative pronoun could be either Samyntha or Aphrodite.

**4. ᾿Άδωνα:** Adonis, one of Aphrodite's human consorts, a youth of extraordinary beauty who died young tragically when he was gored by a wild boar while hunting. A festival mourning the death of Adonis was celebrated annually by the women of ancient Greece.

**Nossis 6 G-P = *A.P.* 9.605**

τὸν πίνακα ξανθᾶς Καλλὼ δόμον εἰς ᾿Αφροδίτας
  εἰκόνα γραψαμένα πάντ᾿ ἀνέθηκεν ἴσαν.
ὡς ἀγανῶς ἕστακεν· ἴδ᾿ ἁ χάρις ἁλίκον ἀνθεῖ.
  χαιρέτω, οὔ τινα γὰρ μέμψιν ἔχει βιοτᾶς.

*Meter: Elegiac Couplets*

—

**ἀγανός, -ή, -όν:** gentle, mild
**ἀνθέω, ἀνθήσω, ἤνθησα, ἤνθηκα, —, —, —:** bloom; blossom; flourish
**βιοτή, -ῆς, ἡ:** life
**εἰκών, -ονος, ἡ:** image; representation; semblance
**ἡλίκος, -η, -ον:** how great; how much; how greatly
**ἴσος, -η, -ον:** equal; like
**μέμψις, -εως, ἡ:** blame; censure; fault
**ξανθός, -ή, -όν:** golden (esp., golden-haired)
**πίναξ, -ακος, ὁ:** a votive tablet hung on the image of a god; painting; picture
**χάρις, -ιτος, ἡ:** beauty; grace; charm
**χαίρω, χαιρήσω, ἐχαίρησα, κεχάρηκα, κεχάρημαι, ἐχάρην:** rejoice in; take pleasure in; delight in; often used as a greeting, "be well" or "hello" or "farewell"

—

**1–4:** This epigram calls attention to a painting commissioned by the woman Kallō ("Beauty"), probably a courtesan, left as a dedicatory object to Aphrodite. Is the painting of Aphrodite or of Kallō? Perhaps the vagueness in the Greek text about the painting's subject (lines 1–3) implies a likeness in beauty and grace between the dedicator and the dedicatee. The deictic way in which the narrator draws attention to the features of the painting involves both the reader and the imaginary addressee (or addressees) in an appreciation of the painting's subject. The epigram concludes with a comment on the blamelessness of Kallō's life and, perhaps, livelihood.

**1. ξανθᾶς ... ᾿Αφροδίτας** = ξανθῆς ...᾿Αφροδίτης (Att.)

**2. πάντ᾿ ... ἴσαν** = πάντ᾿ ... ἴσην (Att.): "like (to the original) in every way"

**3. ἴδ᾿:** aor. imper. of εἶδον (the aorist form used for ὁράω): "behold"; "look there"

**3. ἁλίκον** = ἡλίκον (Att.)

**4. χαιρέτω**: Third person sing. imperative; literally, "may she rejoice" or "may she be well", although some translators (e.g.,Plant, 2004, p. 65) see in this imperative "farewell". Either Kallo is alive and should rejoice because she is leading a blameless life or the narrator bids farewell to a deceased woman whose likeness appears in a painting dedicated to Aphrodite. It is far more likely in the context of the poem that a general expression of benevolence is intended, particularly given that Nossis 9 G-P, line 4 (see below) uses the same word (χαίροις πολλά) to express goodwill rather than a last farewell.

**4. βιοτᾶς** = βιοτῆς (Att.)

**4. χαιρέτω… βιοτᾶς:** Skinner (2005, p. 118–119) suggests that, given the woman's name (Καλλὼ, "Beautiful") and the fact the dedicatory painting is a dedication to Aphrodite, the poem celebrates a courtesan or *hetaera* (like Nossis 4) and her way of life. See the introduction for Nossis in this volume for a discussion of historical sources that indicate that in Epizephyrian Locris, sacred prostitution of aristocratic women constituted a form of community sacrifice to avert the brutal consequences of losing war. It may be that Nossis celebrates the women associated with the cult of Aphrodite in her community.

**Nossis 7 G-P = *A.P.* 9.604**

Θαυμαρέτας μορφὰν ὁ πίναξ ἔχει· εὖ γε τὸ γαῦρον
  τεῦξε τό θ' ὡραῖον τᾶς ἀγανοβλεφάρου.
σαίνοι κέν σ' ἐσιδοῖσα καὶ οἰκοφύλαξ σκυλάκαινα
  δέσποιναν μελάθρων οἰομένα ποθορῆν.

*Meter: Elegiac Couplets*

—

**ἀγανοβλεφάρος, -ον:** having gentle or tender eyes
**γαῦρος, -ον:** haughty; prideful; splendid; disdainful; exultant
**μελάθρον, -ου, τό:** house
**μορφή, -ῆς, ἡ:** form; appearance; shape; beauty
**οἰκοφύλαξ, -ακος, ὁ, ἡ:** guard of the house
**οἴομαι, οἰήσομαι, ᾠϊσάμην, —, —, ᾠήθην:** think; suppose; believe
**πίναξ, -ακος, ὁ:** a votive tablet hung on the image of a god; painting; picture
**σαίνω, —, ἔσηνα, —, —, —:** wag the tail; fawn upon
**σκυλάκαινα, -ας, ἡ:** (fem. of σκύλαξ, -ακος, ὁ): puppy (female)
**τεύχω, τεύξω, ἔτευξα, τέτευχα, τέτυγμαι/τέτυκμαι, ἐτεύχθην:** make, build; produce (by work or artistry)
**ὡραῖος, -α, -ον:** prime of youth; seasonable; at the proper time; beautiful; graceful

—

**1–4:** Another dedicatory epigram in which the narrator draws attention to a painting. The subject of the painting is beautiful Thaumaretē, whose shapeliness, eyes, and youthfulness are rendered in it in a captivating way. The painting is so life-like that Thaumaretē's puppy would wag her tail as she gazed upon the painting, believing her mistress to be present in the room.

1. **Θαυμαρέτας** = Θαυμαρέτης (Att.); the name of "Thaumaretē" is a compound noun consisting of θαῦμα ("marvel") and αρέτη ("excellence").
2. **τᾶς** = τῆς (Att.)
2. **μορφὰν** = μορφὴν (Att.)
3. **κέν** = ἄν (Att.)
3. **ἐσιδοῖσα:** from εἰσοράω (nom. s. fem. participle, aorist)
3. **σκυλάκαινα:** This is the only instance of this particular feminine iteration of σκύλαξ in extant Greek literature. See Anyte 10 G-P = Poll. 5.48 in this volume for another Hellenistic epigram featuring a puppy.
4. **δέσποιναν** = δεσποίνην (Att.)
4. **οἰομένα** = οἰομένη (Att.)
4. **ποθορῆν:** infinitive of προσοράω ("to gaze upon")

### Nossis 8 G-P = *A.P.* 6.353

Αὐτομέλιννα τέτυκται· ἴδ' ὡς ἀγανὸν τὸ πρόσωπον.
ἁμὲ ποτοπτάζειν μειλιχίως δοκέει.
ὡς ἐτύμως θυγάτηρ τᾷ ματέρι πάντα ποτῴκει·
ἦ καλὸν ὄκκα πέλῃ τέκνα γονεῦσιν ἴσα.

*Meter: Elegiac Couplets*

—

**ἀγανός, -ή, -όν:** gentle, mild
**γονεύς, -έως, ὁ, ἡ:** parent; ancestor
**ἔτυμος, -η, -ον:** true
**ἴσος, -η, -ον:** equal to; like
**μειλιχίος, -α, -ον:** soothing, mild, gentle, gracious
**πέλω πέλομαι:** (only the pres., imperf., and aor. [usually aorist 3rd s., ἔπλετο] forms occur), be; come into existence; become
**προσέοικα:** (perf. with pres. sense; only the perf. and pluperf. forms occur), resemble, be like (a dative object)
**πρόσωπον, -ου, τό:** face, countenance
**τεύχω, τεύξω, ἔτευξα, τέτευχα, τέτυγμαι/τέτυκμαι, ἐτεύχθην:** make, build; produce (by work or artistry)

—

**1–4:** A lovely quatrain epigram celebrating a painting of Melinna. The exactitude of the likeness to its subject is given a particularly imaginative life with the metaphors of "daughter" (painting) and "mother" (Melinna). Verbal echoes, repetitions of sound, and balanced word placement within the epigram emphasize this verisimilitude.[20]
1. **ἴδ':** aor. imper. of εἶδον (the aorist form used for ὁράω): "behold"; "look there"
2. **ἁμὲ:** Doric for ἧμας

**2. ποτοπτάζειν:** Doric verb for infinitive of προσοράω ("to gaze upon" or "to look upon")
**3. τᾷ ματέρι** = τῇ μητέρι (Att.)
**3. ποτῴκει:** Doric for προσέοικει (Att.)
**4. ὄκκα:** Doric for ὅτε (Att.)

**Nossis 9 G-P = *A.P.* 6.354**

γνωτὰ καὶ τηλῶθε Σαβαιθίδος εἴδεται ἔμμεν
  ἅδ' εἰκὼν μορφᾷ καὶ μεγαλειοσύνᾳ.
θάεο· τὰν πινυτὰν τό τε μείλιχον αὐτόθι τήνας
  ἔλπομ' ὁρῆν. χαίροις πολλά, μάκαιρα γύναι.

*Meter: Elegiac Couplets*

—

**αὐτόθι:** (adv.) from this spot; on the spot
**γνωτός, -ή, -όν:** perceived; known; understood
**γυνή, γυναῖκος, ἡ:** woman
**εἰκών, -όνος, ἡ:** image, likeness, representation (often in art)
**ἔλπω:** (related to Attic ἐλπίζω): (act.), cause to hope or expect; (med.), expect; hope
**θεάομαι, θεάσομαι/θεήσομαι, ἐθεασάμην, —, τεθέαμαι, —:** contemplate; observe as a spectator; see clearly
**μάκαρ (masc., neut.), μάκαιρα (fem.):** blessed; fortunate; happy
**μειλιχίος, -α, -ον:** soothing, mild, gentle, gracious
**μορφή, -ῆς, ἡ:** form; appearance; shape; beauty
**ὁράω, ὄψομαι, εἶδον, ἑώρακα ἑόρακα, ἑώραμαι ὦμμαι, ὤφθην:** see; gaze upon; perceive (through sight); observe
**πινυτή, -ῆς, ἡ:** understanding; insight; wisdom
**τηλόθεν:** (adv.), from afar; far from
**χαίρω, χαιρήσω, ἐχαίρησα, κεχάρηκα, κεχάρημαι, ἐχάρην:** rejoice in; take pleasure in; delight in; often used as a greeting, "be well" or "hello" or "farewell"

—

**1–4:** The narrator points to an artistic representation of the woman Sabaithis—either a painting or a sculpture—which stands at some distance from the speaker, drawing the reader's attention to the beauty and magnificence, wisdom and gentleness of its subject. Such characteristics captured in the artwork make it impossible for the viewer to mistake the identity of the woman the *eikōn* represents.
**1. τηλῶθε** = τηλόθε(ν) (Att.); that is, one can recognize from a fair distance that the image is that of Sabaithis.
**1. ἔμμεν** = εἶναι (Att.)
**2. ἅδ'** = ἥδε (Att., without the crasis)

**2. μορφᾷ** = μορφῇ (Att.)

**2. μεγαλειοσύνᾳ** = μεγαλειοσύνῃ (Att.), but the noun does not occur elsewhere in Greek literature. It probably means something like "magnificence" or "splendor" or "greatness" (as per μεγαλεῖος, "magnificent", "splendid").

**3. θάεο:** Doric 2nd s. imperative of θεάομαι.

**3. τὰν πινυτὰν** = τὴν πινυτὴν (Att.)

**3. τήνας** = Doric for ἐκείνης (Att.)

**4. ἔλπομ' ὁρῆν:** crasis (ἔλπομαι) and the present infinitive of ὁράω. The painting is so life-like that the narrator expects to see in it the very characteristics of the living person who is its subject.

**4. χαίροις πολλά:** This is most certainly a general wish of goodwill, rather than an expression of solemn farewell, as per Gow and Page (1965, vol. 2, p. 441), which gives strength to a similar reading for Nossis G-P 6, line 4 above.

**4. γύναι:** the vocative sing. form of γυνή

**Nossis 10 G-P = *A.P.* 7.414**

καὶ καπυρὸν γελάσας παραμείβεο καὶ φίλον εἰπών
　ῥῆμ' ἐπ' ἐμοί. 'Ρίνθων εἰμ' ὁ Συρακόσιος,
Μουσάων ὀλίγα τις ἀηδονίς, ἀλλὰ φλυάκων
　ἐκ τραγικῶν ἴδιον κισσὸν ἐδρεψάμεθα.

*Meter: Elegiac Couplets*

—

**ἀηδονίς, -ίδος, ἡ:** nightingale

**γελάω, γελάσομαι γελάσω, ἐγέλασα, —, γεγέλασμαι, ἐγελάσθην:** laugh

**δρέπω, δρεψεῦμαι (Dor. only), ἔδρεψα, —, —, ἐδρέφθην:** (act.), pluck; gain possession or enjoyment of a thing; (med.) pluck for one's self

**ἴδιος, -α, -ον:** one's own; personal; private

**καπυρός, -ά, -όν:** crackling; dry; brittle; clear-sounding; loud

**κισσός, -οῦ, ὁ:** ivy

**ὀλίγος, -η, -ον:** little; small; few

**παραμείβω, παραμείψω, παρήμειψα, —, —, παρημείφθην:** (act.) change, alter; (med.) pass by; go by

**ῥῆμα, -ματος, τό:** word; line of verse

**τραγικός, -ή, -όν:** pertaining to dramatic tragedy; tragic

**φλύαξ, -ακος, ὁ:** also called the ἱλαροτραγῳδία, a form of tragic burlesque

—

**1–4:** This funerary epigram calls upon the passerby of Rhinthon's tomb to laugh and say a friendly greeting to the deceased, Syracusan writer of *phlyax* dramas.

1. **παραμείβεο** = παραμείβου (Att.), pres. 2nd s. imper.
2. **῾Ρίνθων...ὁ Συρακόσιος:** Rhinthon was a Hellenistic (early 3rd century BCE) writer of *phlyax*-plays. Nine titles of his plays are preserved of a total of 38 attributed to him by ancient authors. Only the barest fragments survive, and, like the epigrams of Nossis, these are written in the Doric dialect. *Phlyakes* (also called *hilarotragoidiae*, or "merry tragedies") were farcical tragi-comedies performed chiefly in southern Italy in the 4th and 3rd centuries BCE and they featured erotic themes and scenes from daily life and mythology subjected to comic distortion. Rhinthon, Nossis tells us, is from Syracuse in Sicily, a major theatrical center of the Hellenistic world. He appears to have mixed burlesque elements of farcical mime and pantomime with material from Greek tragedy, and especially Euripides. Fountoulakis (2000) demonstrates through inscriptional evidence that writers (like Rhinthon) of south Italian and Syracusan mime, pantomime, and *phlyakes* formed a professional guild dedicated to Aphrodite. See also Piqueux (2006) for a discussion of representations (especially costuming) of *phlyakes* productions on Apulian red-figure vases.
3. **ὀλίγα** = ὀλίγη (Att.)
4. **κισσὸν:** ivy was an iconographic symbol of Dionysus, the god of theater, and especially of tragedy and comedy.

### Nossis 11 G-P = *A.P.* 7.718

ὦ ξεῖν', εἰ τύ γε πλεῖς ποτὶ καλλίχοραν Μιτυλήναν
  τᾶν Σαπφοῦς χαρίτων ἄνθος ἐναυσόμενος,
εἰπεῖν ὡς Μούσαισι †φίλαν τῆνᾳ τε Λόκρις γᾶ
  τίκτε μ'· ἴσαις δ' ὅτι μοι† τοὔνομα Νοσσὶς ἴθι.[21]

*Meter: Elegiac Couplets*

—

**ἄνθος, -ους, τό:** flower, bloom; brilliancy; brightness
**ἐναύω, ἐναύσομαι, ἔναυσα, —, —, —:** (act.) kindle; light; (med.) draw inspiration from (an acc. object); light a fire for oneself
**καλλίχορος, -α, -ον:** characterized by beautiful dances; with beautiful dancing-grounds (as an epithet for a city)
**ξένος, -ου, ὁ:** foreigner; wayfarer; wanderer; stranger; guest-friend
**ὄνομα, -ματος, τό:** name
**πλέω, πλεύσομαι, ἔπλευσα, πέπλευκα, πέπλευσμαι, ἐπλεύσθην:** sail
**τίκτω, τέξω, ἔτεξα/ἔτεκον, τέτοκα, τέτεγμαι, ἐτέχθην:** give birth to; bear, produce, beget; engender
**χάρις, -ιτος, ἡ:** grace, beauty, elegance; gratitude; favour

—

**1–4:** A common motif in Hellenistic funerary epigram is the request that a passerby pause to appreciate the life of the deceased, taken by death from her or his beloved native land. Nossis adapts this motif to appeal to a (male) wayfarer (who is also, of course, a stand-in for the reader) sailing to Sappho's homeland of "beautiful choruses" to announce there that the Locrian land bore Nossis, who is also dear to the Muses. Skinner (2005, p. 126–127) suggests that this quatrain served as an epilogue to her published collection, comprising a ring-composition with Nossis 1 G-P of allusions to Sappho, and signaling that she is Sappho's literary equal and descendant. As Snyder (1989, p. 79) deftly put it, "The message is clear enough: 'Locri has produced a second Sappho, and I am she.'"

**1. ξεῖν'** = ξένε (Att., without the crasis)

**1. ποτὶ** = πρός (Att.)

**1. Μιτυλήναν** = Μιτυλήνην; Mitylene, one of the principle cities of the island Lesbos, was said to be the home of Sappho.

**2. τᾶν** = τῶν (Att.)

**3. εἰπεῖν:** an infinitive functioning as an imperative

**3. φίλαν** = φίλην (Att.)

**3. τῆνα** = Doric for ἐκείνη (Att.); the referent is Σαπφοῦς (line 2).

**3. γᾶ** = γῆ (or γαῖα) (Att.)

**4. ἴσαις:** fem., voc. s. participle of οἶδα—"having seen that" and, thus, "learning that"

**Nossis (?) 12 G-P = *A.P.* 6.273**

῎Αρτεμι Δᾶλον ἔχοισα καὶ ᾿Ορτυγίαν ἐρόεσσαν,
τόξα μὲν εἰς κόλπους ἅγν' ἀπόθου Χαρίτων,
λοῦσαι δ' ᾿Ινωπῷ καθαρὸν χρόα βᾶθι δ' †ἐς οἴκους
λύσουσ' ὠδίνων ᾿Αλκέτιν ἐκ χαλεπῶν.

*Meter: Elegiac Couplets*

—

**ἁγνός, -ή, -όν:** holy; chaste; pure

**ἐρόεις, -εσσα, -εν:** lovely, charming

**καθαρός, -ά, -όν:** clean, clear, pure

**κόλπος, ου, ὁ:** lap; bosom; loose folds of a woman's robe

**λούω, λούσω, ἔλουσα, —, λέλουμαι, ἐλούθην:** (act.) wash (an object); (med.) bathe (oneself)

**τόξον, -ου, τό:** bow

**χαλεπός, -ή, -όν:** difficult; hard to deal with

**χρώς, χρωτός, ὁ:** skin; flesh

**ὠδίς, ὠδῖνος, ἡ:** pains of child-birth

—

**1–4:** We are in doubt as to whether or not Nossis is the true author of this epigram, since its heading in the *A.P.* (ὡς Νοσσίδος) could mean either "*as* Nossis" (i.e., "in the style of Nossis") or "*supposedly* Nossis".[22]

In this cletic epigram addressed to Artemis, the narrator appeals to the goddess to put away her hunting bow, bathe herself in the pure waters of the Inopus stream, and come to give relief to Alcetis, who is suffering from the labor pains of childbirth.

**1. Ἄρτεμι:** voc. case; Artemis, a goddess of childbirth was born on the island of Ortygia (*Homeric Hymn to Apollo* 3.15–16), while her twin brother was born on Delos. The Inopus (mentioned in line 3) is a river or stream on this island.

**1. Δᾶλον** = Δῆλον (Att.)

**1. ἔχοισα** = ἔχουσα (Att.)

**2. ἀπόθου:** aor. imper. 2nd s. of ἀποτίθημι; "put away"

**3. χρόα:** Epic, Ionic, and Aeolic acc. s. = χρῶτα (Att.)

**3. βᾶθι:** Doric, 2nd s. aor. imper. of βαίνω

### Nossis 1 G-P = *A.P.* 5.170

Nothing is sweeter than *eros*, all other blessings are
second; I spit even honey from my mouth.[23]
This Nossis says: the one whom the Cyprian goddess has not favored
does not know what kind of flowers are her roses.

### Nossis 2 G-P = *A.P.* 6.132

This quatrain reads like a dedicatory epigram giving voice to enemy shields, thrown away by their "cowardly" owners (the Brettioi, an indigenous people of southern Italy) and dedicated to the gods after they were retrieved by the narrator's fellow Locrians' victory in battle. The epigram may serve as a dedication to actual Brettian shields, or it may be artificially dedicatory. Either way, the objects the epigram animates are given personified feeling.

These shields the Brettian men threw from their ill-fated shoulders,
struck by the hands of the swift-battling Locrians,
as a testament to whose bravery they were placed in the god's temple,
and they do not miss the forearms of the cowards whom they abandoned.

### Nossis 3 G-P = *A.P.* 6.265

Honored Hera, you who ever gaze down upon your aromatic Lacinian
temple[24] as you descend from the heavens,
accept this linen robe, woven – along with her noble daughter
Nossis – by Theuphlis, daughter of Cleocha.

**Nossis 4 G-P = *A.P.* 9.332**

Let us go to the temple to gaze upon Aphrodite's
statue—how intricately it has been adorned with gold.
Polyarchis, has dedicated it in honor of the very great wealth
she has acquired reaping the fruits of her body's beauty.

**Nossis 5 G-P = *A.P.* 6.275**

It is good that Aphrodite, delighting in this hair-net from the locks of Samytha,[25]
accepts it as a votive offering,
for it is intricately woven and smells like the sweet ambrosia
with which she also anoints handsome Adonis.[26]

**Nossis G-P 6 = *A.P.* 9.605**

This painting Kallō[27] placed in the temple of golden-haired Aphrodite,
a likeness painted in every way equal to herself.[28]
How gently she[29] stands there; Look—how much gracefulness is in bloom.
May she flourish,[30] since she leads a life without reproach.

**Nossis G-P 7 = *A.P.* 9.604**

This painting possesses the beautiful form of Thaumaretē. How well it has
captured the dignity and youthfulness of her tender eyes.
Looking upon you, your watchdog puppy would wag her tail,
supposing that she gazed upon the mistress of the house.

**Nossis G-P 8 = *A.P.* 6.353**

A lovely quatrain epigram celebrating a painting of Melinna, whose similitude to her "mother" (the painting itself)[31] is given every emphasis.

Melinna herself has been recreated; Look at how gentle is her face.
She seems to gaze upon us graciously.
How truly the daughter resembles her mother in every way;
Ah, what a good thing it is when a child is the very picture of her parent.

**Nossis 9 G-P = *A.P.* 6.354**

Recognizable even from far off, one can see by the beauty and magnificence
that this painting is of Sabaithis.
Observe: even from here I expect to see her wisdom and graciousness.
You have much reason to rejoice, blessed woman.

**Nossis 10 G-P = *A.P.* 7.414**

This epigram calls upon the laughing passerby of Rhinthon's tomb to say a friendly greeting to the deceased, Syracusan writer of burlesque tragi-comedies. Notice the balance between comic elements (laughing raucously) and tragic elements (nightingale) in the epitaph.

Laughing—and raucously—pass by and speak a kindly
word to me. Rhinthon am I, from Syracuse,
and something of the Muses' little nightingale,[32] but I plucked for myself
my own ivy from my tragic burlesques.[33]

**Nossis 11 G-P = *A.P.* 7.718[34]**

Wayfarer, if you sail to Mitylene, city of beautiful choral dances,[35]
to draw inspiration from the bloom[36] of Sappho's graces,
say that the Locrian[37] earth bore me,
dear to the Muses and to her. Having learned that my name is Nossis, go.

**Nossis (?) 12 G-P = *A.P.* 6.273[38]**

Women who died in childbirth in the ancient Greek world were said to have died by the "arrows of Artemis," a virgin, huntress, and goddess associated with childbirth. This cletic epigram calls upon Artemis to leave her bow in the care of the Graces, perform ritual ablutions in the Inopus stream, and come to Alcetis's home to release her from the pains of a difficult childbirth.

Artemis, you who possess Delos and lovely Ortygia,[39]
put away your sacred hunting bow into the laps of the Graces,
and bathe your holy skin in the Inopus stream, and go into the home
of Alcetis to release her from the hard pains of child-birth.

## Notes

1. Snyder (1989, p. 64–84) provides a good overview of the ways in which the poems of Nossis reflect the aesthetic and cultural complexities of the Hellenistic period.
2. For good overviews of Rhinthon's phlyax plays and the Greek dramatic tradition that influenced them within a Sicilian context, see Fountoulakis (2000), Deardon (2004), Piqueux (2006), Corrente (2017), and Jendza (2020), p. 254–264.
3. Barnard (1978) argues that there was a tradition of women's poetry in Greece that particularly followed in the wake and tradition of Sappho. Hallett (1979) argues for a female audience of Sappho's poetry, while Skinner (1996) argues for a wide-spread female oral tradition of poetry. Gutzwiller (1998, p. 86 and 1997a, p. 219–220) argues that Nossis's epigram 11 may be viewed as an attempt

to procure a place in the tradition of women's poetry in the Greek world. See also Bowman (2004), who argues that both orally transmitted and textually transmitted women's poetry probably had its own "subculture" and tradition of song, but that (p. 3) "there is no certain evidence for the influence of a segregated oral tradition of women's poetry on the extant female-authored poems."

4. The historian Polybius (*Histories*, 12.5.7–10) offers a lengthy discussion of Aristotle's comments on the founding of Epizephyrian Locris by fugitive slaves, on which Aristotle offers no discussion in his brief commentary on Epizephyrian Locris in the *Politics* (2.1274a). Clement of Alexandra (*Stromata* 1.26.170) mentions a now lost work by Aristotle, *The Polity of Locrians*, and this may have been Polybius's source. In the *Politics* (2.1274a), Aristotle merely notes that the Epizephyrian Locrians were given their laws by Zaleucus, a pupil of the philosopher Thales. There were three somewhat independent, but culturally unified regions of Locris in mainland Greece: Ozolian Locris on the Gulf of Corinth; Epicnemidian Locris near the pass of Thermopylae, opposite the island of Euboea; and Opuntian Locris, just to the east of Epicnemidian Locris.
5. Polybius, *Histories* (12.5.7–10).
6. Cazzaniga (1972) traces the uncommon and aristocratic name Cleochos to an association with Miletus, Zankle and Kalè Akte on Sicily, and Epizephyrian Locri through filiations of colonial foundings, suggesting that it would not be absurd to assume that the Milesian Cleochos became an aristocratic household in Epizephyrian Locris, connected with the cult of Hera.
7. A point stressed by Plant, 2004, p. 63.
8. Ps.-Apollodorus (*Epitome* 6.20–21) claims that the first women to whom this lot fell were Periboea and Cleopatra (not the Macedonian queen of Egypt) after the Locrians experienced a plague. He notes that the Locrians were first prompted to send *hierodoulai* when a plague struck. These "slaves of the goddess" had their hair cropped after being chased into the sanctuary by locals, and they were responsible for cleaning the sanctuary and purifying it by sprinkling it with water. They did not go out of the temple, according to the author, and only wore single garments and went barefoot.
9. Aelian, *Varia Historia* fr. 47.
10. See Domínguez (2007) for a thorough discussion of the historical sources involving *hierodoulai* among the Locrians. He quotes Justin 21.3.1: *die festo Veneris virgines suas prostitutueren.* Domínguez builds heavily on the work of Manuela Mari (1997), who collects and discusses "sacred prostitution" by Locrians in both Troy and Epizephyrian Locris.
11. Diodorus Siculus, 12.76.4. See Domínguez (2007).
12. Plutarch, *De Alex. fort.* 5.338c and *Dion.* 6.1. For discussion of the ways in which Dionysius II employed the political symbolism of his daughters' names, see Mitchell (2012, p. 12–13).
13. Gutzwiller (1997b) is a "must read" for the editorial choices Meleager made as he was compiling the *Stephanos.* Gutzwiller (1998) provides an authoritative overview of the genre of Hellenistic epigram in its literary and social contexts.
14. See Skinner (2005, p. 124–125) for a discussion of poems 1 and 11, which, Skinner argues, served as the preface and epilogue to Nossis's book of poems. See Skinner (1989) and Gosetti-Murrayjohn (= Pitts, 2006, p. 22–24 and 27–30) for the ways in which Nossis stylizes herself as a literary descendant of Sappho and for the ways in which the "rose" flower is particularly resonant of Sappho's poetic persona.
15. See Skinner (2005) and Gosetti-Murrayjohn (= Pitts, 2006, p. 38–40) for discussion of the epithet *thēlyglossos,* or "female-tongued" as an economical

characterization of Nossis's women-centered poetry. Gosetti-Murrayjohn (=Pitts) also discusses at some length Antipater's description of Sappho as the "female Homer."

16. See also Skinner (1989 and 2001) for discussions of Herodas's burlesque representation of Nossis.
17. The text is largely that of Gow and Page (1965, vol. 1, p. 151), except for the crux at line four, elegantly solved by Degani (1981), whose solution appears here in the form of τῆνας τἄνθεα.
18. For discussion of the literary tradition associating the Muses with Pieria and the rose with Sappho, see Gosetti-Murrayjohn (= Pitts, 2006, p. 21–24).
19. Relevant is Hōschele's (2007) study of the ways in which literary epigrams invite the reader to journey to a monument or artifact, thus evoking a three-dimensional space as the reader becomes a "metaphorical traveler" journeying through the two-dimensional space of the papyrus scroll.
20. Some scholars interpret this epigram literally, believing that Melinna's resemblance to her mother in the painting is the point. Skinner (2005, 121), for example, interprets the opening word, "Automelinna" ("Melinna herself") as a verbal play intended to evoke the sense that she is the "genetic reincarnation of her parent." Parker (2004), however, has cogently asserted another convincing interpretation: that "the 'daughter' is, of course, the painting" and the similarity between the subject of the painting (the woman Melinna) and the painting (i.e., the "daughter") is the point.
21. The Greek text of the lemma supplied by Gow and Page (1965, vol. 2, p. 442), which offers elegant solutions to the problems of the text published in vol. 1 of the same.
22. Some scholars (Plant, 2004, p. 66, esp. note 4) view this epigram as consistent with the style of Nossis. Others, however, are dubious. Balmer (1996) did not include the epigram in her collection of translations of classical era women poets; and, Skinner (2005) did not include it in her discussion of the epigrams of Nossis, though every other epigram receives detailed attention.
23. That is, even honey tastes poorly in comparison to erotic desire. Compare this opening priamel to that in the opening stanza of Sappho fr. 16.
24. A single Doric column is all that survives of this temple, six miles southeast of Croton (now called "Capo Colonna" in honor of that column). This temple of Hera was of sufficient beauty and fame that the Roman historian Livy commented upon it considerably (*Ab Urbe Condita*, 24.3.1–9) and reported (*AUC*, 28.46.15–16) that the Carthaginian general Hannibal erected an altar beside it when his army spent the summer in the surrounding vicinity, afflicted by a disease epidemic and hunger.
25. Hair-nets were woven by women—especially by prostitutes—on handheld sprang-frames placed on the lap (Jenkins and Williams, 1985).
26. Raised by Persephone, Adonis in Greek and Roman myth was the exceptionally attractive human lover of Aphrodite. He died young having been gored to death by a boar while hunting. Both Persephone and Aphrodite adored Adonis and fought over him so avidly that Zeus had to intervene. The father of gods and men ruled that Adonis would spend four months of the year with Persephone, four months with Aphrodite, and the remaining four however the lad chose (Ps.-Apollodorus, *Bibliotheca* 3.183). So smitten was he with Aphrodite that he elected to spend his four free months with her also. As he lay dying from his hunting wound, Aphrodite poured ambrosial nectar into his wound. Although he did, nevertheless, die, the ambrosially redolent Anemone flower grew in the spot where his blood mixed with nectar (Ovid, *Metamorphoses*, 10.708–739). An annual spring festival called the Adoneia (or, Adonia) was

celebrated by women throughout the ancient Greek world in which ritual mourning for Adonis occurred. Athenian women celebrated this festival largely on the rooftops of their houses, where dancing, singing (including the singing of mourning songs), and the planting of "Gardens of Adonis" (quick-growing celery and fennel) were planted in potsherds, wherein they sprouted, withered, and died before growing into full-sized plants. Women carried images of Adonis in a mock funeral procession, and then buried both the images and the "gardens" in springs or at sea.

27. The name "Kallō" literally means "Beauty" in Greek (much like "Bella" in English and Italian), and is likely fashioned here as the sobriquet of a prostitute or celebrant of Aphrodite. Skinner (2005, p. 119) suggests that the final line of the epigram "must be construed as a bold defense of her way of life."
28. The Greek text does not make it clear whether the image is the very likeness of Kallō or of Aphrodite. Perhaps this ellipsis is intentional, blurring the distinctions between the beauty of the dedicator and the dedicatee. As Skinner (2005, p. 119) put it, "this portrait, then, could be either like the sitter or like the divinity who receives it," since beauty is one of the reigning attributes of Aphrodite and one of the great gifts she bestows on mortals (as per Nossis 4).
29. In Greek, the subject of the verb is not expressed, but left implied. Technically, it could be the painting, Kallō, or Aphrodite, while Kallō is probably the foregrounded referent. Once again, there is a (perhaps intentional) ellipsis between the portrait, its dedicator, and its dedicatee.
30. The Greek verb, *xairetō,* could mean several things: (a) "may she be well"; (b) "hello"; (c) "farewell" (and, thus, "good-bye"); or, even, (d) "may she rejoice". It signifies (as per Gow and Page, 1965, p. 441) "general benevolence" and is often used in greetings, coming and going. While the verb could, of course, mean that its subject (probably Kallō, but left implied rather than expressed) is deceased ("farewell" for good), the general tone and timbre of the poem make that interpretation less appealing.
31. While quite a few scholars (Barnard, 1978, p. 213; Plant, 2004, p. 66; and, Skinner, 2005, p. 120–121,for ex.) believe the epigram expresses how much the daughter Melinna resembles her mother, Parker (2004) notes that the "similarity of mother and daughter" are "the actual subject" of the poem, since the 'daughter' "is, of course, the painting." Nossis 6, 7, and 9 G-P share the same emphasis on verisimilitude between painting and painted subject.
32. The nightingale is associated with female laments in Greek tragedy and is often evoked as a symbol of lamentation, grief, loss, and mourning.
33. The Greek word used here specifies a specific type of tragi-comedy called *phlyakes* (also called *hilarotragoidiae*, or "merry tragedies"). These were farcical tragi-comedies performed chiefly in Southern Italy in the 4th and 3rd centuries BCE, and they featured erotic themes and scenes from daily life and mythology subjected to comic distortion. Rhinthon was a particularly well-known writer of this particular kind of drama. Nossis renders Rhinthon as stating that he plucked for himself ivy because ivy was sacred to Dionysus, the god of the theater—especially of tragedy and comedy.
34. Skinner (2005, p. 126–127) suggests that this quatrain served as an epilogue to Nossis's published collection, signaling that she is Sappho's literary equal and descendant. Snyder (1989, p. 79) suggests that Nossis is announcing that "Locri has produced a second Sappho" by the name of Nossis. If it is the case that this poem served as the closing piece to her collection, the last word of the poem, the imperative "go" (*ithi,* in Greek), is as much addressed to the reader as to the imagined wayfarer. The message is, "Go, remembering the name of Nossis, another Sappho, dear to the Muses."

35. Mitylene is the principle city of the island of Lesbos and Sappho's home town. Many of Sappho's songs were composed for and performed by choruses of young girls and women. Likewise, the choral poems of her compatriot and fellow Mitylinean, Alcaeus.
36. The Greek word for "bloom" or "flower" is *anthos,* from which the word *anthologia* ("anthology") is derived. The word *anthos* is frequently used as a metaphor for poetry, especially brilliant poetry. An anthology is, in a metaphorical way, a collection of flowers assembled into a garland. Thus, the 1st-century BCE Meleager entitled his anthology collection of clever poems by various writers (including himself) "The Garland", and many of these poems were epigrams containing erotic themes.
37. Epizephyrian Locris was a Doric (Greek) colony in south Italy from the 7th century BCE onward. Southern Italy was known as "Magna Graecia" since much of the area contained Greek colonies. See the introduction to Nossis in this volume for a discussion of Epizephyrian Locris and its relationship, through social structure and religious practice, to mainland Locris.
38. There is some doubt about the authenticity of this epigram, since its label in the *Anthologia Palatina* offers a qualifying phrase that may mean something like, "supposedly Nossis" or "in the style of Nossis". Gow and Page (1965, vo. 2, p. 443). Plant (2004) includes the poem in his translations of Nossis's poetry (duly noting its questionable authenticity), while Balmer (1996) and Skinner (2005) do not.
39. Ortygia, is the birth-site of Artemis. The reference to Ortygia and Delos brings to mind the *Homeric Hymn to Apollo* (*Hymn* 3), wherein Artemis's own mother, Leto, suffered a very difficult birth-pain, being forced by a jealous Hera to wander to the earth in labor. Whereas other localities had been warned (or, rather, bullied) by Hera not to allow Leto to lie down in them to give birth, only Delos allowed her to do so in exchange for becoming a famous for the establishment on it of a sanctuary to Apollo. Thus, the evocation of Leto's painful child-bearing through the mention of Ortygia and Delos parallels that of Alcetis.

# 6 Anyte

Writing somewhere between 290 and 310 BCE, Anyte has, in the last several decades of scholarship, been recognized as one of the first (if not the first) Hellenistic poets to use bucolic, idyllic landscapes. Such landscapes, replete with refreshing springs, fountains, and vineyards, serve as settings for pastoral vignettes where encounters occur between shepherds and nature deities like Pan and Nymphs. Thus, Anyte may have influenced later bucolic poets like Theocritus (*Idylls*) and Vergil (especially the *Eclogues*). She was heavily imitated by the Hellenenistic epigrammatist Mnasalces in both style and subject matter.[1] Although she apparently also wrote epic poetry which did not transmit through the ages to us,[2] a substantial collection of epigrams has survived through the medium of the *Palatine* and *Planudean* anthologies. We are in a fortunate position of having more complete poems of Anyte than of any other female poet of Greco-Roman antiquity, and only from Sappho do we have more actual words that survive.[3] There exist 19 epigrams of certain authorship by Anyte and an additional two that were most likely written by her, bringing the total of extant poems that were very likely composed by her to 21. A few additional epigrams were incorrectly attributed to Anyte in antiquity and are not included in this volume.[4] Drawing upon epic language, dialect, and themes, Anyte's epigrams offer a range of type, from dedicatory to funerary, and their topics center not only on young girls and women, children, animals, and pastoral landscapes, but also on war, war-horses, spears, and the death of male soldiers in battle.

Gutzwiller (1993, p. 71–72) makes a convincing argument for a contemporary publication of Anyte's poems in book form, particularly given that the later anthologizer Meleager had a collection of her poems at his disposal for the collation of his *Garland*. Stehle (1997, p. 114–118) and Bowman (2019, p. 77–79) have suggested that the Hellenistic genre of epigram afforded to female poets an opportunity to compose poetry in private that could be circulated in book form publicly, thus taking advantage of a "loophole" that would allow "female-authored texts … to appear in public space, in dedications and funeral epitaphs, provided the 'speaker' was absent" (Bowman, 2019, p. 78).

DOI: 10.4324/9781003031727-8

About Anyte's life we know almost nothing for certain. Pollux tells us that she was from a settlement called Tegea in Arcadia on the Peloponnesus (i.e., not the same place of origin as Corinna's Tegea in Boeotia), but no other ancient author gives us corroborating information about her origins, and we know nothing about her parents or family.[5] All we have beyond Pollux's suggestion that she was a native of Tegea in Arcadia is an apocryphal anecdote by the 2nd-century CE Greek travel-writer and geographer Pausanias, famous for his descriptions of the local lore of various sites in Greece. The story pertains to Pausanias' description of Naupactus, a coastal town on the north shore of the Corinthian Gulf.[6] The city, he notes, got its name from either a woman or a Nymph and was the titular eponym for a (now lost) epic poem about women called *Naupactia*, whose uncertain authorship Pausanias discusses.[7] The city, according to the geographer, boasts a coastal temple of Poseidon fitted with a bronze statue of the god, as well as a sanctuary of Artemis containing a marble statue of the goddess (called the "Aetolian") hurling a javelin. Naupactus also possesses, he tells us, a subterranean cave-sanctuary devoted to Aphrodite wherein, among other forms of ritual worship that take place there, widows ask the goddess to grant them marriage. The sanctuary of the physician-god Aesclepius in Naupactus, however, was in ruins when Pausanias visited the site, and its legendary founding by one Phalysius involved an apocryphal tale about Anyte. According to Pausanias, Anyte was inspired by the god Aesclepius to sail to Naupactus. She carried with her a sealed wax tablet to Phalysius, who had sent prayers to the god to alleviate his blindness. Surprised at being able to read its contents when he was told by Anyte to break the seal, he found that they instructed him to give two thousand gold-staters to the poet. Phalysius gave the huge sum to Anyte and then founded the sanctuary to Aesclepius at Naupactos in thanksgiving to the god.

Etiological explanations for the origins of sanctuary-complexes are quite common, and Pausanias' founding myths often involve some element of the supernatural. The vehicle for the expression of divine manifestation in this narrative is the poet herself, whom the legend credits with inspirational knowledge of the kind soothsayers and poets frequently possess in ancient Greek literature. Moreover, the narrative centers on the disability of blindness, which is a standard biographical element in apocryphal representations of Homer, *the* itinerant poet (or *aoidos*) par excellence, who was frequently called "divine" and shown achieving apotheosis in art. Françoise Létoublon (2007) has suggested that while some victims of mythic tales receive blindness as a punishment for gazing upon an image forbidden to human eyes, the gods grant to poets and soothsayers special, supra-human, divine insight that is inaccessible to ordinary humans. While Anyte in Pausanias's narrative is not blind, she is portrayed as a human surrogate of Asclepius and she is both imbued with and the purveyor of divine knowledge. That knowledge imparts the healing of vision and is conveyed through a written text enclosed with a *sphragis*, or seal. The *sphragis* itself is a literary device frequently found in Greco-Roman literature in which an author names or otherwise identifies himself or herself, particularly at the beginning or end of a collection of poems, to mark out a collection of poems as stylistically distinctive and frequently to associate a written collection with poetic immortality.[8] Moreover, while male bards are frequently represented as itinerant, stories in ancient Greece about women travelling independently, especially female poets, are relatively rare.[9]

## Select Bibliography

Barnard, S. 1978. "Hellenistic Women Poets," *Classical Journal* 73: 204–213.

———. 1991. "Anyte: Poet of Children and Animals," in F. De Martino (ed.), *Rose di Pieria*, Bari: Levante, p. 165–176.

Beecroft, A. 2011. "Blindness and Literacy in the *Lives* of Homer," *CQ* 61.1: 1–18.

Bowman, L. 2019. "Hidden Figures: The Women Who Wrote Epigrams," in Christer Henriksén (ed.), *A Companion to Ancient Epigram*. Hobonek, NJ: Wiley-Blackwell, p. 77–92.

Geoghegan, D. 1979. *Anyte: The Epigrams*. Rome: Edizioni dell' Ateneo & Bizzarri.

Gow, A. S. F. and D. L. Page. 1965. *The Greek Anthology: Hellenistic Epigrams, vols. 1–2*. Cambridge: Cambridge University Press.

Greene, E. 2005. "Playing with Tradition: Gender and Innovation in the Epigrams of Anyte," in Ellen Greene (ed.), *Women Poets in Ancient Greece and Rome*, Norman, OK: University of Oklahoma Press, p. 139–157.

Gutzwiller, K. J. 1993. "Anyte's Epigram Book," *Syllecta Classica* 4: 71–89.

Létoublon, F. 2007. "To see or not to see: Blind People and Blindness in Ancient Greek Myth," in M. Christopoulos, E. Karakantza and O. Levaniouk (eds.), *Light and Darkness in Ancient Greek Myth and Religion*. Lanham, MD: Lexington Books, p. 167–180.

Lulli, L. 2014. "Local Epics and Epic Cycles: The Anomalous Case of a Submerged Genre," in G. Colesanti and M. Giordano (eds.), *Submerged Literature in Ancient Greek Culture. vol. 1*. Berlin: Walter de Gruyter, p. 76–89.

Pratt, L. 1995. "The Seal of Theognis, Writing, and Oral Poetry," *AJP* 116.2: 171–184.

Rehm, R., 1994. *Marriage to Death: The Conflation of Wedding and Funeral Rituals in Greek Tragedy*. Princeton, NJ: Princeton University Press.

Rutherford, I. 2009. "Aristodama and the Aetolians: An Itinerant Poetess and Her Agenda," in Richard Hunter and Ian Rutherford (eds.), *Wandering Poets in Ancient Greek Culture*. Cambridge: Cambridge University Press, p. 237–249.

Snyder, J. 1989. *The Woman and the Lyre: Women Writers in Classical Greece and Rome*. Carbondale, IL and Edwardsville, IL: Southern Illinois University Press.

Stehle, E. 1997. *Performance and Gender in Ancient Greece: Nondramatic Poetry in Its Setting*. Princeton, NJ: Princeton University Press.

Vara, J. and J. Weatherby. 1992. "The Sources of Theocritean Bucolic Poetry," *Mnemosyne* 45.3: 333–344.

## Anyte 1 G-P (*A.P.* 6.123)

ἕσταθι τᾷδε, κράνεια βροτοκτόνε, μηδ' ἔτι λυγρόν
  χάλκεον ἀμφ' ὄνυχα στάζε φόνον δαΐων,
ἀλλ' ἀνὰ μαρμάρεον δόμον ἡμένα αἰπὺν 'Αθάνας
  ἄγγελλ' ἀνορέαν Κρητὸς 'Εχεκρατίδα.

*Meter: Elegiac Couplets*

—

**ἀνορέα, -ας, ἡ:** poetic word for ἀνδρεία; manliness, prowess, courage
**αἰπύς, -εῖα, -ύ:** sheer, lofty, high, steep
**βροτοκτόνος, -ον:** mortal-slaying, man-killing
**δάϊος, -ου:** enemy, foe
**δόμος, -ου, ὁ:** house
**ἧμαι:** sit
**ἵστημι, στήσω, ἔστησα/ἔστην, ἕστηκα/ἕστατον, ἕσταμαι, ἐστάθην:** make stand (transitive); stand (intransitive)
**κράνεια, -ας, ἡ:** spear made of cornelian cherry wood (a type of dogwood tree)
**Κρής, Κρητός, ὁ:** Cretan, from the isle of Crete
**λυγρός, -ά, -όν:** baneful, mournful
**μαρμάρεος, -α, -ον:** made of marble
**φόνος, -ου, ὁ:** murder, slaughter
**ὄνυξ, -υχος, ὁ:** claw, talon
**στάζω, στάξω, ἔσταξα, —, ἐνέσταγμαι, ἐπεστάχθην:** let fall, drop, drip

—

**1–4:** On the spear of a Cretan warrior which was given to the temple of Athena in dedication to the goddess. One common type of Hellenistic literary verse is the dedicatory epigram, in which an object, dedicated to a deity, is given voice or addressed by the narrator-speaker about how and why it came to be placed in a temple. The votive object is often personified to some degree and given *pathos*. While some dedicatory epigrams may commemorate actual objects, some are merely literary, intended to evoke the experience of standing before the object while reading from a papyrus book-roll.

**1. ''Εσταθι:** intransitive, 2nd perfect, 2nd sing. imperative of ἵστημι ("Stand"). This appears to be an intensive perfect, denoting an *action* rather than a state which is the result of an action (see Smyth #1947).

**2. κράνεια βροτοκτόνε:** the placement of this vocative phrase in the very center of the opening hexameter line gives it emphasis, *pathos*, and personification as the addressee of the poem. The fact that Aeschylus's chorus of Furies, in stichomythia dialogue with Athena, used the participle (βροτοκτονοῦντας, from βροτοκτονέω, "man-slaying") in the *Eumenides* (421) is worth mentioning, given that the *LSJ* lists that occurrence as the only instance of the verb in surviving Greek literature. In that scene, Athena appears before the Furies, claiming that she heard their summons from far off at the river Scamander (on the Trojan plain) while the goddess was being assigned a portion of spears obtained from the spoils of war. Like the spear in Anyte's poem, Athena in the Aeschylean tragedy claims that the (presumably Trojan) spears were in the process of being dedicated to the goddess when she was summoned to make an epiphany into the dramatic space of the tragedy. When Athena asks of the Furies to state their reason for calling her, the Furies respond, "βροτοκτονοῦντας ἐκ δόμων ἐλαύνομεν", or, "we drive murderers from their home". Perhaps Anyte consciously drew upon the adjective βροτοκτόνε to evoke tragic *pathos* in connection with Athena, the Furies, and the spear as dedicatory object to Athena from spoils of war.

**3. ἡμένα:** present tense participle, nominative, feminine, singular of ἧμαι, a verb which is only inflected in the present tense (see Smyth #789).
**Ἀθάνας** = Doric for Attic Ἀθήνης

**4. ᾽Εχεκρατίδα** = acc. m. sing., patronymic, "son of *Echekratos*"

**Anyte 2 G-P (*A.P.* 6.153)**

Βουχανδὴς ὁ λέβης· ὁ δὲ θεὶς ᾽Εριασπίδα υἱός
Κλεύβοτος, ἁ πάτρα δ᾽ εὐρύχορος Τεγέα·
τἀθάνᾳ δὲ δῶρον, Ἀριστοτέλης δ᾽ ἐπόησεν
Κλειτόριος, γενέτᾳ ταὐτὸ λαχὼν ὄνομα.

*Meter: Elegiac Couplets*

—

**βουχανδής, -ές:** holding an ox; big enough to hold an ox
**γενέτης, -ου, ὁ:** father, ancestor
**εὐρύχορος, -ον:** spacious, with wide open space
**λαγχάνω, λήξομαι, ἔλαχον, εἴληχα, εἴληγμαι, ἐλήχθην:** obtain by lot, get by chance, come into possession of
**λέβης, -ητος, ὁ:** kettle, cauldron
**πάτρα, -ας, ἡ:** fatherland
**τίθημι, θήσω, ἔθηκα, τέθηκα, τέθειμαι, ἐτέθην:** put, place, set down, dedicate

—

**1–4:** On the dedication by Kleobolus of a large cauldron. Another dedicatory epigram, celebrating both the dedicator and the artist he commissioned to fashion it. The patrilineal genealogies of both dedicator and artist occupy most of the quatrain, apart from the two and a half metrical feet before the caesura of the opening line.

**1. Βουχανδὴς:** this compound adjective (from the base verb, χανδάνω, "hold" or "contain"), appears to contain within it possible allusions to Homer, and especially to vessels awarded as prizes in funerary games (Hom. *Iliad* book 21, lines 267–268, 885–886, and 700–703; Geoghegan, 1979, p. 31).

**1. θείς:** aorist, active participle, nominative, masculine, singular of τίθημι
**2. ἁ** = Doric ἡ (Att.)
**2. Τεγέα:** a *polis* in the Peloponnesian region of Arcadia
**3. τἀθάνᾳ** = crasis and Doric for τῇ Ἀθήνῃ
**4. Κλειτόριος:** of *Kleitor*, another town in Arcadia
**ταὐτὸ** = crasis for τὸ αὐτὸ

**Anyte 3 G-P (*A.Pl.* 291)**

φριξοκόμᾳ τόδε Πανὶ καὶ αὐλιάσιν θέτο Νύμφαις
  δῶρον ὑπὸ σκοπιᾶς Θεύδοτος οἰονόμος
οὕνεχ᾽ ὑπ᾽ ἀζαλέου θέρεος μέγα κεκμηῶτα
  παῦσαν ὀρέξασαι χερσὶ μελιχρὸν ὕδωρ.

*Meter: Elegiac Couplets*

—

**ἀζαλέος, -α, -ον:** parched, dry, withered
**θέρος, -εος, τό:** summer
**κάμνω, καμοῦμαι, ἔκαμον, κέκμηκα, —, —:** toil, labor, fall sick
**μελιχρός, -ά, -όν:** honey-sweet
**οἰονόμος, -ου, ὁ:** shepherd
**ὀρέγω, ὀρέξω, ὤρεξα, ὤρεγμαι, —, ὠρέχθην:** reach out, hold out, hand, give
**Πάν, Πάνος, ὁ:** Pan, god of the rustic wilderness, shepherds, and flocks; frequent companion of nymphs
**σκοπιά, -ᾶς ἡ:** hilltop, peak, a look-out place that commands a view of the surrounding area
**τίθημι, θήσω, ἔθηκα, τέθηκα, τέθειμαι, ἐτέθην:** put, place, set down, dedicate
**φριξοκόμης, -ου, ὁ:** with shaggy or bristly hair
**ὕδωρ, ὕδατος, τό:** water

—

**1–4:** On an (unidentified) object dedicated to Pan and the Nymphs by Theudotos for the gift of a drink of water in the summer heat. That the gift itself (i.e., the dedicatory object, τόδε … δῶρον) is not identified nor described suggests that the reader's attention is rather directed to the charming and numinous bucolic setting wherein "shaggy-haired Pan" and "Nymphs who protect the herd" supply sweet water for the relief of shepherds laboring in the summer heat. Shrines in such countryside locations, particularly near springs, were commonplace. Other non-dedicatory, pastoral epigrams of Anyte include 16 and 19.
**1. φριξοκόμᾳ:** this may be an epithet of Pan invented by Anyte.
**1. αὐλιάσιν…Νύμφαις:** the word αὐλιάσιν may be intended to refer to one of several words, and it may contain intentional echoes of all of them:

1. αὖλις—a tent or a place for passing the night; 2. αὐλή—a barn or place where cattle reside; or, a courtyard or dwelling; 3. αὔλιον—a grotto or cave. Sanctuaries of nymphs were often to be found in grottoes and caves, and they were protectors of cattle and those traveling through rural areas. See Geoghegan (1979, p. 44–45) for a discussion of the various etymologies that have been proposed for this word, wherein it is noted that Anyte may intend to be "deliberately ambiguous". Given the strong association between Nymphaea (sanctuaries consecrated to water-nymphs) with natural grottoes and springs, the English translation below reflects the αὔλιον evocation.

**3. κεκμηῶτα:** acc., masc. sing. perfect tense, active participle

**4. παῦσαν:** in poetry, the epsilon augment of past tense, indicative verbs is often lacking.

**Anyte G-P 4 (*A.P.* 7.724)**

Ἥβα μέν σε, πρόαρχε, ἕσαν· παίδων ἅτε ματρός
  Φειδία ἐν δνοφερῷ πένθει ἔθου φθίμενος,
ἀλλὰ καλόν τοι ὕπερθεν ἔπος τόδε πέτρος ἀείδει
  ὡς ἔθανες πρὸ φίλας μαρνάμενος πατρίδος.

*Meter: Elegiac Couplets*

—

**ἅτε:** as if, just as
**δνοφερός, -ά, -όν:** dark, murky
**Ἥβη, -ης, ἡ:** youth, prime of youth
**ἵζω, εἵσομαι, εἷσα/ἵζησα, ἵζηκα, —, —:** (act.) cause to sit; place; set; seat; (med.) set up and dedicate (in honor of the gods)
**μάρναμαι, —, —, —, —, —, ἐμαρνάσθην:** (this verb usually only appears in the present and imperfect tenses); fight, strive, contend
**πένθος, -εος, τό:** sorrow, grief
**πέτρος, ου, ὁ:** rock, stone
**πρόαρχος, -ου, ὁ:** captain, chief

—

**1–4:** Evoking commemorative inscriptions placed upon grave monuments, funerary epigrams like this one give voice to a (real or imaginary) tombstone honoring the deceased. The stone itself (τόδε πέτρος, line 3) sings (ἀείδει, an epicizing word, for example, Hom. *Iliad* 1.1) the glory of a soldier who died young in defense of his beloved country. The narrator-speaker addresses the deceased, or, rather, the deceased's tombstone, which serves as the deceased's "voice", singing the ἔπος (line 3) young captain's martial glory.[10]

**1–2.** This poem presents several philological challenges, particularly in the first couplet. Geoghegan (1979, p. 57) translates the first couplet: "The youth (sc. of the city) buried you, captain. When you died, Pheidias, you cast them into dark mourning, as of children for their mother". In another evocation of Aeschylean tragedy, this funerary epitaph for a soldier contains an echo (line 2) of Aeschylus' *Persians*, 535–536: ἄστυ τὸ Σούσων ἠδ' Ἀγβατάνων/**πένθει δνοφερῷ κατέκρυψας.** Geoghegan's text (1979, p. 57) has been used here. Notice the balanced syllabic structure of line 1.

**1.῞Ηβα** = Doric for῞Ηβη. Geoghegan (1979, p. 57) suggests that῞Ηβα, a singular nominative, functions as a collective noun (i.e., the youth of the city) governing the plural, ἕσαν.

**1. ἕσαν:** another difficult word, which Geoghegan (1979, p. 58–9) argues is an aorist form of ἵζω, having an equivalent meaning of θέσαν (the aorist of τίθημι), which, in one of its many idioms, means "lay in the grave, bury". Geoghegan points out that ἕσαν does appear once as a *hapax legomenon* in the *Iliad* (19.393) and that ancient critics viewed the Homeric occurrence of ἕσαν as equivalent to θέσαν.

**1. παίδων ἅτε ματρός:** ἅτε usually takes an accusative, so we must understand πένθος as the unstated object of it from πένθει in the next line. The genitive παίδων indicates whose grief is referenced in this simile, while ματρός serves as an objective genitive ("just as [the grief] of children for their mother"). While grammatically speaking either genitive may serve as the objective genitive, the grief of children (for their mother) makes unifying sense in a couplet in which "the youth" has done the action of burying a captain.

**3. ἔπος τόδε πέτρος ἀείδει:** the πέτρος is the tombstone set upon this soldier's grave, and upon it is etched a line of verse that "sings" that he died defending his fatherland. Both ἀείδει and ἔπος are words closely associated with epic poetry and epic stories. Consider, for example, *Iliad* 1.1 (μῆνιν ἄειδε θεὰ Πηληϊάδεω Ἀχιλῆος) and *Od.* 8.83 (ταῦτ' ἄρ' ἀοιδὸς ἄειδε περικλυτός...), as well as *Od.* 8.91, wherein the Phaeacians urge the "divine bard" Demodocus to sing since they delight in his songs (...ἐπεὶ τέρποντ' ἐπέεσιν...).

**Anyte 5 G-P (*A.P.* 7.486)**

πολλάκι τῷδ' ὀλοφυδνὰ κόρας ἐπὶ σάματι Κλείνα
  μάτηρ ὠκύμορον παῖδ' ἐβόασε φίλαν,
ψυχὰν ἀγκαλέουσα Φιλαινίδος, ἃ πρὸ γάμοιο
  χλωρὸν ὑπὲρ ποταμοῦ χεῦμ' Ἀχέροντος ἔβα.

*Meter: Elegiac Couplets*

—

**ἀνακαλέω,-καλῶ,-ἐκάλεσα,-κέκληκα,-κέκλημαι,-ἐκλήθην:** summonback, call back again and again; summon the dead
**βοάω, βοήσομαι, ἐβόησα, βεβόηκα, βεβόημαι, ἐβώσθην:** cry aloud, call for, shout
**γάμος, -ου, ὁ:** wedding, marriage
**κόρη, -ης, ἡ:** young girl, usually of marriageable age; daughter
**ὀλοφυδνός, -ή, -όν:** lamenting; here, used as an adverb
**πολλάκι (adv.):** often, many times
**σῆμα, -ματος, τό:** sign; sign by which a gravesite is marked; grave; tomb
**χεῦμα, -ματος, τό:** that which is poured; stream
**χλωρός, -ά, -όν:** pale, pallid, greenish yellow
**ὠκύμορος, -ον:** dying too swiftly; dying at a young age

—

**1–4:** On the grief of Cleina for the loss of her daughter, Philaenis, who died before marriage. The fiction of the epigram provides a setting before the sepulchral image of Cleina's daughter, where mother expresses grief in the public space occupied by Philaenis's tombstone. The mother's grief for her child, taken from her by death, evokes the grief experienced by Demeter at the loss of Persephone (Greene, 2005).

**1. ὀλοφυδνὰ:** In the *Iliad* (23.102), Achilles speaks aloud an "ἔπος ὀλοφυδνὸν" addressed to the departing ghost of Patroclus, who chastised the hero for neglecting his due burial rites. In his address, Achilles marvels that even in the house of Hades a soul and a phantom image (ψυχὴ καὶ εἴδωλον) remain, but there is no conscious life (φρένες οὐκ) of the deceased. There is general agreement (Gow and Page, 1965, p. 94; Geoghegan, 1979, p. 65–68; Greene, 2005, p. 142) that Anyte is probably alluding to this passage.

**1. κόρας:** = Doric genitive (= Attic κόρης). Even though this noun's base ends in (-ρ), the nominative and genitive forms of this noun in Attic take "pure" (-η) forms.

**1. σάματι:** = Doric equivalent of Attic σήματι
**2. παῖδ':** = crasis for παῖδα
**3. ἀγκαλέουσα:** = (Attic) ἀνακαλέουσα
**3. ἅ:** = Attic ἥ
**3. γάμοιο:** = Attic γάμου
**4. χεῦμ':** = crasis for χεῦμα

**4. 'Αχέροντος:** the Acheron is one of the rivers of the underworld. Others include Styx, Periphlegethon, Lethe, and Kokytos.
**4. ἔβα:** = 3rd sing. aorist active indicative of βαίνω

### Anyte 6 G-P (*A.P.* 7.490)

παρθένον 'Αντιβίαν κατοδύρομαι, ἇς ἐπὶ πολλοί
νυμφίοι ἱέμενοι πατρὸς ἵκοντο δόμον
κάλλευς καὶ πινυτᾶτος ἀνὰ κλέος· ἀλλ' ἐπὶ πάντων[11]
ἐλπίδας οὐλομένα Μοῖρ' ἐκύλισε πρόσω.

*Meter: Elegiac Couplets*

—

**δόμος, -ου, ὁ:** house
**ἐπίπας, -πασα, -παν:** all (of something) together; the whole or sum of something
**ἐφίημι, -ἥσω, -ἧκα/-εῖτον, -εἶκα, -εἶμαι, -εἵθην:** (+ gen.) long for, desire
**ἱκνέομαι, ἵξομαι, ἱκόμην, —, —, —:** come to or arrive at a place
**κάλλος, -ους, τό:** beauty
**κατοδύρομαι:** mourn
**κλέος, τό:** (this noun only appears in the nom. or acc.): fame, (good) reputation
**κυλίω** (a later form of κυλίνδω): roll (an accusative object) along
**Μοῖρα, -ας, ἡ:** death, fate, destiny
**ὄλλυμι, ὀλέσω, ὤλεσα, ὄλωλα, —, ὠλέσθην:** destroy, ruin, make an end of (act.); die, perish, come to an end (mid.)
**νυμφίος, -ου, ὁ:** bridegroom; male suitor for a woman's hand in marriage
**παρθένος, -ου, ἡ:** unmarried, young woman or girl
**πινυτής, -ῆτος, ἡ:** discretion, prudence
**πρόσω:** (adv.), far off, far away from (a genitive object)

—

**1.** A funerary epigram on the (unidentified) speaker's grief for the maiden Antibia's death. The trope of the girl facing the promise of marriage to an illustrious spouse, whose hopes are taken away and replaced by death was common in Greek literature, and especially in Greek tragedy (Iphigenia in Aeschyus' *Agamemnon* and Euripides' *Iphigenia at Aulis*; the titular character of Sophocles's *Antigone*, for example).[12] In an innovative inverse of the trope, Moira ("Death") has stolen away the hopes of her many suitors. One might pay particular attention to word balances and oppositions: the relative positions (surely, ironic) of παρθένον and νυμφίοι (lines 1 and 2), for example, and ἐπὶ πολλοί/ἐπὶ πάντων in lines 1 and 3.
**1. ἇς:** = Attic ἧς: the genitive relative pronoun here is a little tricky. The preposition ἐπί takes a dative or accusative object, not a genitive.Gow and Page (1965, p. 94) suggest that tmesis may be understood (ἐπὶ… ἱέμενοι) and that genitive is dependent upon the participle, ἐφιέμενοι (i.e., "desiring whom…").

**3. κάλλευς:** Doric gen. of the neuter noun, κάλλος
**3. πινυτᾶτος:** = Doric form of the Attic πινυτῆτος; note: this is a genitive singular noun (and not a superlative adjective)
**3. κάλλευς καὶ πινυτᾶτος ἀνὰ κλέος:** The language here is quite Homeric. In the *Iliad* (13.364ff), for example, a soldier (Othryoneos) has come to Troy in the wake of the rumor of war (πολέμοιο μετὰ κλέος). Cf., *Od.* 20.70–71.
**3. ἀνὰ κλέος:** the preposition is being used somewhat idiosyncratically here to suggest motion to/toward.Gow and Page (1965, p. 94) suggest "drawn by" the fame…
**4. Μοῖρ':** = crasis for Μοῖρα
**4. οὐλομένα:** = Doric for Attic form, οὐλομένη; middle present participle

**Anyte 7 G-P (*A.P.* 7.646)**

λοίσθια δὴ τάδε πατρὶ φίλῳ περὶ χεῖρε βαλοῦσα
εἶπ' Ἐρατὼ χλωροῖς δάκρυσι λειβομένα,
ὦ πάτερ, οὔ τοι ἔτ' εἰμί, μέλας δ' ἐμὸν ὄμμα καλύπτει
ἤδη ἀποφθιμένας κυάνεος θάνατος.

*Meter: Elegiac Couplets*

—

**ἀποφθίνω, -φθίσω, -ἔφθισα, —, —, —:** perished, destroyed
**δάκρυ, τό:** (does not appear in the genitive case) tear
**καλύπτω, καλύψω, ἐκάλυψα, —, κεκάλυμμαι, ἐκαλύφθην:** cover, veil, conceal, hide
**κυάνεος, -α, -ον:** dark blue, black
**λείβω, —, ἔλειψα, —, —, —:** pour forth (act.); be running (with tears) (pass.)
**λοίσθιος, -α, -ον:** last, final, remaining
**μέλας, μέλαινα, μέλαν:** dark, murky, black
**ὄμμα, -ματος, τό:** eye
**χείρ, χειρός, ἡ:** hand
**χλωρός, -ά, -όν:** pale, pallid; fresh, blooming, sparkling, glistening

—

**1–4:** On a dying girl, Erato ("Lovely"), speaking tearful last words as she embraces her father. Perhaps as imagined or represented on a sepulchral relief sculpture.
**1. χεῖρε:** "her (two) hands"—a dual accusative (object of περιβαλοῦσα); **περὶ…βαλοῦσα:** tmesis; βαλοῦσα = Doric form of Attic βαλοῦση; Geoghegan (1979, p. 83) sees potential allusions to Aeschylus, *Agamemnon*, 1556–1559 and Euripides, *Andromache*, 115.
**2. χλωροῖς δάκρυσι:** "glistening" or "fresh" rather than pallid or pale in color (c.f., Euripides' *Medea*, 906 and 922), where both the chorus and Jason remark on Medea's weeping.

**2. λειβομένα:** = Attic λειβομένη
**4. ἀποφθιμένας:** = Attic ἀποφθιμένης ("of me already dead")

**Anyte 8 G-P (*A.P.* 7.649)**

ἀντί τοι εὐλεχέος θαλάμου σεμνῶν θ' ὑμεναίων
μάτηρ στᾶσε τάφῳ τῷδ' ἔπι μαρμαρίνῳ
παρθενικὰν μέτρον τε τεὸν καὶ κάλλος ἔχοισαν,
Θερσί, ποτιφθεγκτὰ δ' ἔπλεο καὶ φθιμένα.

*Meter: Elegiac Couplets*

—

**ἀντί:** (+ gen.) instead of, in place of
**εὐλεχής, -ές:** bringing happiness in marriage
**ἐφίστημι, -στήσω, -ἔστησα/-ἔστην, -ἕστηκα, -ἕσταμαι, -ἐστάθην:** erect, set in place, place upon
**θαλάμος, -ου, ὁ:** bedroom, bridal chamber
**κάλλος, –ους, τό:** beauty
**μαρμάρινος, -η, -ον:** marble, made of marble
**μέτρον, -ου, τό:** measure (of life)
**παρθενική, -ῆς, ἡ:** a young, unmarried woman
**πέλω (and πέλομαι), —, ἔπελον and ἐπελόμην, ἔπλε and ἐπλόμην, —, —, —:** be
**προσφθέγτός, -ή, -όν:** capable of being called by name; capable of being or able to be addressed
**σεμνός, -ή, -όν:** holy
**τάφος, -ου, ὁ:** grave, tomb, statue marking a gravesite
**τεός, -ά, -όν:** Doric for σός, your
**ὑμεναίος, -ου, ὁ:** wedding, wedding song
**φθίνω, φθίσω, ἔφθισα, —, ἔφθιμαι, ἐφθίθην:** waste, perish, die

—

**1–4:** On the image of a dead maiden represented on a sepulchral relief sculpture and placed there on the tomb by her mother, which the girl received instead of the marriage-bed she ought to have enjoyed. Another instance of Anyte's elaboration of the "marriage to death" motif, a motif particularly prevalent in Greek tragedy (of which, Rehm (1994) provides a useful exegesis).
**1. ἀντί:** governs both εὐλεχέος θαλάμου and σεμνῶν … ὑμεναίων
**2. μάτηρ:** = Doric for Attic form of μήτηρ
**3. στᾶσε … ἔπι:** tmesis (from ἐφίστημι); στᾶσε is Doric for Attic στῆσε, and the epsilon augment signifying past (aorist) tense has been omitted, as often happens in poetry; this compound verb takes a dative object.
**3. ἔχοισαν:** = Doric for Attic ἔχουσαν
**4. Θερσί:** this is the only attested instance of this name for a woman or girl.

**4. ποτιφθεγκτὰ:** = Doric for Attic προσφθεγκτὴ
**4. ἔπλεο:** = imperfect or aorist 2nd sing. indicative mid. of πέλω
**4. φθιμένα:** = Doric for Attic φθιμένη, aor. mid. participle

**Anyte 9 G-P (*A.P.* 7.208)**

Μνᾶμα τόδε φθιμένου μενεδαΐου εἵσατο Δᾶμις
ἵππου, ἐπεὶ στέρνον τοῦδε δαφοινὸς ᾽Άρης
τύψε· μέλαν δέ οἱ αἷμα ταλαυρίνου διὰ χρωτὸς
ζέσσ᾽, ἐπὶ δ᾽ ἀργαλέᾳ βῶλον ἔδευσε φονᾷ.

*Meter: Elegiac Couplets*

—

**αἷμα, -ματος, τό:** blood
**ἀργαλέος, -α, -ον:** painful, grievous
**Ἄρης, -εως, ὁ:** Ares, the god of war and the blood-lust of battle
**βῶλος, -ου, ἡ:** clod of earth, soil
**δαφοινός, -όν:** savage, cruel
**δεύω, δεύσω, ἔδευσα, —, δέδευμαι, ἐδεύθην:** wet, drench
**ζέω, ζέσω, ἔζεσα/ζέσσα, —, —, —:** boil or bubble up, seethe (of water or liquids)
**μέλας, μέλαινα, μέλαν:** black, dark, murky
**μενεδήιος, -ον:** staunch, steadfast, especially in the face of battle or danger
**μνῆμα, -ματος, τό:** a memorial or monument in honor of the dead, grave
**φθίνω, φθίσω, ἔφθισα, —, ἔφθιμαι, ἐφθίμην:** destroy (act.); perish, die, pass away (pass.)
**στέρνον, -ου, τό:** chest, breast, heart
**ταλαύρινος, -ον:** thick, tough as a bull's hide
**τύπτω, τύψώ τυπτήσω, ἔτυψα, —, τετύφθαι, ἐτύφθην:** strike down, smite
**φονή, -ῆς, ἡ:** murder, slaughter
**χρώς, χρωτός, ὁ:** skin, hide

—

**1–4:** On an epitaph memorializing a horse whose heart was pierced in battle. Damis erected the memorial to commemorate his deceased equine battle-partner's fearlessness in battle. Epigrams like this and Anyte 1 and 4 have led most scholars to conclude that Anyte's representation of men's military actions reflect fairly conventional and traditional attitudes toward war. Geoghegan (1979, p. 97) notes, "Anyte's approach is not in any way mitigated by the consideration that the epitaph is to a horse rather than a human being. Both in tone and subject matter, the epigram is comparable to 1 and 4 and, if anything, exceeds them in epic grandiloquence". This is one of several epigrams by Anyte on animals (see Barnard, 1991). See also Mnasalces, *A.P.* 7.212 for an epigram honoring a race-horse.
**1. μνᾶμα:** = Doric for μνῆμα
**1. μενεδαΐου:** = Doric for μενεδηίου

**1. εἴσατο:** = 3rd s., causal aorist of ἵζω/ἕζομαι: to set up, place, put, lay.

**2. δαφοινὸς:** Geoghegan (1979, p. 99) notes that Homer uses the word three times, each time to describe the hide of a beast of prey (*Iliad* 2.308; 10.23; 11.474), and suggests that "Anyte probably had the Homeric contexts in mind".

**3. οἱ:** dat. sing. masc. personal pronoun of the 3rd person ("his").

**4. ζέσσ':** = epic for ἔζεσα, 1st sing. aor. indic. act. of ζέω.

**4. ἐπὶ δ' ἀργαλέᾳ βῶλον ἔδευσε φονᾷ:** "and (the black blood) drenched the soil amid the grievous slaughter".

**4. φονᾷ:** = Doric for φονῇ.

**Anyte 10 G-P (Pollux 5. 48)**

ὤλεο δή ποτε καὶ σὺ πολύρριζον παρὰ θάμνον,
 Λόκρι, φιλοφθόγγων ὠκυτάτα σκυλάκων·
τοῖον ἐλαφρίζοντι τεῷ ἐγκάτθετο κώλῳ
 ἰὸν ἀμείλικτον ποικιλόδειρος ἔχις.

*Meter: Elegiac Couplets*

—

**ἀμείλικτος, -ον:** without pity, harsh, cruel
**ἐγκατατίθημι, -θήσω, -ἔθηκα, -τέθηκα, -τέθειμαι, ἐτέθην:** lay or put in
**ἐλαφρίζω:** be light and nimble
**ἔχις, -εως, ὁ:** viper, poisonous serpent
**θάμνος, -ου, ὁ, ἡ:** bush, shrub, copse of bushes or shrubs
**ἰός, -οῦ, ὁ:** venom of a serpent
**κῶλον, -ου, τό:** limb
**ὄλλυμι, ὀλέσω, ὤλεσα, ὄλωλα, —, ὠλέσθην:** destroy, ruin, make an end of (act.); die, perish, come to an end (mid.)
**ποικιλόδειρος, -ον:** with a mottled or variegated neck
**πολύρριζος, -ον:** with many roots
**σκυλάκη, -ης, ἡ:** puppy
**φιλοφθόγγος, -ον:** fond of making noise, noisy
**ὠκύς, -εῖα, -ύ:** swift

—

**1–4:** On the death of a puppy whose paw was struck by a poisonous viper. The epigram is rife with allusions to Homer, and its language is epicizing. Geoghegan (1979, p. 105) points out that there are no fewer than 24 recurrences of lugubrious, lamentation-like ω and ο sounds, amid frequent instances of assonance and alliteration.

**1. ὤλεο:** 2nd person sing., aorist ("you died"). Geoghegan (1979, p. 105–106) notes that this particular form of ὄλλυμι appears only once in Homer (*Iliad* 24.725), wherein Andromache begins her lament for Hector; and, the word sequence of ποτε καὶ σὺ is also Iliadic (11.441; 19.315).

**2. ὠκυτάτα:** = Doric for Attic ὠκυτάτη

**2. Λόκρι:** vocative; the poem addresses a Locrian puppy. Locris is both a region of northwestern Greece and the name of an ancient breed of hunting dogs cited by Xenophon in the *Cynegeticus* (10.1).
**3. τεῷ:** = Attic σοι (dat. sing. 2nd pers. pronoun): "your"
**3. ἐγκάτθετο:** 3rd sing. aorist mid. indicative with the epsilon augment syncopated.

### Anyte 11 G-P (*A.P.* 7.202)

οὐκέτι μ᾽ ὡς τὸ πάρος πυκιναῖς πτερύγεσσιν ἐρέσσων
ὄρσεις ἐξ εὐνῆς ὄρθριος ἐγρόμενος·
ἦ γάρ σ᾽ ὑπνώοντα σίνις λαθρηδὸν ἐπελθὼν
ἔκτεινεν λαιμῷ ῥίμφα καθεὶς ὄνυχα.

*Meter: Elegiac Couplets*

—

**ἐγείρω, ἐγερῶ, ἤγειρα, —, ἐγήγερμαι, ἠγέρθην:** wake, rouse
**ἐρύω [ep., ἐρύσσω], ἐρύσω, εἴρυσα [Ep. εἴρυσσα], —, —, —:** draw, pull, row
**εὐνή, -ῆς, ἡ:** bed
**λαθρηδόν:** adv., indecl., secretly, by stealth, treacherously
**λαιμός, -οῦ, ὁ:** throat, gullet
**ὄνυξ, -υχος, ὁ:** claw, talon
**ὄρθριος, -α, -ον:** at daybreak, at dawn, in the early morning
**ὄρνυμι, ὄρσω, ὦρσα, ὄρωρα, ὀρώρεγμαι ὤρεγμαι, ὠρέχθην:** (act.) urge, excite, make (a direct object) to rise up; (med.) arise, rise up
**οὐκέτι:** adv., no longer
**πττέρυξ, -υγος, ἡ:** wing
**πυκινός, -ή, -όν = (Attic) πυκνός, -ή, -όν:** close, compact, thick, dense, crowded; moving quickly back and forth
**ῥίμφα:** adv., lightly, swiftly
**σίνις, -ιδος, ὁ:** ravager, plunderer, destroyer
**ὑπνόω, ὑπνώσω, ὕπνωσα, ὕπνωκα, ὑπνωμαι, ὑπνώθην:** (act.) put to sleep, fall asleep, sleep; (pass.), be made to sleep

—

**1–4:** Another quatrain epigram offering a lament for a deceased animal, in this case, either (as per Geoghegan, 1979, p. 110–113) a cicada (which produces a stridulating sound by vibrating membranes in its thorax) or grasshopper or cricket (which produce very similar sounds by rubbing their wings together), killed by a child's fingernail. Given the plentiful associations in Greek poetry between the cicada (τέττιξ) and song and poetry as early as Hesiod (*Works and Days* 582–583), Geoghegan's argument for a stridulating insect is tempting, and is buttressed by the fact that the preceding 11 of 13 epigrams in the *Anthologia Palatina* (7.189–201) concern grasshoppers and cicadas. See also Anyte 20 G-P in this volume. Gow and Page (1965, vol. 2, p. 97) believe that the deceased animal is a rooster, killed by the claw or talon of a prowling predator (such as a fox or large cat).

**1. τὸ πάρος:** an accusative adverbial phrase, "as before" (see Smyth #1611)

**1. πτερύγεσσιν ἐρέσσων:** Aeschylus uses a similar phrase to describe vultures (*Agamemnon* 52, πτερύγων ἐρετμοῖσιν ἐρεσσόμενοι).

**2. ἐγρόμενος:** a later form of the verb ἐγείρω; this is a present tense, middle participle.

**Anyte 12 G-P (*A.P.* 7.215)**

οὐκέτι δὴ πλωτοῖσιν ἀγαλλόμενος πελάγεσσιν
  αὐχέν' ἀναρρίψω βυσσόθεν ὀρνύμενος,
οὐδὲ περὶ σκαρθμοῖσι νεὼς περικαλλέα χεῖλη
  ποιφύξω, τἀμᾷ τερπόμενος προτομᾷ,
ἀλλά με πορφυρέα ποντου νοτὶς ὦσ' ἐπὶ χέρσον
  κεῖμαι δὲ ῥαδινὰν τάνδε παρ' ἀιόνα.

*Meter: Elegiac Couplets*

—

**ἀγάλλω, ἀγαλῶ, ἤγηλα, —, —, —:** in the passive voice, take delight in or exult in a dative object
**ἀναρρίπτω, -ρίψω, -ἔρριψα, -ἔρριφα, -ἔρριμμαι, -ἐρρίφθην:** to throw up
**αὐχήν, -ένος, ὁ:** neck, throat; narrow strait or narrow passage of the sea
**βυσσόθεν:** adv., from the bottom (of the sea)
**ἠϊών, -όνος, ἡ:** shore, beach
**κεῖμαι, κείσομαι, —, —, —, —:** lie
**ὄρνυμι, ὄρσω, ὦρσα, ὄρωρα, ὀρώρεγμαι ὤρεγμαι, ὠρέχθην:** (act.) urge, excite, make (a direct object) to rise up; (med.) arise, rise up
**ναῦς, νεώς, ἡ:** ship
**νοτίς, -ίδος, ἡ:** moisture, wetness
**πέλαγος, -εος, τό:** open sea, high sea, the sea
**περικαλλής, -ές:** very beautiful
**πλωτός, -ή, -όν:** navigable
**ποιφύσσω:** a reduplicated, onomatopoetic form φυσάω, blow, snort, or puff out (with accus.); fut., ποιφύξω
**πορφύρεος, -α, -ον:** dark, dark-gleaming
**προτομή, -ῆς, ἡ:** figurehead (carved decoration found on the bow of a ship)
**ῥαδινός, -ή, -όν:** slim, narrow
**σκαρθμός, -οῦ, ὁ:** a leap, a leaping
**τέρπω, τέρψω, ἔτερψα, —, —, ἐτέρφθην:** delight, gladden; in middle and passive, to enjoy or delight oneself (with a dative of instrument)
**χεῖλος, -εος, τό:** prow of a ship; beak or bill of a bird; or, gunwales (pl.)
**χέρσος, -ου, ὁ:** dry land
**ὠθέω, ὠθήσω, ἔωσα ὦσα, ἔωκα, ἐώσθην:** force onwards, thrust, push, shove

—

**1–4:** Another of Anyte's animal epigrams, this is the only poem of hers that does not consist of a quatrain, but rather of three elegiac couplets. Funerary in tone, the epigram commemorates the death of an unnamed marine animal—perhaps a dolphin—found dead on the shore. It is imagined to be voicing its fate to a passer-by.

**1. πλωτοῖσιν ἀγαλλόμενος πελάγεσσιν:** literally, "delighting in the navigable seas", but πλωτοῖσιν might be reasonably read either as a transferred epithet ("delighting as *I* navigate the seas") or in a passive sense ("delighting in the seas being navigated" [by me]).

**3. περὶ ... περικαλλέα χεῖλη:** "around the beautiful gunwales of a ship as I leap"; Geoghegan (1979, p. 123–124) rejects σκαρθμοῖσι as a reading (as per Gow and Page, 1965, vol. 1, p. 38) and offers σκαλμοῖσι. If Geoghegan's reading is correct, the translation he offers is, "Nor shall I blow around the gunwales of the ship, lovely with their tholes". The tholes (σκαλμοῖσι) of a ship are the pinholes for the oars. The singular νεώς is poetic. Dolphins were sometimes to be found swimming about ships (Euripides, *Electra* 432–435, for example).

**4. τἀμᾷ** = (through crasis) τε + ἐμᾷ, which is Doric for ἐμῇ

**4. προτομᾷ** = Doric for προτομῇ

**4. τἀμᾷ τερπόμενος προτομᾷ:** the figurehead on the prow of the ship is the head of a dolphin.

**5. ὦσ'** = (through crasis) ὦσα, which is the epic or Doric for ἔωσα, the aorist 1st person sing., active voice indicative of ὠθέω

**6. ἀιόνα** = Doric for ἠϊόνα (= Att.); the preposition παρά + acc. can be used to suggest that past motion has come to rest upon or beside an acc. object. For a comprehensive list of prepositions and their objects in Anyte's body of poetry, see Geoghegan (1979, p. 129).

**Anyte 13 G-P (*A.P.* 6.312)**

ἡνία δή τοι παῖδες ἐπί, τράγε, φοινικόεντα
  θέντες καὶ λασίῳ φιμὰ περὶ στόματι
ἵππια παιδεύουσι θεοῦ περὶ ναὸν ἄελθα,
  ὄφρ' αὐτοὺς ἐφορῇ νήπια τερπομένους.

*Meter: Elegiac Couplets*

—

**ἆθλον, -ου, τό:** contest, game in which contestants compete for a prize
**ἐφοράω, ἐπόψομαι, -εῖδον, —, —, -ὄφθην:** look at or upon, observe, see, behold
**ἡνία, -ων, τὰ:** bridle, reins
**ἵππιος, -α, -ον:** of horses or horse-races
**λάσιος, -α, -ον:** shaggy, wooly
**ναός, νεώς, ὁ:** temple or shrine
**νήπιος, -α, -ον:** childish, foolish
**στόμα, -ματος, τό:** mouth
**τέρπω, τέρψω, ἔτερψα, —, —, ἐτέρφθην:** delight, gladden; in middle and passive, to enjoy or delight oneself (with a dative of instrument)
**τράγος, -ου, ὁ:** goat
**φιμά, -ῶν, τά:** any instrument that keeps the mouth closed, such as a bit, bridle, or muzzle
**φοινικόεις, -εσσα, -εν:** dark, dark-red, crimson

—

**1–4:** This poem may present an idyllic scene in which children play with a goat beside a temple of an unnamed deity, placing purple reins on it and pretending the goat is a race-horse. The poem may be an ekphrasis of a votive painting or relief sculpture. Parallelism in the hexameter and pentameter lines is especially strong in this epigram and worthy of notice. See Barnard (1991) for a thorough discussion of Anyte's epigrams involving animals and children.
**1. τοι** = Doric form for Attic σοι
**1–2. ἐπί … θέντες**: tmesis
**3. ἄελθα** = epic form for Attic ἆθλα
**4. ὄφρα** = epic for Attic ἵνα and introduces a purpose clause; ἐφορῇ is a present tense, active, 3rd sing. subjunctive (the implicit subject of which is θεός).
**4. νήπια** is an adverb modifying the participle τερπομένους.

**Anyte 14 G-P (*A.P.* 9.745)**

θάεο τὸν Βρομίου κεραὸν τράγον, ὡς ἀγερώχως
  ὄμμα κατὰ λασιᾶν γαῦρον ἔχει γενύων,
κυδιόων ὅτι οἱ θάμ᾽ ἐν οὔρεσιν ἀμφὶ παρῆδα
  βόστρυχον εἰς ῥοδέαν Ναΐς ἔδεκτο χέρα.

*Meter: Elegiac Couplets*

—

**ἀνέρωχος, -ον:** high-spirited, arrogant, lordly
**βόστρυχος, -ου, ὁ:** hair, curl, lock of hair
**Βρομίος, -ου, ὁ:** an epithet (and alternate name) of Bacchus, Dionysus
**γαῦρος, -ον:** haughty, exultant
**γένυς, -υος, ἡ:** jaw
**δέχομαι, δέξομαι, ἐδεξάμην, —, δέδεγμαι, ἐδέχθην:** accept, receive, take
**θαμά:** (adv.) often
**θεάομαι, θεάσομαι, ἐθεασάμην, —, τεθέαμαι, —:** gaze at, behold
**κεραός, -ά, -όν:** horned
**κυδιάω/κυδιόω:** (this verb appears in the present tense only) bear oneself proudly, exult
**λάσιος, -α, -ον:** shaggy, bushy
**Ναΐς, -ΐδος, ἡ:** a Naiad, or river nymph, spring nymph
**ὄμμα, -ματος, τό:** eye
**ὄρος, -εος, τό:** mountain
**παρηΐς, - ΐδος, ἡ:** cheek, jaw
**ῥόδεος, -α, -ον:** rosy
**τράγος, -ου, ὁ:** goat
**χείρ, χειρός, ἡ:** hand

—

**1–4:** On a painting or sculpture of the goat of Dionysus seducing a river nymph. The opening word involves the reader in the imaginary act of gazing upon the work of art. Goats were traditional symbols of Dionysus and evoked lusty behavior appropriate to the god of wine and revelry. Satyrs (half he-goat/half human followers of Dionysus) are frequently represented in Greek art erotically pursuing fleeing nymphs.
**1. θάεο:** Doric, 2nd sing. imperative of θεάομαι
**2. λασιᾶν:** genitive pl. fem. (Doric)
  **κατὰ...ἔχει:** tmesis; the implicit subject is the "horned goat": "how spiritedly he casts his haughty eye down upon his shaggy jaw"
**3. κυδιόων ὅτι:** "reveling" or "taking pride in the fact that"
  **οὔρεσιν** = epic form of Attic ὄρεσιν
  **παρῆδα** is a contracted (accusative singular) form of παρηΐδα
**3–4. ἀμφὶ παρῆδα/βόστρυχον:** i.e., a tuft of hair around the jaws (of the goat)
**4. ἔδεκτο:** 3rd sing. imperfect indicative of δέχομαι
  **χέρα** = poetic form of Attic χείρα

**Anyte 15 G-P (*A.P.* 9.144)**

Κύπριδος οὗτος ὁ χῶρος, ἐπεὶ φίλον ἔπλετο τήνᾳ
αἰὲν ἀπ' ἠπείρου λαμπρὸν ὁρῆν πέλαγος,
ὄφρα φίλον ναύτῃσι τελῇ πλόον· ἀμφὶ δὲ πόντος
δειμαίνει λιπαρὸν δερκόμενος ξόανον.

*Meter: Elegiac Couplets*

—

**δειμαίνω:** (only in present and imperfect tenses): fear
**δέρκομαι, δέρξομαι, ἔδρακον, δέδορκα, —, ἐδέρχθην:** see, see clearly (perfect tense has a present sense)
**ἤπειρος, -ου, ἡ:** land, earth, mainland
**Κύπρις, -ιδος, ἡ:** "Cyprian" is an epithet of Aphrodite that appears as early as Homer
**λαμπρός, -ά, -όν:** bright, brilliant, clear
**λιπαρός, -ά, -όν:** bright, brilliant; oily smoothness; shiny
**ναύτης, -ου, ὁ:** sailor
**ξόανον, -ου, τό:** wooden statue, image of a god
**ὁράω, ὄψομαι, εἶδον, ἑώρακα, ἑώραμαι, ὤφθην:** see, look at, gaze upon
**πέλαγος, -εος, τό:** sea
**πέλω (and πέλομαι), —, ἔπελον and ἐπελόμην, ἔπλε and ἐπλόμην, —, —, —:** be
**πλόος, πλοῦς, ὁ:** sailing, marine voyage
**πόντος, -ου, ὁ:** sea
**τελέω, τελῶ, ἐτέλεσα, τετέλεκα, τετέλεσμαι, ἐτελέσθην:** accomplish, complete, fulfill, bring to an end
**χῶρος, -ου, ὁ:** land, country

—

**1–4:** On a wooden statue of Aphrodite facing the sea from the position of her sanctuary. The epigram imagines the beautiful ocean view from the perspective of the statue, subtly evoking Aphrodite's cosmogonic origins. The Hellenistic epigrammatist Antipater likely used this poem as a model for his own *A.P.* 9.143.

**1. Κύπριδος:** Hesiod (*Theogony* 173–205) provides a birth narrative of Aphrodite: Cronos overthrows his father Ouranos by castrating him with a sickle; while the blood falls to the earth and generates the Erinyes (a.k.a., Furies) and the Giants, the castrated genitals of the male sky god fall into the sea and mix with sea foam, amid which formed the goddess Aphrodite. Hesiod recounts that she first drew near the island of Cythera (from which she received the epithet, Cytherian), but then drifted to sea-girt Cyprus, where she set her feet upon the ground in anthropomorphic form and underneath her lovely feet grass grew. Because she was born on Cyprus, Hesiod notes, she is called "Cyprogenes". Among gods and humans she was given the province of smiles, deception, love, grace, and the whisperings of maidens.

**1. ἔπλετο** = imperfect/aorist indicative, 3rd sing. of πέλω

**1. τῆνᾳ** = Doric form for Attic ἐκείνῃ

**1. φίλον ἔπλετο τήνᾳ:** "it is dear to her"

**2. ὁρῆν** = ὁράειν

**3. ὄφρα** = epic form for Attic ἵνα; ὄφρα…τελῇ is a purpose clause; ὄφρα probably also governs the subjunctive δειμαίνῃι.

**Anyte G-P 16 (*A.P.* 9.313)**

῞Ιζε' ἅπας ὑπὸ καλὰ δάφνας εὐθαλέα φύλλα
ὡραίου τ' ἄρυσαι νάματος ἁδὺ πόμα
ὄφρα τοι ἀσθμαίνοντα πόνοις θέρεος φίλα γυῖα
ἀμπαύσῃς πνοιᾷ τυπτόμενα Ζεφύρου.

*Meter: Elegiac Couplets*

—

**ἀναπαύω, -παύσω, -ἔπαυσα, -πέπαυκα, -πέπαυμαι, -ἐπαύθην:** let rest, take a rest
**ἅπας, ἅπασα, ἅπαν:** all, the whole, the entire, all together (in pl.)
**ἀρύω, —, ἤρυσα, —, —, ἠρύσθην:** draw water
**ἀσθμαίνω:** breathe hard, pant (only appears in the present tense)
**γυῖον, -ου, τό:** limb
**δάφνη, -ης, ἡ:** bay or laurel tree
**εὐθαλής, -ές:** blooming, flourishing, thriving
**ἡδύς, -εῖα, -ύ:** sweet, pleasant
**θέρος, -εος, τό:** summer, summer heat
**ἵζω, εἵσομαι, εἷσα/ἵζησα, ἵζηκα, —, —:** (act.) cause to sit; place; set; seat; (med.) set up and dedicate (in honor of the gods)
**νᾶμα, -ματος, τό:** river, stream, spring, anything that flows
**πνοιή, -ῆς, ἡ:** (poetic form of πνοή, -ῆς): wind, breeze
**πόνος, -ου, ὁ:** labor, toil, physical exertion, trouble, distress
**πῶμα, -ματος, τό:** drink, draught
**τύπτω, τύψω, ἔτυψα, τέτυφα, τέτυμμαι, ἐτύφθην:** beat, strike, smite
**φύλλον, -ου, τό:** leaf, foliage (in pl.)
**ὡραῖος, -α, -ον:** seasonable

—

**1–4:** A bucolic epigram calling upon the passerby to rest from labor in an idyllic summer landscape. The speaker is unidentified, which has the effect of giving voice to the bucolic setting itself charmingly idealized in the poem. Perhaps the epigram is intended to evoke an inscription for a fountain or spring. See also Anyte 3, 17, and 18 G-P for springs or fountains set in idyllic landscapes. There is a strong repetition of "alpha" sounds in the poem, perhaps evocative of relaxing sighs ("ahhhh....").

**1. Ἵζε':** the middle voice, imperative ἵζευ, by which Anyte may be echoing Homer, *Iliad* 3.162, wherein Priam addresses Helen, inviting her to sit beside him so that they may gaze together upon her former countrymen arrayed on the battlefield.Geoghegan (1979, p. 151–152).

**1. δάφνας:** = Doric form for Attic δάφνης; the first alpha is metrically short.

**2. ἁδὺ:** = Doric form for Attic ἡδὺ

**2. πόμα:** = Doric form for Attic πῶμα

**2. ἄρυσαι:** aorist, 2nd, sing. active imperative

**3. ὄφρα** = Homeric for Attic ἵνα; introduces a purpose clause with the (aorist tense) subjunctive ἀμπαύσῃς (Ionic form = Attic ἀναπαύσῃς)

**4. πνοιᾷ τυπτόμενα Ζεφύρου:** πνοιᾷ = poetic and Doric form for Attic πνοῇ. The phrase is reminiscent of Homer's ἅμα πνοιῇ Ζεφύροιο (*Iliad* 19.415). Zephyrus is the west or westerly wind.

### Anyte 17 G-P (*A.P.* 9.314)

Ἑρμᾶς τᾷδ' ἕστακα παρ' ὄρχατον ἀνεμόεντα
  ἐν τριόδοις πολιᾶς ἐγγύθεν αἰόνος
ἀνδράσι κεκμηῶσιν ἔχων ἄμπαυσιν ὁδοῖο,
  ψυχρὸν δ' †ἀχραὲς κράνα ὑποιάχει†.

*Meter: Elegiac Couplets*

—

**ἀνάπαυσις, -εως, ἡ:** rest, repose (from a thing in the genitive)
**ἀχραής, -ές:** pure
**ἐγγύθεν:** nearby; an adverb that is frequently complemented by a genitive noun indicating what something is close to
**Ἑρμῆς, -οῦ, ὁ:** a Herm statue; the god Hermes
**ἠιών, -όνος, ἡ:** beach, shore
**ἠνεμόεις, -εσσα, -εν:** windy, stirred or waved by the wind
**ἵστημι, στήσω, ἔστησα/ἔστην, ἕστηκα, ἕσταμαι, ἐστάθην:** erect, set in place, place upon, make stand (transitive); stand (intransitive)
**κάμνω, καμοῦμαι, ἔκαμον, κέκμηκα, —, —:** toil, labor, be weary or sick
**κρήνη, -ης, ἡ:** well, fountain, spring, source of water
**ὄρχατος, -ου, ὁ:** orchard, row of trees
**τρίοδος, -ου, ἡ:** a meeting of three roads
**ὑποϊάχω:** (this verb only appears in the present tense): resound, echo, sound forth a little or in answer

—

**1–4:** An inscription for a fountain or spring beside which is a statue of Hermes or a Herm. The bucolic scene, with its breeze, orchards, and resounding trickle of flowing water provide respite for the weary traveler and the toils of mid-day.

**1. Ἑρμᾶς:** = Doric for Attic Ἑρμῆς. This may refer to a statue of Hermes or, more likely, a Herm. Hermes was, of course, the god of travelers, boundaries, and comings and goings. Herms were widely used to mark boundaries and stood in the entrances to private homes and temples and alongside roadways. The typical herm statue seems quite curious to modern eyes, since it boasts a male head (usually bearded), which stands poised upon a rectangular shaft for a body carved into which are erect, male genitalia.

**1. τᾷδ':** = Doric for Attic τῇδε ("here, in this place")

**1. ἀνεμόεντα:** = Doric for Attic ἠνεμόεντα

**2. ἀιόνος:** = Doric for Attic ἠιόνος

**3. κεκμηῶσιν:** Dative pl., perfect tense participle of κάμνω

**3. ἔχων:** here, this participle probably means something like "having charge of" or "being in charge of". ἀνδράσι κεκμηῶσιν ἔχων ἄμπαυσιν ὁδοῖο thus means something like, "being in charge of rest for weary way-travelers".

**3. ἄμπαυσιν:** = Doric for Attic ἀνάπαυσιν

**4.** This line is difficult to make out and the text is uncertain.Gow and Page (1965, p. 100) suggest that there may be an ellipsis of the word ὕδωρ ("water") governing the adjectives ψυχρὸν and ἀχραὲς ("pure, cold water"). The whole line may read something like, "and the spring makes the pure, cold water echo". Alternatively,Gow and Page (1965, p. 100) suggest that the verb ὑποιάχει may be a corruption of some kind of compounded form of χέω ("pour"), in which case, the line would read something like "and the spring pours forth pure, cold water". For a thorough discussion of the textual difficulties and history of proposed emendations, see Geoghegan (1979, p. 157–158).

**4. κράνα:** = Doric for Attic κρήνη

### Anyte 18 G-P (*A. Pl.* 228)

Ξεῖν', ὑπὸ τὰν πέτραν τετρυμένα γυῖ' ἀνάπαυσον—
   ἁδύ τοι ἐν χλωροῖς πνεῦμα θροεῖ πετάλοις –
πίδακά τ' ἐκ παγᾶς ψυχρὸν πίε, δὴ γὰρ ὁδίταις
   ἄμπαυμ' ἐν θερμῷ καύματι τοῦτο φίλον.

*Meter: Elegiac Couplets*

—

**ἀνάπαυμα, -ματος, τό:** respite, repose, rest

**ἀναπαύω, -παύσω, -ἔπαυσα, -πέπαυκα, -πέπαυμαι, -ἐπαύθην:** let rest, take a rest

**γυῖον, -ου, τό:** limb

**ἡδύς, -υῖα, -ύ:** sweet, pleasant

**θερμός, -ή, -όν:** hot
**θροέω, —, ἐθρόησα, —, —, —:** utter, speak, murmur
**καῦμα, -ματος, τό:** burning heat of the sun
**ὁδίτης, -ου, ὁ:** wayfarer, traveller
**πέταλον, -ου, τό:** leaf
**πέτρα, -ας, ἡ:** rock
**πηγή, -ῆς, ἡ:** running water, stream, spring, fountain
**πῖδαξ, -ακος, ἡ:** spring, fountain
**πίνω, πιοῦμαι, ἔπιον, πέπωκα, πέπομαι, ἐπόθην:** drink, sip
**πνεῦμα, -ματος, τό:** breeze, wind
**τρύω, τρύσω, —, —, τέτρυμαι, —:** (usually found in the perfect passive) wear out, distress (act.); worn out, distressed (pass.)
**χλωρός, -ά, -όν:** green, pale green, yellowish green
**ψυχρός, -ά, -όν:** cold, cool

—

**1–4:** An inscription upon a spring or fountain addressed to a passerby, inviting them to pause and enjoy the cool breeze and the drink the cold and refreshing water. The vocative Ξεῖν' which opens the poem is frequently used in funerary epigrams to call attention to the life of a deceased person commemorated by a tombstone epitaph. See Nossis 11 (G-P) in this volume as a good example. It is worth noting that the hexameter lines are exactly metrically parallel, while first half of the final pentameter is heavily spondaic, perhaps to give lengthened pause to the relief evoked in it. There is also a strong repetition of "π" sounds in the poem.

**1. τὰν:** = Doric for Attic τὴν
**ἀνάπαυσον:** 2nd pers., sing., act., aorist imperative
**2. ἁδύ:** = Doric for Attic ἡδύ
**3. παγᾶς:** = Doric for Attic πηγῆς
**πίε:** imperative of πίνω
**4.** The antecedent of τοῦτο is the action (from line 3) of drinking cool water.

**Anyte 19 G-P (*A. Pl.* 231)**

—Τίπτε κατ' οἰόβατον, Πὰν ἀγρότα, δάσκιον ὕλαν
ἥμενος ἁδυβόᾳ τῷδε κρέκεις δόνακι
—'Όφρα μοι ἑρσήεντα κατ' οὔρεα ταῦτα νέμοιντο
πόρτιες ἠυκόμων δρεπτόμεναι σταχύων.

*Meter: Elegiac Couplets*

—

**ἀγρότης, -ου, ὁ:** rustic country-dweller
**δάσκιος, -ον:** thickly shaded, bushy
**δόναξ, -ακος, ὁ:** reed-stalk, anything made of reeds (such as a pan-pipe)
**δρέπτω:** (usually appears in the middle voice of the present and imperfect tenses): pluck, crop (a genitive object)
**ἑρσήεις, -εσσα, -εν:** dewy, fresh
**εὔκομος, -ον:** lovely-haired; with good foliage
**ἡδυβόης, -ες** (Doric, ἁδυβόας): sweet-sounding
**ἧμαι:** (appears only in the present and imperfect tenses) sit, be seated
**κρέκω, —, ἔκρεξα, —, —, —:** play an instrument (which, in this instance, appears in the dative case)
**νέμω, νεμῶ, ἔνειμα, νενέμηκα, νενέμημαι, ἐνεμήθην:** graze, feed on pasture; deal out, distribute
**οἰόβατος, -ον:** lonesome
**ὄρος, -εος, τό:** mountain, hill
**Πάν, Πανός, ὁ:** Pan
**πόρτις, -ιος, ἡ:** calf, young heifer
**στάχυς, -υος, ὁ:** ear of corn, grain, meadow grasses
**ὕλη, -ης, ἡ:** forest, woodland

—

**1–4:** This epigram evokes two voices in dialogue: the first voice (lines 1–2) is an anonymous figure (perhaps an imagined traveler) addressing a statue of Pan playing a reed-pipe in a woodland setting; the second (lines 2–3) voice iterates Pan's response.

**1. Τίπτε:** the epicizing and syncopated form of τί ποτε

**1. ὕλαν:** = Doric form of Attic ὕλην

**1. Πὰν:** a deity associated with the mountain wilderness, rustic countryside, shepherds, and flocks. He possesses the legs, hindquarters, and horns of a goat and is often found in the company of nymphs. He is associated with the mountainous region of Arcadia and with the rustic music produced by a so-called "pan-pipe" or "syrinx", a wind-pipe made of reeds. Ovid (*Metamorphoses* 1. 689ff.) narrates the story of Syrinx, a follower of Artemis who, while praying for escape from the sexual predations of Pan, was transformed into river-reeds. Pan fashioned his iconic instrument from them.

**1. δάσκιον:** this two-termination adjective modifies ὕλαν

**2. ἥμενος:** nom. sing. masc. present tense participle of ἧμαι
**2. ἁδυβόᾳ:** Doric, dat., sing., masc. form of Attic ἡδυβόης
**3. ὄφρα...νέμοιντο:** a purpose clause introduced by ὄφρα, the Doric and epicizing equivalent of ἵνα. We might have expected the verb to be subjunctive rather than optative. Gow and Page (1965, p. 101) note, "the opt., if correct, must be explained on the supposition that the first couplet means in effect 'why was your statue put up here?'"
**3. οὔρεα:** poetic nom. and acc. pl. form of ὄρος
**4. πόρτιες:** nom. pl. (πόρτις is a 3rd declension noun)
**4. ἠυκόμων:** is an epicizing form of εὔκομος (from ἠΰκομος, -ον).

### Anyte (or Leonidas) 20 G-P (*A. P.* 7.190)[13]

'Ακρίδι τᾷ κατ' ἄρουραν ἀηδόνι, καὶ δρυοκοίτᾳ
  τέττιγι ξυνὸν τύμβον ἔτευξε Μυρὼ
παρθένιον στάξασα κόρα δάκρυ, δισσὰ γὰρ αὐτᾶς
  παίγνι' ὁ δυσπειθὴς ᾤχετ' ἔχων 'Αΐδας.

*Meter: Elegiac Couplets*

—

**Ἅιδης, -ου, ὁ:** Hades, the netherworld to which the spirits of the departed go; also, Hades, the deity who lives in and rules over the netherworld.
**ἀκρίς, -ίδος, ἡ:** grasshopper
**ἄρουρα, -ας, ἡ:** earth, ground, land
**ἀηδών, -όνος, ἡ:** songstress, nightingale (used as a metaphor here)
**δάκρυ, τό:** (this noun does not appear in the gen. case) tear
**διττός, -ή, -όν:** double; two-fold; both
**δρυοκοίτης, -ου, ὁ, ἡ:** dwelling in or on oak trees or trees generally
**δυσπειθής, -ές:** hard to persuade, unyielding, implacable
**κόρη, -ης, ἡ:** unmarried girl; daughter
**ξυνός, -ή, -όν:** common; public
**ὀχέω, ὀχήσω, ὤκχησα, —, —, —** (usually appears in the present and imperfect tenses): carry, bear, carry away
**παίγνιον, -ου, τό:** play thing, pet; sport, game
**παρθένιος, -α, -ον:** belonging to an unmarried girl, maidenly
**στάζω, στάξω, ἔσταξα, —, —, ἐστάχθην:** let (an accusative object) drop or fall; shed drop by drop
**τέττιξ, -ιγος, ὁ:** a cicada, known for its chirping "songs"
**τεύχω, τεύξω, ἔτευξα, τέτευχα, τέτυγμαι, ἐτύχθην:** make, prepare
**τύμβος, -ου, ὁ:** tomb, grave, sepulchral mound

—

**1–4:** A playful, mock-tragic funerary epigram for a grasshopper and cicada, given a common tomb by a young girl named Myro. The grasshopper is called the "nightingale", evoking the association in Greek tragedy between the nightingale and the lament song. The lost tragedy *Tereus* by Sophocles, for example, features two sisters, one of whom (Procne) is changed into a nightingale after she avenges her sister Philomela's rape and glossectomy by her husband Tereus by killing their son, Itys. Procne *qua* nightingale perpetually mourns her dead child. See also Anyte 11 for a possible funerary epigram on an unidentified stridulating insect.

**1. τᾷ:** = Doric form for Attic τῇ (adverb, "here, in this place")

**1. δρυοκοίτᾳ:** Hesiod (*Works and Days* 529) calls the cicada a ὑληκοῖτα ("forest-dweller"), and Anyte may have this reference in mind.

**2. ξυνὸν...δισσά:** the (singular) grave that the girl Myro made for both the grasshopper and the cicada is "common" to both of them, since they were "both" her play-things or pets.

**3. κόρα:** = Doric form for Attic κόρη

**3. δισσά:** = Doric form for Attic διττά

**3. αὐτᾶς:** = Doric form for Attic αὐτῆς

**4. Ἀΐδας:** = Doric form for Attic Ἅιδης; the alpha and iota are pronounced separately as two short syllables (Ᾰ-ῐ-δᾱς) to complete the second half of the pentameter.

**Anyte (or Antipater of Sidon) 21 G-P (*A. P.* 7.232)**[14]

Λύδιον οὖδας ἔχει τόδ' Ἀμύντορα, παῖδα Φιλίππου,
πολλὰ σιδηρείης χερσὶ θιγόντα μάχης,
οὐδέ μιν ἀλγινόεσσα νόσος δόμον ἄγαγε νυκτός
ἀλλ' ὄλετ' ἀμφ' ἑτάρῳ σχὼν κυκλόεσσαν ἴτυν.

*Meter: Elegiac Couplets*

—

**ἀλγινόεις, -εσσα, -εν:** painful, grievous
**θιγγάνω, τεθίξομαι, ἔθιγον, —, —, ἐθίχθην:** reach; win; touch upon; touch, take hold of; engage in
**ἴτυς, -υος, ἡ:** shield; outer rim of a shield
**κυκλόεις, -εσσα, -εν:** circular
**νόσος, -ου, ἡ:** disease; sickness
**νύξ, νυκτός, ἡ:** night; darkness; metaphor of death
**οὖδας, οὔδεος, τό:** ground, earth
**σιδήρεος, -α, -ον:** made of iron; hard as iron

—

**1–4:** A funerary epigram in honor of Amyntor, the son of Philippus, who died defending his native Lydia and protecting his comrade in arms with his shield in battle. The epigram features strong traditional correlations between honor and death in battle.

**2. σιδηρείης** = Ep. for σιδηρέας

**2. θιγόντα:** "having engaged in", as per Gow and Page, 1965, vol. 2, p. 102.

**3. δόμον ... νυκτός:** i.e., Hades
**4. σχὼν:** 2nd aor. part. of ἔχω

**Anyte 1 G-P (*A.P.* 6.123)**

Stand there, murderous spear, and stop dripping
the blood of enemies around your bronze talon.
But, resting in the high marble house of Athena,
proclaim the bravery of the Cretan son of Echecratos.

**Anyte 2 G-P (*A.P.* 6.153)**

The cauldron is big enough to hold an ox. Cleubotos the son of Eriaspis,
who lives in spacious Tegea dedicated it
as a gift to Athena. Aristotle of Cleitor made it-
he has the same name as his father.

**Anyte 3 G-P (*A. Pl.* 291)**

For wooly-haired Pan and the Nymphs of the grottoes,
Theudotos, the shepherd, placed beneath the hilltop this dedicatory offering,
since they stopped to give him honey-sweet water with their own hands
while he was laboring away under the parching sun.

**Anyte 4 G-P (*A.P.* 7.724)**

The youth buried you here, captain. When you died, Pheidias, you put them in
dark mourning, just as orphaned children for their mother.
But the tombstone above you sings in verse
that you died fighting for your beloved fatherland.

**Anyte 5 G-P (*A.P.* 7.486)**

Many times has Cleina wept in grief at this tomb of her daughter,
her dear child who died too young,
calling out again and again for Philaenis's soul, who journeyed beyond the pale stream
of the river Acheron before her wedding day.

**Anyte 6 G-P (*A.P.* 7.490)**

I mourn the loss of the young woman Antibia, whose many
suitors came to her father's house wanting to marry her,
lured there by the fame of her beauty and prudence. But,
destructive Fate wheeled far away the hopes of all of them.

**Anyte 7 G-P (*A.P.* 7.646)**

Throwing her hands around her beloved father,
Erato spoke these last words, wet with glistening tears,
"Father, I am no longer your own, but murky, black death
covers my eyes and I have already perished..."

**Anyte 8 G-P (*A.P.* 7.649)**

In place of a blissful marriage bed and sacred wedding hymns
your mother set upon your tombstone a marble statue,
the image of a young woman, possessing your likeness in age and beauty,
Thersis. And, so, you are able to be spoken to even though you are dead.

**Anyte 9 G-P (*A.P.* 7.208)**

Damis set this monument as a memorial for his horse, fearless in battle,
since cruel Ares pierced him in the heart.
Dark blood bubbled up through his leathery
hide and drenched the earth amid the devastating slaughter.

**Anyte 10 G-P (Pollux 5. 48)**

You, too, perished once upon a time beside the tangle-rooted thicket,
Locrian hunter, the swiftest of yipping puppies.
How cruel was the venom the speckle-necked viper
injected into your agile paw.

**Anyte 11 G-P (*A.P.* 7.202)**

No longer, as before, will you rouse me from bed at the break of dawn,
rowing the air with your fast-moving wings;
for, a predator stealthily came upon you as you were sleeping
and slaughtered you, nimbly sinking his nail into your throat.

**Anyte 12 G-P (*A.P.* 7.215)**

No longer will I feel joy navigating the ocean,
nor will I launch my neck out of the water as I emerge from the depths,
nor will I blow around the gunwales of a ship, beautiful with their tholes,[15]
delighting that its figurehead is made in my image;
but, the dark-gleaming water of the sea thrust me onto dry land,
and I lie upon this narrow strand of beach.

**Anyte 13 G-P (*A.P.* 6.312)**

Children, having placed a crimson bridle as a muzzle
upon your shaggy mouth, O goat,
pretend that they are racing horses around the temple of the god
so that he may look upon them delighting in childhood games.

**Anyte 14 G-P (*A.P.* 9.745)**

Regard the horned goat of Bacchus, how spirited
his eyes as he gazes down at his shaggy beard,
reveling in the fact that often in the mountains a river nymph takes
a lock of his hair into her rosy hand.

**Anyte 15 G-P (*A.P.* 9.144)**

This is the land of the Cyprian goddess, since she loves
ever to gaze upon the bright sea from dry land
so that she may bring to port the mariners who love sailing;
the surrounding sea, gazing upon her smooth wooden statue, fears her.

**Anyte 16 G-P (*A.P.* 9.313)**

Sit right down under the beautiful laurel tree whose leaves are in full bloom
and drink in a sweet sip of the summer spring
to let your dear body rest, exhausted as it is by the exertions of heat
and pummeled by the westerly wind of Zephyrus.

**Anyte 17 G-P (*A.P.* 9.314)**

I, a Herm, have been erected here beside an orchard billowed by the wind
at a crossing of three roads near the grey sea's beach.
I serve as a respite for weary travelers of the road
and a spring pours forth cool, pure water.[16]

**Anyte 18 G-P (*A.Pl.* 228)**

Stranger, rest your wearied body under this rock—
a breeze murmurs sweetly among the green leaves –
and drink cool water from the fountain, for this is welcome respite
from the blazing hot sun for travelers on the road.

**Anyte 19 G-P (*A.Pl.* 231)**

"Why ever, rustic Pan, seated within this lonely, shaded woodland
do you play upon your sweet-sounding reed pipe?"

"So that my heifer calves may graze along these dewy hillsides,
cropping the long-haired meadow-grasses."

### Anyte or Leonidas 20 G-P (*A. P.* 7.190)[17]

For a melodious grasshopper and a tree-dwelling
cicada, Myro here made a common tomb beneath the earth
as she shed the tears of a young girl. For, implacable Hades carried away both
of her pets, taking them for himself.

### Anyte or Antipater of Sidon 21 G-P (*A. P.* 7.232)[18]

The Lydian earth holds this man, Amyntor, the son of Philippus,
who engaged in hard battle many times with his hands,
nor did painful disease lead him to the home of death,
but he died defending his companion with his circular shield.

## Notes

1. Snyder (1989, p. 67) and Vara and Weatherby (1992, esp. p. 341–343), for example, on the influence of Anyte on Theocritus and bucolic poetry in general, while Gutzwiller (1993, p. 72) carefully discusses the history of scholarship demonstrating Mnasalces's imitation of Anyte.
2. Pausanias, *Description of Greece* 10.38.7.
3. A point made by Snyder (1989, p. 66).
4. Of dubious attribution to Anyte are G-P 22 (*A.P.* 7.236), G-P 23 (*A.P.* 7.492), and G-P 24 (*A.P.* 7.538). See Gow and Page (1965, vol. 2, p. 101–104) for discussions of each poem's problems of authorship.
5. Pollux, *Onomasticon,* 5.48. The Greek Anthology (*AP* 7.492) does mention that she is from Mytilene on Lesbos, but there is general consensus that this is an artificial attribution consciously intended to link her to Sappho.
6. Pausanias, *Description of Greece* 10.38.13. See Snyder (1989), p. 66, 67–68, and 97–98for further discussion.
7. He claims that the author was either a poet of Miletus (as most people think) or (as he thinks) Carcinus of Naupactus. Based on the very few fragments of this poem that do survive, it has been established that its contents involved a catalog of women *qua* Hesiod's *Ehoiai,* and included several narrative digressions on various sagas, including the story of the Argonauts. Elsewhere in his *Description of Greece* (2.3.9) Pausanias claims that in the epic *Naupactia* it is written that Jason migrated to Corcyra from Iolchus after Pelias' death, and that his eldest son Mermerus was killed by a lioness while hunting in Epirus. For a discussion of the *Naupactia* as a localized epic, see Lulli (2014).
8. Some examples include Theognis, *IEG* 19–26, Nicander, *Theriaca,* 957–958, Vergil, *Georgics,* 4.563–6, Horace, *Odes* 3.30, Propertius 1.22, and Ovid, *Amores* 1.15. For summary discussions of the *sphragis* motif, first appearing in the poetry of Theognis, see Pratt (1995).
9. A point made by Rutherford (2009) in his survey of female poets who were said to have been itinerant. For a review of seminal studies of Homer as an itinerant, blind bard see Beecroft (2011).

10. Greene (2005) offers a useful analysis of the Homeric vocabulary and language used by Anyte. While most of her discussion centers on Anyte's more domestic themes, she notes (p. 140) that Anyte "transforms traditional epigram through her application of the heroic language of Homeric verse..."
11. Gow and Page (1965, vol. 1, p. 36) have ἐπιπάντων, while Geoghegan (1979, p. 73 and 78) offers ἐπὶ πάντων. The text is otherwise Gow and Page, but Geoghegan's discussion of the common use of anaphora in prepositions (lines 1 and 3, ἐπὶ, also in poems 12, 3, 13, 17, and 18-G-P) is persuasive, and the balance with ἐπὶ πολλοί in line 1 too graceful to be anything else, in our view.
12. For a useful examination of the "Marriage to Death" motif in Greek tragedy, see Rehm (1994).
13. The epigram is ascribed to both Anyte and Leonidas of Tarentum (another epigrammatist). However, Gow and Page (1965, vol. 2, p. 101) argue, largely on the basis of poetic style, that the attribution to Leonidas is an error. Geoghegan (1979, p. 171) states strongly, "despite the double ascription ... there can be no doubt of Anyte's authorship." See *A.P.* 7.364 for an imitation of this epigram by Marcus Argentius.
14. Planudes ascribes the epigram to Antipater of Sidon, while the scribe J attributes it to Anyte. Most scholars (Gow and Page, 1965, vol. 2, p. 102 and Argentieri, 2003, p. 201–202) are in agreement that the author is likely Anyte.
15. Tholes are the pinholes for the oars on a ship; the gunwale is the upper edge or side of a boat.
16. The text of this line is uncertain.
17. While this epigram has been ascribed to both Anyte and Leonidas, Gow and Page (1965, vol. 2, p. 101) believe that the attribution to Leonidas is an error.
18. Gow and Page (1965, vol. 2, p. 102) make a convincing argument that this quatrain belongs to Anyte rather than Antipater of Sidon.

# 7 Praxilla

Praxilla was a lyric poet whose fame as a versatile composer of *skolia* (sympotic drinking songs), dithyrambs (choral songs associated with festivals in honor of the god Dionysus), and other hymns appears to have been substantial in her day. Yet, we know lamentably little about Praxilla's poetry and even less about Praxilla the person. No papyri have come to light bearing Praxilla's poetry, as they have in the cases of Sappho, Corinna, and Erinna. Unlike the epigrams of Anyte, Nossis, Moero, and Erinna, Praxilla's works were not preserved through the millenia in anthologies like the *Anthologia Palatina*. Nor was the name Praxilla employed as a sobriquet for a *puella* of Latin elegy, as in the case of Ovid's Corinna. What little we do have comes in the form of passing quotations handed down to us by ancient authors who either quoted her work directly or made indirect claims about Praxilla's mythographic content. Eight fragments in total exist, and only five of them are direct quotations attributed to Praxilla. The other three (*PMG* 751, 752, and 753) are indirect claims: (a) Praxilla claims that Aphrodite rather than Semele was the mother of Dionysus; (b) Praxilla of Sicyon says that Chrysippus was carried away by Zeus, not Laius;[1] and (c) Praxilla wrote that a festival called the Carneius celebrated in Sparta and other Peloponnesian cities was named after Carneius, a son of Zeus and Europa who was raised by Apollo and Leto.[2]

Of the direct quotations that are quoted by other ancient authors, one appears to originate from a Hymn to Adonis; one is from a Dithyramb; one may be from a wedding song or *skolion*; and, the remaining two are *skolia*. Two of these direct attributions to Praxilla have recently come under scrutiny (Cazzato, 2016), potentially dwindling down from five to three our holdings of snippets of poems that are securely in Praxilla's own words. Also contested are inferences that a 5th-century Boeotian vase with sympotic scenes currently held in the British Museum in London contains four words of one of her poems etched into the tondo (fr. 3 = *PMG* 749). Cazzato's study, furthermore, casts some doubt on the supposition (Page, 1962, p. 388; Plant, 2004, p. 38) that the 5th-century Athenian comic playwright Aristophanes parodied her works in both the *Wasps* (line 1238) and

DOI: 10.4324/9781003031727-9

the *Thesmophoriazusae* (line 528).[3] If Cazzato is correct, the evidence traditionally marshalled in support of the idea that an Athenian audience in 5th-century Athens would have known and recognized her poetry may not, unfortunately, be heavily relied upon.[4]

That she was popular, however, is attested by several converging sources. Athenaeus, a 2nd-century, CE writer of anecdotes who frequently quotes literary excerpts, states that Praxilla of Sicyon was admired for the *skolia* she composed.[5] He then launches into an excursus on the three types of songs that were sung by symposiasts at drinking parties, distinguishing between *skolia* (the third type) and other types of verse. He notes that everyone in the party sang together the first type; the second, everyone sang not as a group, but in rotation, one symposiast after another; the third, however, came after all the others, and only those regarded as the most intelligent or witty would sing them, regardless of where each of the singers was seated in relation to the other symposiasts. *Skolia*, he notes, are in this last group, and they were called "crooked songs" (*skolia* means "crooked" in Greek) because of the disordered progression of singers.[6] He then provides a catalogue of 25 such *skolia*, which range in content from brief hymns to various deities (*PMG* 884, 885, 886, and 887, for example) to gnomic sentiments (such as *PMG* 889 and 890) to mythological subjects (*PMG* 898 and 899) to invitations to drink wine (*PMG* 902). One of the *skolia* he cites without directly naming its presumed composer echoes *verbatim* Praxilla 4 (= *PMG* 749), which a scholiast of Aristophanes' comedy, *The Wasps*, attributes to Praxilla directly while commenting on a comic scene containing a parody of a *skolia* competition between two characters, Bdelycleon and his father, Philocleon.

The association of drinking songs with Praxilla has led to some modern scholars to conclude that Praxilla must have been a *hetaera* on the assumption that respectable 5th-century women of Greece did not have anything to do with symposia, and that the only women who attended them were prostitutes, flute-playing sex-workers called *aulides*, and *hetaerae*. As Snyder has discussed in some depth (1989, p. 56 and note 35), Wilamowitz argued on the basis of no other evidence that Praxilla must have been a *hetaera*. Two verses preserved by Hephaestion about a girl seen from a window (Praxilla 3 = *PMG* 749) and composed in the *praxilleion* meter, a meter reputed to have been Praxilla's invention, have subsequently been treated as evidence in this controversy. Also invoked as evidence in the debate is a Boeotian vase (c. 450 BCE) containing a series of sympotic scenes and an inscription of four words that correspond to the first four words of that poem. Halporn (1983, p. 500), for example, views the inscription as supporting evidence for reading the Praxilla fragment through the lens of prostitution, interpreting the gaze referenced in the first line of the fragment as "the sweet glance which makes the prostitute of Praxilla appear virginal in her *kephalē* ["head"] despite what the poet knows of the condition of the lower part of her body."

More recent scholarship, however, has generally rejected such interpretation. Certainly, no ancient author has attested that Praxilla was believed to have been a *hetaera*. Synder (1989, p. 56) simply notes that there is no evidence to support such a claim. Other scholars have benefitted from a plethora of more recent studies elucidating the complicated relationships between oral and literary culture. Plant (2004, p. 38), for example, suggests that Praxilla may have been a professional musician, composing original *skolia* on commission, and perhaps performing them herself. Cazzato's (2016) argument involves several layers. She argues: that Praxilla 3 should be read as a wedding song, not as a *skolion*; that the inscription on the Boeotian vase ought to be interpreted on its own terms as evidence for sympotic culture rather than as a direct quotation of a *skolion* authored by Praxilla; that ancient attributions of Praxilla with the writing of *skolia* were probably wrong, and that she appears to have composed songs appropriate to performance in ritual settings; and, as a consequence, that arguments identifying Praxilla as a *hetaera* are deeply problematic.[7] Jones (2016), furthermore, argues that *skolia* attributed to individual artists were, in fact, often generically derived from a continuous tradition within non-elite, oral culture. While taken quite seriously as ritualized components of the symposium, he argues, *skolia* were "free-floating, ambient oral material" that contained stock elements, multiple versions of individual songs, and repetitive content derived from popular folklore. An implication of Jones's analysis is that *skolia* attributed to specific poets like Praxilla may have, in fact, obtained from (p. 257) a "coherent repertoire of songs performed in a common culture of popular symposia."

Whether or not Praxilla actually composed a repertoire of *skolia* for which Athenaeus claims she was famous, the high regard in which Praxilla's poetry was esteemed in antiquity may also be gleaned from both an epigram and a sculpture. Antipater of Thessalonica, a 1st-century BCE epigrammatist who lived under the Roman regime of Augustus, lists Praxilla's name in an epigram that canonizes and celebrates nine ancient Greek female poets (*A.P.* 9.26):

> These divinely-tongued women Mt. Helicon fed
> with songs, as did the rocky outcrop of Macedonian Pieria:
> Praxilla, Moero, the mouth of Anyte, the female Homer,
> Sappho, the adornment of the women of Lesbos with beautiful hair,
> Erinna, and glorious Telesilla, and you, Corinna,
> who sang about the surging shield of Athena,
> and woman-tongued Nossis, and sweet-voiced Myrtis,
> all of these women are crafters of eternal songs.
> Great Ouranos fathered nine Muses, and these nine
> Gaia bore, an immortal delight for mortals.[8]

Antipater's epigram casts nine female poets (Praxilla, Moero, Anyte, Sappho, Erinna, Telesilla, Corinna, Nossis, Myrtis) as the mortal parallels of the nine Muses, born on earth (Gaia) and nourished by Mount Helicon and Pieria, both of which have well established connections with the Muses in Greek literature. The epigram, however, states nothing about the nature of the poetry that warranted Praxilla's inclusion in a canonical list of nine female poets. It does, however, place Praxilla's name first in the list of nine, although it is unclear whether that placement should be interpreted as a corroborating indication of a greater aesthetic value placed upon her *oeuvre* than on those of the other eight poets. As we will see below, a famous bronze statue was also cast of her.

So much for Praxilla's poetry and reputation. About her life, we are equally in the dark. Eusebius (who lived in the 3rd and 4th centuries CE) records that Praxilla lived in the mid-5th century (451/2 BCE).[9] We also know that she was a native of the ancient Greek *polis* Sicyon on the Peloponnesus about eleven miles northwest of Corinth. Throughout the classical period and especially during the 4th century BCE, Sicyon was renowned as a center of artistic excellence, particularly in the fine arts of sculpture and painting. It was home to the revered Sicyonic school of painting founded by Eupompus in roughly a generation after Praxilla, if Eusebius's dating of her is to be believed.[10] One of these famous 4th-century Sicyonian sculptors, Lysippus, made a bronze statue of Praxilla, which may have found its way to the Portico of Pompey in Rome.[11] This statue probably depicted Praxilla in a homogenously conventional manner rather than as a portrait intended to replicate in statuary her exact physical features. A viewer would likely have known that the statue represented Praxilla by an inscription on its base. In an essay discussing the fate of a statue of Sappho by Silanion in Sicily seized by Verres,[12] Rosenmeyer (2007, p. 279) discusses the various ways in which Greek statuary made its way to Rome in the 1st century BCE. While some statues could be purchased legally, others were looted as booty in conquests of war, and still others (like the statue of Sappho by Silanion) could be purchased at obscenely low prices through extortion or intimidation. The demand in the Roman art market for Greek originals and for foreign luxuries in general was fueled by not only by the goal of symbolizing conquest, but also, through seizure and sale, to help finance it (Weis, 2003, p. 365–367). The Portico of Pompey, erected to commemorate Pompey's victories in the east, contained some statues that Pompey himself commissioned and many that were appropriated while on campaign.

## Select Bibliography


Burnett, A. 2012. "Brothels, Boys, and the Athenian Adonia," *Arethusa* 45.2: 177–194.

Cameron, A. 1995. *Callimachus and His Critics*. Princeton, NJ: Princeton University Press.

Cazzato, V. 2016. "'Glancing Seductively Through Windows': The Look of Praxilla fr. 8 (*PMG* 754)," in Vanessa Cazzato and André Lardinois (eds.), *The Look of Lyric: Greek Song and the Visual*. Leiden: Brill, p. 185–203.

Collins, D. 2004. *Master of the Game: Competition and Performance in Greek Poetry.* Hellenic Studies Series 7. Washington, D.C.: Center for Hellenic Studies. https://chs.harvard.edu/chapter/8-aristophanes-wasps-1222-49/. Accessed 11/1/21.
Halporn, J. 1983. "A Note on Praxilla Fr. 754 PMG," *Hermes* 111.4: 499–500.
Jones, G. S. 2016. "Observing Genre in Archaic Greek Skolia and Vase-Painting," in V. Cazzato and A. Lardinois (eds.), *The Look of Lyric: Greek Song and the Visual.* Leiden: Brill, p. 146–184.
Page, D. L. 1962. *Poetae Melici Graecae.* Oxford: The Clarendon Press.
Paris, H. S., M-C. Daunay, and J. Janick. 2012. "Occidental Diffusion of Cucumber (*Cucumis sativus*) 500-1300 CE: Two Routes in Europe," *Annals of Botany* 109.1: 117–126. doi: 10.1093/aob/mcr281.
Plant, I. (ed.). 2004. *Women Writers of Ancient Greece and Rome: An Anthology.* Norman, OK: University of Oklahoma Press.
Renehan, R. 1987. "Praxilla Fr. 8 [= PMG 754]," *Hermes* 115.3: 373–377.
Rosenmeyer, P. 2007. "From Syracuse to Rome: The Travails of Silanion's Sappho," *TAPA* 137.2: 277–303.
Synder, J. M. 1989. *The Woman and the Lyre: Women Writers in Classical Greece and Rome.* Carbondale, IL and Edwardsville, IL: Southern Illinois University Press.
Thornsen, T. S. 2012. "Sappho, Corinna and Colleagues in Ancient Rome: Tatian's Catalogue of Statues (*Oratio ad Graecos*) 33–34 Reconsidered," *Mnemosyne* 65.4/5: 695–715.
Weis, H. A. 2003. "Gaius Verres and the Roman Art Market: Consumption and Connoisseurship in *Verrine* II.4," in Andreas Haltenhoff, Andreas Heil, and Fritz-Heiner Mutschler (eds.), *O tempora, o mores! Römische Werte und römische Literatur in den letzten Jahrzehnten der Republik.* Leipzig and München: K.G. Sauer, p. 365–400.

## Praxilla 1 = *PMG* 747

κάλλιστον μὲν ἐγὼ λείπω φάος ἠελίοιο,
δεύτερον ἄστρα φαεινὰ σεληναίης τε πρόσωπον
ἠδὲ καὶ ὡραίους σικύους καὶ μῆλα καὶ ὄγχνας·

*Meter: Dactylic Hexameter*

—

**ἄστρον, -ου, τό:** (usu. in plural) star
**ἡλίος, -ου, ὁ:** sun
**μῆλον, -ου, τό:** apple
**ὄχνη, -ης, ἡ:** pear; pear-tree
**πρόσωπον, -ου, τό:** face; countenance
**σελήνη, -ης, ἡ:** moon
**σίκυος, -ου, ὁ:** cucumber; snake-melon
**φαεινός, -ή, όν:** bright; radiant
**φάος, φάεος, τό:** light
**ὡραῖος, -α, -ον:** ripe; seasonable; in the prime of life; at the right time

—

**1–3:** An excerpt of a *Hymn for Adonis* attributed to Praxilla and preserved by the paroemiographer Zenobius in 2nd century CE. Zenobius quotes this three-line passage to explain the meaning of the proverb "sillier than Praxilla's Adonis" (4.21). Adonis was the son of Myrrha, who conceived him during incestuous sexual relations with her own father. Adonis was extraordinarily beautiful and was beloved by both Persephone and Aphrodite. When he came of age, he became Aphrodite's lover. He was gored to death by a boar while hunting. Women of Athens celebrated a festival in honor of Adonis that involved, among other things, ritual obscenity, climbing onto roofs with pots containing tender seedlings of lettuce plants, and ritual lamentations over the dying lettuce leaves. See Burnett (2012) for an interpretation of the Adoneia as a festival celebrating Athenian boys' introduction into sexuality by prostitutes in brothels. Zenobius explains that when in the Underworld, Adonis was asked by those below about the most beautiful thing that he had left behind in the upper world. According to Zenobius, Praxilla had him reply in a way that Zenobius deemed foolish, since "whoever deems *sicyoi* and such equal to the sun and the moon is a silly man." Cazzato (2016, p. 194–195) suggests that this passage was transmitted in antiquity through sympotic reperformances. She notes that the σικύους (line 3) may be a pithy word-play on Praxilla's hometown (Sicyon) and that the fruits and vegetables listed in the final line may be subtle double-entendres for sexual organs. While translators usually render σικύους as "cucumbers" according to the listing in the *LSJ*, Paris, Daunay, and Janick (2012) argue that the *sikyos* is nearly always mistranslated in Greek. It is not, they argue, a cucumber, but a snake-melon, which is long, hairy, and often coiled like a snake.

**1. φάος:** in Attic, this third declension noun forms a contraction: φῶς φωτός, τό. We have provided in the vocabulary the uncontracted form listed in the *LSJ*.

**1. ἠελίοιο** = ἡλίου (Attic)

**2. σεληναίης** = σελήνης (Attic)

**Praxilla 2 = *PMG* 748**

ἀλλὰ τεὸν οὔποτε θυμὸν ἐνὶ στήθεσσιν ἔπειθον

—

**στῆθος, -εος, τό:** breast; chest

—

**1:** This line is preserved by Hephaestion, a 2nd-century CE grammarian of Alexandria who wrote a manual of Greek meters. He notes that the line appears in a dithyrambic poem by Praxilla entitled, *Achilles.*

Dithyrambs were choral poems performed in honor of the god Dionysus, usually at festivals.

**1.** τεὸν = epic possessive adjective, "your". The Attic equivalent = σόν, from σός, -ή, -όν

**Praxilla 3 = *PMG* 749**

ὦ διὰ τῶν θυρίδων καλὸν ἐμβλέποισα
παρθένε τὰν κεφαλὰν τὰ δ' ἔνερθε νύμφα

*Meter: Praxilleion*

—

**ἐμβλέπω, —, —, ἐμβέβλοφα, —, —:** look directly at; gaze intently upon; look
**θυρίς, -ίδος, ἡ:** window
**κεφάλη, -ης, ἡ:** head

—

**1–3:** Hephaestion (*Enchiridion* 7.8), who preserves this brief two-line fragment, states that it is part of a *scholion* (or, *paroinion*), a genre of songs sung in ancient Greek symposia. Cazzato (2016, p. 185–186) begins her analysis of this two-line snippet thus: "This tantalizing fragment addressed to a woman glancing seductively through a window leaves us wondering who this woman might be and what kind of situation might have prompted the speaker to remark on her gaze. Since this couplet is all we have of the poem, it has been tempting to see a simple ironic contrast between the first line and the second…which is understood as a revelation of the woman's true nature: her face may look innocent, but 'down below' she is well practiced—she is, in other words, a whore or a *hetaira.*" Such interpretations, Cazzato argues, have been supported by an identification of the first three lines of this fragment on a vase-inscription etched into the tondo of a 5th-century (possibly Boeotian) kylix currently residing in the British Museum in London (95.10-27.2) and which depicts a series of sympotic scenes, albeit, not very adeptly. Moreover, there has been a tendency, Cazzato argues, to assume that because Praxilla wrote *skolia*, she must have been an *hetaira.* However, Cazzato argues that the inscription may not be connected to Praxilla. Instead, she views Praxilla's *oeuvre* as a whole as centered around civic ritual rather than sympotic contexts and views this fragment as part of a wedding song, and specifically a wedding song sung before or at the groom's house after the wedding night. Cameron (1995, p. 499) also expresses doubts about the traditional interpretation, since the duality between the "head of a virgin" and a "bride beneath" could very well refer to marriage, which brings about the end of virginity for young girls and women. Halporn (1983) suggests that the line on the vase (mentioned above) indicates that the phrase was both proverbial and popular and may not, by extension, have belonged to Praxilla specifically. See also Renehan (1987).

**1. ἐμβλέποισα** = ἐμβλέπουσα (Attic)

**1. διὰ τῶν θυρίδων:** Halporn (1983) offers the suggestion that the "windows" are a metaphor for the "eyes". Moreover, he suggests (p. 500), "It is the sweet glance which makes the prostitute of Praxilla appear virginal in her κεφάλη despite what the poet knows of the condition of the lower part of her body." However, if Cazzato's (2016) reading is correct, the poem is not from a *skolion*, but a wedding hymn, wherein the wedding celebrants see the bride looking out from the "windows" of the groom's house after she and her bridegroom have consecrated their marriage.

**2. παρθένε ... νύμφα:** Both are vocative.

**2. τὰν κεφαλὰν** = τὴν κεφάλην (Attic); accusative of respect with regard to body part ("maiden, with respect to your head")

**2. τὰ δ' ἔνερθε:** "the things below"; τὰ is an accusative of respect with regard to body part

**Praxilla 4 = *PMG* 749**

᾿Αδμήτου λόγον, ὦ ἑταῖρε, μαθὼν τοὺς ἀγαθοὺς φίλει,
τῶν δειλῶν δ᾽ ἀπέχου γνοὺς ὅτι δειλῶν ὀλίγα χάρις.

*Meter: Greater Asclepiad*

—

**ἀπέχω, ἀφέξω ἀποσχήσω, ἀπέσχον, —, —, —:** (act.) keep (an accusative object) off or away from; (med.) hold one's self away from; keep (one's self) away from; abstain from

**δειλός, -ή, -όν:** cowardly; vile; worthless

**ὀλίγος, -η, -ον:** little; small; few

**χάρις, -ιτος, ἡ:** outward grace; kindness; goodwill; gratitude

—

**1–2:** Bdelycleon, one of the heavily caricaturized characters of Aristophanes's comedy, *The Wasps*, utters the first line of this two-line extract (at line 1238) while teaching his father Philocleon the techniques and etiquette of singing *skolia* at symposia in the hopes that Philocleon will abandon his addiction to jury-duty in favor of more aristocratic pursuits. Each character competes by capping his opponent's *skolion* with another that is intended to be both apropos and humorous. The ancient scholiast who commented on line 1238 states that while some say it is by Alcaeus and others by Sappho, it is in fact by Praxilla of Sicyon. The scholiast then cites the second line. Cazzato (2016, p. 193) points out that quite apart from the scholiast's citation of alternative authors, the fact that a male speaker is addressing a male *hetairos* "sits uncomfortably with authorship" by Praxilla. She also points out that the fragment occurs in nearly identical form among the general *skolia* relayed by Athenaeus (15.695c). Cazzato's study casts doubt on the traditional attribution of this *skolion* to Praxilla. See Collins (2004) for a summary of how this competition works in symposia and how Aristophanes parodies proper sympotic etiquette.

**1. 'Αδμήτου λόγον:** Admetus was a king of Thessaly and one of the Argonauts. When Apollo was forced to endure enslavement for a time under a mortal, the god served as Admetus's herdsman and was treated kindly by the king, in recompense for which Apollo made his herd double in size. Admetus was known for his hospitality, geniality, and kindness. Euripides dramatizes one of the many stories about the hero in the "happy ending" tragedy, *Alcestis*, wherein Herakles retrieves from Hades the wife of Admetus (Alcestis), who had willingly sacrificed her life so that her husband may live longer.

**1. φίλει:** an imperative (2nd person singular).

**2. ἀπέχου:** an imperative (2nd person singular).

**2. γνοὺς:** a nominative singular participle of γιγνώσκω ("knowing that…")

**Praxilla 5 = *PMG* 750**

ὑπὸ παντὶ λίθῳ σκορπίον, ὦ ἑταῖρε, φυλάσσεο

—

**λίθος, -ου, ὁ:** stone
**σκορπίος, -ου, ὁ:** scorpion
**φυλάττω, φυλάξω, ἐφύλαξα, πεφύλαχα, πεφύλαγμαι, ἐφυλάχθην:** (act.) guard; keep watch; defend; (med.) be on one's guard; watch out for

—

**1:** This single line is preserved by a scholiast to Aristophanes, who cites it while explaining a few lines of a choral song from the *Thesmophoriazusae* (lines 529–530). The chorus in this passage proclaims that it loves the old *paroimia* (or, proverb), "one should look under every stone, lest an orator bite." The scholiast, who quotes *PMG* 750, suggests that Aristophanes' joke is adapted from verses ascribed to Praxilla. Cazzato (2016, p. 193) once again casts considerable doubt on the attribution to Praxilla of a "widespread generic sentiment" that was endlessly adaptable to situations in everyday life and in myth. Indeed, she cites *PMG* 903, another *skolion*, which offers a similar sentiment: "a scorpion creeps under every stone, friend; take care that it doesn't strike you, for every manner of trickery keeps it invisible." She concludes, "the ascription seems unconvincing and this seems rather another case of a generic tradition being tied to a named author, perhaps because of the existence of a Sicyonian collection which would naturally have been associated with Sicyon's most famous singer."

**1. φυλάσσεο** = φυλάττου (Attic)—a middle voice imperative.

**Praxilla 1 = *PMG* 747**

The most beautiful thing I leave behind is the light of the sun,
second, the shining stars and the face of the moon,
and then, ripe snake-melons[13] and apples and pears.

**Praxilla 2 = *PMG* 748**

but I (or they) did not ever persuade the heart in your breast.

**Praxilla 3 = *PMG* 749**

You who are gazing charmingly through the windows,
your head is maiden, but below, you are a bride.

**Praxilla 4 = *PMG* 749[14]**

Learning the saying of Admetus,[15] my friend, take up with good people,
and stay away from contemptible people, knowing that they have little social grace.

**Praxilla 5 = *PMG* 750**

beware, friend, of a scorpion under every stone

## Notes

1. Chrysippus was a hero of Elis in the Peloponnesus and the son of the eponymous legendary figure, Pelops. According to ps.-Apollodorus (3.5.5), Chrysippus was kidnapped by Laius, the boy's tutor and the Theban father of Oedipus, while journeying together to the Nemean games. Laius raped Chrysippus, a crime for which the gods punished Laius and his city. Athenaeus (13.79) claims that while other sources feature Laius as Chrysippus's kidnapper, Praxilla makes Zeus himself the kidnapper.
2. In a work called the *Bibliotheca* (*Library*), Photius of Constantinople (9th century CE) provides a summary of a work by the Augustan era mythographer Conon called the *Diēgēseis* (*Narrations*), which was composed in Attic Greek. In paragraph §26 of the *Bibliotheca*, Photius reports that Conon treated the story of Carnus. According to the legend as reported by Conon, a spectral phantasm (or, according to other writers, a lover of Apollo) named Carnus, a seer for the Dorians, followed them as they invaded the Peloponnesus. One of these Dorians, a descendant of Heracles named Hippotes, killed this specter during the invasion. A plague fell upon the Dorians as a consequence, and they exiled Hippotes from the camp. His outcast son raised an army, invaded Corinth, and attacked Attica. In his descriptions of notable tourist sites in the Peloponnesus, Pausanias (3.13.3-5) claims that Carnus, an Arcadian by birth, was honored as a seer of Apollo. After Hippotes was banished for killing the seer, the Dorians propitiated him in cult practice. Pausanias goes on to say that the poet Praxilla makes him the son of Europa, while Leto and Apollo are his nurses.

3. Cazzato (2016) argues that Praxilla 4 and 5 of this volume (= *PMG* 749 and 750) are erroneous attributions.
4. As suggested by Plant (2004, p. 38).
5. Athenaeus 694a.
6. See Jones (2016) for a discussion of the generic components of *skolia*.
7. Following a systematic critique of the arguments linking the vase-inscription to Praxilla, Cavatto (2016, p. 193) summarizes the main thrust of her interpretation of Praxilla's poetry: "…I take a different tack by speculating on the impression of Praxilla as a poet by what remains of her corpus (though it is admittedly very little indeed). This suggests that, rather than being an author of racy sympotic songs, Praxilla in the main composed civic ritual songs. The sympotic compositions which go under her name appear to be generic convivial ditties which came to be ascribed to her at some later stage; this in turn may have affected the transmission of her civic poetry through sympotic reperformance."
8. Antipater of Thessalonica (*A.P.* 9.26):

   Τάσδε θεογλώσσους ῾Ελινὴν ἔθρεψε γυναῖκας
   ὕμνοις, καὶ Μακεδὼν Πιερίας σκόπελος,
   Πρήξιλλαν, Μοιρώ, ᾽Ανύτης στόμα, θῆλυν ῞Ομηερον,
   Λεσβιάδων Σαπφὼ κόσμον εὐπλοκάμων,
   ῎Ηρινναν, Τελέσιλλαν ἀγακλέα, καὶ σέ, Κόριννα,
   θοῦριν ᾽Αθηναίης ἀσπίδα μελψαμέναν,
   Νοσσίδα θηλύγλωσσον, ἰδὲ γλυκυαχέα Μύρτιν,
   πάσας ἀενάων ἐργάτιδας σελίδων.
   ἐννέα μὲν Μούσας μέγας Οὐρανός, ἐννέα δ᾽ αὐτὰς
   Γαῖα τέκεν, θνατοῖς ἄφθιτον εὐφροσύναν.

9. Eusebius, *Chron. Ol.* 82.2.
10. Pliny the Elder (*Natural History* 35.36.6), discussing a painting by Eupompus of a victor in an athletic contest holding a palm branch, digresses to say more about the painter. He claims that prior to Eumpompus's tenure as the head of the Sicyonic school of painting, there had previously been two major schools of art in the greater Mediterranean world—the Helladic (or Grecian) and the Asiatic. The Helladic division had consisted of two major branches, the Ionic and the Attic. Eupompus's influence, Pliny notes, was so powerful that a new division of the Helladic school emerged—the Sicyonian. Pliny goes on to say that under his influence, free-born children were given drawing lessons, but enslaved and unfree individuals were forbidden from being instructed in art. This accounts for the fact that (again, according to Pliny) no famous works of painting or sculpture were made by any enslaved person.
11. Tatian, *Oratio ad Graecos,* 33.2, a Christian evangelist (120–180 CE) who offers a tirade against (mostly) female poets whom the Hellenes represented in statues and which he claims to have seen himself in Rome (33.2-5; 35.1-7), argues that Lysippus cast Praxilla in a bronze statue, "although she said nothing useful in her poems." Other sculptures that Tatian polemicizes include those of Sappho, Corinna, Erinna, Myrtis, Myro, Anyte, Telessila. Thornsen (2012, p. 699–700) suggests that Tatian saw these statues in the Portico of Pompey on the evidence of Pliny the Elder (*Natural History* 7.34). See also Rosenmeyer (2007, p. 293–294).
12. Cicero, *Against Verres* 2.4.126–127.
13. While translators usually render the Greek noun *sikyos* as "cucumber" in accordance with the listing in the *LSJ*, Paris, Daunay, and Janick (2012) argue that that the *sikyos* is nearly always mistranslated in Greek. It is not, they

argue, a cucumber, but a snake-melon, which is long, hairy, and often coiled like a snake.

14. This two-line fragment is supplied by a scholiast of Aristophanes's *Wasps* (line 1238) in response to one of the characters of the comedy citing the first line of it in a competition between son (Bdelycleon) and father (Philocleon), wherein each tries to cap each other's *skolion*, or sympotic drinking song. While the scholiast claims that the *skolion* belongs to Praxilla, a recent study (Cazzato, 2016) has cast considerable doubt on that attribution.
15. Admetus was a king of Thessaly and one of the Argonauts. When Apollo was forced to endure enslavement for a time under a mortal, the god served as Admetus's herdsman and was treated kindly by the king, in recompense for which Apollo made his herd double in size. Admetus was known for his hospitality, geniality, and kindness. Euripides dramatizes one of the many stories about the hero in the "happy ending" tragedy, *Alcestis*, wherein Herakles retrieves from Hades the wife of Admetus (Alcestis), who had willingly sacrificed her life so that her husband may live longer.

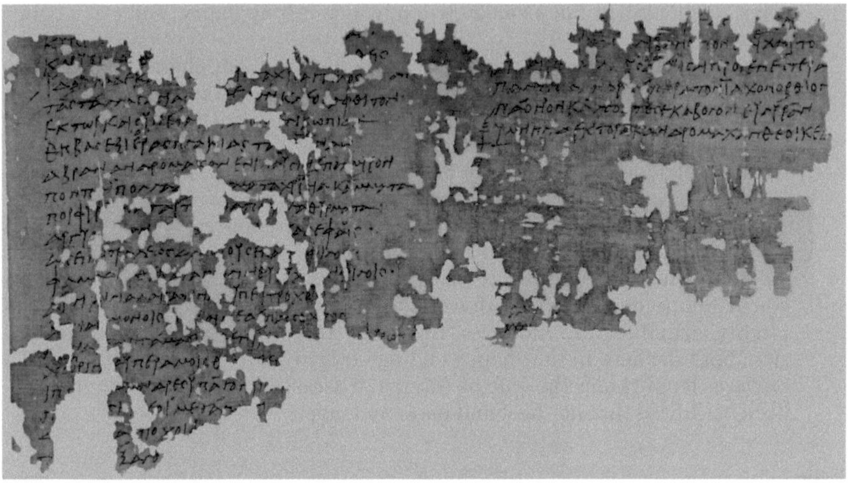

*Figure 1* Sappho fr. 44 L-P. Detail of P.Oxy. X 1232 fr. 1.

Source: Grenfell, B. P. and A. S. Hunt. 1914. *The Oxyrhynchus Papyri: Part X.* London: The Egypt Exploration Fund.

*Figure 2 Urbs Roma* Commemorative Coin. Fourth century CE.

Source: Wikimedia Commons.

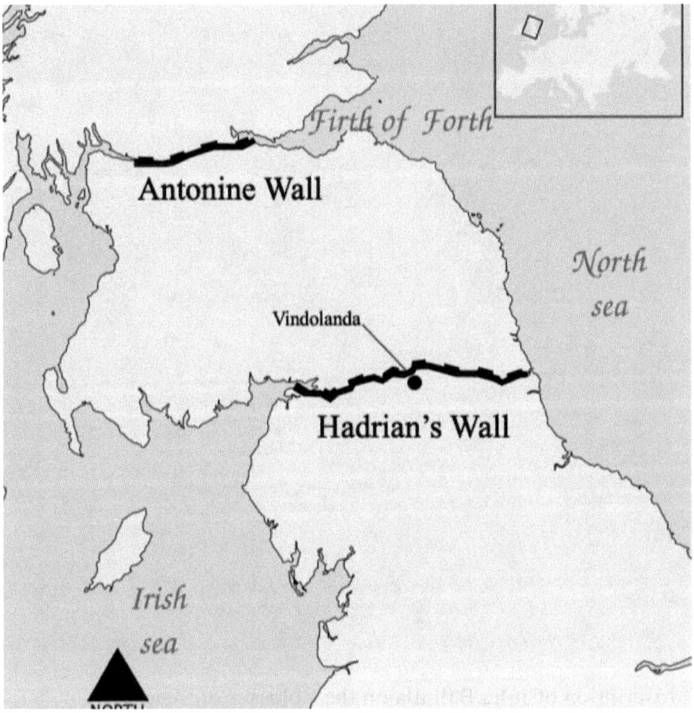


*Figure 3* Map of Britain.

Image Credit: Bartolo A. Natoli.

*Figure 4* Letter of Claudia Severa to Sulpicia Lepidina. Vindolanda Tablet II 291.

Source: Wikimedia Commons.

*Figure 5* Inscription of Julia Balbilla on the Colossus of Memnon.

Photo Credit: Mary Beard and Robin Cormack.

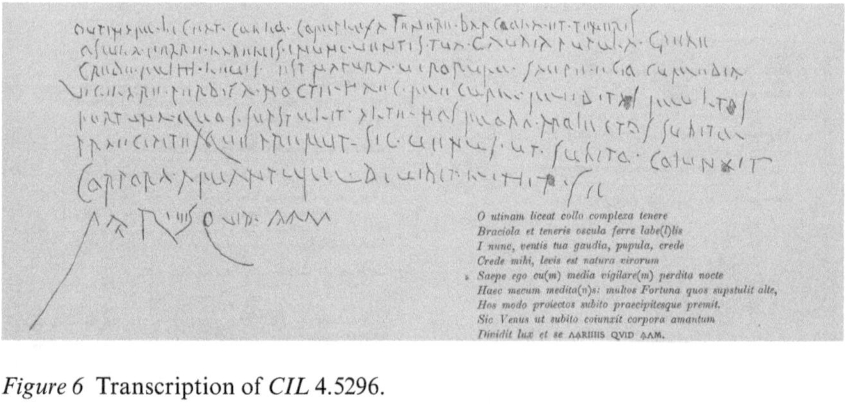


*Figure 6* Transcription of *CIL* 4.5296.

Source: Wikimedia Commons.

# Part II

# Rome

# 8 Melinno

The poetry of Melinno comes down to us only through a reference to her and a quotation of one of her poems in a compilation book. The 5th-century CE compiler Stobaeus records Melinno's poetry in his selection of poems on manliness (περὶ ἀνδρείας). However, the inclusion of Melinno in this section seems to have been an error first noted by Hugo Grotius in his 1623 edition of Stobaeus. The main misunderstanding centers around the opening of the poem and the entity to which the poem is dedicated. Stobaeus read the word ῥώμα as the Doric form of ῥώμη, which in Greek means "strength" (Μελλιοῦς Λεσβίας εἰς ῥώμην, *Ecl.* 3.7.12). However, as Grotius noted, the same word ῥώμη was the Greek word for the city of Rome, Ῥώμη (*Putavit haud dubie Stobaeus ῥώμην heic esse ἀνδρείαν. At mihi tamen valde se probat eorum opinio qui posterioris aevi hoc poema putant urbi Romae dicatum*, 522). The reference to Ῥώμη as the daughter of Ares (line 1) and the existence of a cult of Dea Roma seems to confirm this reading.

Of Melinno herself we know nothing other than what Stobaeus mentions, and that is limited to his statement that she was from Lesbos. However, no further evidence exists to support that claim, and scholars have cast serious doubts on this assertion, arguing that the only reason Melinno is associated with Lesbos is that the poem she wrote was written in a meter connected to Sappho. Of her relative dating, there has been some debate on whether to ascribe Melinno a date in the Hellenistic period (Bowra, 1957; Plant, 2004; Gutzwiller, 2017) or a later date in the 1st century CE. However, the general consensus among scholars is that she composed c. 200–150 BCE. The main evidence for this is the reference to the Dea Roma cult in the poem. That cult began to expand across the Greek world at the beginning of the 2nd century BCE as Rome's power began to become stronger and more consolidated. However, this growth seems to have stopped after the middle of the 2nd century. Thus, an early 2nd century BCE date seems most likely. Beyond this, all we can say with any degree of certainty is that she was likely

DOI: 10.4324/9781003031727-11

well-educated, as she has mastered the meter of the Sapphic stanza and makes multiple allusions to other literary works of authors such as Sappho, Homer, and Hesiod.

The poem itself is unique, although it seems to show a definite connection to a Sapphic model. Like many of the poems of Sappho, Melinno's poem is composed in stanzas and in Sappho's meter. Yet, unlike the stanzas of Sappho, Melinno's stanzas do not flow into one another, but instead break off into separate, distinct units. Likewise, Melinno does not employ Sappho's Aeolic dialect, but the artificial, mixed dialect typical of choral poetry (cf. Appendix A). Her vocabulary is filled with weighty and serious adjectives, the result of which is a poetic flow that is much more formal and rigid than that of Sappho, or even Alcaeus. This gravity has led some to critique Melinno's poetry rather harshly. Bowra (1957) sums up this viewpoint well, stating "If we compare [Melinno's poetry] with the hymns of Sappho and Alcaeus, from which it is remotely and insecurely descended, it looks stiff and stilted; and indeed it lacks their ease and grace of movement and their immediate response to the calls of the heart...Melinno is not a distinguished poet, but she did something" (28). Yet, perhaps, this slow, deliberate seriousness with which the poem proceeds is not the result of some stylistic failing, but a deliberate attempt by Melinno is capture the religious weight and formality that would accompany a hymn to a divinity.

The structure of the poem resembles a traditional hymn and has at least two of the formal features of a hymn (invocation, praise, and prayer). The first stanza (lines 1–4) is an invocation and establishes contact between the speaking persons and the addressee (Furley and Bremer, 2001, p. 51). It consists of many the general aspects that make up that formal portion: direct address, name, genealogy, epithets, and the location of the god. The remaining four stanzas (lines 5–20) provide the praise portion, presenting many of the traditional features of this formal section, including: repeated (anaphoric) addresses, predication of powers, and narratives (Furley and Bremer, 2001, p. 58–59). Most notably, this section makes frequent use of the *Du-Stil*, addressing the goddess in the second person on multiple occasions (σοὶ μόνᾳ, 5; σᾷ δ᾽ ὑπὰ σδεύγλᾳ, 9; σὺ δ᾽, 11; σοὶ μόνᾳ, 15; σὺ μόνα, 17). The final portion of the hymn structure, the prayer proper, is missing. This may reflect that the poem is incomplete; however, it may also be the case that the poem is more of a praise poem in the loose style of a hymn and not a hymn *per se* (Gutzwiller, 2017, p. 401).

## Select Bibliography

Alekniené, T. 2006. "Le Poème de Mélinno dans l'Anthologie de Jean Stobée: une erreur d'interprétation?," *Philologus* 150.2, 198–202.

Bowra, C. M. 1957. "Melinno's Hymn to Rome," *JRS* 47.1/2, 21–28.

Furley, W. and J. M. Bremer. 2001. *Greek Hymns: Greek Texts and Commentary*. Mohr Siebeck.

Gutzwiller, K. 2017. “Melinno,” in D. Sider (ed.), *Hellenistic Poetry: A Selection*. Ann Arbor, MI: University of Michigan Press, p. 400–404.

Mellor, R. 1975. *Thea Rome: The Worship of the Goddess Roma in the Greek World*. Gottingen: Vandenhoeck & Ruprecht.

Norden, E. 1929. *Agnostos Theos. Untersuchungen sur Formengeschichte religiöser Rede*. Leipzig-Berlin: Teubner.

Plant, I. 2004. *Women Writers of Ancient Greece and Rome*. Routledge.

Raimondi, V. 1995–1998. “L'Inno a Roma di Melinno,” in *Helikon*. p. 35–38, 283–307.

### *Melinno (Stobaeus Ecl. 3, 7, 12)*

χαῖρέ μοι ῾Ρώμα, θυγάτηρ Ἄρηος,
χρυσεομίτρα δαΐφρων ἄνασσα,
σεμνὸν ἃ ναίεις ἐπὶ γᾶς Ὄλυμπον
αἰὲν ἄθραυστον.

σοὶ μόνᾳ, πρέσβιστα, δέδωκε Μοῖρα
κῦδος ἀρρήκτω βασιλῇον ἀρχᾶς,
ὄφρα, κοιρανῇον ἔχουσα κάρτος
ἀγεμονεύῃς.

σᾷ δ᾽ ὑπὰ σδεύγλᾳ κρατερῶν λεπάδνων
στέρνα γαίας καὶ πολίας θαλάσσας
σφίγγεται· σὺ δ᾽ ἀσφαλέως κυβερνᾷς
ἄστεα λαῶν.

πάντα δὲ σφάλλων ὁ μέγιστος αἰὼν
καὶ μεταπλάσσων βίον ἄλλοτ᾽ ἄλλως
σοὶ μόνᾳ πλησίστιον οὖρον ἀρχᾶς
οὐ μεταβάλλει.

ἦ γὰρ ἐκ πάντων σὺ μόνα κρατίστους
ἄνδρας αἰχματὰς μεγάλους λοχεύεις
εὔσταχυν Δάμαρτος ὅπως ἀνεῖσα
καρπὸν †ἀπ᾽ ἀνδρῶν.
—

*Sapphic Stanzas*

**ἄθραυστος, ον:** unbroken, unbreakable
**αἰχμητής, οῦ:** spear-wielding; warlike
**αἰών, ῶνος, ὁ:** time, life, age
**ἄλλοτε:** **(adv.)** at another time, sometimes
**ἄλλως:** **(adv.)** otherwise
**ἄνασσα, ἡ:** queen
**ἀνέχω:** to come forth; hold up
**ἄρρηκτος, ον:** unbroken
**Ἄρης, ὁ:** Ares
**ἄστυ, ἄστεος/ἄστεως, τό:** city
**ἀσφαλέως:** **(adv.)** certainly, firmly, surely
**βᾰσῐ́λειος, α, ον:** royal
**γαῖα, ἡ:** earth
**δαΐφρων, ον:** warlike, fiery; wise
**Δημήτηρ, τερος/τρος, ἡ:** Demeter
**εὔστᾰχυς, υ:** rich in corn; blooming, fruitful
**ζεύγλη, ἡ:** loop attached to the yoke (through which the animals' head was placed)
**ἡγεμονεύω:** to lead the way; rule, command
**κάρτος, εος, τό:** strength
**κοιράνειος, ον:** belonging to a sovereign
**κρᾰτερός, ά, όν:** strong, mighty, fierce
**κυβερνάω:** to steer
**κῦδος, εος, τό:** glory, renown
**λέπαδνον, τό:** broad leather strap (fastening the yoke to the neck)
**λοχεύω:** to bring forth; bear, give birth

**μεταβάλλω:** to throw into a different position
**μεταπλάσσω:** to mold differently; to remodel
**μοῖρα, ας, ἡ:** fate, lot
**ναίω:** to dwell, live
**Ὄλυμπος, ὁ:** Olympus, Mt. Olympus
**οὖρος, ὁ:** fair wind
**πλησίστιος, ον:** filling/swelling the sails
**πολιός, ά, όν:** gray
**πρέσβιστος, η, ον:** eldest, most august, most reverend
**Ῥώμη, ἡ:** Rome
**σεμνός, ή, όν:** revered, holy, august
**στέρνον, τό:** breast, chest
**σφάλλω:** to cause to fall, overthrow
**σφίγγω:** to bind tight
**χρυσομίτρης, ου:** with girdle or headband of gold

—

1. **Ῥώμα:** The ambiguity over this word is a major contention in the history of this poem. Stobaeus seems to have originally included this poem in his section on manliness (περὶ ἀνδρείας) because he read this word as ῥώμη, "physical force" or "might". However, it is also the Greek word for the city of Rome. It is most likely that both meanings are operative, as Rome is lauded in this poem for her physical might as a daughter of Ares.
1. **θυγάτηρ Ἄρηος:** The deified Roma is not typically described as a daughter of the god Ares in any extant sources. The reason for including the phrase here seems to be twofold. First, it draws a close connection between the battle-ready Roma and the Amazons, famous warrior women from classical mythology. In particular, the phrase θυγάτηρ Ἄρηος seems to allude to the Amazon queen Penthesilea, who is described with the same epithet in a fragment of the *Aethiopis* (fr. 1.2a PEG): ἦλθε δ' Ἀμαζών, Ἄρηος θυγάτηρ μεγαλήτορος ἀνδροφόνοιο ("And came an Amazon, a daughter of Ares the greathearted man-slayer"). Secondly, it activates the traditional founding myth of the city of Rome by making the deified Roma a sister of the twins Romulus and Remus, who were the children of Ares and Rhea Silvia. Such a connection between these two disparate strands—the Amazonian Roma and the close connection between Roma and the twins—can be found on Republican coinage, but became even more popular in the 4th century CE with the *urbs Roma* coins commemorating Rome and celebrating the rise of Constantinople (Figure 2).
2. **χρυσεομίτρα:** The scansion of this word requires the -o to be long, but it is unclear how that syllable, otherwise short by nature, can be lengthened. Therefore, there may be a potential transmission error in the manuscripts here. The meaning of the word is also problematic, as it can be used to describe either a golden girdle or a golden headband. In the Hellenistic period, the latter was a typical use of the word (Plut. *Demetr.* 41; Theocr. 17.19; Call. *Hymn* 4.166). However, when used to describe Amazons, the term seems to refer more to their girdle (Apollo. *Bibl.* 2.5.9). Bowra (1957) explains that "the girdle seems to have been

regarded as the seat of an Amazon's strength or superiority … when Rome is given a golden girdle, it is a sign of her unusual and special strength" (23).

**2. δαΐφρων:** This may be another allusion drawing a relationship between Roma and the Amazon queen Penthesilea. In the opening lines of his epic, Quintus of Smyrna describes Penthesilea with the same adjective (δαΐφρονι Πενθεσιλείῃ, 1.47).

**3. ἅ:** Aeolic form of the relative pronoun ἥ.

**3. γᾶς:** Aeolic form of the genitive γῆς. Construe with ἐπὶ.

**3–4. ἐπὶ γᾶς Ὄλυμπον … ἄθραυστον:** The description of Olympus as the last place untrodden by Rome underlines the fact that Rome has conquered everywhere on land and sea; only Olympus is left beyond her control (cf. Alpheius of Mytilene *AP* 9.526 for a similar sentiment).

**4. ἄθραυστον:** Construe with σεμνὸν … Ὄλυμπον.

**5. πρέσβιστα:** Aeolic form of the vocative πρέσβιστη.

**5. Μοῖρα:** (Gutzwiller 2017) points out that the connection of Μοῖρα with political rule began to become more prevalent in the early Hellenistic period (403). This increased association of Μοῖρα thus helps us to date this poem more securely to the Hellenistic period.

**6. κῦδος … ἀρχᾶς:** Synchesis (ABAB word order). Construe κῦδος with βασιλῆον and ἀρρήκτω with ἀρχᾶς.

**6. ἀρρήκτω:** Aeolic form of the genitive ἀρρήκτου.

**6. βασιλῆον:** Aeolic form of βασίλειον.

**6. ἀρχᾶς:** Aeolic form of the genitive ἀρχῆς.

**7. κοιρανῆον:** Aeolic form of κοιράνειον.

**8. ἀγεμονεύῃς:** Aeolic form of ἡγεμονεύῃς, present active subjunctive of ἡγεμονεύω. Construe with ὄφρα in a purpose clause (Smyth §2193ff.).

**9. σᾷ δ' ὑπὰ σδεύγλᾳ:** Aeolic form for σῇ δ' ὑπὸ ζεύγλῃ.

**13–14. πάντα δὲ … ἄλλοτ' ἄλλως:** A somewhat complex word order. A more prosaic word order would be: ὁ μέγιστος αἰὼν σφάλλων πάντα καὶ μεταπλάσσων βίον ἄλλοτ' ἄλλως…

**14. ἄλλοτ' ἄλλως:** This double adverb is somewhat cumbersome to translate. Perhaps "some in one way, others in another" is a smoother option in English.

**15. πλησίστιον οὖρον:** The image of the fair wind filling the sails is borrowed from a formulaic phrase in Homer: ἵκμενον οὖρον ἵει πλησίστιον, ἐσθλὸν ἑταῖρον (*Od.* 11.7 and 12.149).

**15. ἀρχᾶς:** Aeolic form of the genitive ἀρχῆς.

**17–18. κρατίστους ἄνδρας αἰχματὰς μεγάλους:** The noun ἄνδρας is modified by three adjectives exemplifying the might of Rome's soldiers.

**17–20.** The final stanza of this poem is a simile comparing the mighty warriors begotten by Roma to the Spartoi, or "Sown men", of Thebes. The story goes that the hero Cadmus had been instructed by an oracle to follow a cow across the countryside and to stop and found a city wherever the cow stopped. When the cow stopped at a spring, Cadmus and his men were attacked by a dragon who lived there. Although this dragon was sacred to Ares, Cadmus killed it. He then took some of the dragon's teeth and sowed them into the ground. Fierce warriors sprang up from these teeth and became known as the Spartoi. Five of these men helped Cadmus to found the city of Thebes. Cadmus later had to serve eight years of slavery to Ares in order to atone for the death of the dragon. At the end of his service, Cadmus was given Harmonia, the daughter of Ares and Aphrodite, to be his wife. The link to Ares and his daughter Harmonia here thus creates a tidy response to the opening lines of this poem for Roma, another daughter of Ares.

**19–20. εὔσταχυν ... κα ρπὸν:** The poem ends with a simile in complex word order. A more prosic order would be: ὅπως ἀνεῖσα εὔσταχυν καρπὸν Δάμαρτος.

**19. Δάμαρτος:** Aeolic spelling for the genitive Δημήτερος.

**19. ὅπως** = ὡς

**19. ἀνεῖσα:** present active participle from ἀνίημι.

**19–20. ἀνεῖσα καρπὸν:** This image of crops sprouting forth is borrowed from the *Homeric Hymn to Demeter* (2.333 and 2.472): καρπὸν ἀνῆκεν.

**20. †ἀπ' ἀνδρῶν:** The final line of the poem is problematic, and no editors have been able to provide a satisfactory emendation. The provided text ἀπ' ἀνδρῶν is difficult and hard to understand in context. Another conjecture (Bassus Lollius 6.5 *GP*) provides ἐν ὅπλοις, a phrase that makes the apparent reference to the sown men of Thebes more clear.

### *Melinno (Stobaeus Ecl. 3, 7, 12)*

Hail Rome, daughter of Ares[1],
war-like queen with girdle of gold,
you who live upon holy and ever-unbroken
Olympus[2] on earth.

To you alone, most revered one, has Fate given
royal glory of unending rule,
so that, wielding sovereign strength,
you may lead the way.

Beneath your yoke of strong straps
the breasts of the land and white sea
are bound tight. Safely you steer
the cities of men.

Although all-powerful time conquers all things,
remolding some in one way, others in another,
for you alone the sail-filling fair wind of rule
does not change.

For indeed you alone of all beget
the most powerful, great spear-wielding men,
bringing them forth just as Demeter's[3] fruitful
crop[4] from men(?).[5]

## Notes

1. Ares is the god of war in classical Greek mythology. The deified city of Rome is not typically described as a daughter of the god Ares in any extant sources. The reason for including the phrase here seems to be twofold. First, it draws a close connection between the battle-ready Rome and the Amazons, famous warrior women from classical mythology. In particular, the phrase "daughter of Ares" seems to allude to the Amazon queen Penthesilea, who is described with the same epithet in a fragment of the epic poem *Aethiopis*. Secondly, it activates the traditional founding myth of the city of Rome by making the deified Rome a sister of the twins Romulus and Remus, who were the children of Ares and Rhea Silvia. Romulus went on to kill his twin and found the city of Rome.
2. Originally, Olympus referred to Mount Olympus in northern Greece. However, the mountain was so high and threatening, it was thought to be the dwelling of the gods.
3. Demeter is the goddess of fertility and agriculture in Greek mythology.
4. The reference here appears to be to the "sown men" from Thebes. The story goes that the hero Cadmus had been instructed by an oracle to follow a cow across the countryside and to stop and found a city wherever the cow stopped. When the cow stopped at a spring, Cadmus and his men were attacked by a dragon who lived there. Although this dragon was sacred to Ares, Cadmus killed it. He then took some of the dragon's teeth and sowed them into the ground. Fierce warriors sprang up from these teeth and became known as the Spartoi, or the sown men. Five of these men helped Cadmus to found the city of Thebes. Cadmus later had to serve eight years of slavery to Ares in order to atone for the death of the dragon. At the end of his service, Cadmus was given Harmonia, the daughter of Ares and Aphrodite, to be his wife. The link to Ares and his daughter Harmonia here thus creates a tidy response to the opening lines of this poem for Roma, another daughter of Ares.
5. The ending of this line is problematic and no scholars have yet to offer a satisfactory emendation. Therefore, the text has been marked with a (?).

# 9 Sulpicia

## Historical Background

Sulpicia is perhaps the most famous female writer in Latin literature, as her elegies are the only complete poems in Latin by a woman that have survived from classical antiquity. Yet, she is also one of the most difficult to pin down. Everything we know about Sulpicia is the result of piecing together a variety of accounts from antiquity with comments she makes in her own poetry. Sulpicia's poetry associates her with the literary world of Marcus Valerius Messalla Corvinus, consul in 31 BCE and a literary patron of poets such as Tibullus and Ovid. A reference by the 4th-century CE writer Jerome (*Adversus Iovinianum* 1.46) provides more background for Sulpicia's identification. Jerome reports that Messalla's sister, Valeria, married the legal scholar Servius Sulpicius Rufus and did not remarry after her death. Further evidence comes from Sulpicia's own poetry. In Sulpicia 4, Sulpicia identifies herself as Sulpicia, daughter of Servius. Likewise, in Sulpicia 11, Sulpicia intimates that she is keeping her romantic relationships secret from her mother. Finally, in Sulpicia 2, Sulpicia complains that Messalla is too interested in her and that he has some legal control over her. Taken together, this evidence has led scholars to conclude that the Sulpicia who wrote these poems was a historical figure and that she was the daughter of Valeria and Servius Sulpicius Rufus. After her father's death in 43 BCE, her uncle Messalla became her legal guardian. Through her interactions with Messalla's circle, she was well-educated and exposed to Roman and Greek literature, particularly the genre of elegy, which was prominent in the last half century of the millennium. For this reason, scholars usually date her poetry to around 19 BCE, at which time the elegist Tibullus died.

## The Poetry and the Text

The poetry usually associated with Sulpicia is a series of 11 poems that have come down from antiquity in Book 3 of Tibullus' elegies. Six of the poems are considered to be authentically Sulpician (Sulpicia 1–6). They are told from the first-person perspective of Sulpicia and are generally short, ranging

DOI: 10.4324/9781003031727-12

from four to ten lines in length. There is scholarly debate regarding the other five poems, commonly referred to as the Garland of Sulpicia (Sulpicia 7–11). These poems are much longer, ranging from 20 to 26 lines. These poems alternate their point of view between first and third person narratives. Scholars are divided regarding the authorship of the entire Sulpician corpus. Some, like Hallett (*passim*), believe all 11 poems are authentically by Sulpicia. Others, like Gruppe (1838) and Rossbach (1855), believe Sulpicia wrote the shorter six poems and not the Garland. Still others, like Parker (1994) and Lowe (1988), believe Sulpicia 1–6, 8, and 10 are authentic, and the rest written by another. Holzberg (1998) and Hubbard (2004–2005) perhaps presents the most extreme viewpoint, arguing that Sulpicia did not write any of the poems ascribed to her.

The debate is fueled, in part, by the nature of the transmission of Sulpicia's poems. For they did not come down from antiquity as a stand-alone book of poetry, but as a part of Book 3 of Tibullus. Tibullus Book 3 is a collection of poems not by Tibullus, but by poets associated with him. For example, the first six poems of the book is the work of a poet who refers to himself as Lygdamus and the seventh is a praise poem for Messalla. The Sulpician corpus follows this poem, with the Garland poems coming first and the six shorter elegies following. This volume leaves the ultimate question of authorship up to the reader, but presents the poems as two independent, yet connected, cycles. Since the majority of scholars currently consider the six shorter elegies more likely to be authentic than the five longer poems, the six shorter elegies (Tib. 13–18) are presented first, followed by the five Garland poems (Tib. 8–12). The reader is encouraged to grapple with the question of authorship, to compare the style and content of the two cycles, and to think through how the order in which the poems are presented could change their interpretation.

Regardless of the question of authorship, certain themes and motifs are constant across all 11 poems. At the heart of the poetry is a romantic relationship between Sulpicia and a young man she calls Cerinthus. The pair are depicted as traditional elegiac lovers (see below), grappling with issues of faithfulness, secret trysts, potential rivals, and what society thinks of them and their love. Sulpicia herself seems to be most exercised by this last issue; for as a respectable Roman woman her reputation was of the upmost importance and any inappropriate actions would result in adverse social consequences. As the poetry progresses, the reader can see Sulpicia working through the competing ideas of writing erotic poetry and maintaining the proper social norms for a Roman woman. In the end, however, she decides to bare her feelings for Cerinthus and to eschew propriety, asking only that Cerinthus act in kind and join her in a mutual, equal love.

The final poem in this volume's collection of Sulpicia's elegies is the so-called Petale Epitaph, an epitaph in elegiac couplets from the city of Rome, dated to c. 20 BCE. The epitaph is written for a *lectrix* (a woman who read and performed poetry aloud) by the name of Sulpicia Petale. Due to the striking similarities in word play and ambiguity to the Sulpician corpus, it is thought that this epitaph was written by Sulpicia herself for her own *lectrix*. If this is the case, the Petale Epitaph confirms many of the conclusions drawn about Sulpicia from her own poetry and the reference of Jerome: she was a member of the wealthy upper class and well-steeped in literary studies.

## Roman Elegy

It is nearly impossible to understand Sulpicia's poetry without some basic background in the genre in which she wrote: Roman elegy. Roman elegy is defined as a style of poetry written in couplets (one dactylic hexameter and one dactylic pentameter) that has at its core an erotic situation: the poet longs for the affection of a beloved girl or boy. In declaring his love for the beloved, the poet-lover eschews all trappings of normative masculinity. Traditionally, Roman men were expected to be active, rational, serious citizen-soldiers who were always in control of the situation. Moreover, Roman men were allowed to have multiple sexual partners, provided that they maintained an active role in the relationship and that the partner was not under the control of another Roman man. Conversely, the poet-lover in elegy was the opposite of nearly all of these norms. He is frequently depicted as overly-emotional and love-sick, willingly in bondage to his beloved, and completely faithful to the beloved.

These core ideas often were described in the twin concepts of *servitium amoris* (slavery to love) and *militia amoris* (the service to love). The poet-lover willingly gives himself into the service of his beloved and abandons any active control of his life. He wishes to be beaten, shackled, and mistreated, so long as the beloved shows affection to him. Likewise, the poet-lover trades in his duty to military service for Rome for a new service to love. He rejects the norms of controlled masculinity and prefers to lead a life in service to love.

The description of the beloved continues the theme of inversion. Frequently described as *puella* (girl) or *puer* (boy), the beloved takes on all of the traditional masculine roles in the poet-lover's stead. Elegiac beloveds frequently are forceful, demeaning, and dominant. However, most distressing to the poet-lover is the fact that the beloved often has multiple sexual partners and is not faithful to the poet-lover, no matter what he does.

Sulpicia's elegies add a new wrinkle to the traditional elegiac setup. Whereas the elegies of other prominent authors in the genre such as Propertius, Tibullus, Ovid all feature a male poet-lover, the elegies of Sulpicia present a female poet-lover. As such, the traditional inversion of gender norms is given an additional twist. She, a woman, is fulfilling the male role of poet-lover, a role that is marked by non-male gender norms. Yet, she is not simply undoing the original inversion and returning to conventional feminine norms. Sometimes, Sulpicia depicts herself as the poet-lover, sometimes as the *puella* herself. Moreover, she often rejects the traditional one-sided *servitium amoris* in favor of a *mutuus amor*, an equal love. She does not limit herself to blindly following her beloved, even if he does not love her. Instead, she frequently threatens to leave him should he do so, but far more often tries to chastise him into loving her or praying to the gods for their assistance.

One final note about Sulpicia's twist on elegy must be noted. Male authors of elegy enjoyed the privilege of slipping out of their adherence to masculine norms and writing poetry about erotic and non-normative themes. Sulpicia, on the other hand, may have faced more backlash for doing so as a woman. Her poetry often remarks on questions of private vs. public, and she outwardly wrestles with the question of the effect of her poetry on her reputation. This tension between loyalty to a non-normative, erotic genre and one to acceptable social mores is present throughout the corpus in Sulpicia's tendency to use ambiguity, convoluted word order, and double-meanings to create plausible deniability for herself. Although the effect is a heighted frequency of difficult syntax, it perhaps is a marker of one of the absolute great stylists of Roman elegy.

## Overview of the Poems

**Sulpicia 1:** As the first poem in the six-poem Sulpicia cycle, this poem is filled with programmatic importance and sets the tone for the poems that follow. The two major themes introduced in this poem are (1) Sulpicia's place in the genre of Roman elegy and the lineage of female authors, and (2) Sulpicia's place in the sociocultural context of Augustan Rome. To the first point, this poem seeks to set up Sulpicia as the Roman Sappho, a woman who writes the type of love poetry for which Sappho is known but in the Latin language. Moreover, Sulpicia positions herself in the genre of Roman elegy, as she plays the role of the poet-lover traditionally occupied by male poets. Likewise, the object of her desire can be construed both as a real lover and as the poetry itself, an ambiguity made famous by Roman elegists. To the second point, Sulpicia shows herself as keenly aware of her place as a woman in Roman society. It was considered improper for elite women to have romantic involvements outside of marriage, and even more so to speak freely about them in publicly-consumed literature. Therefore, Sulpicia is faced with the problem of how she is to write love poetry as a Roman elegist while still remaining silent about her relationships due to her status as a privileged woman. This tension is present throughout the poem, as it oscillates between clear, bold statements of her love and more hidden depictions of it through complex syntax and word order. Sulpicia tries to speak of her love through ambiguities and code, but eventually discards those pretenses in the final couplet of the poem.

**Sulpicia 2:** After calling attention to her place, both generically and socioculturally, in her first poem, Sulpicia continues these twin themes in this second poem, cast as a genethliacon, a birthday poem. Sulpicia opens the poem by lamenting that she is being forced to spend the occasion not in the city with her beloved, but in the countryside. She concludes by complaining to her uncle Messalla that he is too controlling in forcing her to do so. Again, as in Sulpicia 1, Sulpicia highlights the plight of a Roman woman, who was to be under the constant guardianship of some man, by describing the power dynamics in her own relationship with Messalla. Yet, in this poem such a guardianship may extend beyond mere social control, and into generic control, as well. As in the first poem, Sulpicia places herself squarely with the world of elegy, in which the *puella* frequently departs the city—and the poet/lover—for another location, a fact that causes the poet to worry about her faithfulness. Here, Sulpicia is simultaneously the departing *puella* and the poet/lover worrying about the faithfulness of Cerinthus. Beyond Sulpicia's use of the elegiac departure poem, this poem also hints at her removal from elegy by Messalla: for she is forced to forgo the *urbs*, the traditional locus of elegy, for the more pastoral location of Arretium, which is unsuitable for an elegiac *puella*.

**Sulpicia 3:** Sulpicia follows her poem lamenting her departure from the city on her birthday with this brief, two couplet poem. Here, she is delighted at a turn of events that has allowed her to stay in Rome to celebrate. The poem concludes with the introduction of another person—or persons—into the relationship between Sulpicia and Cerinthus; for it is not only those two who will be celebrating, but a larger community (*omnibus nobis*).

**Sulpicia 4:** After two poems celebrating her ability to stay in Rome for her birthday and to see Cerinthus, Sulpicia switches gears and tells us about Cerinthus' potential infidelity. She chastites him for not acting as a proper Roman man and for engaging in some sort of relationship with a lower-class girl toting a spinning basket. Sulpicia then states that he should know better and ought not to continue in his relationship with her, the daughter of an upper class Roman family, if he continues such behavior. After all, Sulpicia has members of her family that are worried about her getting into a potential relationship with another man.

**Sulpicia 5:** In this poem, Sulpicia evokes the traditional elegiac theme of concern over a sick beloved. Oftentimes, the Roman elegists try to prove their love and devotion for their beloveds through their offerings and prayers to the gods to restore the beloved's health. Here, Sulpicia casts herself as the beloved *puella* and chastises Cerinthus for his seeming indifference to her sickness. However, instead of letting her anger inspire her to leave Cerinthus, Sulpicia dramatically states that she would not wish to recover or even live any longer if Cerinthus does not care for her. In so doing, she simultaneously points out Cerinthus' lack of concern and demonstrates the proper loyalty to the relationship that she expects from him. This makes even more sense if Sulpicia's sickness is read not as a true sickness, but as a love sickness: in this metaphorical sense, Sulpicia would not wish to continue in her love for Cerinthus if he does not have an equal desire for her.

Some scholars see this poem as connected to Sulpicia 9, in which Sulpicia lies ill and Cerinthus shows his genuine concern for her (see below).

**Sulpicia 6:** This poem, which features some of the most difficult syntax in the entire Sulpician corpus, again plays with the idea of mutual love so prevalent in Sulpicia. Sulpicia states how ashamed she is over her actions during the night before, when she rebuffed Cerinthus' advances and did not show reciprocal love. She explains, however, that she did this not out of indifference or lack of desire for Cerinthus, but out of nervousness and fear. The reader is left to wonder what the cause of Sulpicia's hesitancy is, but it may be the prospect of the relationship moving from a verbal one to a physical one.

**Sulpicia 7:** This poem introduces the second cycle of Sulpicia poems and does so in a completely different manner than the first cycle. The poem is told from the third person point of view and spends the entire time focusing not on the inner emotions of Sulpicia or on her love of Cerinthus, but on her outward beauty and the effects it has on those who gaze upon her. The first portion of the poem addresses the god Mars and encourages him to come and to see the beautiful *puella* and not to worry about causing Venus to be jealous; for even she will forgive him. In fact, the poem is crafted in such a manner as to imbue Sulpicia with many of the qualities of Venus herself through the use of ambiguity. This section ends with a simile in which the beauty of Sulpicia, which is becoming in all seasons and manner of dress, is compared with the god of the seasons, Vertumnus. The second portion of the poem furthers the description of Sulpicia's beauty by arguing that she alone of girls is worthy to be decorated with the most beautiful and expensive objects from all the reaches of the Roman world. This section is full of colorful imagery and engages all of the senses of the reader in order to make the reader see, feel, and smell Sulpicia's presence. At last, the poem concludes with a final section in which the Pierides and Apollo are encouraged to join in singing Sulpicia's praises; for she is the most worthy of that song and will bring glory to their sacred rites.

**Sulpicia 8:** In this poem, Cerinthus has gone on a hunting trip, and Sulpicia worries aloud about what will happen to him in the first person. Sulpicia's worries can be divided into two primary concerns. First, she is concerned for the physical health of Cerinthus as he hunts boar, deer, and other wild beasts. Such an endeavor will undoubtedly run the risk of marring Cerinthus' flesh, or result in something even worse. On another level, however, Sulpicia is also consumed with the traditional elegiac concern about the beloved's faithfulness. She worries about what exactly is happening on Cerinthus' hunt and whether or not he is falling in love with another person. To prevent this from occurring, Sulpicia suggests that she accompany Cerinthus on the hunt. However, as he has already left, she resorts to praying that no love find him on his trip and that any female rival attempting to take him from Sulpicia be torn to pieces by wild animals.

**Sulpicia 9:** This poem returns to the third-person perspective and describes a traditional elegiac situation: illness. Sulpicia has fallen ill and Cerinthus has prayed to the gods for assistance in healing her. The third-person narrator also calls for assistance, but specifically to Apollo, who is traditionally associated with medicine. The poem is broken into three distinct portions: In the first, the narrator sets the scene of Sulpicia's illness and asks Apollo to come and heal her. Sulpicia is objectified and sexualized throughout, as the narrator states that it will not disgust Apollo to lay hands upon her and that her beauty should not be allowed to be destroyed by illness. In the second, Cerinthus is addressed directly and encouraged to take heart, as the gods have heard his prayers and that Sulpicia will recover. In the final, the narrator turns the attention to Apollo, outlining the praise and glory that will await the god if he saves Sulpicia and restores the two lovers to one another.

**Sulpicia 10:** This poem returns the reader to first-person poetry placed into the mouth of Sulpicia and takes the form of a genethliacon, a birthday poem (cf. Sulpicia 2, 3, 12). Sulpicia commemorates Cerinthus' birthday with a prayer for a mutual love between her and Cerinthus. She enlists both Venus and Cerinthus' Genius to accomplish her goal. In addition to praying for this love, Sulpicia interestingly acknowledges the existence of potential rivals who would try to steal Cerinthus away from her (cf. Sulpicia 4 and 8). Should these rivals be successful, Sulpicia asks Cerinthus' Genius to abandon him and to leave him to fend for himself.

**Sulpicia 11:** This final poem of the Garland of Sulpicia cycle returns the reader to a third-person narrative and includes many of the same themes of the other five poems in the cycle: birthdays, prayers for a mutual love, lovesickness, and the *paraclausithyron*. The poem is set up as an elaborate prayer to Juno, the goddess of marriage, and she is asked to help Sulpicia and Cerinthus find a mutual love and a means of being together. The context of the poem seems to indicate that Sulpicia has been betrothed to another man and has come to the Temple of Juno to ask the goddess for her help in achieving a relationship with Cerinthus. The poem employs imagery of public vs. private throughout (cf. Sulpicia 10, line 20, *clamne palamne*), especially in the juxtaposition between the public displays of marriage as defined by Sulpicia's mother and Sulpicia's secret desire for Cerinthus.

**Sulpicia 12:** This verse epitaph, written in elegiac couplets, was discovered in the late 1920s in the center of Rome. Since it begins with the name of Sulpicia and is a funerary inscription for a *lectrix*, or female reader, scholars such as Stevenson (2005) have suggested that the inscription is for a *lectrix* of the writer Sulpicia by the name of Petale. Certain features of the text seem to confirm this suggestion by dating the epitaph to the mid-20s BCE, the same time as Sulpicia was active. Archaic forms found in the Latin inscription, such as *quoi* and *longinquom*, fell out of fashion soon after the 20s BCE. Moreover, after the 20s BCE, it became customary to end the pentameter lines of elegiac poetry with only two-syllable words. This inscription only uses a two-syllable word once (*colus*), a fact that dates the inscription to before this shift in stylistic taste. Beyond the dating, the inscription also has many hallmarks of Sulpician poetry, including ambiguity, double-meaning, and a focus on the literary ability (*arte*, *ingenio*) of the woman. A key example of this Sulpician ambiguity is the first word of the poem, the genitive *Sulpiciae*. Because of its placement at the beginning of the poem and away from the other genitive word of the line, *lectricis*, *Sulpiciae* can simultaneously have multiple meanings: on the one hand, it can be taken with *lectricis* to describe the name of the *lectrix* (the reader named Sulpicia), likewise, it can be taken as a possessive and describe her owner (the reader of Sulpicia), and it even can be taken objectively to describe the person's work that she read (the reader of Sulpicia's work). Since it was customary for freed slaves to take the name of their former owners, it is most likely that all three of these meanings are active at once: this is the epitaph for Sulpicia Petale, the *lectrix* of Sulpicia who read the works of Sulpicia.

## Select Bibliography

Batstone, W. 2018. "Sulpicia and the Speech of Men," in S. Frangoulidis and S. Harrison (eds.), *Life, Love and Death in Latin Poetry.* Berlin and Boston, MA: De Gruyter, p. 85–110.

Bradley, J. R. 1995. "The Elegies of Sulpicia: An Introduction and Commentary," *New England CJ* 22.

Churchill, L. J., P. R. Brown and J. E. Jeffrey, eds. 2002. *Women Writing Latin from Roman Antiquity to Early Modern Europe 1: Women Writing Latin in Roman Antiquity, Late Antiquity and the Early Christian Era.* New York and London: Routledge.

Currie, H. MacL. 1983. "The Poems of Sulpicia," *ANRW* 30.3: 1751–1764

Davies, C. 1973. "Poetry in the 'Circle' of Messalla," *Greece & Rome* 20: 25–35.

Fatucchi, A. 1976. "Le ferie aretine di Sulpicia (Nota topografia)," *Orpheus* 23: 145–160.

Fear, T. 2002. "The Poet as Pimp: Elegiac Seduction in the Time of Augustus," *Arethusa* 33.2: 217–240.

Fielding, I. 2020. "The Authorship of Sulpicia," in T. Franklinos and L. Fulkerson (eds.), *Constructing Authors and Readers in the Vergiliana, Tibulliana, and Ovidiana.* Oxford, p. 186–197.

Flaschenriem, B. L. 1999. "Sulpicia and the Rhetoric of Disclosure," *CP* 94: 36–54.

Frederick, D. 1997. "Reading Broken Skin: Violence in Roman Elegy." In Hallett and Skinner (eds.), *Roman Sexualities*, 172–93.

Fulkerson, L. 2017. *A Literary Commentary on the Elegies of the 'Appendix Tibulliana'. Pseudepigrapha Latina.* Oxford; New York: Oxford.

Gruppe, O. 1838. *Die romische Elegie.* Vol. 1. Leipzig.

Hallett, J. 1990. "Contextualizing the Text: The Journey to Ovid," *Helios* 17: 187–195.

———. 1993. "Martial's Sulpicia and Propertius' Cynthia," in Mary DeForest (ed.), *Woman's Power, Man's Game: Essays in Classical Antiquity in Honor of Joy K. King.* Wauconda, IL, 322–353

———. 2002a. "*The Eleven Elegies of the Augustan Elegist Sulpicia*," in Churchill, Brown and Jeffrey: 45–65.

———. 2002b. "Sulpicia and the Valerii: family ties and poetic unity," in Henrik Fich, Gorm Tortzen, Pernille Flensted-Jensen, Adam Schwartz and Thomas Heine, eds. *Noctes Atticae: 34 Articles on Graeco-Roman Antiquity and its Nachleben. Studies Presented to Jorgen Mejer on his Sixtieth Birthday, March 18, 2002.* Copenhagen: 141–149.

———. 2002c. "The Role of Women in Roman Elegy; Counter-cultural Feminism" in P.A. Miller (eds.), *Latin Erotic Elegy: An Anthology and Reader*, 329–347.

———. 2006. "Sulpicia and her fama; an intertextual approaches to recovering her Latin literary image." *CW* 100.1: 37–42.

———. 2009a. "Absent Roman Fathers in the writings of their daughters: Cornelia andSulpicia," in S. Huebner and D.M. Ratzan, eds. *Growing Up Fatherless in Antiquity.* Cambridge: 175–191.

———. 2009b. "Sulpicia and Her Resistant Intertextuality," in Danielle van Mal-Maeder, Alexandre Burnier and Loreto Nunez, *eds. Jeux de Voix: Enonciation, intertextualite et intentionnalite dans la literature antique. Special issue of Echo.* Collection de L'Institute d'Archaeologie et de Sciences de l'antiquite de l'Universite de Lausanne: 141–155.

———. 2009c. "Ovid's Thisbe and a Roman Woman Love Poet," in Barbara W. Boyd and Cora Fox eds, *Approaches to Teaching the Works of Ovid and the Ovidian Tradition.* Approaches to Teaching World Literature, Modern Language Association: 170–177.

———. 2009d. "Corpus Erat: Sulpicia's Elegiac Text and Body in Ovid's Pygmalion Narrative (Metamorphoses 10.238–297), in Thorsten Foegen and Mireille Lee, eds. *Bodies and Boundaries in Graeco-Roman Antiquity.* Berlin and New York: DeGruyter: 111–124.

———. 2009e. "Ovid's Sappho and Roman Women Latin Poets", Dictynna 4. https://doi.org/10.4000/dictynna.269

———. 2010. "Human Connection and Paternal Evocations: Two Elite Roman Women Writers and the Valuing of Others," in Ralph Rosen and Ineke Sluiter, eds. *Valuing Others in Classical Antiquity.* Leiden: 353–373.

———. 2011. "Recovering Sulpicia: the value and limitations of prosopography and intertextuality," in Jan Nelis, eds. *Receptions of Antiquity.* Ghent: 297–311.

———. 2012. "Authorial Identity in Latin Love Elegy: Literary Fictions and Erotic Failings," in Barbara K. Gold, ed. *A Companion to Roman Love Elegy.* Malden, Oxford and Chichester: Wiley-Blackwell: 269–284.

Hallett, J., and S. Dickison, 2014. *A Roman Women Reader: Selections from the 2nd Century BCE- BCE 2nd Century CE.* Bolchazy-Carducci.

Hemelrijk, E. 1999. *Matrona Docta: Educated women in the Roman Elite from Cornelia to Julia Domna*: Routledge.

Hinds, S. 1987. "The Poetess and the Reader: Further Steps toward Sulpicia," *Hermathena* 143: 29–46.

Holzberg, N. 1998. "Four Poets and a Poetess or Portrait of the Young as a Young Man? Thoughts on Book 3 of the *Corpus Tibullianum*," *CJ* 94: 169–191.

Hubbard, T. 2004–2005. "The Invention of Sulpicia," *CJ* 100.2: 177–194.

Keith, A. 1997. "Tandem venit amor: A Roman Woman Speaks of Love," in Judith P. Hallett and Marilyn B. Skinner (eds.), *Roman Sexualities.* Princeton, NJ: Princeton University Press, p. 295–310.

Lowe, N. J. 1988. "Sulpicia's Syntax," *CQ* 38: 193–205.

Martinon, P. 1895. *Les Élégies de Tibulle, Lygdamus et Sulpicia.* Paris.

Merriam, C. U. 1990. "Some Notes on the Sulpicia Elegies," *Latomus* 49: 95–98.
———. 1991. "The Other Sulpicia," *CW* 84: 303–305.
Miller, P.A. 2002. *Latin Erotic Elegy; An Anthology and Reader.* Routledge.
Parker, H. 1992. "Other Remarks on the Other Sulpicia," *CW* 86: 89–95.
———. 1994. "Sulpicia, the Auctor de Sulpicia, and the Authorship of 3.9 and 3.11 of the Corpus Tibullianum," *Helios* 21: 39–62.
Richlin, A. 1992. "Sulpicia the Satirist," *CW* 86.2.
Roessel, D. 1990. "The Significance of the Name Cerinthus in the Poems of Sulpicia," *Transactions of the American Philological Association* 120: 243–250.
Rossbach, A. 1855. *Albii Tibulli libri quattor.* Leipzig.
Santirocco, M. 1979. "Sulpicia Reconsidered," *CJ* 74: 229–239.
Skoie, M. 2002. *Reading Sulpicia: Commentaries 1475–1990*, Oxford: Oxford University Press.
Snyder, J. M. 1989. *The Woman and the Lyre. Women Writers in Classical Greece and Rome*, Carbondale, IL and Edwardsville, IL: Southern Illinois University Press.
Stevenson, J, 2005. *Women Latin Poets: Language, Gender & Authority from Antiquity to the Eighteenth Century.* Oxford.
Wyke, M. 1987. "Written Women: Propertius' *Scripta Puella*," *JRS* 77: 47–61.
———. 1995. "Taking the Woman's Part: Engendering Roman Love Elegy," in A. J. Boyle (ed.), *Roman Literature and Ideology: Ramus Essays for J.P. Sullivan* Bendigo, Australia: Aureal Publications, p. 110–128.

### *Sulpicia 1 (Tib. 3.13)*

Tandem venit amor, qualem texisse pudori
  quam nudasse alicui sit mihi fama magis.
Exorata meis illum Cytherea Camenis
  attulit in nostrum deposuitque sinum.
Exsolvit promissa Venus: mea gaudia narret,
  dicetur si quis non habuisse sua.
Non ego signatis quicquam mandare tabellis,
  ne legat id nemo quam meus ante, velim,
sed peccasse iuvat, vultus conponere famae
  taedet: cum digno digna fuisse ferar.

*Meter: elegiac couplets*

—

**Camena, Camenae, *f.*:** Muse
**conpono, conponere, conposui, compositum:** to put, place together; to arrange
**Cytherea, Cythereae, *f.*:** Cytherean, the Cytherean one (i.e., Venus)
**depono, deponere, deposui, depositum:** to put aside, put down
**exoro, exorare, exoravi, exoratum:** to persuade, entreat
**exsolvo, exsolvere, exsolvi, exsolutum:** to undo, loosen; pay, discharge
**iuvat:** (*impers.*) it delights, pleases
**mando, mandare, mandavi, mandatum:** to order, command
**nemo, neminis, *m./f.*:** no one
**nudo, nudare, nudavi, nudatum:** to strip, lay bare, expose
**pecco, peccare, peccavi, peccatum:** to do wrong, offend, cheat (in a relationship)

**promissum, promissi, *n*.:** promise
**qualis, quale:** what kind of, of such kind, such as
**signo, signare, signavi, signatum:** to mark, designate
**tabella, ae, *f*.:** small (writing) tablet
**taedet, taeduit:** (*impers.*) it disgusts, offends, wearies
**Venus, Veneris, *f*.:** Venus, goddess of (sexual) love

—

**1–2: Tandem ... magis:** The opening couplet states clearly the problem facing Sulpicia as a woman writing elegy: she wants to tell of her love, but is prohibited from doing so due to her sex. This tension is mimicked by the clear, bold statement *tandem venit amor*, and the subsequent complex syntax designed to portray the manners in which Sulpicia must hide her love due to her normative, feminine *pudor*. This oscillation between complex and simple syntax continues throughout the poem, as Sulpicia uses complex syntax when speaking about social expectations and simple syntax when revealing her private feelings.

**1. qualem ... magis:** difficult syntax aimed at portraying Sulpicia's attempts at hiding her love. A more prosaic word order would be: *qualem mihi magis fama est texisse pudori quam nudasse alicui.* Translate as: "the sort of love it would be more reputable for me to have covered for shame's sake than to have bared to someone."

**1. pudori:** double dative construction with *sit mihi fama magis* (line 2). Double datives pair a dative of reference (here, *mihi*) with a dative of purpose (here, *pudori*). Literally "It is more reputable for me for the purpose of shame."

**2. nudasse:** syncopated form of *nudavisse*

**2. sit:** present subjunctive in a relative clause of characteristic with *qualem* (cf. Allen and Greenough §535).

**2. fama magis:** Literally, "fame would be more". A smoother translation would construe *fama* as an adjective made comparative by *magis*: "more reputable".

**3–6: Exorata ... sua:** In these couplets, Sulpicia returns to a clearer style of syntax and claims her place in the lineage of female poets with a direct reference to Sappho 1. In that poem, Sappho calls upon Aphrodite to come to her aid and be her ally in the battles of love. Here, Sulpicia states that she has called upon Aphrodite and that she has delivered on her promises, bringing a love into her lap. In addition to alluding to Sappho, Sulpicia also makes clear that she is doing something entirely different, as she invokes the native Italian *Camenae* in an effort to claim her heritage in Latin literature. As such, Sulpicia, through her allusions and word choice, depicts herself as new Sappho, one who does what Sappho did, but brings that style of poetry into Latin. This transition is completed in line 5 wherein the Greek *Cytherea* is transformed into the Latin *Venus.*

**3. illum:** Refers to the *amor* in line 1 and is the object of *attulit* and *deposuitque* (line 4). The reader is left to wonder what kind of *amor* Sulpicia is describing: is she referring to an actual person whom Venus has led to her embrace or physical sexual fulfillment or a reference to the love poetry she is writing on the wax tablets situated on her lap? Or all three?

**3. Cytherea:** A traditional epithet for Venus, who held the south Aegean island of Cythera as sacred to her. It occurs as early as Homer (*Od.* 8.288), but is particularly associated with Sappho (*fr.* 86 and 140a). Thus, Sulpicia's use of the epithet here highlights the allusion she is making to Sappho, and the transition from *Cytherea* to *Venus* in line 5 depicts the transition from the Greek Sappho as female writer of love poetry to the Roman Sulpicia.

**3. Camenis:** The Camenae were traditionally Roman water-nymphs associated with the Porta Capena. However, early Latin literature associated them with poetic inspiration and set them up as Roman analogs to the Greek Muses (cf. Liv. Andron. *Od.*, Enn. *Ann.* fr. 487).

**5. gaudia:** In Roman elegy, *gaudia* most typically referred to sexual exploits and enjoyments. So, perhaps, a proper translation here would be "trysts".

**5. narret:** present jussive subjunctive of *narrare*. Translate as "let him tell." The subject is left unstated, but it appears to be the *quis* from the protasis in line 6. If so, the couplet is a challenge to the reader: "let him tell of my trysts, if someone will be said not have had his own." Such a challenge emphasizes Sulpicia's hedging of responsibility because of the requirements of her *pudor*: it is not she who tells the story, but another, yet only if he is able to understand her coded messages.

**7–8: Non … velim:** Sulpicia returns to her complex syntax, almost as if she recalls the pressures put on her by *pudor*. She has spent lines 3–6 clearly speaking of her loves, but now returns to an anxious apprehension at the prospect of someone else reading either her *gaudia* or her notes to her beloved. A more prosaic order of the complex syntax would be: *Non ego quicquam tabellis signatis mandare velim ne nemo id legat antequam meus [vir].*

**7. tabellis:** A *tabella* is similar to the modern notebook. Fulkerson (2017) explains, "They are flat, thin sheets of wood covered over with wax and scratched into with a stylus to write short notes and poetry" (277). In Roman elegy, they are the typical means of communication between lovers (cf. Ov. *Am.* 1.11.7 and 15, 1.12.1 and 7).

**8. velim:** potential subjunctive. Translate as "I would [not] want".

**8. ne … nemo:** A double negative. Literally "not no one". Translate as "lest someone".

**8. quam … ante:** tmesis of *antequam.*

**9–10: sed … ferar:** In this final couplet of the poem, Sulpicia eventually throws off the limitations of *pudor* and determines to tell her story, despite social pressures. The dangers of rumor are embraced, as she ends the poem with the provocative *ferar* (see note 10 *ferar* below).

**9. peccasse:** syncopated form of *peccavisse.*

**9. vultus conponere famae:** perhaps a more modern translation would be "to keep up the appearance of good repute"

**10. digna:** This feminine adjective describing the narrator is the first moment in the poem—or in the sextet of Sulpicia's poetry—that we learn the narrator is a woman.

**10. digno digna:** An instance of the literary device *figura etymologica*, the placing of different forms of the same word in close proximity to each other. It is a favorite device of Sulpicia.

**10. ferar:** Sulpicia ends her poem of double meaning and ambiguity with another loaded word. The form *ferar* can either be future indicative or present subjunctive. So, Sulpicia leaves it to the reader to determine whether it is "I will be said" (future indicative) or "let me be said" (jussive subjunctive) or even "I may be said" (potential subjunctive). In such a way, Sulpicia again provides some distance between the reader and Sulpicia's true feelings. The definition of *fero* here is not the simple one of "to carry/bear" but "to carry/bear [in rumor]."

***Sulpicia 2 (Tib. 3.14)***

Invisus natalis adest, qui rure molesto
  et sine Cerintho tristis agendus erit.
Dulcius urbe quid est? an villa sit apta puellae
  atque Arretino frigidus amnis agro?
Iam, nimium Messalla mei studiose, quiescas;
  heu tempestivae saepe, propinque, viae!
Hīc animum sensusque meos abducta relinquo,
  arbitrio quamvis non sinis esse meo.

*Meter: elegiac couplets*

—

**abduco, abducere, abduxi, abductum:** to lead away, carry off, remove
**amnis, amnis, *m.*:** stream, river
**arbitrium, i, *n.*:** judgment, free will; presence, company
**Arretinus, a, um:** Arretian, pertaining to the town of Aretium
**Cerinthus, i, *m.*:** Cerinthus
**frigidus, a, um:** cold, chilling, frigid
**invisus, a, um:** hated
**Messalla, ae, *f.*:** M. Valerius Mesalla Corvinus
**molestus, a, um:** troublesome, annoying
**natalis, is, *m.*:** birthday
**propinquus, a, um:** near, neighboring
**quamvis:** as much as you like; although
**quiesco, quiescere, quievi, quietum:** to rest, relax; keep quiet
**relinquo, relinquere, relicui, relictum:** to leave behind, abandon
**rus, ruris, *n.*:** the country(side)
**sino, sinere, sivi, situm:** to let, allow, permit
**studiosus, a, um:** eager, attentive, devoted
**tempestivus, a, um:** belonging to the right time, timely, seasonable, appropriate
**villa, ae, *f.*:** country house

—

**1–4. invisus … agro:** The first half of this poem identifies Sulpicia's complaint in generically-charged terms. On one level, the lines can be read as a straightforward lament of an elegiac *puella* who is being forced to leave the city and her beloved. Such departure poems are a commonplace in Propertian elegy (Prop. 1.8, 2.19, 4.3), and Fulkerson (2017) points out that such a close connection between this poem and Propertian elegy may represent a tacit rejection of Tibullan elegy, which is typically pastoral in nature (281). On another level, the vocabulary used in these lines may suggest that Sulpicia is being separated from writing her elegies. She states that she (a *puella*) is being forced from the city (*urbs*), the traditional location for elegy, and into a more pastoral one (*Arretino agro*). Moreover, she is to go without Cerinthus (*sine Cerintho*), who may be a corporeal person, but also a representative of elegy itself.

When taken together, we may read these lines as a complaint that she is being forced from writing elegy and from her poetry itself by departing to a location of a more pastoral genre.

1. **invisis natalis:** It is unclear whose birthday it is to which the poem is referring. The implication here is that it is Sulpicia's, but the subsequent poem (Sulpicia 3) claims that it is Cerinthus's (cf. Sulpicia 3, note 2 *suo* below).

2. **Cerinthus:** This is the first mention of the name of Cerinthus in this construction of the eleven poem cycle. According to the manuscripts and standard editions, there are several poems before this one that refer to her beloved by this name. The name Cerinthus may be the name of an actual individual, pseudonymous, or both. Traditionally, scholars have connected his name to the Greek word κήρινθος, meaning "bee-bread", and have argued a further connection between bees and their production of wax. Since wax was typically used by Romans to make the *tabellae* on which Sulpicia is writing her poetry, it is thought that Cerinthus may represent Sulpicia's poetry itself. If Cerinthus is, indeed, a historical figure, the name is thought to be a pseudonym for Cornutus, an individual referenced by Tibullus in 2.2–3 as about to be married and celebrating a birthday. Connections to this or a Cornutus make some sense, as well, seeing as the juxtaposition between Cornutus and Cerinthus produces a bilingual pun (cornus = κέρας) and there was a historical Cornutus in the circles of Messalla and Sulpicia in the form of Marcus Caecilius Cornutus, who was in the Arval college with Messalla, or his son.

2. **tristis:** nominative modifying *qui* (i.e., *natalis*).

2. **agendus erit:** passive periphrastic in the future tense. Translate as "will have to be spent".

3. **urbe:** ablative of comparison.

3. **sit:** present deliberative subjunctive of *esse*. Translate as "would be".

3. **aptus puellae:** *aptus* takes a dative to describe the thing for which one is fit/suitable.

4. **Arretino … agro:** ablative of place where. Arretium was approximately 100 miles north of Rome in modern Tuscany. Maecenas, the famous patron of the arts under Augustus, is thought to have been from Arretium (Hor. *Carm.* 3.29.1, *Sat.* 1.6.1). Fatucchi (1976) suggests that inscriptional evidence exists that the Sulpicii had property there, as well.

4. **Arretino frigidus amnis agro:** The chiasmus (ABBA word order) here cleverly paints the image of a cold river in the middle of the Arretian field.

5. **mei studiose:** *studiosus* most frequently takes the objective genitive to describe the thing for which one is eager.

5. **Messalla:** Valerius Messalla Corvinus (64 BCE-8 CE), a prominent soldier, orator, statesman, and patron of the arts. He also may have been Sulpicia's legal guardian (cf. Introduction).

**5. quiescas:** present jussive subjunctive of *quiescere.* 2nd singular, jussive subjunctives often are construed as polite commands and are translated as imperatives. Translate as "relax!".

**5–6. Messalla … studiose … propinque:** The vocative *Messalla* is followed by its two adjectives *studiosus* and *propinquus*. This repeated use of the vocative makes the syntax of this couplet difficult.

**6. heu tempestivae … viae:** supply *sunt.* The entire line is problematic. At issue is the initial word *heu.* Most manuscripts and modern editions print *neu* instead, as that provides the appropriate negative meaning required by the line. However, as Fulkerson (2017) points out, *neu* would add a connective that does not refer back to anything else and, thus, would be grammatically out of place. In this edition, we follow Fulkerson (2017) and retain *heu*, despite the interpretative problems.

**6. propinque:** This adjective is frequently used, as it is here, to describe closeness in terms of relationships (cf. Sall. *J.* 10.3; Verg. *A.* 2.86; Cic. *Off.* 1.17.53; Hor. *S.* 2.3.218). We, perhaps, would translate it as "kindred", "kinsman", or "relative".

**8. arbitrio:** The *arbitrium* was the legal term for the power of free will an individual had over another. In this situation, since Messalla is here depicted as Sulpicia's guardian, he would have *arbitrium* over her. In the literary realm, the term also extends to poetic judgment (Ov. *EP* 3.9.48, *arbitrio variat multa poeta suo*). The tension between these two legal and literary meanings is present in this final line: Sulpicia, because of Messalla's *arbitrium* over her, has no legal means of making her own decisions (*arbitrium*) and following her own poetic judgment (*arbitrium*) in writing elegy.

### *Sulpicia 3 (Tib. 3.15)*

Scis iter ex animo sublatum triste puellae?
  natali Romae iam licet esse suo.
Omnibus ille dies nobis natalis agatur,
  qui nec opinanti nunc tibi forte venit.

*Meter: elegiac couplets*

—

**natalis, is, *m*.:** birthday

**opino, opinare, opinavi, opinatum:** to think, believe, imagine; to be of opinion

**Roma, ae, *f*.:** Rome

**subfero, subferre, sustuli, sublatum:** to endure, suffer; to carry under

—

**1. iter:** Sulpicia cleverly reminds the reader of the threat of her forced travel to Arretium in the previous poem, Sulpicia 2.

1. **ex animo:** Usually translated as an idiom meaning "from the heart, truly", Fulkerson (2017) sees this as a more literal meaning: the journey's concern has been lifted off of Sulpicia's heart.
1. **triste:** the description of the journey (*iter*) as *tristis* directly responds to the opening of Sulpicia 2 in which the hated birthday is described as *tristis* (line 2).
1. **puellae:** An ambiguous word. Some editors have taken *puellae* with *iter*: "the girl's journey"; others, however, have taken *puellae* with *ex animo* in the sense of "in accordance with the wish of the girl". The latter reading is strengthened by the position of the words in the line, as *ex animo* stands at the caesura, and *puellae* at the line end.
2. **Romae:** locative case. Translate as "at Rome".
2. **licet:** impersonal phrase with a dative (*natali suo*) and an infinitive (*esse*). Translate as "it is allowed for X to Y."
2. **suo:** There is great debate among editors regarding this word. The most reliable manuscripts read *tuo*; however, this does not seem to be correct as it would make Cerinthus' birthday the subject of the poem and disrupt the unity of the birthday poem pair Sulpicia 3 forms with Sulpicia 2. Therefore, editors generally accept that *tuo* is incorrect. The debate arises regarding the correct emendation. Later medieval manuscripts preserve a tradition that reads *suo*, a reading that maintains the unity of Sulpicia 2 and 3 by keeping the focus on Sulpicia's birthday (Miller, 2002). Other later editors (Bradley, 1995) have emended the text to *meo*, which, although sensible, has no manuscript attestation. Therefore, we have chosen to followFulkerson (2017) and to keep *suo* in this edition.
3. **omnibus ... nobis:** A surprise inclusion, as until this point Sulpicia has only discussed her relationship with Cerinthus. Here, a third party is invited to join them in the celebration of her birthday. Fulkerson (2017) suggests that a larger community, perhaps the *sollicti* of Sulpicia 4, is invoked here. However, this may also be a nod to the audience of Sulpicia's poetry, who have been drawn into her relationship with Cerinthus by virtue of their reading her poetry. If so, Sulpicia invites us as readers to celebrate her birthday by taking part in her relationship with Cerinthus, who may also represent her poetry.
3. **agatur:** present jussive subjunctive from *agere*. Translate as "let it be spent". The choice of *ago* here directly corresponds to the same verb to describe the hated birthday in Sulpicia 2 (*invisus natalis ... agendus erit*).
4. **qui:** refers to *dies*. Translate as "which".
4. **opinanti:** dative participle agreeing with *tibi*. Cerinthus is described as surprised or unsuspecting here, and, perhaps, Sulpicia hopes that he will be excited to learn of her unexpected arrival.

***Sulpicia 4 (Tib. 3.16)***

Gratum est, securus multum quod iam tibi de me
permittis, subito ne male inepta cadam.
Sit tibi cura togae potior pressumque quasillo
scortum quam SERVI FILIA SULPICIA.
Solliciti sunt pro nobis, quibus illa dolori est
ne cedam ignoto maxima causa toro.

*Meter: elegiac couplets*

—

**ignotus, a, um:** ignorant, unknown; low-born, vulgar
**ineptus, a, um:** silly, foolish, senseless
**quasillum, i, *n*.:** small basket for wool
**scortum, i, *n*.:** prostitute, harlot; piece of hide, skin
**Servius, i, *m*.:** Servius Sulpicius Rufus, Sulpicia's father
**sollicitus, a, um:** disturbed, agitated, worried
**Sulpicia, ae, *f*.:** Sulpicia
**toga, ae, *f*.:** toga
**torus, i, *m*.:** couch, sofa, marriage-bed

—

**1. Gratum est:** "it is deserving of thanks". The unstated subject of the clause is the *quod* in the following clause.
**1–2. securus multum quod tibi de me permittis:** Translate as "the fact that you, too confident about me, permit yourself so much (about me)." This clause is quite ambiguous. Key to the meaning is *securus*, which should be construed with *de me* to mean "confident about me" (i.e., confident that Sulpicia won't cheat or, alternatively, that Cerinthus won't be caught in his own affairs). *Multum* could be construed with *securus* (overly-confident) or as the object of *permittis* (you allow much to yourself) or both.
**2. ne … cadam:** present subjunctive of *cadere* in a negative purpose clause.
**3. togae:** The toga was the traditional clothing of citizen men and prostitutes in ancient Rome. Fulkerson (2017) sees the use of toga here as a pun that activates both meanings: Sulpicia is both urging Cerinthus to think of his status as a citizen and to stop getting into trysts with low-class women (i.e., Let the (citizen) toga be a care for you) and also, exasperated, is telling him to go ahead, keep his affairs, and leave her alone (i.e., Let the (whore's) toga be a care for you).
**3. Sit tibi cura togae potior:** *Sit* is a present jussive subjunctive of *esse*, translated as "let be". The subject of *sit* is both *cura togae* and *pressumque … scortum. Tibi* is a dative of reference or possession with *sit. Potior* is a comparative adjective in the predicate position after *sit*. Translate as "let the care of the toga be more important for you."
**3. pressumque quasillo:** literally "having been forced to the basket". This is a demeaning phrase meaning that the *scortum* is so poor than she must carry spun wool in baskets to make a living.

**4. scortum:** This term is used to refer to a male or female paid for sexual services. The modern English word 'escort' derives from it. Perhaps best translated as "call girl" in this instance.

**4. SERVI FILIA SULPICIA:** "Sulpicia, daughter of Servius". Sulpicia here refers to herself in the formal, public style of an aristocratic inscription in order to create a juxtaposition with the *scortum*. The text has been marked in capital letters to highlight the inscriptional quality of the line, but the manuscripts themselves have no such capitalization for emphasis. However, as Batstone (2018) has noted, *filia* is often used to describe prostitutes in such phrasings. So, Sulpicia, although trying to marshall her aristocratic status to draw a distinction between herself and Cerinthus' potential other lovers, simultaneously draws attention to her own illicit relationship with Cerinthus.

**5. quibus illa dolori est … maxima causa:** Difficult and ambiguous word order. *Illa* is the subject of *est*, and looks ahead to and agrees with *maxima causa*. *Dolori* is a dative of cause. Translate as "for whom that is the highest cause of pain." However, *maxima causa* could also be taken in apposition to the understood "I" that is the subject of *cedam*. If taken thus, the meaning shifts to "for whom it is a cause of pain that I, their greatest concern, fall in an unknown bed." This reading is strengthened by the ABBA word order of line 6 in which the greatest concern (i.e., Sulpicia) is in the middle of the unknown bed (*ignoto maxima causa toro*).

**6. ne cedam:** present subjunctive of *cedere* in a fear clause built off of either *dolori* or *sollicitti sunt*.

### *Sulpicia 5 (Tib. 3.17)*

Estne tibi, Cerinthe, tuae pia cura puellae,
  quod mea nunc vexat corpora fessa calor?
A! Ego non aliter tristes evincere morbos
  optarim, quam te si quoque velle putem.
At mihi quid prosit morbos evincere, si tu
  nostra potes lento pectore ferre mala?

*Meter: elegiac couplets*

—

**calor, caloris, *m*.:** warmth, heat; fever; heat of passion
**Cerinthus, i, *m*.:** Cerinthus
**evinco, evincere, evici, evictum:** to overcome completely, conquer
**lentus, a, um:** slow, lazy; calm, indifferent, unconcerned
**vexo, vexare, vexavi, vexatum:** to shake, agitate, plague, torment

—

**1–2. Estne … calor:** Sulpicia opens the poem with a couplet describing her exasperation at Cerinthus' seeming indifference to her suffering. This indifference, however, is only Sulpicia's interpretation of Cerinthus' actions. In Sulpicia 9, Cerinthus is depicted as anxiously worrying over the health of a suffering Sulpicia. As such, these two poems may be responding to one another.

**1–2: tibi … tuae … mea:** The entirety of the poem centers around the juxtaposition of the actions of Sulpicia with those of Cerinthus. To emphasize this "me vs. you" drama, Sulpicia makes constant use of personal pronouns *ego* and *tu* throughout the poem.

**1. tuae pia cura puellae:** A tidy instance of Neoteric Latin style. The two adjective-noun pairs *pia cura* and *tuae puellae* are organized via chiasmus (ABBA word order). Likewise, the adjectives are thrust forward and the nouns pushed backwards, an effect that creates suspense in the readers, as we know the the descriptive words before we discover what they are describing.

**2. quod:** here translate as "because".

**2. calor:** This is the standard medical term for 'fever'; however, in elegy, it also takes on the meaning of the heat of amatory passion. Here, the word is placed into a position of emphasis, as it is delayed until the last position of the couplet.

**3–4. A! … putem:** After asking her incredulous question about Cerinthus' apathy toward her situation in the opening couplet, Sulpicia gets even more dramatic. Beginning with the exclamatory *A!*, Sulpicia states that she would not wish to conquer her ailment if Cerinthus did not want her to do so. This statement is, indeed, extreme and shows a glimpse into Sulpicia's highly emotional state.

**3. A! Ego:** there is most likely a hiatus in the scansion here. Therefore, do not elide the *A!* and the *Ego.*

**3–4. aliter … quam:** literally "not otherwise". Translate here as "except".

**4. optarim:** syncopated form of *optaverim.*

**4. optarim … putem:** an inverted conditional with a protasis in the present subjunctive (*putem*) and a potential subjective in the perfect tense (*optarim*). In the perfect tense, potential subjunctives may be translated as "would" (cf. Allen and Greenough §447.1). Therefore, construe as "I would not wish … if I should think …"

**5–6. At … mala:** Sulpicia hits peak drama in the final couplet. It is not enough to state that she wouldn't want to overcome her illness if Cerinthus did not want her to, as she did in the middle couplet of the poem. She follows this with the statement that she shouldn't even try to conquer the illness if he shows such apathy.

**5. mihi quid prosit:** present deliberative subjunctive of *proesse.* Translate as "what would it benefit me?"

**5. evincere:** subjective infinitive with *prosit.*

**6. nostra … mala:** More neoteric stylings in this line. The two adjective-noun pairs *nostra mala* and *lento pectore* are arranged in a chiastic order (ABBA) and are balanced throughout the line. Moreover, the two adjectives are pushed forward in the line, emphasizing the descriptors of the pairs before the reader learns the objects they modify.

**6. lento:** *lentus* is the standard term used to mark a insufficiently amorous lover in Roman elegy. Often, it is juxtaposed with the overexuberance of the *amator* (cf. Tib. 2.6.36, Prop. 1.6.12, Ov. *Ars* 1.732). Here, the *lentum pectus* of Cerinthus is juxtaposed with the *calor* of Sulpicia.

***Sulpicia 6 (Tib. 3.18)***

Ne tibi sim, mea lux, aeque iam fervida cura
  ac videor paucos ante fuisse dies,
si quicquam tota commisi stulta iuventa
  cuius me fatear paenituisse magis,
hesterna quam te solum quod nocte reliqui,
  ardorem cupiens dissimulare meum.

*Meter: elegiac couplets*

—

**ardor, ardoris, *m.*:** flame; desire, passion
**dissimulo, dissimulare, dissimulavi, dissimulatum:** to conceal, disguise, keep secret
**fervidus, a, um:** burning, fiery, raging
**hesternus, a, um:** yesterday's, of yesterday
**iuventa, ae, *f.*:** youth, the age of youth
**paeniteo, paenitere, paenitui, —:** to grieve one (acc.) of something (gen.)
**stultus, a, um:** foolish, simple, stupid

—

**1–6. Ne … meum:** This is, perhaps, the most difficult poem of the six shorter Sulpicia elegies in terms of syntax, as the entire poem is a single, winding sentence of multiple subordinate clauses. As is typical of Sulpicia, she uses convoluted syntax to hide the true meaning of her poems, especially when they describe something against social expectations. In this poem, Sulpicia describes a tryst between the two lovers that got a bit too heated for Sulpicia in the moment. When the temperature rose, Sulpicia pretended to be disinterested (*stulta*) and left Cerinthus alone. However, Sulpicia only pretended to be disinterested because she wanted to disguise her true feelings of passion (*ardorem meum*). Such an erotic situation would not be something for a Roman woman to discuss in public; thus, it is appropriate for Sulpicia to disguise with complex syntax. As for the syntax proper, the poem can be generally described as an inverted condition with the protasis beginning in line 3 and the apodosis replaced by the hortatory subjunctive *ne sim* in line 1. However, the negative subjunctive adds a twist to the condition: Sulpicia states that *if* she committed something of which she was more ashamed than the fact that she left Cerinthus alone, then she *wouldn't want* to be as much of a care to him as she had been that night. However, if she presumably has not done something worse than leave Cerinthus alone, then the opposite of the subjunctive clause would be the truth: she *has not done* anything worse and thus she *would want* to be as much of a care to Cerinthus as she had been that night. A more prosaic word order of the entire poem would be: *si stulta quicquam tota iuventa commisi, cuius me magis paenituisse fatear, quam quod te solum nocte hesterna reliqui, cupiens ardorem mean dissimulare, ne sim aeque iam fervida cura tibi, mea lux, ac ante paucos dies fuisse videor.*

**1. Ne ... sim:** present hortatory subjunctive of *esse*. Translate as "may I not be"

**1–2. aeque ...ac:** "as burning a care now as"

**2. paucos ante ... dies:** Translate as "a few days ago".

**3. si ... iuventa:** Translate as "If I, foolish, did anything in my entire youth".

**3. stulta:** referring to Sulpicia. As Fulkerson (2017, *ad loc.* points out, *stultus* is used regularly in elegy to describe individuals either uninterested in or incompetent at love (cf. Tib. 1.2.68, 1.4.34, 1.9.45, 1.9.65). In this poem, it is Sulpicia who states that she pretended to be disinterested in order to disguise her passion for Cerinthus.

**4. cuius ... bold:** Lowe (1988, p. 198) translates this as "of which I can say I have been more repentant...".

**4. cuius:** genitive object of *paenitere.*

**4. paenituisse:** perfect active infinitive of *paenitere* in indirect statement with *fatear.*

**4. fatear:** subjunctive in a relative clause of characteristic (cf. Allen and Greenough §534–535).

**5. hesterna ... reliqui:** A bit of a word picture describing Cerinthus abandonment by Sulpicia. The two adjective noun pairs *hesterna nocte* and *te solum* are separated from one another and placed into a chiastic structure (ABBA). The *te solum* (i.e., Cerinthus) is placed in the middle of the line, isolated from the other words by the two *q*-words *quam* and *quod.*

**5. quam:** Translate as "than" and construe with *magis* (line 4).

**5. quod:** Translate as "the fact that".

**6. cupiens:** referring to Sulpicia.

**6. ardorem ... meum:** More word pictures here. The identification of the *ardor* as belonging to Sulpicia is delayed until the end of the sentence, disguising whose *ardor* it is until the end of the line. Such a disguising mimics the sense of the sentence that Sulpicia wanted to hide her passion.

### *Sulpicia 7 (Tib. 3.8)*

Sulpicia est tibi culta tuis, Mars magne, kalendis:
  spectatum e caelo, si sapis, ipse veni.
Hoc Venus ignoscet: at tu, violente, caveto
  ne tibi miranti turpiter arma cadant.
illius ex oculis, cum volt exurere divos,
  accendit geminas lampadas acer Amor.

Illam, quidquid agit, quoquo vestigia movit,
componit furtim subsequiturque Decor.
Seu solvit crines, fusis decet esse capillis:
seu composit, comptis est veneranda comis.
Urit, seu Tyria voluit procedere palla:
urit, seu nivea candida veste venit.
Talis in aeterno felix Vertumnus Olympo
mille habet ornatus, mille decenter habet.
Sola puellarum digna est, cui mollia caris
vellera det sucis bis madefacta Tyros,
possideatque, metit quidquid bene olentibus arvis
cultor odoratae dives Arabs segetis,
et quascumque niger rubro de litore gemmas
proximus Eois colligit Indus aquis.
Hanc vos, Pierides, festis cantate kalendis,
et testudinea Phoebe superbe lyra.
Hoc sollemne sacrum multos consummet in annos:
dignior est vestro nulla puella choro.

*Meter: elegiac couplets*

—

**accendo, accendere, accendi, accensus:** to set on fire, to light
**annus, anni, *m.*:** year, age
**Arabs, Arabis (gen.):** Arabian
**bis:** (adv.) twice
**capillus, capilli, *m.*:** hair; single hair
**chorus, chori, *m.*:** chorus, dancing and singing performance
**colo, colere, colui, cultus:** to adorn, to decorate; to live in, to inhabit
**como, comere, compsi, comptus:** to arrange, to adorn
**consummo, consummare, consummavi, consummatus:** to complete, perfect, bring together
**crinis, crinis, *m.*:** hair
**decenter:** (adv.) becomingly, properly, decently
**Decor, Decoris, *m.*:** charm, grace, beauty
**dignus, a, um:** appropriate; worthy, deserving
**Eous, a, um:** eastern, oriental
**exuro, exurere, exussi, exustus:** to burn; to destroy
**festus, a, um:** festive, joyous
**fundo, fundere, fudi, fusus:** to pour, pour out, shed
**furtim:** (adv.) secretly, stealthily
**geminus, gemina, geminum:** double, twin
**gemma, gemmae, *f.*:** jewel, gem, precious stone; bud
**ignosco, ignoscere, ignovi, ignotus:** to pardon, to forgive
**Indus, a, um:** Indian
**kalens, kalendis, *f.*:** Kalends (the first day of the month)
**lampada, lampadae, *f.*:** torch; lantern
**litus, litoris, *n.*:** shore, coast; beach, landing place
**lyra, lyrae, *f.*:** lyre, lyric poetry
**madefacio, madefacere, madefeci, madefactus:** to make wet, to soak, to dip

**Mars, Martis, *m*.:** Mars (god of war)
**meto, metere, messui:** to reap, collect
**niveus, a, um:** snowy; white
**odoratus, a, um:** perfumed, fragrent
**oleo, olere, olui:** to smell of, to smell like
**ornatus, us, *m*.:** furnishing, decoration
**palla, pallae, *f*.:** palla, a woman's outer garment
**Pierides, um, *f.pl*.:** (the) Muses
**possideo, possidere, possedi, possessus:** to seize, to hold
**proximus, a, um:** nearest, closest, next
**quoquo:** **(adv.)** whithersoever, to whatever place
**ruber, rubra, rubrum:** red, ruby-colored
**sapio, sapere, sapivi:** to understand; to be wise
**seges, segetis, *f*.:** crop, field of grain
**solemne, sollemnis, *n*.:** religious ceremony, ritual offerings, rite
**specto, spectare, spectavi, spectatus:** to look at, to observe
**subsequor, subsequi, subsecutus sum:** to follow close; to pursue
**sucus, suci, *m*.:** juice, sap; dye
**testudineus, a, um:** made of tortoise-shell
**Tyros, Tyri, *f*.:** Tyre (city of the Phoenicians famed for its purple dye)
**uro, urere, ussi, ustus:** to burn
**vellus, velleris, *n*.:** fleece, wool
**venero, venerare, veneravi, veneratus:** to adore, to pay homage to; to worship
**Venus, Veneris, *f*.:** Venus (goddess of (sexual) love)
**Vertumnus, i, *m*.:** Vertumnus (god of seasons and change)
**violentus, a, um:** violent, impetuous, boisterous

—

**1–8:** The poet sets the scene for this poem by announcing its elegiac intentions and drawing a clear connection between Sulpicia and the goddess Venus. The poem opens with an invocation of Mars, the god of war, inviting him to come see the beauty of Sulpicia for himself. The poet argues that Venus herself will not begrudge him as much because Sulpicia's beauty is so outstanding. The poem then continues to highlight Sulpicia's beauty by blurring the lines between her and Venus through the use of ambiguous pronouns that could conceivably refer to either Sulpicia or Venus.

**1. tibi:** Either a dative of reference (Sulpicia has been decorated *for you*) or dative of agent (Sulpicia has been worshipped *by you*).

**1. tuis ... kalendis:** March 1st. Traditionally, the Kalends of March was the occasion of the Matronalia, a festival honoring the role of the Sabines—the first Roman 'wives'—in reconciling the Romans to their Sabine neighbors. Although the myth at the core of the Matronalia is well-known, it is less certain what the actual events of the festival were. Moreover, the role of the reference to the Matronalia here is uncertain. On one level, it serves to activate the backdrop of marriage against which the poet will develop a number of elegiac themes. Immediately, the poet encourages Mars to leave his lover Venus, with whom he famously has an affair, to admire the beauty of Sulpicia, stating that Venus will forgive the transgression (*hoc Venus ignoscet*, 3). It is Sulpicia's beauty and charm that will drive Apollo—and his Muses—to sing of her for years to come (*in multos annos*, 23).

**1. Mars magne:** Although it is surprising at first blush to see a reference to the god of war in poetry about love, this was commonplace in Roman elegy. Known as *militia amoris* (the warfare of love) and made most popular by the poet Ovid, this trope describes the experience of the poet-lover as similar to that of a soldier on the battlefield. The poet-lover is constantly fighting against *Amor* and, at times, the object of the poet-lover's desire. This can take a variety of forms from complaints about the loss of the traditional roles the poet-lover had played before falling in love to actual violent acts perpetrated by the poet-lover against his beloved. Here, the poet is communicating to the reader that this poem will be an elegy, with a blend of love and war (*Mars* and *Venus*) so common in *militia amoris.*

**2. spectatum:** supine of purpose (cf. Allen and Greenough §509). Translate as "for the purpose of watching" or "to watch".

**2. veni:** present imperative of *venire.*

**3. Hoc:** This refers to the potential act of seeing Sulpicia (*spectatum*) on line 2.

**3. caveto:** future imperative of *cavere* (cf. Allen and Greenough §163b and 449).

**4. ne … cadant:** negative purpose clause built off of *caveto.*

**4. miranti:** dative participle agreeing with *tibi.*

**5–6. illius … Amor:** Amor causes gods to fall in love by kindling the flames of love in them via the eyes of objects of their gaze. When the gods look upon these individuals, they become inflamed with passion.

**5. illius:** An ambiguous word, as it can plausibly refer to either Venus, the most recent goddess referenced, or Sulpicia, the topic of the poem. The ambiguity here draws the two individuals together and imbues Sulpicia with some of the qualities of the beautiful Venus.

**5. volt:** Archaic spelling of *vult.* As with *illius* above, this word, too, is ambiguous, as it can refer either to Venus, Sulpicia, or—as it turns out in the subsequent line—Cupid. Again, the ambiguity gives Sulpicia some of the qualities of these divinities of love, but it also highlights the difficulty in pinning down the exact nature of love. Does gazing upon Sulpicia cause passion to arise in those watching or does Cupid shoot them with an arrow? How does Venus factor in, as well?

**6. Amor:** the personified Cupid.

**7. illam:** Again, the lines between Sulpicia and Venus are blurred, as the *illam* is ambiguous and can be said to describe both (cf. note 5 *illius* above).

**9–14:** The description of Sulpicia's beauty gets even more detailed in this second portion of the poem, as the poet portrays her beauty as one suitable for each and every season. No matter how she does her hair or what clothes she chooses to wear, Sulpicia is stunning. This section concludes with a simile comparing Sulpicia to Vertumnus, the god of seasons and change, as both are able to change their adornments to look beautiful in every season.

**10. est veneranda:** passive periphrastic construction. Translate as "ought to be worshipped".

**11–12. urit ... venit:** This couplet is replete with stark imagery and flashes of color. The purple hues of the Tyrian garment are elegantly juxtaposed against the radiant brightness of the snow-white clothing. One can even catch a glimpse of the flashes of fire present in the repeated verb *urit*. Altogether, the poet seeks to emphasize Sulpicia's beauty by vividly painting her for the reader so that the reader may come and see her as Mars does.

**13. Vertumnus:** Vertumnus is the god of seasons and change, thought of as originating as an Etruscan god (cf. Varro *DLL* 5.46, Prop. 4.2.4, Plin. *NH* 34.34). He is oftentimes depicted as crossing the lines of gender: a male god dressed in female clothing. His appearance here in a comparison to Sulpicia may speak to Sulpicia's own gender trouble, as she, a female, engages in the traditionally male task of writing poetry. Moreover, the juxtaposition of the Italic Vertumnus with the more Greek Olympus shows the same mixing of Greek and Italic elements that Sulpicia plays with in Sulpicia 1, wherein she announces herself as the Roman Sappho through the combination of the Greek *Cytherea* and the Italic *Camenis* (line 3).

**15–20:** The beauty of Sulpicia is elaborated upon in this third portion of the poem in which the poet takes the reader on a tour of the Roman world, listing places each more and more distant from Rome: Phoenicia, Arabia, and India. As earlier with Sulpicia's attire, the vivid colors and scents are emphasized, as the poet seeks to engage all of the reader's senses.

**15. digna:** The description of Sulpicia as *digna* is a common thread in the Sulpician corpus, looking back to her statement in the last line of Sulpicia 1: *cum digno digna fuisse ferar.* She is also referred to as *dignior* in the final line of this poem (cf. Sulpicia 11, line 10).

**15–16. digna est ... det:** The statement *digna est* (she is worthy) introduces a relative clause of characteristic (cf. Allen and Greenough §535). Translate as "she is worthy to be the one to whom (Tyre) gives". *Det* is the present subjunctive of *dare.*

**15–16. cui ... Tyros:** This relative clause features complex word order. A more prosaic order would be *cui Tyros mollia vellera, sucis caris bis madefacta, det.*

**17. possideatque:** Present potential subjunctive from *possidere.* Translate as "she (alone) should possess". The enclitic *-que* joins the verb back to the original phrase *sola puellarum digna est* (line 15) and alerts the reader that the subject of the verb is still *sola puellarum.* The objects of *possideat* are the two subsequent relative clauses *metit quidquid … segestis* and *quascumque … aquis.*

**17–18. metit … segetis:** Convoluted word order. The *cultor* is modified by both *dives* and *Arabs.* A more prosaic order would be *quidquid dives Arabs cultor segetis odoratae arvis bene olentibus metit.*

**17. olentibus … odoratae:** The references to the fragrant smell of the crops and fields indicate that this is a reference to perfume. It was a frequent motif in Roman elegy to describe perfumes and perfume-producing lands in such a manner (cf. Cat. 68.144, Tib. 1.5.36, Prop. 2.29.17 and 3.13.8).

**19–20: et quascumque … aquis:** Yet more convoluted word order. The *Indus* is modified by both *proximus* and *niger.* A more prosaic word order would be *quascumque gemmas niger Indus proximus aquis Eois de litore rubro colligit.*

**20. Eois … aquis:** In Roman elegy, the eastern waters were typically connected with the Indian Ocean. Fulkerson (2017, p. 235) points out that the Indian Ocean was "traditionally considered the border between West and East, and is regularly connected with its native Indians" (cf. Tib. 2.2.15-16, Prop. 4.3.10, and Ov. *Ars* 1.53).

**21–24:** The poem concludes with a return to the divine world with which it started. Whereas Mars is addressed at the beginning of the poem, here the Muses and Apollo are invoked in their role as patrons of poetry and song. The poet argues that Sulpicia's beauty, so artfully described throughout the poem, is singularly deserving of being remembered in song for generations to come.

**21. Pierides:** The epithet *Pierides* is frequently given to the nine Muses in Greco-Roman mythology. It is a reference to the Muses' birth on Mt. Pierus, a mountain in Thessaly.

**22. testudinea … lyra:** Can be construed as either a ablative of means or ablative of specification with *superbe.*

**23. hoc sollemne … annos:** The poem concludes with a strange image: a mortal woman being praised in song by the gods. If we imagine that Sulpicia here is cast a traditional elegiac *puella* and, thus, as both a corporeal girl and the poetry itself, this closing image may create an *inclusio* with the opening lines that evoked *militia amoris.* Descriptions of *militia amoris* in Roman elegy oftentimes blended generic elements of love poetry (i.e., elegy) with those of violent poetry (i.e., epic) (for more on this, see Frederick, 1997). Moreover, the invocation of the muses, was a standard trope to open most epics. Therefore, here, the poet may be adding the epic invocation of the muses to the end of the poem as a means not only to harken back to the blend of *Venus* and *Mars* in lines 1–3, but also as an opening invocation to this cycle of poems about Sulpicia.

**23. consummet:** present jussive subjunctive of *consummare.* Translate as "let [this solemn rite] continue into many years".

**24. dignior … vestro choro:** the adjective *dignus* frequently takes the ablative of specification (cf. Allen and Greenough §418b). Translate as "worthy of you chorus". Again, Sulpicia is described in terms of worth (cf. note 15 *digna* above).

### *Sulpicia 8 (Tib. 3.9)*

Parce meo iuveni, seu quis bona pascua campi
seu colis umbrosi devia montis aper,
nec tibi sit duros acuisse in proelia dentes,
incolumem custos hunc mihi servet Amor.
Sed procul abducit venandi Delia cura:
o pereant silvae, deficiantque canes!
Quis furor est, quae mens densos indagine colles
claudentem teneras laedere velle manus?
Quidve iuvat furtim latebras intrare ferarum
candidaque hamatis crura notare rubis?
Sed tamen, ut tecum liceat, Cerinthe, vagari,
ipsa ego per montes retia torta feram,
ipsa ego velocis quaeram vestigia cervi
et demam celeri ferrea vincla cani.
Tunc mihi, tunc placeant silvae, si, lux mea, tecum
arguar ante ipsas concubuisse plagas:
tunc veniat licet ad casses, inlaesus abibit,
ne Veneris cupidae gaudia turbet, aper.
Nunc sine me sit nulla venus, sed lege Dianae,
caste puer, casta retia tange manu,
et, quaecumque meo furtim subrepit amori,
incidat in saevas diripienda feras.
At tu venandi studium concede parenti
et celer in nostros ipse recurre sinus.

*Meter: elegiac couplets*

—

**acuo, acuere, acui, acutum:** to make sharp, to sharpen, to whet; to incite, arouse
**aper, apri, *m.*:** boar
**arguo, arguere, argui, argutum:** to prove, to argue; to accuse, to blame
**cassis, cassis, *m.*:** hunting net, snare, trap
**cervus, cervi, *m.*:** stag, deer
**concumbo, concumbere, concubui, concubitum:** to lie together, to lie with
**crus, cruris, *n.*:** leg, shin
**cupidus, a, um:** eager, passionate, desirous
**demo, demere, dempsi, demptum:** to take away, to cut off, to remove
**dens, dentis, *m.*:** tooth; ivory
**densus, a, um:** dense, thick; packed; frequent
**devius, a, um:** out-of-the-way; distant
**diripio, diripere, diripui, direptum:** to tear apart, to tear to pieces; to lay waist, to plunder
**ferreus, a, um:** iron, made of iron; cruel, unyielding

**furtim:** (adv.) secretly, stealthily
**hamatus, a, um:** hooked, crooked
**incolumis, is, e:** unharmed, uninjured; safe
**indago, indaginis, *f.*:** an enclosing, surrounding; investigation, hunt
**latebra, latebrae, *f.*:** hiding place, lair, cave
**noto, notare, notavi, notatum:** to mark; to record; to write, to inscribe
**pascuum, i, *n.*:** pasture; grazing-land
**plaga, plagae, *f.*:** hunting net, snare, trap
**recurro, recurrere, recucurri, recursum:** to run back; to return
**rete, retis, *n.*:** net, snare
**rubus, rubi, *m.*:** bramble, briar; thorn
**subripio, subripere, subripui, subreptum:** to snatch away secretly, to steal
**torqueo, torquere, torsi, tortum:** to twist, to turn; to bend, to distort; to torture
**umbrosus, a, um:** shady, shadowy, dark
**vagor, vagari, vagatus sum:** to wander, to roam
**velox, velocis (gen.):** swift, quick, speedy
**venor, venari, venatus sum:** to hunt
**vinclum, vincli, *n.*:** chain, bond

—

**1–4:** The poem opens with Sulpicia's direct address to a wild boar (*aper*) and an appeal that it not harms her beloved Cerinthus while he takes part in a hunting trip. In addition to setting the scene as one of hunting, these lines also activate multiple elegiac themes through their word choice. First, the verb *acuere* and the noun *proelium* are often used in elegy to describe the battles of love. Likewise, the figure of the *custos* is a frequent character in elegy, as he stands outside the door of the beloved and blocks the entrance of the poet-lover. Taken together, these lines seem to belie Sulpicia's worry that Cerinthus get ensnared in another love while on his hunting trip; thus she asks Cupid himself to stand guard and prevent that from happening.

**1. meo iuveni:** object of *parce*, which takes a dative object.

**2. colis:** 2nd singular present of *colo, colere*.

**2. aper:** nominative subject of both *colis* and *parce*, delayed for suspense.

**3. nec … sit:** present, jussive subjunctive. Translate as "let/may it not be".

**3. acuisse:** perfect active infinitive from *acuere*. Construe as the subject of *sit*.

**4. incolumem … Amor:** interlocked word order: *incolumem* custos *hunc* mihi servet Amor. This, perhaps, is meant to depict Sulpicia's hope that Cupid figuratively lock Cerinthus up and keep him from harm.

**4. servet:** present jussive subjunctive of *servare*. Translate as "let/may Cupid protect".

**5–10:** Sulpicia follows her initial statement of her dual worries that Cerinthus be injured on the hunt or be ensnared in another love with the realization that he has already gone away, driven by concern for the hunt (*cura venandi*). As a result, Sulpicia writes two couplets of incredulous exasperation: why would anyone in their right mind willingly put themselves in the danger of the hunt? She peppers these couplets with elegiac vocabulary, heightening the sense that it is not as much the danger to Cerinthus' person that worries her, as it is the potential that he is suffering from a love-madness (*furor*) for another that is driving him away from her.

**5. Sed ... cura:** There is an unstated *illum* here, as Sulpicia says that Delia has led Cerinthus away.

**5. venandi:** genitive singular gerund of *venare*. Construe with *cura* and translate as "by/with care of hunting".

**5. Delia:** a word with multiple meanings. On the one hand, Delia is frequently a reference to the goddess Diana, who was born on the island of Delos. On the other hand, Delia was the name of the *puella* of the elegist Tibullus. Here, both meanings are operative, as Sulpicia bemoans the fact that Cerinthus has already been led away to the hunt. The question is: has Delia the huntress or Delia the elegiac *puella* led him away?

**5. cura:** ablative of means/manner.

**6. pereant ... deficiantque:** present jussive subjunctives of *perire* and *deficere*. Translate as "let perish" and "let fail".

**7. furor:** A frequent word in both Roman elegy and epic. In the epic, martial context, *furor* is a madness associated with blind rage or single-minded obsession. In elegy, *furor* is closer to a love-madness for a beloved. Here, Sulpicia seems to be activating both senses of the word: on one level, she cannot comprehend why Cerinthus would be crazy enough to want to take part in the dangerous activity of the hunt. On another, she worries that it is a love-crazed desire for another beloved that drives Cerinthus to the woods and away from her.

**7–8. densos ... manus:** complex word order. The entire phrase is an accusative-infinitive construction with *claudentem velle* at its core. *densos indagine colles* is built off of the *claudentem*. *teneras manus* is the object of *laedere*, which itself is the complement of *velle*. Translate as "what madness is it? what mindset is it that one, encircling the dense hills in the hunt, would wish to harm his tender hands?"

**9. quidve:** Translate as "why". This is an accusative of respect literally translated as "with respect to what".

**9. latebras intrare ferarum:** A seeming reference to the story of Io in Ov. *M.* 1.593. In that story, the god Jupiter tries to convince the maiden Io with these exact words that she go into the forests and into the lairs of the wild beasts so that they can have sex. She, however, flees from him, but is unable to escape him and is raped. Sulpicia, here, may be emphasizing the amatory dangers that await Cerinthus on the hunt and worries that he will engage in a sexual relationship with another lover.

**10. candida crura:** Cerinthus is depicted as having bright, pale legs. Typically, female objects of desire are given this attribute, not men. Thus, Sulpicia's depiction of Cerinthus not only places him into the role of object of her desire, but it may also serve to effeminize him.

**10. notare:** This verb not only can mean to mark flesh by scraping or wounding, but also to scratch poetry into wax tablets. By using this term, Sulpicia highlights the aspect of Cerinthus as *scriptus puer*, a personification of her elegiac poetry, and complains that he has left her to hunt rather than stay and engage in poetry with her.

**11–18:** After complaining about Cerinthus' departure for the hunt and wondering aloud why one would want to do so, Sulpicia states that it wouldn't be so bad for her if she could come and participate in the hunt. She begins by listing hunting activities she could help Cerinthus with—carrying the hunting nets, looking for deer tracks, and taking the leashes off of the hunting dogs—but ends with her true purpose: she isn't interested in participating in the hunt as much as preventing Cerinthus from finding another lover and engaging in amatory relations with him herself.

**11. ut … liceat … vagari:** purpose clause with the present subjunctive of *licere*. Translate as "so that it may be allowed to wander with you".

**12–14. feram … quaeram … demam:** These three verbs are wonderfully ambiguous. They can either be future indicative or present subjunctive. If taken as the former, Sulpicia is making a clear and definite statement: she will come along on the hunt, and Cerinthus has no choice in the matter. If the latter, the subjunctive would be jussive, and Sulpicia would, instead, be making a polite request of Cerinthus to allow her to accompany him.

**15–16. tunc … plagas:** future-less-vivid condition with the apodosis (*tunc placeant silvae*) preceding the protasis (*si arguar concubisse*). Translate as "should … would".

**15. mihi:** dative of reference with *placeo*.

**15. mea lux:** Sulpicia's reference to Cerinthus as *mea lux* matches the manner in which she refers to him in Sulpicia 6.1 (*mea lux*). In that context, Sulpicia is describing a night in which the two lovers were together and engaging in a tryst that she broke up before it could get too far because she feared for her reputation. Here, the two lovers are also imagined in a tryst; however, this time, she cares not about her reputation and proudly states "let me be accused of lying with you".

**16. concubuisse:** perfect active infinitive of *concumbere*. Construe with *arguar*.

**17. veniat licet ad casses:** Here, *licet* is translated as "even though" because it is construed with a subjunctive. Translate as "Even though the boar may come to the snares".

**18. ne … turbet:** present subjunctive in a negative purpose clause. Translate as "so that the boar may not disturb".

**18. aper:** delayed subject of *veniat*, *abibit*, and *turbet*.

**19–24:** Sulpicia ends the poem with a return to her current situation: left behind by Cerinthus as he goes off on the hunt. She implores that Cerinthus remain loyal to her and refrain from any affairs while away. She even goes so far as to curse any potential woman thinking about taking

Cerinthus away, praying that any rival be torn apart by beasts. To conclude, she turns to Cerinthus and asks him to leave hunting for his parent, and return to her lap.

**19. sit:** present, jussive subjunctive. Translate as "let (no love) be".

**19. Dianae:** Diana was the Roman equivalent to Artemis, the goddess of the hunt and the wilderness. Diana was also a virgin goddess. Therefore, her followers were expected to be chaste, as well, and to eschew any amatory encounters. Here, Sulpicia hopes that Cerinthus will follow Diana's law, *lege Dianae*, and keep from any erotic relationships, since Sulpicia cannot be with him on the hunt.

**20. casta:** ablative construed with *manu.*

**21. meo … amori:** dative object of the compound verb *subrepit.*

**21. subrepit:** Another double-meaning. On the surface level, Sulpicia curses any female (*quaecumque*) who tries to steal her beloved Cerinthus. However, the verb *subripere* is frequently used in Latin poetry to describe literary theft (i.e., one author stealing an idea or story from another). Cf. Cic. Brut. 19.76: *qui a Naevio vel sumpsisti multa, si fateris, vel, si negas, surripuisti* (You, who either took many things from Naevius, if you confess it, or, if you deny it, stole them.) or Sen. Ep. 108.34: *Ennium hoc ait Homero surripuisse, Ennio Vergilium* (He says Ennius stole this from Homer, Vergil from Ennius.). Therefore, when taken together with the motif of Cerinthus as *scriptus puer*, Sulpicia may also be hinting at a curse against any female who tries to write poetry with Cerinthus or even in that elegiac style.

**22. diripienda:** nominative, singular, gerundive agreeing with *quaecumque.*

**23. venandi:** genitive gerund construed with *studium.* Translate with *studium* as "the pursuit of hunting".

**23. parenti:** dative of reference with the compound verb *concede.*

**24. et … sinus:** interlocked word order to create the word picture of Cerinthus in Sulpicia's lap, engaging in an embrace: *et celer* ***in nostros*** *ipse recurre* ***sinus***. The imagery calls to mind Sul. 1.4, in which Venus places Cerinthus into Sulpicia's lap (*attulit in nostrum deposuitque sinum*). The image of Cerinthus in Sulpicia's lap again heightens the motif of Cernithus as the *scriptus puer*, as that is where Sulpicia would be holding her wax tablets to write poetry.

***Sulpicia 9 (Tib. 3.10)***

Huc ades et tenerae morbos expelle puellae,
  huc ades, intonsa Phoebe superbe coma;
crede mihi, propera, nec te iam, Phoebe, pigebit
  formosae medicas applicuisse manus.
Effice ne macies pallentes occupet artus,
  neu notet informis candida membra color,
et quodcumque mali est et quidquid triste timemus,
  in pelagus rapidis evehat amnis aquis.

Sancte, veni, tecumque feras, quicumque sapores,
quicumque et cantus corpora fessa levant; *10*
neu iuvenem torque, metuit qui fata puellae
votaque pro domina vix numeranda facit;
interdum vovet, interdum, quod langueat illa,
dicit in aeternos aspera verba deos.
Pone metum, Cerinthe: deus non laedit amantes; *15*
tu modo semper ama: salva puella tibi est;
nil opus est fletu: lacrimis erit aptius uti, *21*
si quando fuerit tristior illa tibi. *22*
At nunc tota tua est, te solum candida secum *17*
cogitat, et frustra credula turba sedet.
Phoebe, fave: laus magna tibi tribuetur in uno
corpore servato restituisse duos. *20*
Iam celeber, iam laetus eris, cum debita reddet *23*
certatim sanctis laetus uterque focis;
tunc te felicem dicet pia turba deorum, *25*
optabunt artes et sibi quisque tuas.

*Meter: elegiac couplets*

—

**applico, applicare, applicui, applicitus:** to connect, to place near, to bring together; to apply
**aptus, a, um:** fit, apt, appropriate
**artus, artus, *m*.:** arm, leg, limb
**asper, aspera, asperum:** rude; cruel, harsh, savage
**cantus, cantus, *m*.:** song, chant; poem
**celeber, celebris, celebre:** famous, celebrated
**Cerinthus, i, *m*.:** Cerinthus
**certatim:** **(adv.)** with rivalry, in competition
**credulus, a, um:** trustworthy, credible
**eveho, evehere, evexi, evectum:** to carry away
**expello, expellere, expuli, expulsum:** to drive out, banish
**faveo, favere, favi, fautum:** to befriend, to support, to favor
**focus, foci, *m*.:** altar; hearth, fireplace
**formosus, a, um:** beautiful, fine, finely formed, fair, handsome
**informis, is, e:** deformed; formless, shapeless
**interdum:** **(adv.)** meanwhile
**intonsus, a, um:** uncut, unshaved
**langueo, languere:** to be unwell, to be ill; to be tired
**levo, levare, levavi, levatum:** to lift up; to lessen, to lighten; to comfort; to free from, to release
**macies, maciei, *f*.:** leanness, meagerness; poverty
**medicus, a, um:** healing, curative, medical
**noto, notare, notavi, notatum:** to mark; to record; to write, to inscribe
**numero, numerare, numeravi, numeratum:** to count, to add up; to consider, to reckon
**palleo, palette, pallui:** to be pale, to look pale; to fade
**pelagus, pelagi, *n*.:** sea

**Phoebus, i, *m.*:** Phoebus Apollo
**piget, pigere, piguit, pigitum est (*impers.*):** to pain, to afflict, to grieve, to disgust
**rapidus, a, um:** rapid, swift
**restituo, restituere, restitui, restitutum:** to restore; to receive; to bring back
**salvus, a, um:** well, unharmed, safe; alive
**sapor, saporis, *m.*:** taste, flavor; smell; good taste
**torqueo, torquere, torsi, tortum:** to twist, to turn; to bend, to distort; to torture
**tribuo, tribuere, tribui, tributum:** to divide, to assign; to present; to grant, to allot, to bestow
**voveo, vovere, vovi, votum:** to vow, to dedicate, to consencrate

—

**1–14:** In the first portion of the poem, the third-person narrator sets the scene for the reader: Sulpicia has fallen ill and is in need of divinc intervention. The poet thus calls upon Apollo, the god of medicine, to come to her aid and to bring all of his healing arts to revive her (lines 9–10). Cerinthus is also present and is depicted as distraught at Sulpicia's state, praying constantly to the gods for assistance (lines 11–14). However, for as straightforward as the section seems, there are multiple ambiguities and double-meanings that give the poem a much more elegiac flair. First, the emphasis throughout is not on Sulpicia's illness, but on her objectification. The poet's fear is not for Sulpicia's well-being, but that her beauty not be harmed by the disease (lines 5–8). Moreover, even when asking Apollo for help, the poet appeals to Sulpicia's beauty, stating that Apollo should come because he would not be disgusted to lay his hands upon one so beautiful (lines 3–4). Second, the ambiguities around the type of sickness that has befallen Sulpicia hints at the potential that Sulpicia has fallen for another lover and is displaying signs of lovesickness for that individual. In particular, the references to *morbus* and *macies* as descriptors of Sulpicia's disease point to lovesickness as the potential cause, as both terms are frequent indicators of lovesickness in Roman elegy.
**1. ades:** present active imperative of *adesse*. Translate as "be present".
**2. intonsa … coma:** ablative of specification with *superbe*. Cf. the similar use of this construction to describe Apollo in Sulpicia 7.22 (*testudinea Phoebe superbe lyra*).
**3–4. te … pigebit … applicuisse:** The impersonal verb *piget* typically takes an accusative-infinitive construction, as here. Translate as "it will not digust you to have placed".
**4. formosae:** dative singular with compound verb *applicare*. The adjective refers to an unstated Sulpicia.
**4. applicuisse:** perfect active infinitive of *applicare*. Construe as a subjective infinitive with *pigebit*.
**5. effice ne … occupet … neu notet … et evehat:** The imperative *effice* introduces three noun clauses, the first two that negated by *ne* and *neu*,

and the third which begins with *et*. Translate as "bring it about that (thinness) not seize ... and that (an unseemly color) not mark ... and that (the river) carry away". *Occupet, notet*, and *evehat* are all present subjunctives.

**5. macies:** Although this word typically describes a leanness or thinness of an individual who is ill or unhealthy, it also can be used to describe lovesickness (cf. Prop. 4.3.27, Ov. *Met.* 9.536, 11.793) and the poverty of language (cf. Tac. *Or.* 21.1). Fulkerson (2017) sees a potential meta-poetic comment on the desire for slim poetry espoused by the Hellenistic poet Callimachus, a style that was popular with many late Republican and Augustan poets. Here, it seems to hint that the cause of Sulpicia's illness is lovesickness over another lover. This lovesickness consequently keeps her from Cerinthus and, metaphorically, the writing of poetry with and about him.

**5–8:** The juxtaposition of *pallor* and *candidus*, although seemingly repetitive, is poignant. *Pallor* is a whiteness associated with illness; whereas *candidus* denotes a bright and blemish-free appearance of someone healthy and attractive, and is typically used to describe elegiac beloveds. Here, due to her illness, Sulpicia runs the risk of losing her healthy glow for a sickly pallor and changing from a *formosus* indiviual to an *informis* one.

**6. notet:** The image of the marring of bright, blemish-free complection is similar to the manner in which Sulpicia described her worries over the dangers of Cerinthus going on a hunt in Sulpicia 8.9–10: *quidve iuvat ... candidaque hamatis crura notare rubis?*

**7. quodcumque mali:** Partitive genitive *mali* construed with *quodcumque*. Translate as "whatever evil" (literally, "whatever of evil").

**8. in pelagus ... aquis:** Artistic word order. A more prosaic order would be *amnis in pelagus aquis rapidis evehat.*

**9. feras:** present jussive subjunctive of *ferre*. Jussives are often used as polite requests, as would be appropriate here. Translate as "please bring".

**9–10. quiqumque sapores, quicumque cantus:** nominative plural subjects of *levant*.

**11. neu torque:** *ne* + present imperative for a command. This construction is, perhaps, more colloquial and is frequent in comedy (cf. Allen and Greenough §450a). Translate as "do not torture".

**12. votaque ... vix ... numeranda:** Accusative neuter plural *vota* modified by the gerundive *numeranda* and its adverb *vix*. Translate as "prayers scarcely (able) to be counted". The countlessness of a lover's desires or actions is a typical motif in Roman elegy from Catullus (Cat. 5 and 7) onward.

**13. langueat:** present subjunctive in a causal clause (cf. Allen and Greenough §540). The verb *languere* typically has erotic undertones in Roman elegy, and it's frequently used to describe the feeling of satiety and exhaustion the lover feels after a romantic encounter. Thus, the choice of the verb to describe Sulpicia's suffering and Cerinthus' anger may point to the potential involvement of Sulpicia with another lover.

**14. in aeternos ... deos:** *in* + accusative frequently has the sense of "against", as it does here.

**15–18:** After setting the stage of Sulpicia's illness and the potential of her involvement in another relationship, the poem shifts its focus to Cerinthus. In particular, the poet tells Cerinthus not to worry about Sulpicia's potential involvement with another lover, as it is not true and she remains entirely his (*at nunc tota tua est*, 17). Moreover, she will recover from her illness; therefore, he should save his tears for a time in which she may actually be cheating on him with another.

**16. tibi:** dative of possession with *est*.

**21–22:** Although most manuscripts have this couplet after line 20, there is nearly universal agreement that there has been in error in transmission and that it makes much more sense after line 16.

**21. nil opus est fletu:** The impersonal phrase *opus est* typically is combined with the object needed in the nominative or ablative. Here, *fletu* is in the ablative. Translate as: "There is no need for weeping".

**21. lacrimis erit aptius uti:** A difficult clause. The neuter comparative adjective *aptius* is used impersonally with *erit*. The present deponent infinitive *uti* is construed as the subject of *erit*. *Lacrimis* is the ablative object of *uti*. Translate as "It will be more fitting to make use of tears".

**21. lacrimis erit ... illa tibi:** A mixed future condition. The protasis (si-clause) has a verb in the future perfect indicative (*fuerit*), and the apodosis has a verb in the future indicative (*erit*). It is typical to place the verb of the protasis in the future perfect if that action is thought to have been completed before the action of apodosis (cf. Allen and Greenough §516c). Here, since Sulpicia's potential action occurs before Cerinthus' potential crying, the future perfect is appropriate.

**22. si quando:** syncopation for *si aliquando*. Translate as "if at some point".

**17. candida:** The description of Sulpicia as *candida* indicates that she has begun to recover from the illness that ran the risk of destroying her bright complexion (cf. ll. 5–6).

**18. credula turba:** This seems to refer to a crowd of suitors or admirers of Sulpicia. Such a reading makes sense with the previous couplet, as the narrator juxtaposes the loyalty to Cerinthus that is in Sulpicia's mind with the crowd of admirers surrounding her that think they can win her.

**18. sedet:** Fulkerson (2017) sees a potential connection between the admirers of Sulpicia sitting in awe of her and those of Lesbia in Catullus 51.3. Catullus 51 is a refashioning of Sappho 31 (cf. this volume); thus there may be a connection drawn here between Sulpicia and Sappho.

**19–26:** After reassuring Cerinthus that Sulpicia remains loyal to him, the poet turns the attention back to Apollo, arguing that great glory awaits the god if he is successful in healing Sulpicia and restoring the two lovers back to one another.

**19–20. laus magna ... duos:** An extremely difficult clause grammatically, although the sense is clear. At the heart of the issue is how to construe *restituisse*. The best solution seems to be to construe it as a Greek Infinitive (i.e., Infinitive of Respect). As such, it would translate as "great praise will be given to you for having saved two in one saved body".

**20. restituisse:** perfect active infinitive of *restituere*.

**23. debita:** perfect passive participle taken substantively. Translate as "the things owed" or "debts".

**24. sanctis ... focis:** either dative with *reddet* ("to the holy hearths") or ablative of place ("at the holy hearths").

**24. laetus:** Some editors have proposed that *laetus* here is problematic, as it is applied here to mortals, but to an immortal in line 23. This point of view is, perhaps, strengthened by the fact that *laetus* occurs in successive lines at roughly the same location in the line. Such close proximity increases the chance for transmission errors. Martinon (1895) has put forth the conjecture *gratus*.

**24. laetus uterque:** Although this could be a reference to the two lovers, Sulpicia and Cerinthus, this also could indicate that the scope of thankful lovers has expanded beyond them. We thus should imagine that Apollo will gain a full following of lovers by listening to the prayers of one, Cerinthus.

**25. pia turba deorum:** The following of devoted lovers in line 24 now extends to the gods themselves, who have become a devout crowd of worshippers of Apollo.

**26. optabunt ... tuas:** Another difficult clause. The subject is the singular *quisque* ("each"), but the sense is plural in nature, as it is describing each/all of the gods. The plural verb *optabunt* belies this sense. *Sibi* finishes the clause as a plural dative of reference. Translate as "Each (of the gods) will choose your arts for themselves."

***Sulpicia 10 (Tib. 3.11)***

Qui mihi te, Cerinthe, dies dedit, hic mihi sanctus
  atque inter festos semper habendus erit.
Te nascente novum Parcae cecinere puellis
  servitium et dederunt regna superba tibi.
Uror ego ante alias: iuvat hoc, Cerinthe, quod uror,
  si tibi de nobis mutuus ignis adest;
mutuus adsit amor, per te dulcissima furta
  perque tuos oculos per Geniumque rogo.
Magne Geni, cape tura libens votisque faveto,
  si modo, cum de me cogitat, ille calet.
Quod si forte alios iam nunc suspiret amores,
  tunc precor infidos, sancte, relinque focos.
Nec tu sis iniusta, Venus: vel serviat aeque
  vinctus uterque tibi vel mea vincla leva;
sed potius valida teneamur uterque catena,
  nulla queat posthac quam solvisse dies.
Optat idem iuvenis quod nos, sed tectius optat:
  nam pudet haec illum dicere verba palam.
At tu, Natalis, quoniam deus omnia sentis,
  adnue: quid refert, clamne palamne roget?

*Meter: elegiac couplets*

—

**adnuo, adnuere, adnui, adnutum:** to indicate, to declare; to nod assent, to indicate by a nod
**caleo, calere, calui:** to be warm, to feel warm
**catena, ae, *f.*:** chain, fetter, shackle
**clam:** **(adv.)** secretly, in secret; privately
**faveo, favere, favi, fautum:** to befriend, to support, to favor
**festus, a, um:** festive, joyous
**focus, foci, *m.*:** altar; hearth, fireplace
**furtum, furti, *n.*:** theft; trick, deception
**mutuus, a, um:** mutual, reciprocal
**palam:** **(adv.)** openly, publicly
**queo, quere, quivi, quitum:** to be able
**rogo, rogare, rogavi, rogatum:** to ask, to ask for; to invite
**suspiro, suspirare, suspiravi, suspiratum:** to sigh; to utter with a sigh
**tus, turis, *n.*:** frankincense
**uro, urere, ussi, ustus:** to burn
**votum, voti, *n.*:** vow, pledge, promise; prayer, wish

—

**1–8:** The organization of this poem is generally structured around the invocation of multiple individuals. The first such section is addressed to Cerinthus, and Sulpicia describes his effect on her in specifically elegiac terms. According to Sulpicia, when Cerinthus was born, he caused all girls to instantly desire to give themselves to him through a *servitium amoris*. Sulpicia contends that she, however, is the girl most in love with Cerinthus and that she desires his affection. Yet, the type of affection she wants is not the traditional *servitium amoris*, which is one-sided and dominated by the beloved, but a *mutuus amor* between the two.

**1. qui mihi … dies dedit:** The *qui* is proleptic and comes before its antecedent *dies*. A more prosaic word order would be *dies, qui mihi te, Cerinthe, dedit*.

**1 hic:** Refers to *dies*.

**1–2:** The opening couplet presents an ambiguous situation to the reader that is not resolved until *te nascente* on line 3. The day to which Sulpicia could be referring is either Cerinthus' birthday or the day on which the two lovers met. The reader discovers in line 3 that the former is the correct reading.

**2. festos:** Supply *dies*. The *festi dies* are typically translated as 'holidays' because they are associated with celebrations, feasting, and the absence of work.

**2. habendus erit:** a passive periphrastic in the future tense. Such constructions are awkward to translate into English, but one literal possibility is "will have to be held". The presence of *semper* in the line creates the possibility that we can render the periphrastic into the normal present form while still retaining the future feel: "must always be held".

**3. Te nascente:** ablative absolute. Translate as "when you were born".

**3. novum:** Construe with *servitium* on l. 4. *Novum* is placed much before the noun it modifies in order to emphasize the novelty of the *servitium* Cerinthus is imposing upon girls. Typically in Roman elegy, it is the *puella* who causes the male poet to fall into *servitium amoris*; yet, in Cerinthus' case, he places the *puellae* into *servitium*.

**3. Parcae:** The Parcae were the fates from Greco-Roman mythology, three old women who weaved the threads of life for mortals. They are often depicted as singing as they weave.

**3. cecinere:** syncopated form of the perfect active *cecinerunt*.

**5. iuvat hoc … quod uror:** The *quod* here is substantive and responds back to the *hoc*. Translate as "the fact that" (cf. Allen and Greenough §572).

**6. de nobis:** The *de* here is slightly ambiguous. It could be rendered as "from" in the sense of the fire has come from Sulpicia, or it could be rendered as "about" in the sense of the passionate fire Cerinthus feels is about Sulpicia. I am inclined to prefer the latter.

**8. adsit:** present, jussive subjunctive. Translate as "let (it) be present."

**8–9. per te … rogo:** Although it seems that *te* is the object of *per*, it is not. Instead, *te* is the object of *rogo*, and *dulcissima furta* is the object of *per*. Such an enclosing of *te* within a request is typical in Roman elegy (cf. Tib. 1.5.7–8: *per te furtivi foedera lecti, per venerem quaeso conpositumque caput*) (I ask you by the bonds of the secret bed…).

**8. Geniumque:** The Genius is a murky topic in Roman religion. It is generally regarded as a guardian angel type spirit, although the later theologian Augustine associated it with the concept of the soul (*C.D.* 7.13). The Genius was the divine portion of an individual and stayed with that individual from birth and throughout their life.

**9–12:** The section of the poem shifts away from Cerinthus and is addressed to Cerinthus' Genius. Sulpicia asks the Genius to assist her in helping to secure a *mutuus amor* with Cerinthus. However, she also includes the threat that, if he should fall in love with another, the Genius should abandon him and his house.

**9. Magne Geni:** vocative singular of direct address. It is noteworthy here that Sulpicia appeals directly to Cerinthus' Genius, a unique and otherwise unattested instance in Latin poetry.

**9. libens:** The participial form of *libet* is rare and makes best sense here in an adverbial sense. Translate as "willingly".

**9. faveto:** future imperative. Translate as "Be favorable".

**10. si modo:** Translate as "if only".

**11. Quod si:** Translate as "but if" (cf. Allen and Greenough §324d).

**11. suspiret:** present subjunctive of *suspirare* in a future less vivid condition. Translate as "he should sigh".

**12. relinque:** present active imperative of *relinquere*.

**13–18:** In the third section of the poem, Sulpicia moves on from Cerinthus and his Genius and appeals directly to Venus herself. Again, Sulpicia's address centers on the desire for a *mutuus amor*, as she asks Venus to either bind them both together (*vinctus*) or release Sulpicia from her feelings for Cerinthus. However, immediately after asking to be freed from Cerinthus, Sulpicia changes her mind and redoubles on her position for a shared love. She concludes the section by trying to understand why Cerinthus is not as vocal about their love as she is, convincing herself that he loves her secretly.

**13. sis:** present jussive subjunctive used as a polite command. Translate as "(do not) be".

**13–14. vel … leva:** Sulpicia presents the two alternatives for Venus in an unparallel manner. The first option is constructed using a jussive subjunctive (*serviat*), the second using a present imperative (*leva*).

**14. tibi:** Construe as the dative object of *serviat*.

**15. sed potius:** The comparative *potius* is frequently used to build upon an argument, as in this instance. Although a literal translation would be "but rather", the context of the previous couplet would require a sense closer to "no, rather", as Sulpicia rejects her initial thought of being freed from love (ll. 13–14) in favor of the thought of being bound with Cerinthus by a strong, everlasting, and mutual love (ll. 15–16).

**15. teneamur:** present jussive subjunctive. Translate as "let us be held".

**16. nulla … dies:** An intricately balanced line with much hyperbaton. A more prosaic word order would be *quam nulla dies posthac soluisse queat*.

**16. queat:** present subjunctive of *quere* in a relative clause of characteristic (cf. Allen and Greenough §535). Translate as "may be able".

**16. quam:** refers to *catena* on line 15.

**16. solvisse:** perfect active infinitive of *solvere.*

**17. optat idem ... quod nos:** The meter necessitates that *idem* have a short -i, making the word neuter accusative singular. *Quod* opens its own relative clause, and refers back to *idem*, making it neuter accusative singular. *Nos* is the subject of the relative clause, and its verb is an understood *optamus.* Translate the sentence as "The youth desires the same thing that we (desire)".

**18. nam pudet ... verba palam:** The *nam* introduces Sulpicia's reasoning for why Cerinthus desires her in secret and not in the open: it is because he is ashamed to do so. It is left unstated why he would be hesitant to do so, but various theories have posited differences in social status. One would be remiss not to note the similarities to Sulpicia 1, in which Sulpicia eschews such shame and decides to bare her relationship to the world.

**18. pudet haec illum dicere verba:** The impersonal form *pudet* is often built with an accusative-infinitive construction in which the accusative is the person who is ashamed and the infinitive is the action that is shameful. This is the case here, as well. Translate as "it shames him to speak these words."

**19–20:** Sulpicia seems to ask *Natalis* to grant Cerinthus' wish. Yet, it is odd that she would ask this, as the difference between Cerinthus declaring his love publicly and keeping it a secret would be immense.

**20. adnue:** present imperative of *adnuere.*

**20. quid refert:** Idiomatic expression. Translate as "What does it matter?" or "Why is it important?"

**20. roget:** present subjunctive of *rogare* in an Indirect Question.

***Sulpicia 11 (Tib. 3.12)***

Natalis Iuno, sanctos cape turis acervos,
quos tibi dat tenera docta puella manu.
Tota tibi est hodie, tibi se laetissima compsit,
staret ut ante tuos conspicienda focos.
Illa quidem ornandi causas tibi, diva, relegat;
est tamen, occulte cui placuisse velit.
At tu, sancta, fave, neu quis divellat amantes,
sed iuveni, quaeso, mutua vincla para.
Sic bene compones: ullae non ille puellae
servire aut cuiquam dignior illa viro.
Nec possit cupidos vigilans deprendere custos
fallendique vias mille ministret Amor.
Adnue purpureaque veni perlucida palla:
ter tibi fit libo, ter, dea casta, mero;
praecipit et natae mater studiosa, quod optat:
illa aliud tacita, iam sua, mente rogat;
uritur, ut celeres urunt altaria flammae,
nec, liceat quamvis, sana fuisse velit.
Sis iuveni grata ac, veniet cum proximus annus,
hic idem votis iam vetus exstet amor.

*Meter: elegiac couplets*

—

**acervus, acervi, *m*.:** mass, heap, pile; treasure, stock
**altaria, altarium, *n.pl*.:** offerings
**castus, a, um:** pure, moral; chaste
**como, comere, compsi, comptum:** to arrange, adorn
**conspicio, conspicere, conspexi, conspectum:** to observe, to see; to notice
**deprendo, deprendere, deprendi, deprensum:** to seize, to catch; to surprise; to interrupt
**divello, divellere, divelli, divulsum:** to separate, to compel apart; to alienate, to estrange
**exsto, exstare:** to exist; to stand forth, to stand out
**faveo, favere, favi, fautum:** to befriend, to support, to favor
**libum, libi, *n*.:** cake, pancake, ritual offering
**ministro, ministrare, ministravi, ministrum:** to attend to, to serve; to supply
**mutuus, a, um:** mutual, reciprocal
**natalis, is, *m*.:** birthday
**occulte: (adv.)** secretly
**orno, ornare, ornavi, ornatum:** to equip; to dress; to decorate
**palla, pallae, *f*.:** palla, a woman's outer garment
**perlucidus, a, um:** transparent, pellucid
**purpureus, a, um:** purple, dark red
**relego, relegare, relegavi, relegatum:** to ascribe; to remove, to separate, to relegate
**servio, servire, servivi, servitum:** to serve, to be a slave to

**tacitus, a, um:** silent, secret
**tus, turis, *n*.:** frankincense
**ullus, a, um:** any, any one
**uro, urere, ussi, ustus:** to burn
**vigilans, vigilantis (gen.):** watchful, vigilant, alert; wakeful

—

**1–6:** The opening three couplets introduce Sulpicia to the reader and depict her coming to the Temple of Juno with offerings (*sanctos turis acervos*) and to show her loyalty to the goddess (*tota tibi est*). The description of Sulpicia, however, is done in an objectifying manner, focusing on her beauty and outward ostentatious display. Juxtaposed with this outward, public display is the other major aspect of the poem: Sulpicia's secret love for Cerinthus (*occulte cui placuisse velit*).

**1. cape:** present active imperative of *capere*.

**2. quos … manu:** Chiastic word order (tenera *docta puella* manu).

**2. docta puella:** This refers to Sulpicia, but the *docta puella* is a loaded elegiac term. In Roman elegy, the *docta puella* typically described the woman who was the object of the poet-lover's desire. She is described as a non-normative Roman woman in many ways: she is skilled in poetry, music, and the arts; she is often a courtesan or an individual who had some level of financial and sexual control over her life. All of these aspects make sense to describe Sulpicia, who is skilled in poetry, involved in an elegiac relationship, and is striving in this poem to have some modicum of control over her sexual life (lines 15–18) (cf. also Catullus 35.16–17).

**3. Tota tibi est hodie:** The unstated subject is the *docta puella* from line 2. The dative *tibi* here is a Dative of Reference, best taken with *tota* as "all yours" (literally, "all for you").

**4. staret ut:** Inverted word order, with *ut* delayed until after *staret*, the verb in its clause. *Staret* is imperfect active subjunctive in a Purpose Clause.

**4. conspicienda:** An ambiguous word with an ambiguous form. If taken as a passive periphrastic, it carries the meaning "ought to be seen". If taken literally as a future passive participle, it means "about to be seen". The intended meaning here seems to be a bit of both, as the reader imagines Sulpicia, elegantly adorned (*se compsit*, line 3) and standing outside the temple of Juno both waiting to be seen by Cerinthus and as a sight that ought to be seen because of her beauty.

**5–6:** It is revealed that Sulpicia has gotten dressed up not to visit the temple of Juno, but for Cerinthus. However, the fact that she has done so for Cerinthus is kept a secret, as indicted by both the adverb *occulte* and the fact that Cerinthus is not directly stated as the subject of line 6.

**5. ornandi:** gentive gerund, taken with *causas*. Translate as "of dressing (up)".

**5. causas tibi … relegat:** The verb *relegare* is often used with *causas* and the dative with the meaning "to ascribe X to Y".

**6. est tamen … velit:** The poet does not come out and name Cerinthus directly, and instead uses a more impersonal construction. *Est … velit* should be translated as "There is one whom she secretly wishes to have pleased." *Est* is translated impersonally because it is the first word in the sentence and no subject is given. *Cui* is dative with the verb *placuisse*, the perfect infinitive of *placere*, which takes a dative object. Finally, *velit* is a present subjunctive in a relative clause of haracteristic with *Est … cui* (cf. Allen and Greenough §535a).

**7–14:** The poem shifts to the prayer to Juno, and Sulpicia explicitly asks for two things: a mutual love between herself and Cerinthus (*ullae … viro*), and a variety of means for the two lovers to be with each other in secret (*fallendi vias*). This section concludes with highly ritualized language: the existence of traditional offerings (*libum* and *merum*), as well as the alliteration of *t*, *p*, and *l* that is indicative of incantations.

**7. fave:** present active imperative of *favere.*

**7. neu quis:** *et non (ali)quis.* Translate as "and (may) no one".

**7. divellat:** A strangely emphatic word in this context, as it typically refers to a violent tearing, slaughter, or dismemberment, but it seems to mean something like "forcibly separate" here. It is a present jussive subjunctive. Translate as "may (no one) separate".

**8. para:** present active imperative of *parare.*

**9–10:** The prayer continues with a complex couplet. Translate as "May you arrange it well thus: let him be no more worthy to serve any girl; let her be no more worthy to serve any man." At the heart of the construction is an understood jussive *sit*, construed with *dignior*. The sentiments here call to mind the end of Sulpicia 1 (*cum digno digna fuisse ferar*) and play with the strong juxtaposition between the high status of *dignus* and the low status of *servire.*

**9. compones:** present jussive subjunctive. The sense of *componere* here is closer to "arrange". Translate as: "may you arrange".

**10. ullae puellae:** This is the only instance in Latin literature of *ullae* as a dative, feminine, singular (typically, it is formed as *ulli*). Fulkerson (2017) postulates that it is a medieval corruption in the manuscript. Here, it is construed with *puellae*, which is the dative object of *servire* (line 10).

**10. servire:** present active infinitive of *servire.* Here, the infinitive is functioning as the complement of *dignior* (cf. Allen and Greenough §461). Such a construction is Greek in origin, but is seen frequently in Roman Elegy, particularly in Ovid.

**11–12:** The poet continues the prayer to Juno and references the traditional elegiac trope of the *paraclausithyron*, in which the poet-lover is hindered from reaching the beloved by a guard, a door, or some other blocking figure. Here, the poet prays that the guard not be able to catch the lovers and that Cupid give the lovers multiple ways of deceiving the guard. One may also detect a reference to Sulpicia 8, line 4, in which Cupid himself acts as a guard to protect Cerinthus on the hunt.

**11. Nec possit:** present jussive subjunctive of *posse*. Translate as "may (the guard) not be able).

**11. cupidos:** substantive adjective acting as the object of *deprendere*. Translate as "lovers/desirous ones".

**11. custos:** nominative singular subject of *possit*.

**12. fallendi:** genitive gerund of *fallere*. Construe with *vias* and translate as "ways of deceiving".

**12. ministret:** present jussive subjunctive of *ministrare*. Translate as "let (Love) supply".

**13. adnue:** present active imperative of *adnuere*.

**13. puepureaque ... perlucida palla:** Translate as "shining in a purple palla". The *purpurea palla* is an Ablative of Specification construed with *perlucida*.

**14. ter tibi fit libo, ter ...mero:** The verb *fieri* typically is construed as the passive form of *facere* in Latin. However, it can also have a specialized meaning in the religious sphere, as here. It is often used impersonally and with the ablative with the meaning "to sacrifice" or "to make an offering" (cf. Cic. Att. 1.13.3; Liv. 37.3.5). Here, translate as "thrice an offering is made to you with cake, thrice with wine".

**14. libo:** The *libum* was a type of honey cheesecake used by the Romans in a variety of offering settings. Ovid relates that it was a type of cake associated with the discovery of honey by Bacchus. In Roman elegy, it is typically used in sacrificial offerings as a method of pleasing the gods. Although at least twice, the *libum* is used to describe a sort of birthday cake (Ov. *Am.* 1.8.94 and *A. A.* 1.429). A recipe for the cake is given by Cato at *de Agricultura* 75.

**14. mero:** For the Romans, it was traditional to dilute wine with water to cut some of the sweetness of the taste. *Merum* referred to wine that went undiluted by water and was generally regarded as appropriate for provincials and barbarians to drink. Otherwise, it was frequently used in libations to the gods.

**15–20:** In the final section of the poem, it gradually becomes clearer that Juno is operating as the goddess of marriage in the poem and that the poet is asking for her help in deceiving Sulpicia's parents, as Sulpicia burns with a secret love for Cerinthus. The section concludes with a final prayer that Juno brings it about that the love between the two lovers continues for at least another year.

**15. natae mater studiosa:** The adjective *studiosa* both describes the *mater* and takes the objective genitive *natae*. Translate as "mother attentive to her daughter". The reference to Sulpicia 2, line 5, in which Messalla is described as overbearing regarding Sulpicia (*nimium Messalla mei studiose*), is made clear.

**16. illa aliud ... rogat:** A difficult line. At the center of the difficulty is how to construe *iam sua*. Based on its placement in the line, *sua* must have a short *a*, rendering it nominative singular feminine or neuter accusative plural. If taken as a nominative, *iam sua* would be rendered something like "now her own (woman)". If as an accusative, the *sua* would be "now her own things" and would be in apposition to *aliud* "another thing". The latter option is more difficult to make sense of, so the former reading is preferable. Translate as "she, now her own woman, asks for another thing with a silent mind".

**17. ut:** Translate as "as", since it is followed by the indicative verb *urunt*.

**18. liceat quamvis:** *Liceat* is the present active subjunctive of *licet* in a concessive clause with *quamvis* (cf. Allen and Greenough §527e).

**18. nec … sana fuisse velit:** *Velit* is the present active subjunctive of *velle* and is a potential subjunctive. Translate as "she would not wish to have been healthy". Here, treat *sana* as the opposite of love-sick. Fulkerson (2017) suggests the archaic adjective "heart-whole".

**19–20:** Although this couplet is fraught with manuscript issues, the poem appears to conclude with a wish that Juno hear the prayer, be kind to Cerinthus, and grant that the love between Cerinthus and Sulpicia carry on until the next year.

**19. Sis iuveni grata:** *Sis* is a present jussive subjunctive from *esse*. Translate as "may you be". The adjective *gratus*, here with a meaning close to "agreeable" or "favorable", takes the dative *iuveni*.

**20. hic idem … amor:** A difficult line to end the poem. The words *hic idem amor* are all in agreement, and *vetus* is best suited as the predicate. The verb of the sentence, *exstet*, is the present jussive subjunctive from *exstare*. Finally, *votis* is best construed as an ablative of means or cause. Translate as: "May this same love through her prayers be old then".

### *Sulpicia 12 (L'Année Epigraphique 1928.73)*

Sulpiciae cineres lectricis cerne viator
  quoi servile datum nomen erat Petale.
Ter denos numero quattuor plus vixerat annos
  natumque in terris Aglaon ediderat.
Omnia naturae bona viderat arte vigebat.
  splendebat forma, creverat ingenio.
Invida fors vita longinquom degere tempus
  noluit hanc fatis defuit ipse colus.

*Meter: elegiac couplets*

—

**Aglaos, Aglaon (acc.), *m.*:** Aglaos (son of Sulpicia Petale)
**colus, colus, *f*:** distaff
**dego, degere, degi:** to pass/spend time; to live, continue, endure
**deni, ae, a:** ten each; ten at a time
**invidus, a, um:** envious; hostile, inimical
**lectrix, lectricis, *f*:** reader
**longinquus, a, um:** long, extensive

**Petale, Petalis, *f*.:** Sulpicia Petale
**plus, pluris:** more, additionally; further
**servilis, servile:** of a slave, servile
**splendeo, splendere, splendui:** to shine, glitter, gleam; to be bright
**Sulpicia, ae, *f*:** Sulpicia
**ter:** **(adv.)** three times, thrice
**viator, viatoris, *m/f*:** a traveler, wayfarer
**vigeo, vigere, vigui:** to thrive, flourish; to prosper; to live

—

**1–2: Sulpiciae ... Petale:** The epitaph opens in a traditional fashion, as it calls to passersby (*viator*) to acknowledge (*cerne*) the remains (*cineres*) of Sulpicia Petale. The word order, however, is intricate and evocative of Sulpicia's poetry. It opens with *Sulpiciae cineres*, identifying the remains as those of a certain Sulpicia. The next word, *lectricis*, adds more detail, as it agrees with the genitive *Sulpiciae* and informs the audience that this certain Sulpicia was a *lectrix*, or female reader. However, the separation of *Sulpiciae* and *lectricis* also allows for *Sulpiciae* to be both the object of *lectricis* (read as "the reader of Sulpicia") and the possessor of *lectricis* (read as "Sulpicia's *lectrix*"). It is not until the end of the couplet that the audience learns that this Sulpicia was known as Petale when she was a slave. Thus, the couplet neatly introduces Sulpicia Petale by starting with her free name and ending with her slave name.
**1. cerne:** present active imperative of *cernere.*
**2. servile...Petale:** Intricate word order marked by synchesis (ABAB). A more prosaic order would be: *servile nomen Petale datum erat.*
**2. quoi:** Archaic form of *cui*, dative singular of *qui, quae, quod.*
**2. Petale:** The slave name of Sulpicia Petale is derived from the Greek word *petalon* (πέταλον, τό), meaning "leaf" or "wreath". This is an apt name for a *lectrix*, as Greek and Latin authors frequently describe collections of poetry with words for flowers or garlands.
**3–4:** The second couplet of the epitaph gives the audience more information about Petale, specifically regarding her age and her family. We learn that she died at thirty-four years of age and that she had a son by the name of Aglaos. Yet, even these biographical details are imbued with an air of artistic production befitting a *lectrix.*
**3. ter ... annos:** A poetic description of Petale's age. Translated literally as "she had lived thrice ten plus four years".
**3. ter denos quattuor plus annos:** Accusative of Time Duration (cf. Allen and Greenough §423).
**3. numero:** Ablative of Specification (cf. Allen and Greenough §418). Translate as "in number".
**4. Aglaon:** Greek accusative, singular, masculine of Aglaos. It is in apposition to *natum.* The name means "splendid", "noble", or "beautiful" (ἀγλαός).

**4. ediderat:** This verb depicts Sulpcia Petale's labor with Aglaon as an act of artistic production. For *edere* can both mean "to beget, give birth" and "to produce, publish".

**5–6:** The third couplet of the epitaph continues the description of Sulpicia Petale by moving from the biographical details of the second couplet to a description of her personal characteristics. In particular, there is an emphasis on her physical beauty (*forma*), as well as her skill (*arte*) and talent (*ingenio*) in artistic creation.

**5–6. viderat ... vigebat ... splendebat ... creverat:** The four verbs that describe Sulpcia Petale's actions are linked together in asyndeton, and their tenses are artistically arranged in a chiastic structure: pluperfect (*viderat*), imperfect (*vigebat*), imperfect (*splendebat*), pluperfect (*creverat*).

**5–6. arte, forma, ingenio:** Ablatives of Specification (cf. Allen and Greenough §418).

**7–8:** The final couplet of the epitaph with a traditional lament regarding the fleeting nature of life and that Sulpicia Petale was not fated to live longer than she did. However, the theme of artistic creation, so prevalent throughout the epitaph, is also manifest here in the references to spinning that conclude the text.

**7. vita:** Ablative of Specification (cf. Allen and Greenough §418). The position of the word in the line—before the caesura that divides the line—creates some ambiguity. Although it makes most sense to take *vita* with *tempus* ("time in life"), it can also be construed with *fors* ("fate/lot in life"). Therefore, as with so much of Sulpician poetry, ambiguity is embraced, and words can be used twice in a line. Here, we can translate the line thus: "Envious fate in life did not want her to spend a long time in life."

**7. longinquom:** Archaic spelling of *longinquum*. The adjective modifies *tempus*.

**7. degere:** present active infinitive from *degere*. Construe as an Objective Infinitive with *noluit* and *hanc*. Translate as "[envious fate] did not want her to spend".

**8. fatis defuit ipse colus:** The final image of the epitaph portrays the traditional image of the three Fates spinning the thread of life for humans. Whenever the Fates cut someone's thread that individual's life ends. Here, the epitaph seems to state that the Fates were unable to extend Sulpicia Petale's thread of life, although it is left unspoken whether or not they wanted to do so. The image of the distaff, the last word of the epitaph, leaves the audience with the final image of the two major aspects of Sulpicia Petale's—and the Sulpicia the elegist's!—identity: artistic production and gender. For oftentimes in Roman literature, the production of poetry was depicted as spinning or weaving words together. Likewise, the work of spinning on the distaff was a traditional image associated with the Roman *matrona*. Taken together, the epitaph leaves the reader with an image associating poetic production with women's work, an apt description for Sulpicia and her *lectrix*.

**8. fatis:** dative object of *defuit.*

**8. colus:** The term *colus* is traditionally a feminine word, but here it is construed as masculine, agreeing with *ipse*. The ending of *ipse* could easily have been changed to *ipsa* without upsetting the meter of the line; so, the change to masculine seems to have a purpose. Hallett and Dickison (2014) suggest that it may be in order to connect the epitaph to an elegiac context, as the masculine *colus* is used in at least two other contexts: Catullus 63.311 (to describe the distaff of the spinning Fates) and Propertius 4.9.28 (to describe the distaff of Hercules, when he once worked wool himself).

### *Sulpicia 1 (Tib. 3.13)*

At last a love has come! A love that it would better suit my reputation
to hide under modesty than to lay bare to anyone.
Beseeched by my songs, Cytherea[1] has carried him to me
and placed him into my lap.
Venus[2] has kept her promises: let that man tell of my pleasures,
who is said to have not had pleasures of his own!
I shouldn't wish to commit anything to writing
that is meant for my lover's eyes only;
Yet, it is fun to be bad; pretending to be proper is wearisome.
Let me only be said to have been a worthy partner to a worthy man.

### *Sulpicia 2 (Tib. 3.14)*

The hated birthday has come, and I must spend it – sadly –
in the dreadful countryside and without Cerinthus[3].
For what is sweeter than the city? Can a country-house and
a cold stream in the Arretian[4] field really be appropiate for a girl?
Please relax, Messalla[5]; you care about me too much;
Journeys are often undertaken at the wrong time, uncle.
Here in Rome I, snatched away, leave my heart and soul;
although you prevent me from even having my own opinions.

### *Sulpicia 3 (Tib. 3.15)*

Remember that sad journey truly endured by your girl?
Now she can spend her birthday in Rome!
May that birthday be celebrated together by all of us,
a birthday that perhaps has come to you unexpectedly!

### *Sulpicia 4*

I should really thank you that you are taking so many pains over me
lest I suddenly make a mistake, silly girl that I am.
Why don't you go ahead and pay more attention to the toga[6]
and that call girl with her wool basket than you do to

SULPICIA, THE DAUGHTER OF SERVIUS.[7]
There are those who are worried about me, who take the greatest pains
to ensure that I not wander into a commoner's bed.

### *Sulpicia 5*

Cerinthus, do you have a genuine concern for your girl
because now a fever[8] rages through my tired limbs?
I would not wish to conquer this sad sickness
if I should think that you too did not want me to recover.
Yet what good would it do for me to conquer my sickness,
if you are able to bear my sorrows without a care?

### *Sulpicia 6*

May I not kindle, o light of my life, your heart's passion
as much as I seem to have done a few days ago,
if I ever in my whole life have done something so foolish
that I would admit shamed me more
than the fact that I left you alone last night
because I wanted to hide my feelings for you.

### *Sulpicia 7*

Sulpicia has been adorned for you, great Mars[9], on your Kalends[10]:
Come down from heaven and see for yourself, if you are wise.
Venus[11] will forgive this: but you, violent one, take care
Lest your arms fall shamefully, as you admire her.
For harsh Cupid, when he wishes to enflame the gods,
Kindles twin torches from her[12] eyes.
Whatever she does and wherever she goes,
She is secretly attended by grace and charm.
If she lets down her hair, she is charming with flowing locks;
If she does up her hair, she ought to be worshipped as well.
She sets people afire, whether she wish to go out in a Tyrian[13] *palla*[14];
She sets them afire, whether she come shining in clothes of snow.
In such a way lucky Vertumnus[15] on eternal Olympus
Has thousands of decorations, and looks graceful in them all.
She alone of girls is worthy of receiving the soft wool from Tyre[16],
Twice washed in expensive dye,
She alone is worthy of possessing whatever the rich Arabian
Tiller of fragrant crops reaps from the sweet-smelling fields,
And whatever jewels the dark Indian, closest to the Indian Ocean,
Collects from the tawny shoreline.
Sing of this girl, o Pierides[17], on your Kalends[10],
And you, proud Phoebus[18], on your tortoise-shell lyre.

This solemn rite will endure for many years:
No girl is more worthy of your chorus.

***Sulpicia 8***

Spare my boyfriend, o boar, whether you inhabit the good pastures
of the field or the unbeaten paths of the shady mountain.
Do not sharpen your harsh teeth for battle;
Let Love guard him and keep him safe for me.
And yet, Delia[19] has taken him far away with a desire for hunting.
O let the forests perish! The dogs pass away!
What madness, what mindset is it to want to wound tender hands
by surrounding the dense hills with hunting parties?
Why does it please to enter the lairs of beasts secretly
and to mark your unblemished limbs with thorny brambles?
Still, Cerinthus[3], in order that I wander the countryside with you,
let me carry the twisted nets through the mountains;
Let me search out the tracks of the swift stag;
Let me release the quick dog from his iron chains.
Then, then, the forests would be pleasing to me, o light of my life,
If I were said to have embraced you before the traps themselves.
Then, although the boar fell into the traps, it would leave unharmed,
lest it disturb the joys of our passionate embrace.
But now, without me let there be no love, but by the law of Diana[20],
chaste boy, grab your nets with a chaste hand.
Moreover, if any girl tries to steal my love in secret,
May she be torn to pieces by savage beasts.
But you, my love, leave the desire for hunting to your father
And quickly run back into my embrace.

***Sulpicia 9***

Be present and send away the illness of the tender girlfriend;
Be present, Phoebus[18] proud of your uncut hair.
Hurry and believe me, Phoebus[18], it will not disgust you
to touch her beautiful body with your healing hands.
Do not allow emaciation to seize her paling limbs;
Do not allow an unsightly color to mar her unblemished body,
And whatever evil and whatever sadness we fear,
May the river carry into the sea with rapid waters.
Holy one, come and bring with you whatever scents
and whatever songs raise tired bodies.
Do not torture her boyfriend, who fears the fates of his girl
and makes prayers scarcely able to be counted for his mistress.
At times he prays, at times he speaks harsh words against the gods
because she is utterly exhausted.

Calm your fear, Cerinthus[3]: god does not harm lovers.
You just love as always: your girlfriend has been saved.
There is no need for weeping. It will be better to make use of tears,
if ever she will be unfavorable towards you.
But now she is totally yours; you alone she thinks of in her mind,
and the hopeful crowd waits on her in vain.
Phoebus[18], be favorable! Great praise will be given to you
For rescuing two in saving one.
Now your shines will be crowded, now you will be happy,
when each lover will earnestly repay their debts at your hearths.
Then the pious crowd of the gods will call you blessed,
and will wish your arts were their own.

***Sulpicia 10***

The day, Cerinthus[3], that gave you to me
I will always hold as special and sacred.
When you were born, the Muses sang love-bondage for girls
and gave proud kingdoms to you.
But I burn beyond all others, Cerinthus[3], and it is pleasing that I burn,
as long as a mutual fire burns for you, as well.
May there be a mutual love! By our sweetest of secret delights!
by your eyes, and by your spirit, I beg you!
Great Genius[21], take my frankincense and hear my prayers,
If only he grows warm when he thinks of me.
But if, by chance, he now sighs with another love,
I pray, holy one, that you abandon his unfaithful hearth.
You, too, O Venus[11], do not be unjust: either let each of us serve
Equally bound to you or release me from my love-bond.
No, rather let us each be held by a strong chain,
Which no day after will be able to break.
My youth wants the same thing as I, but he wants it secretly;
For he is ashamed to say these words out loud.
But you, Birthday, since as a god you know all things,
Nod assent. What does it matter if he asks openly or in secret?

***Sulpicia 11***

Birthday Juno[22], take the holy heaps of frankincense
that the learned girl gives to you with a tender hand.
Today she is all yours; for you she most happily dressed up,
so that she might stand before your temple as a sight to behold.
Indeed, goddess, that girl publicly professes that you are the reason for her adornment;
However, there is one for whom she secretly wishes to have pleased.

But you, holy one, favor her. I beg you, do not allow anyone to tear apart the lovers,
but prepare a mutual bond for the young man.
You would arrange it well thus: may that man not be more worthy to serve any other girl,
and may that girl not be more worthy to serve any other man.
May the vigilant guard be unable to seize upon their desires.
May a thousand tricks be provided by Love itself.
Nod your approval and come, resplendent in your purple *palla*[14]:
thrice the sacred cake[23] is given to you, chaste goddess, thrice the wine.
The meddling mother tells her daughter what to ask for,
yet she, now her own woman, requests something else in her tacit mind.
She burns with passion, as the nimble flames burn your offerings,
and she does not wish her love-sickness to be healed, though it is allowed.
May you be kind to the young man and, when the next year will have come,
through her prayers may this same love be then long-lasting.

### *Sulpicia 12*

See, traveler, the ashes of Sulpicia's reader
Whose given slave name was Petale[24].
For thrice ten and four years she had lived
and had given birth to a son, Aglaon[25].
She had seen all good things of nature; she was prospering in her craft.
She was gleaming in her beauty; she had grown in her talent.
Hateful destiny did not wish to grant her a longer time of life;
The distaff itself failed the Fates.

## Notes

1. A traditional Greek epithet for Venus, the goddess of love, who held the south Aegean island of Cythera as sacred to her. It occurs as early as Homer, but is particularly associated with Sappho. Thus, Sulpicia's use of the epithet here highlights the allusion she is making to Sappho, and the transition from Cytherea to Venus in line 5 depicts the transition from the Greek Sappho as female writer of love poetry to the Roman Sulpicia.
2. The goddess of love in classical mythology.
3. This is the first mention of the name of Sulpicia's beloved in the cycle. The name Cerinthus may be the name of an actual individual, pseudonymous, or both. Traditionally, scholars have connected his name to the Greek word κήρινθος, meaning "bee-bread", and have argued a further connection between bees and their production of wax. Since wax was typically used by Romans to make the tablets on which Sulpicia is writing her poetry, it is thought that

Cerinthus may represent Sulpicia's poetry itself. If Cerinthus is, indeed, a historical figure, the name is thought to be a pseudonym for Cornutus, an individual referenced by Tibullus in 2.2-3 as about to be married and celebrating a birthday. Connections to this or a Cornutus make some sense, as well, seeing as the juxtaposition between Cornutus and Cerinthus produces a bilingual pun (the Latin word *cornus* = the Greek word κέρας) and there was a historical Cornutus in the circles of Messalla and Sulpicia in the form of Marcus Caecilius Cornutus, who was in the Arval college with Messalla, or his son.

4. Arretium was approximately 100 miles north of Rome in modern Tuscany. Maecenas, the famous patron of the arts under Augustus, is thought to have been from Arretium, and inscriptional evidence suggests that the Sulpicii had property there, as well.
5. Valerius Messalla Corvinus (64 BCE-8 CE), a prominent soldier, orator, statesman, and patron of the arts. He also may have been Sulpicia's legal guardian (cf. Introduction).
6. The toga was the traditional clothing of citizen men and prostitutes in Ancient Rome. The reference to it here seems to be a pun that activates both meanings: Sulpicia is both urging Cerinthus to think of his status as a citizen and to stop getting into trysts with low-class women and also, exasperated, is telling him to go ahead, keep his affairs, and leave her alone.
7. Sulpicia here refers to herself in the formal, public style of an aristocratic inscription in order to create a juxtaposition with the low-class prostitute. The text has been marked in capital letters to highlight the inscriptional quality of the line, but the manuscripts themselves have no such capitalization for emphasis.
8. The Latin word for "fever" here is *calor*, and it can both denote the physical fever of illness and the amatory fever of passion. Sulpicia is activating both meanings here.
9. Mars is the god of war in classical mythology. Here, his presence also tells us that the month this poem is discussing is the month of March, which was named for him.
10. March 1st. Traditionally, the Kalends of March was the occasion of the Matronalia, a festival honoring the role of the Sabines—the first Roman "wives"—in reconciling the Romans to their Sabine neighbors. Although the myth at the core of the Matronalia is well-known, it is less certain what the actual events of the festival were. Moreover, the role of the reference to the Matronalia here is uncertain. On one level, it serves to activate the backdrop of marriage against which the poet will develop a number of elegiac themes. Immediately, the poet encourages Mars to leave his lover Venus, with whom he famously has an affair, to admire the beauty of Sulpicia, stating that Venus will forgive the transgression. It is Sulpicia's beauty and charm that will drive Apollo—and his muses—to sing of her for years to come.
11. Venus is the god of love in classical mythology. In many myths, she is depicted as cheating on her husband and having an affair with the god Mars.
12. The Latin leaves the identity of this female ambiguous, leaving it to the reader to decide whether the poem refers to Venus, Sulpicia, or both. The effect is that slippage is created between the two women and Sulpicia is imbued with the amatory qualities of Venus.
13. Tyre was famous in antiquity for the production of a purple dye made from murex shellfish. Because of the difficult process of its extraction, the purple dye was expensive.
14. The *palla* was the outer garment for Roman women. It was formed by wrapping or draping a rectangular piece of cloth over the woman.

15. Vertumnus is the god of seasons and change, thought of as originating as an Etruscan god. He is oftentimes depicted as crossing the lines of gender: a male god dressed in female clothing. His appearance here in a comparison to Sulpicia may speak to Sulpicia's own gender trouble, as she, a female, engages in the traditionally male task of writing poetry. Moreover, the juxtaposition of the Italic Vertumnus with the more Greek Olympus shows the same mixing of Greek and Italic elements that Sulpicia plays with in Sulpicia 1.
16. Tyre was a city in Phoenicia (modern-day Lebanon) famous for its trade, ship-building, and purple dye from murex shellfish.
17. The epithet Pierides is frequently given to the nine Muses in Greco-Roman mythology. It is a reference to the Muses' birth on Mt. Pierus, a mountain in Thessaly.
18. Phoebus is an epithet for Apollo, the god of music, medicine, prophecy, and the sun in classical mythology. The word itself is from the Greek word φοῖβος (*phoibos*), which means "pure", "bright", or "radiant". He is frequently depicted as a young man with long, flowing hair.
19. A word with multiple meanings. On the one hand, Delia is frequently a reference to the goddess Diana, who was born on the island of Delos. On the other hand, Delia was the name of the puella of the elegist Tibullus. Here, both meanings are operative, as Sulpicia bemoans the fact that Cerinthus has already been led away to the hunt. The question is: has Delia the huntress or Delia the elegiac *puella* led him away?
20. Diana was the Roman equivalent to Artemis, the goddess of the hunt and the wilderness. Diana was also a virgin goddess. Therefore, her followers were expected to be chaste, as well, and to eschew any amatory encounters. Here, Sulpicia hopes that Cerinthus will follow Diana's law and keep from any erotic relationships, since Sulpicia cannot be with him on the hunt.
21. The Genius is a murky topic in Roman religion. It is generally regarded as a guardian angel type spirit, although the later theologian Augustine associated it with the concept of the soul (*C.D.* 7.13). The Genius was the divine portion of an individual and stayed with that individual from birth and throughout their life.
22. Juno was the wife of Jupiter, the protectress of community, and the goddess of marriage and childbirth.
23. The sacred cake referred to here is the *libum*, a type of honey cheesecake used by the Romans in a variety of offering settings. Ovid relates that it was a type of cake associated with the discovery of honey by Bacchus. In Roman elegy, it is typically used in sacrificial offerings as a method of pleasing the gods. Although at least twice, the *libum* is used to describe a sort of birthday cake (Ov. *Am.* 1.8.94 and *A. A.* 1.429). A recipe for the cake is given by Cato at *de Agricultura* 75.
24. The slave name of Sulpicia Petale is derived from the Greek word *petalon* (πέταλον, τό), meaning "leaf" or "wreath". This is an apt name for a *lectrix*, as Greek and Latin authors frequently describe collections of poetry with words for flowers or garlands.
25. The name Aglaon means "splendid", "noble", or "beautiful" in Greek (ἀγλαός).

# 10 Sulpicia Caleni

In one of the stranger happenstances from classical antiquity, the only two instances of Latin poetry written by women that have survived were both composed by women named Sulpicia. As opposed to the Augustan elegist Sulpicia, this Sulpicia is known as Sulpicia Caleni, and is dated to the last two decades of the 1st century CE. The evidence for Caleni's identification and dating comes chiefly from two places. First, two poems of the Roman poet Martial (86–101/2 CE) provide a reference to her identification and dating. In Martial 10.35 and 10.38, Martial refers to a female poet by the name of Sulpicia who had a devoted husband named Calenus. As such, scholars have concluded that this Sulpicia Caleni was a contemporary of Martial and composed in the later decades of the 1st century CE. The second major source for Sulpicia Caleni comes from the reception of her poetry, which seems to have been popular and provocative. The 4th-century CE rhetorician Ausonius lists her works alongside those of Apuleius, Pliny, and Cicero, remarking that although her poetry was provocative, in her private life, she was proper (*pruire opusculum Sulpiciae, frontem caperare*, Wedding Cento 139.5-6). Likewise, Fulgentius (5th–6th century CE) also marked her as provocative, calling her shameless and listing her poetry among works of elegy and erotic romance (*Sulpicillae procacitas*, Myth 1.4). The 5th-century CE bishop Sidonius Apollinaris, too, singles her out for her smooth-talking wit and associates her with Thalia, the muse of comedy and short, witty poems (*quod Sulpiciae iocus Thaliae scripsit blandiloquum suo Caleno*, Carmina 9.261-2).

Yet, perhaps the most important reference to Sulpicia Caleni is that found in Giorgio Valla of Piacenza's Renaissance commentary on Juvenal, itself purportedly a copy of a more ancient commentary by a certain Probus. In that commentary, Juvenal's use of the rare word *cadurcum* in *Sat.* 6.537 is explained with a two-line quotation from the poetry of Sulpicia Caleni (Caleni 1 in this volume). These two lines are the only authentic lines from Caleni's poetry that have survived to modernity. Moreover, the lines seem to confirm the provocative nature of Caleni's poetry reported by the references above, as they describe her as naked on her bed with her husband.

DOI: 10.4324/9781003031727-13

In addition to the two-line quotation from Caleni, this volume also includes the so-called *Sulpiciae Conquestio* (The Complaint of Sulpicia), a long satire whose authorship is debated, but some ascribe to Caleni. The satire is a critique of the reign of Emperor Domitian (ruled 81–96 CE) and, in particular, his expulsion of the philosophers between 88–94 CE. The text of the *Conquestio* survived antiquity on a single manuscript from northwestern Italy as part of the texts of the *Epigrammata Bobiensia.* None of the manuscripts containing the *Conquestio* survive today, and scholars rely on transcripts made in 1493 to piece together the text. Because of the difficult manuscript history, the text is full of errors, including misspelled words and lines that appear out of order. Despite this, the text is of great importance, as it could be the longest extent piece of Latin literature written by a woman, and the only piece of verse satire. Some scholars, such as Plant (2004), believe that it is not the work of Caleni, but the work of a 4th or 5th century CE author who knew Caleni's work well. Other scholars, such as Butrica (2000) and Richlin (1992), see no reason why the work cannot be that of Caleni. The text of the *Conquestio* in this volume is that of Butrica (2000).

## Select Bibliography

Butrica, J. L. 2000. *Sulpiciae Conquestio*: http://www.curculio.org/Sulpiciae

———. 2006. "The Fabella of Sulpicia ("Epigrammata Bobiensia" 37)," *Phoenix* 60.1/2: 70–121.

Hallett, J. P. 1992. "Martial's Sulpicia and Propertius' Cynthia," *CW* 86.2: 99–123.

———. 2013. "The Fragment of Martial's Sulpicia". In Churchill, Laurie J.; Brown, Phyllis R.; Jeffrey, Jane E. (eds.). *Women Writing Latin From Roman Antiquity to Early Modern Europe. Volume 1: Women Writing Latin in Roman Antiquity, Late Antiquity, and the Early Christian Era.* New York: Routledge.

Parker, H. 1992. "Other Remarks on the Other Sulpicia," *CW* 86.2: 89–95.

Plant, I. 2004. *Women Writers of Greece and Rome.* Norman, OK.

Richlin, A. 1992. "Sulpicia the Satirist," *CW* 86.2: 125–139.

### *Sulpicia Caleni 1 (scol. at Juv. 6.537)*

Si me cadurci restitutis fasciis
nudam Caleno concubantem proferat.

*Meter: iambic trimeter*

—

**cadurcum, i, *n.*:** marriage bed
**Calenus, i, *m.*:** Calenus (Sulpicia's husband)
**concubo, concubare:** to lie with
**fascia, ae, *f.*:** band, binding
**profero, proferre, protuli, prolatum:** to bring forth; to reveal
**restituo, restituere, restitui, restitutum:** to restore; to replace; to put back in place

—

**1–2:** The fragmentary nature of this poem makes interpretation nearly impossible. However, it is noteworthy that Sulpicia Caleni speaks with a frankness about herself that is almost the diametrical opposite of Sulpicia the elegist. Whereas Sulpicia the elegist's poetry is marked by hedging and a certain level of restraint, this poem of Sulpicia Caleni is remarkably frank. Notice the progression in the two lines that tantalizes the reader by gradually revealing the naked poetess. She begins with marking herself as the object of the gaze (*me*), places herself in the erotic location of her bedroom (*cadurci restitutis fasciis*), reveals her nude body (*nudam*), and finally depicts herself laying nude next to her husband in bed (*Caleno concubantem*).

**1. cadurci restitutis fasciis:** Ablative Absolute.

**2. nudam … concubantem:** Modifying *me.* Hallett (2013) sees parallels between these lines and Propertius 2.15.

**2. Caleno:** Dative with compound verb *concubantem* (cf. Allen and Greenough §370).

**3. proferat:** Present subjunctive in a si-clause. Because this sentence is fragmentary, it is unclear who or what the subject of the verb is. Hallett (2013) suggests that the subject could be Venus.

### *Sulpicia Caleni 2 (Epigrammata Bobiensia* **37)**

Musa, quibus numeris heroas et arma frequentas,
fabellam permitte mihi detexere paucis.
Nam tibi secessi, tecum penetrale retractans
consilium; quare neque carmine curro Phalaeco
nec trimetro †iambo nec qui pede fractus† eodem
fortiter irasci discit duce Clazomenio,
cetera quin etiam, †quod denique† milia lusi
________________________________________

primaque Romanas docui contendere Graiis  
et salibus variare novis, constanter omitto  
teque quibus princeps et facundissima calles 10  
aggredior: precibus descende clientis et audi.  
Dic mihi, Calliope: quidnam pater ille deorum  
cogitat? An terras in patria saecula mutat  
quasque dedit quondam mortalibus eripit artes  
nosque iubet tacitos et iam rationis egenos 15  
non aliter, primo quam cum surreximus aevo, 19  
glandibus et purae rursus procumbere lymphae? 20  
An reliquas terras conservat amicus et urbes,  
sed genus Ausonium †Romulique† extirpat alumnos? 22  
Quid reputemus? Enim duo sunt quibus extulit ingens 16  
Roma caput: virtus belli et sapientia pacis. 17  
Stabat in his, neque enim poterat constare sine istis: 32  
Aut frustra uxori mendaxque Diespiter olim 33  
“imperium sine fine dedi” dixisse probatur. 34  
Sed virtus, agitata domi et Latialibus armis, 18  
in freta Sicaniae et Carthaginis exilit arces 23  
ceteraque imperia et totum simul abstulit orbem.  
Deinde, velut stadio victor qui solus Achaeo 25  
languet et immota secum virtute fatiscit,  
sic itidem Romana manus, contendere postquam  
destitit et pacem longis frenavit habenis,  
ipsa domi leges et Graia inventa retractans  
omnia bellorum terra quaesita marique 30  
praemia consilio et molli ratione regebat. 31  
Nunc igitur qui rex Romanos imperat inter, 35  
non trabe sed tergo prolapsus et ingluvie albus,  
et studia et sapiens hominum nomenque genusque  
omnia abire foras atque urbe excedere iussit.  
Quid facimus? Graiorum nonne revicimus urbes,  
ut Romana foret manus his instructa magistris: 40  
nunc, Capitolio veluti et turbante Camillo  
ensibus et trutina Galli fugere relicta,  
sic nostri palare senes adiguntur et ipsi  
ut ferale suos onus exportare libellos.  
Ergo Numantinus Libycusque erravit in isto 45  
Scipio, quod Rhodio crevit formante magistro,  
ceteraque illa manus bello facunda †secundo†,  
quos inter prisci sententia dia Catonis 48a  
———————————————— 48b  
scire deos magni fecisset, utrumne secundis  
an magis adversis staret Romana propago. 50  
Scilicet adversis: nam, cum defendier armis  
suadet amor patriae et caritura penatibus uxor,

convenit, ut vespis, quarum domus arce Monetae, *53a*
——————————————— *53b*
turba rigens strictis per lutea corpora telis;
ast ubi apes secura redit, oblita suorum *55a*
——————————————— *55b*
plebs<que> patresque una somno moriuntur obeso:
Romulidarum igitur longa et gravis exitium pax.
Hoc fabella modo pausam facit. Optima, posthac,
Musa, velim moneas, sine qua mihi nulla voluptas *59a*
——————————————— *59b*
vivere, uti quondam †smyrnalibusque† peribat,
†nunc itidem migrare velit vel denique quidvis
ut dea quaere aliud tantum Romana Caleno
moenia iucundos† pariterque averte Sabinos."
Haec ego. Tum paucis dea me dignarier infit:
"pone metus aequos, cultrix mea: summa tyranno
ecce instant odia et nostro periturus honore est.
Nam laureta Numae fontisque habitamus eosdem
et comite Egeria ridemus inania coepta.
Vive, vale. Manet hunc pulchrum sua fama dolorem:
Musarum spondet chorus et Romanus Apollo."

*Meter: Dactylic Hexameter*

—

**Achaeus, a, um:** Achaean, Greek
**adigo, adigere, adegi, adactum:** to force, compel
**aggredior, aggredi, aggressum sum:** to approach, go toward
**alumnus, i, *m.*:** nursling, pupil; foster-child
**apes, apis, *f.*:** bee
**ast:** but; moreover, yet
**Ausonius, a, um:** Ausonian
**averto, avertere, averti, aversus:** to turn away
**Calenus, i, *m.*:** Calenus (Sulpicia's husband)
**calleo, callere:** to be experienced, skilled; to be hardened, calloused
**Calliope, Callipoes, *f.*:** Calliope (chief of the Muses)
**Camillus, i, *m.*:** Camillus
**Capitolius, a, um:** Capitoline, of the Capitoline Hill
**careo, carere, carui, cariturus:** (+ abl.) to lack
**carmen, carminis, *n.*:** song, poem
**Carthago, Carthaginis, *f.*:** Carthage
**Cato, Catonis, *m.*:** M. Porcius Cato (234–149 BCE)
**Clazomenius, a, um:** Clazomenian; of Clazomenae
**cliens, clientis, *m./f.*:** client, dependent
**conservo, conservare, conservavi, conservatum:** to preserve
**constanter:** (adv.) without change
**contendo, contendere, contendi, contentum:** to stretch, strain; to fight, contend
**convenit:** (impersonal) it is appropriate, it is fitting
**cultrix, cultricis, *f.*:** female worshipper, devotee
**desisto, desistere, destiti, destitum:** to set down; to cease from

**detexo, detexere, detexui, detextum:** to weave; describe
**Diespiter, Diespitris, *m*.:** Diespater; Jupiter
**digno, dignare, dignavi, dignatus:** to deem worthy
**dius, a, um:** divine, god-like
**effero, efferre, extuli, elatum:** to bear out, to carry out
**egenus, a, um:** bereft, void of
**ensis, ensis, *m*.:** sword
**excedo, excedere, excessi, excessum:** to go out; depart
**exilio, exilire, exilui:** to spring up; to rise up
**exitium, i, *n*.:** ruin, destruction
**exporto, exportare, exportavi, exportatum:** to carry out
**exturpo, exturpare, exturpavi, exturpatum:** to pluck up, root out; to eradicate
**fabella, ae, *f*.:** story, narrative
**facundus, a, um:** eloquent, fluent
**fatisco, fatiscere:** to grow weak, become exhausted
**feralis, e:** deadly, fatal
**foras:** (adv.) out of the doors; abroad
**formo, formare, formavi, formatum:** to form, mould, shape
**fortiter:** (adv.) bravely
**freno, frenare, frenavi, frenatum:** to bridle
**frequento, frequentare, frequentavi, frequenatum:** to assemble, gather together; to celebrate
**fretum, i, *n*.:** strait; sea
**Galli, Gallorum, *m.pl*.:** the Gauls
**glando, glandinis, *f*.:** acorn
**Graius, a, um:** Greek
**habena, ae, *f*.:** rein
**habito, habitare, habitavi, habitatum:** to live, dwell, inhabit
**heros, herois, *m*.:** hero
**honor, honoris, *m*.:** honor
**iambus, i, *m*.:** iambic
**immotus, a, um:** unmoved, motionless
**inanis, is, e:** empty, pointless
**infit:** (impersonal) he/she/it begins
**ingluvies, ei, *f*.:** maw
**insto, instare, insteti, instatum:** to stand upon, threaten
**instruo, instruere, instruxi, instructum:** to prepare, teach; to set in order
**inventum, -i, *n*.:** device, invention
**itidem:** (adv.) in like manner; in the same way
**iucundus, a, um:** pleasant, agreeable
**langueo, languere:** to be weary, worn out
**libellus, i, *m*.:** little book, booklet
**Libycus, a, um:** Libyan
**ludo, ludere, lusi, lusum:** to play
**luteus, a, um:** yellow
**lympha, ae, *f*.:** water; spring water
**mendax, mendacis:** lying, deceptive
**migro, migrare, migravi, migratum:** to depart; migrate
**Moneta, ae, *f*.:** (Juno) Moneta
**musa, ae, *f*.:** muse
**nonne:** (adv). not? (interrogative *non*, expecting an affirmative answer)
**Numantinus, a, um:** Numantine (surname given to Scipio Africanus)
**obesus, a, um:** fat, heavy; stuffed, overeaten
**obliviscor, i, oblitus sum:** (+ gen.) to forget
**omitto, omittere, ommisi, omissum:** to let go, give up; to pass over, omit
**optimus, a, um:** best
**palo, palare, palavi, palatum:** to wander
**pariter:** (adv.) equally

**patria, ae, *f.*:** fatherland, homeland
**patrius, a, um:** paternal, fatherly; native
**pausa, ae, *f.*:** pause, stop, end
**Penates, Penatium, *m.pl.*:** Penates
**penetralis, e:** piercing, penetrating; inward, internal
**Phalaecus, a, um:** Phalaecian
**plebs, plebis, *f.*:** the common people; the whole people, the nation
**posthac:** (adv.) henceforth, after this time.
**priscus, a, um:** old, ancient; old-fashioned
**procumbo, procumbere, procubui, procubitum:** to fall forward, sink down
**prolabor, prolabi, prolapsus sum:** to fall down; to fail
**propago, propaginis, *f.*:** offspring, descendants
**purus, a, um:** pure
**quidvis:** whatever (you wish)
**quin etiam:** furthermore
**quod:** because
**quondam:** once
**ratio, rationis, *f.*:** reason
**reputo, reputare, reputavi, reputatum:** to think over, ponder
**retracto, retractare, retractavi, retractatum:** to take hold of again; to undertake anew
**revinco, revincere, revici, revictum:** to conquer, subdue
**Rhodius, a, um:** Rhodian
**rigens, rigentis:** stiff, rigid; stubborn, unyielding
**Roma, ae, *f.*:** Rome
**Romanus, a, um:** Roman
**Romulidae, arum, *f.pl.*:** the Romans; posterity of Romulus
**Romulus, i, *m.*:** Romulus (mythical first king of Rome)
**Sabinus, a, um:** Sabine
**sal, salis, *m.*:** salt; wit; good taste
**Scipio, Scipionis, *m.*:** Scipio
**secedo, secedere, secessi, secessum:** to go apart, to separate, to withdraw
**Sicania, ae, *f.*:** Sicania; Sicily
**smyrnalis, e:** Smyrnian
**socialis, e:** social; allied
**stadium, i, *n.*:** stadium
**stringo, stringere, strinxi, strictum:** to draw (in hostility); to bind
**suadeo, suadere, suasi, suasum:** to persuade, urge
**–, sui:** him/her/it/self; themselves
**summus, a, um:** highest, tallest
**surgo, surgere, surrexi, surrectum:** to raise, erect; to arise, get up
**trabs, trabis, *f.*:** beam, timber
**trimetrus, i, *m*:** trimeter
**trutina, ae, *f.*:** balance, pair of scales
**tyrannus, i, *m.*:** tyrant
**una:** (adv) as one; together
**vario, variare, variavi, variatum:** to diversify, change; to vary
**vespa, ae, *f.*:** wasp

—

**1–11:** In the introductory section of the poem, the poet invokes Calliope, the muse of epic poetry, to assist her in singing her satire. She states that she is coming to Calliope not in the meters of satire with which she is most adept and famous, but in hexameter, the meter of epic and in which Calliope is the most well-versed.

**1–2. Musa … paucis:** The opening lines feature fairly straightforward grammar, but the *quibus numeris* is slightly proleptic. A more prosaic word order of these lines would be: *Musa, permitte mihi fabellam paucis [verbis et] numeris, quibus heroas et arma frequentas, detexere.*

**1. Musa:** In the opening two lines, the poet evokes the content and meter of heroic epic before asking the Muse to permit this current poem not to reach the length of a traditional epic, but a shorter length. Epic is immediately evoked by the opening word, *Musa,* as traditional epic begins with some sort of invocation of the Muse to inspire their verses. As the reader discovers on line 12, this muse is Calliope, the chief of the Muses and the muse of epic poetry.

**1. numeris:** Here, the *numerus* meant by the poet is poetic meter (cf. Ovid, *Amores* 1.1-2: *arma gravi numero violentaque bella parabam/edere*). Construe *numeris* as an ablative of manner with *fabellam detexere* on line 2.

**1. heroas et arma:** An allusion to the famous opening of the *Aeneid*: *arma virumque cano.* The poet evokes the *Aeneid* in a request that the muse allow the poet to use epic meter for the poem.

**2. mihi:** Dative with *permitte.*

**2. detexere:** In Roman poetry, the act of writing poetry was commonly described with images of weaving. As the weaver weaves strands of material to create a coherent work of art, the poet weaves words and phrases together into a coherent poem.

**2. pacuis:** Supply *verbis.* The contrast is between the length of poems in traditional epic (line 1) and the shorter aims of this satirical poem.

**3–6:** The poet yields to the desire of the Muse and abandons earlier plans at composing the poem in hendecasyllabics, iambic trimeter, or choliambs. Along with dactylic hexameter, all of these had been frequent meters for satire in antiquity. Thus, it becomes clear to the reader that this poem will be satirical in nature.

**4. carmine … Phalaceo:** The Phalacean meter was commonly referred to by Roman poets as the hendecasyllabic meter. It was named after the Alexandrian poet, Phalaikos, who was fond of using the meter.

**5. †iambo nec qui pede fractus†:** The entirety of this line seems to be corrupt. The parallel structure started by the ablatives *carmine Phalaeco* and *trimetro iambo* is not completed with the *qui* clause that completes the clause. Moreover, the antecedent of *qui fractus* is obscure. The sense of the line, however, is clear: the poet does not write satires in the Phalacean meter, the Iambic Trimeter, or in Choliambs.

**6. duce Clazomenio:** This is a reference to the Greek poet Hipponax, famed in antiquity for his biting and irreverent satire. He wrote much of his work in choliambs, which is marked by a long third beat in the final metrical foot. After he had been expelled from his native Ephesus, he moved to the city of Clazomenae.

**7a–11:** The poet reveals an earlier career in writing more frivolous poetry (*cetera … milia lusi*), but asks the muse to assist with writing this poem in a different style: hexameter satire.

**7a. †quod denique†:** Another seemingly corrupt line, as *quod denique* does not make sense in the line. Heinsius has put forth the conjecture *quondam quae*, which makes some sense with *cetera ... quae*. The sense of the line appears to be that the poet will not even make use of the other thousands of meters, which she once has employed.

**7a. milia:** Plural of *mille*. Translate as "thousands".

**7b:** The link between lines 7 and 8 is unclear and sudden. Therefore, editors have suggested that a line may be missing here. Thus, this edition marks the potential missing line.

**8–9:** The poet claims to have been the first to teach Romans to compete with the Greeks in poetry and to vary poetry with novel witticisms. The phrasing is reminiscent of a similar claim made by Horace in *Odes* 3.30.13–14: *princeps Aeolium carmen ad Italos deduxisse modos* (I was the first to lead forth an Aeolian poem to Italian meters). Key here is the adjective *prima* and the noun *salibus*. By using the feminine, nominative *prima*, the poet identifies herself as a female and the feminine counterpart to Horace. The connection with Horace gets even closer with the introduction of *sal*, used frequently in Latin literature to refer to satire.

**9–11:** The poet states that, although she has enjoyed fame and glory in her earlier lyric works, she will give them up (*constanter omitto*) in favor of hexameter poetry. Thus, she asks for the help of the muse.

**10. teque:** Object of *aggredior*. The *-que* separates the two main clauses *constanter omitto* and *te aggredior*.

**10. quibus:** Supply *numeris*, as the poet is describing the meters in which Calliope is superior.

**10. calles:** A clever play on Calliope, the name of the muse invoked by the poet.

**11. precibus ... audi:** An apparent allusion to Horace, *Odes* 3.4.1-2: *descende caelo et dic age tibia/regina longum Calliope melos* (Descend from heaven and, come, speak the tibia and a long song, queen Calliope).

**11. precibus:** Either Ablative of Attendant Circumstance or Dative of Direction with *descende*.

**11 clientis:** The poet describes her relationship with her muse as a patron-client relationship with the poet as the client.

**12–34:** After beginning the poem with an invocation of Calliope, the poet now turns directly to the muse and asks her why Rome has seemingly fallen out of favor with her father Jupiter. Has he left Rome in search of other cities to patronize? Is he planning to send the human race back to its very beginnings? These two questions are marked by the repetition of *an*. This section then concludes with the poet's assertion that the two foundational ideals that have always butressed Rome have fallen by the wayside: valor in war and wisdom in peace (*virtus belli et sapientia pacis*, 17). Without them the power without end (*imperium sine fine*), which was promised by Jupiter, is in danger of being lost.

**14. quasque ... artes:** Prolepsis. The antecedent *artes* is delayed until the end of the line for emphasis.

**14. morientibus:** Dative, present, deponent participle from *morior.*

**15. nosque ... egenos:** Supply *esse* as the infinitive in the accusative-infinitive construction started by *iubet.*

**15. rationis egenos:** *egens* takes a genitive object of which one is bereft. Here, the object is *rationis.*

**19. non aliter ... quam:** Translate as "not otherwise than...".

**20. procumbere:** infinitive with *iubet.*

**20. glandibus ... purae ... lymphae:** Datives with the compound verb *procumbo.*

**22. †Romulique†:** This appears to be another corruption in the manuscript, as *Rōmulīque* cannot scan in the line. Pithou has suggested *Remulique*, and Butrica *lupulaeque*, "the nurslings of the little she-wolf".

**16. Enim:** Although *enim* is nearly always postpostive, in early comedic writers, it can be used in the primary position to add extra emphasis to the subsequent words and means something like "to be sure" (cf. Pl. *Poen.* 4.2.33).

**16. duo:** Neuter plural. Supply "things".

**16. quibus:** Ablative of Means.

**17. virtus belli et sapientia pacis:** *belli* and *pacis* are limiting genitives. Translate as "virtue in war and wisdom in peace".

**32. Stabat in his:** The poet includes a potential complex allusion. The same phrase occurs in the same metrical position at Ovid *M.* 8.743 (*Stabat in his ingens annoso robore quercus*). In that passage, Ovid uses *stabat* to describe a huge, sacred oak (*quercus*) that Erysichthon chops down in a sacrilegious act. Ovid also echos the famous passage from Vergil, *Aeneid* 4.441 in which the *quercus* stands as a symbol for the steadfast and everlasting power of Roman power. Against this intertextual background, the poet of *Epigramata Bobiensia* 37 evokes the image of Roman *imperium*, but also foreshadows the potential sacrilegious destruction of that *imperium* when Domitian expels the philosophers from Rome (lines 35–40).

**32. his:** Refers to *consilio et molli ratione* on 31.

**33. uxori:** This word is problematic. Since Jupiter says this quotation to Venus at *Aeneid* 1.279 (see note 34 below), and not to Juno, two possibilities have been suggested: either the poet gets the mythology wrong, or the text is incorrect. Some editors, led by Burmann, have replaced *uxori* with *Veneri*. This is paleographically possible, but, as Butrica 2000 has noted, may be editorial overreach. Thus, this text has retained *uxori.*

**34. imperium sine fine dedi:** The poet quotes Vergil, *Aeneid* 1.279, in which Jupiter assures his daughter, Venus, that he has granted *imperium sine fine* to the Romans. The quotation is placed in the same metrical position as the original.

**18–38:** The poet launches into a brief review of Roman history, one that is rife with the theme of decline of virtue and *Romanitas*, a theme quite prevalent throughout Roman literature. Beginning with the rise of Rome and her gradual domination of the Italian peninsula, Carthage, and the rest of the world, the poet depicts Rome resting on her laurels and losing sight of her core values. Rome's fall culminates with the rise of Domitian, who expels the philosophers from Rome.

**18. domi:** Locative case (cf. Allen and Greenough §427).

**18. Latialibus armis:** The poet seems to be describing the gradual growth of Roman *imperium*, beginning with battles with neighboring Italic peoples, but the original manuscript adjective *socialibus* evokes the Social Wars of the 1st century BCE. That chronology, however, would be impossible, as the Punic Wars preceded the Social Wars. Therefore, this must refer to pre-3rd century BCE wars with the Italic peoples that later would become allies of Rome. Thus, we have accepted the emendation of Butrica (2000) of *Latialibus*.

**23. in freta ... arces:** The poet references both the First Punic War (264–241 BCE), which was punctuated with naval battles off the coast of Sicily, and the Second (218–201 BCE) and Third Punic Wars (149–146 BCE), which ended with the Battle of Zama and the sacking of Carthage itself, respectively.

**23. freta Sicaniae:** The word *fretum* was the typical word used to describe the Strait of Messina, which separates the eastern coast of Sicily from the Italian peninsula. Since one major impetus of the First Punic War was the dispute over Messina and eastern Sicily, *fretum Sicaniae* may refer to the Strait of Messina itself rather than to a more generic sea around Sicily.

**23–24. et ... que ... et:** The sequence of these conjunctions is key. The poet uses *et* to separate the two actions of the main clauses (*exilit*, *abstulit*). The -*que* joins the objects of *exilit* (*Carthaginis arces, ceteraque imperia*).

**25–35:** The poet moves from the expansion of Roman power through warfare to the manner in which the Romans maintained their empire. In short, the poet argues that the Romans were able to do so by balancing the harsh, masculine *virtus* of their conquests with the "softer", more effeminate virtues of wisdom, reason, and law, all of which were learned from the Greeks. This is a fuller version of the concise statement on line 17: *virtus belli et sapientia pacis*. The poet sets this balance against the portrayal of Domitian, who engages in sexual deviance and expels the proponants of wisdom from Rome.

**25. velut stadio ... Achaeo:** Chiastic structure that creates a clever picture of the victor actually inside the stadium: *stadio* ***victor qui solus*** *stadio*.

**27–28. contendere ... destitit:** Construe together. *Desistere* can take an infinitive to complete its meaning. Translate as: "ceased from fighting".

**29. ipsa:** Refers to *Romana manus* on line 27.

**29. domi:** Locative case (cf. Allen and Greenough §427). See also line 18.

**30. omnia ... quaesita ... praemia:** Extremely proleptic construction. *Omnia* is thrown ahead in the sentence for emphasis, but agrees with *quaesita* and *praemia*. The effect is a gradual reveal of the antecedent *praemia* that is preceded by the descriptive phrases *omnia bellorum* and *terra quaesita marique*. A more prosaic order would be: *ipsa [Romana manus], domi leges et Graia inventa retractans, omnia praemia bellorum, quaesita terra marique, consilio et ratione molli regebat.*

**30. terra quaesita marique:** This image evokes the famous description of Aeneas' travels in the proem to the *Aeneid*: *multum ille et terris iactatus et alto* (*Aen.* 1.3). The poet thus describes the gradual increase of Roman *imperium* in the same terms by which Aeneas, the mythological founder of the Romans, gradually consolidated his own *imperium*.

**30. marique:** Ablative, singular, i-stem.

**31. molli ratione:** The adjective *mollis* was one regularly attributed to effeminate individuals or concepts, particularly in Roman elegy. Here, it describes reason and learning (*ratio*), the direct opposite of the masculine *virtus* (22) that led to the conquest of the Mediterranean.

**35. qui rex:** The exact emperor is not named, but the reference is to Domitian (81–96 CE). Domitian expelled Stoic philosophers from Rome in 88/89 CE and from all of Italy in 93/4 CE. Perhaps the most famous of those expelled was the philosopher Epictetus.

**35. qui rex ... inter:** The poet creates a word order with hyperbaton (*Romanos ... inter*) in order to place two antithetical concepts, *rex* and *Romanos*, next to one another. Traditional Roman thought equated kings with the polar opposite of all that Rome and the Republic represented. The poet thus twists the word order of the line to create something that doesn't quite fit in the same manner as the depiction of Domitian as king distorts normative Roman order.

**36. non trabe ... albus**: An erotic and graphic image aimed at questioning Domitian's Roman masculinity. *Trabs* is used as a metaphor for the penis throughout Latin literature, most pointedly, perhaps, in Catullus 28.9-10 (*O Memmi, bene me ac diu supinum/tota ista trabe lentus irrumasti*). Likewise, *tergum* is oftentimes used as a euphemism for the anus in anal penetration. As such, describing Domitian as sliding forward (*prolapsus*) not with his penis (*trabs*), but his buttocks (*tergum*), places him in the passive role in anal penetration. Since Roman sexuality was generally constructed on an active-passive dichotomy with the masculine role constructed as the penetrative one, showing Domitian as the penetrated in anal intercourse throws his masculinity into doubt. Moreover, the image gets more graphic in the final portion of the line, as Domitian is described as white with respect to his throat (*ingluvie albus*). On the heels of the overly sexual depiction with *prolapsus*, this also may paint Domitian having a white throat due to swallowing semen. If so, Domitian's masculinity is even more degraded.

**37. sapiens ... nomenque genusque:** In agreement as neuter, singular, accusative objects of *abire*.

**38. omnia:** Hyperbaton. Agrees with *studia* on line 37. The resulting word order is chiastic: *et studia et* ***sapiens hominum nomenque genusque****/omnia*.

**39–40. Graios... magistris:** The transmission of these lines in the original text seems to be corrupted, as the grammar does not make sense: *Graios hominumque relinquimus urbes,/ut Romana foret magis his instructa magistris.* In particular, the imperfect subjunctive *foret* cannot follow the present indicative *relinquimus* and adhere to sequence of tenses. Likewise, it is unclear what the function of *hominumque* is and how it relates to *Graios urbes*. Finally, the role of *magis* and the antecedent of *Romana* are problematic. Therefore, the text provided here includes the emendations of Butrica (2000).

**40. foret = esset** (cf. Allen and Greenough §170a).

**41–42. Capitolio ... relicta:** The reference here is to the expulsion of the Gauls by Camillus and M. Manlius Capitolinus in 390 BCE. When the Gauls took the Capitoline Hill, the Romans agreed to pay a ransom in order to free themselves. However, at the moment in which scales were brought out to measure the ransom, Camillus arrived with the Roman cavalry and put the Gauls to flight (cf. Livy 5.48–49 and Plutarch, *Camillus* 28–29).

**42. ensibus:** Butrica (2000) suggests an emendation to *censibus* (cash), but we have retained the transmitted reading here. The change to *censibus* sets up the awkward and un-parallel phrasing of *censibus et trutina relicta* (with cash and the abandoned scale). By retaining *ensibus*, the swords add to the description of Camillus on line 41 and the *et* now can separate two Ablatives Absolute (*turbante Camillo/ensibus* and *trutina relicta*).

**42. fugere:** Syncopated form of *fugerunt*.

**44. ferale ... libellos:** Chiastic word order (*ferale* ***suos*** *onus exportare* ***libellos***).

**45–46. Numantinus Libycusque ... Scipio:** The reference is to P. Cornelius Scipio Aemilianus Africanus Numantinus (185–129 BCE), who gained the title Numantinus by defeating Numantia in 134–133 BCE and Africanus by defeating Carthage in the Third Punic War. The poet has apparently changed Scipio's title of Africanus to Libycus. In addition to his exploits in combat and politics, Scipio Aemilianus is also well-known for his patronage of Greek learning and philosophy in Rome and his central role in the so-called Scipionic Circle. Therefore, he makes an ideal exemplum for the balance of Roman *virtus* with Greek learning.

**45–46. in isto ... quod:** Take *isto* with *quod* on line 46. Translate the phrase as "in this, namely that...".

**46. Rhodio ... magistro:** The reference here is to Panaetius of Rhodes, who was a friend of Scipio Aemilianus and is regarded as a part of the Scipionic Circle. Cicero *de Officiis* 1.90.12 and Porphyrio's commentary on Horace *Odes* 1.29.13 refer to the relationship between Panaetius and Scipio as one of mutual learning and respect rather than of teacher-student. Butrica (2000) *ad loc* notes that "Panaetius could not have taught Scipio as a child, and so *crevit* in the next line must be used in the sense 'flourished in his career', though no no doubt the idea of intellectual 'growth' into a sort of philosophical adulthood is present as well".

**47. cetera illa manus ... facunda:** *Manus* here is better translated as "force".

**47. †secundo†:** *Secundo* is transmitted in the manuscript tradition, but Butrica (2000) raises questions based on the chronology of the poem. If this is to be taken as a reference to the Second Punic War, it seems out of place to skip backward from Scipio Aemilianus and the Third Punic War and forward from a reference to Camillus and the Gallic invasion of 390 BCE. However, with no clear solution, the transmitted *secundo* has been retained.

**48a. quos inter:** Anastrophe. A more prosaic word order would be *inter quos*.

**48a. prisci Catonis:** The Cato referenced here is M. Porcius Cato (234–149 BCE), who famously was not a lover of the influx of Greek ideas into Rome during his lifetime. Plutarch, in his *Cato* 22, recounts that, when an embassy came to Rome from Athens, the Roman youth became enamored of the speeches the members of the embassy gave. Cato, on the other hand, became more and more suspicious of the embassy and feared that Roman youth would come to love reputation based more on words than on deeds (φοβούμενος, μὴ τὸφιλότιμον ἐνταῦθα τρέψαντες οἱνέοι τὴν ἐπὶ τῷ λέγειν δόξανἀγαπήσωσι μᾶλλον τῆς ἀπὸ τῶνἔργων καὶ τῶν στρατειῶν). Thus, Cato spoke out in the Senate that Rome should finish its business with the embassy as quickly as possible so that the Roman youth could return to heeding the laws and magistrates of Rome (οἱ δὲ Ῥωμαίων νέοιτῶν νόμων καὶ τῶν ἀρχόντων ὡσπρότερον ἀκούωσι).

**48a. sententia dia:** This is a reference to a line from Horace *Sat.* 1.2.31-32, in which Cato's *sententia* is spelled out: *quidam notus homo, cum exiret fornice, 'macte/virtute esto' inquit sententia dia Catonis.* ("When a certain man he knew was coming out of the brothel, Cato made the divine statement: go on in your manliness!") The situation in *Sat.* 1.2 is that Cato made this statement to young man exiting a brothel instead of seeking sexual gratification in the form of an extramarital affair. The relationship to this poem is that Cato, like Scipio, is standing as another examplum of proper Roman masculinity: he is describing a time when Roman men (a) were the active participants in the sex act and (b) controlled their desires with reason and restraint. Again, these stand in direct opposition to the portrayal of the sexual deviant Domitian.

**48b:** There is a lacuna in the text at this point. We have marked it with a line.

**49. scire deos:** This phrase appears to be the object of *magni fecisset*. Translate as "[he/she/it had considered it of great value] that the gods know".

**49. magni fecisset:** The verb *facio* can take a Genitive of Value to describe value or worth. Here, the word *magni* fulfills that role. Translate as "he/she/it had considered of great value".

**49. fecisset:** Pluperfect, active, subjunctive of *facere*. It is difficult to identify the function of the verb, as the lacuna in the previous line most likely includes grammatical information necessary to explain the subjunctive nature of the verb.

**49–50. utrumne … propago:** Complex word order. A more prosaic order would be *utrumne propago Romana secundis magis staret an adversis*. Translate as "whether the Roman offerspring would be more steadfast in prosperity or in adversity".

**50. magis staret:** The adverb *magis* is best construed with *staret*. Literally, this translates as "would stand firm more", but a smoother English translation would be "would be more steadfast".

**50. staret:** imperfect active subjunctive of *stare* in an Indirect Question with *utrumne … an*.

**51–57:** The poet shifts here to a traditional motif in satire: the decline of virtues from age to age. In particular, the poet pinpoints the cause of the current state of affairs as the lack of a proper enemy to create enough adversity for the Romans to maintain their manliness and courage. A similar motif can be found in the opening of Sallust's *Bellum Catilinae*, but also throughout Latin literature. Sallust argues that Rome was at its height when it followed *virtus* through the twin ideals of audacity in war and justice in peace (*Duabus his artibus, audacia in bello, ubi pax evenerat aequitate seque remque publicam curabant, BC* 9). However, once Rome had destroyed its enemies and rested on its laurels, gluttony, avarice, and sloth began to cause the city to decline (*Qui labores, pericula, dubias atque asperas res facile toleraverant, eis otium, divitiae, optanda alias, oneri miseriaeque fuere, BC* 10). To illustrate the point, the poet concludes with an evocative metaphor comparing the battle-ready wasp and the gluttonous and lazy bee. However, the lines containing the metaphor contain multiple *lacunae*, which make it difficult to understand its entire intent.

**51. defendier:** archaic form for the present passive infinitive. The more expected form would be *defendi*. Here, it is best construed with *armis* as the object of *suadet*, literally translated as "[the love of country persuades]" to be defended with arms. It is, perhaps, better translated with the noun "defense". This use of *defendier* may be an allusion to Juv. *Sat.* 15.157, where the same word is used in the same metrical position in a passage describing how Roman citizens had used to come together for the common good, but in Juvenal's time that sense of community had declined into rampant individualism and greed.

**52. caritura penatibus uxor:** *Caritura* is the future active participle of *carere*, a verb which takes an ablative object, as *penatibus*. This phrase literally translates as "a wife about to lack penates". However, the sense of the phrase is, perhaps, better translated as "the thought/threat of a homeless wife".

**53. ut vespis:** *Ut* here is construed as "as" not as "that". *Vespis* is the dative plural of *vespa*, construed with *convenit*, "it is fitting". Translate as "as for wasps".

**53a. arce Monetae:** The text here is uncertain. Two manuscripts give the reading *arce movente*, and two others have *arce monetae.* This text follows Butrica (2000) in his reading of *arce Monetae*, as not only does the phrase *arce movente* seem meaningless, but a reference to the Temple of Juno Moneta is appropriate in the context of the poem. The Temple of Juno Moneta was located on summit of the citadel located on the Capitoline Hill, and was the site of the mint of Rome until the time of Domitian. It was said to have been built on the site of the house of Manlius, who famously drove the Gauls away from the city in 390 BCE (cf. Ov. *F.* 6.183–186). He is referenced earlier in this poem as Capitolinus in line 41. The force of the image is to depict how Romans like Manlius used to perform proper masculinity and protect their country and family as wasps. Moreover, there may be an oblique reference to Domitian's removal of the mint from the Temple of Juno Moneta to a site near the Colosseum, construed here as another instance of Domitian failing to live up to the traditions of his Roman ancestors and distorting what it meant to be a proper Roman.

**53b:** There is a lacuna in the text at this point. We have marked it with a line.

**54. strictis ... telis:** A chiastic structure, with *strictis* modifying *telis* and the prepositional phrase *per lutea corpora* sandwiched inside. *Strictis telis* is an Ablative of Specification (cf. Allen and Greenough §418), construed with *rigens.*

**55a: oblita suorum:** *Oblita* is the perfect participle of *oblivisci*, a deponent verb of forgetting that takes a Gentive object of the thing forgotten (cf. Allen and Greenough §350).

**55b:** There is a lacuna in the text at this point. We have marked it with a line. Butrica (2000) suggests that there may, in fact, be multiple lines missing at this point due to the brevity of the bee metaphor.

**56. patres:** These are not fathers, *per se*, but the patricians. Roman writers typically refer to the members of the patrician class as *patres.*

**56. somno ... obeso:** Ablative of Manner (cf. Allen and Greenough §412). Themes of gluttony and sloth are prevalent ones in all of Roman satire. However, nowhere in canonical satire (Lucilius, Horace, Persius, Juvenal) are these two terms paired together so closely.

**57. Romulidarum ... pax:** Complex word order arranged thus to delay *pax* for maximum emphasis. A more prosaic word order would be: *Pax longa et gravis [erat] exitium Romulidarum.* By delaying *pax* until the end of the line, the poet brings this section of the poem, devoted to the reasons why Roman *virtus* has degenerated so far, to a tidy conclusion with a verdict: excessive peace has dulled Roman virtue.

**58–63:** This section of the poem is the most challenging, as the text has been corrupted at multiple places. The sense of the section seems to suggest that the poet is asking Calliope for advice: should the poet remain at Rome or emigrate from the city to avoid the problems caused by Domitian?

**58. Optima:** A challenging word due to its ambiguity. It can either be nominative singular feminine, vocative singular feminine or accusative plural neuter. If the first, it is construed with *fabulla* (the best little story); if the second, with *Musa* (the best Muse); and if the third, as a substantive object of *moneas* (the best [things]). We think the third option is the most likely here, as *Musa optima* in the vocative is unattested, and *fabulla optima* seems out of place. Moreover, the sense of the passage seems to be that the poet is asking the Muse about the best course of action to take.

**59a. velim:** present, active subjunctive of *velle*. This appears to be a potential subjunctive, but it is difficult to be certain due to lacuna on the following line. If a potential subjunctive, it would translate as "I should wish".

**59a. moneas:** present active subjunctive of *monere*. Construe with *velim* as a Substantive Clause of Purpose (cf. Allen and Greenough §563b). Translate with *velim* as "I should wish that you advise".

**59a. sine qua … voluptas:** Supply *est*.

**59b:** There is a lacuna in the text at this point. We have marked it with a dashed line.

**60. uti** = *ut*

**60. †smyrnalibusque†:** This word is uncertain. One of the manuscripts of the text has the reading *smyrnalibus* without the enclitic *-que*. However, the line does not scan properly with that reading. The remaining manscripts all have the enclitic *-que*, which fixes the meter, but does not make sense in the line. We are, perhaps, missing the rest of the picture with the lacuna in the previous line. Therefore, we have left the text with the enclitic *-que*.

**61–63. †nunc … iucundos†:** Another highly uncertain text. As transmitted, the grammar does not make sense. Various attempts at emendation have tried to aid our understanding, but none seemingly address all the issues. This is, again, most likely due to the lacuna in 59b, which would probably add much to our understanding of these lines. Therefore, we have left the text as-is.

**61. velit:** present active subjunctive of *velle*.

**62. Caleno:** This reference to a certain Calenus is one of the chief reasons that this poem has been attributed to Sulpicia Caleni. However, no further mention is made of him in the poem.

**63. Sabinos:** The Sabines are a seemingly odd reference to make at this point of the poem. However, it may have something to do with the fact that Domitian's family was descended from the Sabines.

**64–70:** At this point, the poet concludes and cedes the way for Calliope herself to make a statement. Calliope calms the poet's fears and states unequivocally that Domitian will pay the price for his faults and that his bad reputation will follow him into the future.

**64. Haec ego:** Supply *dico.*

**64. paucis:** Supply *verbis.*

**64. dignarier:** archaic form for the present deponent infinitive. The more expected form would be *dignari.* Construe as a complementary infinitive with *infit.*

**65–66: summa ... odia:** A complex word order. A more prosaic word order would be: *ecce, summa odia tyranno instant. Instare* here has a meaning close to "threaten" or "impend".

**66. periturus est:** active periphrastic of *perire.* Translate as "about to die/ perish".

**67–68:** In Roman mythology, Egeria was a water nymph who also was the divine counselor and wife of Numa Pompilius, the second king of Rome. According to Livy 1.21.3, Numa was accustomed to meet Egeria in a grove just outside the Porta Capena in Rome. Here, the poet seems to refer to Egeria and Numa as a means of connecting back to the Roman past, depicting famous Romans from a more virtuous time making fun of Domitian. This reference is also taken as evidence for Sulpicia Caleni as author; for in Martial 10.35.13-14 Martial brings up Egeria and Numa as an analog for Sulpicia Caleni and her husband Calenus.

**67. fontisque:** alternative ending of the accusative plural in the 3rd declension (*-īs*).

**68. comite Egeria:** These two ablatives are in apposition and should be translated as "with Egeria as companion".

**69. Manet ... dolorem:** A curious and awkward line. The sense is that Domitian's bad reputation will follow him wherever he goes, but the reflexive possessive adjective *sua* is awkward as the subject. Literally, this translates as "His own reputation remains for this pretty pain".

**70. Musarum ... Apollo:** The final image of the poem is an evocative one: Calliope gives her sacred word that Domitian will receive a bad reputation and that his reputation will continue to be sung to future generations through poetry and song. The reference to the Muses makes a nice *inclusio* to the poem, bringing back the same image with which the poem opened (*Musa, quibus* ...). Moreover, it is also strangely similar to the end of Sulpicia 7, in which the narrator states that Sulpicia's reputation for beauty will sung solemnly and for many years by Apollo and the Muses (lines 21–24).

### *Sulpicia Caleni 1 (scol. at Juv. 6.537)*

If, with the bindings of my marriage bed restored,
me nude and lying with Calenus she(?)[1] should reveal…

### *Sulpicia Caleni 2* (*Epigrammata Bobiensia* 37)

O Muse, in the meter[2] in which you celebrate heroes and arms,
allow me to weave together a story of peace in a few words.
For I have come to you for advice, reconsidering my inmost
plan. Therefore, I neither run with a Phalaecean song[3]
nor with iambic trimeter[4] nor with that same meter which, broken,
learned to rage bravely with the Clazomenian guide.[5]
Indeed, I have played a thousand others…
[*one line missing*]
and though I was the first woman to teach Roman women to contend with Greeks
and to be different in their new wit, I steadfastly give it up
and I come to you in the meter in which you are best and most experienced:
come down and harken to the prayers of your client.
Tell me, Calliope[6]: what is the famed father of the gods[7] thinking?
Is he changing the lands into his father's age[8]? Is he snatching away
the arts which he once gave to mortals? Is he ordering us, silent and bereft of reason,
just as when we first rose up in the first age of man,
to again stoop down for acorns and pure water?
Or is he preserving the rest of the lands and cities as a friend,
while rooting out the Ausonian race[9] and children of Romulus[10]?
Why should we think about this? For there are two ways in which
Rome raised her huge head: courage in war and wisdom in peace.
On these it stood; for it was not able to exist without them:
Or is Diespater[11] shown to have once told his wife in vain and as a liar:
"I have given you power without end."[12]
But virtue, stirred at home and against Latin arms,
Lept into the strait of Sicily and the citadels of Carthage[13]
And the remaining powers, too, and carried off the entire world at once.
Then, as a victor who, alone in the Achaean[14] stadium,
collapses exhausted with his virtue unmoved,
thus it was for the Roman band, after they stopped fighting
and bridled peace with long reins.
Then, reconsidering at home laws and other Greek inventions,
they began to rule with planning and soft reason
their war-prizes gained on land and sea.
And so now the one who rules among the Romans as king[15],

not sliding forward with his beam, but with his backside,
and whitened in his throat, now orders scholarship,
as well as the name and race of wise men,
to leave and get out of the city.
What are we doing? Didn't we reconquer the cities of the Greece
So that the Roman band might be taught by these teachers?
Now, just as when Capitolius and Camillus rushed the Gauls with swords[16],
And they left behind their weighing-scales,
Thus our old men are forced to wander
And to carry themselves their booklets as a deadly load.
Therefore, Scipio of Numantia and of Libya[17] went wrong in this:
Namely that he grew up with a Rhodian teacher[18] moulding him.
And that other famous force, eloquent in the Second War[19],
Among whom the divine opinion of ancient Cato[20]...
[*one line missing*]
Would have made much of having the gods know
Whether or not the Roman offspring stood in prosperity or in adversity.
Clearly in adversity: for when a call to arms
is what the love of country and the thought of a homeless wife encourages,
it is fitting, as for wasps, whose home is on the citadel of Moneta[21]
[*one line missing*]
a swarm unyielding with swords drawn all over their yellow bodies;
but when the bee has returned safe and sound, forgetful of its own
[*multiple lines missing*]
the plebians and patricians alike die in a gluttonous sleep:
And so the long and deep peace of the children of Romulus has been their undoing.
So in this manner the little tale makes its end. Hereafter, I should like you,
without whom there is no pleasure for me,
to advise me as to the best course of action...
[*one line missing*]
to live, as once (?)for the people of Smyrna was dying(?)[22]
now likewise may wish to move. O finally whatever or, goddess,
seek some other great thing: that you gladden the Roman walls for Calenus
and equally turn back the Sabines[23].
These things I spoke. Then the goddess begins to deem me worthy with a few words of her own:
"Put down your justified fears, my devotee.
Behold, the highest hatred is in store for this tyrant
And he is about to be ruined in our honor.

For the we live in the laurel-groves of Numa[24] and its same springs
And, with Egeria[25] as our companion, we laugh at his vain undertakings.
Live and farewell. This pretty pain retains his reputation:
The chorus of the Muses and Roman Apollo give their sacred promise."

## Notes

1. The subject of this verb is missing; so it is impossible to say who does this action.
2. The epic meter used to sing the deeds of heros and arms is the dactylic hexameter. See Appendix B for more.
3. The Phalacean meter was commonly referred to by Roman poets as the hendecasyllabic meter. It was named after the Alexandrian poet, Phalaikos, who was fond of using the meter. See Appendix B for more.
4. The iambic trimeter was the traditional meter of drama, but frequently was used for satiric poetry, as well. See Appendix B for more.
5. This is a reference to the Greek poet Hipponax, famed in antiquity for his biting and irreverent satire. He wrote much of his work in choliambs, which is marked by a long third beat in the final metrical foot. After he had been expelled from his native Ephesus, he moved to the city of Clazomenae.
6. Calliope traditionally was one of the ancient muses, and was specifically associated with epic poetry.
7. The god Zeus is typically depicted as the father of the gods. He is also the father of the muses, and thus Calliope. Therefore, the poet asks her to explain her father's actions.
8. The father of Zeus is Cronos. Cronos was deposed by his son and banished from Greece. In his exile, he came to Italy. His rule in Italy is typically depicted as an idyllic one in which a more primitive mankind is taught the arts of civilization. Here, the poet seems to be emphasizing the primitive aspect of the age. However, the theme of exile is also introduced, here with Saturn's exile from Greece to Rome, as a means to setup the end of the poem, and the poet's potential exile from Rome along with the Greek philosophers by the god-like Emperor Domitian.
9. Ausonian is a descriptor given by Roman authors to the ancient inhabitants of central Italy.
10. Romulus is the legendary founder and first king of the Romans.
11. Diespiter was originally an Italian god of the sky, but he became associated with Jupiter, the Roman equivalent of Zeus.
12. This a direct quotation from Vergil, *Aeneid* 1.279. However, in that context Jupiter makes this statement to his daughter Venus, the goddess of love, and not to his wife Juno. This error may be due to the poet's misunderstanding of the mythology or to a problem in the transmission of the text.
13. The poet takes us through a brief history of Roman conquests, beginning with wars against the native peoples of Italy. Then, the poet references both the First Punic War (264–241 BCE), which was punctuated with naval battles off the coast of Sicily, and the Second (218–201 BCE) and Third Punic Wars (149–146 BCE), which ended with the Battle of Zama and the sacking of Carthage itself, respectively.
14. Greek.

15. This is a reference to the Emperor Domitian, who ruled Rome from 81–96 CE. Although seemingly a competent ruler, his authoritarian tendencies put him at odds with the Roman Senate. He, consequently, developed a reputation as a tyrant and was eventually assassinated.
16. The reference here is to the expulsion of the Gauls by Camillus and M. Manlius Capitolinus in 390 BCE. When the Gauls took the Capitoline Hill, the Romans agreed to pay a ransom in order to free themselves. However, at the moment in which scales were brought out to measure the ransom, Camillus arrived with the Roman cavalry and put the Gauls to flight.
17. The reference is to P. Cornelius Scipio Aemilianus Africanus Numantinus (185–129 BCE), who gained the title Numantinus by defeating Numantia in 134–133 BCE and Africanus by defeating Carthage in the Third Punic War. The poet has apparently changed Scipio's title of Africanus to Libycus. In addition to his exploits in combat and politics, Scipio Aemilianus is also well-known for his patronage of Greek learning and philosophy in Rome and his central role in the so-called Scipionic Circle.
18. The reference here is to Panaetius of Rhodes, who was a friend of Scipio Aemilianus and is regarded as a part of the Scipionic Circle.
19. The Second Punic War against Carthage (218–201 BCE).
20. The Cato referenced here is M. Porcius Cato (234–149 BCE), who famously was not a lover of the influx of Greek ideas into Rome during his lifetime.
21. The Temple of Juno Moneta was located on summit of the citadel located on the Capitoline Hill, and was the site of the mint of Rome until the time of Domitian. It was said to have been built on the site of the house of Manlius, who famously drove the Gauls away from the city in 390 BCE (cf. line 41.
22. At this point, the text of the manuscript is extremely uncertain, and much of the grammar does not make sense. The reference to Symrna seems to be reference to the forced migration of the people of Symrna (modern-day Izmir, Turkey) to Italy due to extreme famine.
23. The Sabines were an ancient people of central Italy. The Emperor Domitian was said to have been descended from this people.
24. Numa Pompilius was the mythical second king of Rome, associated with the founding of many of Rome's religious rites and offices. He was said to have been of Sabine origin.
25. In Roman mythology, Egeria was a water nymph who also was the divine counselor and wife of Numa Pompilius, the second king of Rome. According to Livy 1.21.3, Numa was accustomed to meet Egeria in a grove just outside the Porta Capena in Rome.

# 11 Claudia Severa

In the 1970s and 1980s, archaeologists excavating near a Roman fort at Vindolanda (located in northern England near Hadrian's Wall, See Figure 3) discovered a cache of more than 500 thin, post-card sized, wooden tablets in various states of fragmentation. To their surprise, these tablets had been folded in half to form into diptychs, and the facing sides of the tablets were covered with messages written in Latin in ink (Figure 4). The writing was on a variety of topics from military matters to personal messages between family members, friends, and slaves. Since the fort at Vindolanda was first constructed c. 85–92 CE and was occupied consistently until c. 104 CE, at which time there was a brief hiatus followed by a reoccupation, the majority of the tablets discovered are dated to the last decade of the 1st century CE.

Among these tablets are two letters that may constitute the oldest extant example of writing in Latin by a woman. The two letters were written by a certain Claudia Severa, identified as the wife of a Roman soldier Gaius Aelius Brocchus, to another woman by the name of Sulpicia Lepidina, the wife of the military prefect Flavius Cerealis. In the first letter, Severa sends Lepidina an invitation to her birthday party (Figure 4). The relationship between the two women is described in intimate terms, and Severa even goes so far as to call Lepidina her sister (*soror*). Yet, due to the differences in their family names, we can be fairly certain that they are not biological sisters and that *soror* is meant as a term of endearment. The second message, rare because more than one diptych survive from the letter, is again from Severa to Lepidina. The letter relates that Severa has asked permission from her husband Brocchus to visit Lepidina, which he seems to have granted. She then states that she will remain in a place called Briga for the time being. Since this second letter is not written for a particular occasion, it is thought to be evidence that the two women engaged in regular correspondence. There is a third letter attributed to Severa (*Tab. Vindol. II 293*), but it is in fragments.

Another interesting aspect of the letters is the handwriting in which they are written. Both letters are written in the same elegant Latin cursive script, except for two three-line portions at the end of each letter. This second

DOI: 10.4324/9781003031727-14

handwriting is less elegant than the first, and it is believed that it belongs to Claudia Severa herself. For in Roman epistolography, it was commonplace for a letter writer to dictate a letter for a scribe to write and then include a small section at the end of the letter written in one's own hand. This was done as a mark of intimacy and as a sign that the letter writer placed a high value on their relationship with the addressee. If these three-line portions are, indeed, written in the hand of Claudia Severa herself, then they are among the earliest examples of writing in Latin by a woman.

## Select Bibliography

Adams, J. N. 1995. "The Language of the Vindolanda Writing Tablets: An Interim Report," *JRS* 85: 86–134.

Bowman, A. K. 1994a. *Life and Letters on the Roman Frontier: Vindolanda and Its People*. British Museum Press.

Bowman, A. K., and J.D. Thomas. 1983. *Vindolanda: the Latin writing-tablets. British Museum Press.*

Bowman, A. K. and J. D. Thomas. 1994b. *The Vindolanda Writing-tablets: (Tabulae Vindolandenses II)*. British Museum Press.

———. 2003. *The Vindolanda Writing-tablets (Tabulae Vindolandenses III)*. British Museum Press.

Hallett, J., and S. Dickison, 2014. *A Roman Women Reader: Selections from the 2nd Century BCE- BCE 2nd Century CE*. Bolchazy-Carducci.

Hallett, J. 2013. "The Vindolanda Letters from Claudia Severa," in L. Churchill et al. (ed.), *Women Writing Latin: Women Writing Latin in Roman Antiquity, Late Antiquity, and the Early Christian Era*. Taylor and Francis, p. 93–99.

### *Claudia Severa 1 (Tab. Vindol. II 291)*

*Left Side of the Letter*

Cl(audia)• Severa Lepidinae [suae
[sa]l[u]tem
iii Idus Septembr[e]s soror ad diem
sollemnem natalem meum rogo
libenter facias ut venias
ad nos, iucundiorem mihi

*Right Side of the Letter*

[diem] interventu tuo factura si
a[deri]s *vacat*
Cerial[em t]uum saluta Aelius meus. [
et filiolus salutant *vacat*
*(m2) vacat* sperabo te soror
vale soror anima
mea ita valeam
karissima et have

*Back of the Letter, Right Side*

(*m1*) Sulpiciae Lepidinae
Cerialis
a S[e]vera

—

**Aelius, i, *m.*:** Gaius Aelius Brocchus (husband of Claudia Severa)
**aveo, avere:** to be eager; (h)ave: greetings!
**Cerialis, is, *m.*:** Flavius Cerealis (husband of Sulpicia Lepidina)
**Claudia Severa, ae, *f.*:** Claudia Severa
**filiolus, i, *m.*:** little son (diminutive)
**Idus, Iduum, *f.pl.*:** Ides (the 15th day of March, May, July, and October; the 13th day of other months)
**interventus, us, *m.*:** arrival, involvement
**iucundus, a, um:** pleasant, agreeable
**libenter:** **(adv.)** warmly, gladly, with pleasure
**natalis, is, *m.*:** birthday
**saluto, salutare, salutavi, salutatum:** to send greetings to
**September, Septembris, *m.*:** September
**sollemnis, sollemne:** solemn, ceremonial
**Sulpicia Lepidina, ae, *f*:** Sulpicia Lepidina

—

The organization of this letter is standard for the Vindolanda tablets. The handwriting is spread across a single double-leaf in a column format:

the left side of the double-leaf contains the opening half of the letter (lines 1–6) and the right side of the double-leaf contains the remainder of the body of the letter (lines 7–14). On the back of the double-leaf on the right side, there is the address of letter (lines 15–17). See Figure 4 for an image of this letter.

**2. Claudia ... salutem:** Supply *dicit.* It was an epistolary commonplace to open a letter with the statement X (nominative) sends greetings (*salutem dicit*) to Y (dative). This is what happening in these lines with *Claudia Severa* in the nominative and *suae Lepidinae* in the dative. The medial dot (•) is unusual, but seems to be serving to mark the abbreviation of Claudia's name to *Cl.*

**3. iii Idus Septembr[e]s:** Literally, "three days before the Ides of September". Since the Ides of September was September 13th and the Romans used inclusive counting to calculate their dates, three days before September 13th would date this letter to September 11th.

**4–8. rogo... si] s:** A complex sentence. A more expected word order would be: *rogo libenter ut facias ut venias ad nos, factura interventu tuo [diem] iucundiorem mihi, si a[deri]s.* Translate as "I warmly ask that you see to it that you come to us, about to make the day more pleasing to me by your presence, if you will be there."

**4. sollemnem natalem:** As Hallett (2013) points out, the adjective *sollemnis* is reserved for ceremonial and formal elements of religion, and "therefore suggests that event to which Severa invites Sulpicia Lepidina is to her an important annual religious occasion" (96). One also can compare this reference to a solemn, religious birthday celebration to a similar celebration by Sulpicia the elegist in this volume (Sulpicia 11). In that instance, Juno is addressed as a birthday goddess, ritual elements of incense, cake, and wine are present, as well as Sulpicia's own mother. Hallett (2013) continues, "It may well have been that Roman women's birthday celebrations—or at least some portion of the day's events—were all-female events, perhaps even restricted to the celebrant and her close female kin" (96). If that is the case, Severa's invitation to have Lepidina join her birthday celebration may mark their relationship as exceedingly close and explain the other markers of intimacy such as writing in one's own hand and references to each other as *soror* and other forms of endearment.

**5. facias:** present active subjunctive of *facere* in an Indirect Command dependent on *rogo* (4).

**5. venias:** present active subjunctive of *venire* in a Substantive Clause of Result with *facias ut* (5) (cf. Allen and Greenough §568).

**5–7. libenter ... si:** These lines have multiple repetitions of forms of *facere (facias, factura*) and *venire* (*venias, interventu*) in close proximity to one another, a literary device commonly known as *figura etymologica*. The presence of such a device may speak to a heightened literary pretense.

**8. a[deri]s:** The text is badly damaged here, making it barely legible. The initial restoration in the *Corpus Epistularum Latinarum (CEL)* is the subjunctive *venias*, and later restorations have suggested the indicative *venies*, which makes more sense grammatically. However, Bowman and Davis (1983) note that the marking at the bottom of the line does not seem to be the strokes of any of the letters in *venie.* Moreover, a stray marking from the beginning of the word resembles the tail of an -a. Taken together, the restoration *a*[*deri*]*s* has been suggested.

**9–10. Cerial[em tu]um saluta ... salutant:** Although no punctuation is present in the text, these are two sentences: *Cerial*[*em tu*]*um saluta. Aelius meus et filiolus salutant.*

**9. saluta:** singular imperative of *salutare*. Translate as "send greetings".

**11–14. sperabo ... have:** These lines are written in a different hand (*m2*), and it is assumed that Claudia Severa herself wrote them. In Roman epistolography, it was commonplace to dictate letters to professional scribes who would, in turn, compose the letters in elegant script. However, to show a heightened level of intimacy with an addressee or to demonstrate a heightened value they placed on their relationship with an addressee, Romans would often write letters or sections of letters in their own hand. Thus, if this is Severa's own hand, she is demonstrating the high value she places on her relationship with Lepidina. Additionally, the word order of these lines is complex. A more expected word order would be: *vale, soror, anima mea, ita valeam, karissima, et have.*

**12–13. vale ... ita valeam:** The sentiment of recipirocal affection and well-wishes is typical at the end of Roman letters. Usually, it takes the form of *si valeas, valeam* ("If you should fare well, I would fare well"), or something similar. Thus, this particular formation of the sentiment is rather unique.

**12–14. vale ... have:** Hallett (2013) suggests that Severa's closure may evoke the famous elegy Catullus 101 on the death Catullus' brother: *ave atque vale* (95).

**12–14. soror anima ... mea ... karissima:** These words of endearment emphasize the intimacy between Severa and Lepidina. Hallett (2013) suggests that there may be a literary allusion here to the close sisterhood between the sisters Dido and Anna in Vergil's *Aeneid.* At the beginning of Book 4, Vergil describes Anna as Dido's *unanimam sororem* ("sister sharing a soul") at 4.8 and has Anna call Dido *luce magis dilecta soror* ("sister more cherished than life") at 4.31. If so, this is another instance of Severa depicting her intimacy with Lepidina through literary means. Beyond the literary nature of the phrase, the phrase *anima karissima/carissima* seems to be a common one, appearing in other Vindolanda letters in the masculine as "*carissime/karissime frater*" (tablets 255, 306, 331) and in Cicero *Epist. ad Fam.* 4.14.2.6 in the plural as "*vos, meae carissimae animae*".

**14. karissima:** Alternative spelling for *carissima*, the superlative of *carus, a, um*.

**14. ita valeam:** *valeam* is the present jussive subjunctive of *valere*. Translate as "thus may I fare well".

**14. have:** Alternative spelling of *ave*, the imperative of *avere*.

**15–17. Sulpiciae ... Severa:** These lines, written on the reverse of the letter, are in the same hand (*m1*) as the first ten lines of the text, presumably that of the scribe.

**15. Sulpiciae Lepidinae:** Dative singular.

**16. Cerialis:** Genitive singular. Supply *uxori* or similar. Translate as "wife of Cerealis".

***Claudia Severa 2 (Tab. Vindol. II 292)***

*Double-Leaf A*

..........
salutem
ego soror sicut tecum locuta fueram et promiseram
ut peterem a Broccho et venirem at te, peti
et res[po]ndit mihi *ta corde semp[erli]citum una*

*Double-Leaf B, Left Side*

..........
*traces*
quomodocumque possim
at te pervenire. sunt enim
necessaria quaedam qua[e]

*Double-Leaf B, Right Side*

..........
*traces?*
rem meum epistulas meas
accipies quibus scies quid
sim actura haec nobis

*Double-Leaf C, Left Side*

*missing*

*Double-Leaf C, Right Side*

..........
*traces*
.ra eram et Brigae mansura.
Cerialem tuum a me saluta

*Double-Leaf B, Right Side, Back*

(*m2*) [val]e m. soror
karissima et anima
ma desideratissima
*vacat traces*

*Double-Leaf C, Right Side, Back*

(*m1*)Sulpiciae Lepidi-
nae Ceria[li]s *traces*?
a Severa B[rocchi

—

**Briga, ae, *f.*:** Briga (a town in northern England)

**Brocchus, i, *m.*:** Gaius Aelius Brocchus (the husband of Claudia Severa)

**Cerialis, is, *m.*:** Flavius Cerealis (husband of Sulpicia Lepidina)

**Claudia Severa, ae, *f.*:** Claudia Severa

**desideratus, a, um:** desired, longed for

**necessarius, a, um:** necessary

**quomodocumque:** (adv.) in whatever way, howsoever

**saluto, salutare, salutavi, salutatum:** to send greetings to

**Sulpcia Lepidina, ae, *f*:** Sulpicia Lepidina

—

The organization of the handwriting on this letter is unique in the collection of the Vindolanda tablets. The letter has been written across three separate double-leaves. The first double-leaf (a) is nearly complete and has text running across the entire width of the double-leaf in one column (lines 1–5). The second double-leaf (b) has text divided into two columns: one across the width of the left half of the double-leaf (lines 6–8), and one across the width of the right half of the double-leaf (lines 9–11). Of the third double-leaf (c), only the right half survives (lines 12–13); so we assume that we are missing a portion of the letter from the left half. On the back of the right side of the second double-leaf (b), there is a salutation written in Claudia Severa's own hand (lines 14–16). On the back of the right side of the third double-leaf (c), there is the address of the letter (lines 17–19).

**1. salutem:** This word is written on the far right side of the tablet. Therefore, it is a fair assumption that words preceded *salutem*. If this letter retains a similar opening to Severa's other letter, we would assume something similar to: *Cl. Severa Lepidinae suae [dicit].*

**2. soror:** vocative singular, referring to Lepidina. It does not agree with *ego*.

**2. locuta fueram** = *locuta eram*. Sometimes, authors use the pluperfect of *sum* instead of the imperfect to create the pluperfect passive form. The result is to emphasize the past nature of the action, particularly when compared with another action in the past, as here with *peti* and *respondit* (cf. Allen and Greenough §184n1).

**3. peterem … venirem:** imperfect subjunctives of *petere* and *venire*. Both are used with *promiseram ut* in an Indirect Command/Substantive Clause of Purpose (cf. Allen and Greenough §563).

**3. at** = *ad*.

**4–5. respondit mihi … licitum una:** This is a complex line made even more difficult by textual issues. The sense of the line is clear: Severa asked her husband Brocchus that she be able to visit Lepidina and he granted her request. The grammar, however, is not. Hallett and Dickison (2014) suggest taking the two phrases *licitum esse* (it is permitted) and *corde [esse]* (it is pleasing) as governed by *respondit*, translating it thus: "he replied that it was at the same time always permitted to me and so pleasing." However, there is an alternative use of *corde* as an adverb meaning "earnestly" (cf. Ver. *A.* 6.675, Pl. *Capt.* 420). This reading of *corde* seems preferable, as it would be construed with *respondit* and would translate as "he earnestly responded thus: that it was always allowed for me to be together [with you]".

**5. licitum:** Supply *esse*. The infinitival construction of the impersonal *licitum est* is governed by the verb *respondit* in an Indirect Statement.

**6–7. quomodocumque ... pervenire:** A more expected word order would be *at te pervenire quomodocumque possim*. The main verb governing *pervenire* is most likely lost in the previous line.

**6. possim:** present, active, subjunctive of *posse*. The subjunctive is governed by *quomodocumque* in an Indirect Question (cf. Allen and Greenough §573–574).

**7. at** = *ad*.

**7–8. sunt enim necessaria quaedam qua[e]:** Translate as "For there are certain necessary matters which". The entirety of the relative clause started by *qua[e]* is missing.

**9. rem meum:** The grammatical relationship between this phrase and the remainder of the line is unclear. It is likely that it to be construed with the previous line, which is not wholly legible.

**11. sim acura:** perfect, passive, subjunctive of *agere*. The subjunctive is governed by *quid* in an Indirect Question (cf. Allen and Greenough §573–574).

**11. haec nobis:** The grammatical relationship of this phrase to the remainder of the line is unclear. The phrase may belong to another line of writing that has been lost.

**12. ra:** The only letters legible at the beginning of this line are *-ra*. Although it is unclear what letters preceded these, due to the presence of the future participle *mansura* later in the line, it may be that the *-ra* is also the end of another future active participle.

**12. Brigae:** Locative case (cf. Allen and Greenough §427.3). Briga is the name of a town, possibly in the vicinity of Vindolanda.

**13. a me:** Translate as "from me".

**14–16. [vale] .... desideratissima:** These lines are written in a different hand (*m2*), and it is assumed that Claudia Severa herself wrote them. In Roman epistolography, it was commonplace to dictate letters to professional scribes who would, in turn, compose the letters in elegant script. However, to show a heightened level of intimacy with an addressee or to demonstrate a heightened value they placed on their relationship with an addressee, Romans would often write letters or sections of letters in their own hand. Thus, if this is Severa's own hand, she is demonstrating the high value she places on her relationship she has with Lepidina.

**14. m..:** The text is unclear at this point, although we may suspect the possessive adjective *mea* or *ma*.

**15. karissima:** Alternative spelling for *carissima*, the superlative of *carus, a, um*.

**15–16. anima ma desideratissima:** Adams (1995) suggests that the combination of *anima* + possessive adjective + adjective may be a particular form of endearment indicative of female speech (p. 120). He postulates a feminine form of speech because there are two instances of this construction in Severa's letters to Lepidina (here and in Severa 1), but no instances of it in the "far more extensive letters written by men".

**16. ma:** Syncopated form of *mea* (cf. the letters of Terrentianus (*P. Mich* VIII.471.34): *mater ma*).

**17–19. Sulpiciae … B[rocchi:** These lines, written on the reverse of the letter, are in the same hand (*m1*) as the first 13 lines of the text, presumably that of the scribe.

**17–18. Sulpiciae Lepidinae:** Dative singular.

**18. Ceria[li]s:** Genitive singular. Supply *uxori* or similar. Translate as "wife of Cerealis".

**19. a Severa B[rocchi:** Translate as "from Severa, wife of Brocchus".

### *Claudia Severa 1 (Tab. Vindo. II 291)*[1]

*Left Side of the Letter*

Claudia Severa to her Lepidina:
Greetings!
On September 11th, sister, for my birthday celebration,
I warmly ask that you see to it that you to us
and make the day more enjoyable for me.

*Right Side of the Letter*

At your arrival, if you will have seen to it…
Say hello to your Cerialis[2] for me.
My Aelius[3] and my little boy send him their greetings.

*(in a second hand)*[4]
I shall hope for your arrival, sister.[5]
Farewell, my sister, soul sweetest to me as I fare well,
and hail.

*Back of the Letter, Right Side*

*(in the first hand)*[6]
To Sulpicia Lepidina
wife of Cerialis
from Severa.

***Claudia Severa 2 (Tab. Vindo. II 292)***[7]

*Double-Leaf A*

.......
greetings.
Just as I had spoken with you, sister, and had promised
that I would ask Brocchus[8] and would come to you,
I asked and he earnestly responded thus:
that it was always allowed for me to be together with you

*Double-Leaf B, Left Side*

.......
in whatever manner I was able to come to you.
For there are certain necessary matters which...

*Double-Leaf B, Right Side*

.......
My business...you will receive my letters
in which you will know what I am about to do...these things to us...

*Double-Leaf C, Left Side*

[missing]

*Double-Leaf C, Right Side*

.......
I was and am going to remain at Briga.[9]
Send greetings to your Cerialis[10] for me.

*Double-Leaf B, Right Side, Back (in a second hand)*[11]

Farewell, my sister,
most dear and my most desired soul...

*Double-Leaf C, Right Side, Back (in the first hand)*[12]

To Sulpicia Lepidina, wife of Cerialis,
from Severa, wife of Brocchus.

## Notes

1. The organization of this letter is standard for the Vindolanda tablets. The handwriting is spread across a single double-leaf in a column format: the left side of the double-leaf contains the opening half of the letter (lines 1–5) and the right side of the double-leaf contains the remainder of the body of the letter (lines 6–11), including a brief portion potentially written by Claudia Severa

herself (lines 9–11). On the back of the double-leaf on the right side, there is the address of letter (lines 12–14). See Figure 4 for an image of this letter.

2. Flavius Cerialis, Sulpicia Lepidina's husband and the Prefect of the Ninth Cohort of Batavians.
3. Gaius Aelius Brocchus, Claudia Severa's husband and a Roman soldier.
4. These three lines are written in a different handwriting than the first portion of the letter, which was presumably written by a scribe. It is most likely that these three lines were actually written by Claudia Severa herself. In Roman epistolography, writing a letter, or a portion thereof, in one's own hand was a manner in which one showed intimacy with the addressee, as well as the level of importance one placed on the relationship. If this is, indeed, Claudia's own handwriting, it would make the handwriting one of the earliest known examples of writing in Latin by a woman.
5. Based on their names, Lepidina and Severa do not appear to be sisters. Instead, this is probably a manner of creating intimacy between the two good friends.
6. These lines are written in the same handwriting as the opening section of the letter, which was presumably written by a scribe.
7. The organization of the handwriting on this letter is unique in the collection of the Vindolanda tablets. The letter has been written across three separate double-leaves. The first double-leaf (a) is nearly complete and has text running across the entire width of the double-leaf in one column (lines 1–5). The second double-leaf (b) has text divided into two columns: one across the width of the left half of the double-leaf (lines 6–7), and one across the width of the right half of the double-leaf (lines 8–9). Of the third double-leaf (c), only the right half survives (lines 10–11); so we assume that we are missing a portion of the letter from the left half. On the back of the right side of the second double-leaf (b), there is a salutation written in Claudia Severa's own hand (lines 12–13). On the back of the right side of the third double-leaf (c), there is the address of the letter (lines 14–15).
8. Gaius Aelius Brocchus, Claudia Severa's husband and a Roman soldier.
9. An unknown site, but one presumably in the vicinity of Vindolanda.
10. Flavius Cerialis, Sulpicia Lepidina's husband and the Prefect of the Ninth Cohort of Batavians.
11. These three lines are written in a different handwriting than the first portion of the letter, which was presumably written by a scribe. It is most likely that these three lines were actually written by Claudia Severa herself. In Roman epistolography, writing a letter, or a portion thereof, in one's own hand was a manner in which one showed intimacy with the addressee, as well as the level of importance one placed on the relationship. If this is, indeed, Claudia's own handwriting, it would make the handwriting one of the earliest known examples of writing in Latin by a woman.
12. These lines are written in the same handwriting as the opening section of the letter, which was presumably written by a scribe.

# 12 An Inscription from Pompeii

It often comes as a surprise to students of antiquity that literature or literary texts come down to us not only through manuscripts, but through inscriptions and graffiti as well. An example of this can be found in the Roman city of Pompeii, buried during the eruption of the nearby Mount Vesuvius in 79 CE. When the city was unearthed, the excavators marveled at the sheer number of inscriptions, graffiti, paintings, and other textual remains that they found. Thousands of inscriptions have been catalogued to date, and some of them purport to have been inscribed or composed by women (Woeckner, 2002). One of these inscriptions, *CIL* 4.5296, is unique in that it claims to have been written by a woman who expresses erotic desires for another woman. Since very little evidence for female same-sex desire comes down to us from the ancient Roman world, save misogynistic, homophobic depictions of lesbians, and other females with non-normative desires as savage, deranged, or terrifying, *CIL* 4.5296 can potentially give us a window into a portion of Roman society, which has hitherto been largely silenced.

## Location and Physical Context

The original graffito of *CIL* 4.5296 is now lost, due to the fact that the plaster upon which it was written has been destroyed. However, notes on the inscription and the original excavation reports provide us with some clues to its original context, though it is far from a clear-cut answer. The *Carmina Latina Epigraphica (CLE)* states that the poem was inscribed on a wall of the house of the doctor in Pompeii (*Pompeis in aedibus medici parieti inscriptum stilo*). The "doctor's house" is located in Insula 9 and faces the *via di Nola*. However, as Graverini (2014) points out, this location is at odds with the excavation reports and the *CIL*, both of which make it "very clear that the graffito is on the right wall of the entryway of another house … the door to this small, nondescript house … opens on a narrow side alley between Insulae 8 and 9 and it is the sixth on the left for those who come from the via di Nola" (15–16).

In addition to the uncertainty over the house in which the graffito was inscribed, there is also some debate over where in the doorway the graffito

DOI: 10.4324/9781003031727-15

was inscribed. Copley (1939), Courtney (1995), and Goold (1998) all suppose the inscription was written on the outside of the doorway, leading many to conclude—following Copley (1939) —that the poem may have been written as a paraclausithyron, a love elegy from the poet-lover, who is locked out of the house of their beloved. Yet, the lack of any of the literary markers of the paraclausithyron in the text of the graffito has led to a reevaluation of the inscription's context. Graverini (2014) points out that none of the original excavation notes indicate the poem was written on the outside of the doorway; in fact, they state that the poem was inscribed on the inside of the doorway.

Either way, the exact location of the graffito matters greatly to questions of author, audience, and intent. If it is outwardly-facing and in a public area, the number and types of individuals available to see and read the graffito are different than if it were written on an inwardly-facing and private area. The different levels of access to individuals that each scenario offers also could affect who had access to this space to write these lines.

## The Nature of the Text

In addition to the questions of occasion and location of the text, there is also great uncertainty about the nature of the text itself. The record of the original inscription shows a graffito of eight lines of text (see Figure 6). The first seven lines are written in one hand, and the last in another. The first seven lines are seemingly presented as a single poem and have traditionally been reorganized into nine lines in order to fit metrical conventions. Yet, there are plenty of problems with the text. First, the lines we have seem to have been inscribed with an eye to meter; however, they are not complete. Only lines 1, 5, and 8 are complete dactylic hexameters. The remaining six are either incomplete dactylic hexameters or incomplete dactylic pentameters. Therefore, it is unclear whether this inscription was intended to be completely in hexameters (Copley, 1939), elegiac couplets, or some irregular variation of hexameters and pentameters (Graverini, 2014). The irregular meter of the inscription raises a second question, that of originality. It is not unusual in Pompeian graffiti to find compositions with incomplete lines, imperfect meter, or irregular allusions. Writing on a wall introduces far more pressures of time, space, and resources than writing in the comfort of one's home or library. As such, two basic schools of thought have dominated the interpretation of this poem. On the one hand, scholars such as Copley (1939) and Graverini (2014, 2017) have argued that this inscription is an original work, but features incomplete meter due to time constraints or ability level and irregular or muddled literary allusions due to memory lapses. One the other hand, Milnor (2014) has suggested that the disjointed grammar, irregular meter, and difficult allusions are due to the fact that this graffito is a cento.[1] Milnor goes on to argue that the point of creating a cento was to disrupt the traditional elegiac genre, which had no models for the culturally-troublesome concept of female same-sex desire (see more below). Whether or not we read this as an entirely original work, as a cento, or as something in between has major implications for how we interpret it, especially in regards to its issues of gender and sexuality.

## Issues of Gender and Sexuality

This poem's major claim to fame, however, is the fact that the narrator identifies herself as a woman, a fact that makes this graffito unique in antiquity. This identification is made clear by the Latin nominative *ego* in line 5 and the appositive *perdita* that has a feminine ending and agrees with the "I" of *ego*. Moreover, the inscription opens with a description of the female poet in an embrace with another woman, whom she identifies with terms of endearment, to whom she describes her bedroom thoughts, and whom she enjoins to beware the fickleness of men. The potential for such an erotic same-sex exchange between two women would set this poem apart from all extant Latin literature. Older scholarship, such as Della Valle (1937) and Della Corte (1976) argued away the identification of the narrator as a woman and promoted a more heteronormative situation of a male poet-lover and female beloved by suggesting that the nominative *perdita* that described the poet-lover was, in fact, an ablative describing *nocte*, and thus should be translated as "ruined night". However, as Graverini (2014) has observed, *perdita* cannot be an ablative for obvious metrical reasons (6). Therefore, more recent scholarship, such as Graverini (2014, 2017) and Milnor (2014), has erased any doubts of the identification of the narrator as a woman. In fact, Milnor has gone so far as to identify this inscription as one of lesbian desire, arguing for the importance of *CIL* 4.5296 in improving our understanding both of the discourse of Roman sexuality and of how that discourse could influence, or even silence, certain voices: "It is clear that a woman who sought to express her desire for another woman, especially if she wished to do it through the medium of poetry, would have been trying to find a voice within a profoundly homophobic cultural context" (213). Hopefully, future scholarship on this poem will continue to give voice to this poet and to all those whose voices are still difficult for us to hear.

## Select Bibliography

Copley, F. 1939. "A Paraclausithryon from Pompeii: A Study of C.I.L. IV, Suppl. 5296," *AjPh* 60.3: 333–349.

Courtney, E. 1995. *Musa Lapidaria. A Selection of Latin Verse Inscriptions*. Atlanta.

Della Corte, M. 1976. *Amori e amanti in Pompei antica. Antologica erotica*. Cava dei Tirreni.

Della Valle, G. 1937. *L'amore in Pompei e nel poema di Lucrezio*. Le Monnier.

Goold, G. P. 1998. "A Paraklausithryon from Pompeii," in P. Knox and C. Foss (eds.), *Style and Tradition. Studies in Honor of Wendell Clausen*. Stuttgart/Leipzig, p. 16–29.

Graverini, L. 2014. "Ovidian Graffiti: Love, Genre and Gender on a Wall in Pompeii. A New Study of CIL IV 5296 – CLE 950," *Incontri di filogia classica* 12: 1–28.
———. 2017. "Further Thoughts on *CIL* IV, 5296 – CLE 950: Textual Problems, Structure, and Gender Issues," *Latomus* 76: 114–126.
Milnor, K. 2014. *Graffiti and the Literary Landscape in Roman Pompeii.* Oxford.
Woeckner, E. 2002. "Women's Graffiti from Pompeii," in L. Churchill et al. (eds.), *Women Writing Latin: Women Writing Latin in Roman Antiquity, Late Antiquity, and the Early Christian Era.* Taylor and Francis Group, p. 67–84.

### *CIL 4.5296*

*(m1)* O utinam liceat collo complexa tenere
braciola et teneris oscula ferre labellis!
I nunc, ventis tua gaudia, pupula, crede.
Crede mihi, levis est natura virorum.
Saepe ego cum media vigilarem perdita nocte,
haec mecum meditans: 'multos Fortuna quos supstulit alte
hos modo proiectos subito praecipitesque premit;
sic Venus ut subito coiunxit corpora amantum,
Dividit lux, et se ...
*(m2)* paries quid ama

—

**braciolum, i, *n.*:** small arm
**collum, i, *n.*:** neck
**complector, complecti, complexus sum:** to clasp, embrace
**coniungo, coniungere, coniunxi, coniunctus:** to join together, unite
**labellum, i, *n.*:** little lip
**meditor, meditari, meditus sum:** to reflect, think upon
**osculum, i, *n.*:** little mouth; kiss
**paries, parietis, *m.*:** wall
**perditus, a, um:** hopeless, ruined, desperate
**praeceps, praecipis (gen.):** headforth, headlong
**proicio, proicere, proieci, proiectus:** to throw forth, to throw down
**pupula, ae, *f.*:** little girl; darling; pupil of the eye
**suffero, sufferre, sustuli, sublatum:** to hold up, support
**utinam:** would that
**Venus, Veneris, *f.*:** Venus, goddess of (sexual) Love
**vigilo, vigilare, vigilavi, vigilatum:** to watch, be wakeful

—

*Meter: varied**

***:** The meter of this poem is irregular. Lines 1, 5, and 8 are hexameters, leading some to believe that this poem was intended to be exclusively in hexameters (Copley, 1939, p. 339). Graverini (2014 and 2017) argues that the poem is a mix of hexameters and quasi-pentameters. Milnor (2014) argues that the mixed meters of the poem indicate that it is most likely a cento, a poem comprised of verses and half-verses taken from other works. Graverini (2014, p. 10–15) gives a full account of the metrical issues of the poem.

**1–2:** The potential opening of this poem begins with an exclamation of desire by the narrator, who wishes to embrace the object of desire. However, multiple aspects of the relationship are left ambiguous. First, it is unclear who is initiating the embrace; the phrase *collo complexa tenere braciola* can be read in multiple ways: is the narrator holding their arms about the neck of the beloved? or is the narrator holding the arms of the beloved about their own neck? Perhaps, the ambiguity in the description is meant to evoke a mutual embrace in which both parties are embracing each other equally. Second, and perhaps more importantly, the identities of the lovers engaged in this embrace are left unstated. We know nothing about them (e.g., sex, gender, class, ethnicity), only that they desire to share a passionate embrace.

**1. liceat:** present, optative, subjunctive of *licet*. Construe with *utinam* and translate as "if only it were allowed".

**1–2. tenere … ferre:** subjective infinitives construed with *licet*.

**3–4:** In the second section of this poem, the narrator addresses the beloved directly with the imperative *I* and the vocative *popula*. At last, the reader learns a bit about the identities of the lovers, as the beloved is described as a *popula*, a little girl. The diminutive need not speak directly to the age of the beloved, as it could simply reflect a term of endearment. The important aspect here, however, is the fact that the beloved is identified as female. The narrator continues by telling the beloved a gnomic statement: "trust me, trivial is the nature of men." The phrase is remarkable for a few reasons. First, the use of the term *vir* identifies the people whose nature is trivial not as males, but elite Roman men; for *vir* was a specialized term describing not merely males, but particularly those in the elite, citizen class who exemplified Roman masculinity. The notion that these men had a trivial nature is a complete inversion of traditional Roman elegy, in which female beloveds (*puellae*) were described as *levis*. The reader, then, is made to consider why the narrator would be warning the beloved to beware the fickle nature of Roman, masculine lovers. However, the reasoning for this is quickly resolved in the subsequent line.

**3. I:** present, second, singular imperative of *eo, ire*.

**3. ventis tua gaudia … crede:** Although the verb *credere* most often takes a dative, it can also take an accusative and a dative with the sense of "entrust X to Y". Using an image of entrusting something to a fleeting act of nature to describe the fickleness of love is a common trope in elegy (cf. Catullus 65.17-18; Catullus 70; Tib. 1.7.20).

**3. gaudia:** In Roman elegy, *gaudia* most typically referred to sexual exploits and enjoyments. So, perhaps, a proper translation here would be "trysts".

**3. pupula:** Graverini (2014, p. 5) points out that the use of *pupula* to mean "darling" or "little girl" and not "the pupil of the eye" is rare, but suggests that it may be a colloquial expression, as it is found on other Pompeiian inscriptions (CIL 4.6842; CIL 4.1234). Copley (1939, p. 345–346) argues that it is a "clear instance of Catullian practice", citing the use of it in Catullus 56.5 as evidence.

**5–6:** The scene of the poem now shifts away from the direct address of the beloved to the narrator's recollection of lying in bed alone in thought. The trope of a lover lying in bed alone and pining for their beloved is a well-known one in antiquity, particularly in Roman elegy (cf. Tib. 1.2.76, 2.4.11; Prop. 1.1.33, 3.15.1-2; Ovid *Ars* 1.735, *Amores* 1.2, 1.3; Sappho fr. 94 Diehl). However, the most important portion of this line is the identification of the poet-lover as a woman with the feminine nominative adjective *perdita*. The identification of the lover as female and the beloved as female potentially makes this one of the only instances of erotic verse between two women from ancient Greece and Rome.

**5. cum ... vigilarem:** imperfect, active, subjunctive of *vigilare* in a cum circumstantial clause. Translate as "when I was lying awake" (cf. Allen and Greenough §546).

**5. media:** Construe with *nocte* as an ablative of time.

**5. perdita:** The meter requires that *perdita* end in a short -a in order to produce the typical dactyl-spondee end to a line of hexameter. Therefore, this word must be construed as a nominative singular. This fact is significant, as it identifies the narrator of the poem as a female. Until this point in the text, the identity of the narrator had remained unstated.

**6–9:** The narrator-lover continues with her recollection of her bedroom musings with a discussion of the fickleness of Fortune, another well-known trope from antiquity (cf. Hor. *Od.* 1.34.14-16, 1.35.1-4, 3.29.49-52; Ovid *Tr.* 3.7.41-42, 3.11.67-68, 5.8.7-8; Tib. 1.2.88). Copley (1939, p. 347) sees parallels between the poem and Catullus 64.139-144. However, the inscription breaks off mid-thought, leaving interpretation nearly impossible.

**6. haec:** neuter plural of *hic, haec, hoc*. Translate as "these things".

**6. meditans:** nominative, singular, feminine, present, deponent participle of *meditari*. It is modifying the *ego* from line 5.

**6. multos Fortuna quos supstulit alte:** The word order is made tricky by the proleptic *quos* which begins its clause, but has been delayed and placed after *Fortuna*. A more prosaic word order would, perhaps, be *multos, quos Fortuna supstulit alte, hos*. The *multos* is not in the relative clause started by *quos*, but rather is the object of *permit* (line 7).

**6. supstulit =** sustulit.

**6. alte:** positive adverb from *altus, a, um*, modifying *supstulit*. Translate as "highly" or "on high".

**7. hos:** The function of *hos* here is to restate the *multos* from the previous line. Construe with *proiectos* and *praecipitesque*.

**7. modo:** Here, *modo* should be translated with the meaning "just now".

**8. subito:** This adverb seems best construed with *proiectos* due to the *-que* on *praecipites* ("suddenly thrown down"). However, the placement between the alliterative *proiectos* and *praecipites* lends itself to a reading of *subito* that construes it with both *praecipites* and *proiectos* ("suddenly thrown down and headlong").

**8. ut:** Translate temporally here as "when" due to the perfect indicative *coiunxit* in its clause (cf. Allen and Greenough §542–543).

**8. amantum:** genitive plural present active participle of *amare*. Literally, this is translated as "of the loving ones", but often this participle is nominalized in usage. Hence, the preferred translation here would be "of lovers".

**9. et se…:** The inscription breaks off here, leaving the poem and sentence unfinished. The *se* could either be a reflexive pronoun or the first syllable of another word (e.g., *secat, separat*).

**10. paries quid ama:** These lines are written in a second hand and, therefore, probably by another writer. The line itself seems incomplete, as *ama* makes little sense as the imperative of *amare*. Graverini (2014) suggests that this line is an allusion to the famous story of the lovers Pyramus and Thisbe from Ovid's *Metamorphoses*. In the story, the two lovers are separated by a wall and call out to the wall, asking it why it stands in their way: *invide—dicebant—* ***paries, quid ama****ntibus obstas?* ("they kept saying, hated wall, why do you stand in the way of lovers?" *Met.* 4.74). If Graverini is correct, the inscriber of this line may have recognized the earlier poem on the wall as elegiac in nature, and made a witty literary allusion to another elegiac story in which a wall played a prominent part.

### *CIL 4.5296*

If only I could hold your dear arms in an embrace about my neck
and bring kisses to your tender lips!
Go now, my dear, trust your trysts to the winds.
But believe me: trivial is the nature of men.
Oftentimes, when I was lying wretchedly awake in the middle of the night,
I thought of how many lovers Fortune has firmly supported in the past
whom now she throws down all of sudden, trampling them underfoot.
Likewise, when Venus has suddenly joined the bodies of lovers,
the daylight divides them and …

(*in a second hand*)
Wall, why lov…

## Note

1. A cento is a poetic composition in which an author creates portions or all of the composition from quotations of other poems. A famous example is Faltonia Proba's cento, *Cento Vergilianus de laudibus Christi,* in which she only used lines of Vergil's poetry, reorganized and repurposed to create a Christian epic.

# 13 Terentia

Terentia was a Roman visitor to Egypt in the early 1st century CE. Her only extant work is a brief hexameter epitaph composed for her brother, Decimus Terentius Getianus, which she had inscribed on the pyramid of Cheops, the largest of the pyramids in Giza. The epitaph itself is six lines in length, but it may have been longer. The reason for this uncertainty is that the epitaph itself is no longer extant because the limestone facing of the pyramid upon which the epitaph was inscribed has been removed. The text of the poem has been preserved mainly by happenstance. In 1335, a German pilgrim, Wilhelm von Boldensele, visited the pyramid and copied down the text of the poem. For the next 500 years, the text was copied into a variety of manuscripts until it was edited in the 19th century by Theodor Mommsen and was included in the *Corpus Inscriptiarum Latinarum* (*CIL* 3.21). Since then, other editors have made further emendations to the text, most notably Franz Bücheler, who included the text in his *Carmina Latina Epigraphica* (*CLE* 270). It is Bücheler's text that is included in this volume.

Although very little can be said about Terentia, we do know some biographical information about her brother thanks to the epigraphical record and to the *Historia Augusta*. According to a stone at Sarmizegetusa, Terentius Gentianus fought alongside Trajan in the Dacian Wars and received a host of honors, including appointments as *consul*, *pontifex*, *quaestor*, tribune, and *censitor* of Macedonia (*CIL* 3.1463). Likewise, Degrassi lists him as *consul suffectus* in 116 CE (34). However, even though these offices indicate that Gentianus had amicable relationships with Trajan and Hadrian, *Historia Augusta* 23 reports that he fell into disfavor with Hadrian, who began to see him as a threat to his power due to his success. *Historia Augusta* 22 also suggests that it was not until Hadrian returned from his tour of Egypt in 130 CE that he began to be displeased with Terentius.

Because of this evidence, some scholars have suggested that Terentia visited Egypt as a member of Hadrian's tour along with Julia Balbilla (see Chapter 14) and that this visit gave her the opportunity to inscribe her

DOI: 10.4324/9781003031727-16

epitaph (Syme, 1984, p. 50–51). However, there is no direct evidence to confirm or deny this possibility. Therefore, most scholars date the epitaph to some point shortly before or after 130 CE.

Beyond the details of biography and dating, the epitaph itself has been met by scholars with mixed reviews. Hemelrijk (1998) sums up the negative viewpoint: "The poem is no literary masterpiece; it seems to be an occasional poem by an upper-class woman who, like so many of her class and time, dabbled in poetry in her leisure-time" (172). However, this sentiment seems too harsh. If not a literary masterpiece, Terentia's poem is still remarkable for the erudition and innovation it displays. Although only six lines are extant, these lines contain no fewer than three allusions to canonical authors of Latin literature: Horace, Ovid, and Catullus. Likewise, it is rendered into clean, crisp lines of hexameter that are not overly laborious. Most of all, however, it is astoundingly audacious; for it is incredible that this Roman woman travelled to Egypt and had her poem inscribed on the tallest of the pyramids in Giza, a profoundly public and grand monument for all to see.

## Select Bibliography

Bücheler, F. 1895–1897. *Carmina Latina Epigraphica.* Teubner.

Churchill, L., P. Brown, and J. Jeffrey. 2013. *Women Writing Latin: Women Writing Latin in Roman Antiquity, Late Antiquity, and the Early Christian Era.* Routledge.

Degrassi, A. 1952. *I fasti consolari dell'impero Romano.* Rome: Edizioni di Storia e Letteratura.

Graefe, E. 1984. "Der Pyramidenbesuch des Guilelmus de Boldensele aus dem Jahre 1335," in Altenmüller, H. and Wildung, D. (eds.), *Festschrift Wolfgang Helk zu seinem 70. Geburtstag.* Hamburg, 569–584.

———. 1990. "A propos der Pyramidenbescreibung des Wilhelm von Boldensele aus dem Jahre 1335," in E. Hornung (ed.), *Zum Bild Aegyptens in Mittelalter und in der Renaissance.* Göttingen, 9–28.

Hemelrijk, E. 1998. *Matrona Docta: Educated women in the Roman Elite from Cornelia to Julia Domna.* Routledge.

Plant, I. 2004. *Women Writers of Ancient Greece and Rome.* Oklahoma, OK.

Stevenson, J. 2005. *Women Latin Poets: Language, Gender, and Authority from Antiquity to the Eighteenth Century.* Oxford.

Syme, R. 1984. "Hadrian and the Senate," in *Athenaeum* 62: 31–60.

### *Terentia*

Vidi pyramidas sine te, dulcissime frater,
Et tibi, quod potui, lacrimas hic maesta profudi,
Et nostri memorem luctus hanc sculpo querelam.
Sic nomen Decimi Gentiani pyramide alta
Pontificis comitisque tuis, Trajane, triumphis
Lustra[que] sex intra censoris consulis exst[et.

—

**censor, censoris, *m.*:** censor (a Roman magistrate)
**Decimus Gentianus, i, *m.*:** Decimus Terentius Gentianus
**exsto, exstare, exstavi, exstatum:** to exist; to stand forth, to stand out
**luctus, luctus, *m.*:** mourning, lament
**lustrum, i, *n.*:** lustrum (a purificatory sacrifice)
**memor, memoris:** (+gen.) mindful, remembering
**pontifex, pontificis, *m.*:** pontifex (a Roman high-priest)
**profundo, profundere, profudi, profusus:** to pour (forth)
**pyramis, pyramidis, *f.*:** pyramid
**querela, ae, *f.*:** complaint
**sculpo, sculpere, sculpsi, sculptum:** to carve, engrave, cut
**sex:** six
**Trajanus, Trajani, *m.*:** Trajan. Emperor of Rome (98–118 CE)
**triumphus, i, *m.*:** triumph, triumphal procession

—

*Meter: dactylic hexameter*

1. **pyramidas:** variant accusative plural of *pyramis, pyramidis* (cf. Plin. 36,12,16 §75 for a similar spelling).
2. **quod potui:** "that which I was able [to do]"
2. **et tibi, quod potui:** There are two potential allusions encapsulated in these words. The first is to Catullus 68.149: "***hoc tibi, quod potui**, confectum carmine munus / pro multis, Alli, redditur officiis*" ("this gift, as I am able, brought about by a poem, is given in return for your many duties, Allius"). Catullus 68 is a complex poem with a troubled textual history, but a clear, consistent theme is that of a brother. In the beginning of the poem, Catullus mourns the death of his own brother. As the poem continues, Catullus gives thanks to Allius for assisting him in visiting his beloved Lesbia's home, an act he compares to the prayers given by sailors to Castor and Pollux, famous brothers from antiquity. In return for such brotherly service, in these lines, Catullus offers Allius the gift of immortality in his song (line 150–151): *ne uestrum scabra tangat rubigine nomen / haec atque illa dies atque alia atque alia* ("lest with corroding rust this day or that day or another or another should touch your name"). Such an allusion is appropriate for Terentia, as she attempts to give her brother a similar immortality through her inscription on the pyramid of Cheops. The second potential allusion is to Ovid, *Fasti* 5.471-2: *noluit hoc frater, pietas aequalis in illo est: **quod potuit, lacrimas** in mea fata dedit* ("my brother did not want this; a loyalty equal to mine is in him: that which he was able, he gave tears onto my fates"). In this context, Ovid reports a speech of Remus in which he states that his brother Romulus cried over his tomb in a display of *pietas*. Such an image is appropriate for Terentia, as she also is performing *pietas* by crying over the funerary epitaph of her brother Gentianus.

**3. et nostri … querelam:** Yet another allusion, here to Horace *Odes* 3.11.50: *I secundo, omine et* ***nostri sepulcro/scalpe querelam***. In the context of *Odes* 3, these lines are spoken by the Danaid Hypermnestra to her husband and nephew Lynceus, the son of Aegyptus. She tells him that she is sparing his life, encourages him to flee her father's rage, and hopes that he will carve a funeral epitaph that remembers her deeds. This allusion is appropriate for Terentia, as she, too, is inscribing an epitaph in Egypt.

**3. memorem … querelam:** It is the complaint itself that remembers the lament, not Terentia. The image of a remembering complaint is appropriate for an inscription that carries with it the memory of Terentia's feelings for her brother.

**4. Gentiani:** To fit the hexameter, this word must be sounded as three syllables (Gen – tian – i).

**5–6. pontificis … comitisque … censoris … consulis:** genitives in apposition to Gentianus.

**6. lustra[que] sex intra:** Translate as "within thirty years." A *lustrum* was a purificatory sacrifice made by the Roman censors after they completed the census. The *lustrum* happened every five years and included a suovetaurilia (i.e., the sacrifice of a pig, sheep, and bull). Here, Terentia includes it to emphasize her brother's role as censor.

**6. censoris:** An apparent embellishment. If this refers to the Gentianus we suspect, Terentia has inflated his office. Gentianus was not a *censor*, but the *censitor* of Macedonia. Whereas there were only two *censores* who oversaw the registration of citizens, taxation, and other duties, a *censitor* was a tax official that fulfilled similar duties in a single province.

***Terentia***

I have seen the pyramids without you, dearest brother.
I, mournful, have poured forth tears for you as I was able.
I am inscribing this complaint as a remembrance of our grief.
Thus may the name of Decimus Gentianus stand out on this high pyramid[1],
he who was the pontifex and companion in your triumphs, O Trajan,[2]
he who was censor and consul within thirty years.

## Notes

1. The pyramid of Cheops, the largest of the pyramids in Giza.
2. Emperor of Rome from 98–118 CE.

# 14 Colossus of Memnon

One of the more unique loci for women's literature in the ancient world is the Colossus of Memnon. In fact, recent analysis has estimated that 6% of all extant literature written by women is located on the Colossus of Memnon (Keegan, 58). Although the Colossus of Memnon leads one to think there was only one statue, there were actually two colossi. These Colossi, located on the Nile plain near Luxor, were two stone statues of quartzite sandstone that stood to a height of approximately 60 feet. The Colossi portrayed the deified Amenhotep III (reigned 1417–1379 BCE), who was depicted in a seated position, with his hands on his knees, and facing East toward the rising sun. These Colossi have sat as guards of his mortuary complex ever since.

However, due to a major earthquake in the area in 27/26 BCE, the northern Colossus lost much of its torso and began to emit a strange sound each morning. It was later understood to be brought about by the change of humidity and temperature caused by the rising sun. Yet, in antiquity, this strange sound brought fame and renown to the statue, and many tourists from across the ancient world began to visit the site for a chance to hear the statue.

Because the northern statue faced the East and the rising sun, it gradually began to be associated not with Amenhotep III, but with the Homeric hero Memnon, the Ethiopian king killed at Troy and the son of Dawn and Tithon. Thus, the northern statue has gained the title the Colossus of Memnon. A mythology grew around the northern statue that included the belief that the strange sound emitted by the statue was the complaint of Memnon to his mother, Dawn. If a visitor was lucky enough to witness Memnon speaking to his mother, it was believed that it was a sign of great favor from the gods.

When visitors came to the Colossus, they marked the occasion by carving commemorative inscriptions on the stone statue. A total of 107 inscriptions still survive, ranging in dates from 20–205 CE, all of which have been catalogued by the French editors Bernand and Bernand (1960). Sixty-one of these inscriptions are in Greek, 45 in Latin, and 1 is bilingual. Likewise, 39 are in verse (35 in Greek and 4 in Latin). Most importantly for our purposes, 11 of

DOI: 10.4324/9781003031727-17

these inscriptions are by women. Nine of these inscriptions are substantial and have been included in this volume. In what follows, a brief introduction to each of the authors of the inscriptions, as well as the inscriptions themselves, will be provided. The original text and numbering of the inscriptions by Bernand and Bernand (1960) have been retained for ease of comparison.

## Select Bibliography


Bagnall, R. and D. Rathbone. 2004. *Egypt from Alexander to the Early Christians: An Archaeological and Historical Guide.* Los Angeles.

Bernand, A. and É. Bernand. 1960. *Les inscriptions grecques et latines du colosse de Memnon.* Paris.

Birley, A.R. 1997. *Hadrian: The Restless Emperor.* London.

Bowie, E. 1990. "Greek Poetry in the Antonine Age." In *Antonine Literature*, edited by D.A. Russell, 53–90. Oxford.

Cirio, A. M. 2003. "Giulia Balbilla: Un ingiusta exclusine," *Grammata* 5, p. 95–102.

———. 2011. *Gli epigrammi di Giulia Balbilla.* Leece.

Hemelrijk, E. 1998. *Matrona Docta: Educated Women in the Roman Elite from Cornelia to Julia Domna.* Routledge.

Keegan, P. 2014. *Graffiti in Antiquity.* Routledge.

Plant, I. 2004. *Women Writers of Ancient Greece and Rome.* Oklahoma, OK

Rosenmeyer, P. 2004. "A Greek Inscription on the Memnon Colossus," *CQ* 54: 620–624.

———. 2008. "Greek Verse Inscriptions in Roman Egypt," *CA* 27: 333–357.

———. 2018. *The Language of Ruin: Greek and Latin Inscriptions on the Memnon Colossus.* Oxford.

West, M. 1978. "Die griechischen Dicherinnen der Kaiserzeit," in H. B. Beck, A. Kambylis, and P. Moraux (eds.), *Kyklos: Festschrift für R. Keydell*, Berlin. 101–115.


## Julia Balbilla

The first and most extensive of the women's literature that we have from the Colossi of Memnon is that of Julia Balbilla. Balbilla's work takes the form of inscriptions carved into the stone left leg of the colossus and consists of four poems in elegiac couplets, written by at least two hands (cf. Figure 5). Likewise, a brief inscription in the name of Empress Sabina is inscribed nearby. In the introduction that follows, extant evidence about Balbilla's biography and the literary aspects of her inscriptions will be discussed. Finally, a brief overview of each poem will be included.

### *Biography*

Julia Balbilla is best described as the quintessential elite, cosmopolitan intellectual of the Roman Empire. On both sides of her family tree, Balbilla was descended from elite families. On her father's side, she was the granddaughter of the last king of Syrian Commagene, King Antiochus. On her mother's side, she was the granddaughter of the astrologer Tiberius Claudius Balbillus, who was prefect of Egypt under Nero (55–59 CE) and the head of the museum in Alexandria. Balbilla's brother was Philopappus, who served as consul in 109 CE, a fact that made him one of the first individuals of Eastern descent to hold the office. Philopappus was also a friend of the famous author Plutarch, who dedicated to Philopappus his treatise on "How to tell a Flatterer from a Friend". This overview paints a picture of Balbilla as a woman of mixed ethnicities with connections to both royalty and the intellectual elite. As a result of this elite status, it is likely that she was well-educated and occupied a position of intimacy in the imperial family during the reign of Emperor Hadrian.

The exact nature of this position, however, has been the topic of considerable scholarly debate. The only aspect of her relationship to the imperial family that is certain is that she was a member of the entourage of Hadrian's wife, Sabina. Moreover, it seems likely that she enjoyed some favor from Hadrian and Sabina because she was allowed to compose public verses commemorating the imperial visit to Memnon. Beyond these facts, all is conjecture. In particular, there has been a strand of scholarship that has posited a potential homoerotic relationship between Balbilla and Sabina. Bowie (1990) encapsulates the view, stating, "[Balbilla's] visit to Memnon with Sabina hints that she was chiefly the empress' companion, perhaps her answer to Hadrian's Antinous" (62).[1] Rosenmeyer (2018), however, counters this potential overreach of evidence by summing up the controversy succinctly: "All these assumptions seem to be based on three facts: Balbilla was female, wrote in an Aeolic dialect, and was traveling with Sabina and Hadrian when they visited the Colossus in Egyptian Thebes" (143).

### *Occasion and Inscription*

Let us now turn from the biographical details of Balbilla's life to the literature itself. Balbilla wrote her four poems to commemorate Hadrian and Sabina's visit to Thebes in November 130 CE as a part of their tour of the Eastern Roman provinces. Three of the poems (28–30) are located close together (cf. Figure 5), and seem to have been inscribed by the same hand. Poem 28 was inscribed on the left ankle of the Colossus, about 1.5 meters from the base. Poem 29 begins underneath poem 28, but continues next to poem 28 in a separate parallel column due to a lack of space. Poem 30 is a inscribed directly underneath the second column of poem 29. Poem 31, however, is written on a different part of the left foot, just above a break in the stone. It is inscribed in much larger letters that have been more deeply carved into the stone, seemingly by a different hand than poems 28–30. All four of the poems are written in elegiac couplets, and three of the poems (28–30) are preceded by a short prose preface that explains the poem's occasion.

In addition to the four poems attributed to Balbilla, there is also a short inscription in the name of Empress Sabina (Poem 32). It is also located on the left leg of the statue, but on the leg rather than the foot, which was considered the best part of the statue for inscribing because it was the first portion touched by the rising sun.[2] It is unclear whether or not Sabina composed or simply commissioned these lines to be inscribed.

The occasion of the poems has also been a topic of scholarly controversy, particularly regarding the order in which the poems should be read. Bernard and Bernard (1960), the original modern editors of the text, postulated that the poems described the following sequence of events and should be read in the following order (scholars have mostly accepted this sequence):[3]

- November 19 (Poem 29): Hadrian and Sabina visit the Colossus of Memnon, but the statue surprisingly stayed silent.
- November 20 (Poem 30): Balbilla and Sabina visited the statue again, without Hadrian, and the statue spoke to them in the first hour.
- November 20 (Poem 28): Hadrian returned to visit the statue and the statue spoke to him three times.
- November 20/21 (Poem 31): Balbilla visited the statue alone and wrote her final epigram.

Rosenmeyer (2018), however, raises questions about this chronology, specifically on two points: (1) It requires the poems to be read out of order, and (2) It is unlikely that Hadrian would want Balbilla to record for future generations Memnon ignoring her patron (148–149). Instead, Rosenmeyer suggests the poems should be read in order and that the chronology was as follows:

- November 19 (Poem 28): Hadrian visits Memnon and the statue speaks three times.
- November 20 (Poem 29): Sabina and Balbilla visit Memnon with Hadrian, and Memnon is silent.
- November 21 (Poem 30): Sabina and Balbilla visit Memnon, and Memnon speaks to Sabina.
- November 21 (Poem 31 and 32): Balbilla and Sabina officially report that Memnon spoke to them, including the date of the occurrence.

### *Dialect and Literary Models*

The most prominent feature of Balbilla's poetry is her use of archaizing forms and the Aeolic dialect (for a detailed overview of Aeolic, see Appendix A). Balbilla's archaizing is indicative of the literary trends in the 2nd century CE to favor older and sometimes artificial dialects. Such a trend can be seen not only in Greek literature (e.g., Lucian's imitation of Herodotean Ionic in his essays), but also in Latin literature (e.g., Fronto's use of archaic Latin forms in his letters to Marcus Aurelius and Lucius Verus). Balbilla's archaizing includes a number of rare poetic forms and Homeric vocabulary.

In addition to her use of Homer, Balbilla's use of Aeolic forms throughout is even more noteworthy. Since the most prominent and famous practitioner of Aeolic in antiquity was the Lesbian poet Sappho, scholars have posited a close relationship between the poetry of the two women, with Balbilla holding up Sappho's poetry as a literary model. The ramifications of taking Sappho as a literary model are far-reaching. As mentioned above, scholars have postulated a potential homoerotic relationship between Balbilla and Sabina based, in part, on Balbilla's selection of Sappho as a model due to the homoerotic and homosocial content of Sappho's poetry. Beyond this, however, Balbilla's use of Sappho as her main literary model may speak to the existence of a literary canon of women writers, all of whom took Sappho as their muse in the same way that the male literary canon looked to Homer as the fount of all literature.

### *Overview of the Poems*

The four poems of Balbilla describe the events of the imperial visit to the Colossus of Memnon from November 19–21, 130 CE. Poem 28 recounts the initial visit of Hadrian to Memnon. Upon Hadrian's arrival, Memnon greets the Emperor by sounding three separate times. Hadrian then returns Memnon's greeting, and the entire event confirms that Hadrian is favored by the gods. Poem 29 describes Sabina and Balbilla's visit to Memnon, but this time without Hadrian's presence. Although the women encourage Memnon to speak, he remains silent. For the rest of the poem, Balbilla shows her intellectual *bona fides*, recounting how King Cambyses mutilated the statue and was subsequently punished, before claiming that she will ensure the statue's immortality through her verses and that she is qualified to do so because of her royal lineage. In Poem 30, the two women visit Memnon again, and again Memnon is silent. However, Balbilla warns the statue not to anger Hadrian by ignoring Sabina's requests for a greeting. After this threat, Memnon greets Sabina. Poem 31 concludes the inscriptions, as Balbilla visits Memnon alone and formally commemorates the occasions of the previous three poems, including the exact dates on which the visit occurred. Poem 32 is the official commemoration of Sabina's visit to Memnon and states that she heard the statue speak twice.

### *Julia Balbilla 1 (Bernand 28)*

Ἰουλίας Βαλ(β)ίλλης·
ὅτε ἤκουσε τοῦ Μέμνονος
ὁ Σεβαστὸς Ἀδριανός.

Μέμνονα πυνθανόμαν Αἰγύπτιον, ἀλίω αὔγαι
  αἰθόμενον, φώνην Θηβαΐ(κ)ω ᾽πυ λίθω.
Ἀδρίανον δ᾽ἐσίδων τὸν παμβασίλη πρὶν αὔγας
  ἀελίω χαίρην εἶπέ (ϝ)οι, ὡς δύνατον.
Τίταν δ᾽ὄττ᾽, ἐλάων λεύκοισι δι ᾽αἴθερος ἴπποις,
  ἐνὶ σκίαι ὠράων δεύτερον ἆχε μέτρον,
ὡς χάλκοιο τύπεντ[ο]ς ἴη Μέμνων πάλιν αὔδαν
  ὀξύτονον· χαίρω[ν κ]αὶ τρίτον ἆχον ἴη.
Κοίρανος Ἀδρίανο[ς τότ᾽ ἄ]λις δ᾽ἀσπάσσατο καὔτος
  Μέμνονα κὰν [στάλ]αι κάλλι[π]εν ὀψ[ι]γόνοις
γρόππατα σαμαίν[ον]τά τ᾽ ὄσ᾽ εὔϊδε κὤσσ᾽ ἐσάκουσε.
  Δῆλον παῖσι δ᾽ἔγε[ν]τ᾽ ὤς (ϝ)ε φίλισι θέοι.

—

**Ἀδρίανος, ὁ:** Hadrian. Emperor of Rome (117–138 CE).
**Αἰγύπτιος, η, ον:** Egyptian
**αἰθήρ, αἰθέρος, ἡ:** the ether, heaven, sky
**αἴθω:** to light up, kindle; to burn, blaze
**ἅλις:** (adv.) sufficiently
**ἀσπάζομαι:** to greet kindly, welcome
**αὐγή, ἡ:** light (of the sun), ray
**αυδή, ἡ:** voice, speech
**ἀχά, ἡ:** sound, noise
**ἐλάω:** to drive
**εἴδω:** to see
**εἰσακούω:** to hear, give ear to
**εἰσοράω:** to look upon
**ἐν:** in (+ dat.)
**θηβαΐκος, η, ον:** Theban
**Ἰουλια Βαλβίλλα, ἡ:** Julia Balbilla
**καταλείπω:** to leave behind
**κοίρανος, ὁ:** king, ruler
**λευκός, ή, όν:** white, bright
**Μέμνων, Μέμνονος, ὁ:** Memnon
**μέτρον, τὸ:** measure, length
**ὀξύτονος, η, ον:** piercing, sharp-sounding
**ὀψιγονος, ον:** late-born; of a later generation
**παμβασιλεύς, -εως, ὁ:** absolute monarch
**σεβαστός, ή, όν:** venerable, august
**σημαίνω:** to show by sign, indicate, point out
**σκιά, σκιᾶς, ἡ:** shadow, shade
**στήλη, ἡ:** block of stone, stone
**Τιτάν, Τιτᾶνος, ὁ:** Titan
**τύπτω:** to beat, strike
**φιλέω:** to love, like
**φωνέω:** to produce a sound; to speak
**χαλκός, ὁ:** bronze
**ὥρα, ἡ:** hour, measure of time
**ὡς:** like, as; that; how

—

*Meter: elegiac couplets*

**1. τοῦ Μέμνονος:** genitive singular of Μέμνων. Verbs of hearing, such as ἤκουσε, take the individual whom is heard in the genitive case and the things that are heard in the accusative case.

**4–7:** The first two couplets of the inscription follow the same basic syntax. Both begin with the accusative object of the sentence (Μέμνονα, Ἀδρίανον), then follow them with a verbal element (πυνθανόμαν, ἐσίδων), then a modifying element describing the accusative object (Αἰγύπτιον, τὸν παμβασίληα), then a phrase about the rays of the sun (ἀλίω αὔγαι αἰθόμενον, πρὶν αὔγας ἀελίω χαίρην), and finally a verbal element about speaking (φώνην, εἶπέ). The effect of this parallel structure is to draw the two principal individuals, Memnon and Hadrian, into comparison with one another, as both are powerful rulers. Moreover, it grants Hadrian a more exalted status, as he is placed on the same level as the mythical Memnon.

**4. πυνθανόμαν:** Aeolic spelling of πυνθανόμην. Imperfect, first singular.

**4. αἴθω:** Homeric spelling of ἡλίου. Genitive, singular.

**4. αὔγαι:** Homeric spelling of αὔγῃ. Dative, singular.

**5. φώνην:** Aeolic spelling of the present, active, infinitive φωνεῖν.

**5. 'πύ = ἀπό:** Protelision of the Aeolic spelling of ἀπό.

**6. ἐσίδων:** Aeolic contraction of εἰσιδών. The subject is an unstated Μέμνων.

**7. ἀελίω:** uncontracted Aeolic spelling of ἡλίου. Genitive, singular.

**7. χαίρην:** Aeolic spelling of the present, active, infinitive χαίρειν. Construe with πρὶν in a temporal clause (cf. Smyth §2431).

**7. (ϝ)οι:** "to him". Aeolic spelling of οἷ, the dative case of the third person personal pronoun. Aeolic forms keep the digamma (ϝ) before initial vowels of the pronoun. Cf. line 15 of this poem.

**7. ὡς δύνατον (ἐστι):** "as much as possible". The stone attempts to greet Hadrian as much as it could.

**8–11:** Having attempted to greet Hadrian as best as he was able, but receiving no reply, Memnon greets Hadrian two more times over the course of the morning.

**8. Τίταν:** Although the general meaning of this word refers to the mythical Titans, it can also be used to describe the Sun-God or Apollo, as it does here (cf. Emp. 38 and Orph. A.512).

**9. ἐνὶ:** Aeolic spelling of ἐν.

**9. ὠράων:** Aeolic/Epic genitive plural of ὥρα.

**9. ἦχε:** Aeolic spelling of εἶχε. Imperfect, third singular of ἔχω.

**10. ὡς χάλκοιο τύπεντ[ο]ς:** Supply an understood αὔδαν. Translate as "like the sound of beaten brass."

**10. χάλκοιο:** Homeric spelling of the genitive singular χαλκοῦ.

**10. τύπεντ[ο]ς:** genitive, singular, aorist, passive participle from ἐτύπην, the poetic 2nd aorist of τύπτω.

**10. ἴη:** Aeolic spelling of ἵει, the imperfect, third singular of ἵημι.

**10. αὐδάν:** Aeolic spelling of αυδήν.

**11. ἄχον:** Aeolic spelling of ἀχάν. Accusative singular.

**11. ἴη:** Cf. note on ἴη on line 10 above.

**12–15:** The inscription concludes with the final comparison of Hadrian and Memnon. As at the beginning, Hadrian and Memnon are placed at the opening of consecutive lines in order to draw their comparison into greater relief (Κοίρανος Ἀδρίανο[ς, Μέμνονα). However, whereas Memnon has been depicted as struggling to communicate and be understood through the entirety of the inscription (ὠς δύνατον, πάλιν, τρίτον), Hadrian is depicted as able to communicate effortlessly in both a verbal and written medium (ἄ]λις, γρόππατα σαμαίν[ον]τά). Because of this, Hadrian is shown to be superior. Rosenmeyer (2018) calls this a "contest of masculine power" that Hadrian wins over Memnon (150).

**12. ἀσπάσσατο:** Aeolic, aorist, middle/passive of ἀσπάζομαι.

**13. κἀν:** crasis of καὶ ἐν

**13. στᾶλαι:** Aeolic spelling of στήλῃ. Dative singular.

**13. καλλι[π]εν:** Aeolic spelling of the aorist κατέλιπεν with apocope.

**14. γρόππατα:** Aeolic spelling of γράμματα (cf. Sappho 112.3, ὄππατα for ὄμματα). The word γράμμα is frequently associated with inscriptions, as it is here (cf. Pl. Phdr. 229e, Chrm. 164d; X. Mem. 4.2.24). However, it also can be used to indicate articulate sounds, a meaning that adds an extra dimension of meaning in this context (cf. Pl. Phlb.18c; Arist. Pr.895a12).

**14. σαμαίνοντα:** Aeolic spelling of σημαίνοντα.

**14. εὔϊδε:** Aeolic, second aorist of εἴδω (οἶδα).

**14. ἐσακούσε:** Epic spelling of the 1st aorist εἰσακούσε.

**15. παῖσι:** Aeolic spelling of the dative πᾶσι.

**15. ἔγε[ν]τ':** Epic spelling of ἐγένετο. Construe with Δῆλον and translate as "It became clear".

**15. (ϝ)ε:** "him". Aeolic spelling of ἕ, the accusative case of the third person pronoun.

**15. φίλισι:** Aeolic spelling of φίλεισι. In Aeolic, contract verbs like φιλέω conjugate as -μι verbs. Hence, this form is a third plural, present. The most familiar Attic form would be φίλουσι.

### *Julia Balbilla 2 (Bernand 29)*

Ὅτε σὺν τῇ Σεβαστῇ Σαβείνη-
ι ἐγενόμην παρὰ τῷ Μέμνονι.

Αὔως καὶ γεράρω, Μέμνον, πάι Τιθώνοιο,
  Θηβάας θάσσων ἄντα Δίος πόλιος,
ἢ Ἀμένωθ, βασίλευ Αἰγύπτιε, τὼς ἐνέποισιν
  ἴρηες μύθων τῶν παλάων ἴδριες,
χαῖρε, καὶ αὐδάσαις πρόφρων ἀσπάσδε[ο κ]αὔτ[αν]
  τὰν σέμναν ἄλοχον κοιράνω Ἀδριάνω.

Γλῶσσαν μέν τοι τμᾶξε [κ]αὶ ὤατα βάρβαρος ἄνηρ,
  Καμβύσαις ἄθεος· τῶ ῥα λύγρῳ θανάτῳ
δῶκέν τοι ποίναν, τὤτωι ἄκ[ρῳ] ἄορι πλάγεις
  τῷ νήλας Ἆπιν κάκτανε τὸν θέϊον.
Ἀλλ᾽ ἔγω οὐ δοκίμωμι σέθεν τόδ᾽ ὄλεσθ᾽ ἂν ἄγαλμα,
  ψύχαν δ᾽ ἀθανάταν λοῖπον ἔσωσα νόῳ.
Εὐσέβεες γὰρ ἔμοι γένεται πάπποι τ᾽ ἐγένοντο,
  Βάλβιλλός τ᾽ ὀ σόφος κ᾽ Ἀντίοχος βασῖλευς,
Βάλβιλλός γενέταις μᾶτρος βασιλήϊδος ἄμμας,
  τῶ πάτερος δὲ πάτηρ Ἀντίοχος βασῖλευς·
κήνων ἐκ γενέας κἄγω λόχον αἶμα τὸ κᾶλον,
  Βαλβίλλας δ᾽ ἔμεθεν γρόπτα τάδ᾽ εὐσέβε[ος].

—

**Ἀδρίανος, ὁ:** Hadrian. Emperor of Rome (117–138 CE).
**ἄγαλμα, -ατος, τὸ:** statue (in honor of a god); glory; honor
**ἄθεος:** godless, god-denying
**Αἰγύπτιος, α, ον:** Egyptian
**ἄκρος, α, ον:** topmost point, top
**ἄλοχος, ου, ἡ:** bed-mate, wife
**Ἀμένωθ, ὁ:** Amenoth
**ἄντα:** opposite to; facing (+ genitive)
**ἄορ, ὁ:** sword, hanger
**Ἆπις, ὁ:** Apis
**ἀσπάζομαι:** to greet kindly, welcome
**αὐδάω:** to speak, utter
**βασιληίς:** royal
**γενεά, ἡ:** race, family, stock
**γενέτης, ὁ:** begetter, father, parent
**γεραρός, η, ον:** majestic, honored
**γραπτός, ή, όν:** written, painted
**δοκιμόω:** to think, suppose
**ἐνέπω:** to say, tell
**εὐσεβής:** pious, religious, righteous
**ἠώς, ἠοῦς, ἡ:** dawn
**θάσσω:** to sit
**Θηβαῖος, η, ον:** Theban
**ἴδρις, ἴδριος:** learned, experienced, knowing
**ἱερεύς, ὁ:** priest
**Καμβύσης, ὁ:** Cambyses
**κατακτείνω:** to kill, slay
**κοίρανος, ὁ:** king, ruler
**λαγχάνω:** to obtain by lot, obtain
**λυγρός, ά, όν:** miserable, mournful
**μῦθος, ὁ:** story, word, speech
**νηλής:** pitiless, ruthless
**ὄλλυμι:** to destroy, die, make an end of
**οὖς, τὸ:** ear
**πάππος, ὁ:** grandfather
**πλήσσω:** to strike, hit
**ποινή, ἡ:** penalty, price, fine
**πρόφρων:** (adjective) kind, kindly
**Σαβεῖνα, ἡ:** Sabina (wife of Hadrian)
**σεμνός, η, ον:** holy, revered, august
**σώζω:** to save
**Τιθωνός, ὁ:** Tithon
**τῶ(ς):** then, therefore, and so

—

*Meter: elegiac couplets*

**3–8:** Balbilla opens this poem with a long greeting to Memnon. As she greets him, she consciously mixes the Homeric tradition with the local Egyptian tradition. Her opening epithet (Αὔως καὶ γεράρω, Μέμνον, πάι

Τιθώνοιο) reminds the reader of the Homeric tradition in which Memnon is identified as the Ethiopian king who is the son of Dawn and Tithon, a prince of Troy. The next lines (ἤ Ἀμένωθ, βασῖλευ Αἰγύπτιε) refer to Amenoth, a name synonomous with the Egyptian pharoah Amenhotep III, who originally had the colossi constructed. After calling upon Memnon by his dual traditions, she asks the hero to welcome a new companion, the revered spouse of Emperor Hadrian, Sabina Augusta (τὰν σέμναν ἄλοχον).

**3. Αὔως:** Aeolic spelling of ἠοῦς. Genitive singular (cf. Sappho fr. 18).

**3. γεράρω:** Aeolic spelling of γεραροῦ. Genitive singular. Construe with Τιθώνοιο.

**3. Τιθώνοιο:** Epic genitive singular ending.

**4. πόλιος:** Aeolic genitive singular.

**5. Ἀμένωθ:** Another name for the pharaoh who constructed the colossi: Amenhotep III.

**5. ἐνέποισιν:** Aeolic spelling of ἐνέπουσιν.

**6. ἴρηες:** Aeolic spelling of ἱερῆς. Nominative plural.

**6. παλάων:** Aeolic spelling of παλαίων.

**7. αὐδάσας:** Aeolic spelling of αὐδήσας. Aorist participle.

**7. ἀσπάσδεο:** Aeolic spelling of ἀσπάζου. Second singular middle imperative.

**7. καὔταν:** crasis of καὶ αὔταν. Translate as "her too".

**8. τὰν:** Aeolic spelling of the article τὴν.

**8. σέμναν:** Aeolic spelling of σέμνην. Accusative singular.

**8. κοιράνω Ἀδριάνω:** Aeolic spelling of κοιράνου Ἀδριάνου. Genitive singular.

**9–12:** Having greeted Memnon and encouraged him to greet Sabina in turn, Balbilla turns again to show off her erudition, as she recounts a legend of how Memnon, in his colossal form, lost the ability to speak. According to Balbilla, Cambyses II, the king of the Achaemenid Empire from 530–522 BCE who led a conquest of Egypt, was to blame, having broken the colossus himself. She goes on to relate another story of Cambyses' atrocities, recounting how Cambyses also travelled to Memphis and killed the Egyptian bull-god Apis. Balbilla's account resemble others from antiquity. According to Pausanias 1.41.3, Cambyses broke the statue of Memnon into two pieces, with the top half of the statue thrown down and the bottom half still remaining intact. Likewise, in Herodotus 3.27ff, Cambyses II, during his conquest of Egypt, had priests bring the Apis bull to him and he stabbed the bull to death. Balbilla, while perhaps not alluding to these sources directly, shows her familiarity of the legends surrounding the colossi and hints at a substantial education.

**9. γλῶσσαν:** Aeolic spelling of γλῶσσην. Accusative singular.

**9. τμᾶξε:** Aeolic form of τέμνω. Aorist, active, third, singular.

**9. ὤατα:** Aeolic spelling of ὦτα. Accusative plural from οὖς, τὸ.

**10. Καμβύσαις:** Aeolic spelling of Καμβύσης. Nominative singular.

**10. ῥα:** Epic form of ἄρα. This enclitic form is used after monosyllables or words ending in a vowel or diphthong.
**10. τῶ:** Epic spelling of τοῦ.
**11. ποίναν:** Aeolic spelling of ποινήν. Accusative singular.
**11. τὤτωι:** Aeolic spelling of τῷ αὐτῷ.
**11. πλαγείς:** Aorist passive participle from πλήσσω.
**12. νήλας:** Aeolic spelling of νηλής. Nominative singular.
**12. κάκτανε:** Epic, aorist, active, indicative form of κατακείνω.
**13–20:** Balbilla concludes the poem with a striking claim: Memnon will not face destruction physically or in memory because she will immortalize him in her poetry (Ἀλλ' ἔγω οὐ δοκίμωμι σέθεν τόδ' ὄλεσθ' ἂν ἀγαλμα,/ψύχαν δ' ἀθανάταν λοῖπον ἔσωσα νόῳ). Moreover, Balbilla backs up her claim by recounting her own genealogy to show her pedigree and bolster her claims. On both sides of her family tree, Balbilla was descended from elite families. On her father's side, she was the granddaughter of the last king of Syrian Commagene, King Antiochus (τῶ πάτερος δὲ πάτηρ Ἀντίοχος βασῖλευς). On her mother's side, she was the granddaughter of the astrologer Tiberius Claudius Balbillus, who was prefect of Egypt under Nero (55–59 CE) and the head of the museum in Alexandria (Βάλβιλλός γενέταις μᾶτρος βασιλήϊδος ἄμμας). Not only does this strengthen her claim to poetic power through her association with elite families, it also provides a clue as to how Balbilla received the education necessary to make the learned allusions with which she opened the poem. Moreover, the multicultural and diverse background of her family and potential upbringing may speak further to her ability to navigate Greek, Roman, and Egyptian cultural references seamlessly.
**13. δοκίμωμι:** Aeolic form of δοκιμόω. In Aeolic, present and imperfect forms of Attic contracted verbs in -άω, -έω, and -όω have -μι conjugations. (e.g., τίμαμι, φῖλημι, δήλωμι).
**13. σέθεν:** Epic genitive form of σύ.
**13. ὀλέσθ':** Shortened form of ὀλέσθαι. Aorist middle infinitive.
**14. ἀθανάταν:** Aeolic spelling of ἀθανάτην. Accusative singular.
**14. λοῖπον:** Adverbial. Translate as "henceforth" (literally, for "the remains of time")
**15. εὐσέβεες:** Epic, nominative, plural of εὐσεβής.
**16. κ'** = καὶ
**17. γενέταις:** Epic spelling of γενέτης.
**17. βασιλήϊδος:** Poetic genitive singular of βασιληίς.
**17. ἄμμας:** Aeolic form of ἐμῆς. Genitive singular.
**19. κήνων:** Aeolic form of ἐκείνων. Genitive plural.
**19. ἔλοχον:** Aeolic spelling of ἔλαχον. Aorist first singular indicative from λαγχάνω.
**20:** Βαλβῖλλας δ' ἔμεθεν γρόπτα τάδ' εὐσέβε[ος]: A profound ending to the poem. Far from remaining in the shadows, Balbilla stakes her claim to

poetic immortality by claiming that the words on the statue are her own (ἔμεθεν γρόπτα τάδ'), even stating her name (Βαλβίλλας).

**20. ἔμεθεν:** Epic genitive form of ἐγώ (cf. σέθεν on line 13 above).

**20. γρόπτα:** Aeolic spelling of γραπτά. Here, construe with τάδ' as "writings".

**20. εὐσέβεος:** Aeolic spelling of εὐσεβοῦς. Genitive singular.

### *Julia Balbilla 3 (Bernand 30)*

Ὅτε τῇ πρώτῃ ἡμέρᾳ οὐκ ἀ-
κούσαμεν τοῦ Μέμνονος.

Χθίσδον μὲν Μέμνων σίγαις ἀπε[δέξατ' ἀκ]οίτα[ν],
    ὠς πάλιν ἀ κάλα τυῖδε Σάβιννα μό[λοι.]
Τέρπει γάρ σ' ἐράτα μόρφα βασιλήϊδος ἄμμας·
    ἐλθοίσαι δ'[α]ὔται θήϊον ἄχον ἴῃ,
μὴ καί τοι βασίλευς κοτέσῃ· τό νυ δᾶρον ἀτά[ρβης]
    τὰν σέμναν κατέχες κουριδίαν ἄλοχον.
Κὼ Μέμνον τρέσσαις μεγάλω μένος Ἀδρι[άνοιο]
    ἐξαπίνας αὔδασ', ἀ δ'ὀΐοισ' ἐχάρη.

—

**ἀΐω:** to hear, perceive by hearing
**ἀκοιτής, ἡ:** bedfellow, wife
**ἄλοχος, ου, ἡ:** bed-mate, wife
**ἀποδέκομαι:** to accept, admit to one's presence
**ἀταρβής:** fearless
**αὐδάω:** to speak, utter
**ἀχά, ἡ:** sound, noise
**βασιληΐς:** royal
**βλώσκω:** to go, come
**δηρός, ά, όν:** too long
**ἐξαπίνης:** (adverb) suddenly
**ἐρατός, ή, όν:** lovely, beloved
**κατέχω:** to detain, hold back
**κουρίδιος, α, ον:** (lawfully) wedded
**κοτέω:** to be angry, bear a grudge
**μένος, τό:** might, force, strength
**μορφή, ἡ:** form, figure, shape
**Σαβεῖνα, ἡ:** Sabina (wife of Hadrian)
**σεμνός, η, ον:** holy, revered, august
**σιγάς, -άδος:** silent
**τέρπω:** to please, delight
**τρέω:** to fear, dread; to flee
**τυῖδε:** hither, to here
**χθίσδον:** yesterday

—

*Meter: elegiac couplets*

**2. τοῦ Μέμνονος:** genitive singular of Μέμνων. Verbs of hearing, such as ἤκουσε, take the individual whom is heard in the genitive case and the things that are heard in the accusative case.

**3–5:** This poem opens with Babilla attributing intent to Memon. She states that he did not make his traditional sound for the Empress Sabina when she first came to visit him in an effort to entice her to return for a second visit. Balbilla suggests that the reason for this is that Memnon is himself enamored of Sabina's beauty, describing her in eroticized terms (Τέρπει γάρ σ' ἐράτα μόρφα). Rosenmeyer (2018, p. 161) points out that this, in fact, may be an oblique reference by Balbilla to Sappho's erotic poetry, particularly Sappho fr. 16 (in this volume). In that poem, Sappho describes her beloved Anactoria in similar terms (βολλοίμαν ἔρατόν τε βᾶμα/κἀμάρυχμα λάμπρον ἴδην προσώπω, ll. 16–17). Such an apparent allusion, coupled with the Aeolicizing throughout the poem, seems to suggest that Sappho was a readily apparent poetic model in Balbilla's mind.

**3. χθίσδον:** Aeolic spelling of χθιζόν.

**3. σίγαις:** Aeolic spelling of σιγάς. Nominative singular.

**3. ἀκοίταν:** Aeolic spelling of ἀκοιτήν. Accusative singular.

**4. ἀ κάλα:** Aeolic spelling of ἡ κάλη.

**4. Σάβιννα:** Aeolic spelling of Σαβεῖνα.

**4. μόλοι:** Aorist optative active third singular from βλώσκω. The optative is used here due to a purpose clause in secondary sequence (cf. Smyth §2196).

**5. ἐράτα μόρφα:** Aeolic spelling of ἐρατή μορφή. Nominative singular. The use of μορφή to describe feminine beauty is a commonly used expression in Greek literature. However, the connection of μορφή with ἐρατή may point to another Sapphic allusion: (μόρφαν ἐπήρατον, 96.22).

**5. βασιλήϊδος:** Poetic genitive singular of βασιληίς.

**5. ἄμμας:** Aeolic form of ἐμῆς. Genitive singular.

**6–10:** Balbilla moves from the eroticization of Sabina and Memnon's attraction to her to a warning for Memnon: next time the Empress comes, be sure to speak to her so as not to anger Emperor Hadrian. Memnon, having been warned and fearing Hadrian's wrath, obliges and speaks to Sabina. Balbilla thus sets up this situation as a contest of masculinities between the two regal males Hadrian and Memnon. By having Memnon oblige Hadrian out of respect for the latter's strength, Balbilla allows Hadrian to be the dominant male in a contest of masculine might.

**6. ἐλθοίσαι δ' αὔται:** Aeolic spelling of ἐλθούσῃ δ' αὐτῃ. Present active participle dative singular feminine from ἔρχομαι. Translate as "to/for her coming".

**6. ἄχον:** Aeolic spelling of ἀχάν. Accusative singular.

**6. ἴη:** Aeolic spelling of ἵει. Second singular imperative of ἵημι (cf. Smyth §777).

**7. τοι:** Aeolic spelling of σοι (cf. Sappho 31.2 Voigt).

**7. κοτέσῃ:** Aorist subjunctive third singular from κοτέω. The subjunctive is used here due to a purpose clause in primary sequence (cf. Smyth §2196).

**7. νυ:** Enclitic form of νῦν

**7. δᾶρον:** Aeolic spelling of δηρόν. Accusative of time duration, "for too long".

**8. τὰν σέμναν:** Aeolic spelling of τὴν σέμνην. Accusative singular.
**8. κατέχες:** Aeolic spelling of κατεῖχες. Imperfect indicative active.
**9. κὠ:** Crasis of καὶ ὁ.
**9. τρέσσαις:** Aeolic spelling of τρεσάς. Aorist active participle nominative singular from τρέω.
**9. μεγάλω:** Aeolic spelling of μεγάλου. Genitive singular.
**9. Ἀδριάνοιο:** Epic genitive singular ending.
**10. ἐξαπίνας:** Aeolic spelling of ἐξαπίνης.
**10. αὔδασ':** Aeolic spelling of ηὔδησ'. Aorist third singular of αὐδάω.
**10. ὀΐοισα:** Aeolic spelling of αἴουσα. Present active participle nominative feminine from ἀίω.

### *Julia Balbilla 4 (Bernand 31)*

Ἔκλυον αὐδήσαντος ἔγω 'πυ λίθω Βάλβιλλα
φώνας τᾶς θείας Μέμνονος ἢ Φαμένωθ.
Ἦλθον ὔμοι δ'ἐράται βασιλήιδι τυῖδε Σαβίννᾳ,
ὤρας δὲ πρώτας ἄλιος ἦχε δρόμος.
Κοιράνωι Ἀδριάνω πέμπτῳ δεκότῳ δ'ἐνιαύτῳ,
φῶτα δ'ἔχεσκεν Ἄθυρ εἴκοσι καὶ πέσυρα.
Εἰκόστῳ πέμπτῳ δ'ἄματι μῆνος Ἄθυρ.

—

**Ἀδρίανος, ὁ:** Hadrian. Emperor of Rome (117–138 CE).
**Ἄθυρ:** Hathyr
**αὐδάω:** to speak, utter
**βασιληίς:** royal
**δρόμος, ὁ:** course, race
**εἰκόσι:** (indeclinable) twenty
**εἰκοστός, ή, όν:** twentieth
**ἐνιαυτός, ὁ:** year; anniversary
**ἐρατός, ή, όν:** lovely, beloved
**κλύω:** to hear
**κοίρανος, ὁ:** king, ruler
**μείς, μηνός, ὁ:** month
**ὁμοῦ:** (adverb) together
**πέμπτος, η, ον:** fifth
**Σαβεῖνα, ἡ:** Sabina (wife of Hadrian)
**τέτταρες:** four
**τυῖδε:** hither, to here
**Φαμένωθ:** Phamenoth
**ὥρα, ἡ:** hour, measure of time

—

*Meter: elegiac couplets*

**1–2:** Balbilla opens this poem with a focus on herself, claiming from the opening word (Ἔκλυον) and emphasizing with the pronoun ἔγω that she herself was in the party that came to Memnon on this day. The first person emphasis may also lend itself to the interpretation that Balbilla herself was making this inscription, or was present as it was being inscribed.
**1. αὐδήσαντος:** The placement of this word is interesting. It seemingly refers to Μέμνονος on line 2. However, it can also agree with λίθω on line 1, which is closer.

**1. λίθω:** Aeolic spelling of λιθοῦ. Genitive singular.

**1. ᾽πύ:** Aeolic spelling of ἀπό with protelision.

**2. φώνας τᾶς:** Aeolic spelling of φωνῆς τῆς. Genitive singular.

**2. Μέμνονος ἢ Φαμένωθ:** Balbilla here may be showing her erudition and awareness of both the contemporary Greek and original Egyptian cultures. Greek and Roman tourists to the colossi frequently associated them with the Homeric hero Memnon. However, the colossi were actually erected to represent the pharaoh Amenhotep III. A colloquial variant of Amenhotep was Amenoth. Some scholars (West, 1978) read Φαμένωθ as a name synonymous with Amenoth, as that was the Egyptian word for the month of March and was thus more recognizable to Greek speakers. In such a reading, Balbilla would here be making a nod to both the Greek and Egyptian traditions of the colossi. Other scholars (Rosenmeyer, 2018; Bagnall and Rathbone, 2004) have suggested that it is actually a mistake and that the inscriber should have written ῥ' Ἀμένοθ.

**3–4:** Balbilla moves from the opening couplet with its first person focus to a second couplet with the attention shifted to her co-traveller, Sabina. Sabina, however, is cast in extraordinarily erotic terms for a public pronouncement of their travel, described as ἐρατός. This eroticization, coupled with the Sapphic Aeolicizing dialect and the focus on the connection between these two women, has led some to suggest that there may have been an erotic dimension to the relationship between Balbilla and Sabina.

**3. ὔμοι:** Aeolic spelling of ὁμοῦ.

**3. ἐράται βασιλήιδι ... Σαβίννᾳ:** Aeolic datives. Translate as "with the lovely, royal Sabina".

**4. ὤρας ... πρώτας:** "during the first hour". Genitive of time within which (cf. Smyth §1444).

**4. ἄλιος:** Aeolic spelling of ἥλιος. Nominative singular.

**4. ἦχε δρόμος:** Aeolic spelling of εἶχε δρόμους.

**5–7:** Balbilla ends the poem with a highly stylized, official record of her visit with Sabina to see Memnon, stating the date and time of day of their visit. As she does to open the poem, she mixes the traditional imperial with the local Egyptian: marking the year in terms of Hadrian's reign and the month and day in a more local manner.

**5. Κοιράνωι Ἀδριάνω πέμπτῳ δεκότῳ δ᾽ἐνιαύτῳ:** The fifteenth year of Hadrian's reign places this inscription in 130 CE.

**5. κοιράνωι Ἀδριάνω:** Aeolic spelling of κοιράνου Ἀδριανοῦ. Genitive singular.

**5. πέμπτῳ δεκότῳ ... ἐνιαύτῳ:** "in the fifteenth year". Dative of time when (cf. Smyth §1528).

**5. δεκότῳ:** Aeolic spelling of δεκάτῳ. Dative singular.

**6–7. φῶτα ... Ἄθυρ:** The Egyptian month of Hathyr generally corresponds to late October through late November. The 24th and 25th days of Hathyr in 130 CE would have been November 20th and 21st (cf. Hemelrijk (1998) p. 165–167 for more).

**6. ἔχεσκεν:** Imperfect active third singular from ἔχω.

**6. πέσυρα:** Aeolic spelling of τέτταρα. Accusative plural neuter.

**7. Εἰκόστῳ πέμπτῳ ... ἄματι:** "on the twenty-fifth day". Dative of time when (cf. Smyth §1528).

**7. ἄματι:** Aeolic spelling of ἤματι. Dative singular.

***Sabina (Bernand 32)***

[Σα]βεῖνα Σεβαστὴ
[Αὐτ]οκράτορος Καίσαρος
[Ἁδρια]νοῦ, ἐντὸς ὥρας
[α? Μέμνονο]ς δὶς ἤκουσε...

—

**Ἀδρίανος, ὁ:** Hadrian. Emperor of Rome (117–138 CE).
**αὐτοκράτωρ, αὐτοκράτορος, ὁ/ἡ:** absolute ruler
**δίς:** (adverb) twice
**ἐντός:** within (+ genitive)
**Καῖσαρ, Καῖσαρος, ὁ:** Caesar
**Σαβεῖνα, ἡ:** Sabina (wife of Hadrian)
**σεβαστός, η, ον:** venerable, august
**ὥρα, ἡ:** hour, measure of time

—

**4. Μέμνονος:** genitive singular of Μέμνων. Verbs of hearing, such as ἤκουσε, take the individual whom is heard in the genitive case and the things that are heard in the accusative case.

## Caecilia Trebulla

Caecilia Trebulla was a visitor to the Colossi and the author of three short epigrams inscribed on the left leg of the statue. Beyond her poems, no external evidence exists regarding her life or literary ambitions. Trebulla's three epigrams are typically dated to the reign of Hadrian (117–138 CE) due to their position on the left leg directly above the inscription of Balbilla 28 (see above). Plant (2004) has suggested that, perhaps, Trebulla's poetry predated that of Balbilla, postulating that Balbilla would have wanted to start her poem higher on the leg, but was prevented from doing so by Trebulla's epigrams (149). However, it is difficult to know for certain, especially because Trebulla seems to be referencing Balbilla's poetry throughout. Thus, the most we can say for certain is that Trebulla's poems were inscribed at approximately the time of Balbilla's, circa 130 CE.

Trebulla's three epigrams are written with a neat simplicity that hides a deeper complexity of allusions and imagery. Each of the epigrams is written in a type of koine Greek with epic vocabulary sprinkled throughout. Likewise, each inscription is comprised of a brief prose preface identifying Trebulla as the author, followed by an epigram in iambic trimeter. Despite the simplistic structure, Trebulla's imagery sparkles with alliteration and chiasmus. As befits poems about a speaking statue, Trebulla's epigrams frequently engage in word play to emphasize her point (e.g., the use of assonance to mimic the statue's droning sound in Poem 94 and the alliterative ἐκμεμαγμένον to mimic indistinct sounds made by the statue with a sound play on the name Memnon). Likewise, Trebulla favors juxtapositions in successive lines, particularly temporal ones (e.g., present vs. past; presence vs. absence).

As with Balbilla's poetry, Trebulla's verses also seem to show a narrative progression. In Poem 92, Trebulla depicts her initial interaction with Memnon, as she hears the statue's voice, an event that calls to mind her desire for mother to take part in the experience. Poem 93 illustrates Trebulla's second encounter with Memnon. This time, she relates how Memnon no longer simply speaks to her and her companions from afar, but greets them kindly as friends. The poem ends with a Trebulla wondering aloud whether it was truly possible for a statue to have the ability to perceive and to speak. In her final poem, Poem 94, Trebulla seemingly answers her own question, writing an epigram in the voice of Memnon and recounting how Memnon came to lose his ability to speak at the hands of King Cambyses.

Throughout the three epigrams, Trebulla blends together a number of literary and historical strands, an action that belies a high level of erudition and poetic skill. She is keenly aware of the Homeric tradition, not only using Homeric vocabulary and phrasing throughout, but also highlighting the Homeric genealogy of Memnon as the son of Dawn and Tithon. Likewise, she has an awareness of history both Greek and Egyptian, referencing not only the story of Cambyses' mutilation of the Colossus recorded in Herodotus and Pausanias, but also alluding to the Colossi's original construction in the image of Amenhotep III. Lastly, and perhaps most interestingly, Trebulla's poetry interacts closely with Julia Balbilla's, as she quotes Balbilla at some points and fills in gaps in Balbilla's narrative at others. This could, perhaps, be seen as a self-awareness on Trebulla's part and an attempt to place herself alongside one of the most conspicuous female poets whose work was featured on the Colossus.

### *Caecilia Trebulla 1 (Bernand 92)*

Τρεβούλλης.

Τῆς ἱερᾶς ἀκούουσα φωνῆς Μέμνονος,
ἐπόθουν σε, μῆτερ, καὶ ἐξακούειν εὐχόμην.

—

**εὐχόμαι, εὔξομαι, εὐξάμην:** to pray
**ποθέω, ποθήσω, ἐπόθησα:** to long for, yearn after
**Τρεβοῦλλα, ης, ἡ:** (Caecilia) Trebulla

—

*Meter: iambic trimeter*

**2–3:** In evoking Memnon's call to Dawn, Trebulla sets up a situation parallel to her own. As Memnon calls to his mother, Dawn, Trebulla is reminded of the absence of her own and she hopes she can hear the call from far away.

**3. ἐπόθουν:** Bernand and Bernand (1960, p. 188) note that this is the only example of ποθέω on the Colossus. They note that, although it is typical for the composers of the Memnon inscriptions to recall someone who is absent, they usually use the verb μιμνήσκομαι.

**3. μῆτερ:** vocative singular of μήτηρ.

**3. καὶ ἐξακούειν:** As inscribed on the stone. However, there must be an elision here to fit the meter. Some editors have emended the text to read κἀξακούειν.

**3. ἐξακούειν:** The verb ἀκούω with the prefix (ἐξ-). The force of the prefix is to emphasize the distance at which a sound is heard. Here, Trebulla wishes that her mother, who apparently is far away, were present to hear the sound. It is left unstated whether Trebulla's mother has died or is simply not present.

### *Caecilia Trebulla 2 (Bernand 93)*

Καικιλία Τρεβοῦλλα
δεύτερον ἀκούσασα
Μέμνονος.

Αὐδῆς τὸ πρόσθεν μοῦνον ἐξακούσαντας,
νῦν ὡς συνήθεις καὶ φίλους ἠσπάζετο
Μέμνον ὁ παῖς Ἠοῦς τε καὶ Τειθωνοῖο.
Αἴσθησιν ἄρα τῷ λίθῳ καὶ φθέγγματα
ἡ φύσις ἔδωκε δημιουργὸς τῶν ὅλων;

—

**αἴσθησις, εως, ἡ:** perception, sense
**ἀσπάζομαι:** to greet kindly, to welcome
**αὐδή, ῆς, ἡ:** voice, sound
**δεύτερον:** (adv.) for a second time
**δημιουργός, ὁ:** maker, craftsman
**Ἠώς, Ἠοῦς, ἡ:** dawn
**Καικιλία, ης, ἡ:** Caecilia (Trebulla)
**Μέμνων, ονος, ὁ:** Memnon
**ὅλα, τά:** the universe
**πρόσθεν:** (adv.) before, former
**συνήθεης, ες:** intimate, familiar
**Τιθωνός, ὁ:** Tithon (brother of Priam, husband of Eos, and father of Memnon).
**φθέγμα, ατος, τό:** voice, speech

—

*Meter: iambic trimeter*

**3. Μέμνονος:** genitive singular of Μέμνων. Verbs of hearing, such as ἀκούσασα, take the individual whom is heard in the genitive case and the things that are heard in the accusative case.

**4–6:** Complex and unexpected word order. A more prosaic order would be Μέμνον ὁ παῖς Ἠοῦς τε καὶ Τειθωνοῖο ἠσπάζετο [ἡμᾶς], αὐδῆς τὸ πρόσθεν μοῦνον ἐξακούσαντας, νῦν ὡς συνήθεις καὶ φίλους. The accusatives, ἐξακούσαντας, συνήθεις, and φίλους all describe an understood ἡμᾶς, a "we" made up of Caecilia Trebulla and her companions. The reader sees the change in the nature of Caecilia's relationship with Memnon change in real time, as she transforms from a mere acquaintance who hears Memnon's voice from afar into a close friend whom Memnon recognizes.

**4. Αὐδῆς:** genitive singular of αὐδή. Construe as the object of ἐξακούσαν τας, which takes the genitive when describing the individual whom is heard (cf. to Μέμνονος on line 3).

**4. τὸ πρόσθεν:** Articular adverb. Translate as "formerly". πρόσθεν is used 72 times in the *Iliad* and 18 times in the *Odyssey.* As such, this may be an attempt by Trebulla to make her verses sound more epic.

**4. μοῦνον:** Epic/Ionic form of the Attic μόνον. In this context, it is being used adverbially as "only". As with πρόσθεν (line 4), another effort to add an epic feel to the verse.

**4. ἐξακούσαντας:** Accusative, plural, aorist, active participle. The penultimate α must be scanned short to fit the meter. The use of this word recalls the previous poem (Caecilia Trebulla 1), when it was used to describe the actions of Trebulla's mother hearing from far away.

**5. ἠσπάζετο:** Reminiscent of Balbilla 28 and 29. This same verb is used to describe both Balbilla's exhortation that Memnon welcome Sabina (29.7) and Hadrian's greetings to the statue (28.12).

**6. Τειθωνοῖο:** The epic genitive singular ending (-οῖο). The use of the ending here shows a knowledge of the *Iliad* and *Odyssey* (cf. *Il.* 11.1 and *Od.* 5.1: *ἠὼς δ' ἐκ λεχέων παρ' ἀγαυοῦ Τιθωνοῖο/ὤρνυθ'*) (But Dawn arose from her bed beside noble Tithon) (cf. also Balbilla 29.3, in which Balbilla calls Memnon Αὔως καὶ γεράρω … πάι Τιθώνοιο). The Homeric ending -οῖο must be scanned short-long in this instance to fit the meter.

**7–8:** Again, as with lines 4–6, the word order is complex, and the objects are placed before the subject and verb of the sentence. A more prosaic word order would be ἡ φύσις ἄρα, δημιουργὸς τῶν ὅλων, ἔδωκε τῷ λίθῳ αἴσθησιν καὶ φθέγγματα; These lines are also littered with philosophically charged terms (αἴσθησις, φθέγμα, φύσις, δημιουργὸς τῶν ὅλων), all of which point to a familiarity with Plato and the Greek philosophical tradition (cf. *Gorgias* 508a and *Lysias* 214b).

**7. φθέγγματα:** cf. Caecilia Trebulla 3, in which the same term is used in the same metrical position.

***Caecilia Trebulla 3 (Bernand 94)***

Καικιλία Τρεβοῦλλα
ἔγραψα ἀκούσασα τοῦδε Μέμνονος.

Ἔθραυσε Καμβύσης με τόνδε τὸν λίθον
βασιλέος ἑῴου εἰκόνα ἐκμεμαγμένον.
Φωνὴ δ'ὀδυρμὸς ἦν πάλαι μοι, Μέμνονος
τὰ πάθη γοῶσα, ἣν ἀφεῖλε Καμβύσης.
Ἄναρθρα δ[ὴ] νῦν καὶ ἀσαφῆ τὰ φθέγγματα
ὀλοφύρομ[α]ι, τῆς πρόσθε λείψανον τύχης.

—

**ἄναρθρος, ον:** inarticulate
**ἀσαφής, ές:** indistinct
**γοάω, γοήσω, ἐγόησα:** to groan, weep
**εἰκών, εἰκόνος, ἡ:** likeness, image
**ἐκμάσσω, ἐκμάξω, ἐκέμαξα, ἐκμέμαχα:** to mould, fashion
**ἑῷος, η, ον:** of the morning, eastern
**θραύω:** to break into pieces; to shatter
**Καικιλία Τρεβοῦλλα:** Caecilia Trebulla
**Καμβύσης, ὁ:** Cambyses
**λείψανον, τό:** remnant, remains
**Μέμνων, Μέμνονος, ὁ:** Memnon
**ὀδυρμός, ὀδυρμοῦ, ὁ:** lamentation
**ὀλοφύρομαι:** to lament, wail, moan
**παλαί:** (adv.) long ago
**πρόσθε:** (adv.) former, before
**φθέγμα, φθέγματος, τό:** voice, sound of the voice, language

—

*Meter: iambic trimeter*

**1–2. Καικιλία Τρεβοῦλλα ἔγραψα:** A profound and provocative statement. Trebulla calls attention to herself as the author of these lines and proudly takes ownership of them with the first person verb ἔγραψα. The exact reason for this is uncertain, but it may be a manner in which Trebulla can ensure that readers ascribe the verses to her, seeing as the remainder of the poem is written with Memnon himself as the speaker.

**2. τοῦδε Μέμνονος:** The use of the demonstrative ὅδε calls attention to the inscriptional nature of the poem, as it is carved onto this here statue of Memnon. The use of the genitive here is as the object of the hearing verb ἀκούσασα, which takes the genitive to describe the individual whom is heard.

**3–6:** Note the intricate, chiastic structure of the first four lines of this poem. Cambyses' destructive behavior (Ἔθραυσε, ἀφεῖλε) brackets the description of Memnon. Moreover, the alliterative ἐκμεμαγμένον both mimics Memnon's name and produces a slurring sound when read aloud, a sound that looks forward to Memnon's description of his voice as inarticulate and indistinct (line 7).

**3–8:** Cf. Balbilla 29.9-12 for the story of Cambyses' mutilation of Memnon. Here, Trebulla seems to be expanding on Balbilla's tale. Whereas

Balbilla simply states the Cambyses cut off Memnon's tongue and ears, Trebulla gives more detail, focusing on the Memnon's speech—or lack thereof—which is now inarticulate and indistinct (Ἄναρθρα ... καὶ ἀσαφῆ τὰ φθέγγματα).

3. **τόνδε τὸν λίθον:** As in line 2, the use of the demonstrative ὅδε calls attention to the inscriptional nature of the poem and to the immediate location of the statue of Memnon.

4–7: The soundplay in these lines is full of assonance that seems to mimic the droning of the statue's voice. Line 4 features -e and -o sounds: βασιλ**έος** **ἑῴου εἰ**κόνα **ἐ**κμ**ε**μαγμ**έ**ν**ο**ν. Line 5 features -o sounds: Φ**ω**νὴ δ' **ὀ**δυρμ**ὸ**ς ἦν πάλαι **μοι**, Μέμν**ο**ν**ο**ς. Line 7, -a sounds: Ἄ**να**ρθρ**α** δ[ὴ] νῦν **καὶ ἀσαφ**ῆ **τὰ** φθέγγματ**α**.

4. **βασιλέος ἑῴου εἰκόνα:** The reference to Memnon as an Eastern king has multiple resonances. First and foremost, as the son of Dawn (Ἠώς), he is quite literally an "eastern" king, and the use of ἑῴου here recalls his mother's name. Secondly, according to *Dictys Cretensis* 4.4, Memnon came to the aid of Troy in the Trojan war with an army of Indians and Ethiopians, generally regarded as Eastern peoples (At sequenti die Memnon, Tithoni atque Aurorae filius, ingentibus Indorum atque Aethiopum copiis supervenit. "On the following day, Memnon, the son of Tithon and Aurora, fell upon them with huge forces of Indians and Ethiopians."). Alternatively, we may also understand that Trebulla knows the original history of the Colossi, which were originally constructed in the image of Amenhotep III (see Introduction to Memnon). As such, potential mention of this history may reveal a knowledge of the history of the statues and an ability to blend Egyptian and Greek elements together into a composite poem.

4. **βασιλέος:** The inscription itself has βασιλέος, but this seems to be an alternative spelling of the genitive singular βασιλέως. Several editors have, in fact, attempted to emend the text to read βασιλέως. However, we have chosen to retain the original spelling from the stone.

4. **ἑῴου εἰκόνα:** As inscribed on the stone. There must be a hiatus between these two words to fit the meter.

5. **ἦν:** imperfect, third, singular, indicative of εἰμί.

5. **μοι:** The diphthong scans short.

6. **γοῶσα ἦν:** As inscribed on the stone. There must be a hiatus between these two words to fit the meter.

7. **Ἄναρθρα δὴ:** The force of the δὴ is to place emphasis on the Ἄναρθρα, resulting in a translation similar to "really inarticulate" or "quite inarticulate". It is this inarticulate nature of his words that leads to the inability for them to be understood (ἀσαφῆ).

7. **καὶ ἀσαφῆ:** As inscribed on the stone. There must be an elision between the two words to fit the meter. Some editors have emended the text to read κἀσαφῆ.

7. **φθέγγματα:** As inscribed on the stone. This appears to be a misspelling of the accusative plural φθέγματα.

## Damo

Damo is the author of one short epigram on the Colossus of Memnon. Her work is a brief poem in two elegiac couplets, inscribed on the left leg of the Colossus. Unlike many of the other authors of poems on the Colossus, we know nothing else about Damo. Her name was a popular one in the ancient world, and it appears in inscriptions throughout Egypt and elsewhere (Bernard and Bernard, 1960, p. 180). Moreover, the name Damo itself is not secure, as the stone has been damaged at the precise place where the name was described (cf. textual notes below). Likewise, the date of the inscription is uncertain. Scholars assume that it was inscribed in early 196 CE or later, but this assumption rests on the position of the inscription on the stone.[4]

Despite the paucity evidence about the biographical details of the author, the epigram itself shares much in common with the poetry of Julia Balbilla, and, indeed, may have been influenced by it, as she appeared to allude to Balbilla 29 with the opening line of the epigram. The most prominent feature of Damo's epigram is that it, like Balbilla's, employs an Aeolic dialect and is peppered by numerous Homeric phrases. Likewise, Damo self-identifies as a lyric poet, depicting herself as "song-loving" and a "beloved of the Muses", both of which are traditional images used by lyric poets to describe themselves. Moreover, she even portrays herself as playing a lyre (*barbitos* in Greek), an instrument already antique and anachronistic by the 2nd century CE.[5] Moreover, there is a lack of any sort of textuality in this epigram, and Damo seems to portray herself as existing in a purely oral culture of singing and listening to poems; in no place is reading or writing ever mentioned.[6] Damo's stance as a lyric poet in this epigram has led some scholars to postulate that she may have been a part of the poetic profession and, perhaps, composed other pieces that are no longer extant.[7]

Damo's emphasis on her status as a lyric poet and her use of the Aeolic dialect immediately brings Sappho into the picture as an obvious model. However, in contrast with Balbilla, Damo depicts her debt to Sappho in exclusively poetic terms, without any of the erotic undertones present throughout Balbilla's poems. As such, Damo seems to look to Sappho as means of creating an alternative reality of the distant past of song culture, a reality in which she is Sappho's poetic peer.

### *Damo (Bernand 83)*

Αὔως ὦ πάι χαῖρε· πρόφρων ἐφθέγξαο γάρ μοι,
   Μέμ[νον], Πειερίδων εἵνεκα, ταῖς μέλομαι
ἀ φιλαο[ιδὸς Δ]αμώ· ἐμὰ δ᾽ἐπὶ ἦρα φέροισα
   βάρβιτος [ἀει]σεῖτ᾽ ἆϊ [σόν], ὧγνε, κρέτος.

—

**ἁγνός, ή, όν:** pure, chaste, pure
**ἀείδω, ἀείσομαι, ἤεισα:** to sing
**βάρβιτος, ἡ/ὁ:** lyre; many-stringed musical instrument
**ἦρα, τα:** gifts, services, offerings
**κράτος, εος, τό:** strength, might
**μέλω, μελήσω, ἐμέλησα:** to be an object of care; to care for
**Πιερίδες, αἱ:** the Pierides, the Muses
**πρόφρων, ονος, ὁ/ἡ:** gracious, kindly
**φθέγομαι, φθέγξομαι, ἐφθεγξάμην:** to utter, creak, speak
**φιλάοιδος [α], ον:** fond of singing; song-loving
**πρόφρων:** (adjective) kind, kindly

—

*Meter: elegiac couplets*

1. **Αὔως:** Aeolic spelling of the genitive singular Ἠοῦς from Ἕως, ἡ.
1. **Αὔως ὦ πάι χαῖρε· πρόφρων ἐφθέγξαο:** Julia Balbilla 29.7 also uses similar phrasing to describe Memnon's greeting (χαῖρε, καὶ αὐδάσαις πρόφρων ἀσπάσδεο). Damo may be intentionally making an allusion to that inscription.
1. **ἐφθέγξαο:** uncontracted form of ἐφθέγξω. Second, singular, middle, aorist.
2. **εἴνεκα** = ἕνεκα.
3. **ἀ φιλαο[ιδὸς Δ]αμώ:** This phrase emphasizes Damo's self-presentation as a skilled lyric poet on par with her Sapphic and Homeric models. She even claims to be a care to the Muses and part of their practitioners. However, the key words φιλαοιδὸς Δαμώ are the most uncertain of the inscription, as they fall in a damaged piece of the stone. Moreover, even the name Δαμώ has been the topic of scholarly debate, as initial vowel of the name is so faintly inscribed that one could also read the name as Δαμώ or Δημώ. However, the use of the Aeolic α throughout the poem has led most to read the name as Δαμώ. For more, cf. Bernard and Bernard (1960), *ad loc.*

3–4. **ἐμὰ δ'ἐπὶ … κρέτος:** Damo here expresses the same desire to immortalize Memnon that Julia Balbilla did in poem 29.

3. **ἀ:** Aeolic spelling of ἡ.
3. **ἐπὶ ἦρα φέροισα:** This is an expression used multiple times by Homer (cf. *Il.* 1.572, 578; 14.132; *Od.* 3.164; 16.375; 18.56).
3. **φέροισα:** Aeolic spelling of φέρουσα.
4. **ἀεισεῖτ':** Aeolic spelling of ἀείσεται.
4. **ἄϊ:** Aeolic spelling of ἀεί.
4. **ὦγνε:** crasis of ὦ ἁγνέ.
4. **κρέτος:** Aeolic spelling of κράτος.

### *Julia Balbilla 1 (Bernand 28)*

By Julia Balbilla.
Whenever the August Hadrian[8] heard Memnon[9].

Egyptian Memnon, I came to find out, speaks from the Theban stone,
Whenever he is warmed by the rays of the sun.
As he saw all-ruling Hadrian[8], before the rays of the sun,
He greeted him, as he was able.[10]
Whenever Titan[11], driving through the heavens with his white horses,
Brought into shadow a second measure of hours,
As sounding bronze, again Memnon[9] sent forth a voice
Sharp-sounding; A third time too, he sent forth a sound.
Emperor Hadrian[8] himself then gave greetings kindly enough
To Memnon[9] and left on stone for future generations
Words signifying what he had seen and had heard.
It became clear to all that the gods love him.[12]

### *Julia Balbilla 2 (Bernand 29)*

Whenever I was in the presence of Memnon[9]
With Sabina Augusta[13].

Son of Dawn and majestic Tithon, Memnon[9],
Sitting opposite to the Theban city of Zeus,
Or Amenoth[14], O Egyptian king, as priests have recounted,
Learned in stories of old,
Greetings, speak kindly and welcome warmly this lady too,
The revered spouse of Emperor Hadrian[8].
A barbarous man cut off your tongue and ears,
Godless Cambyses[15]; yet with a miserable death
He paid the price, struck by the same sword tip
With which he had ruthlessly slain divine Apis[16].
But I do not believe that your statue will be destroyed,
As in my mind I saved for all time your immortal spirit.
For my parents and grandparents were pious,
Balbillus the wise and King Antiochus[17],
Balbillus the father of my royal mother,
And the father of my father, King Antiochus.
From the stock of these I too have received noble blood,
And these words are mine, Balbilla the pious.

### *Julia Balbilla 3 (Bernand 30)*

Whenever we did not hear Memnon[9] on the first day.

Yesterday Memnon[9], silent, received Hadrian's[8] wife[13]
So that noble Sabina[6] might come hither again.
For the lovely form of our royal lady pleases you;[18]

But when she comes again, send forth a divine sound
So that you may not anger the Emperor[8]; for too long already
You have fearlessly detained his lawfully wedded bride.
And so Memnon[9], fearing the might of great Hadrian[8],
Suddenly spoke, and the empress[13], hearing it, was glad.[19]

### *Julia Balbilla 4 (Bernand 31)*

I, Balbilla, heard from the speaking stone
The divine voice of Memnon[9] or Phamenoth[20].
I came together with the lovely royal Sabina[13],
And the sun made its course during the first hour.
In the fifteenth year of the reign of Emperor Hadrian[8],
As Hathyr[21] went through its twenty-fourth day.
On the twenty-fifth day of the month of Hathyr[21].

### *Sabina 1 (Bernand 32)*

Sabina Augusta[16],
Wife of emperor Caesar
Hadrian[8], within one hour
Heard Memnon[9] twice…

### *Caecilia Trebulla 1 (Bernand 92)*

By Trebulla.

When I heard the divine voice of Memnon[8],
I yearned for you, mother, and prayed you could hear it, too.

### *Caecilia Trebulla 2 (Bernand 93)*

Caecilia Trebulla,
Having heard Memnon[8]
A second time.

Although before we only had heard his voice from afar,
Now he greeted us as intimates and friends
Memnon[8], the son of Dawn and Tithon.
Has nature, the maker of all, given to stone
The ability to perceive and to speak?

### *Caecilia Trebulla 3 (Bernand 94)*

I, Caecilia Trebulla,
Wrote this, after hearing Memnon[9].

Cambyses[15] shattered me, this stone,
Molded in the image of an eastern king.
Long ago my voice was lamentation, groaning

The sufferings of Memnon[9], but Cambyses[15] destroyed it.
Now, I moan sounds inarticulate and indistinct,
The remnants of my former fate.

***Damo***

Son of Dawn, greetings! Speak kindly to me,
Memnon[9]; for I am a beloved of the Muses,
I, song-loving Damo. Bearing my gifts, the lyre
Will sing your might, o pure one, forever.

## Notes

1. Birley (1997), 251, puts it bluntly, calls the relationship "a lesbian relationship between the two women.". Other scholars are more hesitant to label it as such (cf. Hemelrijk, 1999, p. 170; Nisbet, 2007, p. 555–558).
2. Rosenmeyer (2018, p. 141); Bernard and Bernard (1960, p. 99).
3. Cf. Fein (1994, p. 83–84); Birley (1997, p. 250–251); Plant (2004, p. 151–152).
4. Plant (2004), 157: "The date of her visit to the Colossus cannot be determined with any certainty, except to note that her epigram was inscribed high on the left leg after the two inscriptions which frame it and so must be dated after them. One of these is dated, and so we can determine Demo's (sic) visit to Memnon was on 25th February AD 196, or some time later."
5. Plant (2004), 157; Rosenmeyer (2018), 165.
6. Rosenmeyer (2018), 165: "Damo presents herself explicitly as a lyric poet, complete with anchronistic lyre, beloved of the Muses; there is no trace of sexuality or, for that matter, textuality in her verses. Damo fashions a fantasy world of a purely oral song culture: Memnon 'speaks' and she 'sings back'.
7. Plant (2004), 157.
8. Hadrian was emperor of Rome from 117–138 CE.
9. According to the Homeric Hymn to Aphrodite ll.215ff, the goddess Dawn fell in love with Tithon, a prince of Troy, and took him away to the ends of the world. The lovers had a son named Memnon, who became the king of the Ethiopians and fought in the Trojan War on behalf of the Trojans (Hesiod, *Theogony* 984).
10. The inscription begins with a comparison of the two regents Hadrian and Memnon (ll.3-6). The effect seems to be to raise Hadrian to the level of the god-like hero Memnon.
11. Although the general meaning of this word refers to the mythical Titans, it can also be used to describe the Sun-God or Apollo, as it does here. The Sun-God was frequently thought to have driven the sun in a curved course across the sky via a chariot pulled by flying horses.
12. The inscription concludes with another comparison of Hadrian and Memnon (ll.11-14). As at the beginning, Hadrian and Memnon are placed at the opening of consecutive lines in order to draw their comparison into greater relief. However, whereas Memnon has been depicted as struggling to communicate and be understood through the entirety of the inscription, Hadrian is depicted as able to communicate effortlessly in both a verbal and written medium. Because of this, Hadrian is shown to be the superior regent.
13. Vibia Sabina (83–136/137 CE) was the wife of Hadrian. The two were married in 100 CE. In 128 CE, she was awarded the title *Augusta* "revered one".

14. Amenoth was another name for the Pharoah Amenhotep III (1417–1379 BCE), who originally constructed the two colossi.
15. Cambyses II was the king of the Achaemenid Empire from 530–522 BCE who led a conquest of Egypt. According to Pausanias 1.41.3, Cambyses broke the statue of Memnon into two pieces, with the top half of the statue thrown down and the bottom half still remaining intact.
16. Apis is an important Egyptian god of fertility, and is usually depicted in the form of a bull. In Herodotus 3.27ff., Cambyses II, during his conquest of Egypt, had priests bring the Apis bull to him and he stabbed the bull to death.
17. On both sides of her family tree, Balbilla was descended from elite families. On her father's side, she was the granddaughter of the last king of Syrian Commagene, King Antiochus. On her mother's side, she was the granddaughter of the astrologer Tiberius Claudius Balbillus, who was prefect of Egypt under Nero (55–59 CE) and the head of the museum in Alexandria.
18. This poem opens with Babilla attributing intent to Memon. She states that he did not make his traditional sound for the Empress Sabina when she first came to visit him in an effort to entice her to return for a second visit. Balbilla suggests that the reason for this is that Memnon is himself enamored of Sabina's beauty, describing her in eroticized terms. Rosenmeyer (2018, p. 161) points out that this, in fact, may be an oblique reference by Balbilla to Sappho's erotic poetry, particularly Sappho fr. 16 (in this volume). In that poem, Sappho describes her beloved Anactoria in similar terms. Such an apparent allusion, coupled with the Aeolicizing throughout the poem, seems to suggest that Sappho was a readily apparent poetic model in Balbilla's mind.
19. Balbilla moves from the eroticization of Sabina and Memnon's attraction to her to a warning for Memnon: next time the Empress comes, be sure to speak to her so as not to anger Emperor Hadrian. Memnon, having been warned and fearing Hadrian's wrath, obliges and speaks to Sabina. Balbilla thus sets up this situation as a contest of masculinities between the two regal males Hadrian and Memnon. By having Memnon oblige Hadrian out of respect for the latter's strength, Balbilla allows Hadrian to be the dominant male in a contest of masculine might.
20. Balbilla here may be showing her erudition and awareness of both the contemporary Greek and original Egyptian cultures. Greek and Roman tourists to the colossi frequently associated them with the Homeric hero Memnon. However, the colossi were actually erected to represent the pharaoh Amenhotep III. A colloquial variant of Amenhotep was Amenoth. Some scholars (West, 1978) read Phamenoth as a name synonymous with Amenoth, as that was the Egyptian word for the month of March and was thus more recognizable to Greek speakers. In such a reading, Balbilla would here be making a nod to both the Greek and Egyptian traditions of the colossi. Other scholars (Rosenmeyer, 2018; Bagnall and Rathbone, 2004) have suggested that it is actually a mistake and that the inscriber should have written Ἀμένοθ.
21. The Egyptian month of Hathyr generally corresponds to late October through late November. The 24th and 25th days of Hathyr in 130 CE would have been November 20th and 21st (cf. Hemelrijk (1998) p. 165–167 for more).

# Appendix A
## An Introduction to Ancient Greek Dialects

The principal dialects of ancient Greek in the Archaic and Classical periods are **Attic-Ionic** (consisting of both Attic and Ionic), **Aeolic** (consisting of Boeotian, Thessalian, and the Aeolic dialect of the Northeast Aegean, including the island of Lesbos), **West Greek** (consisting of Doric, Aetolian, Locrian, and Northwest Greece), and **Arcado-Cypriot** (consisting of Arcadian in the central Peloponnesus and Cypriot).

Most of the female Greek-writing authors in this volume employ their own native dialects as expressions of poetic identity, and several include elements of one or more additional dialects to demonstrate their "studied evocation" of other authors and/or traditions (Coughlan, 2020). Sappho, for example, uses the Aeolic dialect of Lesbos, but includes pepperings of Homeric language and morphology to signal an engagement with epic tradition and epicizing themes. Later female authors like Julia Balbilla signal that they are working within the tradition of Sappho by adopting her Lesbian Aeolic poetic voice. Erinna, who composes largely in the Doric of her native island of Telos in the East Aegean, also includes Aeolic features to express subtly a poetic identity that engages with Sappho and, perhaps, a tradition of women's poetry.

Corinna's utilization of the local Boeotian branch of the Aeolic dialect is an important feature of her epichoric style. The Boeotian dialect of her poetry pairs well with its author's tendency to weave local founding stories and legend together with broader, Panhellenic mythographies. Nossis, who is among the most explicit in this volume in declaring her literary affiliation with Sappho, composes her epigrams in a literary form of Doric appropriate to the conventions of inscriptional funerary epigram.

### Lesbian Aeolic: The Dialect of Sappho

Aeolic refers to a variety of dialects that were prominent in Boeotia, Thessaly, the island of Lesbos in the Northeast Aegean Sea, and some Greek cities on the west coast of what is now modern-day Turkey. Each of these regional areas developed distinctive dialectical characteristics. The dialectical differences between Lesbian Aeolic and Attic are many, but there are a few fundamental guidelines that may be helpful to someone who has become accustomed to the idiosyncracies of Attic.

*Psilosis:* All initial vowels and diphthongs have smooth breathings rather than rough. Examples: ἴππος in Aeolic is equivalent to ἵππος in Attic.

*Recessive Accents:* In Aeolic, the accents of most words (including verbs, nouns, and adjectives) are recessive, meaning the accent will go as far back as it can (to the antepenult, when possible), except in the case of prepositions (περί, ἀμφί) and ἀλλά, οὐδέ, μηδέ, and ἐπεί. In Attic, only the accents of (most) verbs are recessive.

*Vowels:* There are a number of vowel differences that are noteworthy.

*Alpha:*

a Aeolic deploys -ᾱ where Attic frequently uses -η.
b Aeolic frequently deploys –α where Attic uses –ε.
c Aeolic frequently has an -αις where Attic would have an -ας.
d Aeolic frequently has an -αι where Attic would have an -η or -ει

| *Lesbian Aeolic* | *Attic* |
|---|---|
| a. γᾶς μελαίνᾱς (gen., "black earth") | γῆς μελαίνης |
| a. ἆδυ ("sweet/sweetly") | ἥδυ |
| a. βᾶμα (nom./acc. neut. s. "walk") | βῆμα |
| b. ἄτερος ("other") | ἕτερος |
| b. ποτα ("ever") | ποτε |
| c. παῖς (nom., masc., sing. "all/every") | πᾶς |
| d. φώναισαι (aor. infin. "to speak") | φωνῆσαι |
| d. γελαίσας (aor. act. part., m. "laughing") | γελήσας |
| d. αἰ ("if") | εἰ |

*Epsilon:* (a) Aeolic sometimes uses -ε where Attic would use an -α

| *Lesbian Aeolic* | *Attic* |
|---|---|
| a. κρέτην (pres. infin., "to rule") | κρατεῖν |

*Eta:* (a) Aeolic frequently has an -η where Attic would have an -ει.

| *Lesbian Aeolic* | *Attic* |
|---|---|
| a. ἔχην (pres. infin., "to have") | ἔχειν |
| a. ἰππήων (gen. pl. "belonging to horses") | ἱππέων |

*Omicron and Omega:*

a Aeolic frequently has an -ο where Attic would have an -α, particularly after a -ρ.
b Aeolic frequently renders an -οι where Attic would have an -ου.
c Aeolic frequently has an -ο or -ω where Attic would have an -ου.

| *Lesbian Aeolic* | *Attic* |
|---|---|
| a. βρόχυς ("arm") | βραχύς |
| a. στρότος ("army") | στρατός |
| b. λίποισα (nom., f., s., pres., act. participle "leaving behind" | λιποῦσα |
| b. ἐθέλοισα (nom., f., s., pres., act. participle "wanting" | ἐθελοῦσα |
| c. ὄρανος and ὤρανος ("heaven/sky") | οὐρανός |

*Upsilon:* (a) Aeolic frequently has an -υ where Attic would have an -ο, particularly before labials.

| *Lesbian Aeolic* | *Attic* |
|---|---|
| a. δεῦρυ (adv. "hither/to this place") | δεῦρο |
| a. ἀπυστρέφονται ("they turn away from") | ἀποστρέφονται |

*Consonants:* There are a number of consonantal differences that are noteworthy.

- a *σδ:* Where Attic words contain -ζ (except as the first letter of a word), Aeolic has -σδ
- b *π:* Frequently replaces -τ in Attic
- c *μμ and νν:* Frequently appear as doubled consonants where Attic would have singular -μ or -ν
- d *ππ:* Infrequently appears where Attic would have -μμ
- e *πτ:* Sometimes appears where Attic would use -π
- f *βρ:* In place of Attic -ῥ or -ρρ

| *Lesbian Aeolic* | *Attic* |
|---|---|
| a. πέσδων (gen., "of infantry") | πέζων |
| a. ἀπυστρέφονται ("they turn away from") | ἀποστρέφονται |
| b. πήλοι (adv., "far away") | τηλοῦ |
| c. ὔμμες (nom. pl., "you") | ὑμεῖς |
| c. σελάννα ("moon") | σελήνη |
| d. ὄππα ("eye") | ὄμμα |
| e. πτόλιν (acc., "city") | πόλιν |
| f. βροδόπαχυς ("rosy-armed") | ῥοδόπηχυς |
| f. ἐπιβρόμεισι (pres., 3rd pl. indic. act., "buzz") | ἐπιρρόμβεισι |

*Other:*

- a *-μι verbs:* verbs that would, in Attic, sustain contraction in the present and imperfect tenses (i.e., verbs whose first principal parts end in -αω, -εω, or -οω) sometimes have –μι conjugations in Aeolic.

b *prepositions:* See the following table for the most distinctive differences in orthography between Lesbian Aeolic and Attic prepositions.
c *digamma:* ϝ occasionally appears in Aeolic forms of the third person personal pronoun.

| *Lesbian Aeolic* | *Attic* |
|---|---|
| a. φίλημι | φιλῶ |
| b. ὑπά | ὑπό |
| b. ὄν ὄνν | ἀνά |
| b. ἀπύ | ἀπό |
| b. πεδά | μετά |
| c. ϝάν (acc., "her") | Third person personal pronouns in Attic in oblique cases are generally expressed via αὐτός, -ή, -ό, and the Attic equivalent would be αὐτήν. |

## Boeotian Aeolic: The Dialect of Corinna

Corinna composed in a Boeotian dialect that is largely artificial and literary rather than in conformity to a spoken Boeotian dialect of a particular period in time. Although additional idiosyncrasies do occur, the following overview provides the principal vowel, consonantal, and prepositional differences between Boeotian Aeolic and Attic.

*Vowels:* There are a number of vowel and diphthong variations from Attic that are noteworthy.

| *Boeotian* | *Attic equivalent* | *Boeotian example* | *Attic equivalent* |
|---|---|---|---|
| ει | η | Κώρειτες ("Kouretes") | Κουρῆτες |
| η | αι | Κιθηρών ("Kithairon") | Κιθαιρών |
| ι | ει | ἔχι ("has") | ἔχει |
| οι | ῳ | ἄντροι (dat., "cave") | ἄντρῳ |
| ου | υ | ἔκρουψαν ("hid") | ἔκρυψαν |
| υ | οι | λόγυς (dat. p., "words, stories") | λόγοις |
| ω | ου | Κώρειτες | Κουρῆτες |

*Consonants:*

a ϝ occasionally appears in Beotian Aeolic forms.
b –ττ: in some instances where the equivalent in Attic is -σσ.

| *Boeotian Aeolic* | *Attic* |
|---|---|
| a. ϝῖκέ (3rd s., "came" or "arrived") | ἶκε |
| b. λιττάδα (acc., "smooth") | Λισσάδα |

*Prepositions:* The following table outlines the principal differences between Boeotian Aeolic and Attic prepositional orthography.

| *Boeotian Aeolic* | *Attic* |
|---|---|
| ἐν | εἰς |
| ἐς | ἐκ |
| ἐσς | ἐξ |
| ἐν | εἰς |
| ἀππά | ἀνά |

**Doric:** The Doric dialects were spoken in many areas throughout the Peloponnesus, on islands in the Aegean Sea (Crete, Rhodes, Thera, Cos), as well as in several colonized cities in the West (Syracuse and Tarentum, for example) and in Cyrene, Libya, in Northern Africa. Instantiations and incorporations of the Doric dialect occurred in genres as diverse as choral, lyric poetry, Attic drama, and Hellenistic epigram. Regarding the latter, Coughlan (2016) has pointed out that its authors often employed "self-conscious use" of dialect, coloring epigrams with smatterings of various dialects to signal their engagement with inscriptional and literary antecedents. Nossis composed largely in a literary form of Doric in keeping with the conventions of inscriptional sepulchral epigram and with the linguistic reality of her native Epizephyrian Locris (Coughlan, 2020). Some of the common features of literary Doric that appear in this volume include the following.

a *Alpha:* one of the most distinct features of literary Doric is its use of -ᾱ in instances where Attic would use -η and even –ω.
b *Feminine Participles Ending in -οισ*:* in Attic, -ουσ*.
c *Prepositions, Adverbs, and Pronouns:* see (c) below.
d *Middle Imperative Ending:* an ending of -εο for the second person, singular present tense imperative (Attic uses -ου).

| *Doric* | *Attic* |
|---|---|
| (a) Μιτυλήναν (acc., "Mitylene") | Μιτυλήνην |
| (a) ἁδύ | ἡδύ |
| (a) τᾶν (gen., pl. definite article) | τῶν |
| (b) χαίροισαν (acc., fem., pres., act. participle, "rejoicing") | χαίρουσαν |
| (c) ποτί ("to/towards") | πρός |
| (c) ὄκκα ("when") | ὅτε |
| (c) τηλῶθε ("from afar") | τηλόθε |
| (c) τήνα ("that woman; she") | ἐκείνη |
| (d) παραμείβεο ("pass, go by") | παραμείβου |

## Select Bibliography

Coughlan, T. S. 2016. "Dialect and Imitation in Late Hellenistic Epigram," in A. Rengakos and E. Sistakou (eds.), *Dialect, Diction, and Style in Greek Literary and Inscribed Epigram*. Berlin: De Gruyter, p. 37–70.

———. 2020. "The Poetics of Dialect in the Self-Epitaphs of Nossis and Leonidas of Tarentum," *Classical Philology* 115.4: 607–629.

# Appendix B
## Introduction to Ancient Meter

Ancient Greek and Latin poetic verse was composed in lines of long and short syllables in different combinations. These combinations imbued ancient poetry a variety of rhythms that furthered the meaning of the poetry and provided entertainment to the audience of the poems. In antiquity, these rhythms were called *metra* in Greek (μέτρον) and, therefore, have been refered to as **meter** through the present day.

Unlike the meters of English poetry, which are based on word-stress (stressed and unstressed syllables), Greek and Latin poetry relies on the length of syllables (long and short) to determine the rhythm of the meter. Long syllables are considered long because they take twice the time to pronounce as do short syllables. In musical notation, we may consider long syllables to be equivalent to a quarter note (♩) and short syllables equivalent to an eighth note (♪). In traditional metrical notation, long syllables are marked with a (–) above the long syllable and short syllables with a (⏑) above the short syllable.

Reading ancient poetry aloud in meter or analyzing the meter of a given line of poetry is commonly referred to as **scanning**. In order to successfully scan a line of poetry—and thus understand how it is contributing to the meaning of the line of poetry—one needs the ability to complete two tasks: (1) dividing Latin and Greek words into syllables and (2) determining the length of individual syllables.

### Dividing Up Greek and Latin Words into Syllables

A syllable is the smallest unit of sound that can be pronounced. A Latin or Greek word has as many syllables as it has vowels or diphthongs. To divide words into syllables, use the following rules:

1 A single consonant goes with the following vowel. If a word ends in a consonant, it goes with the preceeding vowel.

| | | |
|---|---|---|
| **Examples:** | **furor** | **fu/ror** |
| | **stadium** | **stu/di/um** |
| | **αὔγας** | **αὔ/γας** |
| | **θέοι** | **θέ/οι** |

2 If there are two or more successive consonants, the consonants are split and the final consonant goes with the following syllable.

| | | |
|---|---|---|
| **Examples:** | **Sulpicia** | **Sul/pi/ci/a** |
| | **Consulis** | **con/su/lis** |
| | **Μέμνονα** | **Μέμ/νο/να** |
| | **ὀψιγόνος** | **ὀ/ψι/γό/νος** |

3 If the two consonants combined are a mute followed by a liquid, they are sounded together.

a Mutes

- Greek: π, β, φ, κ, γ, χ, τ, δ, θ
- Latin: p, b, t, d, c, g

b Liquids

- Greek: λ, ρ, μ, ν
- Latin: l, r

| | | |
|---|---|---|
| **Examples:** | **ingluvie** | **in/glu/vi/e** |
| | **agricola** | **a/gri/co/la** |
| | **γλῶσσα** | **γλῶσ/σα** |
| | **ἔκλυον** | **ἔ/κλυ/ον** |

## Determining the Length of Individual Syllables

Determining the length of individual syllables in Latin and Greek words is relatively straightforward and follows standardized rules. To start, assume that all syllables are SHORT (⏑), unless proven otherwise. There are two ways to prove a syllable is LONG (–):

1 A syllable is long (–) by nature if it contains:

a a long vowel (these are all unmarked in the text)

- Greek: η, ω, ᾱ, ῑ, ῡ
- Latin: ā, ē, ī, ō, ū

b a diphthong

- Greek: αι, ει, οι, αυ, ευ, ου
- Latin: ae, au, ei, oe, ui

2 A syllable is long (–) by position if:

a a vowel is followed by two consonants
b a vowel is followed by double consonants

- Greek: ζ, ξ, ψ, or ῥ
- Latin: x

The only exceptions to these rules are:

1 If a vowel followed by mute consonant + a liquid consonant, it is often—but not always!—considered SHORT.

   a Mutes

   - Greek: π, β, φ, κ, γ, χ, τ, δ, θ
   - Latin: p, b, t, d, c, g

   b Liquids

   - Greek: λ, ρ, μ, ν
   - Latin: l, r

2 In Latin, **qu, ch, ph,** and **th** count as a *single* consonant. In Greek, **φ, χ,** and **θ** count as a *single* consonant.

## Elision and Hiatus

To further assist the poet in providing a variety of rhythms and in expanding vocabulary used in the poem, the practice of elision was followed. Elision occurs when the final syllable of a word is not pronounced and is, instead, elided into the beginning syllable of the subsequent word. Elision can occur at the following times:

In Latin:

- If a word <u>ends in a vowel or an -*m*</u> and the subsequent word <u>begins with a vowel or -*h*</u>.

In Greek:

- If a word <u>ends in a vowel</u> and the subsequent word <u>begins with a vowel</u>.

In metrical notation, an elision is typically marked by crossing through the elided syllable and writing the symbol (‿) between the elided words.

**Examples:**

– –  ⏑ ⏑ –
nuda**sse**‿**a**licui

–  ⏑⏑ –  ⏑ ⏑–
Romulidar~~**um**~~‿igitur

– ⏑  – ⏑⏑ –
Κοιράν~~**ωι**~~‿**Ἀ**δριάνῳ

Not every situation in which an elision is possible does the poet choose to employ it. In these situations, no syllable is an elided and every syllable is pronounced. This is termed **hiatus.** Each hiatus that occurs in the text will be marked in the commentary.

## Resolutions

Resolution is the substitution of one long syllable (–) or an anceps (x) with two short syllables (⏑⏑). Poets may choose to use resolution to provide more rhythmic variety or to help fit more words into the poetic line.

## Types of Meters in This Volume

Although these rules provide authors with a great deal of flexibility in crafting poetic lines, there were certain metrical patterns that were standard, and often associated with particular genres of poetry. Below is a listing of the meters used by the poetry in this volume, along with notes on each.

### *Dactylic Hexameter*

The Dactylic Hexameter is, perhaps, the most famous meter of ancient poetry. It is typically used in Greek and Roman epic poetry, as well as in Roman satirical verse. In this volume, the work of Sulpicia Caleni and Terentia are written in dactylic hexameter.

The base of this meter is the **dactyl**, which is one long followed by two shorts (– ⏑ ⏑). The dactyl can resolve its two shorts into a single long. When this occurs, the resulting two longs (– –) is called a **spondee**. This resolution can occur in any dactyl, but is highly unlikely in the fifth foot.

The last beat of each line of dactylic hexameter can be either long or short. In metrical terms, such a beat is called an **anceps** (*anceps* in Latin means "two-headed"). An anceps is notated with an (x).

Dactylic Hexameter: – ⏖ | – ⏖ | – ⏖ | – ⏖ | – ⏖ | – x

**Example:**

– ⏑ ⏑ | – ⏑ ⏑ | – ⏑ ⏑ | – – | – ⏑ ⏑ | – –
Musa, quibus numeris heroas et arma frequentas,
– – | – – | – ⏑ ⏑ | – – | – ⏑ ⏑ | – –
fabellam permitte mihi detexere paucis.
(Sulpicia Caleni 2.1-2)

### *Elegiac Couplet*

The Elegiac Couplet is one of the most frequent meters of ancient poetry. It is used in Greek and Roman Elegiac Verse, as well as in funerary contexts as a meter of emotional expression and lament. In this volume, the poems of Sulpicia, Moero, Erinna, Anyte, Damo, and Julia Balbilla are written in this meter.

The Couplet is comprised of two repeating lines: one dactylic hexameter and one dactylic pentameter.

The dactylic hexameter is discussed above, but the dactylic pentameter is made up of five dactyls, or more accurately four dactyls and two half dactyls. The first two dactyls can resolve, but the last two dactyls and the two half dactyls never change.

– ⏓⏓ | – ⏓⏓ | – ⏓⏓ | – ⏓⏓ | – ⏓⏓ | – x
– ⏓⏓ | – ⏓⏓ | – | – ⏑ ⏑ | – ⏑ ⏑ | –

**Examples:**

– – | – ⏑ ⏑ | – – | – – |– ⏑ ⏑ | – –
Tandem venit amor qualem texisse pudori
– – | – ⏑⏑ | – |– ⏑ ⏑ | – ⏑ ⏑ |–
quam nudasse‿alicui sit mihi fama magis.
(Sulpicia 1.1-2)
– – |– – | – ⏑ ⏑ | – – |– ⏑⏑ |– –
Αὔως ὦ πάι χαῖρε· πρόφρων ἐφθέγξαο γάρ μοι,
– – | – ⏑ ⏑ | – | – ⏑ ⏑ | – ⏑ ⏑ | –
Μέμ[νον], Πειερίδων εἵνεκα, ταῖς μέλομαι
(Damo 83.1-2)

### *Hendecasyllabic*

The Hendecasyllabic meter is popular in Greek and Latin lyric poetry. Hendecasyllabic lines are very regular, as each line has eleven beats (the Greek word for eleven = ἕνδεκα) and features only one place where a resolution can occur. The works of Martial are written in this meter.

Hendecasyllabic: x x | – ⏑ ⏑ | – ⏑ | – ⏑ | – –

**Example:**

– – | – ⏑⏑ | – ⏑ | – ⏑ |– –
Omnes Sulpiciam legant puellae,
– – | – ⏑ ⏑ |– ⏑ |– ⏑ | – –
Uni quae cupiunt viro placere;
(Sulpicia Caleni 3.1-2)

### *Iambic Trimeter*

The Iambic trimeter was the traditional meter of Greek and Roman tragedy, but iambs, in general, were also used in lyric poetry, particularly in lampooning and attacking poetry. This meter is built on three metra of two **iambs** (⏑ –). The first beat of each metron is an anceps. The poems of Caecilia Trebulla are written in this meter.

Iambic Trimeter: x – ⏑ – | x – ⏑ – | x – ⏑ –

**Example:**

– – ⏑ – | – – ⏑ – | ⏑ – ⏑ –
Αὔδῆς τὸ πρόσθεν μοῦνον ἐξακούσαντας,
– – ⏑ – |– – ⏑ – | – – ⏑ –
νῦν ὡς συνήθεις καὶ φίλους ἠσπάζετο
(Caecilia Trebulla 93.4-5)

## *Sapphic Stanza*

As its name suggests, Sapphic stanzas are a frequent meter of the poetry of Sappho. Generally, a sapphic stanza is a four-line stanza of poetry consisting of three Sapphic hendecasyllabic lines and one adonic.

Sapphic Hendecasyllabic: – ⏑ – x – ⏑ ⏑ – ⏑ – –
Adonic: – ⏑ ⏑ – –

**Example:**

– ⏑ – – – ⏑ ⏑ – ⏑ – –
φαίνεταί μοι κῆνος ἴσος θέοισιν
– ⏑ – – – ⏑ ⏑ – ⏑ – –
ἔμμεν' ὤνηρ, ὄττις ἐνάντιός τοι
– ⏑ – – – ⏑ ⏑ – ⏑ – –
ἰσδάνει καὶ πλάσιον ἆδυ φωνεί-
– ⏑ ⏑ – –
σας ὑπακούει
(Sappho 31.1-4)

## *Praxilleion*

The Praxilleion is a meter composed of three dactylic clausulae and a choriamb.

Praxilleion: – ⏑ ⏑ – ⏑ ⏑ – ⏑ ⏑ – ⏑ – x

– ⏑ ⏑ – ⏑ ⏑ – ⏑ ⏑ – ⏑ – ⏑
ὦ διὰ τῶν θυρίδων καλὸν ἐμβλέποισα
– ⏑ ⏑ – ⏑ ⏑ – ⏑ ⏑ – ⏑ – ⏑
παρθένε τὰν κεφαλὰν τὰ δ' ἔνερθε νύμφα

### *Corinna*

Although based in the traditional lyric meters of the **glyconic** and **ionic**, Corinna's poetry is more complex and less regular than the poetry of the other authors in this volume. Therefore, the scansion of each of her poems is given below.

*Corinna 654.iii.12-51*

This fragment features stanzas of five lines. The first four lines of each stanza are **polyschematic**. The final line of each stanza is a **pherecratean**. One can detect the foundational elements of the ionic *a minore* (⏑⏑– –) and the **glyconic** (x x –⏑⏑–⏑–).

Polyschematist: x x – x – ⏑⏑ –
Pherecratean: x x – ⏑⏑– –

**Example:**

– ⏑ – – – ⏑ ⏑ –
τᾶν δὲ πήδω[ν τρῖς μ]ὲν ἔχι
– ⏑ – – – ⏑ ⏑ –
Δεὺς πατεὶ[ρ πάντω]ν βασιλεύς,
– ⏑ – – – ⏑ ⏑ –
τρῖς δὲ πόντ[ω γᾶμε] μέδων
⏑ ⏑ – – – ⏑ ⏑ –
Π[οτιδάων, τ]ᾶν δὲ δουῖν
– – – ⏑ ⏑ – –
Φῦβος λέκτ[ρα] κρατούνι
(lines 12-16)

*Corinna 654.i.12-34*

This fragment features stanzas of six lines. The first five lines of each stanza are dimeters of **ionic *a minore***. The final line of each stanza is a hypermetric **glyconic** clausula.

Ionic *a minore* Dimeter: ⏑⏑– – ⏑⏑– –
Hypermetric Glyconic Clausula: ⏑⏑– – ⏑⏑– ⏑– –

**Example:**

⏑ ⏑ – – ⏑ ⏑ – –
μεγ]άλαν τ' [ἀ]θανάτων ἔσ-
⏑ ⏑ – – ⏑ ⏑ – –
ς] ἕλε τιμάν.' τάδ' ἔμελψεμ·

⏑ ⏑ – – ⏑ ⏑ – –
μάκαρας δ' αὐτίκα Μώση
⏑ ⏑ – – ⏑ ⏑ – –
φ]ερέμεν ψᾶφον ἔ[τ]αττον
⏑ ⏑– – ⏑ ⏑ – –
κρ]ουφίαν κάλπιδας ἐν χρου-
⏑ ⏑– – ⏑ ⏑ – ⏑ – –
σοφαίς· τὺ δ' ἅμα πάντε[ς] ὦρθεν·
(lines 17-22)

*Corinna 655 fr. 1*

This fragment has many lacunae and thus is difficult to fully comprehend. From what remains, the meter appears to be **polychematic**. However, each of the anceps beats has the ability not only be long (–) or short (⏑), but also to resolve into two shorts (⏑ ⏑), as it does in the first feet of each of the lines in the example below.

Polyschematist: x x – x – ⏑⏑ –

**Example:**

⏑ ⏑ ⏑ – ⏑ – ⏑ ⏑ –
ἐπί με Τερψιχόρα [καλῖ
⏑ ⏑ ⏑ – ⏑– ⏑ ⏑ –
καλὰ Fεροῖ' ἀϊσομ[έναν
⏑⏑ ⏑– ⏑ – ⏑ ⏑ –
Ταναγρίδεσσι λ[ευκοπέπλυς,
⏑ ⏑ ⏑ – ⏑ – ⏑ ⏑ –
μέγα δ' ἐμῆς γέγ[αθε πόλις
(lines 1-4)

*Corinna PMG 690*

This fragment uses a traditional **glyconic** meter, but freely resolves the anceps beats into three shorts (⏑ ⏑ ⏑) in lines 1, 3, and 7.

Glyconic: x x – ⏑⏑ – ⏑ –

**Example:**

⏑⏑ ⏑ – ⏑⏑ – ⏑ –
'Ά]ας μὲν ὠκιανῶ λιπῶ-
⏑ ⏑ – ⏑⏑ – ⏑–
σα π[αγὰς] ἱαρὸν φάος

⏑ ⏑ ⏑ –     ⏑ ⏑   – ⏑ –
σελάανας <σ>πάσα[τ' ὠραν]ῷ
– – –   ⏑⏑ –   ⏑ –
''Ωρη δ' ἐς Διὸς ἀμβρότῦ
(lines 1-4)

## Meter Quick Guide

Adonic: – ⏑ ⏑ – –
Dactylic Hexameter: – ⏖ | – ⏖ | – ⏖ | – ⏖ | – ⏖ | – x
Elegiac Couplet: – ⏖ | – ⏖ | – ⏖ | – ⏖ | – ⏖ | – x
– ⏖ | – ⏖ | – | – ⏑ ⏑| – ⏑ ⏑| –
Glyconic: x x – ⏑⏑ – ⏑ –
Greater Asclepidean: x x – ⏑⏑ – – ⏑⏑ – – ⏑⏑ – ⏑ –
Hendecasyllabic: x x | – ⏑ ⏑ | – ⏑ | – ⏑ | – –
Hipponactean: x x – ⏑⏑ – ⏑ – –
Acephalous Hipponactean with Double Coriambic Expression:
x – ⏑⏑ – – ⏑⏑ – – ⏑⏑ – ⏑ – –
Iambic Trimeter: x – ⏑ – | x – ⏑ – | x – ⏑ –
Ionic *a minore* Dimeter: ⏑⏑– – ⏑⏑– –
Hypermetric Glyconic Clausula: ⏑⏑– – ⏑⏑– ⏑– –
Pherecratean: x x – ⏑⏑– –
Polyschematist: x x – x – ⏑⏑ –
Praxilleion: – ⏑ ⏑ –   ⏑ ⏑ –   ⏑ ⏑ –   ⏑ – x
Sapphic hendecasyllabic: – ⏑ – x – ⏑ ⏑ – ⏑ – –

# Appendix C
## The Newest Sappho

In 2014, an American papyrologist and classicist Dirk Obbink, then among the faculty of Classics at Oxford University, published two fragments from papyri (the so-called "Brothers Poem" and the "Kypris Poem") in a journal article entitled, "Two New Poems by Sappho" in the *Zeitschrift für Papyrologie und Epigraphik* vol. 189, p. 32–49. The publication of these and additional fragments of Sappho followed in 2016 in a volume entitled, *The Newest Sappho: P. Sapph. Obbink and P. GC inv. 105, Frs. 1-4, vol. 2*, edited by Anton Bierl and André Lardinois and published by Brill. Chapter One of this volume, authored by Dirk Obbink, "The Newest Sappho: Text, Apparatus Criticus, and Translation," (p. 13–33), published what were widely regarded then as exciting, new fragments of Sappho apparently obtained from mummy cartonnage. Chapter Two of that volume, "Ten Poems of Sappho: Provenance, Authenticity, and the Text of the New Sappho Papyri," also authored by Dirk Obbink, has since been retracted by Brill in a "Retraction Notice" authored by the editors, Bierl and Lardinois, dated March, 2021.

The reasons for the retraction notice "include the serious doubts that have been raised in the years following the publication of this edited volume about the provenance of the newest Sappho papyri (P.Sapph.Obbink and P GC. inv. 105)." These papyri fragments are now alleged to have tainted provenance, and the possibility that they may have been obtained illegally through a Turkish dealer along with fragments from the Museum of the Bible's "Green collection" (P.GC inv. 105), have prompted the editors of the Brill volume to retract Obbink's chapter on the provenance and authenticity of the Sappho papyri (ch. 2). Although Professor Obbink was, according to the editors, given the opportunity to respond to the allegations before a decision was made to retract the essay, he neglected to or chose not to do so. The fragments have been repatriated to Egypt and are now inaccessible for examination by other scholars. In the absence of proof of provenance and in light of the papyri's present inaccessibility, suspicions of forgery have not been suppressed. However, at the time of this writing, no substantial proof that the papyri were forgeries has come to light.

Bierl and Lardinois, the editors of Brill's *The Newest Sappho*, have decided to make available the retracted chapter, both in print and online, with the watermark of "Retracted" on each page. The text and apparatus criticus (published in chapter one of the volume) have not been retracted.

For these reasons, we have made the decision to include several of the fragments published therein, but we do so in this appendix, given that the authenticity of their provenance has been brought under serious question through a series of events involving potential breaches of professional ethics at best and international law at worst. A select bibliography of relevant developments concerning the papyri follows. Especially important are Burris (2017), Sampson (2020), and Hyland (2021).

## Bibliography

Bierl, Anton and André Lardinois. 2021. "Retraction Notice," in Anton Bierl and André Lardinois (eds.), *The Newest Sappho: P. Sapph. Obbink and P.GC inv. 105, Frs. 1-4*, 2016, *Mnemosyne Supplements* vol. 392, vol. 2, Leiden: Brill.

Burris, Simon. 2017. "A New Join for Sappho's 'Kypris Poem': P.GC inv. 105 fr. 4 and P.Sapph.Obbink," *Zeitschrift für Papyrologie und Epigrafik* 201: 12–14.

Burris, Simon, J. Fish, and D. Obbink. 2014. "New Fragments of Book 1 of Sappho," *Zeitschrift für Papyrologie und Epigrafik* 189: 29–31.

Donelli, Giulia. 2021. "Herodotus, the Old Sappho and the Newest Sappho," *Lexis* 39: 13–34.

Ferrari, F. 2014. "Saffo e i suoi Fratelli e altri brani del primo libro." *Zeitschrift für Papyrologie und Epigrafik* 192: 1–19.

Hyland, Bryan. 2021. "A Note on the Provenance of the Sappho Fragments P.GC inv. 105," *Zeitschrift für Papyrologie und Epigrafik* 218: 1–16.

Liberman, G., 2014. "Reflections on aNew Poem by Sappho Concerning Her Anguish and Her Brothers Charaxos and Larichos," Paper delivered at F.I.E.C., Bordeaux, August, 2014. (English version). http://www.papyrology.ox.ac.uk/Fragments/Liberman.FIEC.Bordeaux.2014.pdf (Accessed 10/12/2021).

Lidov, J. B., 2002. "Sappho, Herodotus, and the *Hetaira*." *CP* 97.3: 203–37.

Obbink, Dirk. 2014. "Two New Poems of Sappho," *Zeitschrift für Papyrologie und Epigrafik* 189: 32–49.

———. 2015. "Interim Notes on 'Two New Poems of Sappho," *Zeitschrift für Papyrologie und Epigrafik* 194: 1–8.

———. 2015. "Provenance, Authenticity, and Text of the New Sappho Papyri," Paper read at the *Society for Classical Studies* "New Fragments of Sappho" panel, New Orleans, 9 January, 2015. http://www.papyrology.ox.ac.uk/Fragments/SCS.Sappho.2015.Obbink.paper.pdf

———. 2016. "Ten Poems of Sappho: Provenance, Authenticity, and the Text of the New Sappho Papyri," in Anton Bierl and André Lardinois (eds.), *The Newest Sappho: P.Sapph.Obbink and P.GC inv. 105, Frs. 1-4. Mnemosyne Supplements* vol. 392, vol. 2, Leiden: Brill, p. 34–54. RETRACTED.

———. 2016. "The Newest Sappho: Text, Apparatus Criticus, and Translation," in Anton Bierl and André Lardinois (eds.), *The Newest Sappho: P.Sapph.Obbink and P.GC inv. 105, Frs. 1- 4. Mnemosyne Supplements* vol. 392, vol. 2, Leiden: Brill, p. 13–33.

Sampson, Michael. 2020. "Deconstructing the Provenances of P.Sapph.Obbink," *Bulletin of the American Society of Papyrologists* 57: 143–69.

Smyth, Herbert Weir. 1984. *Greek Grammar*. Harvard University Press. (Original work published in 1920).

Stehle, E. 2016. "Larichos in the Brothers Poem: Sappho Speaks Truth to the Wine-Pourer." In A. Bierl and A. Lardinois (ed.), *The Newest Sappho: P. Sapph. Obbink and P. GC inv. 105, Frs. 1-4: Studies in Archaic and Classical Greek Song, vol. 2.* Leiden: Brill. p. 266–92.
West, M. L. 2014. "Nine Poems of Sappho." *ZPE* 191: 1–12.

### ***Sappho*, fr. 16a (proposed as a possible continuation of fr. 16)[1]**

[ὄλβιον] μὲν οὐ δύνατον γένεσθαι
[πάμπ]αν ἄνθρωπ[ον· π]εδέχην δ' ἄρασθαι
[ἔστιν ἔσλων μοῖραν. ἔγω] δ' ἔμ' αὔται
[τοῦτο σύνοιδα.]

[2-4 stanzas missing]

[.............................] [γέ]νεσθαι
ο [.......................]....βας ἐπ' ἄκρας
τα[.....................]ν χίον'· ἀ δὲ πόλλα
προσ[..................]

ωσδ[.......................]. ων ἀπέλθην
τω. [..........................].[.]. ατ'· ὄττινας γὰρ
εὖ θέω, κῆνοί με μάλιστα σίννον-
τ' ἐξ ἀδοκή[τω.]

*Meter: Sapphic Stanzas*

—

**ἀδοκήτος, -η, -ον:** suddenly, without warning
**ἄκρα, -ας, ἡ:** highest or farthest point; here, possibly "tip-toes"
**ἀπέρχομαι, ἀπελεύσομαι, ἀπήλθον, ἀπελήλυθα, —, —:** depart
**ἀράομαι, ἀράσομαι, ἠρησάμην, —, ἤραμαι, —:** pray
**δύνατος, -η, -ον:** able, powerful; with a pass. verb (such as οὐ δύνατον γένεσθαι), possible
**ἐσθλός, -ά, -όν:** good, noble
**μετέχω, μεθέξω, ——, μετέσκηκα, —, —:** partake of, have a share in
**μοῖρα, -ας, ἡ:** portion, lot, share of
**ὄλβιος, -α, -ον:** happy, prosperous, good
**πάμπαν:** wholly, altogether
**σίνομαι, σινήσομαι, ἐσινάμην, —, —, —:** harm, mistreat, injure
**σύνοιδα (pft. with pres. sense):** know (+ dat. reflexive pronoun= from one's own experience)
**χιών, -όνος, ἡ:** snow

—

**1. οὐ δύνατον γένεσθαι:** "it is not possible" or "it is not within one's power"
**2. πεδέχην** = Aeol. infinitive form of **μετέχω (Attic, μετέχειν)**
**2. ἄρασθαι** = Aeol. infinitive of ἀράομαι
**3. ἔσλων** = Attic ἐσθλῶν

**2–3. πεδέχην... μοῖραν:** The natural word-order in English of this phrase would be rendered into Greek thus: [δύνατον δ'] ἄρασθαι πεδέχην μοῖραν ἔσλων, "but, it is possible to pray to have a share of good things"
**3. ἔμ' αὔται:** = Attic, ἐμοὶ αὐτῇ, "from my own experience"
**5–10.** Lines are lost beyond reasonable reconstruction, but a few words and phrases are worth noting. In line 6, βας may be 2nd pers. s. aorist of βαίνω (you went/walked), in which case, "you went...on tippy-toes...in the snow"; line 7 introduces a subject "she", followed by the adverb or adjective "much/a lot"; finally, there is mention of a departing (ἀπέλθην) in line 9.
**7. ἀ:** = Attic, ἡ
**9. ἀπέλθην:** = Attic, ἀπέλθειν
**10. ὄττινας:** = Attic, οὕστινας
**11. θέω:** = Attic, τίθημι; while this verb has a wide range of semantic meaning, here it means something like "regard" or "treat"
**11. κῆνοί:** = Attic, ἐκεῖνοι
**11. σίννοντ':** = Attic, σίνονται
**12. ἐξ ἀδοκήτω:** = Attic, ἐξ ἀδοκήτως, suddenly, without warning

### *Sappho*, "Kypris Song"[2]

πῶς κε δή τις οὐ θαμέως ἄσαιτο,
Κύπρι, δέσποιν', ὄττινα [δ]ὴ φίλ[ησι,]
[κωὐ] θέλοι μάλιστα πάθαν χάλ[ασσαι;]
[ποῖ]ον ἔχησθα

[νῶν] σάλοισί μ' ἀλεμάτως δαΐσδ[ην]
[ἰμέ]ρω⟨ι⟩ λύ{ι}σαντι γόν' ωμε- [
[...]. α. α. . [.. ]αιμ' οὐ προ [...] ερης [
[...]νεερ. [.]αι

..............[.] σέ, θέλω [....]
[.... τοῦ]το πάθη[ν......]
[........]. αν, ἔγω δ' ἐμ' αὔται
τοῦτο σύνοιδα

[.........]. τοις[......].
[..............] εναμ[
[..................]
[.................]

*Meter: Sapphic Stanzas*

—

**ἀσάω, —,—, —, —, ἠσήθην:** feel nausea at/caused by a surfeit of (an accusative object); feel distressed at (an accusative object)
**γόνυ, γόνατος, τό:** knee
**δαΐζω, δαΐσομαι, ἐδάϊξα, —, —, —:** cleave, rend, tear, divide, slay

**δέσποινα, ἡ:** fem. of δεσπότης; mistress, queen
**ἠλέματος, -ον:** idle, in vain
**θαμέως:** adv., frequently, in a crowded or close-set manner, over and over again
**ἴμερος, -ου, ὁ:** desire, longing
**νόος, -ου, ὁ:** mind, sense, thought
**πάθη, -ης, ἡ:** misfortune, suffering
**σάλος, -ου, ὁ:** tossing motion, turbulence, agitation, restlessness, perplexity
**σύνοιδα (pft. with pres. sense):** know (+ dat. reflexive pronoun = from one's own experience)
**χαλάω, χαλάσω, ἐχάλασα, —, κεχάλασμαι, ἐχαλάσθην:** fall, give way, yield, lessen, release

—

**1. κε:** = Attic, ἄν. When this particle appears (as it does here) with an optative in an independent clause, the optative verb is one of potential, expressing what *could* or *would* happen in a hypothetical situation.

**2. Κύπρι:** vocative and a standard epithet of the goddess Aphrodite (see also, for ex., *Il.* 5.330). The poet Hesiod claims (*Theogony* 192–199) that she is called "Cyprian-born" ("Κυπρογενέα") because she came into being ("γέντο") on the island of Cyprus, where she was washed ashore after first touching upon the island of Cythera following her creation out of the sea-foam that arose when Ouranos' castrated testicles mixed with the sea.

**2. ὄττινα:** = Attic, ὅντινα

**2. φίλησι:** = Attic, φιλεῖ; contracted or vowel-stem verbs in Attic appear as athematic verbs (i.e., -μι verbs) in Aeolic. Thus, the Attic "φιλέω" conjugates as "φίλημι" in Aeolic.

**1–2. πῶς κε δή …ὄττινα δὴ φίλησι:** ὄττινα δὴ φίλησι is, in essence, the object of ἄσαιτο, but it is a bit awkward to capture in English. The following attempts to get at the sense, if not the exact meaning, of these lines: "how could one not, Cyprian Queen, repeatedly be nauseous about whomever one loves…".

**3. κωὐ:** = crasis consisting originally of κε + οὐ

**3. πάθαν:** = Attic, πάθην

**3. χάλασσαι:** aorist act. infin. (Doric and Aeolic)

**3. κωὐ θέλοι μάλιστα πάθαν χάλασσαι:** "And, how could someone not earnestly want release from suffering?"

**4. ποῖον ἔχησθα… νῶν:** 2nd s. med. of ἔχω; νῶν = Attic, νοῦν (acc. s.); the idiom νοῦν ἔχειν, in the sense of "intend, have a purpose, direct one's mind toward" seems to be in operation here, with the infinitive δαΐσδην as the object of that purpose. Perhaps the middle voice of ἔχησθα is intended to suggest that Aphrodite, the verb's addressee and subject (i.e., "you, Cyprian Queen"), keeps her own counsel for her own benefit and to the disadvantage of the narrator ἐγώ. ποῖον modifies νῶν, and literally means "what sort of mind/intention". The overall sense of the syntax of this phrase may be characterized as something like the following: "whatever do you have in mind, that you idly tear me apart in turbulence with desire that has unstrung my knees?"

**5. [νῶν]** = Attic, νόον (acc. s.); ποῖον... νῶν is the direct object of ἔχησθα

**5. σάλοισί:** = Attic, σάλοις

**5. ἀλεμάτως:** = Attic, ἠλεμάτως

**5. δαΐσδην:** = Attic, δαΐζειν

**6–16.** Although the remaining text is quite fragmentary, the few words and phrases that have been salvaged from the damaged papyri are worth examining closely.

**6. λύ{ι}σαντι:** = Attic, λύσαντι?

**6. γόν':** (with the elision of an –α) = Attic, γόνατα

**6. ἰμέρωι λύσσαντι γόν':** ἰμέρωι is perhaps a dative of instrument/means—that is, the means by which the goddess accomplishes the action of tearing the narrator apart (δαΐσδην). The image of desire "loosening" or undoing the strength of the limbs is elsewhere evoked by Sappho. For example, in a brief fragment that has come down to us (fr. 130 V, L-P), Sappho calls Eros "λυσιμέλης" ("loosener of limbs"): it is such a captivating image when set in context that the whole fragment is worth considering in conjunction with the "Kypris" poem:

Ἔρος δηὖτέ μ' ὀ λυσιμέλης δόνει,
γλυκύπικρον ἀμάχανον ὄρπετον.

Eros the limb-loosener once again is shaking me,
a sweet-bitter, irresistible, crawling creature.

**10. πάθην:** = Attic, πάθειν (aor. inf. of πάσχω)

**11–12. ἔμ' αὔται:** = Attic, ἐμοὶ αὐτῇ, "from my own experience"

### The Brothers Poem[3]

[π-(?)
[1 or 5 lines missing]
[3-4] λα[
[2-3]σέμα[

ἀλλ' ἄϊ θρύλησθα Χάραξον ἔλθην
νᾶϊ σὺν πλήαι. τὰ μὲν οἴομαι Ζεῦς
οἶδε σύμπαντές τε θέοι· σὲ δ' οὐ χρῆ
ταῦτα νόησθαι,

ἀλλὰ καὶ πέμπην ἔμε καὶ κέλεσθαι
πόλλα λίσσεσθαι βασίληαν Ἤραν
ἐξίκεσθαι τυίδε σάαν ἄγοντα
νᾶα Χάραξον

κἄμμ' ἐπεύρην ἀρτέμεας. τὰ δ' ἄλλα 13 (9)
πάντα δαιμόνεσσιν ἐπιτρόπωμεν·
εὔδιαι γὰρ ἐκ μεγάλαν ἀήταν
αἶψα πέλονται.

τῶν κε βόλληται βασίλευς Ὀλύμπω 17 (13)
δαίμον' ἐκ πόνων ἐπάρωγον ἤδη
περτρόπην, κῆνοι μάκαρες πέλονται
καὶ πολύολβοι·

κἄμμες, αἴ κε Fὰν κεφάλαν ἀέρρη 21 (17)
Λάριχος καὶ δή ποτ' ἄνηρ γένηται,
καὶ μάλ' ἐκ πόλλαν βαρυθυμίαν κεν
αἶψα λύθειμεν.

*Meter: Sapphic Stanzas*

—

**ἀήτης, -ου, ὁ:** gale, blast of wind
**ἀρτεμής, -ές:** safe and sound
**βαρυθυμία, -ας, ἡ:** heaviness of heart; sullenness; great sadness
**βασίλειος, -α, -ον:** royal; kingly; queenly; regal
**βούλομαι, βουλήσομαι, —, —, βεβούλημαι, ἐβουλήθην:** wish, be willing
**δαίμων, -ονος, ὁ, ἡ:** god or goddess; divine power; deity; the power controlling a person's destiny
**ἐξικνέομαι, —, ἐξίκομην:** arrive at a place
**ἐπαρωγός, -ου, ὁ:** helper; one who provides aid
**ἐπιτρέπω, ἐπιτρέψω, ἐπέτρεψα -ἐπέτραπον, ἐπιτέτραφα, —, ἐπετρέφθην:** commit to; entrust to
**εὐδία, -ας, ἡ:** fair weather
**θρυλέω, θρυλήσω, —, —, —:** repeat over and over; chatter; babble
**κέλομαι, κελήσομαι, ἐκελήσατο, —, —, —:** command; urge; call by name, call upon for aid
**κεφαλή, -ῆς, ἡ:** head
**μάλα:** (adv.) strengthens an assertion; certainly; quite; very
**ναῦς, νεώς, ἡ:** ship
**νοέω, —νοήσομαι, ἔνωσα (Ionic), νενόηκα, νενόημαι, ἐνοήθην:** (act.) think; consider; (pass.) apprehend; understand
**πέλω/πέλομαι, —, ἐπελόμην, —, —, —:** come into existence; become; be
**περιτρόπω:** turn around
**πλέως, πλέα, πλέων:** full, filled
**πολύολβος, -ον:** very blessed; very wealthy
**πόνος, -ου, ὁ:** trouble; pain; hard labor; toil

—

**1–4.** The text is too corrupt to be legible and may contain either four or nine lines (Obbink, 2016, p. 25). In the 3rd line, the letters ΛΑ appear; and, in the fourth, the letters ΣΕΜΑ.

**5. ἄϊ** = ἀεί (Attic) θρύλησθα is present tense ("you are always repeating" or, "you are always prattling on") and introduces indirect discourse (Χάραξον ἔλθην, "that Charaxos is coming…").

**5. Χάραξον:** Herodotus (2.134.1–2.135.6) tells the story of an enslaved Thracian woman named Rhodopis. Herodotus claims that she was the fellow slave of the fable-writer, Aesop, and that both she and Aesop were owned by a Samian son of Hephaestopolis named Iadmon. Rhodopis, Herodotus states, was brought to Egypt by another Samian man named Xanthes, from whom Sappho's brother Charaxos purchased her freedom for a lot of money before returning home to Mytilene. Living as a manumitted and freed woman in Egypt, she accumulated great wealth working as a *hetaera,* and, wanting to leave a memorial of herself in Greece, she dedicated 1/10th of her income in the form of iron bars (a kind of currency in the archaic Mediterranean world) at the sanctuary of Apollo at Delphi. Herodotus claimed that these iron bars still, in his day, could be seen behind an altar erected by the Chians in front of the shrine, and that the name of Rhodopis was still so famous that every Hellene knew her name. Herodotus concludes his narrative by saying that Sappho bitterly attacked Charaxos in one of her poems. See Lidov (2002) for a discussion of Rhodopis, Charaxos, Sappho, and Herodotus. Lidov argues that no such rebuke is to be found in any of the fragments of Sappho that have come down to us, and that Herodotus's story may very well be influenced by 5th century, comic representations of Sappho on the dramatic stage. Liberman (2014), however, suggests otherwise, and provides a biographical reading of several fragments of Sappho's poetry (frs. 5, 15, and 254a V, L-P, for example) that he reads as evidence for a love affair between Charaxos and Rhodopis/Doricha. Liberman (2014, p. 10) rightly points out that "in this poem [i.e., the "Brothers Poem"], it is Larichos who, because of his attitude, causes Sappho concern, whereas if she is worried about Charaxos, it is not related to the affair between Charaxos and Doricha, which may be earlier or later than the time to which our poem refers." Stehle (2016), however, cautions against reading the poem biographically and argues that Sappho (p. 267–268) "is presenting a fictionalized self" as "a woman commenting on the behavior of male relatives." Stehle argues convincingly that the unnamed addressee is Larichos, especially given that the letters ΛΑ are preserved in the otherwise illegible line 3. See also Donelli (2021).

**5. ἔλθην** = ἔλθειν (Attic)

**6. νᾶϊ** = νηΐ (Attic), the dat. sing. form of ναῦς. The noun is the dative object of the preposition σὺν and is modified by the adjective πλήαι (=πλέᾳ, Attic). The phrase νᾶϊ σὺν πλήαι ("with a full ship") suggests that Charaxos was involved in mercantile trade.

**6. οἴομαι:** This verb is parenthetical and does not grammatically introduce standard indirect discourse.

**8. νόησθαι:** a middle/passive infinitive form of the verb, νοέω (Attic), which takes the form of a -μι verb in the Aeolic dialect (νόημι). The infinitive is used in coordination with the impersonal verb χρῆ in line 4.

**9. πέμπην… κέλεσθαι: πέμπην** = πέμπειν (Attic) ("send me and call upon me"); both verbs are infinitives, which may be used in Greek in place of a second person imperative (see Smyth #2013), a construction which is found oftener in poetry than in prose.

**10. λίσσεσθαι:** this infinitive depends upon the infinitives of line 9 (see note above), and initiates the indirect discourse of lines 10–13 ("…to beg queenly Hera that Chraraxos, guiding his ship home, may arrive and find us safe").

**10. βασίληαν** = βασίλειαν (Attic)

**11. σάαν:** reflexive, possessive adjective ("his own")

**12. νᾶα** = ναῦν (Attic), accusative singular of ναῦς.

**13. κἄμμ'** = (crasi) καὶ ὑμᾶς (Attic).

**13. ἐπεύρην** = ἐπεύρειν (Attic), "to find"

**14. ἐπιτρόπωμεν:** a hortatory subjunctive

**15. εὔδιαι** = εὐδίαι (Attic)

**15. μεγάλαν ἀήταν** = μεγαλῶν ἀητῶν (Attic). ἀήτης is a masculine, first declension noun in Attic, but appears here as a feminine noun. The Attic form and gender are listed in the vocabulary above.

**17. τῶν κε βόλληται βασίλευς Ὀλύμπω:** κε = ἄν (Attic); βόλλομαι is the Aeolic form of the Attic verb βούλομαι, and βόλληται is subjunctive. Ὀλύμπω = Ὀλύμπου (Attic). This is an indefinite relative clause (see Smyth #1768), "of those whom the king of Olympus wishes…".

**19. περτρόπην:** from περιτρόπω or περιτροπέω, this is an infinitive. The Attic equivalent would be περιτρόπειν or περιτροπεῖν. It is used in both the *Odyssey* (9.465) and the *Homeric Hymn to Hermes* (line 542) as participles which denote the action of herding livestock by turning them from all sides into the center. Here, it suggests a turning around and away (ἐκ πόνων, "from troubles").

**17–19.** Various suggestions have been offered for these lines. Obbink (2016, p. 33) translates them as follows: "All of those whom the King of Olympus wishes/a divinity as helper to now turn them/from troubles…". West (2014) offers ἐπ' ἄρηον ("prayed for" or "desirable") as an emendation for ἐπάρωγον and translates, "those whose fortune the ruler of Olympus chooses to turn around from hardship for the better…". Liberman (2014, p. 7–8) translates these lines, "deflecting them away from misfortune to a better fate."

**21. κἄμμες** = (crasis) καὶ ὑμεῖς (Attic).

**21. αἴ** = εἰ (Attic)

**21. ἀέρρῃ:** ἀέρρω is the Aeolic form of ἀείρω (Ionic) or αἴρω (Attic) ("lift, raise"). ἀέρρῃ is a present subjunctive, 3rd s. active voice in the protasis of a mixed future condition.

**21. Fὰν:** a reflexive, possessive adjective modifying κεφάλαν ("his own head").

**22. Λάριχος:** According to Athenaeus (425a), Sappho praised her brother Larichos for being a wine-pourer in the prytany among the Mytileneans. Stehle (2016) convincingly argues that the addressee of the poem is Larichos. Others (Ferrari, 2014, p. 4; Liberman, 2014, p. 4; Obbink, 2014, p. 41; West, 2014, p. 8) have suggested that the unnamed addressee is Sappho's mother.

**22. γένηται:** another subjunctive, which, like ἀέρρῃ (line 16) serves as an additional protasis in a mixed future condition.

**23. πόλλαν βαρυθυμίαν** = πολλῶν βαρυθυμιῶν (Attic)

**23–24. κεν αἶψα λύθειμεν:** the apodosis of the mixed future condition begun at line 17. λύθειμεν is an aorist passive optative, first person plural. The basic structure of the condition: "if Larichos lifts his own head and one day becomes a man, we would, indeed, swiftly be released from great heaviness of heart…"

## Notes

1. Greek text derived from: Obbink, Dirk. 2016. "The Newest Sappho: Text, Apparatus Criticus, and Translation," in Anton Bierl and André Lardinois (eds.), *The Newest Sappho: P. Sapph Obbink and P. GC inv. 105, Frs. 1-4*. Brill, p. 13–33, esp. p. 19.
2. Greek text derived from: Obbink, Dirk. 2016. "The Newest Sappho: Text, Apparatus Criticus, and Translation," in Anton Bierl and André Lardinois (eds.), *The Newest Sappho: P. Sapph Obbink and P. GC inv. 105, Frs. 1-4*. Brill, p. 13–33, esp. p. 26-7.
3. Greek text derived from: Obbink, Dirk. 2016. "The Newest Sappho: Text, Apparatus Criticus, and Translation," in Anton Bierl and André Lardinois (eds.), *The Newest Sappho: P. Sapph Obbink and P. GC inv. 105, Frs. 1-4*. Brill, p. 13–33, esp. p. 25–26.

# Greek-English Glossary

ἁβρός, –ά, –όν: graceful, delicate, pretty, luxurious
ἀγάλλω, ἀγαλῶ, ἤγηλα, —, —, —: in the passive voice, take delight in or exult in a dative object
ἄγαλμα, -ατος, τὸ: statue (in honor of a god); glory; honor
ἀγανοβλεφάρος, -ον: having gentle or tender eyes
ἀγανός, -ή, -όν: gentle, mild
ἀγαυός, -ή, -όν: noble, illustrious
ἄγγελος, -ου, ὁ: messenger
ἀγήραος, -ον: ageless, without old age, eternally youthful
ἀγκουλομήτης (gen., –ου): (masc. first decl. adj.) adroitly clever; crooked of counsel; wily
ἀγλαΐα, -ας, ἡ: beauty; splendor
ἁγνός, -ή, -όν: holy, sacred, pure, chaste
ἁγνός, ή, όν: pure, chaste, pure
ἀγρότης, -ου, ὁ: rustic country-dweller
ἀδοκήτος, ον: suddenly, without warning, unexpected
Ἀδρίανος, ὁ: Hadrian. Emperor of Rome (117–138 CE).
ἄδυτον, -ου, τό: innermost sanctuary of a temple
ᾄδω, ᾄσομαι, ᾖσα, —, ᾖσμαι, ᾔσθην: sing
ἀεί: (adv.) always, eternally
ἀείδω ᾄδω, ἀείσομαι ᾄσομαι, ἤεισα/ἄεισα/ᾖσα, —, ᾖσμαι, ᾔσθην: sing; praise; celebrate; sing of (an accusative object); the middle voice often has active voice meaning
ἀζαλέος, -α, -ον: parched, dry, withered
ἀηδονίς, -ίδος, ἡ: nightingale
ἀηδών, -όνος, ἡ: songstress, nightingale (used as a metaphor here)
ἀήτης, -ου, ὁ: gale, blast of wind
ἀθάνατος, -ον: immortal, "without death"
ἄθεος: godless, god-denying
ἆθλον, -ου, τό: contest, game in which contestants compete for a prize
Ἄθυρ: Hathyr
ἄθραυστος, -ον: unbroken, unbreakable
ἄθυρμα, -ματος, τό: beautiful object, an adornment

ἀθύρω, —, —, —, —, —: play, make sport
αἰαῖ: an interjection registering grief or astonishment
Αἰγύπτιος, α, ον: Egyptian
Ἅιδης, -ου, ὁ: Hades, the netherworld to which the spirits of the departed go; also, Hades, the deity who lives in and rules over the netherworld
αἰδώς, -οῦς, ἡ: shame; respect; awe; reverence; sense of honor
αἰετὸς, -οῦ ὁ: eagle, the bird sacred to Zeus
αἰθήρ, -έρος, ἡ: sky; air (i.e., the bright sky between the heavens and earth)
αἰθύσσω: (usu. in present) set in rapid motion, stir up (*act.*); to quiver, of leaves (*pass.*)
αἴθω: to light up, kindle; to burn, blaze
αἷμα, -ματος, τό: blood
αἰνόμορος, -ον: fated to a sad end; fated to doom
αἰπύς, -εῖα, -ύ: sheer, lofty, high, steep
αἱρέω, αἱρήσω, εἷλον, ᾕρηκα, ᾕρημαι, ᾑρέθην: take hold of, grasp, seize
αἴσθησις, -εως, ἡ: perception, sense
αἶψα: quickly
ἀΐω, —, ἐπήϊσα, —, —, —: hear; perceive by hearing; listen to; takes a gen object when the object is a person; acc. object when the object is a thin
αἰών, -ῶνος, ὁ: time, life, age
ἀκοή, -ῆς, ἡ: ear
ἀκοιτής, ἡ: bedfellow, spouse
ἀκοίτης, -ου, ὁ, ἡ: wife, spouse
ἄκρα, -ας, ἡ: highest or farthest point; here, possibly "tip-toes"
ἀκρίς, -ίδος, ἡ: grasshopper
ἄκρος, -α, -ον: topmost point, top
ἀλγινόεις, -εσσα, -εν: painful, grievous
ἀλίπαστος, -ον: sprinkled with salt
ἅλις: (adv.) sufficiently
ἄλλοτε: (adv.) at another time, sometimes
ἄλλως: (adv.) otherwise
ἁλμυρός, -ά, -όν: salty, briny
ἄλοχος, -ου, ἡ: bed-mate, wife
ἄλσος, –ου, τό: sacred grove
ἀμάρυγμα, –ματος, τό: sparkling or flashing, particularly of the eyes
ἀμβροσία, -ας, ἡ: ambrosia, the nourishing substance eaten by the gods
ἀμβρόσιος, -α, -ον: immortal, divine
ἄμβροτος, -ον: immortal, divine
ἀμείβω, ἀμείψω, ἤμειψα, —, ἤμειπται, ἠμείφθην: change; exchange; (med.) answer another person in dialogue; respond
ἀμείλικτος, -ον: without pity, harsh, cruel
Ἀμένωθ, ὁ: Amenoth
ἅμμα, -ματος, τό: clothing

ἀμφιέπω, —, ἀμφίεπον, —, —, —: (verb appears only in pres. and aor. tenses) do honor or reverence to; tend to; go around; be all around; busy one's self about, look after; frequent

ἀνάθεμα, -ματος, τό: dedicatory offering; anything dedicated; votive offering

ἀνακαλέω, -καλῶ, -ἐκάλεσα, -κέκληκα, -κέκλημαι, -ἐκλήθην: summon back; call back again and again; summon the dead; call or summon by name

ἀνακοσμέω: adorn; adorn again

ἀναμίγνυμι, -μίξω, -ἔμιξα, —, -μέμιγμαι, -ἐμίχθην: mix (*act.*); be mixed or mingled together (*pass.*)

ἀναμιμνήσκω, αναμνήσω, —, —, —, ὠμνάσθην: (act.) call to mind again, remind (+ gen. or acc.); (*med.* or *pass.*) remember

ἀνάπαυμα, -ματος, τό: respite, repose, rest

ἀνάπαυσις, -εως, ἡ: rest, repose (from a thing in the genitive)

ἀναπαύω, -παύσω, -ἔπαυσα, -πέπαυκα, -πέπαυμαι, -ἐπαύθην: let rest, take a rest

ἄναρθρος, -ον: inarticulate

ἀνάριθμος, -η, -ον: countless, without number, measureless

ἀναρρίπτω, -ρίψω, -ἔρριψα, -ἔρριφα, -ἔρριμμαι, -ἐρρίφθην: to throw up

ἄνασσα, ἡ: queen

ἄνεμος, -ου, ὁ: wind, breeze

ἀνέρωχος, -ον: high-spirited, arrogant, lordly

ἀνέχω, ἀνέξω / ἀνεσχήσω, ἀνέσχον, ἀνέσχηκα —, —: to come forth; hold up

ἀνθέω, ἀνθήσω, ἤνθησα, ἤνθηκα, —, —, —: bloom; blossom; flourish

ἄνθος, -ους, τό: flower, bloom; brilliancy; brightness; blossom

ἄνθραξ, -ακος, ὁ: charcoal

ἀνορέα, -ας, ἡ: poetic word for ἀνδρεία; manliness, prowess, courage

ἀνορούω, —, ἀνόρουσα, —, —, —: verb form found only in the weak aor. in Homer (as here); start up, leap up

ἄντα: opposite to; facing (+ genitive)

ἀντί: (+ gen.) instead of, in place of

ἄντρον, -ου, τό: cave

ἀοιδή, -ῆς, ᾠδή, -ῆς (Attic), ἡ: song

ἀολλής, -ές: all together, in a crowd, as a horde

ἄορ, ἄορος, τό: sword, hanger

ἁπαλός, -ή, -όν: soft, delicate

ἅπας, ἅπασα, ἅπαν: all, the whole, the entire, all together (in pl.)

ἀπέρχομαι, ἀπελεύσομαι, ἀπῆλθον, ἀπελήλυθα, —, —: depart

ἀπέχω, ἀφέξω ἀποσχήσω, ἀπέσχον, –, –, –: (act.) keep (an accusative object) off or away from; (med.) hold one's self away from; keep (one's self) away from; abstain from

Ἆπις, ὁ: Apis

ἀποδέκομαι: to accept, admit to one's presence

ἀποφθίνω, -φθίσω, -ἔφθισα, —, —, —: perished, destroyed

ἀράομαι, ἀράσομαι, ἠρησάμην, —, ἤραμαι, —: pray
ἀργαλέος, -α, -ον: painful, grievous
ἄργυρος, -α, -ον: made of silver
Ἄρης, -εως, ὁ: Ares, the god of war and the blood-lust of battle
ἅρμα, -ματος, τό: chariot
ἄρουρα, -ας, ἡ: earth, ground, land
ἄρρηκτος, -ον: unbroken
ἀρτεμής, -ές: safe and sound
ἀρύω, —, ἤρυσα, —, —, ἠρύσθην: draw water
ἀρχηγός, -ή, -όν: ancestral hero or heroine; founder; originator
ἀσαφής, -ές: indistinct
ἀσάω, —,—, —, —, ἠσήθην: feel nausea at/caused by a surfeit of (an accusative object); feel distressed at (an accusative object)
ἄση, -ης, ἡ: pain, anguish, distress
ἀσθμαίνω: breathe hard, pant (only appears in the present tense)
ἀσπάζομαι: to greet kindly, welcome
ἀσπάσιος, -α, -ον: glad, well-pleased
ἀστός, -οῦ, ὁ: citizen
ἄστρον, -ου, τό: (usu. in plural) star
ἄστυ, ἄστεος/ἄστεως, τό: city
ἀσφαλέως: (adv.) certainly, firmly, surely
ἀταλός, -ή, -όν: tender; delicate
ἀταρβής, -ές: fearless
ἅτε: as if, just as
ἀτέρωτα: at another time
ἀτρέκεια, -ας, ἡ: precise or absolute truth; certainty
αὖ: again, once more
αὐγή, -ῆς, ἡ: light (of the sun), ray
αὐδάω, αὐδήσω, ηὔδησα, ηὔδηκα, ηὔδημαι, ηὐδήθην: to speak, utter
αὐδή, -ῆς, ἡ: human voice; speech
αὐλή, -ῆς, ἡ: courtyard; enclosed yard wherein domestic animals are kept
αὖλος, -ου, ὁ: a wind instrument consisting of a reed pipe whose sound marginally resembles that of a modern oboe
ἀϋμήν, -μένος, ὁ: scent, fragrance, breath
αὔξω, αὐξήσω, ηὔξησα, ηὔξηκα, ηὔξημαι, ηὐξήθην: make increase, grow
αὐτίκα: immediately, at once
αὐτόθι: (adv.) from this spot; on the spot
αὐτοκράτωρ, αὐτοκράτορος, ὁ/ἡ: absolute ruler
αὐχήν, -ένος, ὁ: neck, throat; narrow strait or narrow passage of the sea
αὔω, ἀΰσω, ἤϋσα, –, –, –: cry out, shout, call upon; call out; cry aloud
ἀφαιρέω, ἀφαιρήσω, ἀφεῖλον, ἀφῄρηκα —, —: to take away
ἄφθιτος, -ον: imperishable, not subject to death
ἀφύσσω, ἀφύξω, ἤφυσα, —, —, —: draw, especially liquids from a vessel with a smaller vessel
ἀχά, ἡ: sound, noise

ἀχραής, -ές: pure
ἄψ: back again
ἀψεύδεια, -ας, ἡ: truth; utter lack of falsehood; inerrant truthfulness
βάρβιτος, ἡ/ὁ: lyre; many-stringed musical instrument
βαρυθυμία, -ας, ἡ: heaviness of heart; sullenness; great sadness
βαρύς, -εῖα, ύ: heavy, grievous, hard to bear, oppressive
βασίλειος, -α, -ον: royal; kingly; queenly; regal
βασιλεύς, βασιλέως, ὁ: king
βασιληίς: royal
βάσκανος, -ον: malicious
βένθος, -εος, τό: depth, of a body of water
βῆμα, –ματος, τό: walk, gait, footfall
βιοτή, -ῆς, ἡ: life
βλώσκω, μολοῦμαι, ἔμολον, μέμβλωκα, —, —: to go, come
βοάω, βοήσομαι, ἐβόησα, βεβόηκα, βεβόημαι, ἐβώσθην: cry aloud, call for, shout
βόστρυχος, -ου, ὁ: hair, curl, lock of hair
βότρυς, -υος, ὁ: grape-cluster; bunch of grapes
βούλομαι, βουλήσομαι, —, —, βεβούλημαι ἐβουλήθην: want, wish, be willing; with ἤ, prefer
βουχανδής, -ές: holding an ox; big enough to hold an ox
βραχύς, -εῖα, -ύ: brief, short
βρέτας, -εος, τό: wooden image of a god or goddess
βρέφος, -εος, τό: infant
Βρομίος, -ου, ὁ: an epithet (and alternate name) of Bacchus, Dionysus
βροτοκτόνος, -ον: mortal-slaying, man-killing
βύσσινος, -η, -ον: made of linen
βυσσόθεν: (adv.) from the bottom (of the sea)
βῶλος, -ου, ἡ: clod of earth, soil
βῶμος, –ου, ὁ: altar
γαῖα, -ας, ἡ: earth; land
γαμέω, γαμῶ/γαμήσω, ἔγημα, γεγάμηκα, γεγάμημαι, ἐγαμήθην: wed, marry
γάμος, -ου, ὁ: wedding, marriage
γαῦρος, -ον: haughty; prideful; splendid; disdainful; exultant
γελάω, γελάσομαι/γελάσω, ἐγέλασα, —, γεγέλασμαι, ἐγελάσθην: laugh
γενεά, -ας, ἡ: race, family, stock
γενέθλη, -ης, ἡ: race, family, line of descendants
γενέτης, -ου, ὁ: begetter, parent; ancestor; father
γένος, -εος, τό: family; tribe; clan; kin
γένυς, -υος, ἡ: jaw
γεραρός, η, ον: majestic, honored
γέρας, -αος, τό, -ή, -όν: reward, prize, gift, privilege
γηθέω, γηθήσω, ἐγήθησα, γέγηθα, —, —: rejoice (perf. tense often used as present tense); rejoice in a dat. object
γῆρας, -αος, τό: old age

γίγνομαι, γενήσομαι, ἐγενόμην, γέγονα, γεγένημαι, ἐγενήθην: to become, be

γλαμφηλαί, -ῶν, αἱ: the maw or jaws of an animal; the beak or bill of a bird

γλῶσσα, -ης, ἡ: tongue

γνωτός, -ή, -όν: perceived; known; understood

γοάω, γοήσομαι γοήσω, ἐγόησα, —, —: groan, weep, bewail

γοερός, -ά, -όν: mournful; wailing; lamenting

γονεύς, -έως, ὁ, ἡ: parent; ancestor

γόνυ, γόνατος, τό: knee

γράμμα, -ματος, τό: drawing; painting; picture; written character; letter; writings (pl.); inscription; anything written or drawn

γραπτός, ή, όν: written, painted

γράφω, γράψω ἔγραψα, γέγραφα, γέγραμμαι, ἐγράφθην: to write, scratch, inscribe

γυῖον, -ου, τό: limb

γυνή, γυναῖκος, ἡ: woman

δαγύς, -ῦδος, ἡ: doll

δαιδάλεος, -α, -ον: cunningly crafted; intricately wrought

δαιδαλόεις, -εσσα, -εν: cunningly crafted; intricately wrought

δαΐζω, δαΐσομαι, ἐδάϊξα, —, —, —: cleave, rend, tear, divide, slay

δαίμων, -ονος, ὁ, ἡ: god or goddess; divine power; deity; the power controlling a person's destiny

δάϊος, -ου: enemy, foe

δαΐφρων, -ον: warlike, fiery; wise

δάκρυ, τό: (does not appear in the genitive case) tear

δαμνάω: subdue, conquer

δάσκιος, -ον: thickly shaded, bushy

δάφνη, -ης, ἡ: bay or laurel tree

δαφοινός, -όν: savage, cruel

δειλός, -ή, -όν: cowardly; vile; worthless

δειμαίνω: (only in present and imperfect tenses) fear

δεξιός, -ά, -όν: the right side; often used in the fem. to refer to the right hand

δέρκομαι, δέρξομαι, ἔδρακον, δέδορκα, —, ἐδέρχθην: see, see clearly (perfect tense has a present sense); look on or at; flash or gleam

δέσποινα, ἡ: fem. of δεσπότης; mistress, queen

δεῦρο: here, thither, to this place

δεύτερον: (adv.) for a second time

δεύτερος, -α, -ον: second

δεύω, δεύσω, ἔδευσα, —, δέδευμαι, ἐδεύθην: wet, drench

δέχομαι, δέξομαι, ἐδεξάμην, —, δέδεγμαι, ἐδέχθην: accept, receive, take

δῆλος, -η, -ον: clear, visible

Δημήτηρ, τερος/τρος, ἡ: Demeter

δημιουργός, -οῦ, ὁ: maker, craftsman

δηρός, -ά, -όν: too long

δηῦτε = δὴ αὖτε: yet again

δίννημι (Aeolic) = δινέω (Attic): whirl, eddy

Διονυσία, -ας, ἡ: Dionysia

δίς: (adv.) twice

διττός, -ή, -όν: double; two-fold; both

διώκω, διώξω, ἐδίωξα, δεδίωχα, δεδίωγμαι, ἐδιώχθην: pursue, chase

δνοφερός, -ά, -όν: dark, murky

δοκιμόω: to think, suppose

δολόπλοκος, -ον: weaver of cunning manipulation or stratagems

δόμος, -ου, ὁ: house

δόναξ, -ακος, ὁ: reed-stalk, anything made of reeds (such as a pan-pipe)

δρέπω, δρεψεῦμαι (Dor. only), ἔδρεψα, —, —, ἐδρέφθην: (usually appears in the middle voice of the present and imperfect tenses) (act.), pluck; gain possession or enjoyment of a thing; (med.) pluck for one's self; pluck or crop (a genitive object)

δρόμος, -ου, ὁ: course, race

δρυοκοίτης, -ου, ὁ, ἡ: dwelling in or on oak trees or trees generally

δρύπτω, δρύψω, ἔδρυψα, –, δέδρυμαι, –: tear, strip

δύνατος, -η, -ον: able, powerful; with a pass. verb (such as οὐ δύνατον γένεσθαι), possible

δυσπειθής, -ές: hard to persuade, unyielding, implacable

δῶρον, -ου, τό: gift

ἔαρ (or, ἦρ), ἔαρος (or, ἦρος), τό: (form appears in both uncontracted and contracted forms in Attic), spring, springtime

ἐγγύθεν: nearby; an adverb that is frequently complemented by a genitive noun indicating what something is close to

ἐγείρω, ἐγερῶ, ἤγειρα, —, ἐγήγερμαι, ἠγέρθην: wake, rouse

ἐγκαταναίω, —, ἐγκατενασσα, —, —, —: make dwell in

ἐγκατατίθημι, -θήσω, -ἔθηκα, -τέθηκα, -τέθειμαι, ἐτέθην: lay or put in

εἴδω: to see (see ὁράω)

εἴκελος, -η, -ον: like (to) or resembling an object in the dat. case

εἰκόσι: (indeclinable) twenty

εἰκοστός, -ή, -όν: twentieth

εἰκών, -όνος, ἡ: image, likeness, representation (often in art)

εἷμα, -ματος, τό: garment, robe

εἶπον: to speak (aorist)

εἰσακούω: to hear, give ear to

εἰσοράω, -ὄψομαι, -ίδω, -όρακα/-ώρακα, -ώραμαι, -ὤφθην: look at, behold, gaze at

ἐκγεννάω: to beget, bear, bring forth

ἐκμάσσω, ἐκμάξω, ἐκέμαξα, ἐκμέμαχα, —, ἐκεμάγην: to mould, fashion

Ἕκτωρ, -ορος, ὁ: prince of Troy whose name means "holding fast". He is the "keep" or "stay" of Ilium.

ἐλαφρίζω: be light and nimble

ἐλάω: to drive (poetic form of ἐλαύνω)

ἐλέφας, -αντος, ὁ: elephant; in the neuter form, used as an adjective meaning "ivory"
ἕλιγμα, -ματος, τό: anything that twists or wraps, such as a bracelet or lock of hair; probably "bracelet" here
ἑλικῶπις, -ώπιδος, ἡ: a distinctively fem. form of the adj. ἑλῑ́κωψ, -ωπος, ὁ, ἡ. Quick-glancing; with eyes that dart about; bright-eyed
ἔλπω: (related to Attic ἐλπίζω): (act.), cause to hope or expect; (med.), expect; hope
ἐμβλέπω, —, —, ἐμβέβλοφα, —, —: look directly at; gaze intently upon; look
ἐν: in (+ dat.)
ἐναντίος, -α –ον: (+ dat.) opposite to, facing
ἔναυλος, –ου, ὁ: dwelling, shelter, haunt (esp. of the gods)
ἐναύω, ἐναύσομαι, ἔναυσα, —, —, —: (act.) kindle; light; (med.) draw inspiration from (an acc. object); light a fire for oneself
ἐνέπω, ἐνισπήσω ἐνίψω, ἔνισπον, —, —, —: to speak or utter; to tell the tale of
ἐνιαυτός, ὁ: lapse of one year; anniversary
ἐνοπή, -ῆς, ἡ: voice; sound of crying or shouting
ἔντεα, -ων, τά: weapons; armor; shields
ἐντός: within (+ genitive)
ἐξαπίνης: (adv.) suddenly
ἐξερύω, ἐξερύσω, ἐξέρυσα, —, —, —: draw out
ἐξικνέομαι, —, ἐξίκομην, —, —, —: arrive at a place; reach a destination
ἔοικε: (an impersonal verb), it is fitting; it is right (that an accusative object do the action of an infinitive)
ἐπαρωγός, -ου, ὁ: helper; one who provides aid
ἐπαυρέω, ἐπαυρήσομαι, ἐπηυρόμην, —, —, ἐπαυρέθην: (act.) partake of, share in a thing; (med.) reap the fruits; enjoy the benefit of a thing
ἔπειτα: (adv.) thereupon, thereafter, then
ἐπήρατος, -ον: charming, lovely
ἐπιδεής, -ές/ἐπιδευής, -ές (poetic form): lacking, deficient in, in need of
ἐπιλαμβάνω, -λήψομαι, -έλαβον, -εἴληφα, -εἴλημμαι, -ελήφθην: seize, attack
ἐπίπας, -πασα, -παν: all (of something) together; the whole or sum of something
ἐπιρρομβέω: make a buzzing or whirring sound
ἐπιτρέπω, ἐπιτρέψω, ἐπέτρεψα ἐπέτραπον, ἐπιτέτραφα, —, ἐπετρέφθην: commit to; entrust to
ἐπιφλέγω, -φλέξω, -ἔφλεξα, —, -πέφλεγμαι, -ἐφλέχθην: kindle; burn
ἔραμαι, ἐράσομαι, ἠρασάμην, —, ἤρασμαι, ἠράσθην: desire passionately, love
ἐρατός, ή, όν: beloved; lovely, charming; desired; alluring
ἐρείδω, ἐρείσω, ἤρεισα, ἔρεικα, ἐρήρεισμαι/ἤρεισμαι, ἐρείσθην: attack, push, thrust

ἔριθος, -ου, ὁ, ἡ: day-laborer; worker in wool; weaver; spinsters
Ἑρμῆς, -οῦ, ὁ: a Herm statue; the god Hermes
ἐρόεις, -εσσα, -εν: lovely, charming
ἔρομαι / ἐρέω, ἐρήσομαι, ἠρόμην, —, —, —: ask
ἔρος, -ου, ὁ: love, desire
ἑρσήεις, -εσσα, -εν: dewy, fresh
ἐρύω [ep., ἐρύσσω], ἐρύσω, εἴρυσα [Ep. εἴρυσσα], —, —, —: draw, pull, row
ἔρχομαι, ἐλεύσομαι, ἦλθον, —, —, —: come, go
ἔρως, ἔρωτος, ὁ: desire, love
ἐσθλός, -ά, -όν: good, noble
ἔσχατος, -η, -ον: furthest, uttermost, extreme
ἑτερόπτολις, ὁ, ἡ: of another city
ἔτι: still, yet
ἔτυμος, -η, -ον: true
εὐδία, -ας, ἡ: fair weather
εὐθαλής, -ές: blooming, flourishing, thriving
εὔκομος, -ον: lovely-haired; with good foliage
εὐλεχής, -ές: bringing happiness in marriage
εὔλυρος, -ον: skilled in the lyre
εὐμαρής, -ές: (it is) easy (+ infinitive)
εὐνή, -ῆς, ἡ: bed
εὐρύοπα, ὁ: far-thundering; this adjective is used in Homer only in the nominative and vocative, and only of Zeus
εὐρύχορος, -ον: spacious, characterized by wide-open spaces
εὐσεβής, -ές: pious, religious, righteous
εὔστᾰχυς, -υ: rich in corn; blooming, fruitful
ἐΰτροχος, -ον: smoothly-running
εὐχόμαι, εὔξομαι, εὐξάμην, —, —, —: to pray
ἐφάπτω, ἐφάψω, ἔφηψα, —, ἐφήμμαι, ἐφήφθην: bind, make fixed or fast; (med.) lay hold of; reach; touch (+ gen.)
ἐφίημι, -ήσω, -ῆκα/-εἶτον, -εἶκα, -εἶμαι, -εἵθην: (+ gen.) long for, desire
ἐφίστημι, -στήσω, -ἔστησα/-ἔστην, -ἕστηκα, -ἕσταμαι, -ἐστάθην: erect, set in place, place upon
ἐφοράω, ἐπόψομαι, -εἶδον, —, —, -ὄφθην: look at or upon, observe, see, behold
ἔχις, -εως, ὁ: viper, poisonous serpent
ἔχω, ἕξω σχήσω, ἔσχησα ἔσχον, ἔσχηκα, ἔσχημαι, ἐσχέθην: to hold
ἑῷος, -η, -ον: of the morning, eastern
ζάθεος, -α, -ον: divine, sacred, holy
ζεύγλη, -ης, ἡ: loop attached to the yoke (through which an animal's head was placed)
Ζεῦς, Δίος: Zeus
ζέω, ζέσω, ἔζεσα/ζέσσα, —, —, —: boil or bubble up, seethe (of water or liquids)

῞Ηβη, -ης, ἡ: youth, prime of youth
ἡγεμονεύω: to lead the way; rule, command
ἡδυβόης, -ες (Doric, Ἁδυβόας): sweet-sounding
ἡδυμελής, -ές: sweetly singing
ἡδύς, -εῖα, -ύ: sweet, pleasant
ἠίθεος, -ου, ὁ: unmarried young man or youth
ἠιών (or, ἠϊών), -όνος, ἡ: beach, shore
ἠλακάτη, -ης, ἡ: distaff, the spindle onto which wool or flax is wound for spinning
ἠλέματος, -ον: idle, in vain
ἡλίκος, -η, -ον: how great; how much; how greatly
ἡλίος, -ου, ὁ/ἡ: sun
ἧμαι: (appears only in the present and imperfect tenses) sit, be seated
ἡμίθεος, -ου, ὁ: demi-god; a being possessed of lesser divine status, such as a minor deity or the offspring of a god and mortal
ἡμίονος, -ου, ἡ: mule (literally, "half-donkey")
ἠνεμόεις, -εσσα, -εν: windy, stirred or waved by the wind
ἡνία, -ων, τὰ: bridle, reins
ἡνίκα: then; at that time; when
ἡνίοχος, -ου, ὁ: chariot-driver (literally, "the one who holds the reins")
ἤπειρος, -ου, ἡ: land, earth, mainland
ἦρα, τα: gifts, services, offerings
ἠρινός, –ή, –όν: of spring
ἠρίον, -ου, τό: tomb
ἥρως, -ος, ὁ: hero; a race of mortals descended from the gods
ἠχή, -ῆς, ἡ: echo; ringing or returning sound
Ἠώς, Ἠόος, ἡ: Eos, the goddess of Dawn
ἠώς, ἠοῦς, ἡ: dawn
θαλάμος, -ου, ὁ: bedroom, bridal chamber
θαλία, –ας, ἡ: good cheer; (in pl.) festivities
θάλλω, θαλήσω, ἔθηλα, τέθηλα,—, —: grow, bloom, flourish
θαμά: (adv.) often
θαμέες, οἱ, dat. θαμέσι, acc. θαμέας, adv. θαμέως: thickly crowded, often, frequently, in a crowded or close-set manner, over and over again
θάμνος, -ου, ὁ, ἡ: bush, shrub, copse of bushes or shrubs
θάσσω: to sit
θεάομαι, θεάσομαι/θεήσομαι, ἐθεασάμην, —, τεθέαμαι, —: contemplate; observe as a spectator; see clearly; gaze at; behold
θείνω, θενῶ, ἔθεινον, —, —, —: (act.), strike; dash; (pass., only in pres. and imperf.), stricken; dashed
θεῖος, -α, -ον: divine
θεός, -οῦ, ὁ: god
θέρμη, -ης, ἡ: heat; when it is hot; summer heat
θερμός, -ή, -όν: hot
θέρος, -εος, τό: summer, summer heat

θεσπέσιος, -α, -ον: divinely sweet, divinely sounding
Θηβαΐκος, -η, -ον: Theban
Θηβαῖος, -η, -ον: Theban
θιγγάνω, τεθίξομαι, ἔθιγον, —, —, ἐθίχθην: reach; win; touch upon; touch, take hold of; engage in
θραύω, θραύσω, ἔθραυσα, —, τέθραυσμαι, ἐθραύσθην: to break into pieces; to shatter
θρῆνος, -ου, ὁ: dirge; lament
θρίξ, τρίχος, ἡ: hair
θροέω, —, ἐθρόησα, —, —, —: utter, speak, murmur
θρυλέω, θρυλήσω, —, —, —: repeat over and over; chatter; babble
θυμιάω, θυμιήσομαι, ἐθυμίησα, τεθυμίηκα, τεθυμίαμαι, —: burn incense or to cause to smoke (*act.*); smoking or burning (with incense) (*med.*)
θυρίς, -ίδος, ἡ: window
θυώδης, -ες: smelling of incense, fragrant
ἰάχω: resound, ring out, shout
ἴδιος, -α, -ον: one's own; personal; private
ἴδρις, ἴδριος: learned, experienced, knowing
ἱδρώς, -ῶτος, ὁ: sweat
ἱερεύς, -έως, ὁ: priest
ἱερός, -ά, -όν: holy, consecrated, filled with divine power, sacred
ἱζάνω: sit
ἵζω, εἵσομαι, εἷσα/ἵζησα, ἵζηκα, —, —: (act.) cause to sit; place; set; seat; (med.) set up and dedicate (in honor of the gods)
ἵημι, ἥσω, ἧκα, εἷκα / ἕωκα, εἷμαι / ἕωμαι, εἵθην: to throw, hurl, send forth
κατέχω: to detain, hold back
ἵκανω (= ἵκω): (this form of the verb appears only in the pres. and imperf. tenses; the fut., aor., and pft. are all derived from a related form of the verb, ἱκνέομαι) come to, arrive; reach; attain; approach as a suppliant; beseech; supplicate
ἱκνέομαι, ἵξομαι, ἱκόμην, —, —, —: come to or arrive at a place
ἵκω, ἵξω, ἶξον/ἶξα, —, ἶγμαι, —: come, come upon
Ἰλιάδαι, -ων, οἱ: descendants of Ilos, Trojans
ἱμείρω: desire
ἱμερόεις, -εσσα, -εν: charming, inducing desire
ἵμερος, -ου, ὁ: desire, longing
ἰόκολπος, -ον: violet-colored, draping robes
ἰός, -οῦ, ὁ: venom of a serpent
Ἰουλια Βαλβίλλα, ἡ: Julia Balbilla
ἱππεύς, –εως, ὁ: member of the cavalry; chariot-fighter; horseman
ἵππιος, -α, -ον: of horses or horse-races
ἱππόβοτος, –ον (βόσκω): grazed by horses
ἵππος, -ου, ὁ: horse
ἴσος, -η, -ον: equal to; equal; like

ἵστημι, στήσω, ἔστησα/ἔστην, ἕστηκα, ἕσταμαι, ἐστάθην: erect, set in place, place upon, make stand (transitive); stand (intransitive)

ἴσχω: (reduplicative form of ἔχω and only found in pres. and imperf. tenses) hold; keep

ἴτυς, -υος, ἡ: shield; outer rim of a shield

καθαρός, -ά, -όν: clean, clear, pure

καθεκτός, -ή, -όν: in the grip of, held back by, restrained by

καθοράω, κατόψομαι, κατώρα, καθεώρακα, κατῶπμαι, κατώφθην: look down upon; perceive; regard

Καικιλία Τρεβοῦλλα: Caecilia Trebulla

Καῖσαρ, Καῖσαρος, ὁ: Caesar

καλλίχορος, -α, -ον: characterized by beautiful dances; with beautiful dancing-grounds (as an epithet for a city)

κάλλος, –ους, τό: beauty

κάλπις, -ιδος, ἡ: urn, pitcher (in this case, used for collecting votes)

καλύπτω, καλύψω, ἐκάλυψα, —, κεκάλυμμαι, ἐκαλύφθην: cover, veil, conceal, hide

Καμβύσης, ὁ: Cambyses

κάμνω, καμοῦμαι, ἔκαμον, κέκμηκα, —, —: toil, labor, fall sick, be weary

καπυρός, -ά, -όν: crackling; dry; brittle; clear-sounding; loud

καρδία, -ας, ἡ: heart

κάρτος, -εος, τό: strength

κασία, -ας, ἡ: cassia, a spice like cinnamon

κατάγνυμι, -ἄξω, -ἔαξα, -ἔαγα, —, -ἐάγην: break

καταίρω/καταέρρω, καταρρήσω, — κατερύηκα, — κατερρύην: flow, stream, or sink down

κατακλαίω, —, —, —, —, —: lament; bewail loudly; weep

κατακτείνω: to kill, slay

καταλείπω, καταλείψω, κατέλιπον, καταλέλοιπα, καταλέλειμμαι, κατελείφθην: leave behind, abandon, forsake

κατάρχω, κατάρξω, κάτηρξα, —, κάτηργμαι, κατήρχθην: make a beginning of; commence; begin

καταχέω, καταχέω, κατέχεα, κατακέχυκα, κατακέχυμαι, κατεχύθην: (note: the present and the future have the same form) pour, shower down (*act.* and *med.*); be poured over (*pass.*)

κατοδύρομαι: mourn

καῦμα, -ματος, τό: burning heat of the sun

κεῖμαι, κείσομαι, —, —, —, —: (only in pres., imperf., and fut.); lie; be placed (regularly used instead of the perfect passive of τίθημι; see Smyth #791); am laid

κεκρύφαλος, -ου, ὁ: hair-net

κελαδέω, κελαδήσομαι, ἐκελάδησα, —, —, —: make the sound of running water

κέλομαι, κελήσομαι, ἐκελήσατο, —, —, —: command; urge; call by name, call upon for aid

κεραός, -ά, -όν: horned
κεφαλή, -ῆς, ἡ: head
κεφάλη, -ης, ἡ: head
κηδεστής, -ου, ὁ: father-in-law; brother-in-law; a family member by marriage
κῆρυξ, κήρυκος, ὁ: herald, public messenger
κισσός, -οῦ, ὁ: ivy
κλέος, τό: (this noun only appears in the nom. or acc.): fame, (good) reputation
κλῆμα, -ατος, τό: twig or branch, especially of the grape vine
κλύω: to hear
κοιράνειος, -ον: belonging to a sovereign
κοίρανος, -ου, ὁ: king, ruler
κόλπος, -ου, ὁ: lap; bosom; loose folds of a woman's robe
κόμη, -ης, ἡ: hair; locks of hair
κόρα, -ας, ἡ: daughter
κόρη, -ης, ἡ: young girl, usually of marriageable age; daughter
κορυφή, -ῆς, ἡ: head
κοσμέω, κοσμήσω, ἐκόσμησα, κεκόσμηκα, κεκόσμημαι, ἐκοσμήθην: adorn; arrange, set in order; embellish
κοτέω: to be angry, bear a grudge
κουρίδιος, -α, -ον: (lawfully) wedded
κράνεια, -ας, ἡ: spear made of cornelian cherry wood (a type of dogwood tree)
κράς, κρατός, τό: head
κρατερός, -ά, -όν: strong, mighty
κρατέω, κρατήσω, ἐκράτησα, κεκράτηκα, κεκράτημαι, ἐκρατήθην: hold sway, hold power over, prevail, conquer, get possession of
κρατήρ, -ῆρος, ὁ: a crater–a large bowl used to mix wine with water from which cups were filled
κράτος, -εος, τό: strength, might
κρατύνω: with an acc. or gen., take possession of, possess; become master of
κρέκω, —, ἔκρεξα, —, —, —: play an instrument (in the dative case)
κρήνη, -ης, ἡ: well, fountain, spring, source of water
Κρής, Κρητός, ὁ: Cretan, from the isle of Crete
Κρήτη, –ης, ἡ: Crete (island in the Aegean Sea)
κρόταλον, -ου, τό: a percussion instrument consisting of two castanet-like clappers held in one hand and struck together with the fingers of that hand; often used in accompaniment with dancing
κρύπτω, κρύψω, ἔκρυψα, κέκρυφα, κεκρύψομαι, ἐκρύφθην: hide, conceal, cover
κρύφιος, -α, -ον: hidden, concealed
κρωσσός, -οῦ, ὁ: an urn holding the cinerary remains of the deceased
κτῆσις, -εως, ἡ: property; wealth; possessions

κυάνεος, -α, -ον: dark blue, black
κυβερνάω: to steer
κυδιάω/κυδιόω: (this verb appears in the present tense only) bear oneself proudly, exult
κῦδος, -εος, τό: glory, renown
κυκλόεις, -εσσα, -εν: circular
κύλιξ, –ικοξ, ἡ: wine-cup
κυλίω (a later form of κυλίνδω): roll (an accusative object) along
κῦμα, -ματος, τό: wave
Κύπρις, -ιδος, ἡ: Cypris, an epithet of Aphrodite
κῶλον, -ου, τό: limb
κῶμα, κώματος, τό: deep sleep
λᾶας, λᾶος, ὁ: stone
λαγχάνω, λήξομαι, ἔλαχον, εἴληχα, εἴληγμαι, ἐλήχθην: obtain by lot, get by chance, come into possession of, get as one's lot in life
λαθράδαν: secretly; a secret; a thing kept hidden; unknown
λαιμός, -οῦ, ὁ: throat, gullet
λαιψηρός, -ά, -όν: nimble, quick, light
λαμπρός, -ά, -όν: bright, brilliant, clear, shining
λανθάνω, λήσω, ἔλαθον, λέληθα, ἐπιλέλησμαι, —: forget; escape one's notice; cause to forget
λάσιος, -α, -ον: shaggy, bushy, wooly
λέβης, -ητος, ὁ: kettle, cauldron
λείβω, –, ἔλειψα, –, –, –: pour forth (act.); be running (with tears) (pass.)
λειμών, –ῶνος, ὁ: grassy meadow
λείψανον, τό: remnant, remains
λέκτρον, -ου, τό: marriage-bed
λέπαδνον, τό: broad leather strap (fastening the yoke to the neck)
λέπτος, -η, -ον: fine, thin, subtle
λευκόπεπλος, -ον: white-robed
λευκός, -ή, -όν: white, bright
λέχος, -εος, τό: bed
λήθη, -ης, ἡ: forgetfulness
λίβανος, -ου, ὁ: frankincense
λιβανωτός, –οῦ, ὁ: incense
λιγυρός, -ά, -όν: clear-toned
λιγύς, λίγεια, λιγύ: clear-sounding, ringing, whistling, or singing
λίθος, -ου, ὁ: stone
λιπαρός, -ά, -όν: bright, brilliant; oily smoothness; shiny
λισσάς, -άδος: bare, smooth
λίσσομαι, —, ἐλισάμην, —, —, —: beg, entreat
λόγιος, -α, -ον: well-versed in stories or tales; eloquent
λοιπός, -ή, -όν: remaining, left
λοίσθιος, -α, -ον: last, final, remaining

λούω, λούσω, ἔλουσα, –, λέλουμαι, ἐλούθην: (act.) wash (an object); (med.) bathe (oneself)
λυγρός, -ά, -όν: baneful, mournful
Λυδός, -οῦ, ὁ: Lydian; Lydia is a region of what is now modern-day Turkey
λύπη, -ης, ἡ: pain, grief
λῷστος, -η, -ον: best; most agreeable
μαίνολης, –ου: frenzied, maddened
μαίνομαι, μανοῦμαι μανήσομαι, ἐμηνάμην, μέμηνα, μεμάνημαι, ἐμάνην: rage, be enraged; be driven mad; be frenzied
μάκαρ, μάκαιρα, μάκαρ: blessed; fortunate; happy
μάλα: (adv.) strengthens an assertion; certainly; quite; very
μάντις, -εως, ὁ: seer, prophet, diviner
μαντόσυνος, -η, -ον: oracular
μαρμάρεος, -α, -ον: made of marble
μαρμάρινος, -η, -ον: marble, made of marble
μάρναμαι, —, —, —, —, —, ἐμαρνάσθην: (this verb usually only appears in the present and imperfect tenses); fight, strive, contend
μάρπτω, μάρψω, ἔμαρψα, —, —, —: seize, reach, catch
μεγαλωστί: (adv.) far and wide, over a vast space
μέδων, -οντος, ὁ: ruler
μεθαρμόζω/μεθαρμόττω, —, μεθηρμοσάμην, —, —, —: change from one mode of music into another
μείγνυμι or μίγνυμι or μειγνύω or μίσγω, μεῖξα, ἔμειξα, μέμειγμαι, —, ἐμείχθην/ἐμίγην: mix with; join with; have sex with
μειδιάω: smile
μειλιχίος, -α, -ον: soothing, mild, gentle, gracious
μείς, μηνός, ὁ: month
μελάθρον, -ου, τό: house
μέλας, μέλαινα, μέλαν: black, dark, murky
μέλι, -ιτος, τό: honey; anything sweet; eloquence
μελιχρός, -ά, -όν: honey-sweet
μέλος, -εος, τό: limb
μέλος, -εος, τό: song
μέλπω, μέλψω, ἔμελψα, —, —, —: to celebrate in song and/or dance
μέλω, μελήσω, ἐμέλησα, μεμέληκα, —, —: to be an object of care; to care for
Μέμνων, Μέμνονος, ὁ: Memnon
μέμψις, -εως, ἡ: blame; censure; fault
μενεδήιος, -ον: staunch, steadfast, especially in the face of battle or danger
μένος, μένεος, τό: might, force, strength
μερίμνα, –ας, ἡ: care, anxiety, distress
μέσσω = μέσου (Attic, μεσός, –ή, –όν)
μεταβάλλω, μεταβαλῶ, μετέβαλον, —, —, —: change; alter; undergo a change
μεταπλάσσω: to mold differently; to remodel

μετέχω, μεθέξω, —, μετέσκηκα, —, —: partake of, have a share in
μέτρον, -ου, τό: length, measure (of life)
μήλινος, -η, -ον: made of apples or quinces
μῆλον, -ου, τό: apple
μητιόεις, -εσσα, -εν: wise in counsel, clever-minded
μιμνήσκω, μνήσω, ἔμνησα, —, μέμνημαι, ἐμνήσθην: (*act.*) call to memory, remind (+ gen. or acc.); (*med.* and *pass.*) remind one's self, remember (+ gen. or acc.)
μνῆμα, -ματος, τό: a memorial or monument in honor of the dead, grave
Μοῖρα, -ας, ἡ: death, fate, destiny
μοῖρα, -ας, ἡ: portion, lot, share of
μολπαῖος, -ον: tuneful
μορφή, -ῆς, ἡ: form; appearance; shape; beauty
μῦθος, -ου, ὁ: story, word, speech
μυριάς, -άδος, ἡ: literally, 10,000 (of something); figuratively, countless
μύρρα, -ας, ἡ: myrrh, the resinous gum of an Arabian tree
Ναΐς, -ΐδος, ἡ: a Naiad, or river nymph, spring nymph
ναίω: to dwell, live
νᾶμα, -ματος, τό: river, stream, spring, anything that flows
ναός, νεώς, ὁ: temple; innermost part of a shrine
ναῦς, νεώς, ἡ: ship
ναύτης, -ου, ὁ: sailor
νεβρίον, -ου, τό: possibly a diminutive of νεβρός, -οῦ, ὁ, fawn
νέκταρ, -αρος, τό: nectar, the nourishing substance that the gods drink
νεκτάρεος, -α, -ον: fragrant, nectarous
νέκυς, -υος, ὁ: corpse
νέμω, νεμῶ, ἔνειμα, νενέμηκα, νενέμημαι, ἐνεμήθην: graze, feed on pasture; deal out, distribute
νέομαι: (pres. and imperf. only), come, go
νηλής, -ές: pitiless, ruthless
νήπιος, -ον: child; childlike; innocent; foolish
νίσομαι/νίσσομαι: (usually in the present or imperf.), come; go
νοέω, νοήσομαι, ἔνωσα (Ionic), νενόηκα, νενόημαι, ἐνοήθην: (act.) think; consider; (pass.) apprehend; understand
νόος, -ου, ὁ: mind, sense, thought
νόσος, -ου, ἡ: disease; sickness
νοτίς, -ίδος, ἡ: moisture, wetness
νύμφη, -ης, ἡ: young woman; bride; newly married wife; daughter; girl of marriageable age
Νύμφη, -ης, ἡ: Nymph, or minor goddess presiding over natural phenomena, such as caves, bodies of water, and woodlands
νυμφίος, -ου, ὁ: bridegroom; male suitor for a woman's hand in marriage
νύξ, νυκτός, ἡ: night; darkness; metaphor of death
ξανθός, -ή, -όν: golden (esp., golden-haired)
ξένος, -ου, ὁ: foreigner; wayfarer; wanderer; stranger; guest-friend

ξόανον, -ου, τό: image carved of wood; statue of a deity; image of a god; wooden statue
ξυνός, -ή, -όν: common; public
ὁδίτης, -ου, ὁ: wayfarer, traveller
ὀδυρμός, -οῦ, ὁ: lamentation
ὄζος, -ου, ὁ: tree-branch, part of a branch where the bud sprouts
ὄζω, ὀζήσω, ὤζησα, ὤζηκα, —, —: smell of; smell sweet
οἶδα, εἴσομαι, ᾔδη or ᾔδειν (plup.), —, —, —: know, know about
οἰκοφύλαξ, -ακος, ὁ, ἡ: guard of the house
οἰκτρός, -ά, -όν: pitiable, to be pitied (adv.: pitifully, piteously)
οἰνοχόη, -ης, ἡ: vessel used in the mixing and pouring of wine
οἰόβατος, -ον: lonesome
οἴομαι, οἰήσομαι, ᾠϊσάμην, —, —, ᾠήθην: think; suppose; believe
οἰονόμος, -ου, ὁ: shepherd
ὀκύτονος, η, ον: piercing, sharp-sounding
ὅλα, τά: the universe
ὄλβιος, -ον: wealthy; rich; prosperous; happy; blessed; good
ὀλίγος, -η, -ον: little; small; few
ὄλλυμι, ὀλέσω, ὤλεσα, ὄλωλα, —, ὠλέσθην: destroy, ruin, make an end of (act.); die, perish, come to an end (mid.)
ὀλολύζω, ὀλολύξομαι / ὀλολύξω, ὠλολύξα, —, —, —: cry out loud or ululate with a loud voice, especially of women praying to the gods
ὅλος, -η, -ον: complete; whole; entire
ὀλοφυδνός, -ή, -όν: lamenting; here, used as an adverb
ὀλοφύρομαι, ὀλοφυροῦμαι, ὠλοφυράμην, —, —, ὠλοφύρθην: to lament, wail, moan
᾿Όλυμπος, -ου, ὁ: Olympus, Mt. Olympus
ὅμαιμος, -ον: brother or sister (as substantive); of the same blood
ὁμαλός, -ή, -όν: equal; on a level with
ὄμμα, -ματος, τό: eye
ὁμοῦ: (adv.) together
ὅμως: yet, still, nevertheless
ὀνία = ἀνία, –ης, ἡ: trouble, misery
ὄνομα, -ματος, τό: name
ὄνυξ, -υχος, ὁ: claw, talon
ὀξύτονος, -η, -ον: piercing, sharp-sounding
ὀπάζω, ὀπάσσω, ὤπασα, —, —, —: give, grant
ὅπῃ: where, in which place, whither
ὅπλα, -ων, τά: armor, weapons
ὀπωπή, -ῆς, ἡ: outward appearance
ὁράω, ὄψομαι, εἶδον, ἑόρακα ἑώρακα, ἑώραμαι ὦμμαι, ὤφθην: see, look upon, perceive with the eyes, behold, gaze, observe
ὀρέγω, ὀρέξω, ὤρεξα, ὤρεγμαι, —, ὠρέχθην: reach out, hold out, hand, give
ὄρθιος, -α, -ον: straight, upright, high-pitched, loud, shrill
ὄρθριος, -α, -ον: at daybreak, at dawn, in the early morning

ὄρθρος, -ου, ὁ: daybreak; just before dawn; dawn

ὁρμάω, ὁρμήσω, ὥρμησα, ὥρμηκα, ὥρμημαι, ὡρμήθην: urge on, set in motion (*act.*); be eager (*med./pass.*)

ὄρνυμι, ὄρσω, ὦρσα, ὄρωρα, ὀρώρεγμαι ὤρεγμαι, ὠρέχθην: (act.) urge, excite, make (a direct object) to rise up; (med.) arise, rise up

ὄρος, -εος, τό: mountain, hill

ὄρχατος, -ου, ὁ: orchard, row of trees

ὀρχέομαι, ὀρχήσομαι, ὠρχησάμην, —, —, —: dance

ὅς, ἥ, ὅ: he, she, it

ὅσος, -η, -ον: as much as, however much

ὅτε: when, whenever

ὀτραλέος, -α, -ον: used by Hom. and Hes. only as the adv., ὀτραλέως (as here); quickly, readily

οὖδας, οὔδεος, τό: ground, earth

οὐκέτι: (adv.) no longer

οὐρανόθεν: from heaven

οὐρανός, -οῦ, ὁ: heaven, sky

οὖρος, -ου, ὁ: fair wind

οὖς, ὠτός, τό: ear

ὀχέω, ὀχήσω, ὤκχησα, —, —, —: (usually appears in the present and imperfect tenses): carry, bear, carry away

ὄχλος, -ου, ὁ: crowd, multitude

ὄχνη, -ης, ἡ: pear; pear-tree

ὀψιγονος, -ον: late-born; of a later generation

πάθη, -ης, ἡ: misfortune, suffering

πάθος, πάθεος, τό: misfortune

παίγνιον, -ου, τό: plaything; toy; pet; darling; children's game

παλαί: (adv.) long ago

παλαιός, -ά, -όν: ancient, old

πάλιν: (adv.) back, again

παμβασιλεύς, -εως, ὁ: absolute monarch

πάμπαν: (*adv.*, πᾶς, πᾶσα, πᾶν) wholly, altogether

Πάν, Πάνος, ὁ: Pan, god of the rustic wilderness, shepherds, and flocks; frequent companion of nymphs

πάντῃ: (adv.) everywhere, in all directions, from all sides

πάππος, -ου, ὁ: grandfather

παράγω, παράξω, παρήγαγον, παραγήγοχα, παρήγμαι, παρήχθην: lead aside from the right path, lead astray, avert

παραμείβω, παραμείψω, παρήμειψα, —, —, παρημείφθην: (act.) change, alter; (med.) pass by; go by

πάρειμι (εἰμί): be present

παρέρπω, —, —, —, —, —, —: pass by

παρηΐς, - ΐδος, ἡ: cheek, jaw

παρθενική, -ῆς, ἡ: a young, unmarried woman

παρθένιος, -α, -ον: belonging to an unmarried girl, maidenly
παρθένος, -ου, ἡ: unmarried, young woman or girl
πᾶς, πᾶσα, πᾶν: all, every
παστάς, -άδος, ἡ: colonnade, such as those which ran around temples
πάσχω, πείσομαι, ἔπαθον, πέπονθα, —, —: suffer, endure
πάτρα, -ας, ἡ: fatherland
πεζομαχέω: fight on land or foot (i.e., of the infantry)
πέζος, -η, -ον: on foot; fighters on foot (as opposed to those on horse or in chariot); infantry
πέκω, —, ἔπεξα, —, —, ἐπέχθην: comb; card (wool)
πέλαγος, -εος, τό: open sea, high sea, the sea
πέλεια, -ας, ἡ: dove
πέλω (and πέλομαι), —, ἔπελον and ἐπελόμην, ἔπλε and ἐπλόμην, —, —, —: be; come into existence; become
πέμπτος, -η, -ον: fifth
πένης, -ητος, ὁ: one who works for a living, day-laborer, poor man
πένθιμος, -ον: made for mourning
πένθος, -εος, τό: sorrow, grief
πεντήκοντα, οἱ, αἱ, τά: (indeclinable) fifty
περ: (*enclitic particle*), adds force to the word which follows it, in the sense of "very much, much, however"
περί = ὑπέρ in Aeolic: above
περιέχω/περίσχω, περιέξω/περισχήσω, περιέσχον, —, —, —: surpass
περικαλλής, -ές: very beautiful
περίοχος, -ον: preeminent, superior
περιτρόπω: turn around
πέταλον, -ου, τό: leaf
πέτρα, -ας, ἡ: rock
πέτρη, -ης, ἡ: rock
πέτρος, -ου, ὁ: rock, stone
πεύκη, -ης, ἡ: pine-torch; anything made of pine
πηγή, -ῆς, ἡ: font or source of light or water; stream; running water; fountain; spring
πήλοι = τηλοῦ: from far away
πῆχυς, -εος, ὁ: arm; the part of the arm from the elbow to the middle finger
πῖδαξ, -ακος, ἡ: spring, fountain
Πιερίδες, αἱ: the Pierides, the Muses
πίμπλημι, πλήσω, ἔπλησα, πέπληκα, πέπλησμαι, ἐπλήσθην: fill, fill up (*act.*); fill for one's self, satiate (*med.*); pass., be filled with/of (*pass.*)
πίναξ, -ακος, ὁ: a votive tablet hung on the image of a god; painting; picture
πινυτή, -ῆς, ἡ: understanding; insight; wisdom
πινυτής, -ῆτος, ἡ: discretion, prudence
πίνω, πιοῦμαι, ἔπιον, πέπωκα, πέπομαι, ἐπόθην: drink, sip
πίτυς, -υος, ἡ: pine

πλείων, -ον: (οἱ πλέονες = nom. pl. m. form): full, complete; in pl., the greater number (of something–in this case, votes)
πλέω, πλεύσομαι/πλεύσω, ἔπλευσα, πέπλευκα, πέπλευσμαι, ἐπλεύσθην: sail
πλέως, πλέα, πλέων: full, filled
πλησίος, -α, -ον: near, nearby
πλησίστιος, -ον: filling/swelling the sails
πλήσσω, πλήξω, ἔπληξα, πέπληγα, πέπληγμαι, ἐπλήχθην: to strike, hit
πλόος, πλοῦς, ὁ: sailing, marine voyage
πλωτός, -ή, -όν: navigable
πνεῦμα, -ματος, τό: breeze, wind
πνέω, πνεύσομαι, ἔπνευσα, πέπνευκα, πέπνυμαι, ἐπνεύσθην: breathe, blow
πνοιή, -ῆς, ἡ: (poetic form of πνοή, -ῆς): wind, breeze
ποθέω, ποθήσω, ἐπόθησα ἐπόθεσα, πεπόθηκα, πεπόθημαι, —: desire; long for; miss
ποία, -ας, ἡ: grass
ποικιλόδειρος, -ον: with a mottled or variegated neck
ποικίλος, -η, -ον: wrought in various colors or patterns
ποινή, -ῆς, ἡ: penalty, price, fine
ποῖος, -α, -ον: of what kind?
ποιφύσσω: a reduplicated, onomatopoetic form φυσάω, blow, snort, or puff out (with accus.); fut., ποιφύξω
πολιά, ᾶς, ἡ: grayness of hair; gray hair
πολιός, -ά, -όν: gray, grizzled
πόλις, πολέως, ἡ: city
πολλάκις (adv.): often, many times, frequently
πολύκλαυστος, -η, -ον: much-lamented
πολύολβος, -ον: very blessed; very wealthy
πολύρριζος, -ον: with many roots
πολυσπερής, -ές: wide-spread over the earth, fruitful
πόνος, -ου, ὁ: labor, toil, physical exertion, trouble, distress, pain
πόντος, -ου, ὁ: sea, open water of the sea
πόρτις, -ιος, ἡ: calf, young heifer
πορφύρεος, -α, -ον: dark, dark-gleaming; purple or blood-red
ποτα = ποτε: ever
ποτήριον, -ου, τό: drinking-cup, wine-cup
πότνια, –ας: mistress (an honorific title)
ποτός, -οῦ ὁ: drink, beverage
πούς, πόδος, ὁ: foot. This irregular noun has some unexpected forms: πόδι (dat. s.), πόδα (acc. s., not πόδυν as one might expect), and both πόσι and πόσσι (esp. in epic and lyric) for the dat. pl.
πτέρυξ, -υγος, ἡ: wing
πραϋλόγος, -ου, ὁ, ἡ: one who is gentle of speech
πρέσβιστος, -η, -ον: eldest, most august, most reverend
Πρίαμος, -ου, ὁ: Priam, aged and noble king of Troy
πρίν: before, until

πρόαρχος, -ου, ὁ: captain, chief
προγενής, -ές (προγενέστερος, -α, -ον = comparative): elder, born earlier
προπάροιθε(ν): (adv.) in time before; before; before the time of (a genitive noun or phrase)
προσέοικα: (perf. with pres. sense; only the perf. and pluperf. forms occur), resemble, be like (a dative object)
πρόσθε(ν): (adv.) former, before
προσκύνημα, προσκύνηματος, τὸ: act of worship
προστίθημι, προσθήσω, προσέθηκα, —, προστέθειμαι, προσετέθην: give besides or also; add on; make an addition
προσφθέγτός, -ή, -όν: capable of being called by name; capable of being or able to be addressed
πρόσωπον, -ου, τό: face, countenance
προτομή, -ής, ή: figurehead (carved decoration found on the bow of a ship)
προφήτης, -ου, ὁ: seer, prophet
πρόφρων, -ονος, ὁ/ἡ: gracious, kindly
πρόφρων: kind, kindly
πρῶτος, -η, -ον: first
πτέρον, – ου, τό: wing
πτοέω, πτοήσω, ἐπτοήσα, —, ἐπτόημαι, ἐπτοιήθην: flutter, excite (by passion)
πτύω, πτύσω, ἔπτυσα, ἔπτυκα, —, ἐπτύσθην: spit out; spit; spew
πυκινός, -ή, -όν = (Attic) πυκνός, -ή, -όν: close, compact, thick, dense, crowded; moving quickly back and forth
πύκνος, -η, -ον: thick, close together
πυνθάνομαι, πεύσομαι, ἐπυθόμην, πέπυσμαι, —: to learn, hear
πυρκαϊά, -ᾶς, ἡ: funeral pyre
πῶμα, -ματος, τό: drink, draught
ῥαδινός, -ή, -όν: slim, narrow
ῥῆμα, -ματος, τό: word; line of verse
ῥίμφα: (adv.) lightly, swiftly
ῥόδεος, -α, -ον: rosy
ῥόδον, –ου, τό: rose
ῥοδόπηχυς, -υ: rosy-armed
ῥοή, -ης ἡ (Doric = ῥοά): stream, river (usually in the plural)
Ῥώμη, ἡ: Rome
σαίνω, —, ἔσηνα, —, —, —: wag the tail; fawn upon
σάλος, -ου, ὁ: tossing motion, turbulence, agitation, restlessness, perplexity
σατίνη, -ης, ἡ: chariot
σεβαστός, -η, -ον: venerable, august
σελήνη, -ης, ἡ: moon
σεμνός, -ή, -όν: holy, solumn, august, reverend
σῆμα, -ματος, τό: sign; sign by which a gravesite is marked; grave; tomb; letter; writing; mark

σημαίνω, σημανῶ, ἐσήμηνα, σεσήμαγκα, σεσήμασμαι, ἐσημάνθην: to show by sign, indicate, point out
σιγάς, -άδος: silent
σιδήρεος, -α, -ον: made of iron; hard as iron
σίκυος, -ου, ὁ: cucumber; snake-melon
σίνις, -ιδος, ὁ: ravager, plunderer, destroyer
σίνομαι, σινήσομαι, ἐσινάμην, —, —, —: harm, mistreat, injure
σκαρθμός, -οῦ, ὁ: a leap, a leaping
σκιά, σκιᾶς, ἡ: shadow
σκιάζω, σκιῶ, ἐσκίασα, —, ἐσκίασμαι, ἐσκιάσθην: cast a shadow (*act.*); to be in shade or shadow (*pass.*)
σκοπιά, -ᾶς ἡ: hilltop, peak, a look-out place that commands a view of the surrounding area
σκορπίος, -ου, ὁ: scorpion
σκυλάκαινα, -ας, ἡ: (fem. of σκύλαξ, -ακος, ὁ): puppy (female)
σκυλάκη, -ης, ἡ: puppy
σπάω, σπάσω, ἔσπασα, ἔσπακα, ἔσπασμαι, ἐσπάσθην: draw, pull
σποδιά, -ᾶς, ἡ: ashes
σπουδάζω, σπουδάσομαι, ἐσπούδασα, ἐσπούδακα, ἐσπύδασμαι, ἐσπουδάσθην: be eager, pursue earnestly
σταγών, -όνος, ἡ: drop
στάζω, στάξω, ἔσταξα, –, ἐνέσταγμαι, ἐστάχθην: let (an accusative object) drop or fall; drip; shed drop by drop
στάχυς, -υος, ὁ: ear of corn, grain, meadow grasses
στείβω, —, ἔστειψα, —, —. —: walk or tread; this verb usually only appears in the present and imperfect tenses
στεναχίζω: Epic lengthened form of στενάχω: groan or lament (about an accusative object)
στέρνον, -ου, τό: chest, breast, heart
στέφανος, -ου, ὁ: wreath, garland
στῆθος, -ους, τό: breast, chest; the seat of feeling and thought
στήλη, -ης, ἡ: a block of carved stone that serves as a funerary monument
στόμα, -ματος, τό: mouth; mouth as the organ of speech; and, thus, voice
στοναχέω, —, ἐστονάχησα, —, —, —: groan, sigh; groan for or over an accusative object
στροῦθος, -ου: sparrow
σύμμαχος, -ον: allied (and, thus, an ally) in battle
συμμείγνυμι, συμμείξω, συνέμειξα, συμμέμιχα, συμμέμειχμαι,—: co-mingle with
συνεταιρίς, -ίδος, ἡ: companion; friend
συνέταιρος, -ου, ὁ: companion, comrade
συνετός, –ή, –όν: intelligible, able to be understood
συνήθεης, -ες: intimate, familiar
σύνοιδα (pft. with pres. sense): know (+ dat. reflexive pronoun = from one's own experience)

σφάλλω, σφαλῶ, ἔσφηλα, ἔσφαλκα, ἔσφαλμαι, ἐσφάλην: to cause to fall, overthrow
σφίγγω, σφίγξω, ἔσφιγξα, —, ἔσφιγμαι, ἐσφίγχθην: to bind tight
σφυρόν, -οῦ, τό: ankle
σῴζω, σώσω, ἔσῳσα, σέσῳκα, σέσῳσμαι, ἐσώθην: save, preserve
σῶμα, -ματος, τό: body
τάλας, τάλαινα, τάλαν: suffering; wretched; in a poor or sorry state
ταλαύρινος, -ον: thick, tough as a bull's hide
τάσσω (Att., τάττω), τάξω, ἔταξα, τέταχα, τέταγμαι, ἐτάχθην: order, command, bid; draw up in order; array
τάφος, -ου, ὁ: grave, tomb, statue marking a gravesite
τελέθω: (cognate with τελέω, τέλλω, and πέλω; τελέθω appears chiefly in the present tense), come into being; to be; to exist
τελέω, τελῶ, ἐτέλεσα, τετέλεκα, τετέλεσμαι, ἐτελέσθην: accomplish, complete, fulfill, bring to an end; make happen
τέμνω, τεμῶ, ἔτεμον, τέτμηκα, τέτμημαι, ἐτμήθην: to cut
τεός, -ά, -όν: Doric for σός, your
τέρπω, τέρψω, ἔτερψα, —, —, ἐτέρφθην: delight, gladden; in middle and passive, to enjoy or delight oneself (with a dative of instrument)
τέτταρες οἱ/αἱ, τέτταρα, τά: four
τέττιξ, -ιγος, ὁ: a cicada, known for its chirping "songs"
τεύχω, τεύξω, ἔτευξα, τέτευχα, τέτυγμαι/τέτυκμαι, ἐτεύχθην: make, build; produce (by work or artistry); prepare
τηλόθεν: (adv.), from afar; far from
τηνίκα: (adv.) then, at that time
τίθημι, θήσω, ἔθηκα, τέθηκα, τέθειμαι, ἐτέθην: put, place, set down, dedicate
Τίθωνος, -ου, ὁ: Tithonus, the mortal husband of Eos (Dawn). Zeus, at her request, granted Tithonus immortal life. However, Eos forgot to ask Zeus to also give her husband eternal youth
Τιθωνός, ὁ: Tithon (brother of Priam, husband of Eos, and father of Memnon)
τίκτω, τέξω, ἔτεξα/ἔτεκον, τέτοκα, τέτεγμαι, ἐτέχθην: give birth to; bear, produce, beget; engender
τιμήεις, -εσσα, -εν: honored, esteemed
Τιτάν, Τιτᾶνος, ὁ: Titan
τοκεύς, –έως, ὁ or ἡ: parent
τόξον, -ου, τό: bow
τότε: (adv.) then
τραγικός, -ή, -όν: pertaining to dramatic tragedy; tragic
τράγος, -ου, ὁ: goat
τρεῖς, τρία: three
τρέω, —, ἔτρεσα, —, —, —: to fear, dread; to flee
τρήρων, -ονος, ὁ, ἡ: trembling, shy, timorous

τρίοδος, -ου, ἡ: a meeting of three roads
τρίπους, -ποδος, ὁ: tripod
τρίτος, -η, -ον: third
τρόμος, -ου, ὁ: trembling, quivering, quaking
τρύω, τρύσω, —, —, τέτρυμαι, —: (usually found in the perfect passive) wear out, distress (act.); worn out, distressed (pass.)
τυίδε = τῇδε: hither, to this place
τύμβος, -ου, ὁ: tomb; grave; sepulchral mound
τύπτω, τύψω, ἔτυψα, τέτυφα, τέτυμμαι, ἐτύφθην: beat; strike; smite
τύχη, -ης, ἡ: fate (good or ill); fortune
τῶ(ς): then, therefore, and so
ὕδωρ, ὕδατος, τό: water
ὕλη, -ης, ἡ: forest, woodland
ὑμεναίος, -ου, ὁ: wedding, wedding song
ὑμνέω, ὑμνήσω, ὕμνησα, –, —, —: sing in praise of, celebrate in song or hymn
ὑπαί = epic form of ὑπό
ὑπακούω, ὑπακούσομαι, —, —, —, —: hear, listen to
ὑπνόω, ὑπνώσω, ὕπνωσα, ὕπνωκα, ὑπνωμαι, ὑπνώθην: (act.) put to sleep, fall asleep, sleep; (pass.), be made to sleep
ὑποζεύγνυμι: yoke; fasten
ὑποϊάχω: (this verb only appears in the present tense): resound, echo, sound forth a little or in answer
ὑποτρέχω, ὑποδραμέομαι, ὑπέδρακον, ὑποδεδράμηκα, —, —: run under
ὑφαίνω, ὑφανῶ, ὕφηνα/ὕφανα, ὕφαγκα, ὕφασμαι, ὑφάνθην: weave; create
ὑψόθεν: (adv.) from above
φαεινός, -ή, όν: bright; radiant
Φαμένωθ: Phamenoth
φάος, φάεος, τό: light, eye
φήμη, -ης, ἡ: speech, utterance, rumor, report
φθέγμα, -ματος, τό: voice, speech, language
φθέγομαι, φθέγξομαι, ἐφθεγξάμην: to utter, creak, speak
φθίνω, φθίσω, ἔφθισα, —, ἔφθιμαι, ἐφθίμην: destroy (act.); perish, die, pass away (pass.)
φιάλη, -ης, ἡ: a flat bowl used for drinking or pouring libations
φιλάοιδος [-α], -ον: fond of singing; song-loving
φιλέω, φιλήσω, ἐφίλησα, πεφίληκα, πεφίλημαι, ἐφιλήθην: love
φιλότης, φιλότητος, –ἡ: love, affection
φιλοφθόγγος, -ον: fond of making noise, noisy
φιμά, -ῶν, τά: any instrument that keeps the mouth closed, such as a bit, bridle, or muzzle
φλόξ, φλόγος, ἡ: flame; fire
φλύαξ, -ακος, ὁ: also called the ἱλαροτραγῳδία, a form of tragic burlesque
φοινίκεος, -έα, -εον: blood-red; crimson; dark-red; dark
φοινικόεις, -εσσα, -εν: dark, dark-red, crimson

φοιτάω, —, —, —, —, —: wander backward and forward; stalk; roam about
φονή, -ῆς, ἡ: murder, slaughter
φόνος, -ου, ὁ: murder, slaughter
φριξοκόμης, -ου, ὁ: with shaggy or bristly hair
φυλάττω, φυλάξω, ἐφύλαξα, πεφύλαχα, πεφύλαγμαι, ἐφυλάχθην: (act.) guard; keep watch; defend; (med.) be on one's guard; watch out for
φύλλον, -ου, τό: leaf, foliage (in pl.)
φύω, φύσω, ἔφυσά ἔφυν, πέφυκα, —, ἐφύην: beget, put forth, make grow
φωνέω, —, ἐφώνησα, —, —, —: speak, produce a sound
φωνή, -ῆς, ἡ: voice, sound of the human voice
φῶς, φωτός, τό: light
χαίρω, χαιρήσω, ἐχαίρησα, κεχάρηκα, κεχάρημαι, ἐχάρην: rejoice in; take pleasure in; delight in
χαίτη, -ης, ἡ: loose, flowing hair
χαλάω, χαλάσω, ἐχάλασα, —, κεχάλασμαι, ἐχαλάσθην: fall, give way, yield, lessen, release
χαλεπός, -ή, -όν: difficult; hard to deal with
χαλκός, -οῦ, ὁ: bronze
χαράττω, χαράξω, ἐχάραξα, —, κεχαράγμαι, ἐχαράχθην: engrave; carve
χαρίεις, -εσσα, -εν: pleasing, beautiful
χάρις, -ιτος, ἡ: beauty; grace; charm; elegance; gratitude; favor; kindness; outward grace; goodwill
χεῖλος, -εος, τό: prow of a ship; beak or bill of a bird; or, gunwales (pl.)
χεῖμα, -ατος, τό: winter
χείρ, χειρός, ἡ: hand
χελώνη, -ης, ἡ: tortoise; tortoise shell; a lyre made from a tortoise shell
χέρσος, -ου, ὁ: dry land
χεῦμα, -ματος, τό: that which is poured; stream
χθίσδον: yesterday
χιών, -όνος, ἡ: snow
χλωρός, -ά, -όν: pale, pallid; green-yellow; fresh, blooming, sparkling, glistening
χορός, -ου, ὁ: chorus, choir, band of dancers and singers
χόρτος, -ου, ὁ: enclosed space, usually one in which domestic animals are kept or fed
χρησμόλογος, -ον: oracular
χρησμός, -οῦ, ὁ: oracular response; oracle delivered by a prophet, seer, priestess or priest
χρίω, χρίσω, ἔχρισα, κέχρικα, κέχριμαι, ἐχρίσθην: anoint; anoint with oil or perfume
χρύσεος, –α, –ον: golden, made of gold
χρυσίος, -ά, -όν: made of gold, golden
χρυσομίτρης, -ου: with girdle or headband of gold
χρυσοφαής, -ές: of shining gold
χρώς, χροός, ὁ: skin, complexion

χρώς, χρωτός, ὁ: skin; hide; flesh
χωρίς: (adv.) separately, apart from
χῶρος, –ου, ὁ: place, land, country
ψῆφος, -ου, ἡ: pebble (placed in an urn) used to cast a vote
ψόφος, -ου, ὁ: sound, especially of musical instruments (and, not of the human voice)
ψυχρός, -ά, -όν: cold, cool
ὠδίς, ὠδῖνος, ἡ: pains of child-birth
ὠθέω, ὠθήσω, ἔωσα ὦσα, ἔωκα, ἐώσθην: force onward, thrust, push, shove
ὠκυμάχος, -ον: swift in battle
ὠκύμορος, -ον: dying too swiftly; dying at a young age
ὠκύς, -εῖα, -ύ: swift, quick
ὥρα, -ας, ἡ: season; hour
ὡραῖος, -α, -ον: prime of youth; seasonable; at the proper time; beautiful; graceful; ripe; in the prime of life
ὠρυγή, -ῆς, ἡ: howling or roaring
ὡς: like, as; that; how

# Latin-English Glossary

a: ah!
abduco, abducere, abduxi, abductum: to lead away, carry off, remove
abeo, abire, abivi, abitum: to depart, to go away; to go forth, to go off
ac/atque: and
accendo, accendere, accendi, accensum: to set on fire, to light
accipio, accipere, accepi, acceptum: to accept, to receive
acer, acris, acre: sharp, piercing
acervus, acervi, *m.*: mass, heap, pile; treasure, stock
Achaeus, a, um: Achaean, Greek
Achilles, Achillis, *m.*: Achilles
acuo, acuere, acui, acutum: to make sharp, to sharpen, to whet; to incite, arouse
ad: (+ acc.) to, toward
adigo, adigere, adegi, adactum: to force, compel
adnuo, adnuere, adnui, adnutum: to indicate, to declare; to nod assent, to indicate by a nod
adsero, adserere, adsevi, adsitum: to sow, plant, weave; (*metaphorically*) to compose poetry
adsum, adesse, adfuī, adfuturum: to be present, at hand
adversus, a, um: opposite, against; unfavorable
Aelius, i, *m.*: Gaius Aelius Brocchus (husband of Claudia Severa)
aeque: equally
aequus, a, um: reasonable, right, fair; equal
aestimo, aestimare, aestimavi, aestimatum: to value, rate, appraise
aetas, aetatis, *f.*: age, time of life
aeternus, a, um: eternal, perpetual
aevum, i, *n.*: age
affero, afferre, attuli, allatum: to bring to, carry to
ager, agri, *m.*: field, open countryside
aggredior, aggredi, aggressum sum: to approach, go toward
agito, agitare, agitavi, agitatum: to drive, move; to rouse up
Aglaos, Agalon (acc.), *m.*: Agalos (son of Sulpicia Petale)
ago, agere, egi, actum: to lead, drive; spend

albus, a, um: white
aliquis, aliquid: some, any
aliter: otherwise, differently
alius, a, ud: other, another
altar, altaris, *n.*: altar; high altar
altus, a, um: high, tall
alumnus, i, *m.*: nursling, pupil; foster-child
amans, amantis, *m./f.*: lover, sweetheart
amicus, i, *m.*: friend
amnis, amnis, *m.*: stream, river
amo, amare, amavi, amatum: to love
amor, amoris, *m.*: love
an: or, whether
animus, i, *m.*: soul, mind
annus, anni, *m.*: year, age
ante: (+ acc.) before
antequam: before
antrum, i, *n.*: cave
aper, apri, *m.*: boar
apes, apis, *f.*: bee
Apollo, Apollinis, *m.*: Apollo
applico, applicare, applicui, applicitus: to connect, to place near, to bring together; to apply
aptus, a, um: fit, apt, appropriate
aqua, aquae, *f.*: water
Arabs, Arabis (gen.): Arabian
arbitrium, i, *n.*: judgment, free will; presence, company
ardor, ardoris, *m.*: flame; desire, passion
arguo, arguere, argui, argutum: to prove, to argue; to accuse, to blame
arma, armorum, *n.pl.*: weapons, armor
Arretinus, a, um: Arretian, pertaining to the town of Aretium
ars, artis, *f*: art; skill
artus, artus, *m.*: arm, leg, limb
arva, arvae, *f.*: plowed field, arid land
arx, arcis, *f.*: citadel, fortress
as, assis, *m.*: as (a Roman coin)
asper, aspera, asperum: rude; cruel, harsh, savageast: but; moreover, yet
at: but
atque/ac: and; also; besides
Atropos, i, *f.*: Atropos, one of the three Parcae
audio, audire, audivi, auditum: to hear, listen
aufero, auferre, abstuli, ablatum: to carry off, carry away
Ausonius, a, um: Ausonian
aut: either, or
aveo, avere: to be eager; (h)ave:greetings!

averto, avertere, averti, aversus: to turn away
Bacchus, i, *m.*: Bacchus
bellum, belli, *n.*: war
bene: (adv.) well
bibo, bibere, bibi, bibitus: to drink
bis: (adv.) twice
bonus, a, um: good
braciolum, i, *n.*: small arm
Briga, ae, *f.*: Briga (a town in northern England)
Brocchus, i, *m.*: Gaius Aelius Brocchus (the husband of Claudia Severa)
Byblis, Byblidis, *f.*: Byblis
cado, cadere, cecidi, casum: to fall; be killed
cadurcum, i, *n.*: marriage bed
caelum, caeli, *n.*: sky, heaven
Calenus, i, *m.*: Calenus (Sulpicia's husband)
caleo, calere, calui,: to be warm, to feel warm
calleo, callere: to be experienced, skilled; to be hardened, calloused
Calliope, Callipoes, *f.*: Calliope (chief of the Muses)
calor, caloris, *m.*: warmth, heat; fever; heat of passion
camelopardus, i, *m.*: giraffe
Camena, ae, *f.*: Muse
Camillus, i, *m.*: Camillus
campus, campi, *m.*: plain, field
candidus, candida, candidum: fair-skinned, pale; bright, clear; innocent, pure, radiant
canis, canis, *m/f*: dog
cano, canere, cecini, cantum: to sing
canto, cantare, cantavi, cantatus: to sing, chant
cantus, cantus, *m.*: song, chant; poem
capillus, capilli, *m.*: hair, single hair
capio, capere, cepi, captum: to capture, seize, take hold
Capitolius, a, um: Capitoline, of the Capitoline Hill
caput, capitis, *n.*: head
careo, carere, carui, cariturus: (+ abl.) to lack
carmen, carminis, *n.*: song, poem
Carthago, Carthaginis, *f.*: Carthage
carus, a, um: dear, precious, expensive
cassis, cassis, *m.*: hunting net, snare, trap
Castrensis, is, *n.*: Castrensis (Roman cognomen)
castus, a, um: pure, moral; chaste
Cato, Catonis, *m.*: M. Porcius Cato (234–149 BCE)
causa, ae, *f.*: cause, reason; case
caveo, cavere, cavi, catus: to beware, take caution
cedo, cedere, cessi, cessum: go, move, yield
celeber, celebris, celebre: famous, celebrated

celer, celeris, celere: swift, quick, fast
censor, censoris, m.: censor (a Roman magistrate)
Cerialis, is, *m.*: Flavius Cerealis (husband of Sulpicia Lepidina)
Cerinthus, i, *m.*: Cerinthus
cerno, cernere, crevi, cretum: to separate, distinguish, perceive
certatim: (adv.) with rivalry, in competition
cervus, cervi, *m.*: stag, deer
ceterus, a, um: other; the rest, remainder
cinis, cineris, m/f: ashes, embers
chorus, chori, *m.*: chorus
clam: (adv.) secretly, in secret; privately
claritas, claritatis, *f.*: brightness, splendor
Claudia Severa, ae, *f.*: Claudia Severa
claudo, claudere, clausi, clausum: to shut, close
Clazomenius, a, um: Clazomenian; of Clazomenae
cliens, clientis, *m./f.*: client, dependent
cogito, cogitare, cogitatvi, cogitatum: to think, consider
cogo, cogere, coegi, coactum: to collect, gather; to urge, force
Colchis, Colchidis, *f.*: Colchian (woman); Medea
colligo, colligere, collegi, collectum: to obtain, collect
collis, collis, *m.*: hill
collum, i, *n.*: neck
colo, colere, colui, cultum: to adorn, decorate; to live in, inhabit
color, coloris, *m.*: color, hue, tint
colus, colus, *f*: distaff; woman's concern; spinning
coma, comae, *f.*: hair
comes, comitis, *m./f.*: companion
como, comere, compsi, comptum: to arrange, adorn
complector, complecti, complexus sum: to clasp, embrace
concedo, concedere, concessi, concessum: to relinquish, to concede; to depart
concubo, concubare: to lie with
concumbo, concumbere, concubui, concubitum: to lie together, to lie with
concupio, concupere, concupivi, concupitum: to desire, wish, long for
condiscipula, ae, *f.*: female school-fellow
coniungo, coniungere, coniunxi, coniunctus: to join together, unite
conpono, conponere, conposui, conpositum: to put, place, bring together
conputo, conputare, conputavi, conputatum: to sum up, compute
conservo, conservare, conservavi, conservatum: to preserve
consilium, i, *n.*: plan, advice; counsel
conspicio, conspicere, conspexi, conspectum: to observe, to see; to notice
constanter: (adv.) without change
consto, constare, constiti, constaturus: to stand together; to agree; to last, endure
consul, consulis, *m.*: consul (a Roman magistrate)

consummo, consummare, consummavi, consummatus: to complete, perfect, bring together
contendo, contendere, contendi, contentum: to stretch, strain; to fight, contend
convenit: (impersonal) it is appropriate, it is fitting
cor, cordis, *n.*: heart
corpus, corporis, *n.*: bodycredo, credere, credidi, creditum: (+ dat.) to trust, believe
credulus, a, um: trustworthy, credible
cresco, crescere, crevi, cretum: to increase, rise; to come to be; to spring from
crinis, crinis, *m.*: hair, lock of hair
crus, cruris, *n.*: leg, shin
cultor, cultoris, *m.*: farmer, planter
cultrix, cultricis, *f.*: female worshipper, devotee
cum (*conj.*): when, since, although
cum (*prep.*): (+ abl.) with
cupidus, a, um: eager, passionate, desirous
cupio, cupire, cupivi, cupitum: to desire
cura, ae, *f.*: care, concern
curo, curare, curavi, curatum: to care
curro, currere, cucurri, cursum: to run
custos, custodis, *m/f*: guard, protector
cytharoedus, i, *m.*: cytharode
Cytherea, ae, *f.*: Cytherean; the Cytherean one (i.e., Venus)
dea, deae, f: goddess, divine being
debitum, debiti, *n.*: debt; duty
decens, decentis (gen.): appropriate; becoming; graceful, pleasing
decenter: (adv.) becomingly, properly, decently
Decimus Gentianus, i, *m.*: Decimus Terentius Gentianus
Decor, Decoris, *m.*: charm, grace, beauty
decorus, a, um: honorable, noble; proper, decent
defendo, defendere, defendi, defensum: to defend, protect
deficio, deficere, defeci, defectum: to fail, to disappoint
dego, degere, degi: to pass/spend time; to live, continue, endure
deinde: (adv.) then
Delia, ae, *f.*: Delia
deliciae, arum, *f.pl.*: charm, pleasure; darling, beloved
demo, demere, dempsi, demptum: to take away, to cut off, to remove
deni, denae, dena: ten each; ten at a time
denique: finally, at last
dens, dentis, *m.*: tooth; ivory
densus, a, m: dense, thick; packed; frequent
depono, deponere, deposui, depositum: to put aside, put down
deprendo, deprendere, deprendi, deprensum: to seize, to catch; to surprise; to interrupt

descendo, descendere, descendi, descensum: to come down
desideratus, a, um: desired, longed for
desisto, desistere, destiti, destitum: to set down; to cease from
desum, deesse, defui, defuturus: to be wanting/lacking; to fail/miss; to abandon/desert; to neglect; to be away/absent/missing
detexo, detexere, detexui, detextum: to weave; describe
deus, dei, *m.*: god, divine being
devius, a, um: out-of-the-way; distant
dico, dicere, dixi, dictum: to say, tell
dies, diēi, *m./f.*: day
Diespiter, Diespitris, *m.*: Diespater; Jupiter
digno, dignare, dignavi, dignatus: to deem worthy
dignus, a, um: worthy, deserving
diripio, diripere, diripui, direptum: to tear apart, to tear to pieces; to lay waist, to plunder
dirus, a, um: fearful, awful, ominous
disco, discere, didici: to learn
dissimulo, dissimulare, dissimulavi, dissimulatum: to conceal, disguise, keep secret
diu: (adv.) for a long time
dius, a, um: divine, god-like
diva, divae, *f.*: goddess
divello, divellere, divelli, divulsum: to separate, to compel apart; to alienate, to estrange
dives, divitis (gen): rich, wealthy; fertile
divido, dividere, divisi, divisum: to divide, separate
divus, divi, *m.*: god
do, dare, dedi, datum: to give; to dedicate; to sell; to pay
doceo, docere, docui, doctum: to teach, to show, to point out
doctus, a, um: learned
dolor, doloris, *m.*: pain, grief
domina, dominae, *f.*: mistress, wife
domus, domus/domi, *f.*: house, home
dulcis, e: sweet, pleasant
duo, duae, duo: two
dupondius, i, *m.*: the sum of two asses
durus, a, um: hard, stern; harsh, rough
dux, ducis, *m.*: leader
e, ex: (+ abl.) (out) from
ebrius, a, um: drunk, intoxicated
ecce: (interjection) behold!, look!
edo, edere, edi, esum: to give out, bring forth; to produce, bear; to give birth to, beget
effero, efferre, extuli, elatum: to bear out, to carry out
efficio, efficere, effeci, effectum: to bring about; to effect

egenus, a, um: bereft, void of
Egeria, ae, *f.*: Egeria
ego, mei: I, me
enim: (postpositive) for
ensis, ensis, *m.*: sword
eo, ire, ii, itum: to go
Eous, a, um: eastern, oriental
epistula, ae, *f.*: letter
ergo: therefore, ergo
eripio, eripere, eripui, ereptum: to take away; snatch away
erro, errare, erravi, erratum: to wander; to err
et: and
eveho, evehere, evexi, evectum: to carry away
evinco, evincere, evici, evictum: to overcome completely, conquer
excedo, excedere, excessi, excessum: to go out; depart
exilio, exilire, exilui: to spring up; to rise up
exitium, i, *n.*: ruin, destruction
exoro, exorare, exoravi, exoratum: to persuade, entreat
expello, expellere, expuli, expulsum: to drive out, banish
exporto, exportare, exportavi, exportatum: to carry out
exsolvo, exsolvere, exsolvi, exsolutum: to undo, loosen; pay, discharge
exsto, exstare: to exist; to stand forth, to stand out
exturpo, exturpare, exturpavi, exturpatum: to pluck up, root out; to eradicate
exuro, exurere, exussi, exustum: to burn; to destroy
fabella, ae, *f.*: story, narrative
facetia, ae, *f.*: jest, witticism, joke
facio, facere, feci, factum: to make, to do; to cause, to bring about
facundus, a, um: eloquent, fluent
Falernus, a, um: Falernian
fallo, fallere, fefelli, falsum: to deceive; to slip up, to fail; to beguile, to drive away
fama, famae, *f.*: rumor, gossip; fame
fascia, ae, *f.*: band, binding
fateor, fateri, fassus sum: to admit, confess, declare
fatisco, fatiscere: to grow weak, become exhausted
fatum, i, *n.*: fate
faveo, favere, favi, fautum: to befriend, to support, to favor
felix, felicis (gen.): happy; blessed; splendid
fera, ferae, *f.*: wild beast, animal
feralis, e: deadly, fatal
fero, ferre, tuli, latum: to bring, carry
ferreus, a, um: iron, made of iron; cruel, unyielding
fervidus, a, um: burning, fiery, raging
fessus, a, um: weary, tired

festus, a, um: festive, joyous
filiolus, i, *m.*: little son (diminutive)
finis, finis, *m.*: limit, boundary, end
fio, fieri, factus sum: to become, happen, be done
flamma, flammae, *f.*: flame, blaze; ardor, fire of passion
fleo, flere, flevi, fletum: to cry, to weep; to cry for
focus, foci, *m.*: altar; hearth, fireplace
fons, fontis, *m.*: spring, fountain
for, fari, fatus sum: to speak, to talk, to say
forma, formae, *f*: form; beauty; appearance; manner, kind, sort
formo, formare, formavi, formatum: to form, mould, shape
formosus, a, um: beautiful, fine, finely-formed, fair, handsome
fors, fortis, *f*: chance
forte: by chance
fortiter: (adv.) bravely
fortuna, ae, *f.*: fortune, fate
frango, frangere, fregi, fractum: to break, shatter
frater, fratris, *m.*: brother
freno, frenare, frenavi, frenatum: to bridle
frequento, frequentare, frequentavi, frequenatum: to assemble, gather together; to celebrate
fretum, i, *n.*: strait; sea
frigidus, a, um: cold, chilling, frigid
frustra (adv.): in vain; pointlessly
fugio, fugere, fugi, fugitum: to flee
fundo, fundere, fudi, fusum: to pour, pour out, shed
furor, furoris, *m.*: madness, rage
furtim: (adv.) secretly, stealthily
furtum, furti, *n.*: theft; trick, deception
Galli, Gallorum, *m.pl.*: the Gauls
gaudium, i, *n.*: joy, delight
geminus, a, um: double, twin
gemma, gemmae, *f.*: jewel, gem, precious stone; bud
genus, generis, *n.*: race, stock; offspring, descendants
glando, glandinis, *f.*: acorn
Graius, a, um: Greek
gratus, a, um: plesant, grateful
gravis, is, e: heavy, serious
habena, ae, *f.*: rein
habeo, habere, habui, habitum: to have, hold, consider
habito, habitare, habitavi, habitatum: to live, dwell, inhabit
hamatus, a, um: hooked, crooked, curved
(h)ave!: greetings!
Hedone, es, *f.*: Hedone
(h)em: indeed! well! alas!

heros, herois, *m.*: hero
hesternus, a, um: yesterday's, of yesterday
heu: oh!, alas!
hic, haec, hoc: this
hīc: (adv.) here
hodie: (adv.) today, nowadays; presently
homo, hominis, *m./f.*: man, person
honor, honoris, *m.*: honor
hora, ae, *f.*: hour
huc: (adv.) hither, to here
iam: at this point, now; already
iambus, i, *m.*: iambic
idem, eadem, idem: the same
Idus, Iduum, *f.pl.*: Ides (the 15th day of March, May, July, and October; the 13th day of other months)
igitur: therefore
ignio, ignire, ignivi, ignitum: to ignite; to make red hot
ignosco, ignoscere, ignovi, ignotum: to pardon, to forgive
ignotus, a, um: ignorant, unknown; low-born, vulgar
ille, illa, illud: that
immotus, a, um: unmoved, motionless
imperium, i, *n.*: (military) power; empire
impero, imperare, imperavi, imperatum: to command, order; rule over
in: in (+ abl.); into (+ acc.)
inanis, is, e: empty, pointless
incido, incidere, incidi, incasum: to fall upon
incolumis, is, e:: unharmed, uninjured; safe
indago, indaginis, *f.*: an enclosing, surrounding; investigation, hunt
indico, indicare, indixi, inductum: to point out, to show, to expose, to reveal
Indicus, a, um: Indian, of India
indulgeo, indulgere, indulsi, indultum: to be courteous; to yield; to allow
Indus, a, um: Indian
ineptus, a, um: silly, foolish, senseless
infidus, a, um: faithless, treacherous
infit: (impersonal) he/she/it begins
informis, is, e: deformed; formless, shapeless
ingenium, ingenii, *n*: natural quality, nature; disposition; natural capacity; talent, ability
ingens, ingentis (gen.): huge, vast
ingluvies, ei, *f.*: maw
iniustus, a, um: unjust, wrongful; severe, excessive
inlaesus, a, um: unhurt, uninjured
insto, instare, insteti, instatum: to stand upon, threaten
instruo, instruere, instruxi, instructum: to prepare, teach; to set in order

inter: (+ acc.) among, between
interdum: (adv.) meanwhile
interventus, us, *m.*: arrival, involvement
intra: (+ acc.) within
intro, intrare, intravi, intratum: to enter, to go into
intonsus, a, um: uncut, unshaved
inventum, -i, *n.*: device, invention
invictus, a, um: unconquered, unsubdued
invidus, -a, -um: envious; hostile, inimical
invisus, a, um: hated
iocus, i, *m.*: jest, joke
ipse, ipsa, ipsum: -self
irascor, irasci, iratus sum: to be angry; to rage
is, ea, id: he, she, it; this, that
iste, ista, istud: this, that
iter, itineris, *n.*: journey, passage
itidem: (adv.) in like manner; in the same way
iubeo, iubere, iussi, iussum: to order, command
iucundus, a, um: pleasant, agreeable
iugalis, e: nuptial
Iuno, Iunonis, *f*: Juno
iuvat (*impers.*): it delights, pleases
iuvenis, iuvenis, *m.*: young man, youth
iuventa, ae, *f.*: youth, the age of youth
iuvo, iuvare, iuvi, iutum: to delight, please
Kalens, Kalendis, *f.*: Kalends (the first day of the month)
labellum, i, *n.*: little lip
lacrima, lacrimae, *f.*: tear, crying
laedo, laedere, laesi, laesum: to strike; to wound, to hurt
laetus, a, um: happy, cheerful, joyful; favorable; successful
lampada, lampadae, *f.*: torch; lantern
langueo, languere: to be unwell, to be ill; to be tired
lapillus, i, *m.*: pebble, small stone
latebra, latebrae, *f.*: hiding place, lair, cave
laus, laudis, *f.*: praise, approval, merit
lectrix, lectricis, *f*: reader
lectulus, i, *m.*: small bed
lego, legere, legi, lectum: to read; to gather, collect
lentus, a, um: slow, lazy; calm, indifferent, unconcerned
levis, e: light, trivial
levo, levare, levavi, levatum: to lift up; to lessen, to lighten; to comfort; to free from, to release
lex, legis, *f.*: law, bill
libellus, i, *m.*: little book, booklet
libens, libentis (gen.): willing, cheerful; glad, pleased

libenter: (adv.) warmly, gladly, with pleasure
libum, libi, *n.*: cake; consecrated cake
Libycus, a, um: Libyan
licet (*conj. with subjunctive*): even though, although
licet (*impers. with dat. and inf.*): it is permitted, allowed
litus, litoris, *n.*: shore, coast; beach, landing place
longinquom: far/long way off; for/after a long while/interval
longus, a, um: long
loquor, loqui, locutum sum: to speak
lucerna, ae, *f.*: lamp, oil-lamp
luctus, luctus, *m.*: mourning, lament
ludo, ludere, lusi, lusum: to play
lustrum, i, *n.*: lustrum (a purificatory sacrifice)
lusus, us, *m.*: game, play
luteus, a, um: yellow
lux, lucis, *f.*: light
lympha, ae, *f.*: water; spring water
lyra, lyrae, *f.*: lyre, lyric poetry
macies, maciei, *f.*: leanness, meagerness; poverty
madefacio, madefacere, madefeci, madefactum: to make wet, to soak, to dip
maestus, a, um: sorrowful, mournful
magis: (adv.) more
magister, magistri, *m.*: teacher, instructor
magistra, ae, *f.*: teacher
magnus, a, um: great, big
malo, mallere, malui: to prefer
malus, a, um: bad, evil, wicked
mando, mandare, mandavi, mandatum: to order, command
maneo, manere, mansi, mansus: to stay, remain
manus, manus, *f.*: hand; band of soldiers
mare, maris, *n.*: sea
maritus, i, *m.*: husband
Mars, Martis, *m.*: Mars (god of war)
mater, matris, *f.*: mother; lady, matron
medicina, ae, *f.*: medicine, cure
medicus, a, um: healing, curative, medical
meditor, meditari, meditus sum: to reflect, think upon
medius, a, um: middle
membrum, membri, *n.*: limb, organ
memor, memoris: (+gen.) mindful, remembering
mendax, mendacis: lying, deceptive
mens, mentis, *f.*: mind; intellect, reason
merum, meri, *n.*: wine (that has not been mixed with water)
Messalla, ae, *f.*: M. Valerius Mesalla Corvinus

meto, metere, messui: to reap, collect
metuo, metuere, metui: to fear, to be afraid of
metus, us, *m.*: fear, dread
meus, a, um: my
migro, migrare, migravi, migratum: to depart; migrate
mille: a thousand
ministro, ministrare, ministravi, ministrum: to attend to, to serve; to supply
miro, mirare, miravi, miratum: to be amazed, to be surprised; to admire, to wonder at
modo: (adv.) only, merely
modus, i, *m.*: way, mode, manner
moenia, moenium, *n.pl.*: (city) walls
molestus, a, um: troublesome, annoying
mollis, is, e: soft; yielding; gentle
moneo, monere, monui, monitum: to remind, admonish
Moneta, ae, *f.*: (Juno) Moneta
mons, montis, *m.*: mountain, hill
morbus, morbi, *m.*: sickness, disease
morior, i, mortuus sum: to die
mortalis, e: mortal
moveo, movere, movi, motum: to move, to stir
multus, a, um: many; large
musa, ae, *f.*: muse
mutuus, a, um: borrowed, lent; mutual, reciprocal
nam: for
namque: for (indeed)
narro, narrare, narravi, narratum: to tell, narrate, report
nascor, nasci, natus sum: to be produced, to come into existence; to spring forth, to grow
nata, natae, *f.*: daughter, child
natalis, is, *m.*: birthday
natura, naturae, *f*: nature; character
natus, nati, *f*: son
ne: in order not, lest; let not
-ne: *untranslatable interrogative particle that introduces a question*
nec/neque: (and) not
nec … nec: neither … nor
necessarius, a, um: necessary
nemo, neminis, *m./f.*: no one
nempe: indeed, certainly, to be sure
nequam: (indeclinable adjective) worthless, good for nothing, naughty
neu: and not
Nicerotianus, a, um: of Niceros
niger, nigra, nigrum: black, dark
nil: nothing; no

nimbus, i, *m.*: cloud; storm-cloud
nimium: too; too much
niveus, a, um: snowy; white
nolo, nolle, nolui: to be unwilling; to refuse; to not want
nomen, nominis, *n.*: name
non: not
nonne: (adv). not? (interrogative *non*, expecting an affirmative answer)
nos, nostrum/nostri: we, us
noster, nostra, nostrum: our
noto, notare, notavi, notatum: to mark; to record; to write, to inscribe
novus, a, um: new, fresh, young; unusual
nox, noctis, *f.*: night
nudo, nudare, nudavi, nudatum: to strip, lay bare, expose
nullus, a, um: none, no, not any
Numa, ae, *m.*: Numa
Numantinus, a, um: Numantine (surname given to Scipio Africanus)
numero, numerare, numeravi, numeratum: to count, to add up; to consider, to reckon
numerus, numeri, *m*: number
nunc (*adv.*): now
nupta, ae, *f.*: married woman, bride, wife
O!: Oh!
ob: (+ acc). on account of
obesus, a, um: fat, heavy; stuffed, over-eaten
obliviscor, i, oblitus sum: (+ gen.) to forget
occulte: (adv.) secretly
occupo, occupare, occupavi, occupatum: to seize; to gain; to overtake
oculus, oculi, *m.*: eye
odium, odii, *n.*: hatred, disdain
odoratus, a, um: perfumed, fragrant
oleo, olere, olui: to smell of, to smell like
olim: (adv.) once
Olympus, i, *m.*: Olympus, Mt. Olympus
omitto, omittere, ommisi, omissum: to let go, give up; to pass over, omit
omnis, e: all, every, as a whole
onus, oneris, *n.*: load, burden
opino, opinare, opinavi, opinatum: to think, believe, imagine; to be of opinion
optimus, a, um: best
opto, optare, optavi, optatum: to choose, select
opus, operis, *n.*: need; work
orbis, orbis, *m.*: world; globe
ornatus, us, *m.*: furnishing, decoration
orno, ornare, ornavi, ornatum: to equip; to dress; to decorate
osculum, i, *n.*: little mouth; kiss
paeniteo, paenitere, paenitui, –: to grieve one (acc.) of something (gen.)

paenitet (*impers.*): it grieves one (acc.) of something (gen.)
palam: (adv.) openly, publicly
palla, pallae, *f.*: palla, a woman's outer garment
palleo, palette, pallui: to be pale, to look pale; to fade
palo, palare, palavi, palatum: to wander
paries, parietis, *m.*: wall
pariter: (adv.) equally
parco, parcere, peperci, parsum: to spare; to refrain from doing
paro, parare, paravi, paratum: to prepare, acquire
parens, parentis, *m./f.*: parent
pascuum, pascui, *n.*: pasture; grazing-land
pater, patris, *m.*: father
patria, ae, *f.*: fatherland, homeland
patrius, a, um: paternal, fatherly; native
paucī, ae, a (*pl.*): few, a few
pausa, ae, *f.*: pause, stop, end
pax, pacis, *f.*: peace
pecco, peccare, peccavi, peccatum: to do wrong, offend; to sin
pectus, pectoris, *n.*: chest, breast
pelagus, pelagi, *n.*: sea
Penates, Penatium, *m.pl.*: Penates
penetralis, e: piercing, penetrating; inward, internal
per: (+ acc.) through, by
perago, peragere, peregi, peractum: to carry through; to complete
perditus, a, um: hopeless, ruined, desperate
pereo, perire, perivi, peritum: to die; to be ruined, to be destroyed
perlucidus, a, um: transparent, pellucid
permitto, permittere, permisi, permissum: to yield, allow, permit
pervenio, pervenire, perveni, perventum: to come to, to arrive at
Petale, Petalis, *f.*: Sulpicia Petale
pes, pedis, *m.*: foot; (metrical) foot
peto, petere, petivi, petitum: to seek, to request
Phalaecus, a, um: Phalaecian
Phaon, Phaonis, *m.*: Phaon
Phoebus, i, *m.*: Phoebus Apollo
Pierides, um, *f.pl.*: (the) Muses
piget, pigere, piguit, pigitum es (*impers.*): to pain, to afflict, to grieve, to disgust
pius, a, um: dutiful, devoted; just, pious
placeo, placere, placui, placitum: to please, to satisfy
plaga, plagae, *f.*: hunting net, snare, trap
plebs, plebis, *f.*: the common people; the whole people, the nation
plus, pluris, *m*: more, additionally; further
pono, ponere, posui, positum: to place, to put
pontifex, pontificis, *m.*: pontifex (a Roman high-priest)

possideo, possidere, possedi, possessum: to seize, to hold
possum, posse, potui, –: to be able; can
posthac: (adv.) henceforth, after this time.
postquam: after, afterward
potis, e: powerful, able
potius: (adv.) rather, more, preferably
praeceps, praecipis (gen.): headforth, headlong
praecipio, praecipere, praecepi, praeceptum: to take in advance; to anticipate
praemium, i, *n.*: reward, booty; profit
prandium, i, *n.*: lunch
precor, precari, precatus sum: to beg, to implore; to wish, to pray for
premo, premere, pressi, pressum: press; pursue, overwhelm
prex, precis, *f.*: prayer
primus, a, um: first
princeps, principis, *m.*: the first one; chief, leader; emperor
priscus, a, um: old, ancient; old-fashioned
pro: (+ abl.) for, before, in front of
probo, probare, probavi, probatum: to prove, test; to show
probus, a, um: proper, appropriate, upright
procedo, procedere, processi, processum: to proceed, to advance
procul: (adv.) distant, far off
procumbo, procumbere, procubui, procubitum: to fall forward, sink down
proelium, proeli, *n.*: battle, conflict
profero, proferre, protuli, prolatum: to bring forth; to reveal
profundo, profundere, profudi, profusus: to pour (forth)
proicio, proicere, proieci, proiectus: to throw forth, to throw down
prolabor, prolabi, prolapsus sum: to fall down; to fail
promissum, i, *n.*: promise
promitto, promittere, promisi, promissum: to promise, to send forth
propago, propaginis, *f.*: offspring, descendants
propero, properare, properavi, properatum: to hurry, to be quick, to hasten
propinquus, a, um: near, neighboring
propitius, a, um: favorable, well-disposed, propitious
proprior, proprius (gen.): close, near
prosum, prodesse, profui: to be of use, do good, profit (+ dat.)
proximus, a, um: nearest, closest, next
pudeo, pudere, pudui, puditum: to be ashamed; to make ashamed
pudicus, a, um: modest, chaste, virtuous
pudor, pudoris, *f.*: modesty, shame
puella, ae, *f.*: girl
puer, pueri, *m.*: boy, young man
pugna, ae, *f.*: fight, battle
pulcher, pulchra, pulchrum: beautiful, pretty

pupula, ae, *f.*: little girl; pupil of the eye
purpureus, a, um: purple, dark red
purus, a, um: pure
puto, putare, putavi, putatum: to think, suppose
Pylius, a, um: Pylian, from Pylos
pyramis, pyramidis, *f.*: pyramid
quaero, quaerere, quaesivi, quaesitus: to search for, to seek; to inquire
qualis, quale: what kind of, of such kind, such as
quam: than
quamvis: as much as you like; although
quare: wherefore; by what means
quarter: (adv.) four times
quasillum, i, *n.*: small basket for wool
quattuor: four
quattus: four
querela, ae, *f.*: complaint
qui, quae, quod: who, which
quidam, quaedam, quoddam: certain
quidvis: whatever (you wish)
quiesco, quiescere, quievi, quietum: to rest, repose, keep quiet
quin etiam: furthermore
quindecim: fifteen
quis, quid (after si, nisi, num, ne): any
quis, quid: who, what
quisnam, quidnam: who? which?
quisquam, quaequam, quidquam/quicquam: any, any one, any thing
quisquis, quidquid: whoever, whatever
quod: because
quomodocumque: (adv.) in whatever way, howsoever
quondam: once
quoque: also, even
quoquo: (adv.) whithersoever, to whatever place
rabidus, a, um: raving, furious
rapidus, a, um: rapid, swift
ratio, rationis, *f.*: reason
recurro, recurrere, recucurri, recursum: to run back; to return
reddo, reddere, reddidi, redditum: to return, to restore; to deliver; to hand over
redeo, redere, redii, reditum: to return; go back
refero, referee, rettuli, relatum: to bright back, to carry back; to move back, to draw back
rego, regere, rexi, rectum: to rule
regnum, regni, *n.*: power; control, sovereignty; royal power
relego, relegare, relehavi, relegatum: to ascribe; to remove, to separate, to relegate
relinquo, relinquere, reliqui, relictum: to leave behind, abandon

reliquus, a, um: remaining, rest
reputo, reputare, reputavi, reputatum: to think over, ponder
res, rei, *f*: thing, matter, affair
respondeo, respondere, respondi, responsum: to answer, reply
restituo, restituere, restitui, restitutum: to restore; to receive; to bring back
rete, retis, *n*.: net, snare
retracto, retractare, retractavi, retractatum: to take hold of again; to undertake anew
revinco, revincere, revici, revictum: to conquer, subdue
rex, regis, *m*.: king
Rhodius, a, um: Rhodian
rideo, ridere, risi, risum: to laugh, smile
rigens, rigentis: stiff, rigid; stubborn, unyielding
rogo, rogare, rogavi, rogatum: to ask, to ask for; to invite
Roma, Romae, *f*.: Rome
Romanus, a, um: Roman
Romulidae, arum, *f.pl*.: the Romans; posterity of Romulus
Romulus, i, *m*.: Romulus (mythical first king of Rome)
ruber, a, um: red, ruby-colored
rubus, rubi, *m*.: bramble, briar; thorn
rursus: (adv.) again
rus, ruris, *n*.: the country(side)
Sabinus, a, um: Sabine
sacer, sacra, sacrum: sacred, holy
saeculum, i, *n*.: generation; race, breed
saepe: (adv.) often
saevus, a, um: savage, fierce, ferocious
sal, salis, *m*.: salt; wit; good taste
salus, salutis, *f*.: health, greetings
saluto, salutare, salutavi, salutatum: to send greetings to
salvus, a, um: well, unharmed, safe; alive
sanctus, a, um: sacred, consecrated
sanus, a, um: sound; healthy
sapiens, sapientis: wise
sapientia, ae, *f*: wisdom
sapio, sapere, sapivi: to understand; to be wise
sapor, saporis, *m*.: taste, flavor; smell; good taste
scilicet: (adv.) clearly, of course
scio, scire, scivi, scitum: to know
Scipio, Scipionis, *m*.: Scipi
scortum, i, *n*.: prostitute, harlot; piece of hide, skin
sculpo, sculpere, sculpsi, sculptum: to carve, engrave, cut
Scylla, ae, *f*.: Scylla
secedo, secedere, secessi, secessum: to go apart, to separate, to withdraw
secundus, a, um (1): second
secundus, a, um (2): favorable

securus, a, um: carefree, untroubled
securus, a, um: free from care, tranquil; careless
sed: but
sedeo, sedere, sedi, sessum: to sit, to remain, to wait
seges, segetis, *f.*: crop, field of grain
senecta, ae, *f.*: old age, senility
senex, senis (gen.): old
sensus, us, *m.*: perception, feeling
sententia, ae, *f.*: opinion, judgment; statement
sentio, sentire, sensi, sensum: to perceive, to feel, to experience; to think, to realize
semper: (adv.) always
September, Septembris, *m.*: September
servilis, servile: of a slave, servile
servio, servire, servivi, servitum: to serve, to be a slave to
servitium, serviti, *n.*: slavery, servitude; slaves (pl.)
Servius, i, *m.*: Servius Sulpicius Rufus, Sulpicia's father
servo, servare, servavi, servatum: to watch over; to protect
seu: or if
sex: six
si: if
sic: (adv.) in this manner, thus
Sicania, ae, *f.*: Sicania; Sicily
sicut: just as
signo, signare, signavi, signatum: to mark, designate
silva, ae, *f.*: forest
simul: (adv.) at the same time; at once
sine: (+ abl.) without
sino, sinere, sivi, situm: to let, allow, permit
sinus, i, *m.*: fold; fold of the toga; lap, bosom
smyrnalis, e: Smyrnian
socialis, e: social; allied
solemne, sollemnis, *n.*: religious ceremony, ritual offerings, rite
sollemnis, sollemne: solemn, ceremonial
sollicitus, a, um: disturbed, agitated, worried
solus, a, um: only, alone
solvo, solvere, solvi, solutum: to loosen, to release; to open
somnus, i, *m.*: sleep; dream
soror, sororis, *f.*: sister
specto, spectare, spectavi, spectatum: to look at, to observe
spero, sperare, speravi, speratum: to hope
splendeo, splendere, splendui: to shine, glitter, gleam; to be bright
stadium, i, *n.*: stadium
sto, stare, steti, statum: to stand, to stand still, to stand firm
studiosus, a, um: eager, zealous, devoted

studium, studi, *n.*: eagerness, enthusiasm, zeal; spirit, devotion, study
stultus, a, um: foolish, simple, stupid
suadeo, suadere, suasi, suasum: to persuade, urge
sub: (+ abl.) under
subfero, subferre, sustuli, sublatum: to endure, suffer; to carry under
subito: (adv.) suddenly
subrepo, subrepere, subrepsi, subreptum: to creep; to steal upon
subripio, subripere, subripui, subreptum: to snatch away secretly, to steal
subsequor, subsequi, subsecutus sum: to follow close; to pursue
sucus, i, *m.*: juice, sap; dye
—, sui: him/her/it/self; themselves
suffero, sufferre, sustuli, sublatum: to hold up, support
Sulpicia, ae, *f.*: Sulpicia
Sulpicia Lepidina, ae, *f*: Sulpicia Lepidina
sum, esse, fui, futurum: to be, exist
sumo, sumere, cumpsi, sumptum: to take up, to begin
superbus, a, um: proud, arrogant, haughty
surgo, surgere, surrexi, surrectum: to raise, erect; to arise, get up
suspiro, suspirare, suspiravi, suspiratum: to sigh; to utter with a sigh
suus, a, um: his (own), her (own), its (own)
tabella, ae, *f.*: small (writing) tablet
taceo, tacere, tacui, tacitum: to be silent
tacitus, a, um: silent, secret
taedet, taeduit (*impers.*): it disgusts, offends, wearies
talis, e: such
Talus, i, *m.*: Talus
tamen: (adv.) however
tandem: (adv.) at last, finally
tango, tangere, tetigi, tactum: to touch, to strike; to influence; to mention
tantum: (adv.) only
tectus, a, um: covered, roofed; hidden, secret; concealed, disguised
tego, tegere, texi, tectum: to cover, hide
telum, i, *n.*: weapon; shaft, spear, dart
tempestivus, a, um: belonging to the right time, timely, seasonable, appropriate
tempus, temporis, *n*: period of time; time; the times, circumstances
teneo, tenere, tenui, tentum: to keep, to hold; to possess; to comprehend
tener, tenera, tenerum: tender; delicate, gentle; immature
ter: three times
tergum, i, *n.*: back
terra, terrae, *f*: ground; earth; world; land
testudineus, a, um: made of tortoise-shell
Themis, Themis, *f.*: Themis
Thyestes, Thyestae, *m.*: Thyestes, son of Pelops and brother of Atreus
tibicina, ae, *f.*: a female flute-player

timeo, timere, timui: to fear, to dread, to be afraid of
tono, tonare, tonui, tonitum: to thunder
torqueo, torquere, torsi, tortum: to twist, to turn; to bend, to distort; to torture
torus, i, *m.*: couch, sofa, marriage-bed
totus, a, um: whole, all, entire, total
trabs, trabis, *f.*: beam, timber
Trajanus, Trajani, *m.*: Trajan. Emperor of Rome (98–118 CE)
tres, trium: three
tribuo, tribuere, tribui, tributum: to divide, to assign; to present; to grant, to allot, to bestow
trimetrus, i, *m*: trimeter
tristis, e: sad, sorrowful
triumphus, i, *m.*: triumph, triumphal procession
trutina, ae, *f.*: balance, pair of scales
tu, tui: you
tum: (adv.) then
tunc: (adv.) then
turba, turbae, *f.*: commotion, uproar, turmoil
turbo, turbare, turbavi, turbatum: to disturb, agitate, confuse
turpiter: (adv.) disgracefully, shamelessly
tus, turis, *n.*: frankincense
tuus, a, um: your, yours
tyrannus, i, *m.*: tyrant
Tyros, Tyri, *f.*: Tyre (city of the Phoenicians famed for its purple dye)
ubi: when; where
udus, a, um: wet, moist, damp, humid
ullus, a, um: any, anyone
umbrosus, a, um: shady, shadowy, dark
una: (adv.) as one; together
unus, a, um: one
urbs, urbis, *f.*: city
uro, urere, ussi, ustus: to burn
ut: (+ subjunctive) so that, that; (+ indicative) as
utor, uti, usus sum: to use, to make use of; to enjoy (+ abl.)
utrimque: (adv.) on both sides, from both sides
utrum: whether
uxor, uxoris, *f.*: wife
vagor, vagari, vagatus sum: to wander, to roam
valeo, valere, valui, valiturus: to fare well, to be healthy
validus, a, um: strong, powerful; valid
vario, variare, variavi, variatum: to diversify, change; to vary
-ve: or
vel: either, or; or else; even
vellus, velleris, *n.*: fleece, wool

velox, velocis (gen.): swift, quick, speedy
velut(i): as, just as
venero, venerare, veneravi, veneratum: to adore, to pay homage to; to worship
veneror, venerari, veneratus sum: to adore, to pay homage to; to worship
venio, venire, veni, ventum: to come, arrive
venor, venari, venatus sum: to hunt
ventus, i, *m.*: wind
Venus, Veneris, *f.*: Venus, goddess of (sexual) Love
verbum, verbi, *n.*: word
Vertumnus, i, *m.*: Vertumnus (god of seasons and change)
vespa, ae, *f.*: wasp
vestigium, vestigi, *n.*: track, trace; footprint, step
vestis, vestis, *f.*: clothing, garment
vetus, veteris (gen.): former; old, aged, ancient
vexo, vexare, vexavi, vexatum: to shake, agitate, plague, torment
via, ae, *f.*: way, road
viator, viatoris, *m/f*: a traveller, wayfarer; an apparitor, messenger
victor, victoris, *m.*: victor; conqueror
video, videre, visi, visum: to see
videor, videri, visus sum: to seem
vigeo, vigere, vigui: to thrive, flourish; to prosper; to live
vigilans, vigilantis (gen.): watchful, vigilant, alert; wakeful
vigilo, vigilare, vigilavi, vigilatum: to watch, be wakeful
villa, ae, *f.*: country house
vincio, vincire, vinxi, vinxtum: to bind, to fetter; to restrain
vinclum, vincli, *n.*: chain, bond
vinco, vincere, vici, victus: to conquer
vinum, i, *n.*: wine
violentus, a, um: violent, impetuous, boisterous
vir, viri, *m.*: man; hero; husband
virtus, virtutis, *f.*: virtue; manliness
vita, vitae, *f*: life
vivo, vivere, vixi, victum: to live; to be alive; to reside
vix: (adv.) hardly, scarcely, barely
volo, velle, volui: to wish, want, be willing
voluptas, voluptatis, *f.*: pleasure, delight, enjoyment
votum, voti, *n.*: vow, pledge, promise; prayer, wish
voveo, vovere, vovi, votum: to vow, to dedicate, to consecrate
Vulcanus, i, *m.*: Vulcan (god of the smith)
vultus, vultus, *m.*: face, public persona

# Index